Peugeot 504
Owners
Workshop
Manual

by J H Haynes
Member of the Guild of Motoring Writers
and B L Chalmers-Hunt
TEng (CEI), AMIMI, AMIRTE, AMVBRA

Models covered:
All Peugeot 504 Saloon and Estate models; Basic L, GL, GR, SL, TI,
Super Luxe and Family with 1796 cc and 1971 cc engines

*Covers fuel injection and carburettor engines, manual and automatic
transmissions*
Does not cover Diesel engine models

ISBN 1 85010 090 X

Printed in England *(161 – 1L2)*

THE
BOOK

Haynes Publishing Group
Sparkford Nr Yeovil
Somerset BA22 7JJ England

Haynes Publications, Inc
861 Lawrence Drive
Newbury Park
California 91320 USA

British Library Cataloguing in Publication Data
Chalmers-Hunt, B. L.
Peugeot 504 owners workshop manual.–
(Owners Workshop Manual)
1. Peugeot automobile
I. Title   II. Series
629.28'722   TL215.P53
ISBN 1–85010–090–X

Acknowledgements

Thanks are due to Peugeot Automobiles UK Limited who provided certain illustrations and much useful technical information, to Castrol Limited who supplied lubrication data, and to the Champion Sparking Plug Company who supplied the illustrations showing the various spark plug conditions.

Special thanks are due to all those people at Sparkford who helped in the production of this manual,

About this manual

Its aims

The aim of this manual is to help you get the best value from your car. It can do so in several ways. It can help you decide what work must be done (even should you choose to get it done by a garage), provide information on routine maintenance and servicing, and give a logical course of action and diagnosis when random faults occur. However, it is hoped that you will use the manual by tackling the work yourself. On simpler jobs it may even be quicker than booking the car into a garage, and going there twice to leave and collect it. Perhaps most important, a lot of money can be saved by avoiding the costs the garage must charge to cover its labour and overheads.

The manual has drawings and descriptions to show the function of the various components so that their layout can be understood. Then the tasks are described and photographed in a step-by-step sequence so that even a novice can do the work.

Its arrangement

The manual is divided into thirteen Chapters, each covering a logical sub-division of the vehicle. The Chapters are divided into Sections, numbered with single figures, eg 5; and the Sections into paragraphs (or sub-sections), with decimal numbers following on from the Section they are in, eg 5.1, 5.2, 5.3 etc.

It is freely illustrated, especially in those parts where there is a detailed sequence of operations to be carried out. There are two forms of illustration: figures and photographs. The figures are numbered in sequence with decimal numbers, according to their position in the Chapter: eg Fig.6.4 is the 4th drawing/illustration in Chapter 6. Photographs are numbered (either individually or in related groups) the same as the Section or sub-section of the text where the operation they show is described.

There is an alphabetical index at the back of the manual as well as a contents list at the front.

References to the 'left' or 'right' of the vehicle are in the sense of a person in the driver's seat facing forwards.

Unless otherwise stated, nuts and bolts are removed by turning anti-clockwise, and tightened by turning clockwise.

Vehicle manufacturers continually make changes to specifications and recommendations, and these, when notified, are incorporated into our manuals at the earliest opportunity.

Whilst every care is taken to ensure that the information in this manual is correct no liability can be accepted by the authors or publishers for loss, damage or injury caused by any errors in, or omissions from, the information given.

Introduction to the Peugeot 504

Considered at one time to be the flagship of the Peugeot range, the 504 is a smart and well-proportioned car. In most respects it is conventional in design; it has a general air of quality and robustness with generous seating capacity and is a satisfying car to drive.

The mechanical specification does not reflect many features of innovative design, the four-cylinder in-line engine driving the rear wheels via a four-speed manual or three-speed automatic transmission.

Front suspension is independent with McPherson struts, coil springs, telescopic shock absorbers and an anti-roll bar. The rear suspension on Estate models is a live axle type with twin coil springs at each side, whereas Saloon models have independent trailing arms and coil springs; in both cases there is an anti-roll bar and telescopic shock absorbers.

The cars have rack-and-pinion steering, and hydraulically operated all disc or disc/drum brakes.

Contents

One of the Peugeot 504 Estate variants - UK specification

Peugeot 504 Saloon - UK specification

Use of English

As this book has been written in England, it uses the appropriate English component names, phrases, and spelling. Some of these differ from those used in America. Normally, these cause no difficulty, but to make sure, a glossary is printed below. In ordering spare parts remember the parts list may use some of these words:

English	American	English	American
Accelerator	Gas pedal	Leading shoe (of brake)	Primary shoe
Aerial	Antenna	Locks	Latches
Anti-roll bar	Stabiliser or sway bar	Methylated spirit	Denatured alcohol
Big-end bearing	Rod bearing	Motorway	Freeway, turnpike etc
Bonnet (engine cover)	Hood	Number plate	License plate
Boot (luggage compartment)	Trunk	Paraffin	Kerosene
Bulkhead	Firewall	Petrol	Gasoline (gas)
Bush	Bushing	Petrol tank	Gas tank
Cam follower or tappet	Valve lifter or tappet	'Pinking'	'Pinging'
Carburettor	Carburetor	Prise (force apart)	Pry
Catch	Latch	Propeller shaft	Driveshaft
Choke/venturi	Barrel	Quarterlight	Quarter window
Circlip	Snap-ring	Retread	Recap
Clearance	Lash	Reverse	Back-up
Crownwheel	Ring gear (of differential)	Rocker cover	Valve cover
Damper	Shock absorber, shock	Saloon	Sedan
Disc (brake)	Rotor/disk	Seized	Frozen
Distance piece	Spacer	Sidelight	Parking light
Drop arm	Pitman arm	Silencer	Muffler
Drop head coupe	Convertible	Sill panel (beneath doors)	Rocker panel
Dynamo	Generator (DC)	Small end, little end	Piston pin or wrist pin
Earth (electrical)	Ground	Spanner	Wrench
Engineer's blue	Prussian blue	Split cotter (for valve spring cap)	Lock (for valve spring retainer)
Estate car	Station wagon	Split pin	Cotter pin
Exhaust manifold	Header	Steering arm	Spindle arm
Fault finding/diagnosis	Troubleshooting	Sump	Oil pan
Float chamber	Float bowl	Swarf	Metal chips or debris
Free-play	Lash	Tab washer	Tang or lock
Freewheel	Coast	Tappet	Valve lifter
Gearbox	Transmission	Thrust bearing	Throw-out bearing
Gearchange	Shift	Top gear	High
Grub screw	Setscrew, Allen screw	Trackrod (of steering)	Tie-rod (or connecting rod)
Gudgeon pin	Piston pin or wrist pin	Trailing shoe (of brake)	Secondary shoe
Halfshaft	Axleshaft	Transmission	Whole drive line
Handbrake	Parking brake	Tyre	Tire
Hood	Soft top	Van	Panel wagon/van
Hot spot	Heat riser	Vice	Vise
Indicator	Turn signal	Wheel nut	Lug nut
Interior light	Dome lamp	Windscreen	Windshield
Layshaft (of gearbox)	Countershaft	Wing/mudguard	Fender

Tools and working facilities

Introduction

A selection of good tools is a fundamental requirement for anyone contemplating the maintenance and repair of a motor vehicle. For the owner who does not possess any, their purchase will prove a considerable expense, offsetting some of the savings made by doing-it-yourself. However, provided that the tools purchased are of good quality, they will last for many years and prove an extremely worthwhile investment.

To help the average owner to decide which tools are needed to carry out the various tasks detailed in this manual, we have compiled three lists of tools under the following headings: *Maintenance and minor repair, Repair and overhaul,* and *Special.* The newcomer to practical mechanics should start off with the *Maintenance and minor repair* tool kit and confine himself to the simpler jobs around the vehicle. Then, as his confidence and experience grows, he can undertake more difficult tasks, buying extra tools as, and when, they are needed. In this way a *Maintenance and minor repair* tool kit can be built-up into a *Repair and overhaul* tool kit over a considerable period of time without any major cash outlays. The experienced do-it-yourselfer will have a tool kit good enough for most repair and overhaul procedures and will add tools from the *Special* category when he feels the expense is justified by the amount of use these tools will be put to.

It is obviously not possible to cover the subject of tools fully here. For those who wish to learn more about tools and their use there is a book entitled *How to Choose and Use Car Tools* available from the publishers of this manual.

Maintenance and minor repair tool kit

The tools given in this list should be considered as a minimum requirement if routine maintenance, servicing and minor repair operations are to be undertaken. We recommend the purchase of combination spanners (ring one end, open-ended the other): although more expensive than open-ended ones, they do give the advantages of both types of spanner.

Combination spanners - 10, 11, 12, 13, 14, 17 mm
Adjustable spanner - 9 inch
Engine sump/gearbox/rear axle drain plug key
Spark plug spanner (with special Peugeot tool)
Spark plug gap adjustment tool
Set of feeler gauges
Brake adjuster spanner (where applicable)
Brake bleed nipple spanner
Screwdriver - 4 in long x ¼ in dia (flat blade)
Screwdriver - 4 in long x ¼ in dia (cross blade)
Combination pliers - 6 inch
Hacksaw, junior
Tyre pump
Tyre pressure gauge
Oil can
Fine emery cloth (1 sheet)
Wire brush (small)
Funnel (medium size)

Repair and overhaul tool kit

These tools are virtually essential for anyone undertaking any major repairs to a motor vehicle, and are additional to those given in the *Maintenance and minor repair* list. Included in this list is a comprehensive set of sockets. Although these are expensive they will be found invaluable as they are so versatile - particularly if various drives are included in the set. We recommend the ½ in square-drive type, as this can be used with most proprietary torque wrenches. If you cannot afford a socket set, even bought piecemeal, then inexpensive tubular box spanners are a useful alternative.

The tools in this list will occasionally need to be supplemented by tools from the *Special* list.

Sockets (or box spanners) to cover range in previous list
Reversible ratchet drive (for use with sockets)
Extension piece, 10 inch (for use with sockets)
Universal joint (for use with sockets)
Torque wrench (for use with sockets)
'Mole' wrench - 8 inch
Ball pein hammer
Soft-faced hammer, plastic or rubber
Screwdriver - 6 in long x 5/16 in dia (flat blade)
Screwdriver - 2 in long x 5/16 in square (flat blade)
Screwdriver - 1½ in long x ¼ in dia (cross blade)
Screwdriver - 3 in long x 1/8 in dia (electricians)
Pliers - electricians side cutters
Pliers - needle nosed
Pliers - circlip (internal and external)
Cold chisel - ½ inch
Scriber
Scraper
Centre punch
Pin punch
Hacksaw
Valve grinding tool
Steel rule/straight edge
Allen keys
Selection of files
Wire brush (large)
Axle-stands
Jack (strong scissor or hydraulic type)

Special tools

The tools in this list are those which are not used regularly, are expensive to buy, or which need to be used in accordance with their manufacturers' instructions. Unless relatively difficult mechanical jobs are undertaken frequently, it will not be economic to buy many of these tools. Where this is the case, you could consider clubbing together with friends (or a motorists' club) to make a joint purchase, or borrowing the tools against a deposit from a local garage or tool hire specialist.

The following list contains only those tools and instruments freely available to the public, and not those special tools produced by the vehicle manufacturer specifically for its dealer network. You will find occasional references to these manufacturers' special tools in the text of this manual. Generally, an alternative method of doing the job without the vehicle manufacturers' special tool is given. However, sometimes, there is no alternative to using them. Where this is the case and the relevant tool cannot be bought or borrowed, you will have to entrust the work to a franchised garage.

> *Valve spring compressor*
> *Piston ring compressor*
> *Balljoint separator*
> *Universal hub/bearing puller*
> *Impact screwdriver*
> *Micrometer and/or vernier gauge*
> *Dial gauge*
> *Stroboscopic timing light*
> *Dwell angle meter/tachometer*
> *Universal electrical multi-meter*
> *Cylinder compression gauge*
> *Lifting tackle (photo)*
> *Trolley jack*
> *Light with extension lead*

Buying tools

For practically all tools, a tool factor is the best source since he will have a very comprehensive range compared with the average garage or accessory shop. Having said that, accessory shops often offer excellent quality tools at discount prices, so it pays to shop around.

Remember, you don't always have to buy the most expensive items on the shelf, but it is always advisable to steer clear of the very cheap tools. There are plenty of good tools around at reasonable prices, so ask the proprietor or manager of the shop for advice before making a purchase.

Care and maintenance of tools

Having purchased a reasonable tool kit, it is necessary to keep the tools in a clean serviceable condition. After use, always wipe off any dirt, grease and metal particles using a clean, dry cloth, before putting the tools away. Never leave them lying around after they have been used. A simple tool rack on the garage or workshop wall, for items such as screwdrivers and pliers is a good idea. Store all normal spanners and sockets in a metal box. Any measuring instruments, gauges, meters, etc., must be carefully stored where they cannot be damaged or become rusty.

Take a little care when tools are used. Hammer heads inevitably become marked and screwdrivers lose the keen edge on their blades from time-to-time. A little timely attention with emery cloth or a file will soon restore items like this to a good serviceable finish.

Working facilities

Not be be forgotten when discussing tools, is the workshop itself. If anything more than routine maintenance is to be carried out, some form of suitable working area becomes essential.

It is appreciated that many an owner mechanic is forced by circumstances to remove an engine or similar item, without the benefit of a garage or workshop. Having done this, any repairs should always be done under the cover of a roof.

Wherever possible, any dismantling should be done on a clean flat workbench or table at a suitable working height.

Any workbench needs a vice: one with a jaw opening of 4 in (100 mm) is suitable for most jobs. As mentioned previously, some clean dry storage space is also required for tools, as well as lubricants, cleaning fluids, touch-up paint and so on which become necessary.

Another item which may be required, and which has a much more general usage, is an electric drill with a chuck capacity of at least 5/16 in (8 mm). This, together with a good range of twist drills, is virtually essential for fitting accessories such as mirrors and reversing lights.

Last, but not least, always keep a supply of old newspapers and clean, lint-free rags available, and try to keep any working area as clean as possible.

Spanner jaw gap comparison table

Jaw gap (in)	Spanner size
0.250	$\frac{1}{4}$ in AF
0.276	7 mm
0.313	$\frac{5}{16}$ in AF
0.315	8 mm
0.344	$\frac{11}{32}$ in AF; $\frac{1}{8}$ in Whitworth
0.354	9 mm
0.375	$\frac{3}{8}$ in AF
0.394	10 mm
0.433	11 mm
0.438	$\frac{7}{16}$ in AF
0.445	$\frac{3}{16}$ in Whitworth; $\frac{1}{4}$ in BSF
0.472	12 mm
0.500	$\frac{1}{2}$ in AF
0.512	13 mm
0.525	$\frac{1}{4}$ in Whitworth; $\frac{5}{16}$ in BSF
0.551	14 mm
0.563	$\frac{9}{16}$ in AF
0.591	15 mm
0.600	$\frac{5}{16}$ in Whitworth; $\frac{3}{8}$ in BSF
0.625	$\frac{5}{8}$ in AF
0.630	16 mm
0.669	17 mm
0.686	$\frac{11}{16}$ in AF
0.709	18 mm
0.710	$\frac{3}{8}$ in Whitworth; $\frac{7}{16}$ in BSF
0.748	19 mm
0.750	$\frac{3}{4}$ in AF
0.813	$\frac{13}{16}$ in AF
0.820	$\frac{7}{16}$ in Whitworth; $\frac{1}{2}$ in BSF
0.866	22 mm
0.875	$\frac{7}{8}$ in AF
0.920	$\frac{1}{2}$ in Whitworth; $\frac{9}{16}$ in BSF
0.938	$\frac{15}{16}$ in AF
0.945	24 mm
1.000	1 in AF
1.010	$\frac{9}{16}$ in Whitworth; $\frac{5}{8}$ in BSF
1.024	26 mm
1.063	$1\frac{1}{16}$ in AF; 27 mm
1.100	$\frac{5}{8}$ in Whitworth; $\frac{11}{16}$ in BSF
1.125	$1\frac{1}{8}$ in AF
1.181	30 mm
1.200	$\frac{11}{16}$ in Whitworth; $\frac{3}{4}$ in BSF
1.250	$1\frac{1}{4}$ in AF
1.260	32 mm
1.300	$\frac{3}{4}$ in Whitworth; $\frac{7}{8}$ in BSF
1.313	$1\frac{5}{16}$ in AF
1.390	$\frac{13}{16}$ in Whitworth; $\frac{15}{16}$ in BSF
1.417	36 mm
1.438	$1\frac{7}{16}$ in AF
1.480	$\frac{7}{8}$ in Whitworth; 1 in BSF
1.500	$1\frac{1}{2}$ in AF
1.575	40 mm; $\frac{15}{16}$ in Whitworth
1.614	41 mm
1.625	$1\frac{5}{8}$ in AF
1.670	1 in Whitworth; $1\frac{1}{8}$ in BSF
1.688	$1\frac{11}{16}$ in AF
1.811	46 mm
1.813	$1\frac{13}{16}$ in AF
1.860	$1\frac{1}{8}$ in Whitworth; $1\frac{1}{4}$ in BSF
1.875	$1\frac{7}{8}$ in AF
1.969	50 mm
2.000	2 in AF
2.050	$1\frac{1}{4}$ in Whitworth; $1\frac{3}{8}$ in BSF
2.165	55 mm
2.362	60 mm

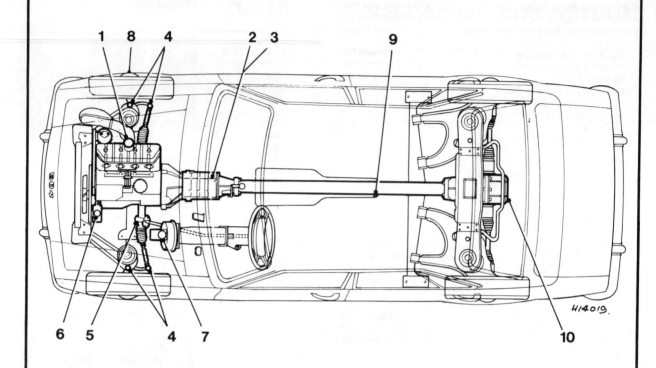

H14019.

Recommended lubricants and fluids

Component or system	Lubricant type or specification
Engine (1)	SAE 10W/40 multigrade engine oil
Manual transmission (2)	SAE 10W/40 multigrade engine oil
Automatic transmission (3)	Dexron ® type automatic transmission fluid
Front suspension/steering balljoint grease nipples (4)	Lithium based multi-purpose grease
Steering gear rack and pinion (5)	Lithium based multi-purpose grease
Power assisted steering gear (6)	Dexron ® type automatic transmission fluid
Clutch and brake master cylinder reservoir (7)	Universal hydraulic fluid to specification SAE J1703/DOT 3
Front wheel bearings (8)	Lithium based multi-purpose grease
Propeller shaft (9)	Lithium based multi-purpose grease
Differential (10)	SAE 80EP hypoid gear oil
Locks, hinges, pivots etc	General purpose light oil

The above are general recommendations only. Lubrication requirements vary from territory to territory and depend on vehical usage. If in doubt consult the operator's handbook supplied with the vehicle, or your nearest Peugeot dealer.

Routine maintenance

Maintenance is essential both for safety and for obtaining the best in terms of performance and economy from your vehicle. Over the years, the need for periodic lubrication — oiling, greasing, and so on — has been drastically reduced, and this has led some owners to think that the various components either no longer exist or will last forever. This is a serious delusion. It follows, therefore, that the largest initial element of maintenance is visual examination.

The following routine maintenance summary is based on the manufacturer's recommendation, but is supplemented by certain checks which the author feels will add up to improved reliability and an increase of component life. The maintenance procedure for more complicated tasks is given in the appropriate Chapter.

Daily
1 Check coolant level.
2 Check engine sump oil level.
3 Check battery electrolyte level.
4 Check tyre pressures. Examine tread depth and generally for other signs of damage.
5 Check operation of all lights.
6 Check windscreen washer fluid level.
7 Check brake and clutch master cylinder hydraulic fluid levels.

Weekly
1 Check tightness of roadwheel nuts.
2 Check automatic transmission oil level (where applicable).

3,000 miles (5,000 km) or 3 months interval

Carry out daily and weekly service plus:
1 Change engine oil.
2 Generally check operation of brake and clutch hydraulic systems. Inspect all pipes and unions for signs of leaks.
3 Check brake pad lining thickness.
4 Check gearbox oil level (manual transmission).
5 Check differential oil level.
6 Clean and reset spark plugs.
7 Inspect driveshaft rubber boots for damage or oil leaks.
8 Clean air cleaner.
9 Bleed the water trap fuel filter (fuel injection models).
10 Bleed fuel injection pump.
11 Check steering system joints for security and backlash.
12 Check handbrake operation. Adjust as necessary.
13 Check operation of horns and windscreen wipers.
14 Check specific gravity of battery electrolyte.
15 Check headlight beam alignment and reset as necessary.
16 Clean windscreen wiper blades and renew if worn or perished.
17 Check exhaust system for security and also for leaks.
18 Check condition and security of seats and seat belts.
19 Lubricate the following points using a grease gun filled with Castrol LM Grease:
   a) *Left-hand steering knuckle pivot*
   b) *Left-hand track arm balljoint*
   c) *Right-hand steering knuckle pivot*
   d) *Right-hand track arm balljoint*
   e) *Steering rack*
   f) *Propeller shaft bearing*
20 Lubricate all door locks and hinges.

6,000 miles (10,000 km or 6 months interval)

Carry out 3,000 miles service, plus:
1 Fit new engine oil filter cartridge.

2´ Drain and refill gearbox.
3 Clean and reset contact breaker points gap.
4 Check ignition timing.
5 Check operation of self disengaging fan.
6 Carefully examine all cooling system and heater hoses for perishing or leaks. Check hose clip security.
7 Lubricate accelerator control linkage and pedal fulcrum with a little engine oil.
8 Lubricate distributor parts.
9 Lubricate handbrake mechanical linkage and cables.
10 Check all fuel lines and joints for leakage. Check tightness of clips.
11 Check tightness of all engine attachments.
12 Check tightness of battery connections. Clean off corrosion and apply vaseline to terminals.
13 Check efficiency of charging system.
14 Check front and rear suspension attachments for security.
15 If wished, change round the roadwheels in a diagonal manner also using the spare to equalise wear. This is not advised if radial tyres are fitted.
16 Balance front wheels.
17 Generally check all electrical cables for damage and the connections for security.
18 Check engine/gearbox/differential units for oil leaks.

9,000 miles (15,000 km) or 9 months interval

Carry out 3,000 miles service (with the exception of service items, 6 and 8), plus:
1 Drain and refill differential unit.
2 Clean fuel pump filter.
3 Renew spark plugs.
4 Renew air cleaner element (when fitted).
5 Clean or renew fuel filter cartridge.
6 Drain and refill fuel injection pump.
7 Change automatic transmission oil.

12,000 miles (20,000 km) or 12 months interval

Carry out 6,000 miles service, plus:
1 Check tightness of engine mountings.
2 Check operation of starter motor and the tightness of all cable attachments.
3 Check tightness of door locks, catches and hinges.
4 Check steering assembly attachments for security.
5 Check operation of brake vacuum servo unit.
6 Tune engine using electronic test equipment.
7 Check HT leads for damage and secure connections. Also check ignition LT leads for security.

24,000 miles (40,000 km) or 2 years interval
1 Renew antifreeze mixture in cooling system.
2 Renew brake fluid. Renew system seals if necessary.

Other aspects of Routine Maintenance
1 Wheel nuts

These should be cleaned and lightly smeared with grease as necessary during work, to keep them moving easily. If the nuts are stubborn to undo due to dirt or overtightening, it may be necessary to hold them by lowering the jack until the wheel rests on the ground. Normally if the wheel brace is used across the hub centre, a foot or knee held against the tyre will prevent the wheel from turning, and so save the wheels and nuts from wear if the nuts are slackened with weight on the wheel. After replacing a wheel make a point of later rechecking the nuts for tightness.

2 Safety

Whenever working, even partially, under the car, put an extra strong box or piece of timber underneath onto which the car will fall rather than onto you.

3 Cleanliness

Whenever you do any work allow time for cleaning when some component is in pieces, or parts removed to improve access to other areas, give an opportunity for a thorough clean. This cleanliness will allow you to cope with a possible future crisis on the road without getting yourself too dirty. During bigger jobs when you expect some dirt it is less extreme and can be tolerated, at least whilst removing a component. When an item is being taken to pieces there is less risk of ruinous grit finding its way inside.

The act of cleaning also focuses your attention onto parts and you are more likely to spot trouble. Dirt on the ignition system is a common cause of poor starting. Large areas such as the engine compartment, inner wings or bulkhead should be brushed thoroughly with a solvent such as Gunk, allowed to soak and then very carefully hosed down. Water in the wrong places, particularly the carburettor or electrical components will do more harm than dirt. Use petrol or paraffin and a small paintbrush to clean the more inaccessible places.

4 Waste oil disposal

Old oil and cleaning paraffin must be destroyed. Although it makes a good base for a bonfire this practice is dangerous. It is also illegal to dispose of oil and paraffin down domestic drains. By buying your new engine oil in one gallon cans you can refill them with the old oil and take the cans back to the local garage who have facilities for disposal or recycling of the oil (for agricultural and industrial use).

5 Long journeys

Before taking the car on long journeys, particularly such trips as continental holidays make sure that the car is given a full visual inspection well in advance so that any faults found can be rectified in time.

Buying
spare parts and vehicle identification numbers

Buying spare parts

Spare parts are available from many sources, for example: Peugeot garages, other garages, accessory shops, and motor factors. Our advice regarding spare part sources is as follows:
Officially appointed Peugeot garages: This is the best source of parts which are peculiar to your car and are otherwise not generally available (eg; complete cylinder heads, internal gearbox components, badges, interior trim etc). It is also the only place at which you should buy parts if your car is still under warranty; non-Peugeot components may invalidate the warranty. To be sure of obtaining the correct parts it will always be necessary to give the storeman your car's engine and chassis number, and if possible, to take the 'old' part along for positive identification. Remember that many parts are available on a factory exchange scheme - any parts returned should always be clean! It obviously makes good sense to go straight to the specialists on your car for this type of part for they are best equipped to supply you.
Other garages and accessory shops: These are often very good places to buy materials and components needed for the maintenance of your car (eg; oil filters, spark plugs, bulbs, fan belts, oils and greases, touch-up paint, filler paste, etc). They also sell general accessories, usually have convenient opening hours, often charge lower prices and can usually be found not far from home.
Motor factors: Good factors will stock all the more important components which wear out relatively quickly (eg; clutch components, pistons, valves, exhaust systems, brake cylinders/pipes/hoses/seals/pads, etc). Motor factors will often provide new or reconditioned components on a part-exchange basis - this can save a considerable amount of money.

Vehicle identification numbers

When ordering spare parts it is essential to give full details of your car to the storeman. He will want to know the car type and serial number, car and engine numbers. When ordering parts for the transmission or body it is best if the transmission number or body number can be quoted.

The locations of the important vehicle numbers are shown in the accompanying illustration.

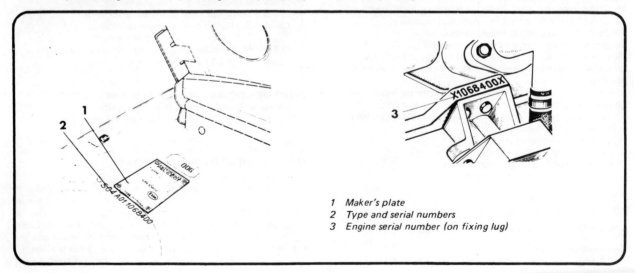

1 Maker's plate
2 Type and serial numbers
3 Engine serial number (on fixing lug)

Chapter 1 Engine

For modifications, and information applicable to later models, see Supplement at end of manual

Contents

Specifications

Engine general

Designation:

Carburettor version:

Saloon	XNI, XM
Station Wagon	XM7

Fuel injection version:

Saloon	XN2
Station Wagon	KF6
Number of cylinders	4

Bore:

1796 cc engine	3.31 in. (84 mm)
1971 cc engine	3.46 in. (88 mm)
Stroke	3.19 in. (81 mm)
Displacement:	1796 cc (109.5 cu in.)
	1971 cc (120.0 cu in.)

Compression ratio:
    XN1, XM, KF6, XN2 ... ...   8.35 : 1
    XM7 ... ...   7.5 : 1
Valve operation ... ...   overhead, rocker operated
Firing order ... ...   1, 3, 4, 2. (No 1 is at REAR)
Compression pressure ... ...   156 lb/in^2 (11 kg/cm^2) at 380 rpm.
Brake horse power (SAE):
    XN1 ... ...   98 at 5600 rpm
    XN2 ... ...   110 at 5600 rpm
    XM ... ...   87 at 5600 rpm
    XM7 ... ...   80 at 5500 rpm
    KF6 ... ...   103 at 5600 rpm

Important: All dimensions to be used in metric form for accuracy; do not attempt to convert to imperial units unless absolutely necessary.

Cylinder block

    Type ... ...   Cast iron with renewable cast iron liners
    Bore diameter ... ...   86.5 mm

Cylinder liners

    Type ... ...   Graded in 4 sizes to match piston diameter. Usually supplied with matching pistons.

Crankshaft

    Type ... ...   Steel
    number of bearings   5
    number of counter weights   4
    main bearing journal diameter (less bearings):
        Front ... ... $63.22 {}^{+\,0.02}_{-\,0.00}$ mm
        Intermediate front ... ... $62.38 {}^{+\,0.02}_{-\,0.00}$ mm
        Centre ... ... $61.00 {}^{+\,0.02}_{-\,0.00}$ mm
        Intermediate rear ... ... $59.97 {}^{+\,0.02}_{-\,0.00}$ mm
        Rear ... ... $55.00 {}^{+\,0.02}_{-\,0.00}$ mm
    Main bearing journal diameter:
        Front ... ...   59.401 - 59.416 mm
        Intermediate front ... ...   58.548 - 58.573 mm
        Centre ... ...   57.174 - 57.189 mm
        Intermediate rear ... ...   56.140 - 56.165 mm
        Rear ... ...   51.166 - 51.181 mm
    Crankpin journal diameter ... ...   49.975 - 49.991 mm
    Crankpin radial clearance ... ...   0.01 mm
    Crankshaft endfloat ... ...   0.08 - 0.20 mm

Main bearing shells

    Type ... ...   Steel-backed aluminium alloy 20% tin
    Bearing thickness:
        Standard ... ...   1.882 - 1.888 mm
        1st regrind ... ...   2.032 - 2.035 mm
        2nd regrind ... ...   2.132 - 2.138 mm
    Radial clearances:
        Front, centre, rear ... ...   0.035 - 0.081 mm
        Intermediate ... ...   0.35 - 0.091 mm
    Thrust washer thickness:
        Standard ... ... $2.30 {}^{+\,0.3}_{-\,0.0}$ mm
        Oversize ... ...   2.40, 2.45, $2.50 {}^{+\,0.3}_{-\,0.0}$ mm

Camshaft

    Type ... ...   Cast iron
    number of bearings   3
    Journal diameters (less bearings):
        Rear ... ... $44 {}^{+\,0.04}_{-\,0.00}$ mm
        Intermediate ... ... $46 {}^{+\,0.04}_{-\,0.00}$ mm
        Front ... ... $48 {}^{+\,0.04}_{-\,0.00}$ mm
    Shaft diameter ... ...   26.5 mm
    Endfloat ... ...   0.05 - 0.14 mm

Connecting rods

Type	Forged steel
Matching	By weight
Weight identification number:	
1	611 - 630 gms
2	631 - 650 gms
3	651 - 670 gms
4	671 - 690 gms
5	691 - 710 gms
6	711 - 730 gms
Maximum weight tolerance	20 gms
Small end bore	24.35 - 24.38 mm
Small end bush:	
Type	Bronze
Fitted diameter	23.005 - 23.018 mm
Big-end bore	53.655 - 53.674 mm
Big-end shells:	
Type	Steel backed aluminium alloy 20% tin
Thickness:	
Standard	1.812 - 1.818 mm
Oversize	1.962 - 1.968 mm
Radial clearance	0.028 - 0.075 mm

Pistons

Type	Aluminium alloy. Elliptical solid skirt
Number of rings	2 compression, 1 oil control
Height of ring grooves:	
Top compression ring	1.50 - 1.55 mm
Bottom compression ring	2.00 - 2.02 mm
Oil control ring	4.00 - 4.02 mm
Piston sizes	Graded in 4 sizes to match cylinder liner diameter. Usually supplied with matching liners
Piston weight variation (maximum)	10 gms

Piston rings

Type:	
Top compression ring	Cast iron. Chrome plated
Bottom compression ring	Cast iron. Bevelled
Oil control ring	Two flexible sections with intermediate expanding section
Height:	
Top compression ring	1.490 - 1.475 mm
Bottom compression ring	1.98 - 1.96 mm
Oil control ring	3.96 ± 0.05 mm
Ring gap:	
Top compression ring	0.40 - 0.55 mm
Bottom compression ring	0.40 - 0.55 mm
Oil control ring	0.20 - 0.50 mm each side of expander ring

Gudgeon pins

Bore diameter	23.00 mm
Clearance in piston bore	0.0 - 0.008 mm
External diameter:	
Standard	$23.005 \begin{smallmatrix} + & 0.0 \\ - & 0.013 \end{smallmatrix}$ mm
1st oversize	$23.5 \begin{smallmatrix} + & 0.0 \\ - & 0.013 \end{smallmatrix}$ mm
2nd oversize	$23.10 \begin{smallmatrix} + & 0.0 \\ - & 0.013 \end{smallmatrix}$ mm

Cylinder head

Type	Aluminium alloy with spherical off-set combustion chambers
Maximum distortion	0.05 mm
Gasket	Metallic sheets with asbestos/rubber compound between and steel rings around the bores
Spark plug tube bore diameter	30.695 - 30.698 mm
Spark plug tube diameter:	
Standard	30.7 mm
Oversize	30.9 mm
Valve guide bores:	
Standard	13.970 - 13.995 mm
1st oversize	14.200 - 14.225 mm
2nd oversize	14.500 - 14.525 mm
Valve guide interference fit	0.04 mm
Valve guide inside diameter	8.02 - 8.04 mm (0.2 mm less than nominal diameter)

Valve guide protrusion on head:
    Inlet valve guides   ...   .   27.5 $\pm$ 0.5 mm
    Exhaust valve guides   ...   .   21.5 $\pm$ 0.5 mm

Valves

Valve head diameter:
    Inlet valve   ...   .   42.5 mm
    Exhaust valve   ...   .   35.5 mm
Valve seat angle (cylinder head):
    Inlet valve   ...   .   120°
    Exhaust valve   ...   .   90°
Valve seat angle (Valve):
    Inlet valve   ...   . $120° {+ 15' \atop - 0.0'}$
    Exhaust valve   ...   . $90° {+ 15' \atop - 0.0'}$
Width of valve bearing face on seat   ...   .   1.5 mm (max)
Valve stem diameter:
    Inlet valve   ...   . $8.02 {+ 0.00 \atop 0.02}$ mm
    Exhaust valve   ...   . $8.00 {+ 0.00 \atop - 0.02}$ mm

Valve springs

Note: A range of valve springs have been fitted and are identified by a colour code. Always check with the supplier of new springs that they are of the correct rating

		XM Engine		XN1, XN2, XM7 Engines
		up to 5/1970	From 5/1970	Since 7/1970
Colour code		Grey	Yellow	Black
Outer spring:				
Height		30.8 mm	30.8 mm	30.8 mm
Under load of		70 kg	66 kg	62 kg
Inner spring:				
Height		26.8 mm	26.8 mm	26.8 mm
Under load of		35.5 kg	33.5 kg	31.5 kg

Pushrods

Length:
    Inlet valve   ...   . $185.4 {+ 0.5 \atop - 0.5}$ mm
    Exhaust valve   ...   . $219.3 {+ 0.5 \atop - 0.5}$ mm

Diameter:
    Inlet valve   ...   . $6.75 {+ 0.15 \atop - 0.05}$ mm
    Exhaust valve   ...   . $6.75 {+ 0.15 \atop - 0.05}$ mm

Valve clearances (cold)

Inlet   ...   .   0.10 mm
Exhaust   ...   .   0.25 mm

Tappets

External diameter:
    Standard   ...   .   23.95 - 23.96 mm
    Oversize   ...   .   24.15 - 24.16 mm
Block bore for tappet:
    Standard   ...   .   24.00 - 24.03 mm
    Oversize   ...   .   24.20 - 24.23 mm
Radial clearance   ...   .   0.04 - 0.08 mm

Valve timing

    Valves set to a clearance of 0.7 mm (inlet and exhaust) on the cylinder being used
Inlet valve opens   ...   .   0° 30' BTDC
Inlet valve closes   ...   .   35° 0' ABDC
Exhaust valve opens   ...   .   35° 30' BBDC
Exhaust valve closes   ...   .   10° 0' ATDC

Lubrication system

Type   ...   .   Pressure feed with renewable canister filter
Oil pump:
    Type   ...   .   Gear
    Depth of gears in body   ...   .   33.95 - 33.98 mm
    Pinion side play   ...   .   0.01 - 0.08 mm

Oil filter type	...	...	...	...	...	...	full flow
Oil pressure (minimum)	...	...	...	...	...	...	800 g/sq cm
Sump capacity	...	...	...	...	...	...	4 litres (7.0 pints, 8.5 US pints)
Filter capacity	...	...	...	...	...	...	0.5 litre (0.875 pints, 1.051 US pints)

Torque wrench settings

							lb f ft	kg f m
Cylinder head bolts	...	...	...	...	...	...	60	8.30
Connecting rod bolts	...	...	...	...	...	...	29	4.0
Main bearing caps	...	...	...	...	...	...	54	7.4
Crankshaft counterweights	...	...	...	...	...	...	49	6.75
Flywheel bolts	...	...	...	...	...	...	49	6.75
Crankshaft pulley	...	...	...	...	...	...	123	17.0
Camshaft pinion	...	...	...	...	...	...	16	2.21
Sump bolts	...	...	...	...	...	...	7	1.0
Spark plugs	...	...	...	...	...	...	16	2.21
Crossmember bolts	...	...	...	...	...	...	33	4.6

1 General description

The engine is a four cylinder overhead valve type and fitted with either a single choke Solex carburettor or Kugelfischer indirect fuel injection. Depending on the system used certain differences do exist between the two engines. Further information will be found later on in this Section.

The engine is mounted at an angle of 45⁰ to the right which results in a lower bonnet line, gives better accessibility to the external engine components and finally lowers the centre of gravity of the car.

Carburettor engine

The cylinder head is of aluminium alloy and has offset hemispherical combustion chambers with a common inlet chamber for all four cylinders. It is fitted with removable cast iron valve guides and seats.

The valves are made of steel and operated by rocker arms. They are held in position by a Teves type safety collet. The exhaust valve stems are chromed and the valve seating stellited so as to resist deterioration due to high temperature operation.

The cylinder block is of cast iron and is fitted with wet type liners to facilitate major engine overhaul.

To ensure a good joint between the cylinder head and cylinder block a special Reinz gasket is used. This is made up of a thin layer of rubber and asbestos between a frame of thin metal sheets.

The pistons are of aluminium alloy and incorporate a steel retaining ring which is inserted during manufacture. This controls piston skirt expansion. Each piston is fitted with three rings: two compression and one oil control ring. The top compression ring is chromium plated whilst the bottom compression ring is of cast iron graphite. The oil control ring is of the "perfect circle" type and consists of two steel rings which are chromium plated on their bearing surfaces. They are held in position by an intermediate steel expander.

The connecting rods are of forged steel and fitted with a bronze small end bush.

The crankshaft is of forged steel and has five large diameter bearings which decrease in diameter from front to rear. The crankshaft main bearings are similar in composition to those used for the big-ends and are coated with an aluminium alloy and tin to withstand high loads. The bearing surface of the journals and crankpins are surface hardened to ensure a long working life. The crankshaft is fitted with four counterweights to provide for static and dynamic balance. Normally once set they need not be disturbed except for regrinding purposes. Crankshaft endfloat is controlled by two bi-metal half flanges fitted on the rear bearing.

A statically and dynamically balanced flywheel is secured to the rear end of the crankshaft by seven bolts.

The camshaft is of cast iron and the cams are case hardened. Also on the camshaft is a helical pinion which drives the distributor and oil pump. There is also an eccentric for operating the mechanical fuel pump. The camshaft is mounted laterally in the cylinder block and rotates through three large section bearings. It is driven by a double link chain and a hydraulic tensioner controls any whip due to slight stretching after high mileages.

The overhead valve rocker assembly is mounted in five substantial cast iron supports.

A high output gear type oil pump is secured to the cylinder block lower mating face and is operated by the camshaft. Further information on the lubrication system will be found later on in this Chapter.

Fuel injection engine

The fuel injection engine differs essentially from the carburettor engine in the following parts:

Cylinder head
Cylinder block
Camshaft
Timing case and timing gear
Distributor and spark plugs
Oil filter body
Oil bath air filter
Inlet manifold
Air distribution chamber
Electric fuel pump
Fuel filters
Injection pump and injectors
Three stage alternator

The aluminium alloy cylinder head is equipped with larger section inlet chambers, one for each cylinder. Located on the inlet side are threaded holes to allow for attachment of the manifold onto which the injectors are mounted.

The cylinder block is basically identical with the exception of the mechanical fuel pump securing flange, which is not fitted to this engine.

The camshaft lobes have a different profile which gives a greater valve lift. It is driven in the same manner to the ⌊carburettor engine.

The fuel injection pump is driven by a SEDIS notched belt from a pinion that is secured to the front of the camshaft.

Obviously care must be taken to ensure that the correct parts are ordered as and when necessary.

2 Major operations possible with engine in place

The following major operations can be carried with the engine in place in the car but it is recommended that whenever possible the unit be removed first, if accessibility is poor.

1   *Removal and replacement of the cylinder head assembly.*
2   *Removal and replacement of the water pump and thermostat.*
3   *Removal and replacement of the magnetic fan clutch.*
4   *Removal and replacement of distributor and fuel system.*
5   Removal and replacement of sump.
6   Removal and replacement of the big-end bearings.
7   Removal and replacement of the pistons and connecting rods.

*8   Removal and replacement of timing chain and gears.
*Definitely, not recommended.

3 Major operations requiring engine removal

The following major operations can only be carried out easily with the engine out of the car, and on a bench or floor.

1   Items 5-8 of Section 2.
2   Removal and replacement of the oil pump.
3   Removal and replacement of the flywheel.

4 Methods of engine removal

The engine can be removed either attached to the gearbox or, disconnected from it, by itself. Both methods are described.

It is easier if a hydraulic type trolley jack is used in conjunction with two pairs of axle stands so that the car can be raised sufficiently to allow easy access to the underside. Overhead lifting tackle will be necessary in both cases.

Because of the weight consideration and the very steep angle to which the engine must be tilted, the do-it-yourself motorist, without the use of a pit or ramp, should remove the gearbox first.

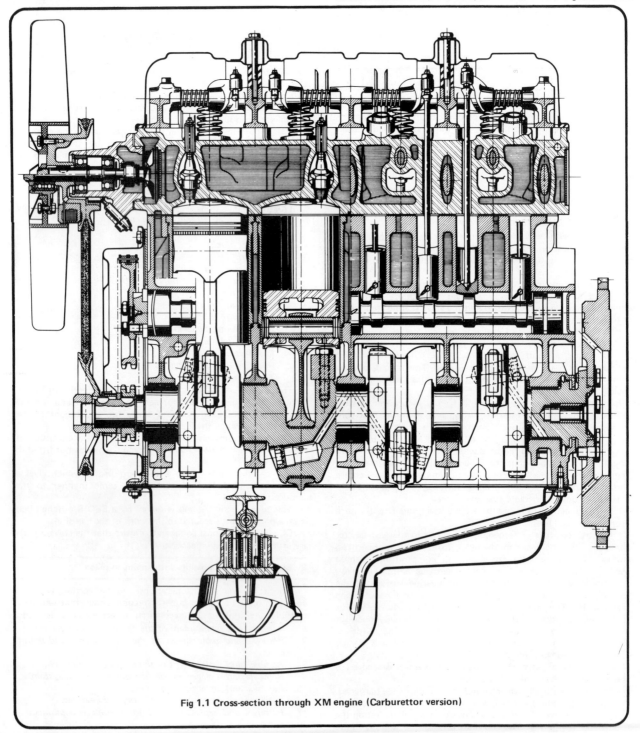

Fig 1.1 Cross-section through XM engine (Carburettor version)

Note: Cars fitted with automatic transmission necessitating engine and transmission removal should have the transmission removed first as described in Chapter 6, and then followed by the engine. This is because of the size and weight of the transmission.

5 Engine (carburettor type) - removal with gearbox

1 The do-it-yourself owner should be able to remove the power unit fairly easily in about 4½ hours. It is essential to have a good

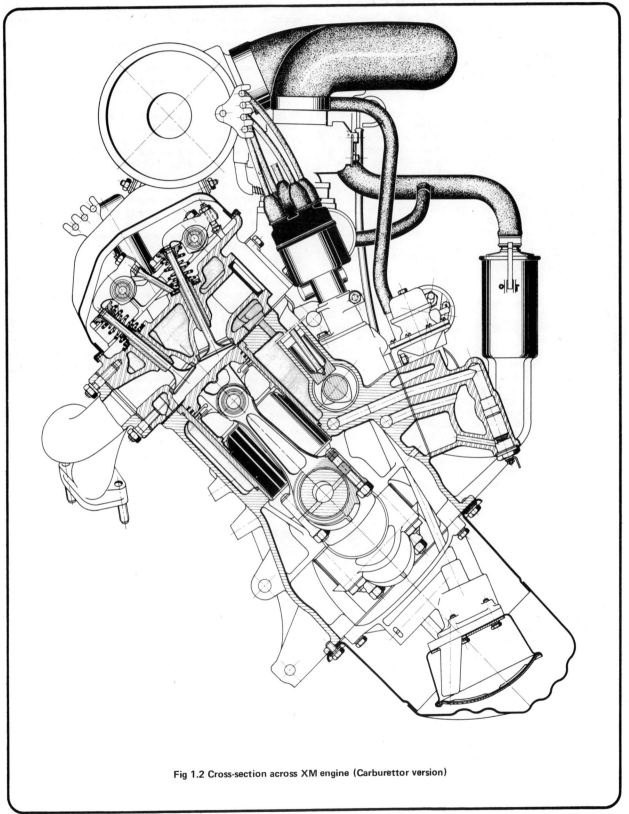

Fig 1.2 Cross-section across XM engine (Carburettor version)

hoist and two axle stands if an inspection pit is not available.

2 The sequence of operations listed in this Section is not critical as the position of the person undertaking the work, or the tool in his hand, will determine to a certain extent the order in which the work is tackled. Obviously, the power unit cannot be removed until everything is disconnected from it and the following sequence will ensure that nothing is forgotten. Obviously various modifications have been made from time-to-time, and if a part not mentioned is fitted make a special note of any connections before removal.

1 Refer to Chapter 12 and remove the bonnet, put in a safe place where it will not become scratched.

2 Remove the battery and tray, as described in Chapter 10. (photo)

3 Refer to Chapter 2, and drain the cooling system.

4 Refer to Chapter 2, and remove the radiator and fan. (photo)

5 Make a note of the electrical connections to the ignition coil and disconnect the terminal connectors. Slacken the nut securing the ignition coil to its mounting bracket and lift away the coil.

6 Make a note of the electrical connections to the starter motor and detach.

7 Detach the cables from the rear of the alternator.

8 To save damage remove the windscreen washer bottle.

9 To give better access remove the air cleaner assembly.

10 Slacken the heater hose clips at the engine and detach the hoses.

11 Disconnect the fuel feed line to the fuel pump and plug the end of the pipe to stop dirt ingress.

12 Make a note of, and disconnect the controls from the carburettor.

13 Disconnect the brake servo unit vacuum hose from the inlet manifold.

14 Disconnect the cables from the temperature indicator and oil pressure sender unit.

15 Detach the exhaust downpipe from the exhaust manifold. Also release the exhaust system front mounting and move the exhaust system to one side. (photos)

16 To give sufficient clearance it is necessary to detach the steering rack assembly from the crossmember. Turn the steering wheel to the left lock and then undo and remove the securing bolts. Note: It is not necessary to disconnect the balljoints. Draw the steering rack assembly downwards from the crossmember and allow to hang on the balljoints. (photo)

17 Working under the car disconnect the speedometer cable and reverse light switch. (photo)

18 Disconnect the engine to body earth strap.

19 Refer to Chapter 7, and disconnect the propeller shaft.

20 Refer to Chapter 6, and with the centre console removed disconnect the gearchange lever assembly. (photos)

21 Refer to Chapter 5, and detach the clutch slave cylinder from the gearbox bellhousing. (photo)

22 Suitably support the weight of the engine and gearbox assembly using an overhead hoist. Do not attempt to raise it from its mounting brackets yet.

23 Suitably support the weight of the gearbox by either using a jack or axle stand.

24 Disconnect the gearbox mounting from the crossmember.

25 Undo and remove the nuts and bolts securing the crossmember to the underside of the body. Lift away the crossmember.

26 Undo and remove the four bolts that secure the engine mountings to the crossmember. (photo)

27 Check that the front left-hand brake line is hard up against the crossmember so that it is not damaged during unit removal.

28 Check that no electrical cables or controls have been left connected and that disconnected cables are tucked well out of the way.

29 Should an air conditioning compressor be fitted this must not be disconnected but simply detached from its mounting and tied back to the wing.

30 The complete engine/gearbox unit may now be removed from the car. Make sure the hoist will stand the weight and also be high enough because the unit must be tilted at rather a steep angle.

31 Commence by removing the support from the rear of the gearbox and carefully lower the end to the ground (applicable if the car is on axle stands).

32 It will be beneficial if a piece of wood planking is placed between the end of the gearbox and the floor to act as a skid.

33 Carefully raise the engine and pull slightly forward. It will now be necessary to tilt the engine at a very steep angle so that the oil pan clears the front grille panels. Continue to raise the engine until the oil sump is just above the front panel.

34 A second person should now lift the rear of the gearbox over the front panel and when all is clear lower the unit to the ground.

35 Thoroughly wash the exterior with paraffin or 'Gunk'. Wash off with a strong jet of water and dry thoroughly.

36 The gearbox may now be separated from the engine if required.

5.2 Disconnect battery positive terminal before starting work

5.4 Removal of fan blades

5.15a Exhaust downpipe detached from manifold

5.15b Exhaust pipe front mounting

5.16 Steering rack and pinion assembly mounting

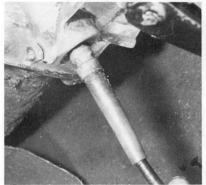

5.17 Removal of speedometer drive assembly

5.19a Removal of propeller shaft assembly securing bolts

5.19b Withdrawing propeller shaft

5.20a Gearchange lever assembly cover

5.20b Gearchange lever top linkage

5.20c Gearchange linkage attached to gearbox

5.20d Detaching linkage balljoint cup

5.21 Clutch slave cylinder

5.26 Engine front mounting

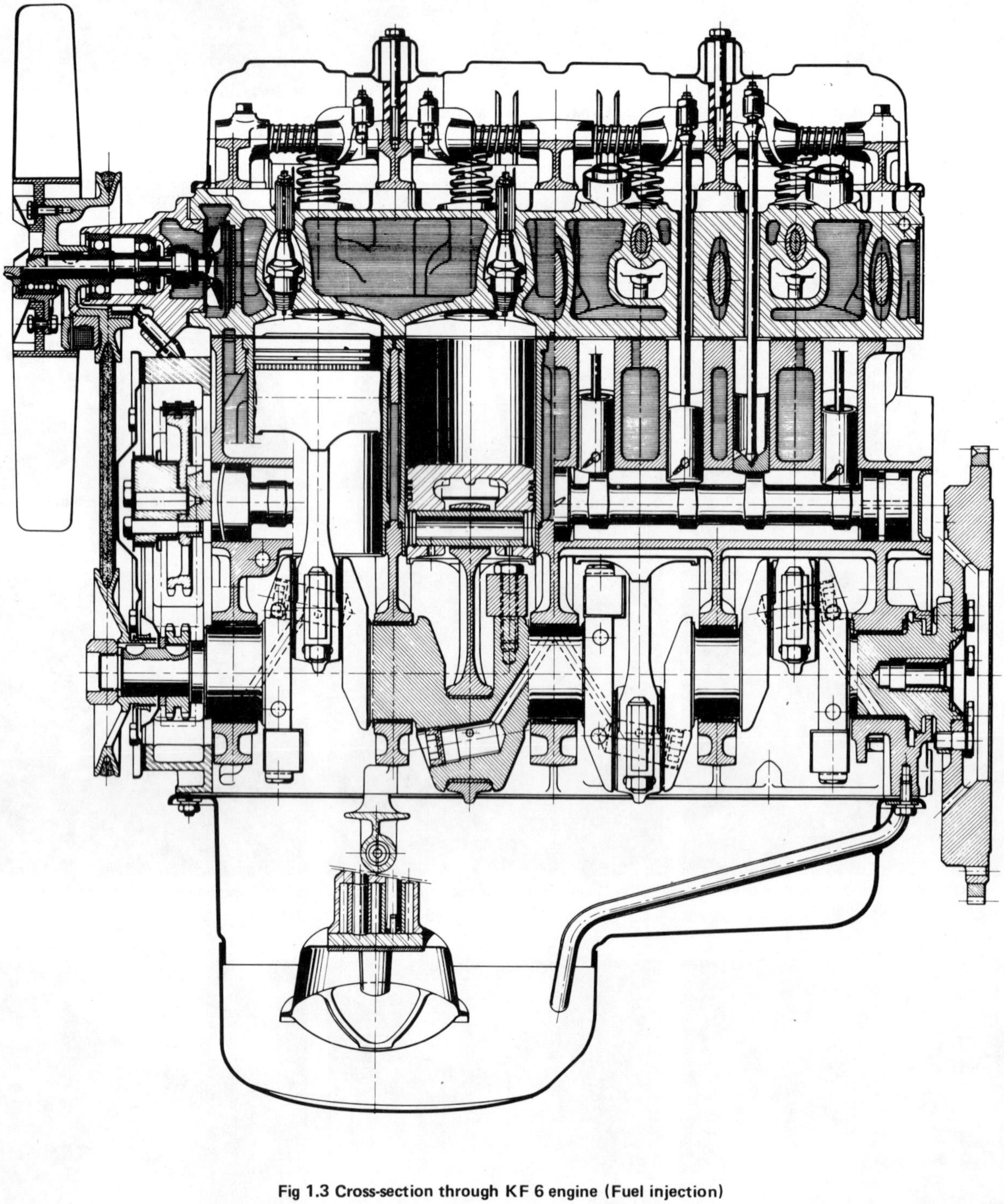

Fig 1.3 Cross-section through KF 6 engine (Fuel injection)

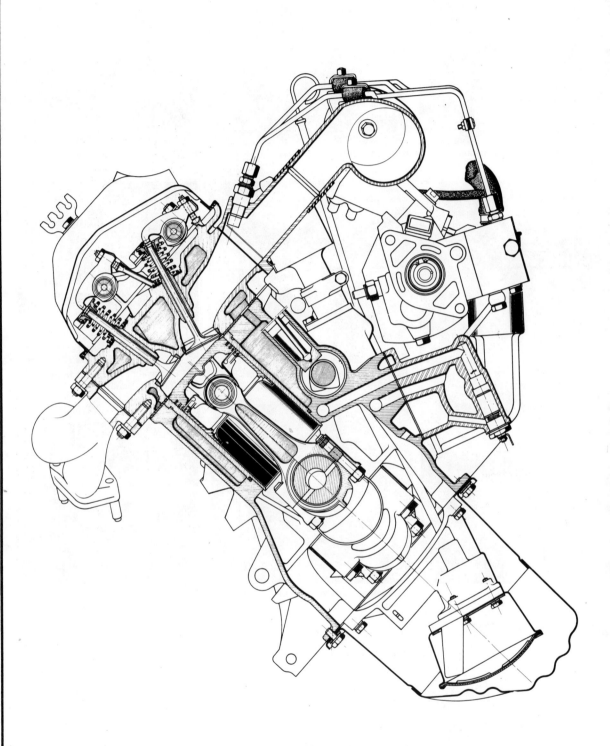

Fig 1.4 Cross-section across KF 6 engine (Fuel injection)

6.1a Removal of air cleaner flexible coupling

6.1b Lifting away air cleaner

6.2 Removal of air duct tube

6.3a Removal of top heater hose

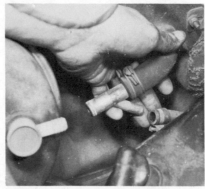

6.3b Removal of bottom heater hose

6.4 Removal of union bolt from rear of fuel injection pump

6.5 Detaching fuel pipe

6.6 Fuel enrichment valve union bolt removal

6.7 Removal of union bolt from front of fuel injection pump

6.8 Fuel injection pump control cable location

6.10a Engine ready for removal

6.10b Engine partially raised in engine compartment

6 Engine (fuel injection type) - removal with gearbox

Follow the instructions in Section 5, but disregard reference to the carburettor and air cleaner. The following additional points should be noted.

1 Remove the air cleaner assembly. (photos)
2 Remove the air duct tube. (photo)
3 Slacken the clips and remove the heater hoses. (photos)
4 Undo and remove the union bolt at the rear of the fuel injection pump. (photo)
5 Detach the fuel pipe located just above the starter motor. (photo)
6 Undo and remove the fuel enrichment valve union bolt shown in this photo.
7 Undo and remove the union bolt at the front of the fuel injection pump. (photo)
8 Make a special note of the control connections to the fuel injection pump and then detach. Tuck the controls well out of the way. (photo)
9 Remove the electro-valve and the altitude corrector located as shown in Fig. 1.5.
10 Removal is now basically identical to that described in Section 5. Refer to the photographs showing final engine removal.

7 Engine (carburettor type) - removal (less gearbox)

1 Follow the instructions given in Section 5, but do not disconnect the propeller shaft, gearchange lever, or gearbox crossmember.
2 Refer to Chapter 10, and remove the starter motor. (photo)
3 Suitably support the weight of the gearbox by either using a jack, axle stand or wood blocks. (photo)
4 Remove the flywheel protector plates and then undo and remove the clutch housing bolts. (photo)
5 The engine may now be detached from the gearbox by drawing forwards until the input shaft is free of the clutch centre plate.
6 It may be necessary to manipulate the gearbox upwards or downwards until it is free of the rear of the engine.
7 Removal of the engine is now similar to that described in Section 5.

8 Engine (fuel injection engine) - removal (less gearbox)

1 Follow the instructions given in Section 6, but do not disconnect the propeller shaft, gearchange lever, or gearbox crossmember.
2 The sequence is now basically identical to that as described in Section 7.

9 Engine - removal (less automatic transmission)

1 Follow the instructions given in Chapter 6, and remove the automatic transmission unit from the car first. This is because of the size and weight of the transmission.
2 Follow the instructions given in Section 5 or 6 as applicable for removal of the engine but disregard reference to the propeller

Fig 1.5 Electro-valve (1) and altitude connector (2) (Sec. 6)

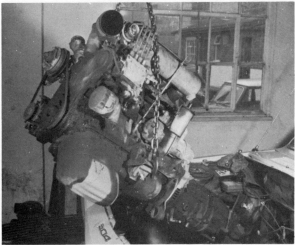

6.10c Engine in fully raised position

7.2 Starter motor removal

7.3 Supporting gearbox

7.4 Flywheel cover plate removal

shaft, gearbox or gear selector mechanism.

10 Separating the engine from gearbox

For full information refer to Chapter 6.

11 Engine - dismantling (general).

1   It is best to mount the engine on a dismantling stand, but if this is not available, then stand the engine on a strong bench so as to be a comfortable working height. Failing this, the engine can be stripped down on the floor.

2   During the dismantling process the greatest care should be taken to keep the exposed parts free of dirt. As an aid to achieving this, it is a sound scheme to thoroughly clean down the outside of the engine, removing all traces of oil and congealed dirt.

3   Use paraffin or a good grease solvent such as 'Gunk'. The latter compound will make the job easier, as, after the solvent has been applied and allowed to stand for a time, a vigorous jet of water will wash off the solvent and all the grease and filth. If the dirt is thick and deeply embedded, work the solvent into it with a stiff paint brush.

4   Finally wipe down the exterior of the engine with a rag and only then when it is quite clean should the dismantling process begin. As the engine is stripped clean each part in a bath of paraffin.

5   Never immerse parts with oilways in paraffin, ie; the crank-shaft, but to clean wipe down carefully with a paraffin moistened rag. Oilways can be cleaned out with nylon pipe cleaners. If an air line is present all parts can be blown dry and the oilways blown through as an added precaution.

6   Re-use of old engine gaskets is a false economy and can give rise to oil and water leaks, if nothing worse. To avoid the possibility of trouble after the engine has been reassembled always use new gaskets throughout.

7   Do not throw the old gaskets away as it sometimes happens that an immediate replacement cannot be found and the old gasket is then very useful as a template. Hang up the old gaskets as they are removed on a suitable hook or nail.

8   When purchasing engine gaskets be particularly careful to state whether the engine is fitted with a fuel injection system or carburettor. Also take care when obtaining a replacement cylinder head gasket as there are at least three different types.

9   To strip the engine it is best to work from the top down. The oil sump and suitable wood packing provides a firm base on which the engine can be supported in an upright position. When the stage where the sump must be removed is reached, the engine can be turned on its side and all other work carried out with it in this position.

10 Whenever possible, replace nuts, bolts and washers fingertight from wherever they were removed. This helps to avoid later loss and muddle. If they cannot be replaced then lay them out in such a fashion that it is clear from where they came.

11 It may be that the engine being worked on has one or more modifications that are not shown in the photographs or illus-trations. Should this occur make a note of any differences.

12 If the engine was removed in unit with the gearbox separate them by undoing the nuts and bolts which hold the bellhousing to the rear of the engine.

13 Carefully pull the gearbox and bellhousing off the engine to separate them.

12 Ancillary engine components - removal

1   Before basic engine dismantling begins the engine should be stripped of all its ancillary components. These items should also be removed if an exchange reconditioned unit is being

purchased. The items comprise:

2   Without exception all these items can be removed with the engine in the car if it is merely an individual item which requires attention. (It is necessary to remove the gearbox if the clutch is to be renewed with the engine in-situ).

3   Remove the alternator after undoing the nuts and bolts which secure it. Remove the alternator securing brackets.

Alternator and alternator brackets
Water pump
Distributor and spark plugs
Inlet and exhaust manifold and carburettor
Air manifold and exhaust manifold
Fuel pump and fuel pipes
Oil filter and dipstick
Oil filler cap
Clutch assembly
Engine mountings
Oil pressure sender unit

4   Remove the distributor by disconnecting the vacuum pipe, unscrew the single bolt and lift out the distributor. (photo)

5   Remove the oil filter assembly by unscrewing it.

6   Unscrew the two bolts securing the mechanical fuel pump. Lift away the pump and gasket.

7   Unscrew the oil pressure gauge unit or the oil pressure sender unit depending on model.

8   On fuel injection models detach the injection pipes and remove the air manifold. (photo)

9   Carburettor models. Remove the inlet manifold together with the carburettor by undoing the bolts and nuts which hold the units in place.

10 Remove the bolts and nuts securing the exhaust manifold to the engine.

11 Unscrew the water pump securing bolts and lift away the water pump. Recover the gasket.

12 Remove the bolts securing the two engine mountings to the sides of the cylinder block. Lift away the mountings.

13 Undo the bolts which hold the clutch cover flange to the flywheel a third of a turn each in a diagonal manner repeating until the clutch and driven plate can be lifted off. (photo)

14 The engine is now stripped of ancillary components and ready for major dismantling.

13 Cylinder head - removal (engine on bench)

1   Mark and then detach the spark plug HT leads and cap assemblies from the spark plugs. (photos)

2   Unscrew the rocker cover securing bolts and lift off the rocker cover and gasket (photo). Recover the plug tube seals and their cups

3   Fuel injection engines. Detach the injector pipes from the injectors and pump. (photos)

4   Fuel injection engine. Release the air manifold attachments and lift off the air manifold. (photo)

5   Carburettor engines. If the inlet manifold and carburettor are still in position these should be removed next. Undo and remove the securing nuts and bolts and lift away the assembly from the side of the cylinder head.

6   Slacken the ignition coil securing nuts and lift away the ignition coil. (photo)

7   Undo and remove the exhaust manifold securing bolts and lift away the exhaust manifold. (photo)

8   Undo and remove the union bolts and lift off the oil transfer pipe linking the cylinder head to the cylinder block. (photo)

9   Undo and remove the bolts securing the rocker assembly and cylinder head to the cylinder block. Undo these bolts half a turn at a time in the order shown in Fig. 1.6. When all the bolts are no longer under tension they may be screwed off one at a time. Lift off the rocker assembly as one unit. (photo)

10 Remove the pushrods keeping them in the relative order in which they were removed. The easiest way to do this is to push them through a sheet of thick paper or thin card in the correct sequence.

12.4 Distributor removal

12.8 Air manifold removal

12.13 Clutch assembly removal

13.1a Withdrawing spark plug caps and tubes

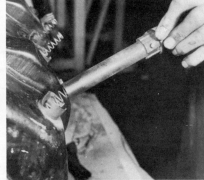
13.1b Note the springs

13.2 Lifting away rocker cover

13.3a Fuel injection pipe detached from injector

13.3b Fuel injection pipe detached from injection pump

13.4 Removal of air manifold

13.6 Removal of ignition coil

13.7 Removal of exhaust manifold

13.8 Location of transfer pipe

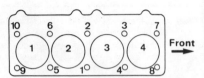

Fig 1.6 Cylinder head bolt slackening and tightening sequence (Secs. 13 and 67)

13.9 Removal of rocker assembly

13.11 Lifting away cylinder head

Fig 1.7 Liners clamped in block (sec 13)

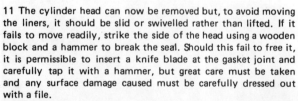

11 The cylinder head can now be removed but, to avoid moving the liners, it should be slid or swivelled rather than lifted. If it fails to move readily, strike the side of the head using a wooden block and a hammer to break the seal. Should this fail to free it, it is permissible to insert a knife blade at the gasket joint and carefully tap it with a hammer, but great care must be taken and any surface damage caused must be carefully dressed out with a file.

12 To stop the cylinder liners moving hold in position with bolts and large washers. Screw the bolts into the cylinder head bolt holes. (Fig. 1.7)

---

14 Cylinder head- removal (engine in car)

To remove the cylinder head with the engine still in the car the following additional procedure to that described in Section

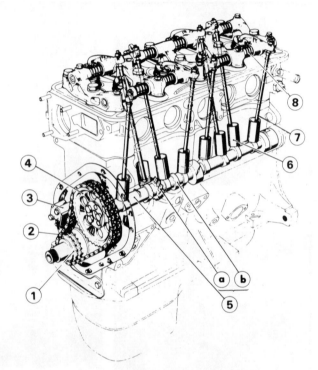

Fig 1.8 Camshaft and valve gear

1   Crankshaft sprocket
2   Timing chain
3   Tensioner
4   Camshaft sprocket
5   Camshaft
6   Tappet (cam follower)
7   Pushrod
8   Rocker assembly
a) Oil pump and distributor drive gear
b) Fuel pump eccentric

13 should be carried out first.
1   Disconnect the battery, for safety reasons.
2   Drain the cooling system, as described in Chapter 2.
3   Take off the air cleaner assembly.
4   Detach the spark plug leads and HT leads from the centre of the ignition coil. Release the distributor cap clips and remove the distributor cap.
5   Slacken the top hose clips and remove the top hose from the cylinder head union and radiator top tank.
6   Slacken the alternator securing bolts and release the fan belt tension. Lift off the fan belt.
7   Detach the fuel pipe and controls from the carburettor.
8   Remove the inlet manifold securing nuts and bolts and lift

the assembly from the side of the cylinder head.

9 Undo the exhaust system downpipe to manifold securing bolts and release the joint. Note a new gasket will be necessary when reconnecting the downpipe to the manifold.

10 On KF6, KF5, and XN2 engines (fuel injection engines) remove the injector pipes. Tape the delivery valves and injector unions to stop dirt ingress. Remove the air manifold chamber from the inlet manifold.

11 Disconnect any electrical leads and hoses directly connected to the cylinder. The actual number and location will depend on the engine application.

12 The procedure is now the same as for removing the cylinder head when on the bench. One tip worth noting is that should the cylinder head refuse to free easily, the battery can be reconnected and the engine turned over on the switch. Under no circumstances turn the ignition on and ensure the fuel inlet pipe

is disconnected from the mechanical fuel pump. Do not try this without someone holding the cylinder head firmly.

15 Valves - removal

1 The valves can be removed from the cylinder head by the following method. Compress each spring in turn with a valve spring compressor until the two halves of the collets can be removed. Release the compressor and remove the springs and spring cup.

2 If, when the valve spring compressor is screwed down, the valve spring retainer refuses to free or expose the split collet, do not continue to screw down the compressor as there is a likelihood of damaging it.

3 Gently tap the top of the tool directly over the retainer with

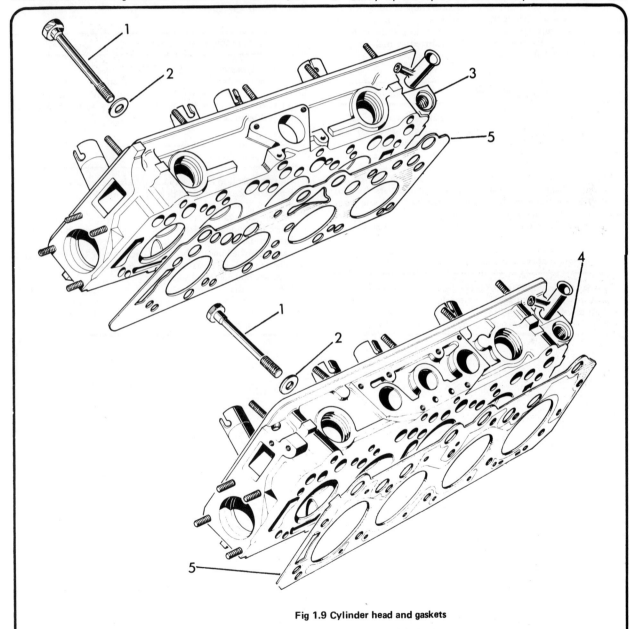

Fig 1.9 Cylinder head and gaskets

1 Cylinder head bolt
2 Washer
3 Cylinder head assembly XM engine

4 Cylinder head assembly XN1 engine
5 Cylinder head gasket (NOT interchangeable between engines)

a light hammer. This will free the retainer. To avoid the compressor jumping off the valve spring retaining cap when it is tapped, hold the compressor firmly in position with one hand.

4   Slide the rubber seal from the valve stem and then drop out each valve through the combustion chamber.

5   It is essential that the valves are kept in their correct sequence unless they are so badly worn that they are to be renewed. If they are going to be kept and used again, place them in a sheet of card having eight numbered holes corresponding with the relative positions the valves were in when fitted. Also keep the valve springs, collets, retainer etc in the correct order. Make No. 1 hole the one at the rear of the cylinder head.

16 Rocker assembly - dismantling

Under normal circumstances this operation should not be necessary unless a worn rocker or shaft is to be renewed. Dismantling is straightforward and will present no problems. Keep all parts in order so that they may be refitted in their original positions. (Fig. 1.10)

17 Timing cover (front) - removal

1   Bend back the crankshaft pulley nut lockwasher.
2   Suitably lock the flywheel and then using a socket, 'T' bar and piece of metal pipe unscrew the pulley securing nut. It is very tight (123 lb f ft/17 kg f m). Lift away the nut and lockwasher.
3   Carefully slide the crankshaft pulley from the end of the crankshaft; if tight, gently lever using two screwdrivers. (photo)
4   Undo and remove the bolts and washers securing the front timing cover. Lift away the front timing cover and recover the gasket (photo). The fuel injection engine application is shown.

18 Fuel injection pump and drive - removal

This Section is applicable to fuel injection models only.
1   Look for the timing marks on the fuel injection pump and camshaft drive pulleys. (photos)
2   Bend back the lockwasher securing the camshaft drive pulley

bolts. Undo and remove the three bolts and lift away the camshaft pulley and drivebelt. Note the bolts are offset to ensure correct fitment.
3   This photo shows the camshaft pulley assembly.
4   Bend back the lockwasher securing the fuel injection pump drive pulley nut.
5   Using suitable means as shown in this photograph lock the drive pulley. Then unscrew the nut, do not remove the nut completely.
6   Undo and remove the fuel injection pump securing nuts and bolts to the rear face of the timing cover.
7   Using a soft-faced hammer release the drive pulley from the taper on the pump shaft. (photo)
8   Unscrew the nut completely, and remove the lockwasher and drive pulley. Don't forget to support the injection pump. (photo)
9   Lift away the injection pump and remove the Woodruff key.

19 Timing chain tensioner - removal

Several types of tensioner have been fitted but all are secured in the same manner. Carefully undo and remove the two securing bolts and lift away the tensioner assembly. Whilst the bolts are being unscrewed hold the tensioner firmly as the slipper pad spring will be in action.

20 Timing gears and chain - removal

1   On fuel injection engines the camshaft gear securing bolts will have already been removed. Bear this in mind in the next paragraph.
2   Rotate the crankshaft until the timing marks on the two gears are in alignment with the bright links in the chain (this is for future reference).
3   Carburettor engines only. Bend back the lockwasher securing the camshaft gear bolts and then unscrew the three bolts. Remove the bolts and lockwasher.
4   Disengage the camshaft gear from the camshaft and detach the chain from the crankshaft gear. In this photograph (20:4) the timing chain tensioner is still in position. It can be removed before or after the timing gears and chain.

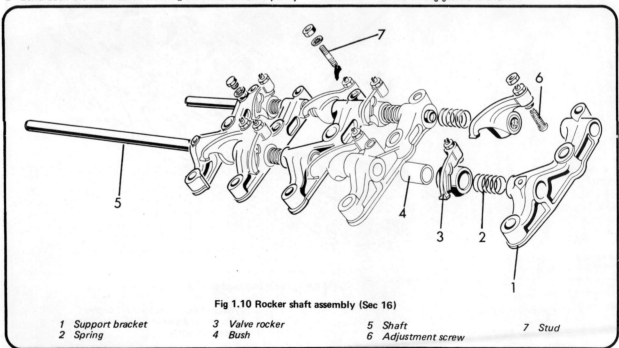

Fig 1.10 Rocker shaft assembly (Sec 16)

1 Support bracket	3 Valve rocker	5 Shaft	7 Stud
2 Spring	4 Bush	6 Adjustment screw	

17.3 Pulling off crankshaft pulley

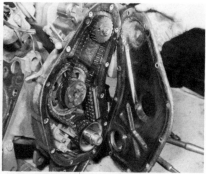
17.4 Removing front timing cover

18.1a Camshaft and injection pump drive chain and belt

18.1b Timing mark - fuel injection pump assembly

18.1c Timing mark - camshaft pulley

18.3 Lifting away camshaft pulley assembly

18.5 One method of locking fuel injection pump pulley

18.7 Releasing drive pulley from pump shaft taper

18.8 Lifting away drive pulley

21 Timing housing - removal

1 On fuel injection models a cast timing housing is fitted whereas on carburettor models a steel plate is used.
2 Undo and remove the timing housing/steel plate securing bolts and washers and lift away the housing. (photo)

22 Camshaft - removal

1 If the cam followers are still in position they should now be removed. Remember they should be kept in order. (photo)
2 Remove the distributor/oil pump driveshaft from its location in the side of the crankcase. It can be released from the camshaft drive-gear using a screwdriver in the slot to 'unwind' it. (photo)
3 Undo and remove the bolt and washer securing the camshaft

retaining plate (thrust plate) to the front face of the cylinder block. Lift away the camshaft retaining plate. (photo)
4 The camshaft may now be withdrawn through the front of the cylinder block. Take great care that the cam lobe peaks do not damage the camshaft bearings as the shaft is pulled forwards. The cam lobes may be sharp so watch the fingers. (photo)

23 Sump - removal

1 With the engine out of the car, first of all drain the oil (if this has not already been done) and then invert the engine.
2 Undo and remove the sump securing bolts, shakeproof and special plain washers.
3 The oil sump may now be lifted off the bottom of the crankcase. (photo)
4 If it is stuck quite firmly because a sealing compound has

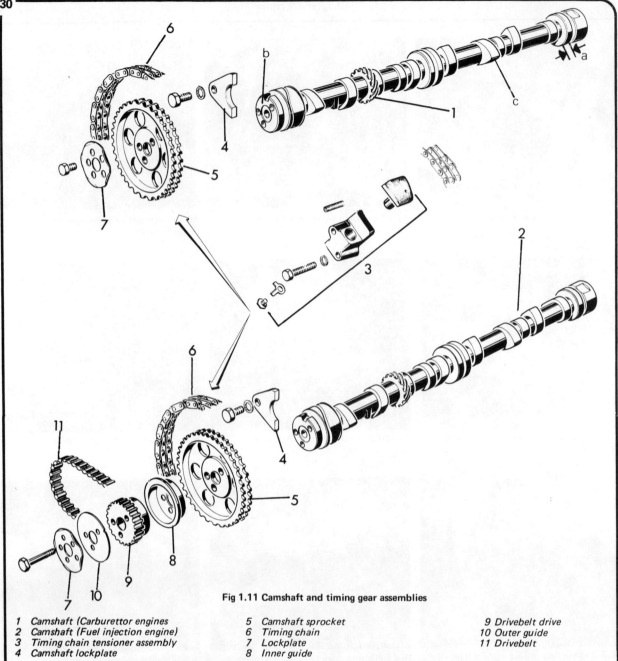

Fig 1.11 Camshaft and timing gear assemblies

1 Camshaft (Carburettor engines	5 Camshaft sprocket	9 Drivebelt drive
2 Camshaft (Fuel injection engine)	6 Timing chain	10 Outer guide
3 Timing chain tensioner assembly	7 Lockplate	11 Drivebelt
4 Camshaft lockplate	8 Inner guide	

Note: For letter caption see text - Section 58

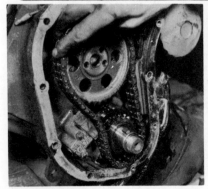

20.4 Lifting away camshaft gear and chain

21.2 Removal of timing housing

22.1 Withdrawing cam follower

Fig 1.12 Main bearing and sump assemblies

| 1 | Front main bearing | 3 | Rear main bearing | 5 | Main bearing cap bolt | 7 | Sump |
| 2 | Intermediate main bearing | 4 | Thrust washers | 6 | Gasket | 8 | Oil return pipe |

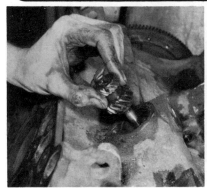

22.2 Removing distributor oil pump driveshaft

22.3 Camshaft retaining plate removal

22.4 Withdrawing camshaft

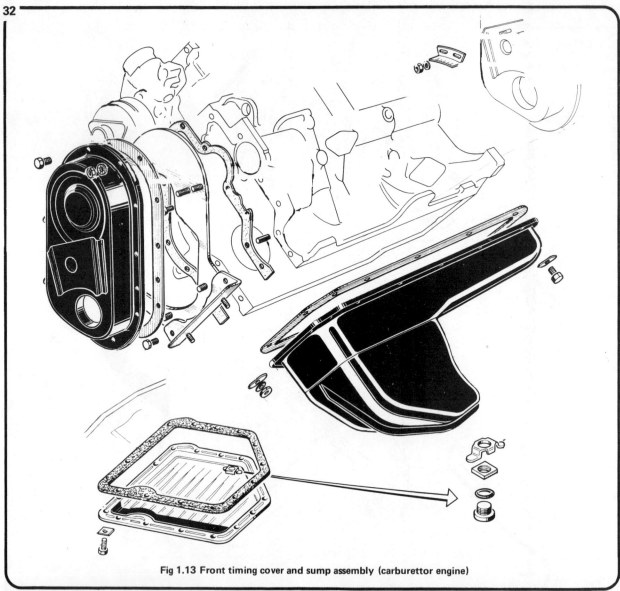

Fig 1.13 Front timing cover and sump assembly (carburettor engine)

23.3 Lifting away oil sump

24.2 Oil pump assembly removal

been previously used, it is in order to lever off in this case. Take care when a cast sump is used. The gasket should be removed and discarded in any case.

24 Oil pump - removal

1 With the sump removed, undo and remove the oil pump assembly securing bolts and washers.
2 Lift away the oil pump. (photo)
3 Note the 'O' ring on the underside of the oil pump body. This must be discarded and a new one obtained ready for re-fitting.

25 Pistons, connecting rods and big-end bearings - removal

1 With the cylinder head and sump removed, undo and remove the big-end nuts.
2 The connecting rods and pistons are lifted out from the top of the cylinder block.
3 Remove the big-end caps one at a time, taking care to keep them in the right order and the correct way round. Also ensure that the shell bearings are kept with their correct connecting rods and caps unless they are to be renewed. Normally the numbers 1 to 4 are stamped on adjacent sides of the big-end caps and connecting rods, indicating which cap fits on which rod and which way round that cap fits. If no numbers or lines can be

found then with a sharp screwdriver, or file, scratch mating marks across the joint from the rod to the cap. One line for connecting rod No. 1, two for connecting rod No. 2, and so on. This will ensure there is no confusion later as it is most important that the caps go back in the correct position on the connecting rods from which they were removed.
4 If the big-end caps are difficult to remove they may be gently tapped with a soft hammer.
5 To remove the shell bearings, press the bearing opposite the groove in both the connecting rod, and the connecting rod caps and bearings will slide out easily.
6 Withdraw the pistons and connecting rods upwards and ensure they are kept in the correct order for replacement in the same bore. Refit the connecting rod caps and bearings to the rods, if the bearings do not require renewal, to minimise the risk of getting the caps and rods muddled.

26 Gudgeon pins - removal

1 The gudgeon pins are retained in the pistons and rods with circlips.
2 Remove one circlip and push out the gudgeon pin.
3 If the gudgeon pin is tight in the piston boss heat the piston in boiling water for a few minutes. On removal the expansion of the aluminium should allow the gudgeon pin to slide out easily.
4 Make sure the pins are kept with the same piston for ease of refitting.

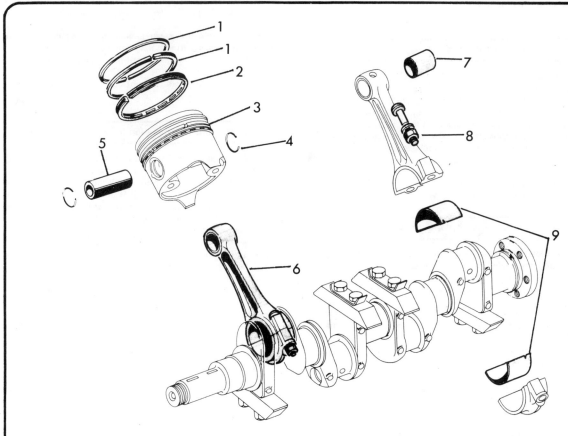

Fig 1.14 Piston and connecting rod assemblies

1 Compression ring	4 Circlip	6 Connecting rod	8 Big end cap nut bolt
2 Oil control ring	5 Gudgeon pin	7 Little end bush	9 Shell bearings
3 Piston			

27 Piston rings - removal

1 To remove the piston rings, slide them carefully over the top of the piston, taking care not to scratch the aluminium alloy. Never slide them off the bottom of the piston skirt. It is very easy to break the iron piston rings if they are pulled off roughly so this operation should be done with extreme caution. It is helpful to use an old feeler gauge.
2 Lift one end of the piston ring to be removed out of its groove and insert the end of the feeler gauge under it.
3 Turn the feeler gauge slowly round the piston and as the ring comes out of its groove apply slight upward pressure so that it rests on the land above. It can then be eased off the piston with the feeler gauge stopping it from slipping into any empty groove if it is any but the top piston ring that is being removed.

28 Flywheel - removal

1 With the clutch removed, mark the flywheel and crankshaft to ensure correct refitment.
2 Bend back the locking plate tabs and then undo and remove the flywheel securing bolts.
3 Lift away the locking plate and then remove the flywheel from the crankshaft flange. (photo)
Note: Some difficulty may be experienced in removing the bolts, by the rotation of the crankshaft every time pressure is put on the spanner. To lock the crankshaft, wedge a block of wood between the crankshaft and the side of the block inside the crankcase.

29 Main bearings and crankshaft - removal

1 Undo and remove the ten bolts that secure the five main bearing caps in place.
2 Lift out the bolts and remove the main bearing caps together with the bottom halves of each shell bearing. Take great care to keep the caps the correct way round and in their right order, and the shells in the right caps. If the caps are not marked make suitable scratch marks to ensure correct replacement.
3 Remove the semi-circular thrust washers fitted to the rear main bearing cap. Note that this bearing cap is dowelled to the crankcase. It also has lateral seals in the sides. (photo)
4 Remove the crankshaft by lifting it out from the crankcase.

30 Lubrication and crankcase ventilation system

1 A forced feed system of lubrication is used, with oil circulated around the engine by a pump drawing oil from the oil sump below the block.
2 The full-flow oil filter is mounted on the left-hand side of the cylinder block.
3 The oil pump is attached to the bottom of the cylinder block and is driven by means of a short shaft and skew gear off the camshaft.
4 Oil reaches the pump by a strainer and steel housing.
5 The oil pump is of the gear type incorporating driving and driven impellers.
6 A spring loaded oil pressure relief valve is fitted and a similar relief valve is incorporated in the external oil filter head which ensures the continued circulation of oil if the filter cartridge becomes blocked.
7 A semi closed positive ventilation system is fitted. A breather and filter is attached to the side of the crankcase (photo). This in turn is connected to the inlet manifold by a hose.

31 Oil filter - removal and replacement

1 The full-flow oil filter is attached to the front right-hand side

of the cylinder block. The element comes in the form of a disposable cartridge, the whole cartridge screwing directly onto a threaded union in the filter head.
2 To remove the filter simply unscrew the cartridge and throw it away.
3 Fitting a new cartridge is the reverse sequence to removal. Lightly lubricate the threads and screw on until hand-tight.

32 Oil pump - overhaul

If the oil pump is worn, or has covered a high mileage it is best to purchase an exchange reconditioned unit as a good oil pump is at the very heart of long engine life. Generally speaking an exchange or overhauled pump should be fitted at a major engine reconditioning.

33 Engine front mountings - removal and replacement

1 With time the bonded rubber insulators, one on each of the front mountings, will perish causing undue vibration and noise from the engine. Severe juddering when reversing or when moving off from rest is also likely and is a further sign of worn mounting rubbers.
2 The front mounting rubber insulators can be changed with the engine in the car.
3 Apply the handbrake firmly, jack-up the front of the car and place stands under the front of the car.
4 Lower the jack, place a suitable wooden block on the jack saddle and place the jack under the oil sump to take the weight of the engine.
5 Undo and remove the lower engine mounting nut, and the two upper mounting securing bolts, spring and plain washers.
6 Raise the engine on the jack until the mounting can be lifted away.
7 Refitting the front engine mounting is the reverse sequence to removal.

34 Engine components - examination for wear (general)

When the engine has been stripped down and all parts properly cleaned decisions have to be made as to what needs renewal and the following Sections tell the examiner what to look for. In any border line case it is always best to decide in favour of a new part. Even if a part may still be serviceable its life will have been reduced by wear and the degree of trouble needed to replace it in the future must be taken into consideration. However, these things are relative and it depends on whether a quick 'survival' job is being done or whether the car as a whole is being regarded as having many thousands of miles of useful and economical life remaining.

35 Crankshaft - examination and renovation

1 Look at the main bearing journals and the crankpins and if there are any scratches or score marks then the shaft will need regrinding. Such conditions will nearly always be accompanied by similar deterioration in the matching bearing shells.
2 Each bearing journal should also be round and can be checked with a micrometer or caliper gauge around the periphery at several points. If there is more than 0.001 in (0.0254 mm) of ovality regrinding is necessary.
3 A Peugeot garage or motor engineering specialist will be able to decide to what extent regrinding is necessary and also supply the special undersize shell bearings to match whatever may need grinding off.
4 Before taking the crankshaft for regrinding check also the cylinder bores and pistons as it may be advantageous to have the whole engine done together.

28.3 Removal of flywheel

29.3 Pulling away rear main bearing cap

30.7 Removal of breather and filter

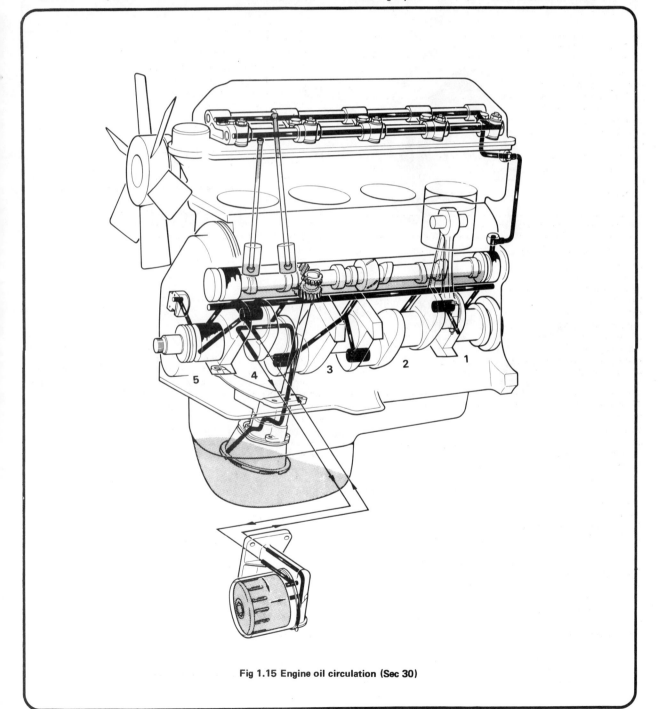

Fig 1.15 Engine oil circulation (Sec 30)

36 Crankshaft, main and big-end bearings - examination and renovation

1 With careful servicing and regular oil and filter changes bearings will last for a very long time but they can still fail for unforeseen reasons. With big-end bearings the indication is a regular rhythmic load knocking from the crankcase. The frequency depends on engine speed and is particularly noticeable when the engine is under load. This symptom is accompanied by a fall in oil pressure although this is not normally noticeable unless an oil pressure gauge is fitted. Main bearing failure is usually indicated by serious vibration, particularly at higher engine revolutions, accompanied by a more significant drop in oil pressure and a 'rumbling' noise.

2 Bearing shells in good condition have bearing surfaces with a smooth, even matt silver/grey colour all over. Worn bearings will show patches of a different colour when the bearing metal has worn away and exposed the underlay. Damaged bearings will be pitted or scored. It is always well worthwhile fitting new shells as their cost is relatively low. If the crankshaft is in good condition it is merely a question of obtaining another set of standard size. A reground crankshaft will need new bearing shells as a matter of course.

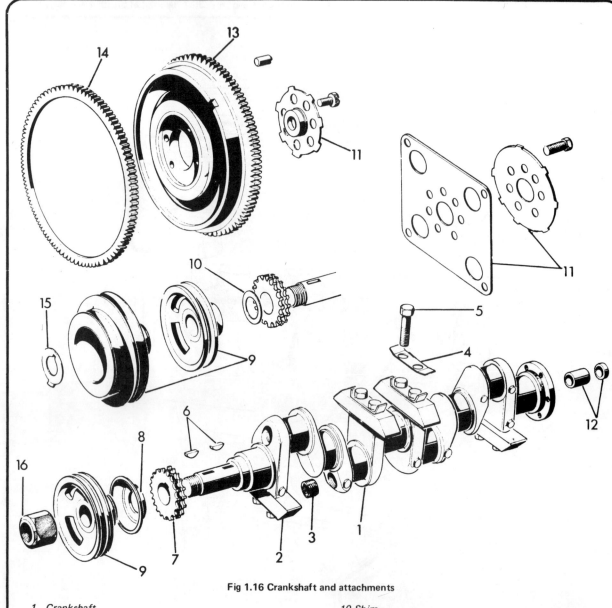

Fig 1.16 Crankshaft and attachments

1 Crankshaft
2 Counterweight
3 Plug
4 Lockwasher
5 Bolt
6 Key
7 Crankshaft sprocket
8 Oil thrower
9 Crankshaft pulley (alternatives shown - NOT interchangeable between engines)
10 Shim
11 Lockplates (alternatives shown - NOT interchangeable between engines)
12 Bush (alternatives shown - NOT interchangeable between engines)
13 Flywheel assembly
14 Starter ring gear
15 Lockwasher
16 Nut

37 Cylinder bores - examination and renovation

1 A new cylinder is perfectly round and the walls parallel throughout its length. The action of the piston tends to wear the walls at right angles to the gudgeon pin due to side thrust. This wear takes place principally on that section of the cylinder swept by the piston rings.

2 It is possible to get an indication of bore wear by removing the cylinder heads with the engine still in the car. With the piston down in the bore first signs of wear can be seen and felt just below the top of the bore where the top piston ring reaches and there will be a noticeable lip. If there is no lip it is fairly reasonable to expect that bore wear is not severe and any lack of compression or excessive oil consumption is due to worn or broken piston rings or pistons (see the next Section).

3 If it is possible to obtain a bore measuring micrometer measure the bore in the thrust plane below the lip and again at the bottom of the cylinder in the same plane. If the difference is more than 0.003 in (0.0762 mm) then it is desirable to fit new liners and matching piston assemblies. Similarly, a difference of 0.003 in (0.0762 mm) or more across the bore diameter is a sign of ovality and calls for the same treatment.

4 Any bore which is significantly scratched or scored will need renewing. This symptom usually indicates that the piston or rings are damaged also in the cylinder. In the event of only one cylinder being in need of liner renewal it is considered best for a complete set of four be fitted.

5 Renewal of the liners is not a difficult job provided that a good puller is available to remove the old ones. If the crankshaft is undergoing regrinding also, it is a good idea to let the same firm renew the liners, renovate and reassemble the crankshaft and pistons to the block. A reputable firm normally gives a guarantee for such work.

38 Pistons and piston rings - examination and renovation

1 Worn pistons and rings can usually be diagnosed when the symptoms of excessive oil consumption and lower compression occur and are sometimes, though not always, associated with worn cylinder bores. Compression testers that fit into the spark plug hole are available and these can indicate where low compression is occurring. Wear usually accelerates the more it is left so when the symptoms occur early action can possibly save the expense of a rebore.

2 Another symptom of piston wear is piston slack - a knocking noise from the crankcase not to be confused with big-end

40.2 A badly worn cam follower and cam lobe

bearing failure. It can be heard clearly at low engine speed when there is no load (idling for example) and is much less audible when the engine speed increases. Piston wear usually occurs in the skirt or lower end of the piston and is indicated by vertical streaks in the worn area which is always on the thrust side. It can also be seen where the skirt thickness is different.

3 Piston ring wear can be checked by first removing the rings from the pistons. Then place the rings in the cylinder bores from the top, pushing them down about 1.5 inches (38.1 mm) with the head of a piston (from which the rings were removed), so that they rest square in the cylinder. Then measure the gap at the ends of the ring with a feeler gauge. If this exceeds 0.55 mm for the two top compression rings and 0.50 mm for each side of the expander ring then they need renewal.

4 The grooves in which the rings locate in the piston can also become enlarged in use. The clearance between ring and piston, in the groove, should now exceed the maximum tolerances as given in the Specifications at the beginning of this Chapter.

5 However, it is rare that a piston is only worn in the ring grooves and the need to replace them for this fault alone is hardly ever encountered.

39 Connecting rods and gudgeon pins - examination and renovation

1 Gudgeon pins are retained in the piston bosses by circlips at each end. Neither the gudgeon pins or circlips need replacement unless the pistons are being changed, in which case the new pistons would automatically be supplied with new gudgeon pins and circlips.

2 Connecting rods are not subject to wear but in extreme circumstances such as engine seizure they could be distorted. Such conditions may be visually apparent but where doubt exists they should be changed. Do not attempt to straighten a bent connecting rod by hammering.

3 The bearing caps should also be examined for indications of filing down which may have been attempted by a previous owner in the mistaken idea that bearing slackness could be remedied in this way. If there are such signs the connecting rod should be renewed.

40 Camshaft and camshaft bearings - examination and renovation

1 The camshaft bearing bushes should be examined for signs of scoring and pitting. If they need renewal they will have to be dealt with professionally as, although it may be relatively easy to remove the old bushes, the correct fitting of new ones requires special tools. If they are not fitted evenly and square they will wear in a very short time. See your Peugeot garage or local engineering specialists for this work.

2 The camshaft itself may show signs of wear on the bearing journals, cam lobes or the skew gear. The main decision to take is what degree of wear justifies replacement, which is costly. Any signs of scoring or damage to the bearing journals cannot be reground. Renewal of the whole camshaft is the only solution. Similarly, excessive wear on the skew gear which can be seen where the distributor driveshaft teeth mesh will mean renewal of the whole camshaft. (photo)

3 The cam lobes themselves may show signs of ridging or pitting on the high points. If ridging is light then it may be possible to smooth it out with fine emery. The cam lobes however, are surface hardened and once this is penetrated wear will be very rapid thereafter.

41 Cam followers - examination

The faces of the cam followers which bear on the camshaft should show no signs of pitting, scoring or other forms of wear. Thoroughly clean them out, removing all traces of sludge. It is most unlikely that the sides of the tappets will prove worn, but, if they are a very loose fit in their bores and can be rocked readily they should be exchanged for new units. It is very unusual to find any wear in the tappets, and any wear present is likely to occur only at very high mileages (see photo 40:2)

42 Valves and valve seats - examination and renovation

1   Examine the heads of the valves for pitting and burning, especially the heads of the exhaust valves. The valve seatings should be examined at the same time. If the pitting on valve and seat is very slight, the marks can be removed by grinding the seats and valves together with coarse, and then fine, grinding paste. Where bad pitting has occurred to the valve seats, it will be necessary to recut them and fit new valves. If the valve seats are so worn that they cannot be recut, then it will be necessary to fit new valve seat inserts. These latter two jobs should be entrusted to the local Peugeot garage or engineering works. In practice, it is very seldom that the seats are so badly worn that they require renewal. Normally, it is the exhaust valve that is too badly worn for replacement, and the owner can easily purchase a new set of valves and match them to the seats by valve grinding.
2   Valve grinding is carried out as follows:
    Smear a trace of coarse carborundum paste on the seat face and apply a suction grinder tool to the valve head. With semi-rotary motion, grind the valve head to its seat, lifting the valve occasionally to redistribute the grinding paste (photo). When a dull matt even surface finish is produced on both the valve seat and the valve, then wipe off the paste and repeat the process with fine carborundum paste, lifting and turning the valve to redistribute the paste as before. A light spring placed under the valve head will greatly ease this operation. When a smooth unbroken ring of light grey matt finish is produced, on both valve and valve seat faces, the grinding operation is completed.
3   Scrape away all carbon from the valve head and the valve stem. Carefully clean away every trace of grinding compound, taking care to leave none in the ports or in the valve guides. Clean the valves and valve seats with a paraffin soaked rag, then with a clean rag, and finally, if an air line is available, blow the valves, valve guides and valve ports clean.

43 Timing gears and chain - examination and renovation

Examine the teeth on both the crankshaft gearwheel and the camshaft gearwheel for wear. Each tooth forms an inverted 'V' with the gearwheel periphery, and if worn, the side of each tooth, ie; one side of the inverted 'V' will be concave when compared with the other. If any sign of wear is present the gearwheels must be renewed.

Examine the links of the chain for side slackness, and renew the chain if any slackness is noticeable when compared with a new chain. It is a sensible precaution to renew the chain at about 30,000 miles (48,000 km) and at a lesser mileage if the engine is stripped down for a major overhaul. The actual rollers on a very badly worn chain may be slightly grooved.

44 Timing chain tensioner - examination and renovation

1   If the timing chain is badly worn it is more than likely that the tensioner will be too.
2   Examine the side of the tensioner which bears against the chain and renew it if it is grooved or ridged.

45 Rockers and rocker shaft - examination and renovation

Remove the threaded plug from the end of the rocker shaft with a screwdriver and thoroughly clean out the shaft. As it acts as the oil passage for the valve gear also, ensure the oil holes in it are quite clear after having cleaned them out. Check the shaft for

straightness by rolling it on the bench. It is most unlikely that it will deviate from normal, but if it does, then a judicious attempt must be made to straighten it. If this is not successful, purchase a new shaft. The surface of the shaft should be free from any worn ridges caused by the rocker arms. If any wear is present, renew the shaft. Wear is only likely to have occurred if the rocker shaft oil holes have become blocked.

Check the rocker arms for wear of the rocker bushes, for wear at the rocker arm face which bears on the valve stem, and for wear of the adjusting ball ended screws. Wear in the rocker arm bush can be checked by gripping the rocker arm tip and holding the rocker arm in place on the shaft, noting if there is any lateral rocker arm shake. If shake is present, and the arms are very loose on the shaft, a new bush or rocker arm must be fitted.

Check the tip of the rocker arm where it bears on the valve head for cracking or serious wear on the case hardening. If none is present, re-use the rocker arm. Check the lower half of the ball on the end of the rocker arm adjusting screw. On high performance engines, wear on the ball and top of the pushrod is easily noted by the unworn 'pip' which fits in the small central oil hole on the ball. The larger this 'pip' the more wear has taken place to both the ball and the pushrod. Check the pushrods for straightness by rolling them on the bench. Renew any that are bent.

46 Starter ring gear - examination and renovation

1   If the teeth on the starter ring gear are badly worn or some are missing, then it will be necessary to remove the ring gear. The old ring can be removed from the flywheel by cutting a notch between two teeth with a hacksaw and then splitting it with a cold chisel. Note which way round the ring gear is fitted!
2   To fit a new ring gear requires heating the ring to 400°F (204°C). This can be done by polishing four equally spaced sections of the gear, laying it on a suitable heat resistant surface (such as fire bricks) and heating it evenly with a blow torch or lamp until the polished areas turn a light yellow tinge. Do not overheat, or the hard wearing properties will be lost. When hot enough place the gear in position quickly, tapping it home if necessary and let it cool naturally without quenching in any way.

47 Cylinder head and piston crowns - decarbonisation

With the cylinder head off, carefully remove with a wire brush and blunt scraper all traces of carbon deposits from the combustion spaces and the ports. The valve head stems and valve guides should also be freed from any carbon deposits. Wash the combustion spaces and ports down with petrol and scrape the cylinder head surface free of any foreign matter with the side of a steel rule, or a similar article.

Clean the pistons and top of the cylinder bores. If the pistons are still in the block, then it is essential that great care is taken to ensure that no carbon gets into the cylinder bores as this could scratch the cylinder walls or cause damage to the piston and rings. To ensure this does not happen, first turn the crankshaft so that two of the pistons are at the top of their bores. Stuff rag into the other two bores, or seal them off with paper and masking tape. The waterways should also be covered with small pieces of masking tape to prevent particles of carbon entering the cooling system and damaging the water pump.

There are two schools of thought as to how much carbon should be removed from the piston crown. One school recommends that a ring of carbon should be left around the edge of the piston and on the cylinder bore wall as an aid to low oil consumption. Although this is probably true for early engines with worn bores, on later engines the thought of the second school can be applied, which is that for effective decarbonisation, all traces of carbon should be removed.

If all traces of carbon are to be removed, press a little grease

42.2 Grinding in valve

Fig 1.17 Spark plug tube removal

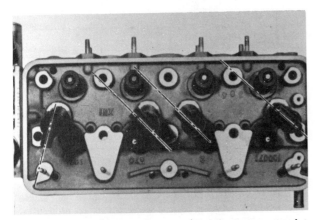

Fig 1.18 Spark plug tube replacement (The plug caps must point in the directions shown)

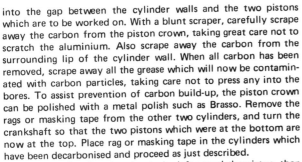

Fig 1.19 Refitting starter ring gear (Sec 46)

1 Firm base with support lip

into the gap between the cylinder walls and the two pistons which are to be worked on. With a blunt scraper, carefully scrape away the carbon from the piston crown, taking great care not to scratch the aluminium. Also scrape away the carbon from the surrounding lip of the cylinder wall. When all carbon has been removed, scrape away all the grease which will now be contaminated with carbon particles, taking care not to press any into the bores. To assist prevention of carbon build-up, the piston crown can be polished with a metal polish such as Brasso. Remove the rags or masking tape from the other two cylinders, and turn the crankshaft so that the two pistons which were at the bottom are now at the top. Place rag or masking tape in the cylinders which have been decarbonised and proceed as just described.

If a ring of carbon is going to be left round the piston, then this can be helped by inserting an old piston ring into the top of the bore to rest on the piston and ensure that carbon is not accidentally removed. Check that there are no particles of carbon in the cylinder bores. Decarbonising is now complete.

48 Valve guides - inspection

Examine the valve guides internally for wear. If the valves are a very loose fit in the guides and there is the slightest suspicion of lateral rocking using a new valve then the guide will have to be reamed and oversize valves fitted. This is a job best left to the local Peugeot garage.

49 Sump - inspection

Wash out the oil sump in petrol and wipe dry. Inspect the exterior for signs of damage or excessive rust. If evident, a new oil sump must be obtained. To ensure an oil tight joint scrape away all traces of the old gasket from the cylinder block mating face.

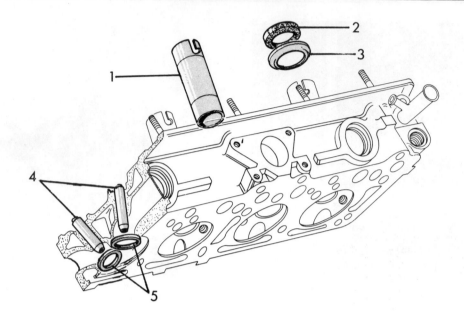

Fig 1.20 Cylinder head valve guides, seats and spark plug tubes

1 Tube   2 Gasket   3 Shoulder   4 Valve guide   5 Valve seat

50 Engine - reassembly (general)

All components of the engine must be cleaned of oil, sludge and old gaskets and the working area should also be cleared and clean. In addition to the normal range of good quality socket spanners and general tools which are essential the following must be available before reassembly begins:

1 *Complete set of new gaskets*
2 *Supply of clean rags*
3 *Clean oil can full of engine oil*
4 *Torque wrench*
5 *All new spare parts as necessary.*

It should be noted that the engine shown in the photographs is of the fuel injection type and, as will have been noted during dismantling, there are some minor differences to the carburettor type. Provided that care was taken to note any differences between the text and the actual engine being worked upon were noted during dismantling no problems will arise. In some instances engine type numbers are given in the text. Identify the engine being worked upon from the data given at the beginning of this manual whenever these occur.

51 Crankshaft - reassembly

1 If the counterweights were removed for any reason their correct locations will have been noted during removal. **Do not** interchange these under any circumstances.
2 Hold the crankshaft in a large bench vice and place the counterweights in position.
3 Refit the counterweight tab washers and bolts and tighten the bolts to a torque wrench setting of 49 lb f ft (6.75 kg f m).
4 Bend up the tab washers, so locking the bolts.
5 If the lubrication hole plugs were removed, obtain new plugs, smear the threads with a suitable sealing compound and refit them to the crankshaft.
6 Tighten the plugs to a torque wrench setting of 40 lb f ft (5.5 kg f m) and lock using a centre punch.

52 Crankshaft - replacement

1 Ensure that the crankcase is thoroughly clean and that all oilways are clear. A thin twist drill or a nylon pipe cleaner is useful for cleaning them out. If possible blow out with compressed air.
2 Treat the crankshaft in the same fashion, and then inject engine oil into the crankshaft oilways.
3 Commence work of rebuilding the engine by replacing the crankshaft and main bearings.
4 Wipe the bearing shell locations in the crankcase with a soft non-fluffy rag.
5 If the old main bearing shells are to be replaced (not to do so is a false economy unless they are virtually new) fit the five upper halves of the main bearing shells to their location in the crankcase. (photo)
6 Apply a little grease to the thrust washer halves and position on the crankshaft journal bearing shell sides. The lubrication slots face the crankshaft. (photo)
7 Lubricate the bearing shell and carefully lower the crankshaft into position. (photo)
8 Fit the bearing half shells onto each main bearing cap having made quite sure that their locations are clean and lay beside the crankcase. (photo)
9 With the rear main bearing, on XN1, XN2 and XM7 engines the diameter of the rear main bearing is 54.92 mm in place of 51.18 mm so make sure the correct bearings have been obtained. There are corresponding differences in the overall width of the thrust washers as well. For these engines they should be 61.5 mm.
10 Apply a little grease to the thrust washer halves and position on the rear main bearing shell.
11 Fit the main bearing caps in position. The rear one should not yet have the lateral seals fitted.
12 Replace the 10 securing bolts and tighten to a torque wrench setting of 55 lb f ft (7.5 kg f m) and check that the crankshaft rotates freely. Should it be stiff to turn or possess high spots a most careful inspection must be made with a micrometer, preferably by a qualified mechanic to get to the root of the trouble. It is very seldom that any trouble of this nature will be experienced

52.5 Fitting crankshaft main bearing shell

52.6 Locating thrust washers

52.7 Lowering crankshaft into position

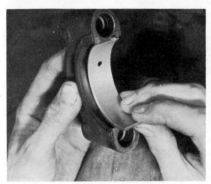

52.8 Fitting shell bearing to main bearing cap

52.13 Lateral seal positioned in rear main bearing end cap

52.14 Refitting rear main bearing end cap

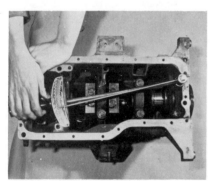

52.15 Tightening end cap bolts

Fig 1.21 Piston and connecting rod components (Sec 53)

when fitting the crankshaft.

13 Next test the crankshaft endfloat. Using a screwdriver ease the crankshaft fully forwards and with feeler gauges check the clearances between the crankshaft journal side and the thrust washer. The clearance should be between 0.08 mm and 0.20 mm. If the endfloat exceeds 0.20 mm:

  a) On XM engines fit new thrust washers.
  b) On XM/2F, XM7, XN1 and XN2 replace the thrust washers using one of the oversize washers. These are available in 2.40 mm, 2.45 mm and 2.50 mm sizes.

13 When all is well, remove the rear main bearing cap and install the two lateral seals. (photo)

14 Carefully smear a jointing compound on the main bearing cap to crankcase mating faces and refit the cap taking care not to dislodge the seals. (photo)

15 Tighten the securing bolts to a torque wrench setting of 55 lb f ft (7.5 kg f m). (photo)

16 Again test for freedom of crankshaft rotation and if all is well test, using feeler gauges that the rear main bearing cap is well seated in the cylinder block.

17 Using a sharp knife cut the lateral seals off 0.5 mm from the block surface.

53 Pistons and connecting rods - reassembly

1 The gudgeon pins are retained in the pistons and connecting rods with circlips.

2 Insert one circlip and with the piston correctly positioned in the connecting rod push in the gudgeon pin until it abuts with the circlip.

3 If the gudgeon pin is a tight fit in the piston which can happen when new pistons are being fitted, heat the pistons in boiling water for a few minutes before sliding in the gudgeon pin.

4 The 'AV' mark and arrow on the piston crown must be at right-angles to the oil thrower.

5 When new liners and pistons are being fitted it is important to keep them in their matched pairs. This is of course also applicable when original parts are being refitted.

6 Refit the second gudgeon pin retaining circlip and double check that both circlips are correctly seated.

54 Piston rings - replacement

1 Check that the piston ring grooves and oilways are thoroughly clean and unblocked. Piston rings must always be fitted over the head of the piston and never from the bottom.

2 The easiest method to use when fitting piston rings is to wrap a thin feeler gauge or piece of shim steel around the top of the piston and place the rings one at a time, starting with the bottom oil control ring over the feeler gauge.

3 The feeler gauge, complete with ring can then be slid down the piston, over the other piston ring grooves until the correct groove is reached. The piston ring is then slid gently off the feeler gauge into the groove.

4 An alternative method is to fit rings by holding them slightly open with the thumbs and both of the index fingers. This method requires a steady hand and great care as it is easy to open the ring too much and break it.

5 It should be noted that gaps of the 'perfect circle' oil scraper (top and bottom sections) must be fitted 20-50 mm either side of the centre of the gudgeon pin hole. The gap for the centre portion of the oil control ring should be set to the centre of the gudgeon pin hole (Fig. 1.22).

6 The gaps for the two compression rings should be set to 120° either side of the centre portion of the oil control ring.

55 Liners - replacement

As was previously stated it is best if the liners are renewed by the local Peugeot garage or engineering works. It is possible for this work to be carried out by an enthusiast but then a dial indicator gauge must be available. Two types of liners are used and once again engine identification is important.

Free expanding liners (XM, KF6 and KF5 engines)

1 With the cylinder block liner locations very clean first fit the liners without their seals. Remember do not mix up the pistons and liners as they are matched pairs.

2 Using a dial indicator gauge check that the liner head (top) protrusion does not exceed 0.07 mm (0.003 in). If it does, remove and look for dirt or other causes.

3 Remove the liners again, fit new seals and refit the liners.

4 Temporarily retain the liners in position with bolts and large washers screwed into the cylinder head mating face.

Compressed liners (XN1, XN2 and XM7 engines)

1 With the cylinder block liner locations very clean first insert the liners without their base gaskets. The flats on the upper shoulders of the liners 1 and 2 also 3 and 4 must be parallel on XN1 and XN2 engines. (Fig. 1.25)

2 Using a dial gauge check each liner at 90° intervals noting the highest point in each case. The maximum difference between

two diametrically opposed points must be less than 0.07 mm (0.003 in).

3 If this figure is exceeded find the reason - usually dirt - or try changing the position of the liners.

4 When all is well mark the liners with their respective cylinder locations.

5 Select a base gasket for each liner which will give a protrusion of as near to 0.11 mm (0.0045 in) as possible. Only use one gasket per liner.

6 Fit the gasket to the liner, engaging the inner tabs in the groove in the liner.

7 Position the tab with the reference mark on it at 90° to the flat and then fit the liners to the cylinder block with the tabs in the position shown in Fig. 1.26

8 Push down on the liners and with the dial indicator gauge check the protrusion at the highest point for all four liners. This should be about 0.11 mm (0.0045 in).

9 The maximum difference between two diametrically opposed points must still be less than 0.07 mm (0.003 in).

10 The maximum deviation in liner protrusion between two adjoining liners must not exceed 0.04 mm (0.0018 in); should this occur select a new base gasket.

11 Retain the liners in position with bolts and large washers screwed into the cylinder head mating face.

56 Pistons - replacement

The pistons complete with connecting rods can now be fitted to the cylinder bores in the following manner:

1 With a wad of clean rag wipe the cylinder bores clean.

2 The pistons complete with connecting rods, are fitted to their bores from the top of the cylinder block.

3 Check the location of the ring gaps as described in Section 54, paragraphs 5 and 6.

4 Well lubricate the piston and rings with engine oil.

5 Fit a universal piston ring compressor and prepare to fit the first piston into the bore. Make sure it is the correct piston/connecting rod assembly for that particular bore, that the connecting rod is the correct way round and that the 'AV' and arrow mark is facing the front of the engine.

6 Again lubricate the piston skirt and insert into the bore up to the bottom of the piston ring compressor. (photo)

7 Gently, but firmly, tap the piston through the piston ring compressor and into the cylinder bore with a wooden or plastic hammer.

57 Connecting rods to crankshaft - reassembly

1 Wipe clean the connecting rod half of the big-end bearing cap, and the underside of the shell bearing. Then fit the shell bearing in position with its locating tongue engaged with the corresponding cutout in the rod. (photo)

2 If the bearings are nearly new and are being refitted then ensure they are replaced in their correct locations on the correct rods.

3 Generously lubricate the crankpin journals with engine oil and turn the crankshaft so that the crankpin is in the most advantagous positon for the connecting rod to be drawn onto it. (photo)

4 Wipe clean the connecting rod bearing cap and back of the shell bearing and fit the shell into positon ensuring that the locating tongue at the back of the bearing engages with the locating groove in the connecting rod cap.

5 Generously lubricate the shell bearing and offer up the connecting rod bearing cap to the connecting rod. (photo)

6 Fit new connecting rod nuts and tighten to a torque wrench setting of 29 lb f ft (4 kg f m). (photo)

7 When all the connecting rods have been fitted, rotate the crankshaft to check that everything is free and that there are no high spots causing binding. The bottom half is now nearly built-up.

Fig 1.22 Correct location for oil control ring gaps (Sec 54)

a) Centre line through gudgeon pin

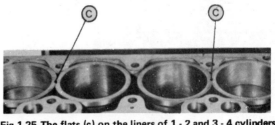

Fig 1.25 The flats (c) on the liners of 1 - 2 and 3 - 4 cylinders must be parallel (Sec 55)

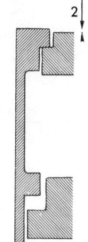

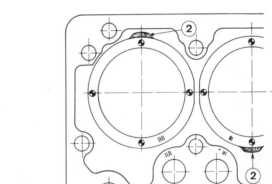

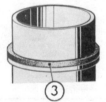

Fig 1.23 Liner protrusion check (Sec 55) (XM, KF6, KF5 engine)

1   *Dial indicator and stand*
2   *Protrusion to be measured*
3   *Seal*

Fig 1.26 Correct cylinder liner gasket fitment (Sec 55)

1   *Inner tabs*
2   *Reference mark on outer tab*
a) *Flat on liner*

HIGHEST POINT ON THE LINER (Without gasket)	GASKET TO BE FITTED	
	Reference	Thickness
from 0.036 to 0.06		0.050
from 0.011 to 0.035		0.075
from 0 to 0.010		0.100
Negative reading		0.125

Fig 1.24 Cylinder liner gasket identification (sec 55) (XN1, XN2 and XM7 engine)   *Note Measurements in metric units*

56.6 Inserting connecting rod into bore

57.1 Fitting big-end shell bearing to connecting rod

57.3 Connecting rod attached to crankshaft

57.5 Fitting big-end bearing end cap

57.6 Tightening big-end bolts

58.2 Replacing camshaft

58.3a Locating camshaft retainer

58.3b Camshaft retainer in position

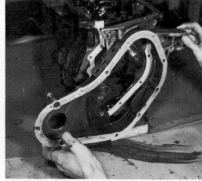
58.5 Refitting timing housing

58.6 Timing housing securing nut and two washers

Fig 1.27 A Camshaft and crankshaft timing (Sec 59)
1 Camshaft   2 Crankshaft

58 Camshaft - replacement

1 Important:
   I On some XM engine camshafts, the groove 'a' (Fig. 1.11) is 8 mm wide instead of 5 mm to ensure correct lubrication of the rocker assembly. Camshafts with the reference 'XN1' or 'XN2' at 'b' (Fig. 1.11) with the boss 'c' (Fig. 1.11) can be fitted on 'XM.', 'KF6' or 'KF5' engines PROVIDED that BLACK valve springs are fitted.
   II On USA models the camshaft marked 'AP' or 'US' at 'b' (Fig. 1.11) is to be used for 1969, 70, 71 and 72 models (emission control standards) and YELLOW valve springs must be fitted.
   III The camshaft marked 'XN1' at 'b' (Fig. 1.11) and with a shoulder at 'c' (Fig. 1.11) is to be used for 1973 models and BLACK valve springs MUST be fitted.
   IV For other USA models consult the Peugeot garage for the latest information.

2 Wipe the camshaft and bearings clean and then lift the camshaft through the bearings taking care not to damage the bearing surfaces with the sharp edges of the cam lobes. Also take care not to cut the fingers. (photo)
3 With the camshaft in position locate the retaining plate (thrust plate) and secure with the bolt and shakeproof washer which should be tightened to a torque wrench setting of 12.0 lb f ft (1.7 kg f m).
4 On carburettor models fit a new paper gasket and then the steel plate. Tighten the retaining bolts securely.
5 Fuel injection engines (KF6, KF5 and XN2):
   Instead of a steel plate being fitted to the front of the cylinder block a timing housing is used. When securing the housing there should be a gap of 0.55 mm or 2.5 mm between the boss and the camshaft end. The gap differential depends on the individual casting. (photo)
6 Do not forget the one retaining nut, shakeproof and plain washer. (photo)

59 Timing gears and chain - replacement

1 When refitting the timing chain round the gearwheels and then to the engine, the bright links in the chain and lines must line up, as was noted during dismantling, on an imaginary line passing through each gearwheel centre.
2 The camshaft gearwheel can only be fitted on one way because the securing bolts are offset to each other.
3 By trial-and-error, line up the crankshaft, and camshaft gearwheels on timing chain rotating the crankshaft and camshaft as necessary until the condition in paragraph 1 has been met.
4 Insert the key into the crankshaft keyway and slide on the crankshaft gearwheel. At the same time take the weight of the camshaft gearwheel.

5 Offer up the locking washer and bolts to the camshaft sprocket and lightly tighten the three bolts.
6 Recheck that the timing marks on the gearwheels and bright links in the chain line up correctly.
7 Tighten the camshaft gearwheel securing bolts to a torque wrench setting of 16 lb f ft (2.25 kg f m) and lock by bending up the locking washer. (photo)

60 Timing chain tensioner - replacement

Several types of tensioner have been fitted but the commonest is that made by Reynolds. In all cases the action of the spring must be neutralised before fitting.
1 If the tensioner is assembled, separate the two halves and with an Allen key inserted into the adjuster turn clockwise to release the spring. Remove the Allen key. (photo)
2 Reassemble the tensioner and offer up to the front of the engine. Push hard on the tensioner body and insert the two securing bolts which should now be fully tightened. (photos)
3 The alternative method is to remove the plug bolt in the tensioner body and tension the spring using the Allen key. Then assemble to the engine, release the spring tension and refit the plug. This is a little difficult on fuel injection engines with the large timing cover because space is limited.

61 Oil pump and sump - replacement

1 Wipe the mating faces of the oil pump and cylinder block clean and fit a new 'O' ring seal to the pump mounting face. (photo)
2 Make sure the two dowel pins are in position and place the oil pump onto the cylinder block. Should the distributor/oil pump drive shaft be in position ensure that the drive dogs engage. (photo)
3 Refit the oil pump securing bolts and tighten to a torque wrench setting of 7.25 lb f ft (1 kg f m).
4 Clean the flanges of the sump and underside of the cylinder block.

Important
   a) Pressed steel or aluminium sump pans which do not have an oil return passage MUST NOT be fitted to 'XM' engines with a rear main bearing cap which incorporates hole 'a' (Fig. 1.27B).
   b) A special rubber/asbestos gasket must be used on USA models fitted with an alloy sump pan.

5 Fit a new gasket and carefully lower the sump into position. (photo)
6 Replace the bolts, special plain washers and shakeproof washers and tighten in a progressive and diagonal manner to a final torque wrench setting of 7.25 lb f ft (1.0 kg f m) (photo)

59.7 Camshaft and timing chain refitted

60.1 Releasing tensioner spring

60.2a Tensioner ready for refitting

60.2b Tensioner positioned ready for inserting securing bolts

61.1 Do not forget the 'O' ring seal

61.2 Oil pump replacement

61.5 Replacing sump

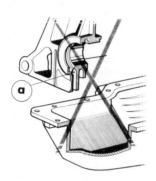

Fig 1.27B Oil sumps in pressed steel or aluminium, which do not have an oil return passage, MUST NOT be fitted on XM engines with a rear main bearing cap incorporating the hole (a) (Sec 61)

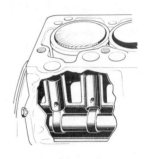

Fig 1.28 Cam lobe position for No 1 piston to be at TDC on firing stroke (Sec 62)

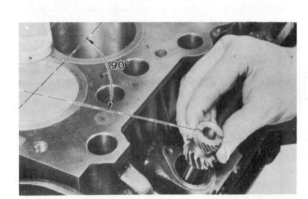

Fig 1.29 Distributor/oil pump driveshaft replacement (XM and XM7 engines) (Sec 62)

Fig 1.30 Distributor/oil pump driveshaft replacement (KF6, KF5, XN1 and XM2 engines) (Sec 62)

62 Distributor/oil pump driveshaft - replacement

Turn the engine until No 1 piston is at TDC (top-dead-centre) on the firing stroke. This may be seen by looking down the tappet holes until the position of No 1 cylinder camshaft lobes are both in the positions shown in Fig. 1.28.

XM and XM7 engines

1 Refer to Fig. 1.29 and hold the driveshaft in the position shown. The large side should be facing the rear of the engine with the slot at 90° to the cylinder block.
2 Carefully insert the drive and when fully engaged with the oil pump it should be more or less in line with No 7 cylinder head bolt hole as shown in Fig. 1.29. If it is difficult to engage turn oil pump spindle with a screwdriver.

KF6, KF5, XN1 and XN2 engines

1 Refer to Fig. 1.30 and hold the driveshaft in the position shown. The large side should be facing away from the cylinder block and the slot parallel with it.
2 Carefully insert the drive and when fully engaged with the oil pump it should be more or less in line with No 2 cylinder head bolt hole as shown in Fig. 1.30. If it is difficult to engage turn the oil pump spindle with a screwdriver.

63 Fuel injection pump and drive - replacement

This Section is applicable to fuel injection models only.
1 Clean the timing cover and injection pump mating faces and offer up the injection pump.

2 Screw in and tighten the two Allen head screws securing the injection pump to the rear face of the timing cover. (photo)
3 Line up the camshaft pulley reference mark and the injection pump reference mark as shown in Fig. 3.36 and slide on the drivebelt.
4 Fit the drive pulley onto the injection pump spindle ensuring that the key is in position and replace the securing nut and lockwasher.
5 Tighten the pump pulley nut to a torque wrench setting of 25 lb f ft (3.5 kg f m) (photo)
6 Turn the crankshaft backwards through one complete turn and then check by rotating through one turn in the normal direction of rotation that the timing marks are still in alignment.

64 Timing cover (front) - replacement

1 Slide the oil slinger over the front of the crankshaft making sure it is the correct way round. (photo)
2 Fit a new gasket to the timing housing and offer up the front timing cover. (photo)
3 Replace the front timing cover securing bolts and washers, but do not tighten yet.
4 With the second Woodruff key in position in the crankshaft slide on the crankshaft pulley. It may be necessary to slightly adjust the position of the front timing cover to allow the pulley to be pushed fully home. (photo)
5 Tighten the securing bolts in a progressive and diagonal manner.
6 Refit the pulley retaining nut and lockwasher. Tighten the nut to a torque wrench setting of 123 lb f ft (17.0 kg f m). If necessary leave this final tightening until the flywheel has been refitted when it can be suitably locked using a bolt and metal bar.

63.2 Replacing injection pump on housing

63.5 Fuel injection pump drive correctly assembled

64.1 Oil thrower (slinger) fitted correct way round

64.2 Refitting cover

64.4 Do not forget the key before sliding on pulley

65 Flywheel - replacement

Important: If a replacement flywheel is being fitted make quite
sure the correct one is to hand. Fig. 1.31 shows four different
types that can be found on models covered by this manual.
1 Wipe the mating faces of the flywheel and crankshaft and
offer up the flywheel, aligning the previously made marks unless
new parts have been fitted.
2 Offer up the flywheel and ensure that it is positioned
squarely on the end of the crankshaft. (photo)
3 Fit the seven crankshaft securing bolts and new tab washer
and tighten the bolts in a progressive and diagonal manner to a
final torque wrench setting of 49 lb f ft (6.75 kg f m). (photo)
4 To stop the crankshaft from turning during tightening of the
flywheel securing bolts it is best to lock the flywheel using a

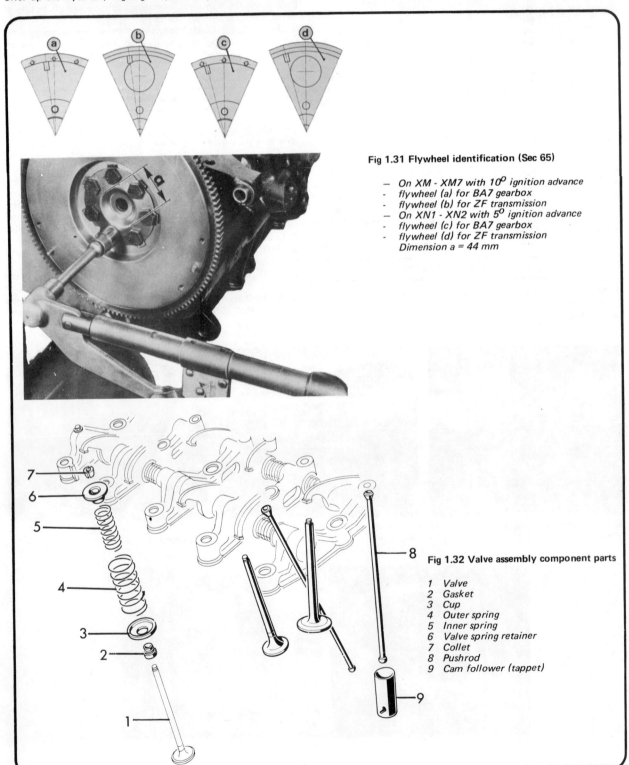

Fig 1.31 Flywheel identification (Sec 65)

— *On XM - XM7 with 10⁰ ignition advance*
- *flywheel (a) for BA7 gearbox*
- *flywheel (b) for ZF transmission*
— *On XN1 - XN2 with 5⁰ ignition advance*
- *flywheel (c) for BA7 gearbox*
- *flywheel (d) for ZF transmission*
Dimension a = 44 mm

Fig 1.32 Valve assembly component parts

1 *Valve*
2 *Gasket*
3 *Cup*
4 *Outer spring*
5 *Inner spring*
6 *Valve spring retainer*
7 *Collet*
8 *Pushrod*
9 *Cam follower (tappet)*

piece of metal engaged in the teeth of the starter ring gear. One method is shown in this photo.

5 Now is a good time as any to refit the clutch. Refer to Chapter 5, for full information on clutch disc centralisation. (photo)

66 Valves - replacement

1 With the cylinder head on its side, lubricate the valve stems and refit the valves to their correct guides. (photos). The valves should previously have been ground-in (see Section 42).
2 Replace the lower valve spring cup. (photo)
3 Position the valve springs over the valve stem. If new springs are being used it is important that the correct springs are fitted. Various springs have been fitted depending on the engine and its application. They are colour coded grey, yellow, or black and must not be interchanged, (see also Specifications). (photo)

4 Position the valve spring retainer over the valve springs. (photo)
5 Compress the valve spring with a compressor as shown in the photograph.
6 Then refit the split collets. A trace of grease will help to hold them to the valve stem recess until the spring compressor is slackened off and the collets are wedged in place by the spring.
7 Release the spring compressor and double check that the collets are correctly in position.

67 Cylinder head - replacement

1 The next step is to thoroughly clean the faces of the block and cylinder head to remove all traces of old cylinder head gasket or jointing compound.
2 If the cam followers have not yet been replaced now is the time to do it. Insert each one into its respective bore and check

65.2 Refitting flywheel

65.3 Tightening flywheel securing bolts

65.4 One method of locking flywheel

65.5 Refitting clutch to flywheel

66.1a Inserting valve into guide

66.1b Oil seal on valve stem

66.2 Lower spring cup fitted

66.3 Refitting both valve springs

66.4 Valve spring retainer replacement

66.5 Collets inserted in spring retainer

Fig 1.33 Correct fitment of cylinder head gasket (Sec 67)

a) *Check diameter*
b) *See caption to fig 1.25*

67.2 Inserting cam follower

67.7 Lowering cylinder head into position

67.8 Inserting pushrods

67.9 Replacing rocker assembly

67.11 Tightening cylinder head and rocker assembly bolts

that it drops down fully. (photo)

3 Remove the liner retaining bolts and large washers that were previously screwed into the top face of the cylinder block.

4 Select the correct gasket, as three are available:

Engine	dimension 'a' (Fig 1.33)
XM	86.5 mm
XN1 and XN2	90.0 mm
XM 7	86.5 mm

5 On 'XN1' and 'XN2' engines make sure that the flats are parallel on liners 1-2 and 3-4.

6 Place the gasket on the top face of the cylinder block. The word 'DESSUS' must face upwards.

7 Carefully lower the cylinder head onto the cylinder block. (photo)

8 Insert the pushrods into the same holes in the block from which they were removed. Make sure the pushrods seat properly in the cam followers. (photo)

9 Carefully lower the rocker assembly onto the top of the cylinder head engaging the rockers with the pushrods. (photo)

10 Insert all the retaining bolts with plain washers and lightly tighten. Then refit the rocker shaft support securing nuts and washers.

11 'XM' engines only: Tighten all securing bolts to a torque wrench setting of 43.5 lb f ft (6 kg f m) in the order shown in Fig. 1.6 in a progressive manner. Then tighten to a final setting of 60 lb f ft (8.25 kg f m). Tighten the rocker shaft support nuts to a torque wrench setting of 11 lb f ft (1.5 kg f m). (photo)

12 'XN1', 'XN2' and 'XM7' engines only: Tighten all securing bolts to a torque wrench setting of 36 lb f ft (5 kg f m) in the order shown in Fig. 1.6 in a progressive manner. Then tighten to a final setting of 60 lb f ft (8.25 kg f m). Tighten the rocker shaft support nuts to a torque wrench setting of 11 lb f ft (1.5 kg f m). It should be appreciated that a special tool for tightening down these cylinder head bolts is really required. Its objective is to accurately tension the bolts but if not available the usual procedure may be used provided that care is taken.

68 Valve clearance adjustment

1 The valve adjustments should be made with the engine cold. The importance of correct rocker arm/valve stem clearances cannot be overstressed as they vitally affect the performance of the engine. If the clearances are set too open, the efficiency of the engine is reduced as the valves open late and close earlier than was intended. If, on the other hand the clearances are set too close there is a danger that the valve stems will expand upon heating or not allow the valves to close properly which will cause burning of the valve head and seat and possibly warping. If the engine is in the car access to the rockers is gained by removing the rocker cover.

2 It is important that the clearance is set when the cam follower of the valve being adjusted is on the heel of the cam, (ie; opposite the peak). This can be ensured by carrying out the adjustments in the following order (which also avoids turning the crankshaft more than necessary).

Valve fully open	Check and adjust (Fig 1.34)	
E 1	A 3	E 4
E 3	A 4	E 2
E 4	A 2	E 1
E 2	A 1	E 3

The correct feeler gauge clearance between valve stem and rocker arm pad with the engine cold is:

	After refitting head	Service adjustment
Inlet	0.006 in (0.15 mm)	0.004 in (0.10 mm)
Exhaust	0.012 in (0.30 mm)	0.010 in (0.25 mm)

3 Working from the rear of the engine the correct clearance is obtained by slackening the hexagon locknut with a spanner while holding the ball pin against rotation with a screwdriver. Then, still pressing down with the screwdriver, insert a feeler gauge in the gap between the valve stem and the rocker arm and adjust the ball pin until the feeler gauge will just move in and out without nipping (photos). Then, still holding the ball pin in the correct position, tighten the locknut.

69 Rocker cover - replacement

1 Before replacing the rocker cover ensure that four spark plug tube sealing rings are serviceable. (photo)

2 Inspect the rocker cover gasket and if it is warped or damaged it should be renewed.

3 Check that the rocker cover securing bolt spacers are correctly located in the cover. (photo)

4 With both mating faces clean fit the rocker cover gasket and carefully lower the cover into position. Retain with the two securing bolts. (photo)

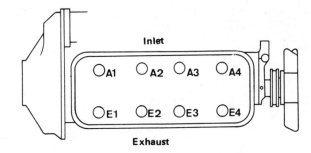

Fig 1.34 Valve clearance adjustment (Sec 68)

E Exhaust   A Inlet

68.3a Checking valve clearance

68.3b Adjustment of valve clearance

69.1 Spark plug tube seal

70 Engine ancillaries - replacement

It should be noted that in all cases it is best to assemble the engine as far as possible before refitting it to the car. The actual items to be refitted will depend largely on what was removed during dismantling but the following list should act as a guide:

a) Engine mounting (photo)
b) Crankcase breather (photo)
c) Dipstick tube (photo)
d) *Fuel injectors (photo)

e) *Air manifold and injector pipes (photo)
f) Water pump (photo)
g) Oil transfer pipe (photo)
h) *Injector pipes to injector pump (photo)
i) Carburettor and inlet manifold (photo)
j) Fuel pump
k) Exhaust manifold
l) Oil filter and head
m) Distributor
n) Spark plugs
* Fuel injection engines

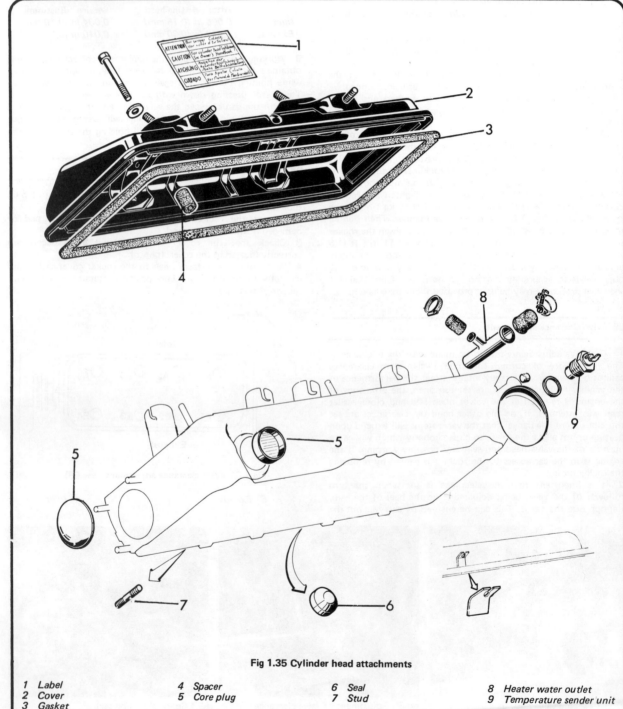

Fig 1.35 Cylinder head attachments

1	Label	4	Spacer	6	Seal	8 Heater water outlet
2	Cover	5	Core plug	7	Stud	9 Temperature sender unit
3	Gasket					

69.3 Spacer on rocker cover bolt

69.4 Refitting rocker cover to cylinder head

70.a Engine mounting

70.b Engine crankcase breather

70.c Dipstick tube

70.d Fuel injector

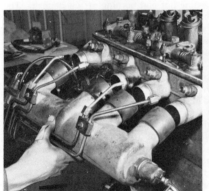

70.e Air manifold assembly

70.f Water pump replacement

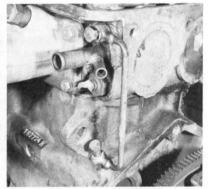

70.g Transfer tube replacement

70.h Fuel filter head

73.2 Lowering engine into compartment

71 Engine - replacement (general)

1 Engine replacement in general is the reverse sequence to removal and will present no problems provided that care was taken during removal to note any cable, hose or pipe connections.
2 Although the engine can be replaced by one man using a suitable winch, it is easier if two are present. One to lower the engine into the engine compartment and the other to guide the engine into position and ensure it does not foul anything.
3 At this stage one or two tips may come in useful. Ensure all the loose leads, cables etc are tucked out of the way. If not, it is easy to trap one and so cause much additional work after the engine is replaced.
4 Always fit a new fan belt and new cooling hoses and jubilee clips as this will help eliminate the possibility of failure while on the road. At extremely high mileages overhaul (or obtain exchange rebuilt units) the carburettor, fuel injector pump, injectors, fuel lift pump and water pump. This will ensure trouble-free service from the rebuilt engine.

72 Engine - replacement (without gearbox)

The sequence for replacement is basically the reverse to that of removal and should present no particular problems. However, the following additional notes should be of assistance.
1 With the engine suitably suspended over the engine compartment carefully lower it until the centre of the flywheel is in line with the gearbox input shaft. Engage top gear. With one person pushing on the engine and the other turning the crankshaft using a 35 mm open-ended spanner engage the input shaft with the clutch disc. Do not use force otherwise the clutch disc could be damaged.
2 Reconnect the gearbox be it manual or automatic transmission to the engine. When automatic transmission is fitted do not forget to rotate the converter using a screwdriver engaged in the cooling fins to line up one of the threaded holes with the coupling plate on the flywheel. Tighten these bolts to a torque wrench setting of 16 lb f ft (2.25 kg f m).
3 Whenever possible use new hoses and clips.
4 When refitting the radiator make sure there is a clearance between the fan hub and radiator matrix of 0.5 - 0.75 in (15 - 20 mm).
5 Reconnect all electrical connections and controls.
6 Check that the drain taps or plugs are closed and refill the cooling system with water and the engine with the correct grade of oil.

73 Engine - replacement (with gearbox)

The sequence for replacement is basically the reverse to that of removal and should present no particular problems. The following additional points should be noted:
1 Refer to Section 72, paragraphs 2-6 inclusive.
2 As the gearbox will be attached to the engine before refitting, it will be necessary to lower the unit into the engine compartment at a rather steep angle. If a pit or lift is not available it will be necessary to jack-up the front of the car and place the front wheels on blocks. (photo)
3 When lowering the unit into position be careful not to damage the rear end of the gearbox.
4 Reconnect the propeller shaft, as described in Chapter 7.
5 When the gearbox controls have been reconnected check their adjustment, as described in Chapter 6.
6 Check the oil level in the gearbox, whichever type is fitted and refill or top-up as necessary.

74 Engine - initial start-up after overhaul or major repairs

1 Make sure that the battery is fully-charged and that all lubricants, coolant and fuel are replenished.
2 If the fuel system has been dismantled it will require several revolutions of the engine on the starter motor to pump the petrol up to the carburettor. On fuel injection engines an electric pump is fitted so this one problem is not applicable except that the injection pipes will have to be filled with petrol from the injection pump. On carburettor engines an initial 'prime' of about 1/3 of a cupful of petrol poured down the air intake of the carburettor will help the engine to fire quickly, thus relieving the load on the battery. Do not overdo this however, as flooding may result.
3 As soon as the engine fires and runs, keep it going at a fast tick-over only (no faster) and bring it up to normal working temperature.
4 As the engine warms up there will be odd smells and some smoke from parts getting hot and burning off oil deposits. The signs to look for are leaks of water or oil which will be obvious, if serious. Check also the exhaust downpipe and manifold connections as these do not always find their exact gastight positon until the warmth and vibration have acted on them and it is almost certain that they will need tightening further. This should be done, of course, with the engine stopped.
5 When normal running temperature has been reached, adjust the engine idle speed as described in Chapter 3.
6 Stop the engine and wait a few minutes to see if any lubricant or coolant is dripping out when the engine is stationary.
7 After the engine has run for 10 minutes remove the engine rocker cover and recheck the tightness of the cylinder head bolts. Readjust the valve clearances to the service adjustment settings given in Section 68.
8 Road test the car to check that the timing is correct and that the engine is giving the necessary smoothness and power. Do not race the engine - if new bearings and/or pistons have been fitted it should be treated as a new engine and run in at a reduced speed for the first 1,000 miles (2,000 km).

75 Fault diagnosis - engine

Symptom	Reason/s	Remedy
Engine fails to turn over when starter control operated		
No current at starter motor	Flat or defective battery	Charge or replace battery. Push start car.
	Loose battery leads	Tighten both terminals and earth ends of earth leads.
	Defective starter solenoid or switch or broken wiring	Run a wire direct from the battery to the starter motor or by-pass the solenoid.
	Engine earth strap disconnected	Check and retighten strap.
Current at starter motor	Jammed starter motor drive pinion	Place car in gear and rock to and fro. Alternatively, free exposed square end of shaft with spanner.
	Defective starter motor	Remove and recondition.

Symptom	Reason/s	Remedy
Engine turns over but will not start No spark at spark plug	Ignition damp or wet	Wipe dry the distributor cap and ignition leads.
	Ignition leads to spark plugs loose	Check and tighten at both spark plug and distributor cap ends.
	Shorted or disconnceted low tension leads	Check the wiring on the CB and SW terminals of the coil and to the distributor.
	Dirty, incorrectly set, or pitted contact breaker points	Clean, file smooth, and adjust.
	Faulty condenser	Check contact breaker points for arcing, remove and fit new.
	Defective ignition switch	By-pass switch with wire.
	Ignition leads connected wrong way round	Remove and replace leads to spark plugs in correct order.
	Faulty coil	Remove and fit new coil.
	Contact breaker point spring earthed or broken	Check spring is not touching metal part of distributor. Check insulator washers are correctly placed. Renew points if the spring is broken.
No fuel at carburettor float chamber or at jets	No petrol in petrol tank	Refill tank!
	Vapour lock in fuel line (in hot conditions or at high altitude)	Blow into petrol tank, allow engine to cool, or apply a cold wet rag to the fuel line.
	Blocked float chamber needle valve	Remove, clean and replace.
	fuel pump filter blocked	Remove, clean and replace.
	Choked or blocked carburettor jets	Dismantle and clean.
	Faulty fuel pump	Remove, overhaul and replace.
Engine stalls and will not start Excess of petrol in cylinder or carburettor flooding	Too much choke allowing too rich a mixture to wet plugs	Remove and dry spark plugs or with wide open throttle, push start the car.
	Float damaged or leaking or needle not seating	Remove, examine, clean and replace float and needle valve as necessary.
	Float lever incorrectly adjusted	Remove and adjust correctly.
No spark at spark plug	Ignition failure - sudden	Check over low and high tension circuits for breaks in wiring.
	Ignition failure - misfiring precludes total stoppage	Check contact breaker points, clean and adjust. Renew condenser if faulty.
	Ignition failure - in severe rain or after traversing water splash	Dry out ignition leads and distributor cap.
No fuel at jets	No petrol in petrol tank	Refill tank!
	Petrol tank breather choked	Remove petrol cap and clean out breather hole or pipe.
	Sudden obstruction in carburettor(s)	Check jets, filter, and needle valve in float chamber for blockage.
	Water in fuel system	Drain tank and blow out fuel lines
Engine misfires or idles unevenly Intermittent spark at spark plugs	Ignition leads loose	Check and tighten as necssary at spark plugs and distributor cap ends.
	Battery leads loose on terminals	Check and tighten terminal leads.
	Battery earth strap loose on body attachment point	Check and tighten earth lead to body attachment point.
Intermittent sparking at spark plug	Engine earth lead loose	Tighten lead.
	Low tension leads to SW and CB terminals on coil loose	Check and tighten leads if found loose.
	Low tension lead from CB terminal side to distributor loose	Check and tighten if found loose.
	Dirty, or incorrectly gapped plugs	Remove, clean and regap.
	Dirty, incorrectly set, or pitted contact breaker points	Clean, file smooth, and adjust.
	Tracking across inside of distributor cover	Remove and fit new cover.
	Ignition too retarded	Check and adjust ignition timing.
	Faulty coil	Remove and fit new coil.
Fuel shortage at engine	Mixture too weak	Check jets, float chamber needle valve, and filters for obstruction. Clean as necessary. Carburettors incorrectly adjusted.

Symptom	Reason/s	Remedy
	Air leak in carburettor	Remove and overhaul carburettor.
	Air leak at inlet manifold to cylinder head, or inlet manifold to carburettor	Test by pouring oil along joints. Bubbles indicate leak. Renew manifold gasket as appropriate.
Lack of power and poor compression **Mechanical wear**	Incorrect valve clearances	Adjust rocker arms to take up wear.
	Burnt out exhaust valves	Remove cylinder head and renew defective valves
	Sticking or leaking valves	Remove cylinder head, clean, check and renew valves as necessary.
	Weak or broken valve springs	Check and renew as necessary.
	Worn valve guides or stems	Renew valve guides and valves.
	Worn pistons and piston rings	Dismantle engine, renew pistons and rings.
Fuel/air mixture leaking from cylinder	Burnt out exhaust valves	Remove cylinder head, renew defective valves.
	Sticking or leaking valves	Remove cylinder head, clean, check, and renew valves as necessary.
	Worn valve guides and stems	Remove cylinder head and renew valves and valve guides.
	Weak or broken valve springs	Remove cylinder head, renew defective springs.
	Blown cylinder head gasket (accompanied by increase in noise)	Remove cylinder head and fit new gasket.
	Worn pistons and piston rings	Dismantle engine, renew pistons and rings.
	Worn or scored cylinder bores	Dismantle engine, rebore, renew pistons and rings.
Incorrect adjustments	Ignition timing wrongly set. Too advanced or retarded	Check and reset ignition timing.
	Contact breaker points incorrectly gapped	Check and reset contact breaker points.
	Incorrect valve clearances	Check and reset rocker arm to valve stem gap.
	Incorrectly set spark plugs	Remove, clean and regap.
	Carburation too rich or too weak	Tune carburettor for optimum performance.
Carburation and ignition faults	Dirty contact breaker points	Remove, clean and replace.
	Fuel filters blocked causing poor top end performance through fuel starvation	Dismantle, inspect, clean, and replace all fuel filters.
	Distributor automatic balance weights or vacuum advance and retard mechanisms not functioning correctly	Overhaul distributor.
	Faulty fuel pump giving top end fuel starvation	Remove, overhaul, or fit exchange reconditioned fuel pump.
Excessive oil consumption **Oil being burnt by engine**	Excessively worn valve stems and valve guides	Remove cylinder head and fit new valves and valve guides.
	Worn piston rings	Fit oil control rings to existing pistons or purchase new pistons.
	Worn pistons and cylinder bores	Fit new pistons and rings, rebore cylinders.
	Excessive piston ring gap allowing blow-up	Fit new piston rings and set gap correctly.
	Piston oil return holes choked	Decarbonise engine and pistons.
Oil being lost due to leaks	Leaking oil filter gasket	Inspect and fit new gasket as necessary.
	Leaking rocker cover gasket	Inspect and fit new gasket as necessary.
	Leaking timing gear cover gasket	Inspect and fit new gasket as necessary.
	Leaking sump gasket	Inspect and fit new gasket as necessary.
	Loose sump plug	Tighten, fit new gasket if necessary.
Unusual noises from engine **Excessive clearances due to mechanical wear**	Worn valve gear (noisy tapping from rocker box	Inspect and renew rocker shaft, rocker arms, and ball pins as necessary.
	Worn big-end bearing (regular heavy knocking)	Drop sump, if bearings broken up clean out oil pump and oilways, fit new bearings. If bearings not broken but worn fit bearing shells.
	Worn timing chain and gears (rattling from front of engine)	Remove timing cover, fit new timing wheels and timing chain.
	Worn main bearings (rumbling and vibration)	Drop sump, remove crankshaft; if bearing worn but not broken up, renew. If broken up strip oil pump and clean out oilways.
	Worn crankshaft (knocking, rumbling and vibration	Regrind crankshaft, fit new main and big-end bearings.

Chapter 2 Cooling system

For modifications and information applicable to later models, see Supplement at end of manual

Contents

Specifications

Type of system	Pressurised assisted by pump and fan	

Thermostat

Type	Bellows	
Location	Water outlet from pump	
	Standard	**Cold climate**
Opening temperature	74° - 76°C	87° - 89°C
Fully open at	87° C	97° C
Valve lift	7.5 mm	57.5 mm
Thermostat height (valve closed)	53 mm	55 mm

Radiator filler cap opening pressure

Colour code white	4 lb/in² (0.28 kg/cm²)
Colour code blue	11.4 lb/in² (0.80 kg/cm²)

Water pump

Type	Centrifugal
Fan hub and water pump pulley clearance	0.012 inch (0.3 mm)
Impeller to body shoulder clearance	0.04 inch (1 mm)

Fan

Type	Electro-magnetic drive
Fan engages	81.0° - 83.5° C (177° - 182° F)
Fan disengages	69.5° - 67° C (157° - 152.5° F)
Number of blades	6 (plastic)
Electromagnetic winding current	0.7 - 0.9 amps at 12 volts

Radiator

Type	Vertical flow, steel tube

Cooling system capacity (with heater)	13.72 pints (7.8 litres, 16.21 US pints)

Torque wrench setting

	lb f ft	**kg fm**
Water pump pulley nut	25	3.5

1 General description

The engine cooling water is circulated by a thermo syphon water pump assisted system and the coolant is pressurised.

The system comprises a radiator, a water pump, a fan, a thermostat, also top and bottom hoses and heater hoses. There is one drain plug located on the right-hand side of the cylinder block towards the rear and another at the bottom of the radiator.

The system functions in the following manner: Cold water from the bottom of the radiator circulates up the lower radiator hose to the water pump where it is pushed round the water passages in the cylinder block, helping to keep the cylinder bores and pistons cool.

The water then travels up into the cylinder head and circulates round the combustion spaces and valve seats absorbing more heat, and then, when the engine is at its correct operating temperature, travels out the cylinder head, past the open thermostat into the upper radiator hose and so into the radiator header tank.

The water travels down the radiator where it is rapidly cooled by the in-rush of cold air through the radiator core which is created by both the fan and the motion of the car. The water, now much cooler, reaches the bottom of the radiator when the cycle is repeated.

When the engine is cold the thermostat (which is a valve which opens and closes according to the temperature of the water) maintains the circulation of the same water in the engine.

Only when the correct minimum operating temperature has been reached does the thermostat begin to open, allowing water to return to the radiator.

In carburettor engines, the carburettor body contains water-ways and is connected to the cooling system by small diameter pipes. This ensures that carburettor warm up is rapid and optimum combustion conditions soon reached.

The fan pulley incorporates an electro magnetic drive which is only energised when the cooling water is hot. By this means the fan is only driven when it is really needed, with a consequent reduction in noise and power consumption.

2 Cooling system - draining

1 If the engine is cold, remove the filler cap from the radiator by turning the cap anticlockwise. If the engine is hot, then turn the filler cap very slightly until pressure in the system has had time to be released. Use a rag over the cap to protect your hand from escaping steam. If, with the engine very hot, the cap is released suddenly, the drop in pressure can result in the water boiling. With the pressure released the cap can be removed.

2 If antifreeze is used in the cooling system, drain into a bowl having a capacity of at least 13 pints (15.6 US pints, 7.4 litres) for re-use.

3 Open the drain plug located on the underside of the radiator bottom tank and also the drain plug located towards the rear right-hand side of the cylinder block.

4 To speed up the draining process set the heater controls to the maximum heat position.

5 When the water has finished draining, probe the drain plug orifices with a short piece of wire to dislodge any particles of rust or sediment which may be causing a blockage.

6 It is important to note that the heater cannot be drained completely during the cold weather so an antifreeze solution must be used. Always use an antifreeze with an ethylene glycol or glycerine base.

3 Cooling system - flushing

In time the cooling system will gradually lose its efficiency as the radiator becomes choked with rust, scale deposits from the water, and other sediment. To clean the system out, remove the radiator filler cap and drain plug and leave water running into the filler cap neck for ten to fifteen minutes.

2 In very bad cases the radiator should be reverse flushed. This can be done with the radiator in position. The bottom hose should be detached from the radiator and a hose with a suitable tapered adaptor placed in the radiator bottom hose union. Water under pressure is then forced through the radiator and out of the top tank filler cap neck.

3 It is recommended that some polythene sheeting is placed over the engine to stop water finding its way into the electrical system.

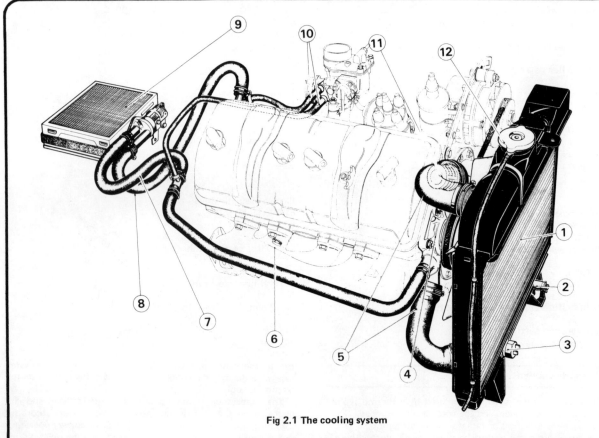

Fig 2.1 The cooling system

1 Radiator	5 Upper and lower radiator hoses	9 Heater radiator
2 Radiator drain tap	6 Cylinder block drain plug	10 Carburettor heater pipes
3 Self-disengaging fan switch	7 Heater intake hose	11 Thermostat
4 Self-disengaging fan and water pump	8 Heater return hose	12 Pressure filler cap

4 The hose should now be removed and placed in the radiator filler cap neck, and the radiator washed out in the usual manner.

4 Cooling system - filling

1 Refit and tighten the cylinder block and radiator drain plugs.
2 Fill the system slowly to ensure that no air lock develops. If a heater is fitted, check that the valve in the heater is open (control at maximum heat), otherwise an air lock may form in the heater. The best type of water to use in the cooling system is rain water; use this whenever possible.
3 Do not fill the system higher than within 0.5 inch (12.7 mm) of the filler neck. Overfilling will merely result in wastage, which is especially to be avoided when antifreeze is in use.
4 Replace the filler cap and turn it firmly in a clockwise direction to lock it in position.
5 Start the engine and allow to idle for two minutes. Carefully remove the radiator cap. Check the level and top-up using warm water or antifreeze or alternatively allow to cool; if cold coolant is added to warm or hot water in the cooling system it can cause internal stress in the water jacket surrounding metal due to sudden temperature changes.
6 Finally inspect for water leaks especially if any part of the cooling system has been disturbed for a new part fitment or overhaul.

5 Radiator - removal, inspection, cleaning and replacement

1 Refer to Chapter 12 and remove the radiator grille.
2 Refer to Section 2 and drain the cooling system.

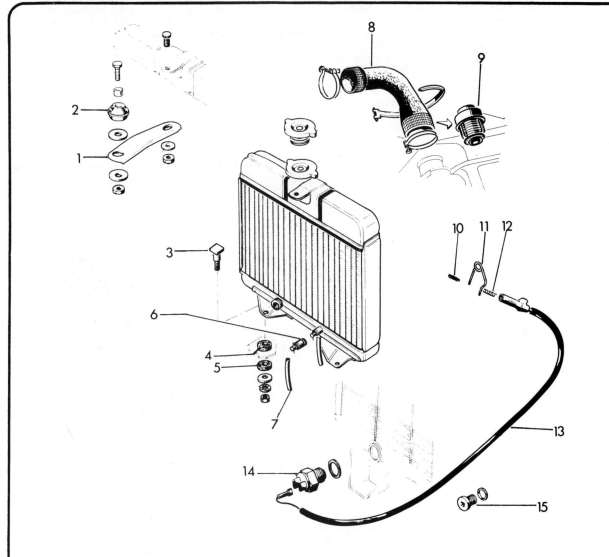

Fig 2.2 Radiator and its attachments (Sec 5)

1 Support bracket	6 Drain tap
2 Rubber washer	7 PVC extension tube
3 Shouldered bolt	8 Top hose
4 Rubber pad	9 Thermostat (located in top hose)
5 Rubber pad	10 Carbon brush

11 Brush holder retaining spring
12 Brush spring
13 Brush holder and electric lead
14 Thermostat switch
15 Radiator plug (when switch is not fitted)

3 Slacken the two clips which hold the top and bottom radiator hoses on the radiator and carefully pull off the two hoses.

4 Slacken the two clips which hold the top and bottom radiator hoses on the water pump and cylinder head outlet union. Carefully remove the two hoses. Note that the thermostat is fitted into the top hose.

5 Disconnect the electrical connector from the switch for the fan. The switch is located at the front of the radiator bottom tank.

6 Undo and remove the nut, bolt and washers securing the upper bracket to the front crossmember.

7 Undo and remove the nuts, bolts and washers securing the two radiator bottom mounting brackets to the body.

8 The radiator may now be lifted upwards and away from the engine compartment. The fragile matrix must not be touched by the fan blades as it is easily damaged. (photo)

9 With the radiator away from the car any leaks can be soldered or repaired with a plastic filler. Clean out the inside of the radiator by flushing, as described in Section 3. When the radiator is out of the car it is advantageous to turn it up-side-down and reverse flush. Clean the exterior of the radiator by carefully using a compressed air jet or a strong jet of water to clear away any road dirt, flies etc.

10 Inspect the radiator hoses for cracks, internal or external perishing and damage by overtightening of the securing clips. Also inspect the overflow pipe. Renew the hoses if suspect. Examine the radiator hose clips and renew them if they are rusted or distorted.

11 Refitting the radiator is the reverse sequence to removal.

12 If new hoses are to be fitted they can be a little difficult to fit on the radiator so lubricate them with a little soap.

13 Refill the cooling system, as described in Section 4.

6 Water pump - removal, inspection and replacement

1 For safety reasons, disconnect the battery.

2 Refer to Section 2, and drain the cooling system.

3 Refer to Section 5, and remove the radiator.

4 Slacken the alternator mountings and remove the fanbelt.

5 Slacken the clip and detach the heater hose from the water pump.

6 Detach the self-disengaging fan brush holder from the water pump fan hub assembly. (photo)

7 Undo and remove the four nuts and washers securing the water pump to the front of the cylinder block. Also undo and remove the one long bolt and washer that is located at the top of the water pump body.

8 Carefully remove the water pump, fan and hub assembly. Recover the gasket. (photo)

9 Once the pump is on the bench, clean the exterior thoroughly. Then give the interior passages and the impeller blades a good clean.

10 Check the pump spindle for smooth rotation in its bearing and for freedom from sideways play. A small amount of endplay may be tolerated. An appreciable amount of sideways play indicates that the spindle bearings should be renewed.

11 If the impeller is severely corroded or runs out-of-true, or if there are any signs of water leaking past the spindle seal, the water pump should be renewed (or overhauled if this is possible — see Section 7).

12 Check that the fan revolves freely on its hub which is carried on the pump spindle. Only a small degree of play is tolerable here. The gap between the fan hub and water pump pulley should be 0.012 inch (0.3 mm). If necessary this can be adjusted with the three screws located on the front of the fan (see Fig. 2.3).

13 To check the winding of the electromagnet in the fan pulley, connect a 12 volt battery and ammeter in the manner shown in Fig. 2.4 but to avoid dismantling put the carbon brush back in the holder temporarily and connect the lead from the positive terminal of the battery to the brush. **Do not** attempt to push a wire or prod through the brush holder direct onto the slip ring. You may scratch or burn it. A higher reading indicates a partial or complete short circuit whilst a lower or zero reading denotes a break in the winding.

14 Refitting the water pump, hub and fan assembly is the reverse sequence to removal and will present no problems.

7 Water pump - renovation

1 If the water pump is found to be faulty it is recommended that it is renewed complete. However, it may be possible to obtain an overhaul kit from a motor factor, in which case overhaul procedures will normally be included in the kit.

8 Fanbelt - tension

1 The correct tensioning of the fanbelt will ensure that it has a long and useful life. Beware, however, of over-tightening as this can cause excessive wear in the water pump and alternator bearings.

2 The tension of the fanbelt is adjusted by altering the position of the alternator which is determined by the slotted support handily placed above it.

3 Peugeot recommend an easy way of checking the tension which has the great merit that something is actually measured. On the fanbelt between the alternator and the water pump make two marks with chalk or wax crayon 100 mm apart with the belt unstretched.

4 Now tighten the belt until these two marks are between 102 and 103 mm apart. It is best to keep the measurements in metric form.

5.8 Removal or radiator

6.6 Brush holder is clipped to water pump casing

6.8 Removal of water pump. (Fan blades removed for clarity)

9 Thermostat - removal, testing and replacement

1 Partially drain the cooling system, as described in Section 2.
2 Slacken the two upper hose clips and carefully remove the top hose. The thermostat is located in the outlet connection from the water pump. (photo)
3 Carefully remove the thermostat from its location, noting which way round it is fitted.
4 Test the thermostat for correct functioning by suspending it on a string in a saucepan of cold water together with a thermometer. Make sure the thermostat or thermometer do not touch the sides or bottom of the saucepan.
5 Heat the water and note the temperature at which the thermostat begins to open. This should be 74 - 76° C and fully open at a temperature of 87°C.
6 Measure the valve lift and this should be 7.5 mm.
7 Allow the thermostat to cool down and ensure that the valve is fully closed when cold.
8 If the thermostat does not fully open in boiling water, or does not close down as the water cools, then it must be discarded and a new one fitted. Should the thermostat be stuck open when cold this will usually be apparent when removing it from the water pump outlet.
9 Refitting the thermostat is the reverse sequence to removal.

10 Antifreeze mixture

1 In circumstances where it is likely that the temperature will drop below freezing it is essential that some water is drained and an adequate amount of ethylene glycol antifreeze such as 'Castrol Antifreeze' is added to the cooling system.
2 If Castrol Antifreeze is not readily available any antifreeze which conforms with Specifications BS 3151 or BS 3152 can be used. Never use an antifreeze with an alcohol base as evaporation

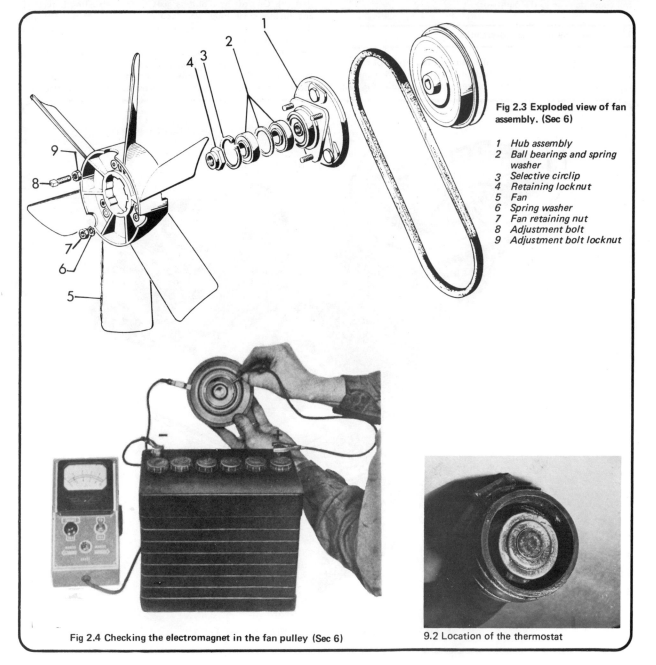

Fig 2.3 Exploded view of fan assembly. (Sec 6)

1 Hub assembly
2 Ball bearings and spring washer
3 Selective circlip
4 Retaining locknut
5 Fan
6 Spring washer
7 Fan retaining nut
8 Adjustment bolt
9 Adjustment bolt locknut

Fig 2.4 Checking the electromagnet in the fan pulley (Sec 6)

9.2 Location of the thermostat

is too high.

3 Castrol Antifreeze with an anti-corrosion additive can be left in the cooling system for up to two years, but after six months it is advisable to have the specific gravity of the coolant checked at your local garage and thereafter once every three months.

4 The table below gives the amount of antifreeze and the degree of protection:

Commences to Freeze		Amount of Anti-freeze
°C	°F	
−5°	23°	1.76 pints (1 litre, 2.3 US Pints)
−12°	10°	3.52 pints (2 litres, 4.6 US Pints)
−21°	−6°	5.28 pints (3 litres, 6.9 US Pints)
−35°	−32°	7.04 pints (4 litres, 9.2 US Pints)

5 Never use antifreeze in the windscreen washer reservoir as it will cause damage to the paintwork.

11 Heating system - general description

The heater unit comprises the usual combination of blower and radiator. Two different makes of heater, the Sofica and the Gelbon, are fitted, but these differ only in detail. Fig. 2.5 shows a cutaway drawing of the Sofica heater whilst Fig. 2.6 shows details of the radiator and the thermostatic control tap associated with it.

All models covered by this manual employ the same basic heater unit though the ducting system varies from model to model.

Fig. 2.7 gives a schematic diagram of the operation of the heater. Referring to the numbers in the illustration, the snutter (1) controls the admission of air to the heater, the air being circulated by the fan (9). On all models except the station wagon, the fan speed is regulated by a thermostat. The station wagon fan is operated by a simple on-off switch.

The air outlet (3), which can be shut off by the flap (2) directs unheated fresh air to outlets at the sides of the dashboard. Air passing though the heater radiator is warmed to a temperature depending on the water flow through the radiator (this is controlled by the thermostatic tap) and can be directed to either or both of two outlets depending on the position of the flap (7). One of these outlets goes to the defrosting louvres (5) and further small louvres at the sides of the dashboard (6) while the other one (8) is underneath the heater itself. The heater control system for saloon models is shown in Fig. 2.8. Referring to the letters in this illustration, (a) controls the thermostatic tap on the heater radiator, (b) controls the air intake shutter and, as it is moved further over to the left, increases the fan speed as it operates the rheostat, (c) controls flap (7)

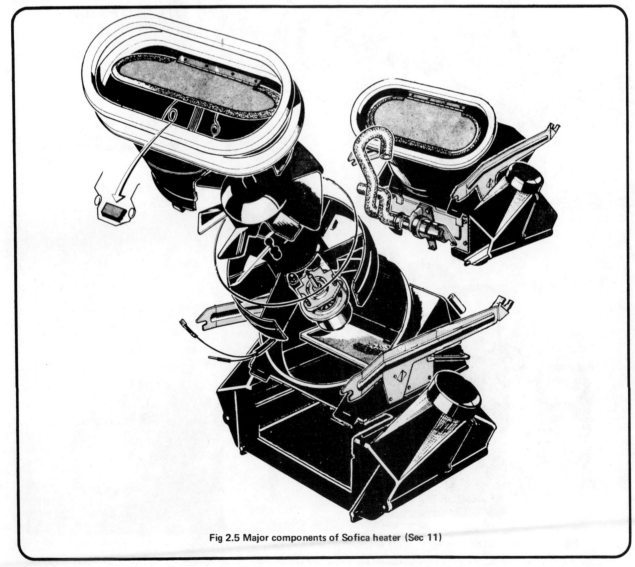

Fig 2.5 Major components of Sofica heater (Sec 11)

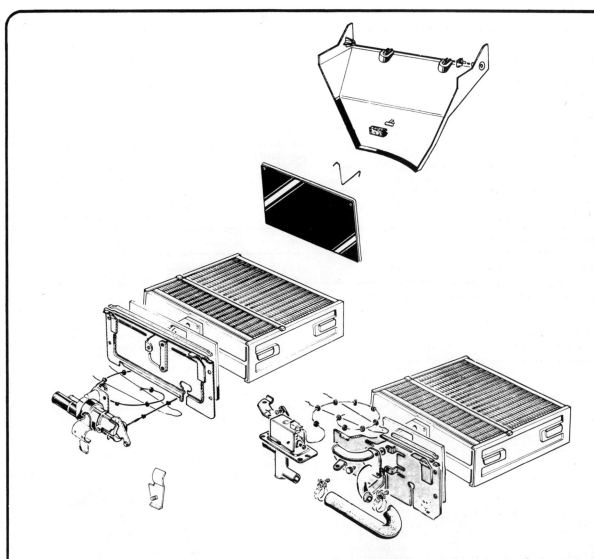

Fig 2.6 Exploded view of heater radiator components showing alternative layouts of thermostatic control system (Sec 11)

Fig 2.8 Heater controls - Saloon models (see text for control lever function) (Sec 11)

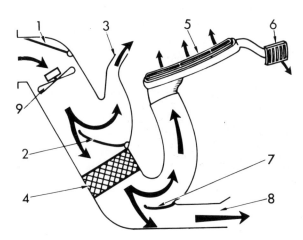

Fig 2.7 Schematic diagram of heater system (Sec 11)

1 Air intake shutter
2 Shutter controlling air flow to 3 and 4
3 Outlet to dashboard central swivelling ventilators
4 Heater radiator
5 De-frosting ducts
6 Heating duct at side of dashboard
7 Shutter controlling air output from underside of heater
8 Air outlet
9 Blower motor

see Fig. 2.7 - shutting off output (8) when it is over to the left and defrosting system when it is over to the right. In addition to the outlets shown in Fig. 2.7 fresh air is directed to vents on either side of the dashboard positioned just below the dashboard louvres, the flow of air to these points being controlled by (a).

12 Heater overhaul

1 Refer to Chapter 13 for details of heater removal. During the removal and dismantling procedures, extreme care must be taken not to damage the long thin pipe which is attached to the thermostatic regulator. This is filled with a special volatile fluid

and once the system has sprung a leak it is useless.
2 If there are signs of coolant leakage at any heater hose junction the hose should be renewed.
3 Take the opportunity of giving the heater radiator a good rinse out. When this has been done check it for leakage by filling it up with water and watching for drips or seepage.
4 On some models it is possible to replace the brushes in the blower motor. Excessive brush wear will lead to armature damage due to poor contact and excessive sparking, and brushes are much cheaper than armatures.
5 Check the bearings for excessive side play (a small amount of end-play is unimportant). Excessive bearing wear is best dealt with by replacing the motor which will probably be in poor condition anyway if this has occurred.

13 Fault diagnosis - cooling system

Symptom	Reason/s	Remedy
Loss of coolant	Leak in system	Examine all hoses, hose connections, drain taps and the radiator and heater for signs of leakage when the engine is cold, then when hot and under pressure. Tighten clips, renew hoses and repair radiator.
	Defective radiator pressure cap	Examine cap for defective seal or spring and renew if necessary.
	Overheating causing rapid evaporation due to excessive pressure in system forcing vapour past radiator cap	Check reasons for overheating.
	Blown cylinder head gasket causing excess pressure in cooling system forcing coolant past radiator cap overflow	Remove cylinder head for examination.
	Cracked block or head due to freezing	Strip engine and examine. Repair as required.
Overheating	Insufficient coolant in system	Top-up.
	Water pump not turning properly due to slack fan belt	Tighten fan belt.
	Kinked or collapsed water hoses causing restriction to circulation of coolant	Renew hose as required.
	Faulty thermostat (not opening properly)	Fit new thermostat.
	Engine out of tune	Check ignition setting and carburettor adjustments.
	Blocked radiator either internally or externally	Flush out cooling system and clean out cooling fins.
	Cylinder head gaskets blown forcing coolant out of system	Remove head and renew gasket.
	New engine not run-in	Adjust engine speed until run-in.
Engine running too cool	Missing or faulty thermostat	Fit new thermostat.

Chapter 3 Fuel system, carburation, fuel injection and emission control

For modifications, and information applicable to later models, see Supplement at end of manual

Contents

Specifications

Part 1 and 2: carburettor engines

Note (1) For identification of engine coding used in this Section - see Chapter 1.
(2) The carburettor specifications given later in this Section, were the latest available from the manufacturer at the time of publication. If your vehicle is a late model consult local dealer for latest carburettor data.

Air cleaner

Type	Replaceable paper element, cleanable, nylon element or oil bath depending on engine specification
Manufacturer	Lautrette

Fuel pump

Type	Mechanical, pushrod operated
Manufacturer	Guiot or AC
Delivery	5.5 gallons (25 litres, 6.6 US gallons) per hour
Delivery pressure	1.06 lb sq in. (75 gm sq cm) at 2000 - 4000 rpm
Maximum pressure (at zero delivery)	3.55 lb/in^2 (250 gm/cm^2)

Fuel pump pushrod:

Diameter	0.315 - 0.0002 in. (8.0 - 0.005 mm)
	- 0.001 in. - 0.027 mm)
Length	1.9192 + 0.0000 in. (48.75 + 0.0000 mm)
	- 0.0062 in. - 0.0160 mm)
Stroke	0.1181 ± 0.004 in. (3.00 ± 0.10 mm)

Solex 34 PBICA carburettor specifications (XM and XM7 engines)

Model series   *504, AO1 and AO3 vehicles*

Engine	XM with BA 7 gearbox		XM with ZF transmission	
Carburettor	34 PBICA 5 l.h.d. (ref. 33) r.h.d. (ref. 34)	34 PBICA 7 (ref. 48) (ref. 49) *(1)*	34 PBICA 5 (ref. 35) (ref. 36)	34 PBICA 7 l.h.d. or r.h.d. (ref. 50) *(2)*
Venturi	27	27	27	27
Main jet	145	145	145	145
Correction jet	170	170	170	160
Emulsion tube	28	28	28	130
Pilot jet	50	50	50	50
Air jet	210 on bowl	210 below choke	210 on bowl	210 below choke
Pump jet	-	50	-	50
Pump injector	45	-	45	-
End of pump stroke for throttle opening of:	3 mm ± 0.5	3 mm ± 0.5	3 mm ± 0.5	3 mm ± 0.5
Air bleed	3 holes 110 diameter	3 holes 110 diameter	3 holes 110 diameter	3 holes 110 diameter
Econostat	—	—	—	—
Enricher jet	—	—	—	—
Choke petrol jet	160	160	160	160
Vacuum jet	—	—	—	—
Needle valve	1.70	1.70	1.70	1.70
Float	5.7 g	5.7 g	5.7 g	5.7 g

Engine	XM7 7.5 : 1 cr	XM7 8.35 : 1 cr	XM USA 1969 BA7 or ZF
Carburettor	34 PBICA 9 l.h.d. or r.h.d. (ref. 54)	34 PBICA 9 l.h.d. or r.h.d. (ref. 65)	34 PBICA 6 BA7 (ref. 43) ZF (ref. 44) *(3)*
Venturi	27	27	27
Main jet	145	145	137.5
Correction jet	200	170	200
Emulsion tube	E.8	28	17
Pilot jet	47.5	50	52
Air jet	210 in choke	210 below choke	210 below choke
Pump jet	50	50	—
Pump injector	50	45	40
End of pump stroke for throttle opening of:	3.5 mm ± 0.5	3 mm ± 0.5	6.5 mm ± 0.5
Air bleed	130/120	3 holes 110 diameter	125/105
Econostat	100	—	100
Enricher jet	—	—	—
Choke petrol jet	160	160	160
Vacuum jet	—	—	0.45
Needle valve	1.70	1.70	1.70
Float	5.7 g	5.7 g	5.7 g

(1) - *34 PBICA 7 on XM engine with BA 7 gearbox since May 1970.*
(2) - *34 PBICA 7 on XM engine with ZF transmission since May 1970, but with ball valve.*
(3) - *34 PBICA 6 on USA XM engine, up to December 1969.*

Solex 32/35 SEIEA carburettor specifications (XN1 engine)

Model series   *504, A11 - A13 vehicles*

Engine	XN1 "Europe-Ralenti"				XN1 "Europe-cycle" *(3)*			
Gearbox used	BA7		ZF		BAZ		ZF	
Carburettor SEIEA 32/35	l.h.d. ref. 57 - 1 *(4)* r.h.d. ref. 58 - 1 *(4)*		ref. 68 - 1 *(4)* ref. 69 - 1 *(4)*		ref. 70 - 1 *(4)*		ref. 71 - 1 *(4)*	
choke	1st	2nd	1st	2nd	1st	2nd	1st	2nd
Venturi	24	27	24	27	24	27	24	27
Main jets	125	137.5	122.5	140	125	137.5	122.5	140
Correction jets	140	150	140	150	140	140	140	150

	ND	S1	ND	S1	ND	S1	ND	S1
Emulsion tubes	ND	S1	ND	S1	ND	S1	ND	S1
Pilot jet	55		55		50		50	
	50(2)	—	50(2)	—	—	—	—	—
Idling air bleed	80	—	80	—	80	—	80	—
Calibrated orifice	200	—	200	—	200	—	200	—
Pump injectors	50(1)	35(1)	50(1)	35(1)	50(1)	35(1)	50(1)	35(1)
Pump stroke (control)	cam		cam		cam		cam	
Progressivity jet	110/100	120	110/100	120	—	120	—	120
Petrol bleed	—	55	—	55	—	55	—	55
Air bleed	—	80	—	80	—	80	—	80
Progressivity slot	7.1 x 0.6 (2)	—	7.1 x 0.6 (2)	—	7.1x0.6	—	7.1x0.6	—
Econostat	—	100	—	100	—	100	—	100
Vacuum jet	—	—	—	—	—	—	—	—
Needle valve	1.80		1.80		1.80		1.80	

Engine	XN1 - 7.6 : 1 compression			
Gearbox used	BA 7		ZF	
Carburettor SEIEA 32/35	ref. 89 ref. 99		ref. 90 ref. 92	
choke	1st	2nd	1st	2nd
Venturi	24	27	24	27
Main jets	125	137.5	122.5	140
Correction jets	140	150	140	150
Emulsion tubes	ND	S1	ND	S1
Pilot jet	60	—	60	—
Idling air bleed	80	—	80	—
Calibrated orifice	200	—	200	—
Pump injectors	50	35	50	35
Pump stroke (control)	cam		cam	
Progressivity jet	—	120	—	120
Petrol bleed	—	55	—	55
Air bleed	—	80	—	80
Progressivity slot	7.1x0.6	—	7.1x0.6	—
Econostat	—	100	—	100
Vacuum jet	—	—	—	—
Needle valve	1.80		1.80	

(1) - Pump injector of 50-35 instead of 40-40 since November 1970 with modified pump cam, with reference XX.
(2) - Progressivity slot of 7.1 x 0.6 instead of 110/100 jet and pilot jet of 50 instead of 55 since January 1971.
(3) - "Europe-cycle" on 504 for Sweden-Norway since July 1970 and for Germany-Austria-Denmark-Switzerland since January 1971.
(4) - Suppression of insulating gasket and float cover with controls on it since March 1972.
Note: The carburettors with the 70-1 and 71-1 reference can be fitted in place of the carburettors with the 57-1/58-1 and 68-1/69-1 reference but the reverse is not to be realised.

Solex 32 - 35 SEIEA carburettor specifications (XN1 USA engine)

Model series   *A91 and A93 vehicles*

Engine	XN1 - 71 standards			
Transmission fitted	BA7		ZF	
Carburettor Reference	32-35 SEIEA 56		32-35 SEIEA 67	
choke	1st	2nd	1st	2nd
Venturi	24	27	24	27
Main jet	122.5	140	120	142.5
Correction jet	140	150	140	150
Emulsion tube	ND	S1	ND	S1
Idling jet	50	—	50	—
Idling air bleed	80	—	80	—
Calibrated orifice	200	—	200	—
Pump injector	40	40	40	40
Pump stroke (control)	cam		cam	
Progressivity jet	—	120	—	120
Petrol bleed	—	55	—	55
Air bleed	—	80	—	80
Progressivity slot	7.1x0.6	—	7.1x0.6	—
Econostat	—	100	—	100
Vacuum jet	0.55	—	0.55	—
Needle valve	1.80		1.80	

Solex 32·BICSA, 34 BICSA and 34 PBIC carburettor specification (XN1 USA ENGINE)

Model series   *A91 and A93 vehicles*

Engine   XN1 - 72 standards

Transmission fitted		BA7		ZF	
Carburettor		32 BICSA2	34 PBIC8	32 BICSA2	34BICSA2
Reference		79	80	81	80
Venturi		24	24	24	24
Main jet		117.5 ± 2.5	112.5 ± 2.5	112.5 ± 2.5	112.5 ± 2.5
Correction jet		210	130	210	130
Emulsion tube		135	17	135	17
Idle electrovalve		55	50	55	50
Idling jet (in choke)		120	210	120	210
Idling air jet		90	—	90	—
Pump injector		40	50	40	50
Main jet cap		3.2 dia.	3.2 dia.	3.2 dia.	3.2 dia.
Vacuum jet		0.55	—	0.55	—
End of pump stroke for throttle opening of:		1.5 mm ± 0.5	6 mm ± 0.5	1.5 mm ± 0.5	6 mm ± 0.5
Air bleed (2 holes)		130 dia.	110 dia.	130 dia.	110 dia.
Econostat		—	—	—	—
Needle valve		1.2	1.5	1.2	1.5
Float		5.7 g	5.7 g	5.7 g	5.7 g

Engine   XN1-73 standards

Transmission fitted		BA7 - ZF	
Carburettor		32 BICSA2	34 PBIC8
Reference			
choke			
Venturi		24	24
Main jet		122.5 ± 2.5	122.5 ± 2.5
Correction jet		180 ± 5	210 ± 5
Emulsion tube		136	137
Idling jet		55	50
Idling air bleed		120	210
Calibrated orifice		90	—
Pump injector		40	50
Pump stroke (control)		3.2 dia.	3.2 dia.
Progressivity jet		—	—
Petrol bleed		—	—
Air bleed		3.5 mm ± 0.5	6 mm ± 0.5
Progressivity slot		130 dia.	110 dia.
Econostat			90
Vacuum jet		1.2	1.5
Needle valve		5.7 g	5.7 g

Solex 34 PBICA carburettor specifications (XM and XM7 USA engines)

Model series   *504, A91 and A93*

Engine

		XM USA 1970 BA7 or ZF	
Carburettor		32 PBICA 8 (ref. 51) *(4)*	34 PBICA 8 (ref. 52) *(4)*
Venturi		24	24
Main jet		120	130
Correction jet		195	200
Emulsion tube		101	17
Pilot jet		55	50
Air jet		210 below choke	210 below choke
Pump jet		—	—
Pump injector		50	50
End of pump stroke for throttle opening of:		4 mm ± 0.5	6 mm ± 0.5
Air bleed		2 holes 115 dia.	2 holes 110 dia.

Econostat	...	...	...	...	...	...	...	—	—
Enricher jet	...	...	...	...	...	...	...	60	—
Choke petrol jet	...	...	...	...	...	...	...	190	—
Vacuum jet	...	...	...	...	...	...	...	0.45	—
Needle valve	...	...	...	...	...	...	...	1.50	1.50
Float	...	...	...	...	...	...	...	5.7 g	5.7 g

(4)   *32 PBICA 8 and 32 PBICA 8 on USA engine since January 1970.*

Fuel tank

Type	...	...	...	...	...	...	...	Flat tank under rear floor
Capacity ...	...	...	...	...	...	...	...	12.3 gallons (56 litres, 16.816 US gallons)

Part 3: fuel injection system

System type	...	...	...	...	...	...	...	Kugelfischer

Air cleaner

Type	...	...	...	...	...	...	...	Oil bath
Capacity ...	...	...	...	...	...	...	...	0.48 Imp. pints (0.270 litres, 0.55 US pints)
Oil grade ...	...	...	...	...	...	...	...	Engine oil

Main line filter

Make	...	...	...	...	...	...	...	Purflux
Type	...	...	...	...	...	...	...	CP 15DE

Fuel feed pump

Type	...	...	...	...	...	...	...	PLF6
Hydraulic part	...	...	...	...	...	...	...	Kugelfischer
Electric part	...	...	...	...	...	...	...	AEG
Capacity (approx.)	...	...	...	...	...	...	...	11 Imp. gallons (50 litres, 15.613 US gallons) under pressure of 17 lb sq in. (1.2 kg sq cm)

Injector pump

Make	...	...	...	...	...	...	...	Kugelfischer
Type	...	...	...	...	...	...	...	PL004 - 104 - 03
Injection pressure	...	...	...	...	...	...	...	42.66 - 54.03 lb sq in. (30.0 - 37.9 kg sq cm)
Fuel capacity (approx.)	...	...	...	...	...	...	0.7 Imp. pint (0.4 litre, 0.8 US pint)

Injectors

Make	...	...	...	...	...	...	...	Kugelfischer
Type	...	...	...	...	...	...	...	DLO 20 B
Calibration pressure (initial)	...	...	...	...	...	42.7 - 54.0 lb sq in. (30 kg sq cm)
Minimum permissible pressure	...	...	...	...	...	21.35 lb sq in. (15 kg sq cm)

Torque wrench settings

	lb f ft	kg fm
Injector holder ...	14.5	2.0
Injector pipe ...	18	2.5
Delivery valve ...	36	5.0
Suction valve ...	18	2.5
Injection pump pulley nut ...	25	3.5
Crankshaft pulley nut ...	123.5	17.0
Pump body to chamber (Allen screw) ...	14.5	2.0
Fuel feed union ...	14.5	2.0
Fuel return union ...	13	1.75

Part 1: Carburettor engines

1 General description

The basic fuel system comprises a single fuel tank located at the rear, from which petrol is pumped to the carburettor system by a mechanically operated pump.

The carburettor installation fitted depends on the model and date of manufacture. A single choke Solex carburettor was fitted to the XM engine series as found in the early saloon and station wagon models. A single twin choke Solex carburettor or pair of matched single choke Solex carburettors were fitted to the later XM engine series.

Incorporated in the carburettor is an acceleration pump which is actuated by the throttle control. This momentarily enriches the mixture supplied to the engine resulting in increased acceleration.

The air filter may be either of the replaceable paper type, cleanable nylon element type or the oil bath type depending on the model.

In order to meet exhaust emission regulations in the USA and elsewhere modifications and improvements to the basic fuel system have been introduced over the years. Vapour from the fuel tank is absorbed in a closed circuit system whilst the products of combustion are dealt with by closed circuit crankcase ventilation. The carburettors have been modified to improve fuel atomisation especially during initial warm-up, idling and acceleration conditions.

2 US Exhaust emission control regulations - their effect on d-i-y servicing

The fuel system of cars for the American market has been modified so that the car will comply with the Federal Regulations covering emission of hydrocarbons and carbon monoxide. To achieve this the ignition system must be set accurately using special equipment (See Chapter 4), before any attempt is made to adjust the carburettor(s) or controls. Thereafter, the fuel system may be reset: but once again special equipment must be used. The information contained in this Chapter is given to assist the reader to clean and/or overhaul the various components but when complete the car must be taken to the local dealer for final adjustments to be made. Failure to do this will mean that the car does not comply with the regulations.

3 Air cleaner - maintenance

A range of air cleaners have been fitted. However, they may be generally divided into two types: renewable element and oil bath. In all cases the dismantling procedure is obvious.

Renewable element (polyurethene foam)

It is recommended the element is changed at the correct mileage interval with the exception that if the car is being used in dusty areas the change interval be brought forward to every 6,000 miles (10,000 km). Do not attempt to wash the element or clean with a compressed air jet.

Renewable element (nylon)

This element should be changed every 24,000 miles (40,000 km) but may be cleaned every 6,000 miles (10,000 km) by washing in paraffin, allowing to drip-dry and then soaking in engine oil.

Oil bath

The filter element should be removed and cleaned in petrol or paraffin. Allow to drip-dry. Remove the old oil from the bowl and thoroughly clean. Refill the bowl up to the mark with 260 cc (approx.) of engine grade oil. Refit the element. If the car is being used in dusty areas the cleaning interval should be brought forward to 3,000 miles (5,000 km) or even sooner.

4 Fuel pump - general description

1 Although the three pumps fitted to 504 models covered by this manual differ in detail the general principle of operation is the same. The basic components of the pump are: a petrol chamber incorporating a filter, an inlet valve, an outlet valve, a diaphragm, a spring which pushes on the diaphragm, a lever which pulls the diaphragm and a small spring against which the lever operates. The inner end of the lever is linked to a rod attached to the diaphragm and its outer end is pushed by a plunger which is in contact with a cam lobe on the engine camshaft.

2 If there is no petrol in the pump the diaphragm is pushed up by the spring so that the space inside the petrol chamber is a minimum. In this case the plunger protrudes from the pump body as far as the cam on the camshaft will permit.

3 As the camshaft rotates it will push the plunger inwards, causing the lever to draw the diaphragm downwards against the pressure of the spring. The space inside the fuel chamber increases and petrol is drawn in by the resulting vacuum. When the cam leaves the plunger, the spring pushes the diaphragm upwards again but the inlet valve stops the petrol from returning to the tank.

4 As this operation is repeated the fuel chamber will soon fill with petrol which passes through the outlet valve and feed pipe to the carburettor float chamber. When the float chamber is full, the needle valve in the carburettor closes so that no more petrol can pass along the pipe.

5 When this happens, the diaphragm cannot return to its

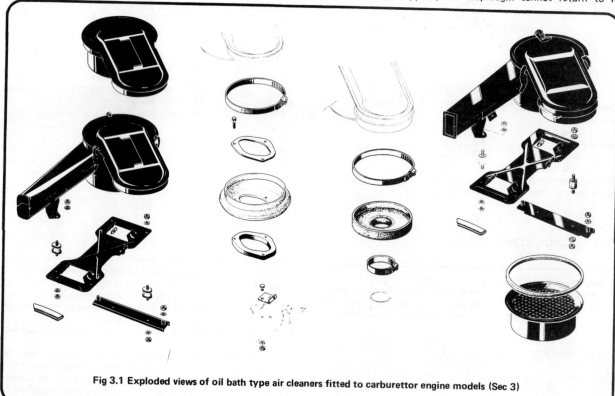

Fig 3.1 Exploded views of oil bath type air cleaners fitted to carburettor engine models (Sec 3)

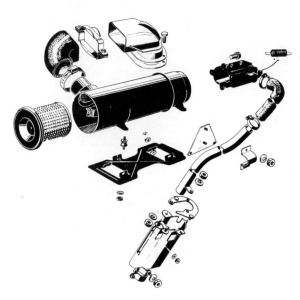

Fig 3.2 Exploded views of renewable element type air cleaners fitted to carburettor engine models (Sec 3)

original position. Once the pump is full of petrol and the diaphragm extended downwards, the lever will be held away from the plunger which in turn no longer bears on the camshaft lobe.

6 With the engine running the level of the petrol in the carburettor drops causing the needle valve to open. Petrol can once more pass along from the pump to the float chamber, continuing to do so until the float chamber is again full.

5 Fuel pump - removal and replacement

1 The fuel pump is located on the crankcase underneath the inlet manifold. It is retained by two bolts.
2 Remove the inlet and outlet connections from the pump and

plug the ends of the pipes to stop loss of fuel and dirt ingress.
3 Undo and remove the two bolts that secure the pump to the crankcase and lift away the pump. Recover the gasket.
4 Whilst the pump is being removed be careful to watch out for the plunger in case it falls out. From experience it will probably stay in the crankcase. If it does not stick out far enough for it to be gripped, turn the engine until the camshaft pushes it out a little further.
5 Refitting the fuel pump is the reverse sequence to removal but there are several additional points that should be noted:
   a) *Do not forget to refit the pushrod.*
   b) *Always fit a new gasket of the same type and thickness.*
   c) *Be careful when reconnecting the hoses that they are fitted the correct way round.*

6 Fuel pump - testing

Assuming that the fuel lines and unions are in good condition and that there are no leaks anywhere, check the performance of the fuel pump in the following manner: Disconnect the fuel pipe at the carburettor inlet union, and the high tension lead to the coil and, with a suitable container or large rag in position to catch the ejected fuel, turn the engine over. A good spurt of petrol should emerge from the end of the pipe every second revolution.

7 Fuel pump - dismantling

1 It will be seen after studying the fuel pump illustrations that two of the three types of pump can be taken apart completely, whereas the third type can only be dismantled to a limited degree, the main body halves being swaged together. (Fig. 3.3)
2 Before starting to dismantle, clear the pump of fuel by operating it a few times.
3 Thoroughly clean the outside of the pump with paraffin or a detergent such as Gunk and then wipe dry.
4 To ensure correct reassembly make alignment marks on the cover, the body and the lower flange.
5 Undo and remove the single screw holding the top cover to the main body. Note the fibre washer under the screw head.
6 Lift away the top cover and gasket followed by the filter element.
7 This is as far as the AC type pump can be dismantled. With

the other two types undo and remove the six screws and washers securing the two halves of the main body together.

8   Carefully part the two halves. Be prepared for the diaphragm to stick to the flanges so, unless it is to be renewed release it with a penknife.

9   Push out the pin holding the lever, being careful not to let the assembly fly apart under the pressure of the lever spring.

8   Fuel pump - inspection and reassembly

1   Thoroughly clean all parts in paraffin. Wipe dry and examine each part for signs of wear. Very little wear is permissible in the mechanical parts and linkages such as the lever and the pin holding it in the body.

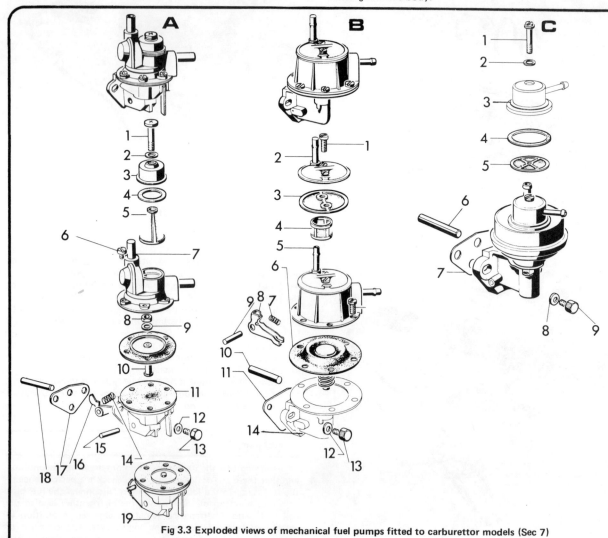

Fig 3.3 Exploded views of mechanical fuel pumps fitted to carburettor models (Sec 7)

Type A

   1 Screw
   2 Fibre washer
   3 Cover
   4 Seal
   5 Filter
   6 Screw
   7 Top cover
   8 Nut
   9 Washer
  10 Diaphragm
  11 Gasket
  12 Washer
  13 Bolt
  14 Spring
  15 Pin
  16 Lever
  17 Gasket
  18 Plunger
  19 Lower body

Type B

   1 Screw
   2 Top cover
   3 Gasket
   4 Filter
   5 Upper body
   6 Diaphragm
   7 Spring
   8 Lever
   9 Pin
  10 Plunger
  11 Gasket
  12 Washer
  13 Bolt
  14 Lower body

Type C

   1 Screw
   2 Fibre washer
   3 Top cover
   4 Seal
   5 Filter
   6 Plunger
   7 Gasket
   8 Washer
   9 Bolt

2 The diaphragm assembly should be renewed if there are any signs of wear, cracking or deterioration.

3 If the inlet or outlet valves are defective, it will be necessary to renew the pump body. From experience however, careful cleaning to dislodge a little particle of dirt will often cure the problem.

4 To reassemble, first install the lever and its pivot pin. Do not forget the small lever return spring.

5 Assemble the diaphragm spring, centre the diaphragm and engage its pull-rod with the lever. Position the diaphragm so that the holes located around its edge are exactly in line with those on the body flange.

6 When all is correctly positioned, check that the pull-rod is properly seated in the lever fork and that everything operates smoothly.

7 To fit the upper half of the body, hold the diaphragm against the flange by pushing on the lever (this is best done with the plunger temporarily installed in the body) whilst the upper body is lowered into position with the marks made on the two flanges in alignment.

8 Insert the six fixing screws and spring washers and tighten them until the heads just engage with their spring washers.

9 Check that the diaphragm is correctly centred and that it does not overlap the edge at any point. Then tighten the screws in a progressive and diagonal manner.

10 Replace the filter element and refit the top cover using new seals. Be careful not to overtighten the screw on the top cover.

9 Carburettor (Solex) - general description

1 Figs. 3:4, 3:5 and 3:6 show cross-sectional views of the Solex Carburettors series 32 BICSA and PBICA. The PBICA is found as a single fitting and also (minus its cold start device) as part of a twin installation of which the 32 BICSA is the other component. The description in the next few paragraphs applies equally to both types unless otherwise indicated.

2 At medium and fast engine speeds the vacuum in the venturi system - there are two concentric venturis (4 and 22 in Figs. 3:4 and 3:5)   causes petrol to be drawn through the emulsion air hole (5) after which it emerges into the venturi system.

3 At lower engine speeds, when the throttle is not very far open, the vacuum above the throttle is insufficient to draw the petrol up the emulsion tube in the manner just described. However, there is always a tendency for it to rise comparatively slowly in the tube to the level of the fuel in the float chamber, because there is a small air jet known as the correction jet or compensating jet (1) at the top of the chamber holding the emulsion tube. The size of this jet is carefully chosen to ensure that the mixture at low speed is neither too lean (as would happen if the jet were too small) or too rich (as would happen if the jet were too large and the petrol could rise too rapidly in the tube).

4 Clearly it is important that the fuel level should be accurately determined. It is set by a float (18) attached to a lever which pushes a needle valve upwards against a seating, cutting off the flow of petrol into the float chamber when it has reached a certain level.

5 When the throttle (11) is almost closed, very little mixture finds its way past it. However, in this condition the vacuum on the engine side of the throttle (which is very high in this condition) draws a small amount of mixture through a hole which is partially blocked by the idling adjustment screw, also called the mixture/volume control screw (10). The petrol arriving at this point has passed through the idling jet (6) whose size is chosen to give the desired idling performance. The passage through which petrol passes to the idling jet is clearly shown in Fig. 3:6 but, only the beginning and the end of the passage from the idling jet to the orifice controlled by the screw (10) appear in the diagram.

6 Many models are fitted with the 'Econostat' device. This consists of a tube with a jet (23) on the end of it, which is submerged in the float chamber and is connected, via a passageway, to an inlet (15) just above the venturi. When the throttle is well open, the vacuum at this point is sufficient to draw petrol through the jet into the ingoing air stream and so enrichen the mixture. By this means the engine is able to run on a weaker mixture at lower speeds without the risk of damage to the exhaust valves etc. which would occur if an equally weak mixture were used at high speeds.

7 In order to provide a momentary enrichment of the mixture when the throttle is open and so to improve acceleration, a diaphragm is made to exert the pressure on petrol in a small chamber connected to the main float chamber by a non-return valve and to the venturi, via a jet (24) and a short injection pipe (16). In fact, there is very little movement of the diaphragm whose actuating lever (17) is not, of course, rigidly connected to the rod (28) attached to the throttle control, but is pushed by a compression spring (29) through which the rod passes.

8 For cold starting the 32 BICSA carburettor is fitted with a conventional choke flap (3) incorporating a poppet-valve (2). When the engine is being turned over by the starter, the poppet valve is closed, but when the engine starts to run the vacuum on the engine side of the flap causes the valve to open and lets enough air in to prevent the engine from choking itself.

9 The PBICA carburettor employs an auxiliary jet system feeding mixture to the engine side of the throttle. The system is controlled by a rotating plate (27) having holes in it at intervals of 120°. When the plate is rotated to the correct position by the lever (25), a hole in the plate appears opposite the passage leading into the carburettor just below the throttle. This permits the flow of air from a passage in the top of the carburettor, through the starting air jet (26), into the small chamber covering the rotating plate and through the hole in the plate. At the same time another hole in the plate appears opposite a passage which is in communication with the starting petrol jet (28), permitting petrol to be sucked through this hole into the small chamber where it mixes with the air being drawn into the carburettor. The plate contains three holes equally spaced apart and progressively increasing in size, and may be set in two possible positions, in each of which the hole opposite the lower passage is larger than that opposite the passage communicating with the starting petrol jet (28); thus two degrees of 'choke' are obtained.

10 Figs. 3:7 and 3:8 shows simplified exploded views of the two carburettors. Although detail differences may appear on different models, study of the exploded views in conjunction with the description given in this Section will enable the owner to tackle work on these carburettors with confidence.

11 On some models an alternative form of enrichment is provided. A diaphragm valve assembly operates at wide throttle openings to permit the passage of petrol through a small jet direct into the venturi.

12 On some models, these carburettors may be fitted with a fuel cut-off solenoid (sometimes called an "electro-valve") which shuts off the fuel supply from the float chamber unless it is energised. By cutting off the fuel supply as soon as the ignition is switched off, the device prevents 'running on' - a source of air pollution.

10 Carburettor (32/35 SEIEA) - general description

1 Although the design of this two barrel carburettor is somewhat different from those described in the previous Section, its operating principles are basically the same. In the following description it will be assumed that the previous Section has been read and the basic principles of operation understood.

2 Figs. 3:9, 3:10, 3:11 and 3:12 show views of the carburettor with various parts indicated by letters and numbers to which reference is made throughout this Section.

3 The two barrels and their jets are not identical, the so called "primary" barrel being of smaller diameter and fed by a smaller main jet. Both barrels are equipped with starter choke flaps, which can be operated manually and are also controlled by a

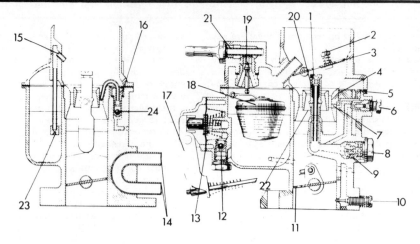

Fig 3.4 Solex 32BICSA Carburettor (Sec 9) [For caption see Fig 3.6]

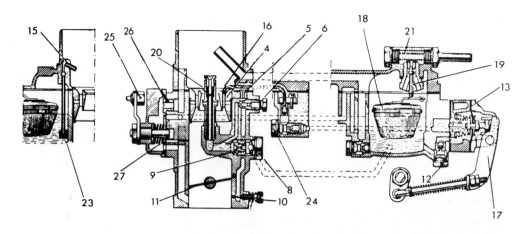

Fig 3.5 Solex 34 PBICA Carburettor (Sec 9) [For caption see Fig 3.6]

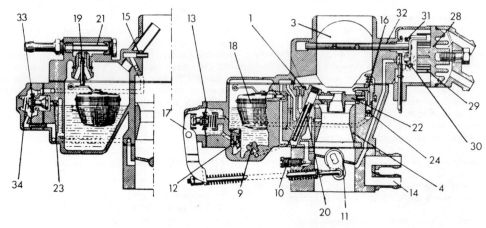

Fig 3.6 Solex 32 BICSA Carburettor (Sec 9)

1 Correction/compensating jet	screw
2 Choke poppet valve	11 Throttle flap
3 Choke flap	12 Non return valve float
4 Main venturi	chamber/accelerator pump
5 Emulsion air calibration hole	13 Accelerator pump diaphragm
6 Idling jet	14 Carburettor heater ducts
7 Emulsion air calibration hole	15 Econostat injector tube
(venturi)	16 Accelerator pump injector
8 Main jet carrier	17 Accelerator pump actuating
9 Main fuel jet	lever
10 Mixture/volume control	

18 Float
19 Needle valve
20 Emulsion tube
21 Petrol inlet gauge filter
22 Minor Venturi - petrol mixture dispersal
23 Econostat metering jet
24 Accelerator pump jet
25 Choke/cold starting system operating lever

26 Starting air jet
27 Starting valve plate
28 Automatic choke thermal head
29 Bi-metal coil strip
30 Choke actuating lever
31 Choke return spring
32 Choke spindle
33 Econostat valve diaphragm
34 Econostat valve spring

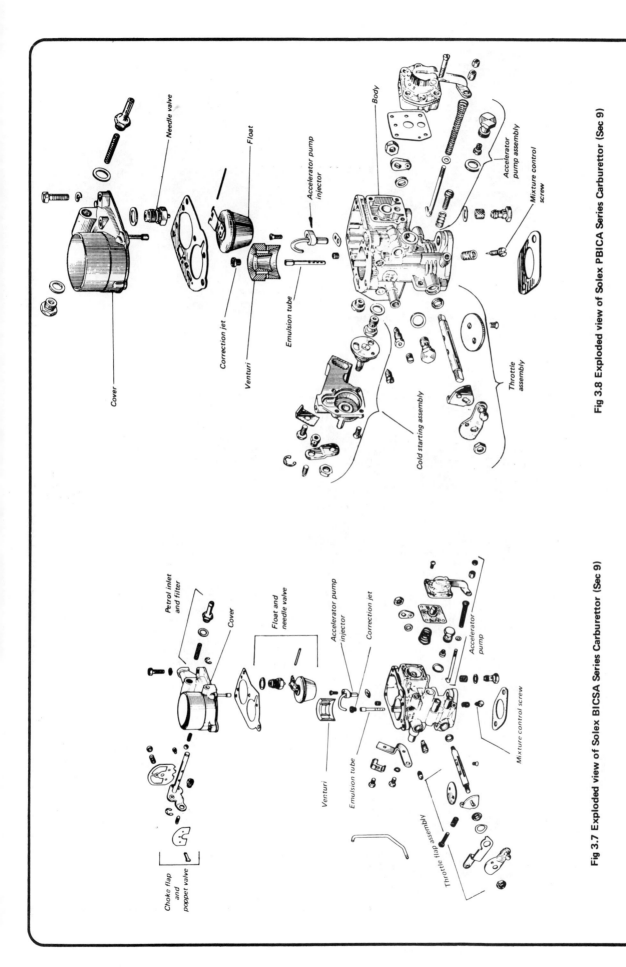

Needle valve

Float

Accelerator pump injector

Body

Accelerator pump assembly

Mixture control screw

Cover

Correction jet

Venturi

Emulsion tube

Cold starting assembly

Throttle assembly

Fig 3.8 Exploded view of Solex PBICA Series Carburettor (Sec 9)

Petrol inlet and filter

Cover

Float and needle valve

Accelerator pump injector

Correction jet

Accelerator pump

Mixture control screw

Choke flap and poppet valve

Venturi

Emulsion tube

Throttle flap assembly

Fig 3.7 Exploded view of Solex BICSA Series Carburettor (Sec 9)

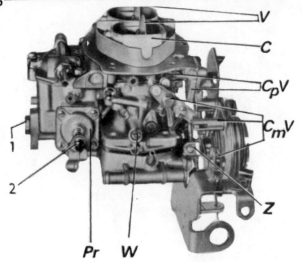

Fig 3.9 Side view of SEIEA Carburettor (Sec 10) [For caption see Fig 3.11]

Fig 3.10 Plan view of SEIEA Carburettor (Sec 10) [For caption see Fig 3.11]

Fig 3.11 Plan view of SEIEA Carburettor showing location of jets and adjustment screws (Sec 10)

1	Float bowl plug (access to main jets)
2	Acceleration pump adjusting screw
C	Plastic Plug
CmV	Manual strangler control
CpV	Preumatic partial strangler opening control
P&	Acceleration pump
V	Strangler flap
W	Mixture screw
Z	Throttle stop screw
a	Correction jets (fixed)
b	Overflow jets (fixed)
D	Sprayers (removable)
E	Econostat jet (removable)
g1	Pilot jet (1st choke)
g2	Bleed jet (2nd choke)
Gg1	Main jet (1st choke)
Gg2	Main jet (2nd choke)
H	Acceleration pump valve (removable)
i	Double acceleration pump injector (removable)
K	Venturis:

1st choke 24 mm
2nd choke 27 mm
idling air jets incorporated

Fig 3.12 SEIEA Carburettor - main and idling jets (Sec 10)

Gg 1 — Main jet   Gg 2 — Idling jet

Fig 3.13 These two screws settings must not be altered (Sec 10)

3 Second throttle flap stop   4 First throttle flap stop

pneumatic device which opens them slightly (if they are closed) when the engine vacuum is high enough, thus producing the same effect as the poppet valve on the 32 BICSA carburettor.

4 The carburettor incorporates an acceleration pump (Pn) which injects fuel into both barrels via an injector (1) just as described previously. This pump is controlled by a cam on the throttle spindle.

5 The spraying system (D) is somewhat different from the vertical emulsion device previously described. It is fed by a horizontal tube and the associated correction jet (a) operates by admitting a controlled amount of air into this tube in the same manner as was described in the previous Section.

6 The carburettor is fitted with an econostat system which functions as described in the previous Section. Instead of a separate tube dipping into the float chamber, the extra fuel is drawn into the barrels through passageways in the body and is controlled by a small jet (E).

7 Although idling is controlled by a single mixture/volume screw (W) and throttle stop screw (Z) it operates on both barrels and is regulated by two jets (g1) and (g2). Note that these two jets are not identical. The same is true of the main jets (Gg1) and (Gg2).

8 Fig. 3:13 shows the carburettor body with various jets and control screws removed. It also shows those which must not be touched.

11 Twin carburettor systems

1 A number of models are fitted with twin carburettor systems: a typical system employing a 32 BICSA and a 34 PBIC-8 is illustrated in Fig. 3:14. Usually these systems have a starting choke and idling controls fitted to only one of the carburettors (the primary in this case to the 32 BICSA-2). Note that in these systems, the carburettors are in tandem, just like the barrels of the SEIEA. The reason for employing two carburettors in this way is to ensure close control of the mixture over a wide range of engine speeds rather than to ensure an even distribution of mixture to the cylinders.

2 In these twin systems, the secondary carburettor may not always be fitted with a full complement of jets.

12 Carburettor - maintenance and adjustment

1 Before blaming the carburettor for any shortcomings in engine performance, remember that there is no reason why the carburettor should lose tune and in fact what usually happens is that as the engine gets older and less efficient, more or less fruitless attempts are made to bring back performance by playing about with the carburettor. This is never very successful and in those parts of the world where exhaust emission is regulated by law it is inadvisable and indeed often forbidden to alter carburettor settings without monitoring exhaust emission levels using special equipment.

2 The ultimate cause of most carburettor troubles is wear in moving parts or dirt in the jets. The Solex carburettor has no continuously operating moving parts except the float and the throttle spindle, which makes it a very reliable device so long as dirt does not enter it. A drop of oil on the various linkages and flap spindles will ensure that they last for years without trouble; this being the case, carburettor overhaul should be no more frequent than major engine overhaul.

3 Routine carburettor maintenance consists only of periodic cleaning of the float chamber and jets, with an occasional look at the small gauze filters associated with the fuel intake union and the acceleration pump valve. These tasks can be carried out without removing the carburettor from the engine. The location of the various jets can be found in the relevant illustration depending on the type of carburettor being dealt with. The small gauze filters are incorporated in the fuel intake union and the pump valve.

4 Before separating the top and bottom parts on the carburettor, or removing the jets, give the outside a good clean with paraffin or a detergent such as 'Gunk'. It is well worth taking this little extra trouble to prevent dirt getting into the carburettor.

5 Clean the jets by blowing air through them. **Never** use pieces of wire.

6 Gently withdraw or drive out (depending on the carburettor type) the spindle on which the float pivots. Remove the float and clean any dirt out of the float chamber with petrol. Use petrol too for washing the small gauze filters from the fuel intake union and the acceleration valve.

7 The work described in this Section together with a little oil on the linkages from time-to-time should be all the carburettor needs to keep it in perfect working order for a considerable time.

13 Carburettor - overhaul

1 There is no great difficulty in removing the carburettor installation from the engine. Disconnect the throttle and choke cables, the vacuum advance pipe, the heating pipes (be ready to block these or clip their ends together unless you have drained the cooling system) and the air hose. Undo and remove the

Fig 3.14 Twin carburettor installation (Secs 11 and 18)

W and 2   mixture screw
Z and 1   throttle stop screw

nuts holding the carburettor to the inlet manifold and simply lift away the carburettor. Do not forget to recover the gaskets. Where there are two carburettors naturally these are removed as a unit and not individually.

2 Once the carburettor is on the work bench, start by cleaning the exterior thoroughly with paraffin or 'Gunk' using a stiff brush where necessary.

3 When taking anything mechanical apart - and this applies particularly to carburettors - it is always sound policy to make sure that the pieces are put back exactly where they came from, even though they may appear to be interchangeable. This can be done by marking or labeling, by putting various pieces into boxes or tins so that they don't get muddled up, or by carefully laying the pieces out on newspaper.

4 Identify the relevant illustrations to the carburettor being dealt with and there will be no difficulty in dismantling. Start by removing the choke valve assembly (where this is fitted) which is held on to the main body of the carburettor by three screws. Follow this by removing the acceleration pump assembly, taking care that the diaphragm is not damaged. This assembly is attached to the main body of the carburettor by four screws except in the case of the SEIEA, but there can be no confusion between the choke valve and acceleration pump on the SEIEA because this carburettor has choke flaps and is not fitted with a choke valve.

5 Take off the top of the carburettor by undoing its fixing screws and lifting away from the main body.

6 The top contains the needle valve (or valves, in the case of the SEIEA) which should be unscrewed from the body, preferably with a small box or socket spanner.

7 The bottom of the main body holds the float or floats, which rest on a spindle set into the body.

8 Remove all jets except the correction jets on the SEIEA which should **never** be touched (See Fig. 3:11).

9 Think twice about removing any adjusting screws, particularly where exhaust emission control devices are fitted. Have a look at the idling adjustment instructions for the particular carburettor and make sure that in no circumstances are the screws altered where the instructions say so.

10 Dismantle the fuel inlet union and remove the acceleration pump valve, being careful not to damage the small gauze filters incorporated in them. The venturi can be removed but there is no real point in doing so.

11 Remove the control linkages from the throttle spindle, making very sure that their locations are noted for correct replacement. Undo the two screws holding the throttle flap to the spindle, supporting it with the other hand to avoid any risk of distortion. Remove the flap and withdraw the spindle, noting how the dustproof sealing rings are fitted.

12 There is little point in taking the dismantling further. The purpose of an overhaul is not to see how many pieces can be produced but to carry out a thorough examination of the component parts - renew these as necessary.

On the SEIEA there is an elaborate linkage mechanism designed to allow partial opening of the throttle flaps under "fast-idle" conditions. If this shows signs of wear it should be dismantled and the offending parts renewed. If it is taken apart make quite sure it can be put back together. Should the bearings for the throttle or choke flaps be worn and indeed if any part of the throttle linkage be worn or defective, it will be necessary to replace the whole carburettor body part in which these are incorporated as no provision is made for rebushing or renewing of individual bits and pieces of the throttle control.

13 Thoroughly clean the dismantled parts in petrol and then carefully examine each moving part for wear. This can be shown by scoring of the casing in which they operate. Check the needle valve by blowing through it while lightly pushing the plunger upwards. If a carburettor overhaul kit is purchased from the local Peugeot dealer it will include a new needle valve assembly as well as an acceleration pump diaphragm so obviously it is best to renew all the parts.

14 There is no provision for adjusting the float level on any of these carburettors except the SEIEA, for which the adjustment

procedure is given in a later Section. Make sure that the metal tag on the float is not bent or distorted; if it is replace the float. Where a metal float is used it may be checked for leakage by submersing it in warm water and looking for air bubbles, though generally speaking if the float is leaking this produces obvious symptoms: the carburettor overflowing with petrol or the mixture being too rich.

15 Reassemble all parts in the reverse of their removal order using new washers and gaskets, as supplied in the overhaul kit, all through and renewing such parts as deemed necessary or supplied automatically in the overhaul kit. Do not overtighten any attachment and do not use any gasket cement.

16 On reassembly, apply a drop of oil to the flap spindle bearings and the various linkages. This is an absolute must since the cleaning of these parts will have removed all traces of lubricant.

17 With reassembly complete, adjust the acceleration pump stroke as described in Section 14 or 15 (depending on the type of carburettor). When this has been completed, the carburettor is ready for refitting to the engine. Always use new gaskets.

14 Acceleration pump - stroke adjustment

1 This Section is applicable to all carburettors other than SEIEA.

2 In order to get the best out of the acceleration pump, its action must be correctly related to the opening of the throttle. The method of achieving this is shown in Fig. 3:15. The throttle flap is held open by a rod (1) whose diameter depends on the carburettor type. This diameter is important and is given in the caption to Fig. 3:15. A drill, as shown in Fig. 3:15 makes an accurate and easily obtained gauge.

3 With the throttle held open, slacken off the nut (2) completely and then tighten it down until it is just in contact with the lever (3). The pump stroke is now correctly set.

15 Acceleration pump (SEIEA) - stroke adjustment

1 This Section is applicable to all SEIEA carburettors.

2 On the SEIEA carburettor the pump stroke is controlled by a cam (6) - Fig. 3:16 - which operates a lever (8) which in turn pushes on the plunger (9).

3 Acceleration pump adjustment on the SEIEA should not be finally carried out until the carburettor is refitted and the idling speed correctly adjusted. Make sure too that the nut (5) holding the cam on the throttle spindle is really tight.

4 To carry out the adjustment, first release the screw (7) until there is a definite gap at (J). Then screw in the screw (7) until it just touches the plunger (9) and the roller (10) is just free of the cam (6).

16 Idling adjustment - XM and XM 7 engines

1 Before adjusting the engine idling speed, make certain that the ignition system is in good condition and properly timed. The engine must be warm (fan engaged). The exciter wire must be disconnected from the alternator to avoid fluctuations of engine speed caused by the varying load imposed by the alternator as its charging rate alters.

2 For engines not fitted with the 'fast idle' system for exhaust emission control first adjust the stop screw (Z) (Fig. 3:17) to obtain an engine speed of approximately 860 rpm.

3 Adjust the mixture screw (W) for maximum engine speed.

4 Reduce the engine speed to 860 rpm by altering the stop screw (Z).

5 Repeat these operations until the maximum engine speed obtainable with the mixture screw is 860 rpm.

6 Screw in the screw (W) until the engine speed drops to 800 rpm and the idling remaining perfectly regular.

7 For engines fitted with the 'fast idling' system, adjust the

idling in exactly the same way except that for engines fitted with a single carburettor (1969 models) the maximum obtainable engine speed should be 825 instead of 860 rpm, making sure that the fast idle system is operational. This can be checked by disconnecting the plug from the electronic control box (see Fig. 3:18) which should immediately produce a faster idling speed.

8 Note that on engines fitted with the 'fast idle' system the setting of the screw just above the mixture screw (W) must never be altered - and where there are two carburettors the setting of the second one must never be touched.

9 Adjustment of the fast idling is dealt with in Section 19.

17 Idling adjustment - XN1 engines with SEIEA carburettor

1 Before adjusting the idling, make certain that the ignition system is in good condition and properly adjusted. The engine must be warm (fan engaged). The exciter wire must be disconnected from the alternator to avoid fluctuations of engine speed caused by the varying load imposed by the alternator as its charging rate alters.

2 Adjust the stop screw (Z) (Fig. 3:17) to produce an engine speed of 840 rpm.

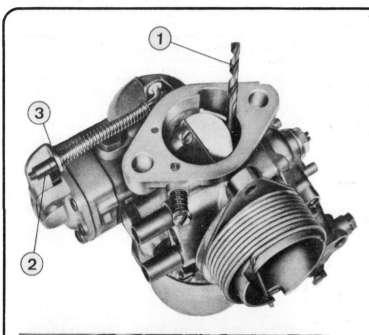

Fig 3.15 Accelerator pump stroke adjustment (Sec 14) [Carburettors except SEIEA]

1 Drill
2 Nut
3 Lever
    Throttle flap opening (drill size):
34 PBICA.5   —   3 mm
34 PBICA.7   —   3 mm
34 PBICA.9   —   3.5 mm
34 PBICA.8   —   4 mm
34 PBIC.8   —   6 mm
34 PBICA.6   —   6.5 mm

Fig 3.16 Acceleration pump stroke adjustment (Sec 15) [SEIEA Carburettor]

5 Nut on throttle spindle
6 Cam
7 Screw
8 Lever
9 Plunger
10 Roller
j Clearance

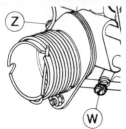

Fig 3.17 Idle speed adjustment (XM and XM7 engines) (Sec 16)

W mixture screw   Z Stop screw

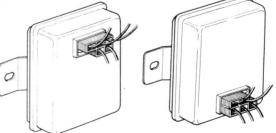

Fig 3.18 Electronic control box showing alternative lead positions (Sec 16)

3   Adjust the mixture screw (W) until the engine speed is at a maximum.

4   Reduce the engine speed to 840 rpm by altering the stop screw (Z).

5   Repeat these operations until the maximum obtainable engine speed is 840 rpm.

6   Screw in the screw (W) until the engine speed drops to 800 rpm without upsetting the regularity of the idling.

7   Be sure that no adjustment screws apart from (W) and (Z) are touched when carrying out these adjustments.

18 Idling adjustment - XN1 engine with twin carburettors

Follow the instructions of the previous Section, the screws (Z) and (W) now being those shown in Fig. 3:14. Instead of a maximum engine speed of 840 rpm set for a figure of 870 rpm for 1972 models or 830-880 rpm for 1973 on models. The final idling speed should be 800 rpm for 1972 models and 800-850 rpm for 1973 on models.

19 Fast idling - adjustment

1   The procedure is the same for all models to which this system is fitted. Start by disconnecting the lead from the electronic control box (See Fig. 3:18). This should immediately produce an increase in idling speed.

2   Where the control diaphragm is of the type shown in Fig. 3.19 (A) Slacken off the locknut (1) and adjust the nut (2) until the fast-idle speed is 1400 rpm. When this is done, tighten the locknut (1).

3   Where the diaphragm is of the type shown in Fig. 3:19 (B). Remove the cap nut (3) revealing the Allen screw (5) and its locknut (4). Slacken the locknut (4) and adjust the Allen screw using a 3 mm key until the engine speed is 1500 rpm.

4   In both cases, when the lead is reconnected to the control box the engine should revert to the normal idling rate.

20 Carburettor (SEIEA) - float level check and adjustment

1   Make up a gauge to the dimensions given in Fig. 3:20.

2   Place the gauge on the float chamber cover as shown in Fig. 3:21. With the gauge resting on the mating surface of the cover (the gasket should be removed) the cross-piece of the gauge should push the float to close the needle valve. The smaller diameter of the float should be in contact with the gauge.

3   If necessary adjust the system by bending the pivot arm (1) (Fig. 3:21).

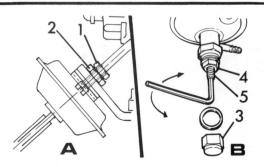

Fig 3.19 Control diaphragm unit (Sec 19) [Alternative types shown]

1   Locknut
2   Adjustment nut
3   Cap nut

4   Locknut
5   Allen screw (with key in position)

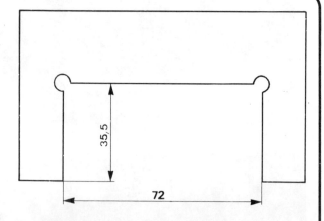

Fig 3.20 Float level setting gauge (Sec 20) [SEIEA Carburettor]

Fig 3.21 Checking float level setting (Sec 20) [SEIEA carburettor]

1   Pivot arm   2   Gauge

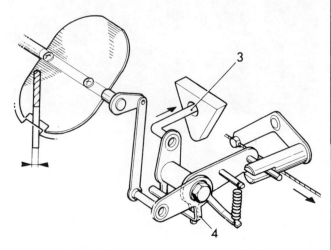

Fig 3.22 Setting choke flap partial opening (Sec 24)

3   Rod   4   Lever

21 Carburettor (SEIEA) - choke flap partial opening - check and adjustment

1 The SEIEA carburettor incorporates a pneumatic system whereby the choke flaps are slightly opened when the engine vacuum reaches a certain level (ie; when the engine reaches a certain speed with the choke flaps closed). This serves the same purpose as the poppet valves often found in choke flaps.

2 To reset the system, pull out the choke knob to its fullest extent. Leaving it in this position, push in the rod (3) (Fig. 3:22) as far as it will go, thus causing the choke flaps to open slightly.

3 The flap in the first choke should be open 0.079 - 0.118 in (2 - 3 mm). A simple way of checking this is to insert a rod or drill of suitable diameter as shown in Fig. 3:15.

4 Adjust if necessary by bending the lever (4) (Fig. 3:22).

22A Fault diagnosis - fuel system and carburation

Unsatisfactory engine performance and excessive fuel consumption are not necessarily the fault of the fuel system or carburettor. In fact they more commonly occur as a result of ignition and timing faults. Before acting on the following it is necessary to check the ignition system first. Even though a fault may lie in the fuel system it will be difficult to trace unless the ignition is correct. The faults below, therefore, assume that this has been checked and sorted out where necessary.

Symptom	Reason/s	Remedy
Smell of petrol when engine is stopped	Leaking fuel lines or unions Leaking fuel tank	Repair or renew as necessary. Fill fuel tank to capacity and examine carefully at seams, unions and filler pipe connections. Repair as necessary.
Smell of petrol when engine is idling	Leaking fuel line unions between pump and carburettor Overflow of fuel from float chamber due to wrong level setting, ineffective needle valve or punctured float	Check line and unions and tighten or repair. Check fuel level setting and condition of float and needle valve, and renew if necessary.
Excessive fuel consumption for reasons not covered by leaks or float chamber faults	Worn jets Over-rich setting Sticking linkages/controls	Renew jets or carburettor body if not removable. Adjust jet. Check correct movement of mechanism.
Difficult starting, uneven running, lack of power, cutting out	One or more jets blocked or restricted Float chamber fuel level too low or needle valve sticking Fuel pump not delivering sufficient fuel	Dismantle and clean out float chamber and jets. Dismantle and check fuel level and needle valve. Check pump delivery and clean or repair as required.

22B Fault diagnosis - emission control system

After reading through Section 22A the following additional points should be checked when investigating a fault in the fuel system which has been modified as described in Sections 23 to 29 inclusive. It is however important to appreciate that a fault located in the engine itself or ignition system can appear as a fault in the fuel system. The local Peugeot garage will have special equipment to locate the fault easily.

Symptom	Reason/s
PCV system Escaping fumes from engine	Clogged PCV valve split or collapsed hoses.
Fuel evaporative emission control system Fuel odour and/or rough running engine	Choked carbon canister. Stuck filler cap valve. Split or collapsed hoses.
Coppolair system Idle speed too low or too high Poor performance Excessive fuel consumption Backfire on acceleration Difficult cold start	Fault in electronic control box, electro-valve, diaphragm unit, vacuum tank or electro-magnetic plug. Seek expert advice.

Part 2: Emission control system

23 Emission control system - general description

1 The three basic causes of atmospheric pollution by the automobile are:

a) *Incomplete combustion of the petrol-air mixture drawn into the engine.*

b) *Fumes emitted from the crankcase breather when the engine is warm.*

c) *Direct evaporation of petrol from the tank.*

2 The first of these three causes is tackled in three different ways - by ensuring that the engine does not receive an over-rich mixture when the driver's foot is released from the accelerator, by maintaining as far as possible a constant temperature of inlet air, and by injecting air into the exhaust system as close to the exhaust valves as possible which has the effect of allowing combustion to continue after the exhaust gases have left the cylinders.

3 There are five approaches to the reduction of pollution, all of which are utilised in varying degree on different versions of the Peugeot 504.

4 There is of course a further way of combating pollution - stringent regulations regarding the adjustment of carburettors. The reader who keeps in mind the warnings given in this manual for setting up the ignition and carburation systems is unlikely to come into conflict with the authorities.

5 In the following Sections the various pollution control devices found on the Peugeot 504 are described and hints are given on their maintenance.

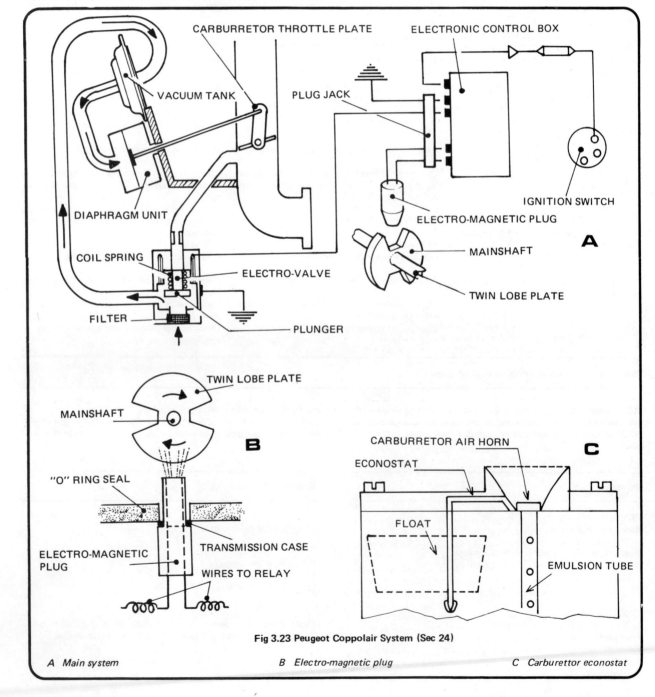

Fig 3.23 Peugeot Coppolair System (Sec 24)

A Main system   *B Electro-magnetic plug*   *C Carburettor econostat*

24 Fast idle system

1 In this sytem (sometimes known as the 'COPPOLAIR' system) the throttle flap of the carburettor is held slightly open under certain running conditions even when the throttle pedal is fully released, ensuring that in these conditions the mixture supplied to the engine is not over-rich. A diagram showing the working of the system is given in Fig. 3:23.

2 Referring to Fig. 3:23 the electro-valve is normally energised, via the electronic control box and in this case it takes up the position shown in Fig. 3:23 and the diaphragm unit controlling the throttle is connected to the atmosphere. This gives the normal idling state.

3 If however the valve is not energised the plunger is pushed down by the coil spring and blocks off the air intake from the pipe to the diaphragm, this now being connected to the pipe from the inlet manifold (ie; to engine vacuum). The diaphragm now operates the throttle control lever and moves the throttle flap into the fast idle position. Obviously, one way of causing the valve to be de-energised is to disconnect the wire leading to it, and this is in fact done when it is necessary to adjust the fast idle speed.

4 The electro-valve is operated by an electronic control box which energises it at low road speeds. As the road speed increases the valve remains energised until the speed reaches 25 mph (40.2 kph) when the current to it is switched off by the control box. When decelerating, the valve remains unenergised until the speed drops to 22 mph (35.4 kph).

5 The control box receives electrical impulses from an electro-magnetic plug fitted into the transmission case. A twin lobe steel plate fitted on the transmission main shaft cuts through the magnetic field of this plug twice per revolution of the main shaft and causes electrical impulses to appear in a coil incorporated in the plug. These impulses are transmitted to the control box and give it the speed information it needs to do its job.

6 In order that the operation of the throttle should not be too abrupt, a vacuum tank is fitted into the pipe between the electro valve and the diaphragm unit.

7 When this system is used in conjunction with dual carburettors it only operates on one of them.

8 The dual carburettors in this case are fitted with electro valves which shut off fuel supplies from the float chambers to the carburettors when the ignition is switched off. These valves - cylindrical with electrical connectors protruding from them - can be seen in Fig. 3:14. They must not be confused with the electro-valve controlling the diaphragm unit although they have the same name.

25 Fast idle pollution control system - maintenance

1 The adjustment of the fast idle controls on the carburettor have already been dealt with (see Section 19). Maintenance here consists of keeping the linkages clean and lubricated.

2 The operation of the electro-valve controlling the diaphragm unit is easily checked by removing and then refitting the lead to it whilst the engine is running. If the engine changes from a slow idle to a fast idle speed and then back again to a slow idle. Be careful not to earth the lead to the valve. If you do the control box will immediately be ruined.

3 **Do not** attempt to check the operation of the control box by connecting a test light across the output lead. This will also ruin the control box. The best plan is to connect a good quality volt-meter between the electro-valve terminal and earth. The speeds at which the valve operates may be checked by jacking-up one rear wheel and chocking the other three really well. Select a low gear, and with the engine running note the speedometer readings at which the valve operates. Do not worry if the readings are not very precise.

4 Replacing the electro-valve, the electronic control box or the vacuum units presents no difficulty. Always disconnect the battery first.

5 The sensing head (electro magnetic plug) is a little more awkard. It is positioned on the underside of the transmission, close to the rear. Look for the electric cable and then the sensing head. Before removing, it will be necessary to drain the transmission oil.

6 The sensing head is held by an inner circlip underneath which there is a washer. Using a pair of circlip pliers remove the circlip, ease out the washer and slide it along the cable. The head may now be easily removed but bear in mind it is sealed into the transmission casing by an 'O' ring. If it does not come out with the head, remove it from the casing.

7 The cable does not disconnect from the plug; withdraw it from the two pin socket at the other end. When fitting a new head, be sure to replace the old 'O' ring with a new one.

8 The small electro-valves fitted to dual carburettor systems can easily be removed from the carburettor bodies and their action checked. A small plunger withdraws into the body when the valve is energised. Replacement, if necessary, is no problem.

26 Inlet air heating system

1 Fig. 3:7 illustrates the system, which is associated with the cylindrical air filter assembly.

2 An air flap inside the blender assembly is controlled by a wax thermostat. When the intake air is cold, the thermostat element contracts and holds the flap closed, cutting off cold air and allowing hot air to flow in from the heat exchanger attached to the exhaust system.

3 As the element warms up, it tends to cut off the supply of heated air, thus regulating the temperature of the air passed to the inlet manifold.

4 The system calls for no special maintenance but should the thermostat fail, which is not likely, the blender assembly must be replaced as a complete unit.

27 Air injection system

1 An exploded diagram of the Peugeot air injection system is shown in Fig. 3:24. The air distribution plate is fitted between the cylinder block and the exhaust manifold, and air is pumped into this through a non-return valve from the air pump. This valve is, of course, a very vital component of the system. It protects the hoses and the pump from any possibility of damage should a back fire occur or should the drive belt of the pump break.

2 As well as ensuring combustion of any unburned fuel carried through to the exhaust system the system also supplies extra air to the inlet manifold during car deceleration. The injection valve is controlled by vacuum from the inlet manifold. Under normal running conditions the valve is closed, but when the vacuum in the inlet manifold increases rapidly, as it does when the driver's foot is lifted from the accelerator pedal, the valve opens and air under pressure is fed into the inlet manifold. This achieves the same objective as the 'fast idle' system in producing a less rich mixture than would otherwise occur on deceleration.

3 Apart from the air pump, the system requires little attention except to ensure that the hoses are satisfactory and that the two valves are operating correctly. The simplest way to check the non-return valve is to disconnect the air hose from the valve run the engine, seeing that no exhaust gases come back from it. A similar check can be carried out on the injection valve; the hose to the non-return valve must, of course, be fitted when the injection valve is checked. Remove the pipe feeding air from the valve to the air intake, run the engine and have an assistant rev up and then take his foot off the accelerator. A puff of air should be felt to come from the injection valve when this is done.

4 The air pump is only serviced as a unit so if it develops an internal fault it is necessary to obtain and fit a new one.

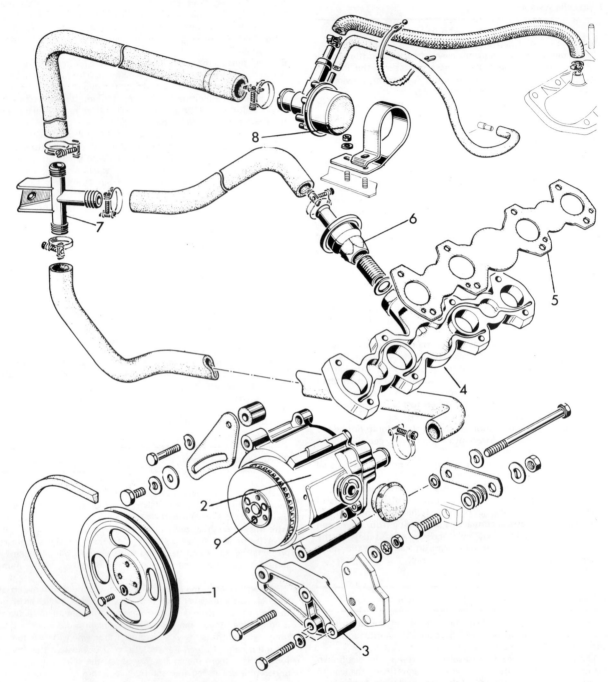

Fig 3.24 Main components of air injection system (Sec 27)

1 *Pulley*	*mounting bracket*	6 *Non-return valve*	8 *Injection valve*
2 *Air pump*	4 *Air distribution plate*	7 *'T' union*	9 *Centrifugal air filter*
3 *Air pump main*	5 *Gasket*	8 *Injection valve*	

28 Crankcase ventilation system

1   The operation of the system is shown in Fig. 3:25.
2   Crankcase fumes are drawn into the inlet manifold through two pipes which branch out from the oil filler cap. The tube leading to the oil filler cap contains a pressure control valve whose object is to limit the back pressure caused by crankcase vacuum which might otherwise affect the performance of the engine by influencing the airflow. When the throttle is closed, the high vacuum on the engine side of the throttle causes fumes to be drawn in through the orifice on the inlet manifold, which is small enough not to affect the idling. At this time the vacuum on the carburettor intake is not very great and relatively few fumes are drawn in at this point; thus the petrol/air mixture is not radically affected by the crankcase fumes.
3   When the throttle is opened, the air inlet vacuum increases and draws fumes into the air intake, but effect is now much less

because of the greater volume of air involved. At intermediate throttle openings, fumes may enter through both systems. Ultimately, the fumes enter the engine where they are burned.

4   Maintenance consists of cleaning and checking the orifice in the inlet manifold, the pressure control valve and the hoses for deterioration every 9,000 miles (1,500 km).

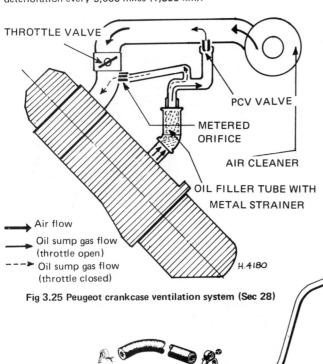

Air flow

Oil sump gas flow (throttle open)

Oil sump gas flow (throttle closed)

H.4180

Fig 3.25 Peugeot crankcase ventilation system (Sec 28)

29 Fuel evaporation control system

1   Fig. 3.26 shows the various parts of the fuel evaporation control system. The 'Separator' is no more than a small tank which has a connection on top taken to an outlet in the petrol tank or its filler tube.

2   Petrol vapour from the fuel tank empties into the separator, where some of it is condensed and fed back, via the connection at the bottom of the separator, to the fuel tank. The remaining vapour finds its way to the canister, which is mounted under the bonnet, containing activated charcoal. This absorbs the remaining vapour. A tube is connected from the canister to the inlet manifold and when the engine is running air is drawn through the carbon in the canister and the petrol or petrol vapour stored in the carbon is drawn out of it and passes into the inlet manifold.

3   The system requires no maintenance apart from keeping an eye on the tubing and its clips to prevent any possibility of leakage, which could be dangerous. Only visible damage can stop the separator and canister from doing their job, and if damaged they must of course be renewed.

4   It is perhaps worth noting the plastic tubing connecting the separator to the canister is taken along the roof of the car and down inside one of the front windscreen pillars.

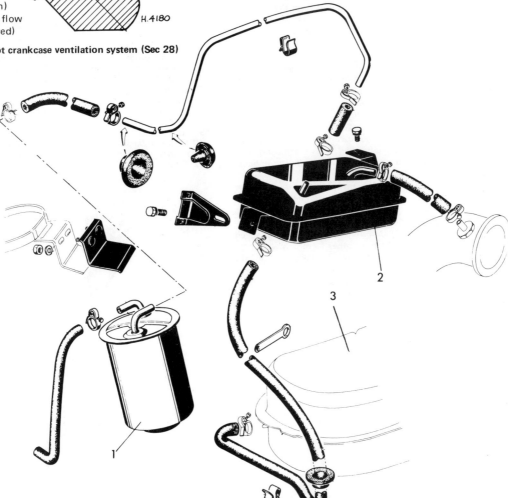

Fig 3.26 Fuel evaporation system - main components (Sec 29)

1   Canister assembly   2   Separator assembly   3   Fuel tank

Part 3: Fuel injection system

30 General description - fuel injection system

1 The best way to understand the operation of the fuel injection system is to consider the basic operation of a conventional carburettor system first.

Obviously, the more fuel an engine burns the more power it will develop within obvious design limitations.

To ensure that the fuel is burnt correctly it must be mixed with air in the correct proportions. If the mixture is too rich, there will not be enough oxygen to support combustion as every motorist who has used the choke control too enthusiastically will know. If it is too weak, the burning process is slow and irregular - sometimes it is still going on when the inlet valve opens and 'spitting back' in the carburettor occurs. The basic function of the fuel system, then, is simply to provide the amount of fuel the engine needs at any given time mixed with the amount of air required to ensure that it is properly burnt.

2 The accelerator pedal, opening and closing the throttle, controls not the amount of fuel entering the engine but the amount of air. A measure of this amount is the suction which occurs on the carburettor side of the throttle (ie; the degree of vacuum set up there). This pressure drop causes the carburettor to release an amount of petrol vapour in ratio to the amount of air going in. This is easier said than done, as is obvious when one looks at the complexity of a modern carburettor as described in Sections 9 and 10.

In the past few years, insistance on the reduction of atmospheric pollution has lead to a demand for tighter control of the petrol/air mixture, and this has made the problems facing the carburettor designer even more difficult. For example, the maximum mixture varies with the temperature of the ingoing air, basically because when air is warm the same weight of air occupies more space and it is the weight of air to weight of fuel that must be considered **not** volume to volume. In the carburettor engine an attempt to improve matters is described in Section 26. However, the problem is dealt with in a different way in the fuel injection engine and the thermostatically operated flap and branch pipe to a hot spot on the exhaust system are not used.

3 The fuel injection system is entirely different from the carburettor because it does not rely directly on engine vacuum to control the amount of petrol drawn in. On each inlet stroke a measured amount of petrol is squirted into the inlet manifold, the amount being principally determined by the engine speed and throttle position, though there are other factors as well.

In the Kugelfisher system fitted to the Peugeot 504, the amount of petrol injected is controlled by varying the stroke of a special pump. The principle of operation is shown in Fig. 3.27.

Referring to the illustration the heart of the system is the hydraulic head (c) containing four metering systems (one of which is shown in section) comprising a piston (1) operating in one branch of a three-way channel whose other branches contain one-way valves. As the piston descends, fuel under pressure enters the system through the inlet valve, and as the piston comes up again petrol is forced out through the outlet valve. The piston is driven, via a tappet, from a camshaft which runs at half engine speed. There are four piston systems, one for each engine cylinder.

The amount of petrol pushed out is determined by the stroke of the piston. The piston is raised by a tappet (5) but its lowest point is determined by the position of the beam (3) on which its lower end rests (the tappet drives the piston through a hole in the beam). Both ends of this beam can be raised or lowered, one end is threaded onto a cranked rod which is attached to the richness lever (14), and if this lever moves downwards as shown in the illustration the end of the beam moves upwards, thus raising the centre part of the beam and shortening the stroke, so reducing the amount of petrol pushed out and making the mixture weaker.

Conversely, when the richness lever (14) is in its highest

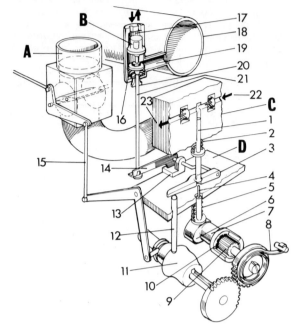

Fig 3.27 Principle of operation of fuel injection pump (Sec 30)

1 Piston	13 Stop
2 Piston spring	14 Richness lever
3 Stroke checking beam	15 Link rod
4 Tappet	16 Thermo control spring
5 Spring	17 Water sleeve in mani-
6 Cam	fold
7 Camshaft	18 Distributor
8 Checking spring	19 Air boost pipe
9 Armature	20 Valve
10 Magnetic bars sleeve	21 Control
11 Adjustment can	22 Inlet valve
12 Finder	23 Delivery valve

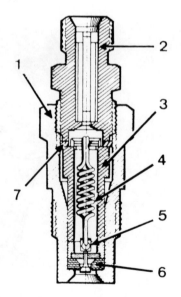

Fig 3.28 Cross-sectional view of injector (Secs 30 and 31)

1 Injector holder	5 Valve
2 Connection	6 Seat
3 Injector body	7 Steel joint washer
4 Spring	

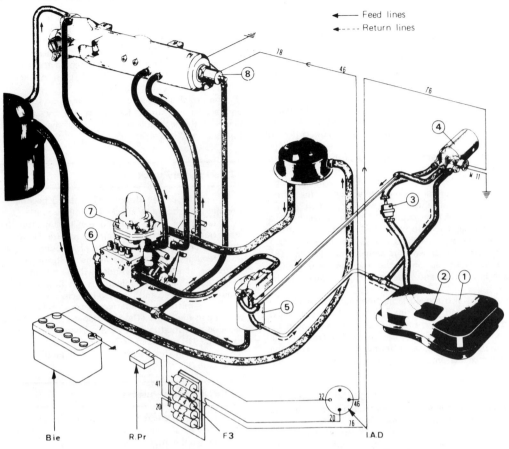

← Feed lines

←---- Return lines

Fig 3.29 Petrol injection system as fitted to KF5 and XN2 engines

Bie	Battery	1AD	Ignition switch	3	Pre-filter	6	Injection pump filter
RPr	Relay	1	Fuel tank	4	Electric lift pump	7	Injection pump
F3	Fuse	2	Fuel strainer	5	Degassing filter (fuel filter)	8	Electrovalve

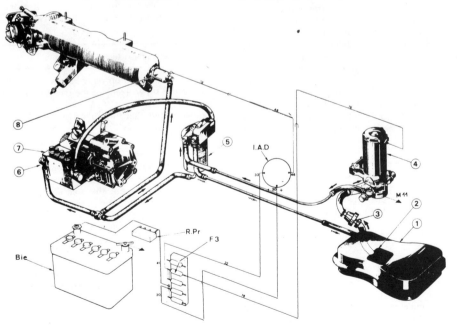

Fig 3.30 Petrol injection system as fitted to KF6 engine [For caption see Fig 3.29]

position the mixture is at its richest. The richness lever is operated by a pushrod (21) which is connected to a thermostat element (B) which is in contact with the coolant. The element expands as it gets warm, gradually pushing down the control rod as the temperature increases until by the time it has reached 50°C the lever has reached its lowest point. Thus below 50°C the richness of the mixture automatically varies with engine temperature.

Also operated by the thermostat is an air valve (20) which gradually closes as the pushrod descends; this allows a little extra air into the manifold when the mixture is rich in order to improve idling.

The other end of the beam is lifted, via a pushrod (12), by a specially shaped cam (11). This cam does not revolve continuously, but the spindle holding it can be turned through about 180° by a gear whose position is altered against the action of a spring (8) by a mechanism very similar to that of the magnetic speedometer. An armature (9) is concentric with a sleeve (10) containing magnetic bars which forms part of the camshaft (7) revolving at half engine speed. The faster the shaft revolves, the further the gear wheel is dragged round against the pull of the spring by the action of the magnetic field. By this means the cam is revolved and a degree of lift it gives to the beam is varied.

This same cam is also moved along the shaft to which it is keyed by a lever operated from a link rod (15) which is attached to the throttle control. Thus the cam is influenced both by engine speed and by the position of the throttle control, and the variation in cam position produces differing degrees of lift on the beam (3) and hence the amount of petrol forced through the outlet valve.

This sytem is employed on 504 models fitted with the KF6 engine. However models fitted with the KF5 or XN2 engines use a pump in which the richness lever is controlled by a pneumatic governor fitted to the top of the pump. This governor performs two functions; in conjunction with the "altitude corrector" which incorporates an aneroid, it adjusts the mixture to compensate for variations in barometric pressure, principally those brought about by altitude, and it adjusts the mixture during deceleration, preventing this from being too rich - thus achieving the same results as the 'fast idle' system on the carburettor engine.

Figs. 3.29 and 3.30 show the fuel feed arrangements for the two systems and in the case of the KF5/XN2 system the air feeds as well. They also illustrate the starting device briefly referred to earlier - an electro-valve which operates only when the starter motor is running to admit a small amount of fuel (under pressure from the primary pumping system) into the manifold to provide a richer mixture. The only components of the system not dealt with so far are the injectors themselves. A diagram is shown in Fig. 3.28. The fuel is simply squirted into the inlet manifold at a point close to the inlet valve port. There must be a nice even squirt and be no dribble at the end of the injection point.

31 Injector - removal, checking and replacement

1   For safety reasons, disconnect the battery.
2   Take off the clamps that hold either end of the injector supply pipe.
3   Undo the nut at the injector end and then the nut at the pump end.
4   Special equipment is required to pressure test an injector so it will be necessary to take all the injectors to the local Peugeot garage for testing. For information however injector performance data is given at the beginning of this Chapter.
5   When replacing an injector always use a new washer between the injector holder and the manifold.
6   Tighten the injector holder to the inlet manifold to a torque wrench setting of 14.5 lb f ft (2.0 kg f m).
7   Connect the pipe at the injector end first and tighten the connection to a torque wrench setting of 18 lb f ft (2.5 kg f m).

Hold the injector holder with a spanner to take the strain whilst tightening otherwise additional torque will be applied to the injector holder as well as the pipe union.
8   If a leakage appears after an injector has been refitted do not attempt to cure this by over-tightening the connections. Start the engine and slightly slacken, then correctly tighten the offending connection.
9   Should this procedure not cure the leak check that the connection is entirely free from dirt by giving it a thorough clean. If the leak still persists change the complete pipe or the injector.

32 Fuel delivery check

When the engine slow running speed becomes irregular the fuel delivery should be checked as follows:
1   Slacken the union nut on one of the injectors slightly; as fuel leaks out the cylinder will start to misfire. Doing this to each of the injectors in turn will indicate which cylinder is at fault.
2   Interchange the injector in the misfiring cylinder with that from one of the other cylinders. If the misfiring now occurs on the other cylinder, the injector is not functioning correctly and should be checked and renewed if necessary.
3   If the misfiring is unaffected by injector change, the fault must be in the pump. The first step is to bleed the pump delivery valve as described in Section 33. Thereafter, it must be checked for leakage as described in Section 34.
4   If misfiring still persists renew the suction valve as described in Section 36.

33 Delivery valve - bleeding

1   Thoroughly clean the area around the valve so there is no possibility of dirt finding its way into the pump.
2   Remove the injector pipe completely.
3   Slacken the delivery valve nut.
4   Switch on the ignition and allow a small amount of fuel to flow out from around the nut.
5   Tighten the nut to a torque wrench setting of 36 lb f ft (5.0 kg f m).
6   Refit the injector pipe and tighten the union to a torque wrench setting of 18 lb f ft (2.5 kg f m).

34 Delivery valve - leakage check

1   With the injection pipes removed, switch on the ignition and check the time taken for the recesses in the valves to fill up with fuel.
2   Any valve that fills up in less than 30 seconds is defective and should be renewed.

35 Delivery valve - removal and replacement

1   Thoroughly clean the area around the valve so there is no possibility of dirt finding its way into the pump.
2   Detach the injector pipes.
3   Unscrew the delivery valve.
4   Clean out the inside of the valve recess and lightly smear it with a little clean oil.
5   Fit the new valve complete with spacer and tighten it to a torque wrench setting of 36 lb f ft (5.0 kg f m) (Fig. 3.31).
6   Refit the injector pipes and tighten the unions to a torque wrench setting of 18 lb f ft (2.5 kg f m).

36 Suction valve - removal and replacement

1   Thoroughly clean the area around the underside of the pump so there is no possibility of dirt finding its way into the pump.

2 Unscrew and remove the suction valve. Recover the 'O' ring and filter (Fig. 3.32).

3 Clean the new valve assembly and lightly lubricate the 'O' ring and the thread with clean oil.

4 Refit the valve but do not fully tighten yet.

5 Switch on the ignition and slacken off the suction valve until petrol is flowing from it. Tighten the valve to a torque wrench settting of 18 lb f ft (2.5 kg f m).

6 Finally bleed the corresponding delivery valve as described in Section 33.

37 Fuel injection pump - removal and replacement

1 In order to remove the fuel injection pump it will be necessary to remove the air chamber. Fig. 3.33 shows it propped up on the rocker cover with the hoses to the thermostat still connected. There is no need to remove them. The rod shown

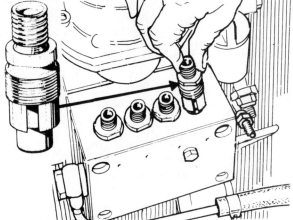

Fig 3.31 Delivery valve complete with spacer

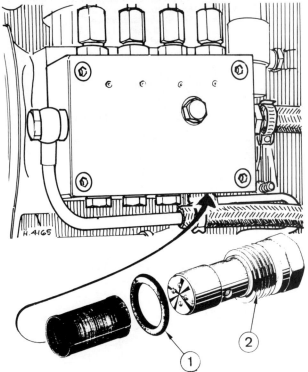

Fig 3.32 Suction valve and its location (Sec 36)

1   'O' ring   2   Valve assembly

sticking up in the air is normally connected to the enrichment lever on the pump. The injection pipes have been removed completely, as have the oil vapour recirculation hose (disconnected at the filter end), the vacuum lines to the distributor and brake servo, the electro-valve petrol line and feed wire, and the throttle cable.

2 On KF5/XN2 installations the system is slightly more complicated, one difference being that the thermostat hoses are connected to the pump instead of to the air chamber so they have to be disconnected. Raise the ends of the hoses above the level of the radiator header tank and it will not be necessary to completely drain the cooling system. Fig. 3.35 shows details of the various hose connections to the pump and the air chambers in case they become muddled.

3 On KF5/XN2 installations there is an oil line between the oil filter mounting and the pump (Fig. 3.34).

4 Remove the fanbelt, the alternator drivebelt, the crankshaft pulley and the timing cover. This will reveal the injection pump pulley driven by a flexible toothed belt from a similar pulley on the camshaft.

5 Before proceeding identify the timing reference marks on the two pulleys and the corresponding small projections on the driving belt as shown in Fig. 3.36. Notice how the two projections straddle a mark on the pump pulley while a single

Fig 3.33 Air chamber detached and supported on rocker cover (Sec 37)

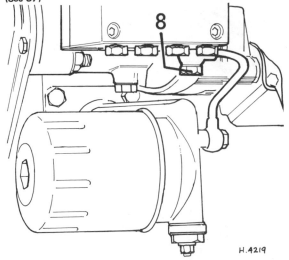

Fig 3.34 Location of oil line between injection pump and filter (Sec 37)

8   Union to underside of pump

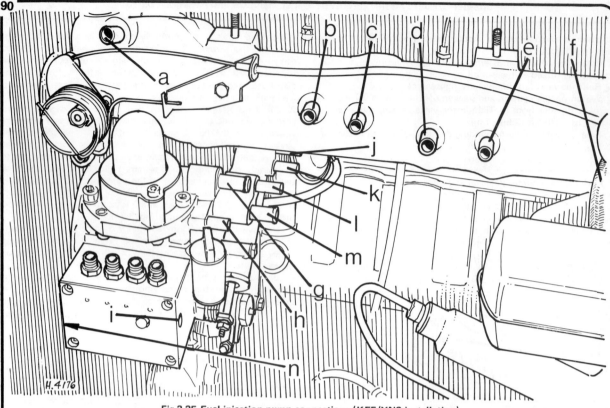

Fig 3.35 Fuel injection pump connections (KF5/XN2 installation)

From	To	Identification
Cylinder head	(j)	Thermostat intake
Water pump	(k)	Thermostat outlet
Air chamber (e)	(l)	Fast idling air intake (O 10 mm)
Air chamber (d)	(m)	Counter pressure line (O 13 mm)
Corrector (f)	(g)	Altitude correction line (O 13 mm)
Air chamber (a)	(h)	Pneumatic governing line (O 10 mm)
Air chamber (b)		Master-Vac vacuum line*
Air chamber (c)		Oil vapour recirculation line*
	(n)	Fuel feed
	(i)	Fuel return

*The removal of these lines is not essential

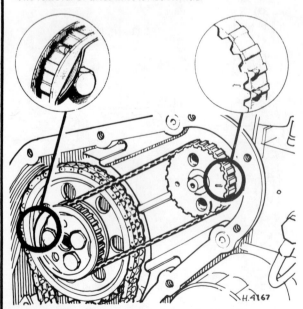

Fig 3.36 Timing reference marks (Sec 37)

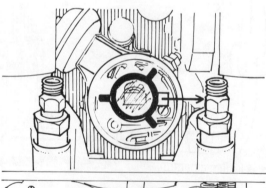

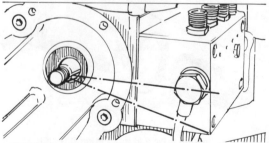

Fig. 3.37 Correct location of keyway and distributor rotor arm (Sec. 37)

projection coincides with a mark of the driving pulley. Notice also which way round the belt is fitted with the projections to the front. It will certainly be necessary to turn the crankshaft to line up the marks to the position shown in Fig. 3.36. Straighten up the lockwashers and remove the fixing nut holding the pump pulley to its spindle.

6 With the pulley removed the position of the keyway on the pump spindle should be as shown in Fig. 3.37. Should the spindle move as the pulley is being drawn replace the pulley and reposition the pulley mark.

The pulley being on a taper should come off quite easily. If it needs a little persuasion obtain and screw in bolts up to the timing case. Alternatively slacken off the two screws which hold the pump to the timing case and withdraw the pump until the pulley rests against the timing case when a gentle tap or two on the end of the spindle with a soft faced hammer will serve to loosen the pulley.

7 Refitting the pump is the reverse sequence to removal. The timing is set up by turning the crankshaft until the rotor arm contact lies between No 1 and No 3 HT terminals this will bring the mark on the driving pulley to the position shown in Fig. 3.36, and the pump pulley (keyed to the pump spindle) is turned until its mark is correctly positioned and the belt projections can be lined up with the marks on the two pulleys. Tighten the pump pulley nut to a torque wrench setting of 25 lb f ft (3.5 kg f m). Always use a new gasket between the pump and the timing case.

8 When the pump is fitted, the timing cover should be carefully entered before being refitted (using a new gasket), and following this the crankshaft pulley should be fitted using a new tab washer and tightening the retaining nut to a torque wrench setting of 123.5 lb f ft (17.0 kg f m).

9 On KF6 installations, replace the air chamber, making sure that the thermostat rod engages with the enrichment lever. Tighten the Allen screws securing the pump body to the chamber to a torque wrench setting of 14.5 lb f ft (2.0 kg f m).

10 Tighten the alternator belt.

11 Tighten the fuel feed union to a torque wrench setting of 14.5 lb f ft (2.0 kg f m), the return union to a torque wrench setting of 13 lb f ft (1.75 kg f m), and the injection line unions to 18 lb f ft (2.5 kg f m).

12 When the engine is running, bleed the oil line (Fig. 3.34) by slackening the upper connector (8) until oil runs steadily past it and then fully tighten.

38 Throttle setting and idling speed - adjustments

1 Adjustment of the system has the following objects:

a) *To ensure that the throttle is opened to the correct small degree when idling.*

b) *In the KF6 system, to maintain correct synchronism between the throttle setting and the pump (in the KF5/XN2 system this is taken care of automatically by the pneumatic governor once the initial throttle opening has been set).*

c) *To ensure a correct relationship between the enrichment lever and the rod which operates it, ie; to ensure that the appropriate enrichment is obtained over the right range of engine temperature.*

d) *To produce the best mixture. The design of the system is such that if the mixture is adjusted to produce correct idling it will be right over the whole range of engine speeds.*

2 Adjustments (a) and (b) are purely mechanical, they are of course an essential preliminary to the mixture adjustment (c). These procedures are devised by the manufacturer to ensure that the engine has the best possible overall performance. If they are departed from, any apparent improvement in engine performance over a restricted range will be offset by a falling off elsewhere.

3 This is particularly important in countries where pollution regulations are rigidly enforced. Incorrect adjustment, even where it makes no significant difference to engine performance, may well produce a degree of pollution outside the acceptable limits.

4 Before commencing work ensure that the **ignition timing** is correctly and accurately set. The contact breaker **points and spark plugs** must be in good order and correctly **adjusted.**

5 Make sure that there are no air leaks and that **the air filter is** in good condition and not blocked by dust and **dirt. This is** doubly important in the KF5/XN2 system which **depends on a** vacuum governor and extra care should be taken **to see that all** lines connected to the air chamber are in first class **condition.**

39 KF6 system - throttle adjustment

1 Check that the distance between centres of the ball heads on the link rod is 3.65±0.004 in (97.3±0.1 mm). If necessary slacken off one of the locknuts and screw the associated ball head in or out until the correct distance is obtained. Be sure that the faces of the ball heads are in line with each other.

2 With the link removed, lock the lever on the pump body by inserting a 0.20 in (5.0 mm) rod through the hole or slot in the pump lever into a blind hole in the pump body (see Fig. 3.38). **Do not** slacken the bolt clamping the lever to its spindle.

3 Slacken the bolt (2) Fig. 3.38 and 3.39. Now insert a strip of metal 0.266±0.001 in (6.75±0.025 mm) in the groove at the

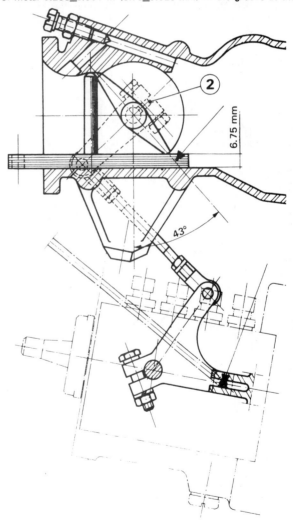

Fig 3.38 Throttle adjustment - KF6 System (Sec 39)

Arrows show metal gauges to be used (See text)

bottom of the throttle entrance. Figs. 3.38 and 3.39 show the gauge used by Peugeot garages in position. The rod sticking out of the metal strip has no critical dimensions, it is simply there to push up against the throttle flap so that this is firmly held against a metal strip when the gauge is pushed into the throttle flap housing.

4 With the throttle flap and the pump lever both locked into their reference positions - the lever by the rod and the throttle flap by the gauge - replace the link, engaging its ball heads with the levers on the pump and on the throttle spindle, and tighten the bolt (2) leaving a clearance of 0.8 ins (2.0 mm) between the lever and the housing. The pump and throttle are now correctly aligned.

5 It now remains to align the throttle drum correctly. This has **three** reference faces as shown in Fig. 3.40. It is secured to the **spindle** by an Allen screw which is accessible after removal of the throttle return spring. Slacken this screw and line the reference face (A) with the lower face (F) of the boss on the air chamber as shown in Fig. 3.41. When tightening the Allen screw, leave a clearance of 0.004 in (1 mm) between the drum and the housing.

6 Alignment of the pump and throttle is now complete. Remove the gauge and the rod. Check that the system operates smoothly. Do not forget to lubricate all moving parts. Finally, do not refit the throttle return spring until the maximum throttle opening adjustment has been completed as described in the next Section.

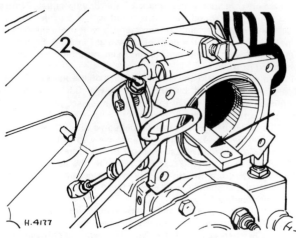

Fig 3.39 Inserting metal strip into groove at bottom of throttle entrance (Sec 39)

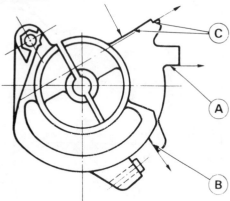

Fig 3.40 Throttle drum setting — Part 1 (Sec 39)

A,B, C — Reference faces

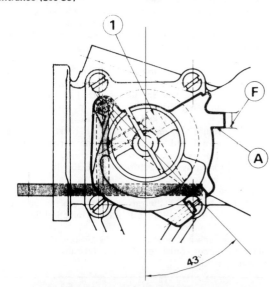

Fig 3.41 Throttle drum setting — Part 2 (Sec 39)

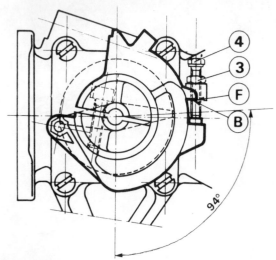

Fig 3.42 Maximum throttle opening (KF6) — Part 1 (Sec 40)

B	*Reference face*
F	*Lower face*

3	*Locknut*
4	*Stop screw*

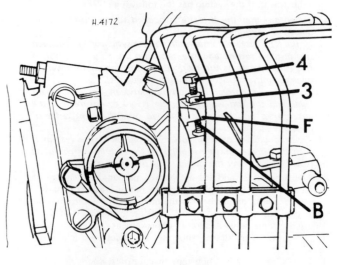

Fig 3.43 Maximum throttle opening (KF6) — Part 2 (Sec 40)
[For caption see Fig 3.42]

40 KF6 system - maximum throttle opening

1   Maximum throttle opening is controlled by a stop screw (4), (Figs. 3.42 and 3.43) and this should be set to bring the reference face (b) into line with the lower face (f) of the boss on the housing.
2   Check that by depressing the accelerator pedal fully maximum throttle opening is obtained. If all is well refit the return spring.

41 KF6 system - minimum throttle opening

1   Minimum throttle opening is controlled by the stop screw (5) (Figs. 3.44 and 3.45). It is set by adjusting this screw until the 10° face of (C) (ie; the longer face) lines up with the lower face (F) of the boss on the air chamber.
2   If it is found that regular idling cannot be obtained with this setting, the minimum opening can set to 12° by aligning the shorter part of face (C) with the boss on the air chamber; this may possibly lead to back firing, in which case the setting should be somewhere between these two positions. Notice that the idling speed is not controlled by the throttle opening, but by the mixture adjustment (See Section 43). The need for a greater degree of throttle opening is only found in new engines as a general rule.

42 Enrichment adjustments

1   For these adjustments the thermostat which controls the enrichment lever must be maintained at a temperature of 77° F (50° C). As well as operating the enrichment lever, this thermostat opens an air valve into the cold air chamber to give a little boost on starting and cold idling conditions.
2   In order to moniter and regulate the thermostat temperature, Peugeot garages use the thermometer and tap arrangement shown in Fig. 3.46. This is connected in series with the hose from the thermostat housing to the water pump. It should not be beyond the ingenuity of a resourceful owner to make up an equivalent.
3   For setting up the enrichment control, the engine should be running and the temperature stabilized to 77° F (50° C). The stabilization is of course, obtained by adjusting the tap.
4   Refer to Fig. 3.47, the nut (7) at the top of the rod operating the enrichment lever must be set so that there is a clearance of 0.004 ± 0.004 in (1.0 ± 1.0 mm) between the nut and the housing when the thermostat temperature is at 77^oF (50^oC). It will be necessary to grip the rod with a pair of pliers or a suitable key whilst the nut is turned using a 10 mm spanner.
5   When the nut is correctly adjusted, stop the engine and close the tap on the thermometer. Hold the feeler gauge in position until it is gripped by the nut as the rod tries to withdraw into the housing when the thermostat cools down.
6   Now slacken the locknut (9) using an 8 mm spanner and adjust the nut (10) using a 10 mm spanner to free off the lever (11) until it comes against the stop (12) on the injection pump. Now screw up the nut (10) until it just touches the enrichment lever and tighten the locknut (9).
7   Adjustment is now complete and the feeler and thermometer can be removed.

43 KF6 system - idling adjustment

1   Run the engine until it reaches its normal operating temperature; at this stage, of course, the electro-magnetic fan will be engaged.
2   Referring to Fig. 3.48 slacken the locknut (13) and adjust the air bleed screw (14) to obtain an engine speed of 800-850 rpm. It will be found that screwing it in decreases the engine speed and screwing it out increases it.

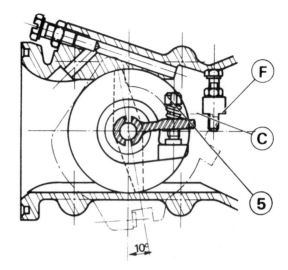

Fig 3.44 Minimum throttle opening (KF6) — Part 1 (Sec 40)

C   Reference face   5   Stop screw
F   Lower face

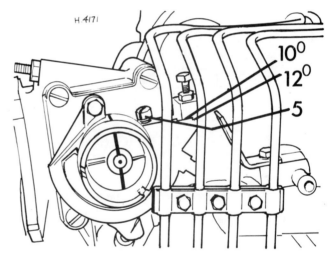

Fig 3.45 Minimum throttle opening (KF6) — Part 2 (Sec 41)

5   Stop screw

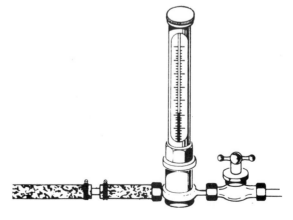

Fig. 3.46 Tap and thermometer arrangement used for enrichment adjustments (Sec 42)

3 Once again it is important that there is no air leakage and that the ignition system is in good operational order. If in despite of this being so it is difficult to obtain an even idling setting it may be necessary to alter the minimum throttle opening as described in Section 41.

44 KF6 engines - running-in - enrichment

In new and reconditioned KF6 engines a washer about 0.02 in (0.5 mm) thick is fitted under the enrichment lever stop (12) (Fig. 3.47). This serves to provide a slightly richer mixture during the running-in period, and should be removed after 600 miles (1,000 km).

45 KF5/XN2 system - initial throttle setting position

1 The initial throttle setting position is set by a stop screw (5),

(Fig. 3.49) which bears against a pad (6) on the air chamber. The setting must be such that as soon as the throttle flap moves it start to uncover a jet housed in the air chamber; Fig. 3.50 shows this and gives an idea of how the setting is checked.

2 Check the setting by first removing the plug (2) (Fig. 3.51) being careful not to lose a thin washer with a small hole in it. It is in fact a correction jet and may become dislodged when the plug is taken out. The various bits and pieces that are located behind this plug are shown in Fig. 3.50.

3 Insert a small light in place of the plug. Fig. 3.51 shows a suitable light holder in-situ and Fig. 3.50 gives a diagrammatic view of the set up.

4 Arrange a mirror so that a reflection of the flap located in the housing can be seen.

5 If the setting is correct a small strip of light must appear as soon as the throttle flap is moved slightly away from the stop position. Should the check show a light all the time or a light does not start to show immediately the flap is moved, the stop

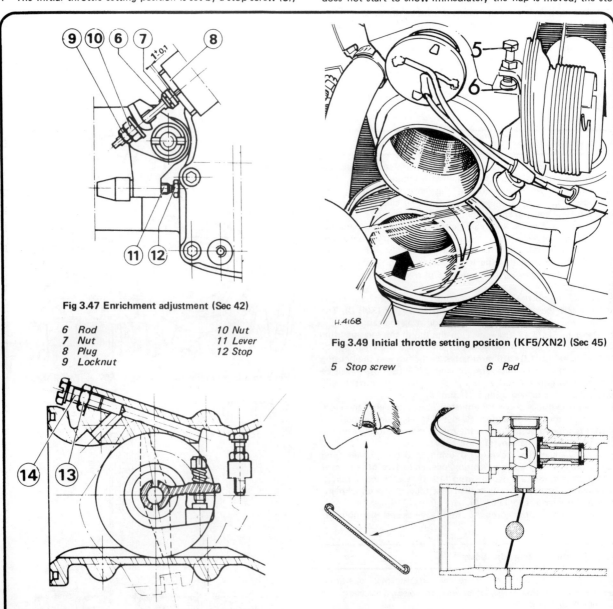

Fig 3.47 Enrichment adjustment (Sec 42)

6 Rod	10 Nut
7 Nut	11 Lever
8 Plug	12 Stop
9 Locknut	

Fig 3.49 Initial throttle setting position (KF5/XN2) (Sec 45)

5 Stop screw   6 Pad

H.4168

Fig 3.48 Idling adjustment (KF6) (Sec 43)

13 Locknut   14 Air bleed screw

Fig 3.50 Cross-section through air chamber showing light and mirror (Sec 45)

screw (5) must be altered.

6   If adjustment is necessary, unscrew the locknut and then screw the stop screw up slightly until a thin strip of light appears above the top edge of the throttle flap. Now slacken the screw off slowly until the light just disappears and then screw it back in a maximum of a tenth of a turn to obtain a slight clearance - the strip of light should just reappear.

7   Retighten the locknut, making sure that the stop screw setting is not altered. Finally recheck the setting.

8   Make sure that the correct jet (paragraph 2) is correctly in place. Refit the plug (2) (Fig. 3.51) oiling the thread and using a new 'O' ring. Finally tighten the plug to a torque wrench setting of 14.5 lb f ft (2.0 kg f m).

46 KF5/XN2 system - enrichment adjustment

1   This adjustment must be carried out with the engine at a temperature of between 75° and 76°C (167-176°F). To check the temperature, Peugeot garages use the thermometer and tap arrangement shown in Fig. 3.46 connected in series with the water return hose from the thermostat - this is the hose connected to outlet (K) (Fig. 3.35)

2   The adjustment is carried out by slackening off the locknut (1) using a 10 mm spanner, gripping the rod (4) with a pair of pliers or a suitable key. Run the engine until the thermometer indicates a temperature of 80°C (176°F) making sure that this figure is reached by a temperature rise and not a temperature

fall. If the engine is hot before this adjustment is commenced allow the temperature to drop to 65°C (149°F).

3   As soon as the temperature reaches 80°C (176°F) switch off the engine. Now adjust the nut (2) (Fig. 3.52) using a 17 mm spanner until it is just possible to insert a special Peugeot gauge numbered '8.0112P' between the nut and the enrichment lever (3). Retighten the locknut. This adjustment must be carried out before the temperature drops to 75°C (167°F). If the temperature drops below this figure before adjustment has been completed, allow the engine to cool down to 65°C (149°F) and warm it up again to 80°C (176°F).

4   When adjustment is complete, the thermometer can be removed and the water hose reconnected.

47 KF5/XN2 system - idling mixture adjustment

1   The idling mixture is controlled by the air bleed screw (1). (Fig. 3.53) and the enrichment stop screw (2) (Fig. 3.54).

2   The adjustment is carried out with the engine hot - approx. 80°C (176°F). At this temperature the electromagnetic fan should be engaged.

3   First adjust the air bleed screw until the engine speed is 900 rpm on a new engine (ie; less than 3,000 miles - 1500 km) or 850 rpm on an engine that has been well run in.

4   Next raise the enrichment lever (3) (Fig. 3.55) slowly. The engine speed should increase slightly to between 1020 and 1050 rpm for a new engine or 950-970 rpm for a well run in engine.

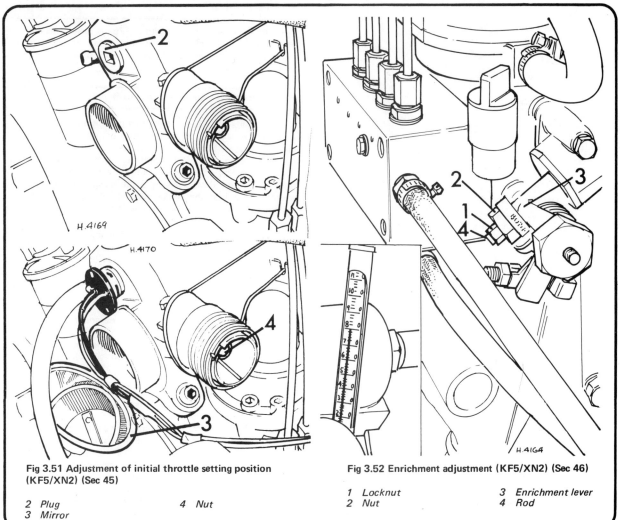

Fig 3.51 Adjustment of initial throttle setting position (KF5/XN2) (Sec 45)

2   Plug   4   Nut
3   Mirror

Fig 3.52 Enrichment adjustment (KF5/XN2) (Sec 46)

1   Locknut   3   Enrichment lever
2   Nut   4   Rod

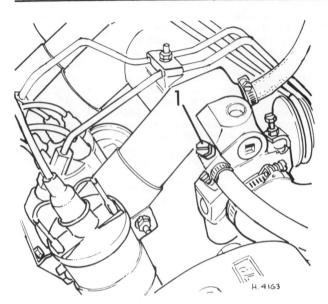

Fig 3.53 Location of air bleed screw (1) (Sec 47)

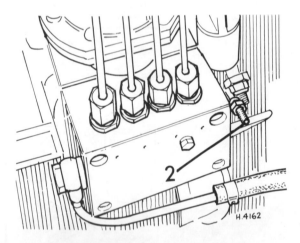

Fig 3.54 Enrichment stop screw (2) (Sec 47)

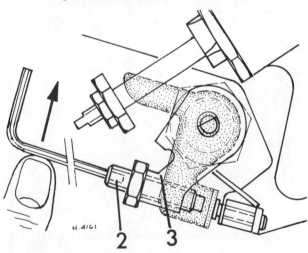

Fig 3.55 Idling mixture adjustment (Sec 47)

2 Allen key in stop screw   3 Enrichment lever

5 If the engine speed with the enrichment lever raised exceeds these figures, the mixture is too lean. In this case, screw in the stop screw (2) a quarter of a turn. If the speed is less, the mixture is too rich and the stop screw should be unscrewed a quarter of a turn.

6 After adjusting the stop screw, reset the engine speed to the original figure and then repeat the procedure just described. Make any further adjustments to the stop screw until the correct speed increase is obtained when the enrichment lever is raised.

48 Fuel lift pump - general description

When fuel injection equipment is fitted an electric lift pump is used instead of the mechanically operated type as found on normal carburettor engines. This lift pump is located at the rear of the car. Removal and replacement of the pump is a straightforward operation and will present no problems. However, for safety reasons, always disconnect the battery before detaching the fuel lines.

49 Air cleaner - maintenance

Generally an oil bath type air cleaner is used. Fig. 3.56 shows two types that have been used. For full servicing information refer to Section 3.

50 In-line fuel filter

An in-line renewable element fuel filter is fitted into the main line from the fuel tank. At the recommended intervals it should be dismantled and cleaned. If the element is blocked with dirt it should be renewed.

51 Fault diagnosis - fuel injection system

Most faults such as excessive fuel consumption, poor engine performance, and erratic running may be blamed on the petrol injection system but after correct diagnosis the cause may be found to be in one of the other systems including ignition, electrical, cooling or that there is insufficient clean petrol in the tank. If none of these systems is the cause of the trouble it is recommended that the car be taken to the agents for further diagnosis. As a guide to fault diagnosis the details below should give an indication as to the cause.

The effect of a fault in the petrol injection system will usually be revealed in one of four ways:
  a) *the engine cannot be started or can be started only with difficulty;*
  b) *the engine starts but runs erratically over the whole or part of the speed range;*
  c) *fuel consumption is excessive;*
  d) *the engine starts but does not respond to movement of the throttle.*

Faults (a), (b) and (c) may be due to incorrect pump adjustments. Refer to the relevant Sections in the text for full information.

a) Engine fails to start or can be started only with difficulty.
1 Switch on the ignition and check (audibly or by touch) that the fuel pump motor is running.
2 If the pump motor is running, disconnect one of the low tension cable connections at the coil but leave the ignition switch on.
3 Grip each injector feed line in turn lightly with the hand and crank the engine. A distinct pulsation should be felt with each line as fuel is injected.
  Note: The feed lines are cleated together and must be separated to avoid the misleading effect of reflected pulsations. If obvious pulsations are felt in each line the petrol injection

Fig 3.56 Exploded views of oil bath type air filters fitted to fuel injection models (Sec 49)

Fig 3.57 Exploded view of in line fuel filter [Fuel injection models only] (Sec 50)

system is unlikely to be the cause of failure to start and some other cause must be found.

If pulsations cannot be felt in any line although the pump motor is working apparently normally, check fuel pressure. If pressure and relief valve settings are satisfactory, switch off the ignition and remove the injection pump for examination of the drive coupling, which may have broken.

Finally, remember to restore the coil low tension connection.

b) Engine starts but runs erratically over the whole or part of the speed range.
1 Check the setting of the injection pump adjustments. Refer to the relevant Sections in the text for full information. Erratic

running may otherwise be caused by:
An irregularity in the fuel supply to one cylinder only or some failing which is affecting all cylinders. In the former case, the fault is most likely to be a stuck open injector and fouling of the associated spark plug will almost certainly have occurred.
2 Short circuit each plug to earth in turn and if one does not affect the engine running note when shorted out, remove, clean and refit this plug.
3 Withdraw the associated injector from the engine and detach from its feed line.
4 Connect the injector to a dry, filtered air supply at a pressure of 80 psi in the forward (injection) direction. This will almost invariably cure a faulty injector (sticking open due to a foreign particle becoming trapped) and if it does so the injector can be refitted to the engine. If it does not, a new injector must be fitted.
Note: Plastic feed pipes must not be heat treated to enable fitment, but must be put on cold.
5 Where the failure affects all cylinders but is more pronounced with higher speed, check pressure and relief valve setting. If the injection pump has recently been removed, check that it has not been fitted 180° out as regards timing.
6 Provided that the timing is correct; the injection pump working correctly; the injectors are in good order; and fuel pressure is satisfactory; then a faulty relay or blown fuse is indicated.

c) Fuel consumption excessive.
This may not necessarily arise from a defect in the petrol injection system and the fault must be correctly traced before taking remedial action. The following checks are therefore given on the assumption that other likely causes have been checked first:
1 Check for correct injection pump adjustments. Refer to the relevant Sections in the text for full information.
2 Check the relief valve setting.
3 If the above 1 and 2 are satisfactory then the control unit is suspect and a replacement metering unit must be fitted. This latter step should be taken only when other likely causes such as plugs, points, leaking pipes, etc., have been eliminated.

d) Engine starts but does not respond to movement of the throttle:
1 Ensure the movement of the accelerator pedal is being relayed to the throttle butterflies.
2 Remove and check that the pipe connecting the manifold to the control unit is air tight.
3 Check the relief valve setting.
4 If both the above 1 and 2 are satisfactory, it will be necessary to fit a replacement injection pump.

Part 4: Controls

52 Accelerator cable - removal and replacement

1 Unscrew the bolt locking the inner cable to the clamp assembly located on the side of the carburettor or fuel injection pump.
2 Detach the outer cable from its support at the carburettor or fuel injection pump end.
3 Working inside the car push the little cup down into the main cup using a small screwdriver and ease the large cup off the end of the pedal control rod.
4 Carefully remove the cable from the car.
5 Before fitting a new cable assembly well lubricate the inner cable with engine oil. Do not use grease as it will cause the cable to stiffen especially in cold weather.
6 Refitting the accelerator cable is the reverse sequence to removal. Before fully tightening the clamp bolt, remove the air cleaner and check for correct butterfly movement on carburettor models. Fuel injection models - refer to Section 39.

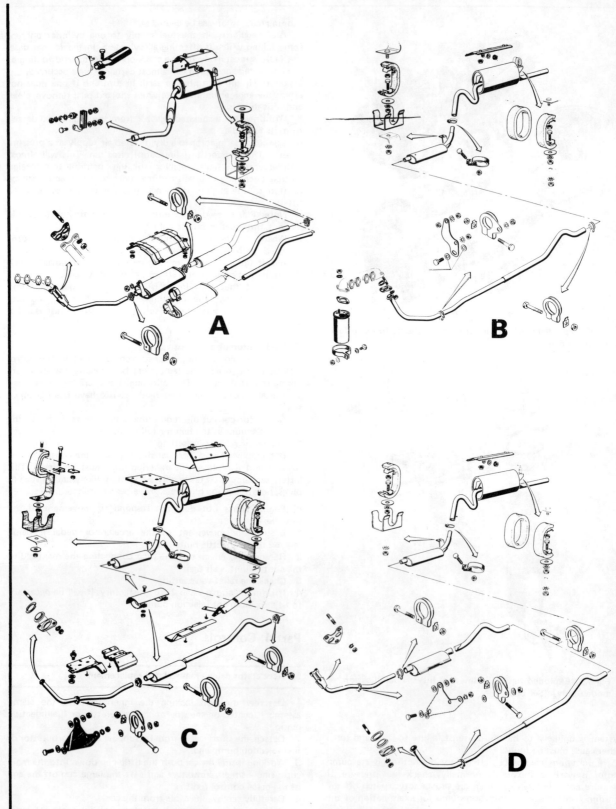

Fig 3.58 Selection of exhaust systems fitted to 504 models

A Saloon, Cabriolet and
   Coupe

B Station wagon (manual
   gearbox)

C Estate (manual and automatic transmission)

D Family car, station wagon and
   estate (automatic transmission)

Note: There are many more so always check under the car before purchasing a new system

53 Accelerator pedal - removal and replacement

1 To remove the pedal footrest undo and remove the two securing screws located at the floor end.
2 Detach the footrest from the pedal control rod.
3 To remove the pedal control rod detach the inner cable from the control rod, as described in Section 52, paragraph 3.
4 Release the spring clip located at the end of the shaft and draw off the control rod.
5 Refitting the accelerator pedal is the reverse sequence to removal. Lubricate the pivot with a little engine oil.

54 Choke cable - removal and replacement

1 This Section is only applicable to carburettor models.
2 Unscrew the bolt locking the inner cable to the clamp on the end of the choke lever.
3 Unscrew the bolt locking the outer cable to the carburettor body.
4 Detach the choke control cable from the carburettor.
5 Slacken the outer cable locknut at the clamp located behind the knob. Slide the cable sideways from the clamp.
6 Carefully remove the cable from the car.
7 Before fitting a new cable assembly well lubricate the inner cable with engine oil.
8 Refitting the choke cable is the reverse sequence to removal. Before fully tightening the clamp bolts remove the air cleaner and check for correct butterfly movement.

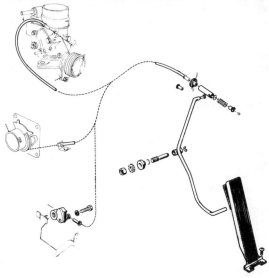

Fig. 3.59. Accelerator pedal and cable assembly (Sec. 53)

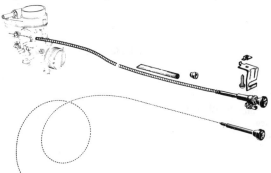

Fig. 3.60. Choke cable assembly (Sec. 54)
(Carburettor models)

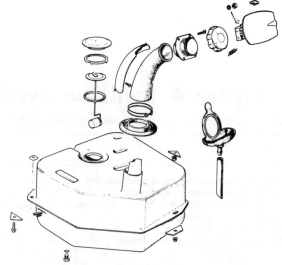

Fig 3.61 Fuel tank assembly [Saloon Car model]

Fig 3.62 Fuel tank assembly [Saloon car (alternative), Cabriolet and Coupe]

Fig 3.63 Fuel tank assembly [utility models]

Chapter 4 Ignition system

For modifications, and information applicable to later models, see Supplement at end of manual

Contents

Specifications

Spark plugs

Size	14 mm, 1.25 pitch, long reach

Type (Carburettor engines only):

Engine series *	XM - XM7, XM and XNI US
Marchal	35 HS
A.C.	44 XL
Champion	N9Y
Engine series *	XNI
Marchal	35 HS
A.C.	44 XL
Champion	N7Y
Electrode gap	0.024 in. (0.6 mm)

Type (Fuel injection engines only):

Engine series *	XM KF6
Marchal	GT 34 HD
Champion	N6Y
Electrode gap	0.020 in. (0.5 mm)
Engine series *	XM KF5 - XN2
Marchal	GT 34 HD
A.C.	42 XL
Champion	N6Y
Electrode gap	0.024 in. (0.6 mm)

* For engine series number identification, see Specifications Chapter 1

Firing order	1 - 3 - 4 - 2 [No. 1 cylinder is nearest flywheel]

Ignition coil

Type	Oil filled
Earlier models:	
Carburettor version	Ducellier 2070B or SEV 3H
Fuel injection version	Ducellier 4112A
Later models:	Ducellier 2772A or SEV 3H 12Y

Spark plug HT leads

Type	Suppressed

Distributor

Type	Ducellier 4161B or SEV - Marchal NA. HC

Advance curve:
USA models:

1969	...	...	...	...	...	...	...	...	M48
1970	...	...	...	...	...	...	...	...	M69
1971	...	...	...	...	...	...	...	...	M69 see Fig. 4.11
1972	...	...	...	...	...	...	...	...	M74
1973 on	...	...	...	...	...	...	...	...	M74

Note: Distributors fitted to USA models have no advance connection.

Other models:

| Carburettor version | ... | ... | ... | ... | ... | ... | M48 |
| Fuel injection version | ... | ... | ... | ... | ... | M53 see Fig. 4.11 |

Dwell percentage	...	...	...	...	...	...	...	$63 \pm 3\%$
Dwell angle	...	...	...	...	...	...	...	$57 \pm 2^{\circ}$
Contact breaker points gap	...	...	...	...	...	0.016 in. (0.40 mm)

Note: With SEV Marchal cassette points sets the contact breaker points gap must be 0.012 in. (0.30 mm)

| Drive ... | ... | ... | ... | ... | ... | ... | ... | ... | Skew gear from camshaft |
| Direction of rotation | ... | ... | ... | ... | ... | ... | Clockwise |

Ignition timing settings *

504 US 1971 Standard	...	...	...	...	...	...	0° TDC
XNI, XN2 (11CV), 504 US — 1970, 72, 73 Standard	...	...	5° BTDC
XM7 (10CV), 504 US — 1969 Standard	...	...	...	...	10° BTDC

These settings are subject to alteration by the vehicle manufacturer, even in retrospect. Check with vehicle handbook or local dealer.

The above figures are to be used on engines fitted with a timing plate above the crankshaft pulley. When not fitted use timing rod in clutch housing hole. [See text]

Torque wrench setting	**lb f ft**	**kg fm**
Spark plug	16	2.25

1 General description

In order that the engine may run correctly it is necessary for an electrical spark to ignite the fuel/air mixture in the combustion chamber at exactly the right moment in relation to engine speed and load.

Basically the ignition system functions as follows: Low tension voltage from the battery is fed to the ignition coil, where it is converted into high tension voltage. The high tension voltage is powerful enough to jump the spark plug gap in the cylinder many times a second under high compression pressure, providing that the ignition system is in good working order and that all adjustments are correct.

The ignition system comprises two individual circuits known as the low tension (LT) circuit and high tension (HT) circuit.

The low tension circuit (sometimes known as the primary circuit) comprises the battery, lead to ignition switch, lead to the low tension or primary coil windings and the lead from the low tension coil windings to the contact breaker points and condenser in the distributor.

The high tension circuit (sometimes known as the secondary circuit) comprises the high tension or secondary coil winding, the heavily insulated ignition lead from the centre of the coil to the centre of the distributor cap, the rotor arm, the spark plug leads and the spark plugs.

The complete ignition system operation is as follows:

Low tension voltage from the battery is changed within the ignition coil to high tension voltage by the opening and closing of the contact breaker points in the low tension circuit. High tension voltage is then fed, via a contact in the centre of the distributor cap, to the rotor arm of the distributor. The rotor arm revolves inside the distributor cap, and each time it comes in line with one of the four metal segments in the cap, these being connected to the spark plug leads, the opening and closing of the contact breaker points causes the high tension voltage to build up, jump the gap from the rotor arm to the appropriate metal segment and so via the spark plug lead, to the spark plug where it finally jumps the gap between the two spark plug electrodes, one being earthed.

The ignition timing is advanced and retarded automatically to ensure the spark occurs at just the right instant for the particular load at the prevailing engine speed.

The ignition advance is controlled both mechanically and by a vacuum operated system. The mechanical governor mechanism comprises two weights which move out under centrifugal force from the central distributor shaft as the engine speed rises. As they move outwards they rotate the cams relative to the distributor shaft, and so advance the spark. The weights are held in position by two light springs, and it is the tension of these springs which is largely responsible for correct spark advancement.

The vacuum control comprises a diaphragm, one side of which is connected, via a small bore tube, to the carburettor, and the other side to the contact breaker plate. Depression in the induction manifold and carburettor, which varies with engine speed and throttle opening, causes the diaphragm to move so moving the contact breaker plate and advancing or retarding the spark.

2 US Exhaust emission control regulations - their effect on d-i-y servicing

In order to conform with the US Federal Regulations which govern the emission of hydrocarbons and carbon monoxide from car exhaust systems, the engine, carburation and ignition system have been suitably modified.

It is critically important that the ignition system is kept in good operational order and to achieve this, accurate analytical equipment is needed to check and reset the distributor function. This will be found at your local dealer.

Information contained in this Chapter is supplied to enable the home mechanic to set the ignition system roughly so at least to start the engine. Thereafter, the car must be taken to the local dealer for final tuning. Failure to do this can result in heavy legal penalties.

3 Contact breaker points - adjustment

1 Release the two clips and lift away the distributor cap. Clean the inside and outside of the cap with a dry cloth and, if the four segments are slightly burned, scrape the deposit away with a screwdriver. Should the segments be badly burned, the cap must be renewed.
2 Check that the carbon brush is free to move in the cap and that it protrudes by at least 0.25 in (6.35 mm).
3 Prise the contact breaker points apart and examine the two faces. If they are rough, pitted, or dirty they must be removed for resurfacing or renewal as described in Section 4. Note that the contour of the fixed contact must be retained for the system to operate successfully.
4 To adjust the contact breaker points accurately, a dwell meter will be required, but to obtain an initial setting first rotate the engine until the heel of the contact breaker arm is on the peak of one of the four cam lobes.
5 Loosen the fixed contact locking screw and position the fixed contact so that a 0.016 in (0.40 mm) feeler gauge just fits between the two points. Tighten the locking screw and recheck the adjustment.
6 Connect a dwell meter and tachometer to the engine, then run the engine at 2000 rpm (vacuum pipe disconnected). The dwell angle must be between 55° and 59°. If this is not the case, stop the engine and reduce the points gap to increase the dwell angle and vice versa. Note that a hole is provided in the baseplate for fitting an eccentric contact point adjuster but this tool is not an essential requirement.
7 The operation of the vacuum advance unit alters the ignition timing by repositioning the moving contact point. This action produces a variation of the dwell angle which will cause uneven timing unless set correctly. If the serrated cam or eccentric adjuster on the distributor baseplate have been disturbed, they must be readjusted by a suitably equipped garage. To make a quick check on the adjustment, move the vacuum control rod through its entire stroke and make sure that the moving contact operates over the central portion of the fixed contact.
8 After adjusting the contact breaker points, refit the distributor cap.

4 Contact breaker points - removal and replacement

1 If the contact breaker points are burned, pitted or badly worn, they should be removed and either replaced or their faces must be filed smooth.
2 To remove the points first detach the distributor cap and rotor arm.
3 Unscrew and lift away the fixed plate locking screw and washer taking care not to drop them into the body of the distributor.

4 Unclip and lift away the hair-pin shaped clip. (photo)
5 Slacken the LT cables securing nuts but do not completely remove. Slide the contact breaker points cable terminal connector up from the terminal. Note it is located between the terminal bolt head and the insulator.
6 Lift off the moving point pivot washer and then very carefully remove the points assembly. Make a note of the location of the insulation washers. (photo)
7 Refitting the contact breaker points is the reverse sequence to removal. Reset the points gap as described in Section 3. (photo)

5 Condenser - removal, testing and replacement

1 The purpose of the condenser (sometimes known as a capacitor) is to ensure that when the contact breaker points open there is no sparking across them which would waste voltage and cause wear.
2 The condenser is fitted in parallel with the contact breaker points. If it develops a short circuit, it will cause ignition failure, as the points will be prevented from interrupting the low tension circuit.
3 If the engine becomes very difficult to start, or begins to misfire after several miles running, and the breaker points show signs of excessive burning then the condition of the condenser must be suspect. A further test can be made by separating the points manually (using an insulated screwdriver) with the ignition switched on. If this is accompanied by a flash it is indicative that the condenser has failed.
4 Without special test equipment, the only sure way to diagnose condenser trouble is to replace a suspected unit with a new one: noting if there is any improvement.
5 To remove the condenser from the distributor, first detach the condenser lead from the LT terminal post on the side of the distributor body.
6 Undo and remove the one securing screw, spring and shakeproof washer noting the locations of the washers. Lift away the condenser.
7 Replacement of the condenser is simply a reversal of the removal procedure.

6 Distributor - lubrication

1 It is important that the distributor cam is lubricated with petroleum jelly and the breaker arm, governor weights and cam spindle with engine oil at the specified mileages.
2 Great care should be taken not to use too much lubricant, as any excess that might find its way onto the contact breaker points could cause burning and misfiring.
3 To gain access to the cam spindle, lift away the rotor arm. Drop no more than two drops of engine oil onto the screw (or felt pad). This will run down the spindle when the engine is hot and lubricate the bearings. No more than one drop's' of oil should be applied to the pivot post.

7 Distributor - removal and replacement

1 For safety reasons, disconnect the battery.
2 Release the clips securing the distributor cap to the body and lift away the distributor cap.
3 Obtain a rod 0.3149 in (8 mm) in diameter and about 6.0 inch (152.4 mm) long. Locate the timing hole on the top right-hand side of the clutch housing. (Fig. 4.2)
4 Remember that the engine has a firing order of 1-3-4-2 and No 1 cylinder is at the **flywheel end** of the engine.
5 Slowly turn the crankshaft in its normal direction of rotation until the rotor arm is pointing to the distributor cap segment which is connected to No. 1 spark plug.
6 Insert the rod into the timing hole and by rocking the crankshaft check that the rod drops into the special timing recess in the flywheel.

3.4 Checking contact breaker points gap

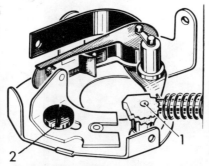

Fig 4.1 Contact breaker points assembly (Sec 3)
1 Adjuster for vacuum control
2 Locking screw

4.4 Main-pin shaped clip removed

4.6 Moving point assembly removed

4.7 Contact breaker points correctly refitted

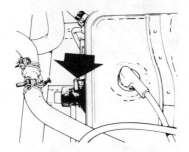

Fig 4.2 Timing rod inserted into clutch housing (Sec 7)

7.9 Distributor removal

7.10 Slot in top of oil pump driveshaft [KF5 and KF6, XN1 and XN2 series only shown]

7 Disconnect the low tension lead from the terminal on the side of the distributor.

8 Detach the vacuum pipe from the distributor advance unit.

9 Undo and remove the bolt and washer securing the distributor clamp plate to the cylinder block. The distributor may now be lifted up and away from the side of the engine. (photo)

10 For future reference note the position of the slot in the top of the oil pump drive shaft. This varies from one engine series to another. (photo)

11 If it is not wished to disturb the ignition timing, then under no circumstances should the engine be turned.

12 Replacement is a reversal of the above sequence. If the engine has been turned it will be necessary to retime the ignition as described in a later Section. **Do not** forget to remove the rod. To prevent any possible leaks smear a little non-setting oil resistance sealer to the machined surface of the distributor support.

8 Distributor - overhaul

It has been found from practical experience that overhauling a distributor is not worthwhile even if all parts are available. The usual items needing attention are such parts as the distributor cap, rotor arm, contact breaker points and condenser (very rare). After these have been considered there is not a great deal left to wear except the shaft assembly, bush and automatic advance system. If one of these parts is worn then it is reasonable to assume the remainder are so all in all it is best to obtain a guaranteed service exchange unit which could work out cheaper than purchasing a complete set of individual parts. For the more ambitious exploded views of various distributors are given and no problems will arise in stripping and rebuilding providing that a) spare parts are readily to hand and b) the exact location of each part however small is noted. (Figs. 4.5 to 4.8).

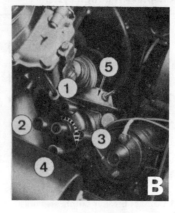

Fig 4.3 Correct fitted position for distributor. Carburettor engine (Sec 7)

A Contact breaker points open
B 1 - 4 HT lead connections
5 Vacuum unit

Fig 4.4 Correct fitted position for distributor. Fuel injection engine (Sec 7)

A Contact breaker points open
B 1 - 4 HT lead connections
5 Vacuum unit

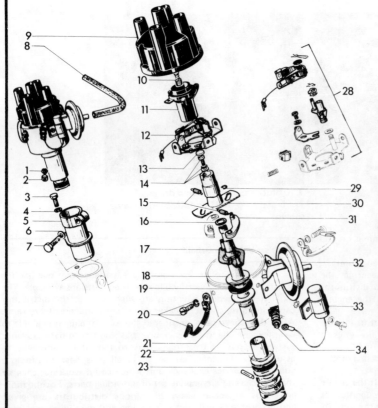

Fig 4.5 Ducellier distributor as fitted to carburettor engines [NOT USA]

1	Washer	20	Spring blade, screw and washer
2	Nut	21	Washer
3	Bolt	22	Bush
4	Washer	23	Plain washer
5	Support	25	Thrust washer
6	Washer	26	Drive dog
7	Bolt	27	Seal
8	Vacuum pipe	28	Exploded view of contact breaker points assembly
9	Distributor cap	29	Clip
10	Carbon brush and spring	30	Cam
11	Rotor arm	31	Control weights
12	Contact breaker points assembly	32	Vacuum unit
13	Felt pad	33	Condenser
14	Screw and washers	34	Terminal assembly
15	Springs		
16	Washer		
17	Action plate		
18	Washer		
19	Thrust washer		

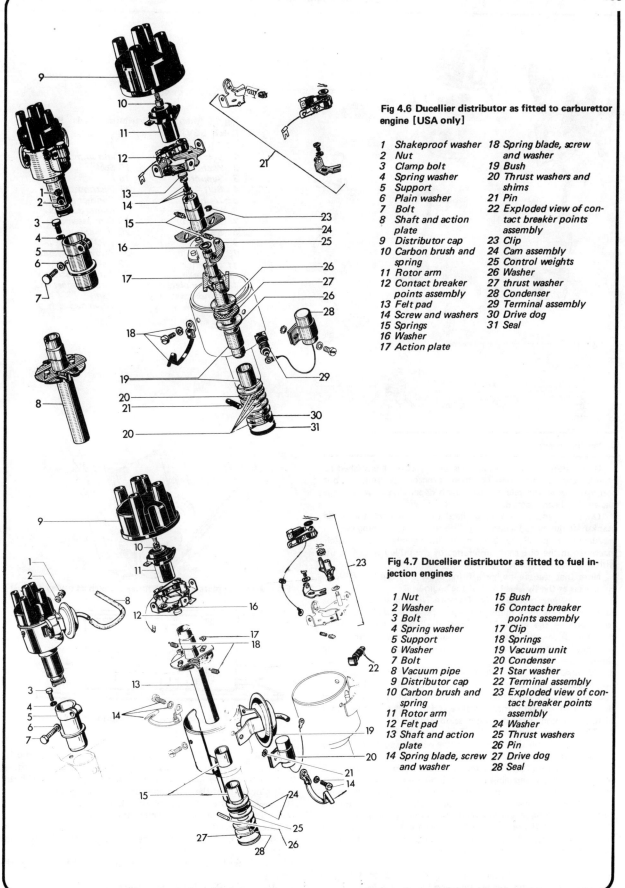

Fig 4.6 Ducellier distributor as fitted to carburettor engine [USA only]

1 Shakeproof washer
2 Nut
3 Clamp bolt
4 Spring washer
5 Support
6 Plain washer
7 Bolt
8 Shaft and action plate
9 Distributor cap
10 Carbon brush and spring
11 Rotor arm
12 Contact breaker points assembly
13 Felt pad
14 Screw and washers
15 Springs
16 Washer
17 Action plate
18 Spring blade, screw and washer
19 Bush
20 Thrust washers and shims
21 Pin
22 Exploded view of contact breaker points assembly
23 Clip
24 Cam assembly
25 Control weights
26 Washer
27 thrust washer
28 Condenser
29 Terminal assembly
30 Drive dog
31 Seal

Fig 4.7 Ducellier distributor as fitted to fuel injection engines

1 Nut
2 Washer
3 Bolt
4 Spring washer
5 Support
6 Washer
7 Bolt
8 Vacuum pipe
9 Distributor cap
10 Carbon brush and spring
11 Rotor arm
12 Felt pad
13 Shaft and action plate
14 Spring blade, screw and washer
15 Bush
16 Contact breaker points assembly
17 Clip
18 Springs
19 Vacuum unit
20 Condenser
21 Star washer
22 Terminal assembly
23 Exploded view of contact breaker points assembly
24 Washer
25 Thrust washers
26 Pin
27 Drive dog
28 Seal

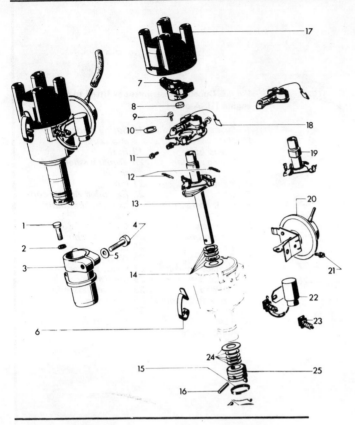

Fig 4.8 Alternative distributor [Paris - Rhone, Bosch, SEV]

1 Bolt	and shims
2 Washer	15 Seal
3 Support	16 Pin
4 Bolt	17 Distributor cap
5 Washer	18 Contact breaker
6 Spring clip	points assembly
7 Rotor arm	19 Cam assembly
8 Felt pad	20 Vacuum unit
9 Screw	[NOT USA]
10 Washer	21 Screw and washer
11 Screw	22 Condenser
12 Spring	23 Terminal assembly
13 Action plate and	24 Plain washers and
spindle assembly	shims
14 Thrust washers	25 Drive dog

9 Ignition timing

If the static ignition timing has been lost or it is wished to check the existing setting then proceed as follows but commencing at the relevant paragraph depending at what stage has already been reached.

On some engines a timing plate was fitted just above the crankshaft pulley to facilitate ignition timing. The timing plate is graduated from 0º to 20º in 2º increments and a notch machined in the outer circumference of the pulley is to line up with the required ignition setting. (Fig. 4.9).

1 Note that the engine has a firing order of 1-3-4-2 and No 1 cylinder is at the **flywheel end** of the engine.

2 *Timing plate models only:* Remove No 4 spark plug (front of engine) then use a metal rod, and if possible a dial test gauge, to determine the exact TDC position of No 4 piston. Check that the 0º mark on the timing plate is exactly in alignment with the notch on the crankshaft pulley. If not, reposition the timing plate.

3 *All models:* Remove No 4 spark plug (front of engine) if not already removed, and place the palm of the hand over the end of the spark plug tube. Turn the crankshaft in its normal direction of rotation until pressure is felt indicating that No 4 piston has commenced its compression stroke.

4 *Timing plate models only:* Turn the crankshaft clockwise until the notch on the pulley is in line with the specified setting on the timing plate (see Specifications).

5 *Models without a timing plate:* Obtain a rod 0.315 in (8.0 mm) in diameter and about 6.0 in (150 mm) long, and insert it in the timing hole located on the top right-hand side of the clutch housing. Slowly turn the crankshaft clockwise until the rod drops into the special timing recess in the flywheel.

6 *All models:* If the distributor has been removed, check that the oil pump driveshaft slot is in the position originally noted (see Chapter 1 if in doubt), then insert the distributor and engage the drive dog.

7 Position the distributor as shown in Fig.4.3 or 4.4, then reconnect the vacuum advance pipe and low tension lead.

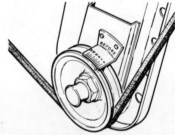

Fig 4.9 Timing plate mounted above crankshaft pulley (Sec 9)

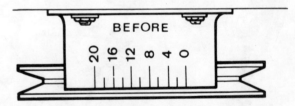

Fig 4.10 Timing plate graduations (Sec 9)

8 Obtain a 12V 5W test lamp and connect it between the LT terminal on the side of the distributor and a good earth point.

9 Switch on the ignition and slowly rotate the distributor body clockwise, if the testlamp is on, until the light goes out.

10 Slowly rotate the distributor body anti-clockwise until the light just comes on then tighten the clamp bolt.

11 Check that the distributor rotor arm is pojnting to the No 4 spark plug segment in the distributor cap. Remove the testlamp.

12 *Models without a timing plate:* Remove the rod from the timing hole.

13 *All models:* Refit No 4 spark plug and HT lead.

Measuring plug gap. A feeler gauge of the correct size (see ignition system specifications) should have a slight 'drag' when slid between the electrodes. Adjust gap if necessary

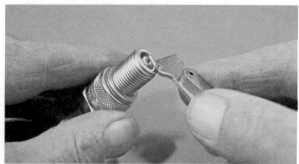

Adjusting plug gap. The plug gap is adjusted by bending the earth electrode inwards, or outwards, as necessary until the correct clearance is obtained. Note the use of the correct tool

Normal. Grey-brown deposits, lightly coated core nose. Gap increasing by around 0.001 in (0.025 mm) per 1000 miles (1600 km). Plugs ideally suited to engine, and engine in good condition

Carbon fouling. Dry, black, sooty deposits. Will cause weak spark and eventually misfire. Fault: over-rich fuel mixture. Check: carburettor mixture settings, float level and jet sizes; choke operation and cleanliness of air filter. Plugs can be re-used after cleaning

Oil fouling. Wet, oily deposits. Will cause weak spark and eventually misfire. Fault: worn bores/piston rings or valve guides; sometimes occurs (temporarily) during running-in period. Plugs can be re-used after thorough cleaning

Overheating. Electrodes have glazed appearance, core nose very white – few deposits. Fault: plug overheating. Check: plug value, ignition timing, fuel octane rating (too low) and fuel mixture (too weak). Discard plugs and cure fault immediately

Electrode damage. Electrodes burned away; core nose has burned, glazed appearance. Fault: pre-ignition. Check: as for 'Overheating' but may be more severe. Discard plugs and remedy fault before piston or valve damage occurs

Split core nose (may appear initially as a crack). Damage is self-evident, but cracks will only show after cleaning. Fault: pre-ignition or wrong gap-setting technique. Check: ignition timing, cooling system, fuel octane rating (too low) and fuel mixture (too weak). Discard plugs, rectify fault immediately

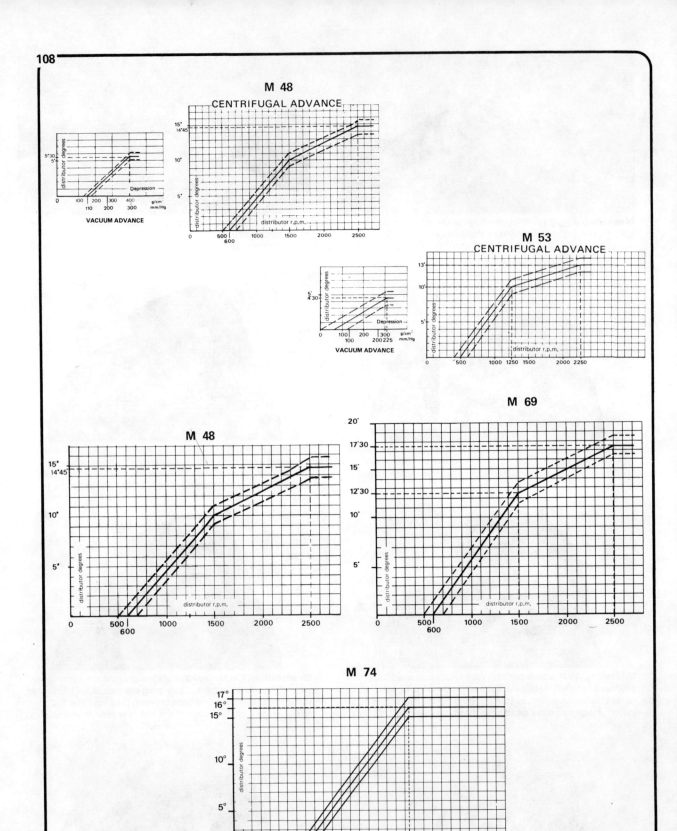

Note: *The two upper advance curves are for distributors with centrifugal and vacuum advance; the three lower advance curves are for distributors with centrifugal advance only. These figures may be subject to local variation; for further information contact your Peugeot dealer*

14 For a more accurate check of the ignition timing, a stroboscopic timing light should be used and connected to the engine in accordance with the manufacturer's instructions. If this method is used always disconnect and plug the pipe from the vacuum unit on the distributor on models incorporating a vacuum unit; also make sure that the engine speed does not exceed 850 rpm during the check. Point the timing light towards the timing plate or timing hole, and make any necessary adjustments by moving the distributor body as previously described. Reconnect the vacuum pipe after completing the check.

10 Spark plugs and HT leads

1 The correct functioning of the spark plugs is vital for the correct running and efficiency of the engine.
2 At the recommended intervals the plugs should be removed, examined, cleaned, and if worn excessively, renewed. Note that the air cleaner must first be removed and the special Peugeot plug spanner will be necessary. The condition of the spark plugs will also tell much about the overall condition of the engine.
3 If the insulator nose of the spark plug is clean and white, with no deposits, this is indicative of a weak mixture, or too hot a plug (a hot plug transfers heat away from the electrode slowly - a cold plug transfers it away quickly).
4 The plugs fitted as standard are as listed in Specifications at the beginning of this Chapter. If the top and insulator nose are covered with hard black looking deposits, then this is indicative that the mixture is too rich. Should the plug be black and oily, then it is likely that the engine is fairly worn, as well as the mixture being too rich.
5 If the insulator nose is covered with light tan or greyish brown deposits, then the mixture is correct and it is likely that the engine is in good condition.
6 If there are any traces of long brown tapering stains on the outside of the white portion of the plug, it will have to be renewed, as this shows that there is a faulty joint between the plug body and the insulator, and compression is being allowed to leak away.
7 Plugs should be cleaned by a sand blasting machine which will free them from carbon more thoroughly than cleaning by hand. The machine will also test the condition of the plugs under compression. Any plug that fails to spark at the recommended pressure should be renewed.
8 The spark plug gap is of considerable importance, as, if it is too large or too small, the size of the spark and its efficiency will be seriously impaired. The spark plug gap should be set to the figure given in Specifications at the beginning of this Chapter.
9 To set it, measure the gap with a feeler gauge, and then bend open, or close, the outer plug electrode until the correct gap is achieved. The centre electrode should never be bent as this may crack the insulation and cause plug failure if nothing worse. On some models special double sided electrodes are fitted. Do not forget to set this gap as well to a clearance of 0.039 in (1 mm).
10 When replacing the plugs, remember to use new plug washers, and replace the leads from the distributor in the correct firing order, which is 1 3 4 2, No 1 cylinder being the one nearest the flywheel.
11 The plug leads require no routine attention other than being kept clean and wiped over regularly.
12 Pull the leads off the plugs and distributor one at a time and make sure no water has found its way onto the connections. Remove any corrosion from the brass ends, wipe the collars on top of the distributor, and refit the leads.

11 Fault diagnosis - ignition system

There are two main symptoms indicating faults. Either the engine will not start or fire, or the engine is difficult to start and misfires. If it is a regular misfire, ie the engine is only running on two or three cylinders the fault is almost sure to be in the secondary, or high tension circuit. If the misfiring is intermittent, the fault could be in either the high or low tension circuit. If the car stops suddenly or will not start at all, it is likely that the fault is in the low tension circuit. Loss of power and overheating, apart from faulty carburation settings, are normally due to faults in the distributor or incorrect ignition timing.

It must however be pointed out that where the engine has been modified to complly with US Federal Regulations the performance of the engine is dependent on the correct functioning of all systems. If a fault arises in one system it is possible that it will show up in another. Therefore other than a major fault, which will be obvious, any intermittent or minor fault will probably require the use of electronic diagnostic equipment to quickly and accurately find the cause.

The suggestions given in the following two sections are for guidance purposes and should not be considered to cover every aspect of the ignition system.

Engine fails to start

1 If the engine fails to start and the car was running normally when it was last used, first check there is fuel in the petrol tank. If the engine turns over normally on the starter motor and the battery is evidently well charged, then the fault may be in either the high or low tension circuit. First check the HT circuit. **Note:** If the battery is known to be fully charged, the ignition light comes on, and the starter motor fails to turn the engine **check the tightness of the leads on the battery terminals** and the secureness of the earth lead at its **connection to the body.** It is quite common for the leads to have worked loose, even if they look and feel secure. If one of the battery terminal posts gets very hot when trying to work the starter motor this is a sure indication of a faulty connection to that terminal.
2 One of the commonest reasons for bad starting is wet or damp spark plug leads and distributor. Remove the distributor cap. If condensation is visible internally dry the cap with a rag and also wipe over the leads. Replace the cap.
3 If the engine still fails to start, check that current is reaching the plugs, by disconnecting each plug lead in turn at the spark plug end, and holding the end of the cable about 3/16 inch (5 mm) away from the cylinder block. Spin the engine on the starter motor.
4 Sparking between the end of the cable and the block should be fairly strong with a strong regular blue spark. (Hold the lead with rubber to avoid electric shock). If current is reaching the plugs, then remove them and clean and regap them to the specified clearance. The engine should now start.
5 If there is no spark at the plug leads take off the HT lead from the centre of the distributor cap and hold it to the block as before. Spin the engine on the starter once more. A rapid succession of blue sparks between the end of the lead and the block indicate that the coil is in order and that the distributor cap is cracked, the rotor arm faulty, or the carbon brush in the top of the distributor cap is not making good contact with the spring on the rotor arm. Possibly, the points are in bad condition. Clean and reset them as described in this Chapter, Section 3 or 4.
6 If there are no sparks from the end of the lead from the coil check the connections at the coil end of the lead. If it is in order start checking the low tension circuit.
7 Use a 12v voltmeter or a 12v bulb and two lengths of wire. With the ignition switched on and the points open, test between the low tension supply lead on the switch side of ignition coil and earth. No reading indicates a break in the supply from the ignition switch. Check the connections at the switch to see if any are loose. Refit them and the engine should run. A reading shows a faulty coil or condenser, or broken lead between the coil and the distributor.
8 Take the condenser lead off the distributor body side terminal and with the points open test between the moving point and earth. If there now is a reading then the fault is in the condenser. Fit a new one and the fault is cleared.
9 With no reading from the moving point to earth, take a

reading between earth and the distributor side of the ignition coil. A reading here shows a broken lead which will need to be replaced between the coil and distributor. No reading confirms that the coil has failed and must be renewed, after which the engine will run once more. Remember to refit the condenser lead to the points assembly. For these tests it is sufficient to separate the points with a piece of dry paper while testing with the points open.

Engine misfires

1   If the engine misfires regularly run it at a fast idling speed. Pull off each of the plug caps in turn and listen to the note of the engine. Hold the plug cap in a dry cloth or with a rubber glove as additional protection against a shock from the HT supply.
2   No difference in engine running will be noticed when the lead from the defective circuit is removed. Removing the lead from one of the good cylinders will accentuate the misfire.
3   Remove the plug lead from the end of the defective plug and hold it about 3/16 inch (5 mm) away from the block. Re-start the engine. If the sparking is fairly strong and regular the fault must lie in the spark plug.
4   The plug may be loose, the insulation may be cracked, or the points may have burnt away giving too wide a gap for the spark to jump. Worse still, one of the points may have broken off. Either renew the plug, or clean it, reset the gap, and then test it.
5   If there is no spark at the end of the plug lead, or if it is weak and intermittent, check the ignition lead from the distributor to the plug. If the insulation is cracked or perished, renew the lead. Check the connections at the distributor cap.
6   If there is still no spark, examine the distributor cap carefully for tracking. This can be recognised by a very thin black line running between two or more electrodes, or between an electrode and some other part of the distributor. These lines are paths which now conduct electricity across the cap thus letting it run to earth. The only answer is a new distributor cap.
7   Apart from the ignition being incorrect, other causes of misfiring have already been dealt with under the Section dealing with the failure of the engine to start. To recap - these are that

a) *The coil may be faulty giving an intermittent misfire;*
b) *There may be a damaged lead or loose connection in the low tension circuit;*
c) *The condenser may be short circuiting; or*
d) *There may be a mechanical fault in the distributor (broken driving spindle or contact breaker spring).*

8   If the ignition timing is too far retarded, it should be noted that the engine will tend to overheat, and there will be a quite noticeable drop in power. If the engine is overheating and the power is down, and the ignition timing is correct, then the carburettor should be checked, as it is likely that this is where the fault lies.

Chapter 5 Clutch

Contents

Specifications

Type	Diaphragm spring, single dry plate, hydraulic operation
Diameter	8.46 in. (215 mm)
Lining material dimensions	5.708 x 8.46 in. (145 x 215 mm)
Spring rating	928 lb (420 kg)
Master cylinder	
Diameter	0.75 in. (19.05 mm)
Slave cylinder	
Diameter	1.125 in. (28.6 mm)
Release bearing	
Type	Thrust, ball bearing race

Torque wrench setting	lb f ft	kg fm
Clutch cover securing screws	11	1.5

1 General description

Peugeot 504 models covered by this manual are fitted with a diaphragm spring clutch hydraulically operated.

The clutch comprises a steel cover which is bolted and dowelled to the rear face of the flywheel and contains the pressure plate and clutch disc or driven plate.

The pressure plate, diaphragm spring, and release plate are all attached to the clutch assembly cover.

The clutch disc is free to slide along the splined first motion shaft and is held in position between the flywheel and pressure plate by the pressure of the diaphragm spring.

Friction lining material is rivetted to the clutch disc which has a spring cushioned hub to absorb transmission shocks and to help ensure a smooth take off.

The clutch is actuated hydraulically. The pendant clutch pedal is connected to the clutch master cylinder and hydraulic fluid reservoir by a short pushrod. The master cylinder and hydraulic reservoir are mounted on the engine side of the bulkhead in front of the driver.

Depressing the clutch pedal moves the piston in the master cylinder forwards so forcing hydraulic fluid through the clutch hydraulic pipe to the slave cylinder.

The piston in the slave cylinder moves forwards on the entry of the fluid and actuates the release arm by means of a short pushrod. The opposite end of the release arm is forked and is located behind the release bearing.

As this pivoted clutch release arm moves backwards it bears against the release bearing pushing it forwards to bear against the release plate, so moving the centre of the diaphragm spring inwards. The spring is sandwiched between two annular rings which act as fulcrum points. As the centre of the spring is pushed out, so moving the pressure plate backwards and disengaging the pressure plate from the clutch disc.

When the clutch pedal is released, the diaphragm spring forces the pressure plate into contact with the high friction linings on the clutch disc and at the same time pushes the clutch disc a fraction of an inch forwards on its splines so engaging the clutch disc with the flywheel. The clutch disc is now firmly sandwiched between the pressure plate and the flywheel so the drive is taken up.

As the friction linings on the clutch disc wear the pressure plate automatically moves closer to the disc to compensate. There is therefore no need to periodically adjust the clutch.

2 Clutch system - bleeding

1   It is not possible to bleed the clutch system in the conventional way, but by reverse feed. Hydraulic fluid under pressure is forced through the bleed nipple until the complete system is full and the fluid level in the reservoir is up to the full mark.

2   Special equipment is used by Peugeot garages to bleed the clutch, and under normal conditions it will be better to take the car to the garage for the work to be completed even if this means towing the car.

3   In an emergency, the following method may be used but extreme care must be taken not to draw air-contaminated fluid into the brake hydraulic system.

4   Obtain a length of rubber or plastic tubing long enough to reach the left-hand brake caliper from the clutch slave cylinder. Fill the tubing with fresh hydraulic fluid and connect it up to both bleed nipples.

5   Loosen both nipples ¼ of a turn each and have an assistant slowly depress the footbrake pedal. Remove the brake/clutch fluid reservoir cap and continue to force fluid into the system until bubbles cease to surface; then tighten the nipples.

6   Top-up the fluid in the reservoir if necessary then check the operation of the clutch and brakes. If air has been drawn into the braking system it will be necessary to bleed the system as described in Chapter 9. Remove the bleed tube from the nipples.

3 Clutch pedal - removal and replacement

The clutch pedal is mounted on the same pedal bracket as that used for the brake pedal. Should it be necessary to remove the clutch pedal, refer to Chapter 13, for further information.

4 Clutch - removal and refitting

1   Access to the clutch can be a little difficult depending on the actual model, the type of engine and transmission fitted. However, the recommended and easiest method is to remove the engine first as described in Chapter 1. The reason for this is that on models with the completely enclosed and rigid torque tube connecting the gearbox to the differential housing, it is necessary to move the differential unit rearwards so that the gearbox can then be removed. This can be a rather long and involved process,

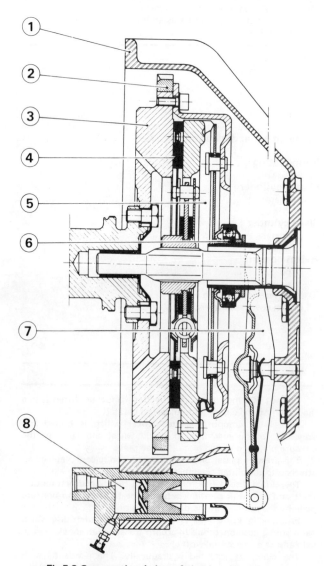

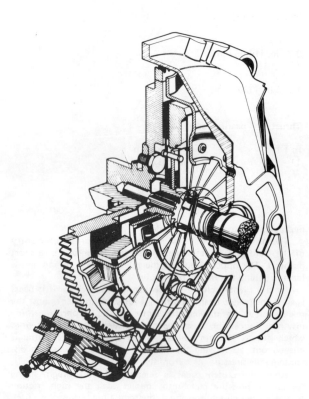

Fig 5.1 Cutaway view of clutch assembly

Fig 5.2 Cross-sectional view of clutch assembly

1	Clutch housing	5	Clutch cover
2	Starter ring gear	6	Release bearing
3	Flywheel	7	Control fork
4	Clutch plate	8	Slave cylinder

whilst the engine can be removed relatively easily.

2 With a scriber or file mark the relative position of the clutch cover and flywheel to ensure correct refitting if the original parts are to be used.

3 Remove the clutch assembly by unscrewing the six screws and special Onduflex washers that secure the cover to the rear face of the flywheel. For this a 6 mm Allen key and wrench will be required. Unscrew the screws, in diagonal order, half a turn at a time to prevent distortion of the cover flange, also to prevent the cover flange binding on the dowels and suddenly flying off.

4 With the screws and washers removed, lift the clutch cover assembly off the locating dowels. The driven plate or clutch disc will fall out at this stage as it is not attached to either the clutch cover assembly or the flywheel. Carefully make a note of which way round it is fitted. (Fig. 5.3).

5 It is important that no oil or grease gets on the clutch disc friction linings, or the pressure plate and flywheel faces. It is advisable to handle the parts with clean hands and to wipe down the pressure plate and flywheel faces with a clean dry rag before inspection or refitting commences.

6 To refit the clutch place the clutch disc against the flywheel with the larger hub boss towards the flywheel. On no account should the clutch disc be replaced the wrong way round as it will be found quite impossible to operate the clutch with the disc incorrectly fitted.

7 Replace the clutch cover assembly loosely on the dowels. Replace the six screws and new Onduflex washers and tighten them finger-tight so that the clutch disc is gripped but can still be moved.

8 The clutch disc must now be centralised so that when the engine and gearbox are mated, the gearbox input shaft splines will pass through the splines in the centre of the hub.

9 Centralisation can be carried out quite easily by inserting a round bar or long screwdriver through the hole in the centre of the clutch, so that the end of the bar rests in the small hole in the end of the crankshaft containing the input shaft bearing bush. Moving the bar sideways or up and down will move the clutch disc in whichever direction is necessary to achieve centralisation.

10 Centralisation is easily judged by removing the bar and viewing the driven plate hub in relation to the hole in the centre of the diaphragm spring. When the hub opens exactly in the centre of the release bearing hole all is correct. Alternatively, if an old input shaft can be borrowed this will eliminate all the guesswork as it will fit the bush and centre of the clutch hub exactly, obviating the need for visual alignment.

11 Tighten the clutch screws firmly in a diagonal sequence to ensure that the cover plate is pulled down evenly and without distortion of the flange. Tighten the screws to a final torque wrench setting of 11 lb f ft (1.5 kg fm).

12 Mate the engine to the gearbox, this being a direct reversal of the procedure decided upon for removal, bleed the hydraulic system (if necessary) and check the clutch for correct operation.

5 Clutch - inspection

1 In the normal course of events 'clutch dismantling and reassembly' is the term used for simply fitting a new clutch pressure plate and friction disc. Under no circumstances should the diaphragm spring clutch unit be dismantled. If a fault develops in the pressure plate assembly an exchange replacement unit must be fitted.

2 If a new clutch disc is being fitted it is false economy not to renew the release bearing at the same time. This will preclude having to replace it at a later date when wear on the clutch linings is very small.

3 Examine the clutch disc friction linings for wear or loose rivets and the disc for rim distortion, cracks and worn splines.

4 It is always best to renew the clutch driven plate as an assembly to preclude further trouble, rather than trying a d-i-y renovation on the existing unit.

5 Check the machined faces of the flywheel and the pressure plate. If either is badly grooved it should be re-machined until smooth, or replaced with a new item (Fig. 5.5). If the pressure plate is cracked or split it must be renewed.

6 Examine the hub splines for wear and also make sure that the centre hub is not loose.

6 Clutch flexible pipe - removal and replacement

1 Wipe the union ends of the flexible pipe to prevent dirt ingress.

2 Using a correctly sized open-ended spanner carefully unscrew the union nuts and lift away the flexible pipe.

3 Plug the holes in the master cylinder and slave cylinder to prevent dirt ingress.

4 Refitting the flexible pipe is the reverse sequence to removal. It will be necessary to bleed the hydraulic system, as described in Section 2.

5 If the pipe between the reservoir and master cylinder is to be removed the same general comments apply. However take care when detaching the union from the master cylinder.

7 Clutch master cylinder - removal and replacement

1 Wipe the top of the master cylinder reservoir and unscrew the cap. Place a piece of polythene sheet over the top of the reservoir and replace the cap. This will stop hydraulic fluid syphoning out during subsequent operations.

2 Wipe the exterior of the master cylinder and then disconnect the pipe that connects the reservoir to the master cylinder. Catch any fluid in a suitable container taking care that hydraulic fluid does not come into contact with paintwork as it acts as a solvent.

3 Disconnect the pipe that connects the master cylinder to the slave cylinder and plug the end to prevent dirt ingress.

4 Working inside the car disconnect the clutch pushrod from the clutch pedal.

5 Undo and remove the two nuts (or bolts) and washers securing the clutch master cylinder to the bulkhead. Lift away the master cylinder.

6 Refitting the master cylinder is the reverse sequence to removal. Bleed the system as described in Section 2.

8 Clutch master cylinder - dismantling, examination and reassembly

Important: On models manufactured up to serial numbers 504. A01/101 4917 and 504. A02/101 2919 the master cylinder contained a residual valve and spring to ensure a constant contact of the thrust bearing on the clutch mechanism and the slave cylinder contained a special cup. The residual pressure is in the region of 11.3 lb/in^2 (0.8 kg/cm^2).

On models manufactured from serial numbers 504 A01/101 4918 and 504. A02/101 2920 and *all* models in the 504. B02 and 504. C02 series the residual pressure valve in the master cylinder was fitted with a special spring in addition to a special cup. This revised arrangement serves the same purpose as the earlier system.

When servicing, the later type slave cylinder may be used with the earlier type of master cylinder but the earlier type slave cylinder **must not** be used with the later type master cylinder.

During dismantling take great care to note the location of each part.

1 To dismantle the master cylinder use a pair of circlip pliers to release the circlip retaining the piston stop washer.

2 Carefully remove the piston stop washer from the cylinder bore and follow this with the piston assembly, main and secondary cups and return spring.

3 If they prove stubborn carefully use a foot pump or air jet on the hydraulic pipe connection and this should move the internal

Fig 5.3 Removal of clutch cover assembly from flywheel (Sec 4)

Fig 5.4 Tightening clutch cover securing screws (Sec 4)

Note: metal rod used to align clutch disc

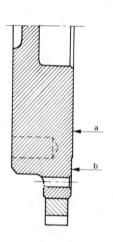

Fig 5.5 If the flywheel is to be machined to remove score marks at 'a', the same thickness must be removed from part 'b' to retain correct diaphragm spring tension (Sec 5)

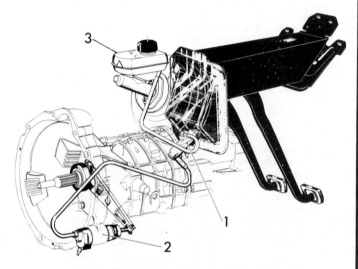

Fig 5.6 Layout of clutch control system

| 1 | Master cylinder | 3 | Reservoir |
| 2 | Slave cylinder | | |

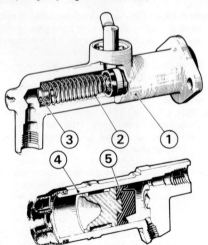

Fig 5.7 Master cylinder and slave cylinder as fitted to earlier models. [For change points see text]

1	Master cylinder	4	Slave cylinder
2	Spring	5	Cup
3	Pressure valve		

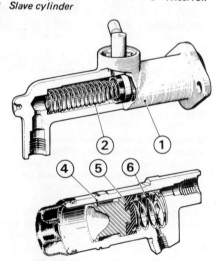

Fig 5.8 Master cylinder and slave cylinder as fitted to later models [For change points see text]

1	Master cylinder	5	Cup
2	Spring	6	Spring
4	Slave cylinder		

parts, but do take care as they will fly out. Place a cloth pad over the end to catch the parts.

4 Note which way round the primary and secondary cups are fitted.

5 Thoroughly clean the parts in brake fluid or methylated spirits. After drying the items inspect the cups for signs of distortion, swelling, splitting or hardening although it is recommended new rubber cups are always fitted after dismantling as a matter of course.

6 Inspect the bore and piston for signs of deep scoring marks which, if evident, means a new cylinder should be fitted. Make sure all drillings are clear by poking gently with a piece of thin wire.

7 As the parts are refitted to the cylinder bore make sure that they are thoroughly wetted with clean hydraulic fluid.

8 Fit the secondary cup onto the piston making sure it is the correct way round.

9 Refit all parts in the reverse order to removal. Make sure that the lips of the cups do not roll over as they enter the bore.

10 Finally replace the circlip and ensure that it is fully seated.

11 The master cylinder is now ready for refitting to the car.

9 Clutch slave cylinder - removal and replacement

1 Wipe the top of the reservoir and unscrew the cap. Place a piece of polythene sheet over the top of the reservoir and replace the cap. This will stop hydraulic fluid syphoning out during subsequent operations.

2 Wipe the area around the hydraulic pipe on the slave cylinder and unscrew the hydraulic pipe union nut.

3 The slave cylinder is retained by a clip located in a groove near to the rubber boot end of the cylinder. This must be released using a screwdriver. Detach the front retaining clip from the gearbox.

4 Temporarily detach the steering rack and pinion from the front crossmember and column, leaving the track rods attached to the steering arms (see Chapter 11).

5 Draw the slave cylinder towards the front of the clutch bellhousing noting that the pushrod will remain connected to the clutch release fork.

6 Refitting the slave cylinder is the reverse sequence to removal. It is important that the bleed nipple is in its lowermost position.

7 Bleed the clutch hydraulic system as described in Section 2.

10 Clutch slave cylinder - dismantling, examination and reassembly

1 Refer to the introduction to Section 8.

2 Clean the outside of the slave cylinder before dismantling.

3 Pull off the rubber dust cover and by shaking hard, the piston and cup assembly should come out of the cylinder bore.

4 If they prove stubborn carefully use a foot pump or air jet on the hydraulic pipe connection and this should remove the internal parts, but do take care as they will fly out. Place a cloth pad over the end to catch the parts.

5 Note which way round the cup is fitted.

6 Wash all internal parts with either brake fluid or methylated spirits and dry using a non-fluffy rag.

7 Inspect the bore and piston for signs of deep scoring which, if evident, means a new cylinder should be fitted.

8 Carefully examine the rubber components for signs of swelling, distortion, splitting, hardening or other wear although it is recommended new rubber parts are always fitted after dismantling.

9 All parts should be reassembled wetted with clean hydraulic fluid.

10 Fit the cup to the piston the correct way round and insert the piston into the bore. Take care not to roll the lip of the cup.

11 Pack the dust cover with a little rubber grease and fit over the end of the slave cylinder body engaging the lips over the groove in the body.

11 Clutch release bearing and fork assembly - removal, overhaul and replacement

1 To gain access it is necessary to remove the engine (See Section 4, paragraph 1).

2 Whilst inspecting the clutch assembly it is worthwhile checking the release bearing assembly. The bearing assembly can be detached without removing the clutch fork.

3 Release the bearing retaining clip and rotate in an anti-clockwise direction.

4 If the bearing is worn or shows signs of overheating it should be renewed. (Fig. 5.9).

5 Should it be necessary to remove the bearing guide sleeve it can be detached using a bench vice and suitable packing. However this is one little job best left to the local Peugeot garage.

6 The clutch release fork can be removed by working inside the housing and removing the rubber cup and fork thrust ball (Fig. 5.10).

7 To reassemble pack the rubber cup with a little grease and slide the release fork from the inside towards the outside of the clutch housing.

8 It will be beneficial to use a screwdriver to lift the clutch release fork backing spring whilst engaging the fork on the ball head. The spring should be backed against the rubber cup.

9 Smear the guide sleeve with a little high melting point grease and engage the new bearing by positioning the retaining jaw towards the starter motor housing.

10 Engage the thrust bearing with the clutch release fork and lock by rotating the bearing clockwise and refitting the retaining clip.

12 Clutch squeal - diagnosis and cure

1 If on taking up the drive, or when changing gear, the clutch squeals, this is a sure indication of a badly worn release bearing. As well as regular wear due to normal use, wear of the clutch release bearing is much accentuated if the clutch is 'ridden', or held down by long periods with a gear selected and the engine running.

2 The clutch release bearing is not an expensive item to renew, but access to it requires engine removal.

13 Clutch slip - diagnosis and cure

1 Clutch slip is a self-evident condition which occurs when the clutch friction plate (driven plate) is badly worn; the release arm free-travel is insufficient, oil or grease has found its way onto the flywheel or pressure plate faces, or the pressure plate itself is faulty.

2 The reason for clutch slip is that, due to one of the faults listed above, there is either insufficient pressure from the pressure plate, or insufficient friction from the friction plate to ensure a solid drive.

3 If small amounts of oil get onto the clutch, they will be burnt off under the heat of clutch engagement, in the process gradually darkening the linings. Excessive oil on the clutch will burn off leaving a carbon deposit which can cause quite bad slip, or fierceness, spin and judder.

4 If clutch slip is suspected, and confirmation of this condition is required, there are several tests which can be made:

a) *With the engine in second or third gear and pulling lightly up a moderate incline, sudden depression of the accelerator pedal may cause the engine to increase its speed without any increase in road speed. Easing off on the accelerator will then give a definite drop in engine speed without the car slowing.*

b) *Drive the car at a steady speed in top gear and, braking with the left foot, try and maintain the same speed by depressing the accelerator pedal. Providing the same speed is maintained, a change in the speed of the engine confirms that slip is taking place.*

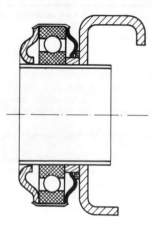

Fig 5.9 Cross-sectional view through clutch thrust bearing assembly (Sec 11)

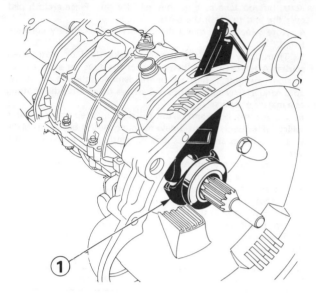

Fig 5.10 Clutch thrust bearing assembly removal (Sec 11)

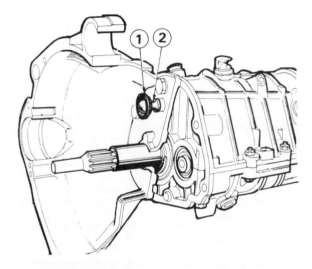

Fig 5.11 Clutch release fork pivot assembly (Sec 11)

1   Rubber cup   2   Ball head

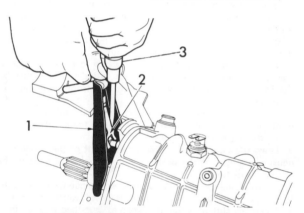

Fig 5.12 Refitting clutch release fork (Sec 11)

1   Clutch release fork   3   Screwdriver
2   Retaining spring clip

c) In extreme cases of clutch slip the engine will race under normal acceleration conditions.

If the slip is due to oil or grease on the linings a temporary cure can sometimes be effected by squirting carbon tetrochloride into the clutch housing. The permanent cure, of course, is to renew the clutch driven plate and trace and rectify the oil leak.

14 Clutch spin - diagnosis and cure

1   Clutch spin is a condition which occurs when there is a leak in the hydraulic actuating mechanism, the release arm free travel is excessive, there is an obstruction in the clutch either on the input shaft splines or in the unit itself, or oil may have partially burnt off the clutch linings and have left a resinous deposit which is causing the clutch disc to stick to the pressure plate or flywheel.
2   The reason for clutch spin is that due to any or a combination of, the faults just listed, the clutch pressure plate is not completely freeing from the centre plate even with the clutch pedal fully depressed.
3   If clutch spin is suspected, the condition can be confirmed by extreme difficulty in engaging first gear from rest, difficulty in changing gear, and very sudden take up of the clutch drive at

the fully depressed end of the clutch pedal travel as the clutch is released.
4   Check the clutch master and slave cylinders and the connecting pipes for leaks. Fluid in the rubber boot fitted over the end of the slave cylinder or fluid around the clutch master cylinder mounting on the bulkhead is a sure sign of a leaking piston seal.
5   If these points are checked and found to be in order then the fault lies internally in the clutch, and it will be necessary to remove it for examination.

15 Clutch judder - diagnosis and cure

1   Clutch judder is a self evident condition which occurs when the power unit mountings are loose or too flexible; when there is oil on the faces of the clutch friction plate, or when the clutch has been assembled incorrectly.
2   The reason for clutch judder is that due to one of the faults just listed, the clutch pressure plate is not freeing smoothly from the friction disc and is snatching.
3   Clutch judder normally occurs when the clutch pedal is released in first or reverse gears, and the whole car shudders as it moves backwards or forwards.

Chapter 6
Manual gearbox and automatic transmission

For modifications, and information applicable to later models, see Supplement at end of manual

Contents

Specifications

Manual gearbox

Gearbox series	BA7
Number of gears	4 forward, 1 reverse
Type of gears	Helical, constant mesh
Synchromesh	All forward gears

Ratios:

First	3.663 : 1 (0.281)
Second	2.169 : 1 (0.475)
Third	1.409 : 1 (0.732)
Top	1.000 : 1 (1)
Reverse	3.747 : 1 (0.275)

Speedometer drive gear ratio:

	ratio	colour
Saloon, family and estate	10 x 20	Black
Station wagon	10 x 21	Blue
Fuel injection models	10 x 19	White

Input shaft

Number of teeth	21
End float adjustment shims:	
Outer diameter	1.6535 in. (42.00 mm)
Inner diameter	1.4645 in. (37.20 mm)
Shim thickness range	0.006 - 0.014 in. (0.15 - 0.35 mm) in increments of 0.002 in. (0.05 mm)

Mainshaft

Front end needle roller bearing	0.071 x 1.02 x 0.622 in. (18 x 26 x 15.8 mm)
Number of teeth:	
First gear wheel	35
Second gear wheel	29
Third gear wheel	26
Reverse gear wheel	31
Adjustment shims:	
Outer diameter	1.8110 in. (46.00 mm)
Inner diameter	1.3858 in. (35.2 mm)

Shim thickness range	...	...	...	...	...	0.006, 0.008, 0.10 and 0.20 in. (0.15, 0.20, 0.25 and 0.50 mm)
Needle roller bearing	...	...	...	...	...	1.53 x 2.29 x 0.394 in. (38.8 x 58.2 x 10 mm)

Layshaft
Number of teeth:
First gear ...	...	...	...	...	...	...	15
Second gear	...	...	...	...	...	...	21
Third gear	...	...	...	...	...	...	29
Constant drive gear	...	...	...	...	...	...	33

Adjustment shims:
Outer diameter	...	...	...	...	...	...	1.102 in. (28.00 mm)
Inner diameter	...	...	...	...	...	...	0.850 in. (21.6 mm)
Shim thickness range	...	...	...	...	...	...	0.085 - 0.134 in. (2.25 - 3.40 mm) in increments of 0.002 in. (0.05 mm)

Idler gear shaft
Diameter	...	...	...	...	...	...	...	0.7874 in. (20.00 mm)
Length	...	...	...	...	...	...	...	3.5433 in. (90.00 mm)

Idler gearwheel
Number of teeth	...	...	...	...	...	...	...	19

Lubricant capacity   ...   .   2.1 pints (2.34 US pints, 1.150 litres)

Automatic Transmission

Type   ...   .   ZF . 3HP . 12., 3 speed epicyclic gear trains with 3 element hydrokinetic torque converter.

Ratios
Converter reduction ratio (max)	...	...	...	...	...	2.29 : 1	

Mechanical reduction ratios:
First	...	...	...	...	...	...	...	0.391
Second	...	...	...	...	...	...	...	0.658
Third	...	...	...	...	...	...	...	1.000

Range multiplication (including converter reduction range):
First	...	...	...	...	...	...	...	0.170 - 0.391
Second	...	...	...	...	...	...	...	0.287 - 0.658
Third	...	...	...	...	...	...	...	0.437 - 1.000

Typical performance data:

Throttle opening   **Gearchanges**

	Up				Down			
	1st to 2nd		2nd to 3rd		3rd to 2nd		2nd to 1st	
	mile/h	km/h	mile/h	km/h	mile/h	km/h	mile/h	km/h
¼	9	15	16	25	14	23	7	12
½	11	17	17	27	16	25	9	15
¾	19	31	55	89	37	60	16	25
Full	24	38	57	92	38	62	19	30
'Kick-down'	37	60	62	100	60	97	33	53
					70*	112*	42**	68**

*Maximum speed for change down to 2nd when selecting 2nd
**Maximum speed for change down to 1st when selecting 1st

Hydraulic fluid capacity:
Transmission unit	...	...	...	...	...	...	8.3 - 9.2 Imp pints (10.0 - 11.2 US pints, 4.75 - 5.25 litres)
Transmission unit and oil cooler	...	...	...	...	...	10 Imp pints (12.00 US pints, 5.5 litres)

Torque wrench settings
							lb f ft	kg f m
Manual gearbox								
Gearbox drain plug	...	...	...	...	...		20	2.75
Gearbox to engine bolts	...	...	...	...	...		43.5	6.0
Radiator mounting bolts	...	...	...	...	...		7.2	1.0
Differential unit (1RS)	...	...	...	...	...		27	3.75
Starter motor	...	...	...	...	...	...		14.5	2.0
Gearbox filler plug	...	...	...	...	...		20	2.75
Detent spring and ball plug	...	...	...	...	...		7.2	1.0
Clutch bellhousing	...	...	...	...	...		20	2.75

							lb f ft	kg f m
Gearbox casing halves nuts and bolts ...	...	...	...				7.2	1.0
Gearbox backing plate screws ...	...	...	...	...			7.2	1.0
Reverse pinion nut	...	...	...	...	...	...	40	5.5
Rear housing nuts and bolts	...	...	...	...	...		11	1.5
Reverse light switch:								
Copper body ...	...	...	...	...	...	...	9.0	1.25
Steel body	...	...	...	...	...	...	20	2.7
Torque tube to gearbox		...	...	...	...	...	16	2.25

Automatic Transmission

							lb f ft	kg f m
Diaphragm securing bolts	...	...	...	...	...		11.6 - 17.4	1.6 - 2.3
Oil sump ...	...	...	...	...	...	...	7.0	1.0

1 General description (manual gearbox)

The gearbox fitted to the 504 models covered by this manual has remained basically the same throughout its production life. There have, however, been some minor detail modifications so whenever spare parts are being ordered always be sure to quote the vehicle chassis number.

Fig. 6.2 shows a cutaway view of the gearbox with the bellhousing and rear extension attached.

The extension houses the speedometer drive pinion which is driven from the wormwheel towards the end of the mainshaft and the two levers on the side operate the gear selectors. As can be seen from Fig. 6.1 the longer of these two levers moves the shaft of the short cranked lever (which sticks out from the underside of the gearbox) up and down causing one of the two short levers on the other end of this shaft to engage with one or other of the selector rods. Once engaged the selector rod is moved in and out by the operation of the lever on the underside of the gearbox to select the gear required.

The two levers are connected by linkages to the gearchange lever - which may be mounted on the steering column or on the floor - so that when the gear lever is moved across the centre of the gate the lever on the side of the gearbox rotates, and when the gearchange lever is moved into one of the gear selection positions the lever on the underside of the gearbox rotates. Originally the selector lever system was designed for a steering column gearchange hence the rather complicated linkage associated with the floor mounted gearchange lever.

The gearbox has four forward speeds and reverse with synchromesh on all forward gears. The split-case construction makes dismantling a simple matter and provided that the layout and operation of the gearbox is understood no problems should arise.

Consider the gear train first. Photo 6:13 shows the whole assembly being lifted from the casing and gives an excellent

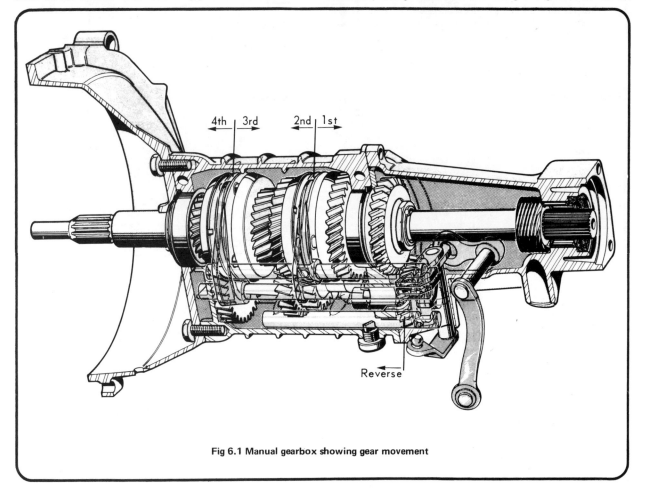

Fig 6.1 Manual gearbox showing gear movement

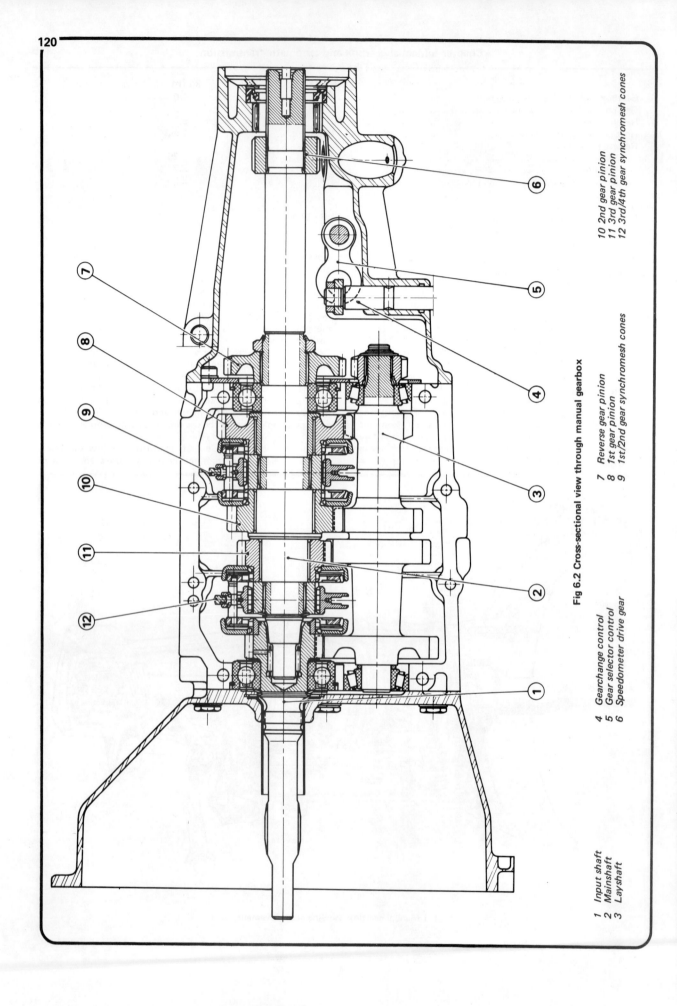

Fig 6.2 Cross-sectional view through manual gearbox

1 Input shaft
2 Mainshaft
3 Layshaft

4 Gearchange control
5 Gear selector control
6 Speedometer drive gear

7 Reverse gear pinion
8 1st gear pinion
9 1st/2nd gear synchromesh cones

10 2nd gear pinion
11 3rd gear pinion
12 3rd/4th gear synchromesh cones

picture of the general arrangement.

It should be appreciated that although the assembly looks as one complete unit in fact the input and output ends are completely independent of each other. This must be so, because the engine drives the input end whilst the output end drives the propeller shaft. The input shaft is sometimes referred to as the driveshaft and the output shaft as the mainshaft.

The input shaft assembly is shown in Fig. 6.3. It carries a single gear which is integral with the shaft. The gear drives the layshaft which is shown in Fig. 6.2. The layshaft assembly is shown in Fig. 6.4 and it carries four gears which are integral with the shaft and a fifth gear - the reverse pinion - which is splined to it. The gear on the input shaft is always in mesh with its opposite number on the layshaft and both rotate when the engine is running whether a gear has been selected or not.

The remaining gears integral with the layshaft drive their opposite numbers on the mainshaft, the exception however, is the reverse pinion which although in mesh with the mainshaft does not drive the mainshaft gear directly but is coupled to it through an intermediate gear when reverse is selected. Selecting a forward speed is a matter of locking the appropriate gear on the mainshaft assembly to the mainshaft (output gear) itself. In the case of the fourth gear the mainshaft is locked directly to the input shaft.

This locking is achieved by moving a splined sleeve which forms part of the synchroniser assembly so that it simultaneously engages with the synchronising hub which is locked to the output shaft and a corresponding hub on the selected gear. The mainshaft, shaft assembly is shown in Fig. 6.5.

To engage third gear, the selector fork pushes the synchroniser over the synchroniser hub towards the hub on the gear. This causes the synchronising cone to engage with the corresponding cone which is fixed to the gear. Friction between these two cones soon makes the gear revolve at the same speed as the synchroniser, and once this has occurred the splines on the synchroniser itself will move over the hub on the gear and the two hubs will be locked together. The synchroniser cone is sprung away from the synchroniser itself so that it makes contact with the cone on the gear before the hubs are locked, and when the synchroniser is fully home the cone clicks into a fixed position.

To engage fourth gear the synchroniser is moved in the other direction and engages with an exactly similar cone and hub on the input shaft, thus locking the input and output shafts together.

The synchroniser for second and first gears is identical in principle but the two synchronisers are not interchangeable.

The arrangements for reverse are quite obvious in Fig. 6.1. An extra pinion - the reverse idler pinion - is interposed between the reverse pinion on the mainshaft and the corresponding gear on the output shaft. It is brought into mesh by the operation of the reverse selector rail which carries a half fork permanently

attached to it which engages in a channel on the idler pinion.

Built into the gearbox are locators for the selector rods and interlock arrangement prevents two gears being engaged at once. These are shown in Fig. 6.6. The locator balls and springs work in notches in the selector rods.

The third/fourth speed selector rod has its locator at the front end while the other two rods are retained by balls and springs which are inserted through plugs on either side of the gearbox casing. The extra ball and two small pieces known as the locking needles and the locking finger form the interlock.

When the third/fourth speed selector rod (the centre one) is moved forwards, or backwards, it will carry with it the interlock needed which is located in a hole in the shaft. At the same time the interlock needle will push the interlock finger and the interlock ball outwards so that these engage with notches in the reverse selector shaft and the first/second speed selector shaft

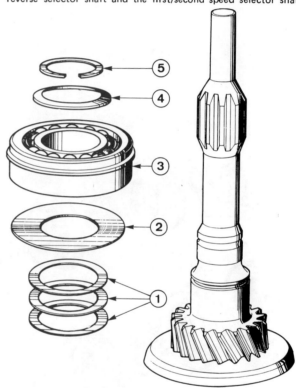

Fig 6.3 Input shaft assembly

1 Shims
2 Deflector washer
3 Ball race

4 Spring washer
5 Snap-ring

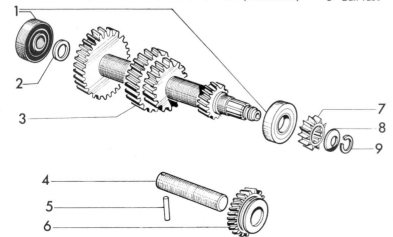

Fig 6.4 Layshaft assembly

1 Bearing
2 Selective shim
3 Layshaft
4 Spindle
5 Lock pin
6 Reverse idler gear
7 Reverse gear
8 Washer
9 Snap-ring

respectively. When this has happened, these two shafts cannot be moved.

If the first/second speed shaft is moved, it will force the interlock ball away, displacing the needle in the third/fourth speed shaft and thus immobilising this shaft. The needle will in turn push the interlock finger firmly into its notch on the reverse selector shaft, making this immovable too. The same thing happens in the opposite direction when the reverse selector shaft is moved.

The neutral position of the selector lever which moves in and out on the underside of the gearbox is located by another ball and spring as shown in Fig. 6.6. The ball used is larger than those used on the selector shafts.

Automatic transmission is fitted as a factory production extra. Further information on this unit will be found in Sections 17 to 20 inclusive.

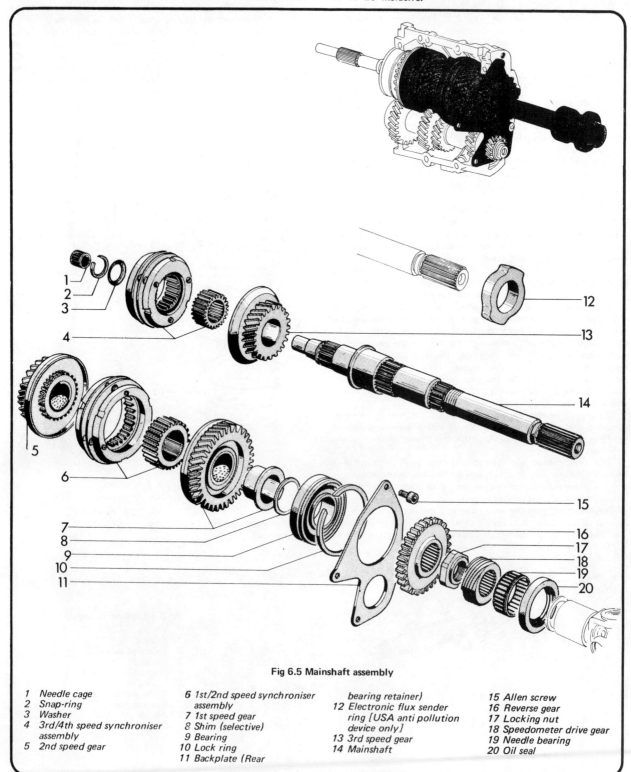

Fig 6.5 Mainshaft assembly

1 Needle cage	5 1st/2nd speed synchroniser assembly	bearing retainer)
2 Snap-ring	6 1st speed gear	12 Electronic flux sender ring [USA anti pollution device only]
3 Washer	7 1st speed gear	
4 3rd/4th speed synchroniser assembly	8 Shim (selective)	13 3rd speed gear
	9 Bearing	14 Mainshaft
5 2nd speed gear	10 Lock ring	
	11 Backplate (Rear	

15 Allen screw
16 Reverse gear
17 Locking nut
18 Speedometer drive gear
19 Needle bearing
20 Oil seal

2 Gearbox (manual) - removal

1 The gearbox is not very easy to remove and involves some fiddly work. The engine is carried on two rubber mountings only and is supported at the rear through the gearbox so facilities must be to hand to take the weight of the engine when the gearbox is being removed. Added to this it will be necessary to turn the engine slightly before the gearbox can be drawn rearwards. This can be carried out without undoing the engine mountings.

The steering housing gets in the way but this can be easily dealt with by releasing it and letting it hang down by its balljoints. These considerations form the basis of the detailed removal procedure described in the rest of this Section.

One other point that needs special mention. When the gearbox is detached from the engine, be sure never to let its weight rest on the input shaft. This can lead to distortion in the shaft or in the clutch which means trouble sooner or later.

2 When removing the gearbox carry out what needs to be done inside the car first whilst you are still clean. With the steering column gearchange there are no inside jobs, but for the floor mounted gearchange it is necessary to remove the console and detach the lever mounting assembly and its linkage from the gearbox. Figs. 6.14, 6.15 and 6.16 give supplementary information on this operation.

3 Using an overhead hoist support the weight of the engine and free it sufficiently to allow it to be turned on its mountings later (see paragraph 1). Start by disconnecting the battery positive lead and then drain the oil from the gearbox. Then remove the following:

  a) *The ignition coil - note all cable connections.*
  b) *The upper radiator mounting.*
  c) *Both bolts of the lower radiator mounting on the front cross member*
  d) *The securing bolts from the starter motor. The motor itself does not have to be removed but do remove the closure plate.*

4 On carburettor engines, remove the air cleaner so preventing damage to the regulator cover whilst working on the engine.

5 On fuel injection engines disconnect the following:

  a) *The electro-valve supply pipe.*
  b) *The air cleaner to air distribution chamber union.*
  c) *The engine oil filler plug. Note: There is no need to undo the oil vapour recirculating rubber hose connections.*

6 The exhaust system does not need to be extensively disturbed when the gearbox is being removed. Disconnect the downpipe from the manifold, and then release the bracket holding the front silencer or the equivalent to this bracket with other exhaust system layouts (Chapter 3). Allow the whole assembly to rest on the rear crossmember. Where a heat dissipation plate is fitted above the front silencer it will be neces-

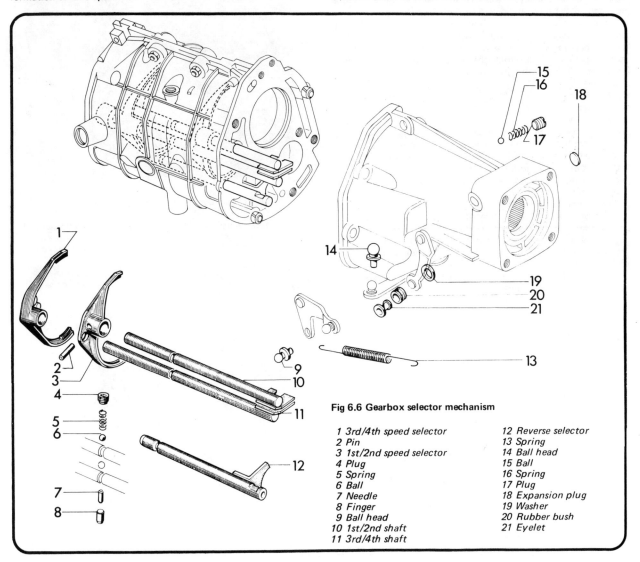

Fig 6.6 Gearbox selector mechanism

1 3rd/4th speed selector	12 Reverse selector
2 Pin	13 Spring
3 1st/2nd speed selector	14 Ball head
4 Plug	15 Ball
5 Spring	16 Spring
6 Ball	17 Plug
7 Needle	18 Expansion plug
8 Finger	19 Washer
9 Ball head	20 Rubber bush
10 1st/2nd shaft	21 Eyelet
11 3rd/4th shaft	

sary to remove this next. **Do not** attempt to separate the exhaust system into its component parts. (Fig. 6.7)

7 Undo and remove the three upper Allen bolts (Key size 8 mm across flats), leaving one of the bottom ones still in position but slackened off.

8 Unless the vehicle is a station wagon or equivalent which has a normal rear axle and more conventional propeller shaft, remove the Allen bolts holding the differential unit under the rear suspension crossmember.

9 On fuel injection engines, free the electric fuel pump from its holding brackets to allow the differential unit to be moved rearwards.

10 Remove the remaining Allen bolt from the underside of the gearbox and push back the torque tube from the gearbox by about 0.75 in (20 mm) and fit the propeller shaft holding plate or a suitable substitute as described in Chapter 7. With the holding plate inserted, remove the propeller shaft assembly from the gearbox and allow it to rest somewhere out of the way.

11 For models with fixed rear axles refer to Chapter 7, for information on detaching the propeller shaft.

12 The rest of the removal sequence really needs two people, one to guide the engine whilst the other works underneath the car. For those concerned about time the next sequence will take about 30 minutes.

13 Raise the front part of the engine, taking care to allow the radiator to come up with it without dragging on the radiator hoses - for example, by supporting it with a piece of rope attached to the sling on the underside of the engine and taken to the hoisting hook or if the whole assembly is being jacked up ensure the radiator as well as the engine is supported by the jack.

14 The gearbox should now be sloping downwards towards the rear, reasonably free from the tunnel and with the three uppermost Allen bolts securing it to the engine reasonably accessible.

15 Check that all connections have been detached (including the speedometer drive cable) and well tucked out of the way to prevent damage.

16 Undo and remove the Allen bolts, disengage the clutch housing from the engine (it is dowelled in two places) and turn it about ¼ turn anticlockwise to enable the starter motor boss to come through the tunnel. (Fig. 6.9).

17 The gearbox should now be drawn rearwards and lifted away from the underside of the car.

3 Gearbox (manual) - replacement

1 Refitting the gearbox is basically the reverse of the removal procedure but there are several points which should be noted.

2 Be sure that the clutch thrust bearing is correctly fitted. It should be offered to the clutch release fork with the retaining tag pointing to the starter motor housing and then turned clockwise so that this tag hooks over the release fork.

3 The guide sleeve of the bearing and the part of the input shaft bearing retainer over which it runs should be smeared with Molycote 321 before the bearing is fitted.

4 Presuming the engine has been left hoisted or jacked-up in the position it was in during gearbox removal replacement of the gearbox is straightforward, the only point to watch being the engagement of the input shaft with the clutch disc on the flywheel. This is a matter of alignment of the mating splines.

5 Once the input shaft has been engaged with the clutch disc the dowels on the housing will make it easy to align the gearbox to the engine and secure it with the three uppermost Allen bolts. It is preferable to use new lockwashers. Tighten the bolts to a torque wrench setting of 43.5 lb f ft (6.0 kg f m). The jack supporting the weight of the gearbox may now be removed.

6 The following items may now be refitted/reconnected as applicable:

    a) *Earth lead to gearbox.*
    b) *Reverse light switch leads.*
    c) *Speedometer drive cable.*
    d) *Steering column gear change only: gearlever connecting*

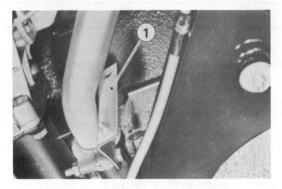

Fig 6.7 Exhaust system front mounting 1 (Sec 2)

Fig 6.8 Items to be detached from gearbox (Sec 2)

1 *Clutch slave cylinder*	4 *Reverse light switch*
2 *Counter lever*	5 *Main earth lead*
3 *Counter lever rods*	6 *Speedometer cable*

Fig 6.9 Turning gearbox anticlockwise to remove (Sec 2)

Note that the steering rack has been detached

rods.

e) Gearbox drain plug. Use a new seal and tighten to a torque wrench setting of 20 lb f ft (2.27 kg fm).

f) Clutch housing closure plate.

g) Clutch release slave cylinder.

h) The steering gear housing. Be sure the wheels point straight-ahead, the steering wheel is correctly positioned and marks on steering rod and universal coupline line up. (See also Chapter 11).

i) Secure the radiator to the front of the car and tighten the bolts to a torque wrench setting of 7.2 lb f ft (1.0 kg fm).

7 Working under the car refit/reconnect the following items:

a) Heat shield to front silencer (where applicable).

b) Reconnect exhaust downpipe to manifold. Always use a new gasket.

c) Reconnect the exhaust system front support bracket.

8 On models with independent rear suspension, bolt the differential unit to the suspension crossmember using new washers. Tighten the bolts to a torque wrench setting of 27 lb f ft (3.75 kg f m).

9 On fuel injection models refit the electric fuel pump.

10 Refit the starter motor securing bolts and tighten to a torque wrench setting of 14.5 lb f ft (2.0 kg f m).

11 Reconnect all other items that were detached from the engine when preparing to remove the gearbox.

12 Floor gearchange models. Refit the gearchange lever, and adjust as described in Section 5.

13 Column gearchange models. Adjust the linkage as described in Section 4.

14 Replenish the gearbox with oil until oil issues from the filler/level hole. Tighten the filler plug to a torque wrench setting of 20 lbf ft (2.75 kgf m).

15 Check for correct operation of the clutch and then road test.

4 Steering column gearchange (manual) - overhaul and adjustment

1 The design of the gearbox is such that the steering column

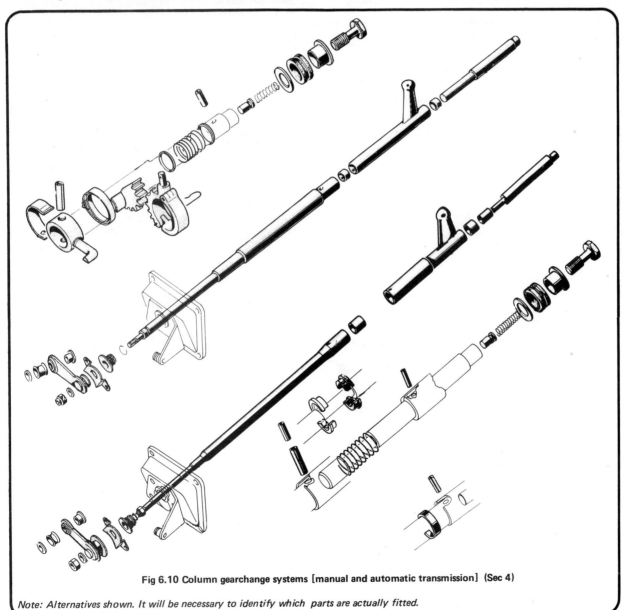

Fig 6.10 Column gearchange systems [manual and automatic transmission] (Sec 4)

Note: Alternatives shown. It will be necessary to identify which parts are actually fitted.

mounted gearchange linkage is comparatively simple. Fig. 6.10 gives an exploded view of the component parts, and in the main access to these requires removal of the steering column as described in Chapter 11.

2 Adjustment starts by checking the relative positions of the gearchange lever and the actuating lever at the bottom of the control rod. There should be an angle of 10° between them as illustrated. If this is not the case, remove the locknut and plain washer and move the lower lever into the correct position on the splines of the rod. Replace the washer and tighten the nut.

3 Check that the dimension 'a' (Fig. 6.12) is 9.76 + 0.04 in (248 $\pm$ 1 mm).

4 With these two adjustments correctly set, refit the selector control link and move the gearchange lever to the neutral position. Refer to Fig. 6.13 and unscrew the nut (2). Ensure that the selector lever (3) is in the neutral position. It will be found that there is a certain amount of free-play in this position. Set the lever centrally between the extreme play positions and retighten the nut (2).

5 Finally check the gear selection in all gears and road test.

---

5 Floor mounted gearchange (manual) - overhaul and adjustment

1 The floor mounted gearchange mechanism is shown in Figs. 6.14 and 6.16. Overhaul consists of checking the various bushes and linkages for wear and/or damage, greasing them and replacing

them as necessary. Unless there has been gross neglect or the car has covered a high mileage it is unlikely that replacement will be necessary.

2 To adjust the system, set the length, of the two control links (dimensions 'a' and 'b' in Fig. 6.17) to 3.51 $\pm$ 0.02 in (89 $\pm$ 0.5 mm) and 11.3 $\pm$ 0.04 in (287 $\pm$ 1 mm) respectively.

3 Lubricate the balljoints before refitting the levers.

---

6 Gearbox (manual) - dismantling

1 Place the complete unit on a firm bench or table and ensure that exterior is clean.

2 Read the whole of this Section before starting work, referring to the illustrations or photographs as applicable.

3 Slacken off the locknut and remove the screw that holds the speedometer drive socket in place. Remove the speedometer drive socket (Fig. 6.18).

4 Remove the clutch release thrust bearing and its lever from the bellhousing. (The lever hides one of the fixing screws), undo the screws and remove the bellhousing. **Do not** try to lever it off with a screwdriver as the mating faces would be damaged resulting in subsequent oil leaks.

5 Set the control lever to the neutral position and pull the selector lever fully to the rear. Undo and remove the seven fixing bolts and remove the rear housing. Tap it gently with a soft faced hammer if it is difficult to part as it is dowelled to the rear face of the gearbox main casing. Once again do not use a screw-

Fig 6.11 Steering column gearchange lever (manual and automatic transmission) [Sec 4]

Fig 6.13 Steering column gearchange adjustment points (Sec 4)

1	Gear selector control link	2	Nut
		3	Selector lever

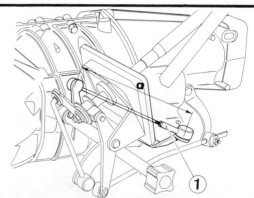

Fig 6.12 Steering column gearchange adjustment (Sec 4)

a = 9.76 $\pm$ 0.04 in. (248 $\pm$ 1 mm)
I = Gear selector control link

Fig 6.14 Floor mounted gearchange lever (Sec 5)

(Saloon de-luxe and utility models)

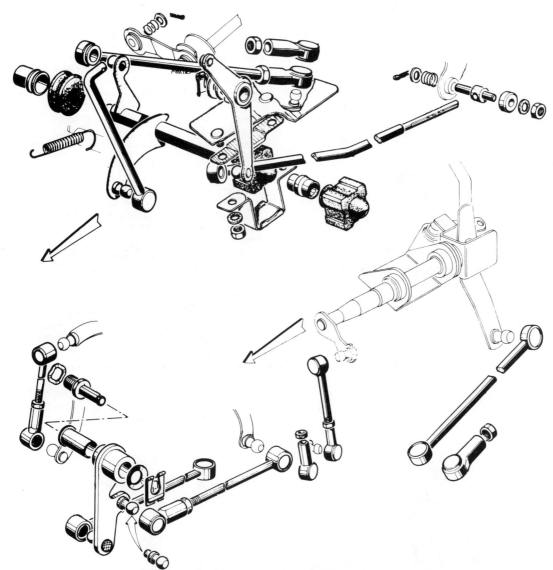

Fig 6.15 Manual transmission control rods and linkage (Sec 5)

Note: Alternatives shown. It will be necessary to identify which parts are actually fitted

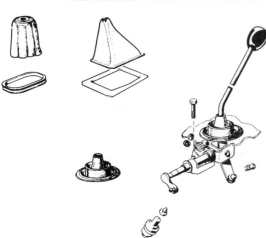

Fig 6.16 Floor mounted gearchange lever (Sec 5)

(Saloon except de-luxe, Cabriolet and Coupe)

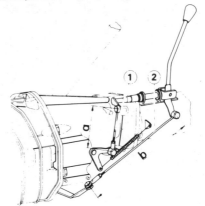

Fig 6.17 Floor mounted gearchange adjustment (Sec 5)

$a = 3.51 \pm 0.02$ in. $(89 \pm 0.5$ mm$)$
$b = 11.3 \pm 0.04$ in. $(287 \pm 1$ mm$)$
1 and 2   Gear selector control links

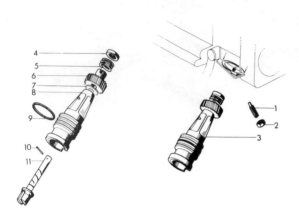

Fig 6.18 Speedometer drive assembly (Sec 6)

1	Screw	7	Washer
2	Nut	8	Housing
3	Speedometer drive assembly	9	'O' ring
4	Cup	10	Pin
5	Spring	11	Shaft
6	Gear		

driver (photo).

6 Note the exact position of the speedometer pinion on the mainshaft and using a universal puller draw off the pinion. (photo)

7 Undo the large nut that secures the reverse pinion to the mainshaft (photo). If it is difficult to move try using two thin screwdrivers gently wedged between the reverse pinion and the bearing locking plate.

8 Slide the reverse pinion off the mainshaft noting which way round it is fitted (photo).

9 Undo and remove the bearing locking plate securing screws using an Allen key and lift off the bearing locking plate (photos).

10 Undo and remove the screws securing the two halves of the gearbox main casing. From this photo note which half is on the table. Lift away the top half of the casing (photo).

11 This photo shows the correct layout of the gear trains.

12 Carefully lift out the layshaft gear assembly (photo)...

13 ... followed by the input shaft and mainshaft assembly (photo).

14 The gearbox itself may now be considered to be dismantled and it now remains for the various sub-assemblies to be attended to, as determined by a thorough inspection for wear or damage.

7 Mainshaft assembly (manual) - dismantling

1 To part the input shaft from the mainshaft, first slide the third/fourth speed synchroniser as far as it will go into the third

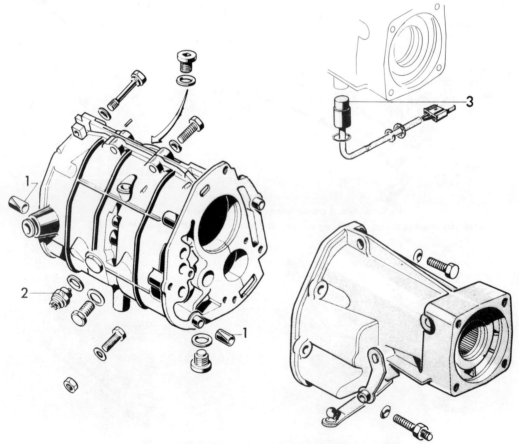

Fig 6.19 Gearbox main casing and rear housing attachments (Sec 6)

1 Dowel
2 Reverse light switch (except station wagon)
3 Speed sensor assembly (USA only)

6.4 Removal of clutch bellhousing

6.5 Removal of rear housing

6.6 Drawing off speedometer pinion

6.7 The nut that retains the reverse pinion on the mainshaft

6.8 Sliding off the reverse pinion

6.9A Removal of bearing locking plate screws with Allen key

6.9B Removal of bearing locking plate

6.10 Parting the two halves of gearbox main casing

6.11 The gear train layout

6.12 Lifting out layshaft assembly

6.13 Removal of input shaft and mainshaft assembly

7.1 Separating input shaft from mainshaft

speed synchroniser cone and simply pull apart (photo).

2 It is important that when the synchronisers are reassembled after having been taken apart the hubs and sliders should go back in exactly the same position as they were found to be in on removal. Before dismantling mark the various components if there is to be any doubt. The other thing to be certain of is that the various shims are put back exactly where they came from. They take up manufacturing tolerances and their number and thickness varies with individual gearboxes.

3 Start dismantling the mainshaft by marking the third/fourth speed sliding gear and hub. Using a pair of circlip pliers release and then remove the snap ring and spring washer from the end of the mainshaft (photo).

4 Slide the third/fourth speed synchroniser assembly from mainshaft (photo).

5 Lift off the third/fourth speed synchroniser assembly hub and gearwheel (photo).

6 Should by chance the reverse pinion and retaining nut still be in position on the rear end of the mainshaft these must be removed. Hold the reverse gear between soft faces in a large bench vice and unscrew the nut. Slide off the reverse pinion.

7 It is now necessary to remove the rear bearing. For this ideally a press is necessary but can be done by judicious levering. Note which way the circlip in the outer track is positioned (photo).

8 Recover any shims from behind the bearing and then slide off the, first speed spacer bushing, needle bearing cage and first speed pinion (photo).

9 Remove the first/second speed synchroniser without parting the sliding gear from the hub (photo).

10 Slide the second speed gear from the mainshaft.

---

8 Input shaft assembly (manual) - dismantling

1 Fig. 6.3 shows an exploded view of the input shaft

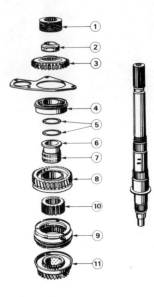

Fig 6.20 Mainshaft assembly (Sec 7)

1	Speedometer drive gear	7	Needle bearing cage
2	Nut	8	1st speed pinion
3	Reverse pinion	9	1st/2nd speed synchroniser sliding gear
4	Rear bearing	10	Hub
5	Shim pack	11	2nd speed
6	1st speed spacer bush		

7.3 Removal of snap-ring from end of mainshaft

7.4 Sliding off third/fourth speed synchroniser

7.5 Lifting away third/fourth speed hub

7.7 The rear bearing on mainshaft being removed

7.8 Sliding off the first speed spacer bushing, bearing and first speed pinion

7.9 Removal of first/second speed synchroniser

components. Dismantling this assembly is perfectly straightforward and should present no problems.
2 First recover the needle bearing from the end of the input
shaft.
3 Using a pair of circlip pliers release the snap-ring and then
remove followed by the dished washer underneath it.
4 Support the bearing between soft faces in a large bench vice
and drive the input shaft assembly through the bearing using a
soft faced hammer.
5 Recover any shims from behind the bearing.

9 Selector and interlock mechanism (manual) - dismantling

1 The selector forks are fixed to their respective shafts by
spring pins which are easily drifted out. In all cases use a
suitable diameter parallel pin punch. The simplest order of
operations is:
  a) *Put first/second gearshaft in the second gear position (ie;
     as far forward as it will go).*
  b) *Drive out the pin from the first/second gear shifting fork.*
  c) *Return shaft to neutral position.*
  d) *Put third/fourth speed shaft in fourth gear position (ie; as
     far forward as it will go).*
  e) *Remove pin from third/fourth gear shifting fork.*

2 Withdraw the third/fourth gear selector shaft from the
gearbox casing, watching for the locking needle which is located
in a hole about half way along it. Put the locking needle in a safe
place. The locating ball which engages with notches at the end of
this shaft will probably have come out and be rolling about
inside the housing. Recover the ball and hook out the spring.
Note in some early models the arrangement is somewhat
different, the spring and ball being retained by a plug.
3 Remove the plugs on either side of the housing which retain
the locking springs and balls for the other two selector rods.
Hook out the springs and with luck the balls will shake out quite
easily. If for any reason they do not, temporarily replace the
retainer plugs.
4 Pull out the two selector rods, sliding the reverse idler pinion
off its spindle as the reverse rod comes out.
5 Remove the retaining plugs again and poke out the retaining
balls if not already removed. Also recover the locking ball and
locking finger which lie between the selectors. By now the
following should have been recovered:

  Three locking springs.
  Four balls.
  One locking finger.

6 The reverse shaft can be removed by drifting out the pin
which holds it in and driving the shaft towards the inside of the
housing.

10 Gearbox (manual) - inspection and overhaul

1 If the gearbox has been stripped because of some obvious
fault such as failure to stay in the selected gear, difficulty in
engaging gear or the sort of noise which can no longer be
ignored, the cause of the fault is usually pretty obvious (see also
Fault diagnosis, Section 21). A not so obvious cause of noise and
trouble is bearing wear, which it is well worthwhile to nip in the
bud by replacing the bearings concerned before things get to
such a state that a shaft has to be renewed.
2 If movement in the bearings exists when they are still well
lubricated it is a fair assumption that when dry movement will
be even worse. Give them a good wash in paraffin and a final
rinse in white spirit. Examine them for signs of wear such as
scoring, blueing or excessive play. If there is any doubt they
should be renewed.
3 If the cones of a synchroniser are obviously worn or heavily
scored or if the synchroniser teeth which engage with the gear
pinions have a battered look, the synchroniser should be
replaced. Replacement synchronisers come complete with the
synchroniser hub and care should be taken to see that the hub

belonging to a particular synchroniser remains with it and that its
position relative to the synchroniser does not get altered (ie; the
hub does not get turned over relative to the synchroniser).
4 Examine the teeth of all gears for signs of uneven or excessive
wear and chipping. If the gear is in a bad state have a good look
at the gear it engages with - this may have to be renewed as well.
5 All gears should be a good running fit on the shaft with no
sign of rocking. The synchronising hubs should not be a
sloppy fit on the shaft splines.
6 Examine the selector rods and forks for damage, wear or
distortion. Replace any item that is doubtful.
7 Examine the control levers in the rear housing for wear or
damage. If any defect is found, this will be expensive because the
levers are not detachable from the rear housing and the whole
housing has to be renewed. The ball heads or adjustable joints
connecting these levers to the link rods of the gearchange
mechanism can, however be replaced.
8 Peugeot recommend that when the gearbox is overhauled,
parallelism of the front and rear faces of the clutch housing
should be checked. Fig. 6.21 shows this being done. This is a very
simple matter if a surface table and dial gauge are to hand. If the
surfaces are not parallel the input shaft to the gearbox will not
be properly aligned with the crankshaft. This can lead to
excessive wear in the gearbox bearings, particularly the front
bearing which supports the input shaft. If bearing wear is
excessive take the housing to the local Peugeot garage or a local
engineering works and get them to check it. Peugeot recommend
that if the lack of parallelism exceeds 0.0039 inch (0.10 mm) the
housing should be renewed. However, to save unnecessary
expense if there is a small lack of parallelism up to say 0.012 in
(0.30 mm) careful maching should be carried out.
9 Replacement of a worn guide sleeve is shown in Fig. 6.22. The
sleeve is held in position by a snap-ring which can be levered out
with a screwdriver. Fig. 6.23 shows the sleeve being pressed out,
but if a piece of wood is held over it, it should be possible to tap
it out with a soft faced hammer. When fitting a new one, be very
careful not to distort it. Fig. 6.22 shows the use of a special
Peugeot tool but no doubt a substitute can be found. Be careful
to drive the sleeve in straight and avoid hitting it directly with
the soft faced hammer. Use a new snap-ring to hold it in
position.
10 Turning now to the rear housing, it has already been stated
that the gear control levers cannot be detached from it and that
the housing must be renewed if these are worn or defective.
Remove the plug retaining the locking ball and spring for the
selector lever (see Fig. 6.24), take out the ball and spring, check
that they are in good condition. Give the plug and the recess a
good clean, smear the ball and spring with oil, put them back
and screw in the plug, smearing its threads with a suitable sealing
compound. The plug should be screwed flush with the housing
and then locked into position by two punch marks.
11 The rear bearing and oil seal should be replaced every time
the gearbox is dismantled. Fig. 6.25 shows the oil seal being
removed. Notice the safety bar secured to the housing to protect
the mating surface.
12 The needle bearing can be drifted out with a suitable
diameter drift and hammer. Be careful when doing this that the
surface at the other end of the housing is not damaged. Stand it
on some cardboard. The replacement rear bearing is fitted with
the engraved face turned outwards (ie; upwards). Here again, a
suitable drift can be used to fit the new bearing. The end of the
bearing should be level with the shoulder in the housing. Well
lubricate the bearing before inserting it. The same applies to the
oil seal which sits on top of the bearing and should be pressed in
as far as it will go.

11 Gearbox (manual) - initial reassembly

1 Although the split case construction makes reassembly a
fairly simple matter, a certain amount of engineering judgement
and common sense is called for, and it is recommended that the
whole of this Section be thoroughly read before work

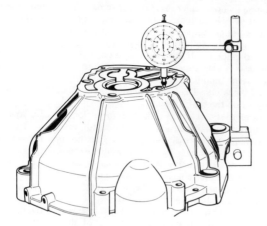

Fig 6.21 Ideal method of checking clutch housing surfaces for parallelism (Sec 10)

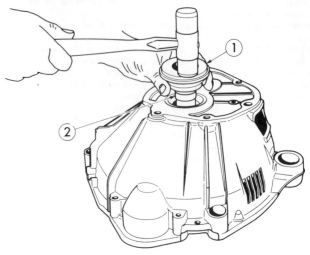

Fig 6.22 Refitting new guide sleeve (Sec 10)

1   *Suitable drift*   2   *Guide sleeve*

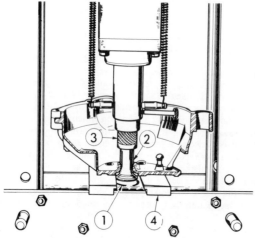

Fig 6.23 Guide sleeve removal (Sec 10)

1   *Snap-ring*   3   *Drift*
2   *Guide sleeve*   4   *Supports*

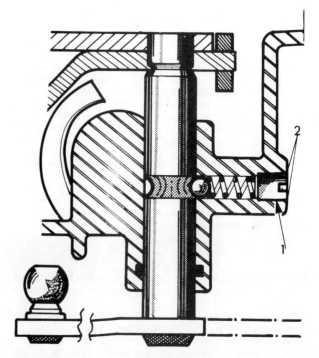

Fig 6.24 Cross-section through neutral ball lock (Sec 10)

1   *Plug*   2   *Punch marks to lock plug*

commences. As discovered during dismantling, both the input shaft and the mainshaft assemblies incorporate adjusting shims which are individually chosen for each gearbox. The function of these shims is to ensure that the synchromesh hubs are correctly positioned. The layshaft also carries adjusting shims which control the distance between the layshaft bearings. These bearings, being taper roller bearings, should be "preloaded" on assembly, that is, they should be squeezed slightly when the gearbox is assembled. Determination of the shim thickness is very easy if all the correct gauges and dial depth indicator are available but these gauges (issued to Peugeot garages by the manufacturers) may well be difficult to come by. However, more often than not they can be done without.

2   Reassembly starts with the refitting of the reverse pinion. First assemble the reverse pinion shaft with the roll pin hole in

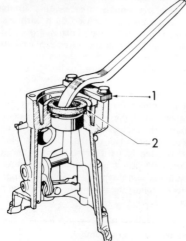

Fig 6.25 Levering out rear housing oil seal (Sec 10)

1   *Fulcrum for lever*
2   *Oil seal*

alignment with the hole in the casing web. Also slide on the reverse pinion and the reverse shift fork assembly, the latter two parts in engagement (photo).

3 Insert the roll pin into the hole in the casing web and tap fully home (photo).

4 Insert the ball into the locking passage leading to the shift rod (photo).

5 Follow this with the spring and having smeared the threads of the plug with a little sealing compound tighten the plug to a torque wrench setting of 7.2 lb f·ft (1 kg f m). (photo)

6 Draw out the reverse shift fork until the neutral position is felt and then insert the third/fourth and reverse locking finger. This must pass through the reverse shift rod (photo).

7 Insert the third/fourth gearchange fork shaft until the hole in the centre is well into the casing and then slide on the third/fourth gearchange fork (photo).

8 Smear the locking needle with a little grease and insert it into the hole in the third/fourth gearchange fork shaft (photo).

9 Do not forget that the third/fourth gearchange fork shaft passes through the first/second gearchange fork so this must be placed in the casing before the shaft is pushed through the centre web of the casing half (photo).

10 Insert the spring into the casing web hole (photo)...

11 ...and follow with the ball bearing. Push the bearing down with a small screwdriver and ease the shaft into position (photo).

12 Line up the holes in the third/fourth gearchange fork and shaft and lock with a roll-pin (photo).

13 Insert the first/second gearchange fork shaft, line up the holes in the fork and shaft and lock with a roll-pin (photo).

14 Move the selector shafts to the neutral position and then insert the last ball bearing into the hole in the side of the casing (photo)...

15 ...and follow this with the spring and plug. The same comments as in paragraph 5 apply. (photo)

16 The description given in this Section is applicable to most gearboxes but should any deviations have been noted during dismantling then obviously they will have to be taken into account during reassembly.

12 Input shaft (manual) - assembly and shim selection

1 The only reason for dismantling the input shaft is usually to fit a new ball bearing assembly or, if the input shaft is being

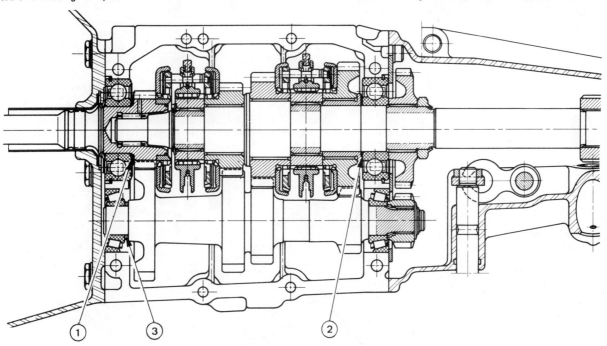

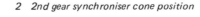

Fig 6.26 Gearbox adjustment points

1 4th gear synchroniser cone position *2 2nd gear synchroniser cone position* *3 Pre-load of layshaft gearshaft conical roller bearings*

11.2 Reverse selector engaged with reverse pinion

11.3 Inserting reverse pinion shaft locking pin

11.4 Inserting ball into locking passage leading to shaft rod

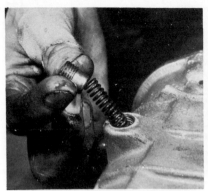

11.5 The spring and plug follow the ball

11.6 Inserting locking finger

11.7 Sliding in third/fourth gearchange fork shaft

11.8 Locking needle inserted into third/fourth gear change fork shaft

11.9 Do not forget that the first/second gearchange fork must be positioned at this stage

11.10 Inserting spring into casing web hole

11.11 Followed by the ball bearing

11.12 Fitting third/fourth gearchange fork locking roll pin

11.13 Inserting first/second gearchange fork shaft

11.14 Inserting the last ball bearing....

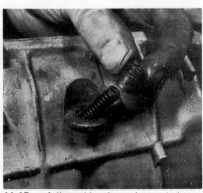

11.15 .... followed by the spring and plug

renewed and the old bearing is in excellent condition then the fitting of a new shaft to an old bearing.

2 During dismantling it was probably found that there were some shims behind the bearing and these should be transferred to the new assembly. There are special gauges to determine any change in shim thickness required and these are at the local Peugeot garage. However, from experience although it is desirable to reassemble all parts "according to the book" it has been found that without using these gauges the job can still be done and in most cases a reasonable result obtained. For those with the necessary equipment however, full information is given.

3 As shown in Fig. 6.3 the input shaft assembly includes shims between the bearing and gear head. These shims determine the distance between the fourth gear synchronizer cone and the end of the case. The thicker the shims, the further away from the case the synchronizer will be.

4 Fig. 6.27 shows how the shim thickness is determined when the special gauges are available. The object is to ensure that the edge of the synchronizer cone is exactly the same height above the end of the case as the gauge 'C'. The adjustment is carried out with the shaft and gauge fitted into the right-hand half of the gearbox case which is assembled to the clutch housing - be sure to tighten the assembling bolts to the correct setting of 14.5 lb f ft (2.0 kg f m) before starting. before starting.

5 The shaft is assembled first of all without any shims and without the oil deflector washer between the bearing and drive pinion. Be sure that the bearing is the correct way round (ie; the groove with the lock ring in it should be furthermost from the drive pinion).

6 This being done, set up the dial indicator in its support resting on the gauge, as shown in Fig. 6.27, rotate the input shaft and set the indicator to zero at the average high spot found for one complete revolution of the input shaft.

7 Move the dial indicator gauge support until the indicator rests on the gauge surface as in Fig. 6.27. The clearance found is the total shim and washer thickness to be inserted between the drive pinion and the bearing. The measured value should be rounded off to the nearest 0.05 mm. For example an indicator reading of 0.58 mm is taken as 0.60 mm and the shims selected accordingly. Shims are available in thicknesses of 0.15 mm, 0.20 mm, 0.25 mm, 0.30 mm and 0.35 mm. The total shim thickness must include the thickness of the deflector washer which is 0.15 mm so in this case choose two shims, one of 0.20 mm and one of 0.25 mm to bring the total thickness of shims and washer to 0.60 mm.

8 This is the official way of selecting shim thickness, for those lucky enough to have access to the gauges.

9 The purpose of this shimming is to take up tolerances in the machining of the gearbox casing and the input shaft.

10 Clearly if neither the shaft nor the gearbox casing has to be replaced the same shims can be used. If the bearing alone is replaced, but the shaft itself shows no signs of wear such as might be caused by a seized bearing moving on the shaft, it is reasonable to assume that the original shims will be satisfactory.

11 If for any reason, the case has to be replaced but the shaft assembly is satisfactory, assemble the shaft complete with its shims and fit it into the old half casing as described in paragraphs 2 and 3, and with whatever equipment is available measure the distance between the synchronizing cone face and the case. Bear in mind that this distance should be within 0.02 mm. This being done, repeat the process using the corresponding half of the new case (Note: if one half of the case requires renewal both halves must be renewed as they are a matched pair) and measure the distance. If the difference between the two distances exceeds 0.05 mm, alter the shim size to make this difference as small as possible.

12 If the input shaft is being renewed, reassemble the bearing and shims on the original shaft and measure the distance between the edge of the synchromesh cone and the back of the bearing. Now repeat the process exactly with the new shaft. If the difference between the measured distances exceeds 0.05 mm alter the shim sizes until the measurement obtained with the new

shaft is, as nearly as possible, the same as that obtained with the old shaft.

13 It will be seen that measurements must be made accurately and it is the difference between two measurements which is important rather than the absolute value of either of them. If necessary use spacing blocks of unknown thickness but always use them the same way round. It is only when damage or wear is involved that problems arise because the original thickness will not be known. In this case the correct gauges will be necessary and if not to hand it may be best to place the gearbox in the hands of the local Peugeot garage.

13 Mainshaft (manual) - shim size selection

1 The purpose of the shims on the mainshaft is to ensure that the second gear synchronizer cone is accurately placed relative to the gearbox casing. The officially recommended setting up procedure is almost identical with that described for the input shaft, except that a longer gauge is used and the dial indicator is positioned on the case, not on the gauge itself.

2 The right-hand half of the gearbox casing should be fixed to the clutch housing exactly as described in Section 12, paragraph 2 and the input shaft correctly assembled. Then fit the following parts:

Mainshaft second gear pinion
1st/2nd gear synchroniser hub
1st gear pinion spacer
Bearing
New snap-ring (fitted to bearing)

Press the bearing fully home until it bottoms against the first gear pinion spacer.

3 Assemble the needle cage into the input shaft end and insert the mainshaft spigot. Place the whole assembly in the right-hand half casing and position the gauge as shown in Fig. 6.28 but with the probe on the top of the gauge.

4 Set the dial indicator gauge to zero when its finger is touching the top of the gauge.

5 Put the indicator finger in contact with the upper edge of the second gear synchronizer cone and obtain the mean reading for this as the input shaft is rotated. Because there are no shims on the mainshaft assembly, the second gear synchronizer cone will be slightly above the gauge surface and the indicator gauge will show by how much. Round off this reading to the nearest 0.05 mm. For example, if the indicator reads 0.47 mm, call this 0.45 mm and use shims of 0.20 mm and 0.25 for the pack, and prepare a shim pack of the appropriate thickness. Shims are available in the following thicknesses; 0.15 mm, 0.20 mm, 0.25 mm and 0.50 mm.

14 Layshaft (manual) - shim size selection

1 The purpose of the layshaft shims is to preload the taper roller bearings on the ends of the layshaft. 'Preloading' means ensuring that they are squeezed slightly when the gearbox is assembled, this being achieved by choosing the correct spacing between them on the shaft. It is important when selecting the shims that everything is properly lined up, hence the somewhat elaborate procedure outlined in this Section.

2 Start by installing the layshaft, equipped with its bearing assemblies in the left-hand housing (see Fig. 6.30).

3 Secure the right-hand housing with the four housing bolts and hand-tighten. Next fix the rear plate with the four Allen screws and again hand-tighten.

4 Support the gearbox as rigidly as possible on the bench with the front part facing upwards. Push down on the layshaft front bearing with a suitable piece of tubing so bedding the bearings well down onto the shaft. (Fig. 6.30).

5 Secure the clutch housing to the gearbox housing with the four bolts and hand-tighten. Now tighten all bolts and Allen screws to a torque wrench setting of 7.2 lb f ft (1 kg fm). Then remove the clutch housing and check that the half housings are not out of flush by more than 0.02 mm. For

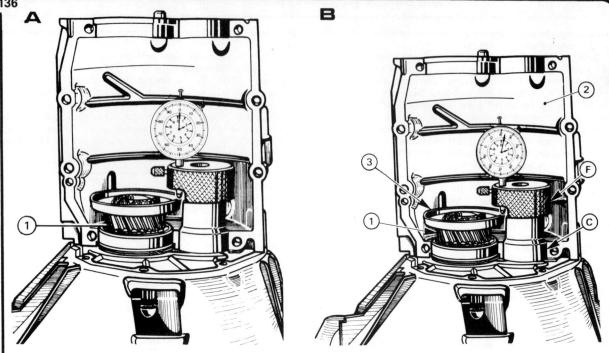

Fig 6.27 Input shaft shim thickness measurement (Sec 12)

1 Input shaft	3 Synchroniser cone	F Support
2 RH housing	C Gauge	

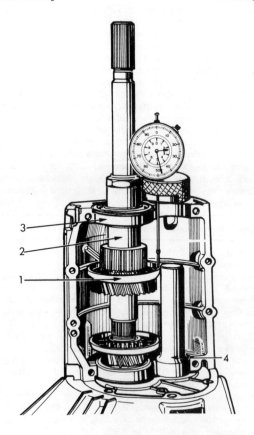

Fig 6.28 Selecting mainshaft shim size (Sec 13)

1 2nd gear synchroniser cone   3 Rear bearing
2 1st gear pinion bushing   4 Gauge

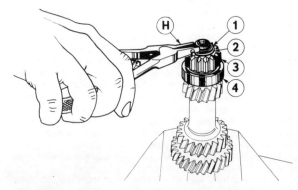

Fig 6.29 Layshaft reverse pinion assembly removal (Sec 14)

H Circlip pliers   3 Reverse pinion
1 Snap-ring   4 Bearing outer race
2 Spring washer

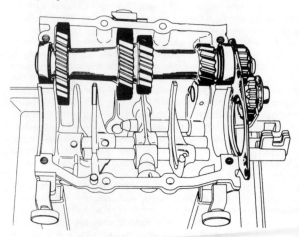

Fig 6.30 Layshaft shim selection (Sec 14)

this a dial indicator gauge is best but feeler gauges and a straight edge can be used. If the housings are too far out of line, go through the procedure described in this paragraph again.

6 Because there are no shims on the layshaft, the outer race of the front bearing will now be slightly below the level of the front face of the housing. Measure this distance using a dial indicator gauge or feeler gauges and a straight edge. This distance should not vary by more than 0.02 mm and if it does try straightening the bearing by gentle tapping. If this tapping causes the layshaft to bind, slacken off the two nearest housing fixing bolts and then retighten. Round off this reading to the nearest 0.05 mm and add 0.10 mm for the preload. For example: depth below housing 2.52 mm, add preload 0.10 mm, total 2.62 mm. Round off to 2.60 mm. This should be the thickness of the shim. Shims are available in thicknesses between 2.25 and 3.25 mm, in increments of 0.05 mm.

7 Draw the front bearing off the layshaft and thread the shim over the shaft with its chamfered side towards the pinion. Replace the bearing ensuring it beds down firmly onto the shim.

15 Mainshaft and input shaft (manual) - reassembly

1 With the mainshaft, start by assembling the components shown in Fig. 6.5. Make sure when assembling the synchronizer hub and its sliding gear that they are in their original positions. Be careful when pressing on the bearing that pressure is exerted only on the part of the bearing that is in contact with the shaft (ie; the inner track).

2 Leave the backing plate, reverse pinion and retaining nut and speedometer drive until later.

3 Working on the other end of the mainshaft, fit the third gear pinion and the third/fourth gear synchronizer, taking note of any previously made marks. Complete this assembly by fitting a new spring washer and snap-ring. It will be necessary to push the snap-ring down the shaft against the action of the spring washer before it will engage in its groove.

4 Fit the third/fourth gear sliding gear, positioning it in accordance with the previously made marks. Push it right home so that third gear is engaged.

5 Fig. 6.3 shows the order in which the components are assembled on the input shaft. There is no particular problem here except making quite sure that the snap-ring is properly engaged in its groove. It will have to be pushed down against the pressure exerted by the spring washer. The spring washer and snap-ring as well as the snap-ring on the bearing should be renewed.

6 Install the needle cage in the end of the input shaft and slip the input shaft over the mainshaft.

16 Gearbox (manual) - final reassembly

1 Assemble the shaft to the mainshaft, not forgetting the needle cage in the end. Put the third/fourth sliding gear in the neutral position.

2 Carefully lower the assembly into the left-hand housing, engaging the selector forks with the synchromesh assemblies.

3 Next mesh and lower the layshaft assembly into the housing.

4 Slide the backing plate (rear bearing retainer) over the mainshaft and layshaft end and up to the housing. (photo)

5 The gearbox should now appear as in the photograph. Check that all mating faces are clean. (photo)

6 Lightly smear the mating surfaces of the half housings with a suitable sealing compound and carefully lower the right-hand housing into position. (photo)

7 Secure the two halves together with the four corner bolts. Tighten to a torque wrench setting of 3.6 lb f ft (0.5 kg f m).

8 Secure the rear backing plate with its four Allen scews and tighten to a torque wrench setting of 7.2 lb f ft (1.0 kg f m).

9 Slide the reverse pinion onto the mainshaft ensuring that it is the correct way round. (photo)

10 Refit the reverse pinion securing nut and tighten to a torque wrench setting of 40 lb f ft (5.5 kg f m).

11 Lock the nut to the mainshaft using a suitable diameter punch to depress part of the nut lip into the mainshaft indentation. (photo)

12 Refit the gearbox oil level and drain plugs. (photo)

13 Smear sealing compound on the rear face of the clutch housing and fasten it to the gearbox housing with six bolts. Tighten in a progressive and diagonal manner to a final torque wrench setting of 20 lb f ft (2.75 kg f m). (photo)

14 Now loosen the four housing bolts and tap the half-housings with a soft-faced hammer whilst rotating the mainshaft. Retighten the four bolts to a torque wrench setting of 11 lb f ft (1.5 kg f m). When this is done the half-housings should not be out of flush at their rear mating surface by more than 0.02 mm. Check this with a dial indicator gauge or feeler gauges and a straight edge. If more than the permitted amount slacken the four bolts and repeat the operation.

15 Replace the remaining nuts and bolts securing the housing halves and tighten to a torque of 7.2 lb f ft (1.0 kg f m). kg f m).

16 Refit the speedometer drive gear onto the end of the mainshaft and tap up to its original position using a suitable diameter tube. (photo)

17 Make sure that the mating surfaces of the rear housing and the main housing are clean and dry. Smear the mating surfaces with a sealing compound and assemble it to the gearbox. (photo) (photo)

18 There will be no problem in engaging the selectors if the external selector lever is pulled fully rearwards. (photo)

19 Replace the rear housing securing nuts and bolts and tighten to a torque wrench setting of 11.0 lb f ft (1.5 kg f m).

20 Turning to the clutch housing, insert the rubber cup in the groove behind the ball head and fill with grease. The guide sleeve should be smeared with a little molybdenum disulphide grease.

21 Attach the clutch release fork to the ball head. (photo)

22 It now only remains to refit the reverse light switch, and the speedometer drive socket assembly. Always use a new 'O' ring smeared with grease before refitting the speedometer drive socket assembly. When tightening the reverse light switch, if the body is of copper tighten to a torque wrench setting of 9 lb f ft (1.25 kg f m) or 20 lb f ft (2.7 kg f m) if it has a steel body.

23 The gearbox is now ready for refitting to the car.

17 Fault diagnosis - manual gearboxes

Symptom	Reason/s	Remedy
Weak of ineffective synchromesh	Synchronising cones worn, split or damaged	Dismantle and overhaul transmission unit. Fit new gear wheels and synchronising cones
Jumps out of gear	Broken gearchange fork rod spring	Dismantle and replace spring.
	Transmission unit coupling dogs badly worn	Dismantle and fit new coupling dogs.
	Selector fork rod groove badly worn	Fit new selector fork rod.
	Selector fork securing pin loose	Dismantle and renew worn parts.
Excessive noise	Incorrect grade of oil in transmission unit or oil level too low	Drain, refill, or top up transmission unit with correct grade of oil.
	Bush or needle roller or ball bearings worn or damaged	Dismantle and overhaul transmission unit. Renew bearings.
	Gearteeth excessively worn or damaged	Dismantle, overhaul and renew gearwheels. new gearwheels.
Excessive difficulty in engaging gears	Clutch fault	See Chapter 5

16.4 Refitting rear bearing retainer

16.5 The gear trains are now in position

16.6 Lowering the right-hand housing into position

16.9 Reverse pinion fitted to mainshaft

16.11 Locking the reverse pinion retaining nut to mainshaft

16.12 Refitting gearbox oil level and drain plugs

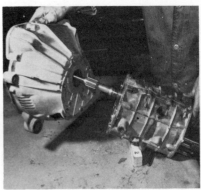

16.13 Refitting clutch housing

16.16 The speedometer drive gear on mainshaft ready to be drifted into position

16.17 Lowering rear housing into position

16.18 The internal selectors which engage with the selector fork rods

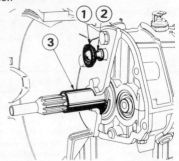

Fig 6.31 Clutch release lever ball head and bearing guide sleeve (Sec 16)

1 Rubber cup   thrust
2 Ball head   3 Guide sleeve

16.21 Clutch release fork and bearing fitted to bell housing

18 General description (automatic transmission)

The automatic transmission unit is fitted as an alternative to the manual gearbox on models covered by this manual. It is manufactured by Zahnradfabrik Friedrichshafen AG and is of the ZF type. The unit comprises three main parts namely, hydraulic torque converter, a gearbox and an automatic control unit.

The torque converter is driven by the engine crankshaft and automatic operation is obtained by the torque converter transmitting its hydrokinetic energy to the propeller shaft, via a hydraulically controlled epicyclic gear train.

The fluid or hydraulic drive is directly employed in all transmission stages which results in the automatic selection of forward low and high gear ranges taking place with a smooth and continuously variable torque output governed by road speed and position of the accelerator pedal.

The gearbox position, as opposed to the torque converter, provides three forward ratios and one reverse which are obtained by manipulating two concentric planetary pinions connected by three pairs of planet gears.

For those unfamiliar with automatic transmissions an epicyclic or planetary gear system is one in which a central sun wheel has smaller planet pinions rotating around it. The planet pinions themselves mesh with an internally toothed ring gear which surrounds the assembly. The drive through an epicyclic gear can give varied output ratios depending on which elements of the gear set are held stationary or driven.

In the ZF automatic transmission unit a Ravignaux or compound planetary gear system is used which combines two sets of planetary pinions and two sun gears. Gear ratio changes are carried out by the locking of the respective gears by disc brakes and two multi plate clutches.

The automatic control unit is housed inside the oil pan located below the main gearbox casing and controls the operation of the multi-plate clutches through a number of hydraulic valves.

The oil filled torque converter has three main parts: an impeller which is driven by the engine, a rotor or turbine which is attached to the gearbox input shaft and a stator which is mounted on a uni-directional clutch (free-wheel) between the impeller and the turbine. The objective of the free-wheel is that the stator can only rotate in the same direction as the impeller. When the impeller is rotated by the engine, the hydraulic fluid with which the torque converter is kept full by a pump, is thrown outwards by centrifugal action through the impeller vanes and is directed onto the turbine. This causes the turbine to rotate as well. The hydraulic fluid then passes through the turbine vanes and is directed backwards into the stator which remains still as it cannot rotate in a reverse direction against the one way clutch. The direction of hydraulic fluid passing through the stator is changed so that on re-entering the impeller the hydraulic fluid assists in driving it and thus provides a multiplication in torque.

The selector lever has six positions and are as follows:

Park (P)   *The gearbox is in the neutral position and the rear wheels are locked by a mechanical device located inside the transmission unit. The starter motor may be operated to start the engine.*

Reverse (R)   *This enables the car to be driven backwards. There is a safety notch to prevent accidental engagement when the car is being driven forwards.*

Neutral (N)   *The gearbox is in the neutral position and the rear wheels are not locked. The starter motor may be operated to start the engine.*

3 (D)   *Drive. Full automatic range for normal road use. Car starts in first and as speed increases automatic changes to second and third speeds. Change point depends on position of accelerator pedal.*

2   *Lock in 2nd ratio. The first two gear ratios are used without passing from second to third. Useful for engine braking for descending steep hills or fast overtaking.*

1   *Lock in 1st ratio. The first gear ratio is used without passing to second. Useful for descending steep hills.*

Note: In 'I' position the car may be started from standstill using the gear selector as with a conventional gearbox. For example: Start and accelerate in 'I', change to position '2' for normal increase in speed and then to 3 for normal driving.

Due to the complexity of the automatic transmission unit, if performance is not up to standard or overhaul is necessary, it is imperative that this be left to the local Peugeot garage or a specialist who will have the special equipment and knowledge required for diagnosis and rectification of faults.

19 Automatic transmission - fluid level and maintenance

1   It is important that transmission fluid manufactured to the correct specification is used. The system should be drained and refilled at intervals of 600 miles (1,000 km), 3,000 miles (5,000 km), 9,000 miles (15,000 km), 18,000 miles (30,000 km) and 27,000 miles (45,000 km).

2   Regularly check the hydraulic fluid level; the manufacturers recommend every 600 miles (1,000 km). The car should be on level ground, the handbrake well applied and the unit at normal operating temperature (after a 5 miles (8 km) run).

3   Select 'N', start the engine and allow to idle for 2-3 minutes. Withdraw the dipstick, wipe it clean and replace it. Quickly withdraw it again, and if the level is below the 'MINI' mark top-up to the recommended 'MAXI' mark. The difference between the two marks is approximately 1 Imp. pint (1.2 US pints, 0.56 litre). Do not overfill the unit as damage can result.

4   When draining the unit remember that if the unit has run recently the hydraulic fluid will be extremely hot so take care.

5   Refit the drain plug and refill with new fluid. It is recommended that 3.5 Imp. pints (4.2 US pints, 2 litres) is poured in first. The engine is then started and allowed to idle. Topping-up is then continued until the level of hydraulic fluid is up to the 'MAXI' mark (paragraph 3).

20 Automatic transmission - removal and replacement

Any suspected fault must be referred to the local Peugeot garage or specialist before unit removal as with this type of transmission the fault must be confirmed, using specialist equipment, before the unit has been removed from the car. As the car will probably be in the hands of the specialist already they will prefer to remove the old unit and fit the new one, making any adjustments as necessary. To act as a guide however a summary of the necessary operations are given in the following paragraphs.

1   For safety reasons, disconnect the battery.

2   Jack-up the car and support on firmly based stands if a lift or pit are not available.

3   Detach the exhaust downpipe from the manifold and release the front support. Tie the system back out of the way.

4   Undo and remove the speedometer drive securing screw located at the rear end of the transmission casing and detach the speedometer drive. Also detach the cables from the starter lock/reverse light switch noting their exact locations.

5   Detach the propeller shaft at the transmission drive flange and move the shaft to one side.

6   Disconnect the starter motor cables and remove starter motor.

7   Disconnect the manual selector lever from the lever on the side of the transmission casing.

8   Using a jack or overhead hoist take the weight of the engine.

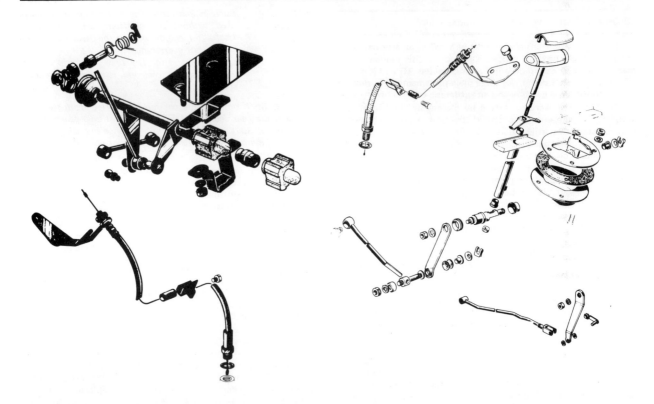

Fig. 6.32 Automatic transmission linkage at gearbox

Fig. 6.33 Automatic transmission gear selector lever assembly

9   Slacken the bolts securing the engine to the torque converter housing.

10 Withdraw the oil filler pipe and plug the hole to prevent loss of hydraulic fluid.

11 Undo and remove the lower torque converter housing cover plate bolts.

12 Undo and remove the four diagphragm securing bolts. Access to these is through the hole in the flywheel. Rotate the crankshaft a quarter of a turn at a time.

13 Very carefully ease the engine upwards and towards the front as far as movement of the rubber mountings will allow.

14 Now remove the previously slackened engine to torque converter housing securing bolts.

15 Using a garage hydraulic jack take the weight of the transmission unit.

16 Make quite sure that the torque converter remains on the transmission unit and does not slip forwards. Remember it will be full of hydraulic fluid.

17 Push back the converter with a screwdriver inserted through the hole in the flywheel as the transmission unit is withdrawn.

18 When the unit is free lower and remove from under the car.

19 Refitting the automatic transmission unit is the reverse sequence to removal but the following additional information should be of use.

20 Note the two dowel sleeves located in the front face of the converter housing. This is important when a factory or specialist exchange assembly is being fitted. A defective sleeve can cause serious damage to the converter and driving disc.

21 Tighten the four diaphragm securing bolts, that are located through the hole in the flywheel, to a torque wrench setting of 11.6 - 17.4 lb f ft (1.6 - 2.3 kg f m).

22 When refitting the cables to the starter lock/reverse light switch, the two opposed pins furthest apart should be connected to the cables coloured green/black and green/white. The other two pins which are closer together should be connected to the cables coloured brown/black and brown.

23 Do not forget to refill the unit with the correct amount of hydraulic fluid before starting the engine.

21 Fault diagnosis - automatic transmission

As has been mentioned elsewhere in this Chapter, no service repair work or adjustments should be carried out by anyone without the specialist knowledge and equipment to undertake the work. This is also relevant to fault diagnosis. If a fault is evident consult the local Peugeot garage or specialist.

Chapter 7 Propeller shaft

For modifications, and information applicable to later models, see Supplement at end of manual

Contents

Specifications

Type

Saloon	Torque tube secured to rear of gearbox and front of differential unit
Estate	As saloon but with thrust bearing at front of torque tube

Shaft diameter ... ... 42 mm

Centre bearing:

Outer diameter of cage	71 mm
Width	62 mm
Needle roller bearing	47 x 55 x 16

Torque wrench settings

	lb f ft	Kg f m
Torque tube to gearbox	41 - 44	5.7 - 6.3
Torque tube to differential	41 - 44	5.7 - 6.3
Differential to crossmember	24 - 30	3.5 - 4.0
Crossmember to body	See text	

1 General description

The propeller shaft arrangement on the saloon models is of a rather unusual layout. The gearbox and differential unit are connected to each other by a rigid tube and it is inside this tube that the propeller shaft rotates. The shaft has splined ends which mate with female splines in the gearbox and differential unit. There are no universal joints.

The shaft is supported at its centre point by a needle bearing assembly located inside the tube. This bearing is lubricated by a grease nipple positioned half way along the tube.

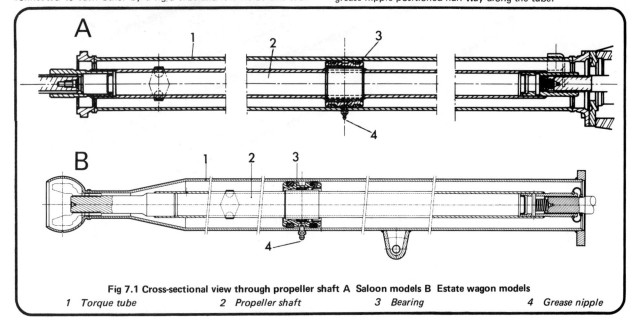

Fig 7.1 Cross-sectional view through propeller shaft A Saloon models B Estate wagon models

1 Torque tube	2 Propeller shaft	3 Bearing	4 Grease nipple

At the end of the shaft which engages with the differential unit a spring is inserted inside the shaft which prevents any fore and aft movement which might otherwise produce wear as well as transmission noise.

This unusual arrangement is only possible when the differential unit is rigidly mounted as in the case with independent rear suspension.

The propeller shaft arrangement for the estate car models and those vehicles with automatic transmission is similar to that fitted to the saloon models and will present no problems provided that the instructions for saloon models are followed and the differences at the gearbox end noted.

2 Propeller shaft (saloon models) - removal

1 Peugeot garages have two special tools which make this work far easier (Fig. 7.3). It is considered worthwhile either borrowing these or making up from odd scraps of metal. For example long bolts can be substituted for the guide rods.

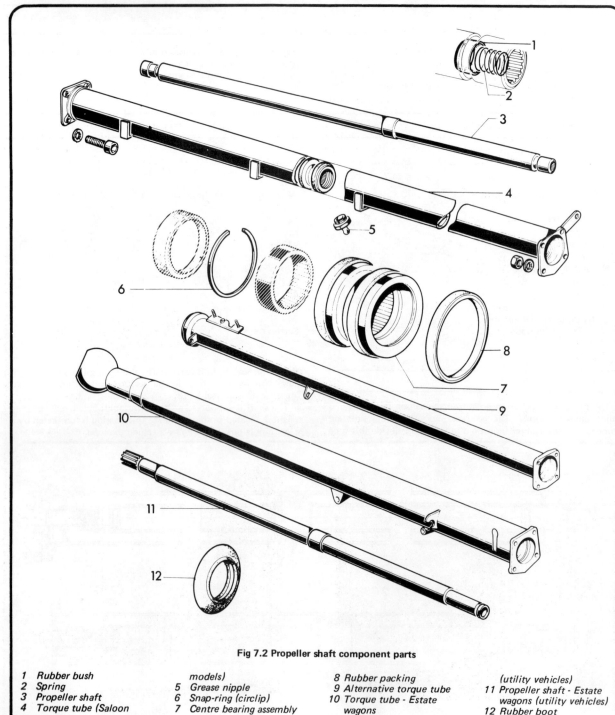

Fig 7.2 Propeller shaft component parts

1 Rubber bush	models)	8 Rubber packing	(utility vehicles)
2 Spring	5 Grease nipple	9 Alternative torque tube	11 Propeller shaft - Estate
3 Propeller shaft	6 Snap-ring (circlip)	10 Torque tube - Estate	wagons (utility vehicles)
4 Torque tube (Saloon	7 Centre bearing assembly	wagons	12 Rubber boot

2 The holding plate will present a little more of a problem but can be made from any material that is not too brittle. For example a hard plywood about 20 mm thick. The thickness is important because the plate engages with a groove in the propeller shaft and holds it steady during reassembly. More important than this perhaps is the fact that when the propeller shaft is held by the holding plate it cannot move from side to side in the tube and thereby impose a strain on the needle bearing. Without the holding plate it is very difficult to prevent this movement taking place.

3 Start by removing the rear seat from inside the car.

4 On the seat pan will be found two groups of three nuts. These nuts secure the rear crossmember, and must not be confused with those for the rear suspension crossmember. These particular nuts are locked by a tab washer.

5 Undo and remove the front nut and raise the tab. This will reveal a hole containing a plastic plug which should next be removed.

6 A threaded hole should now be visible and is in fact in the rear crossmember. Screw the bolt or guide rod into this hole. If a bolt is being used it is wise to place a large diameter plain washer under the head to prevent it pulling through the body panel. If the guide rod and tommy bar is being used leave the tommy bar

in the guide rod (Fig. 7.4).

7 Replace the front nut and tighten.

8 Repeat the operations in paragraphs 4 to 7 inclusive for the other side of the car.

9 Chock the front wheels, raise the rear wheels off the ground and place on blocks so that they are 12-18 inches (304-457 mm) from the ground.

10 Disconnect the exhaust pipe assembly from the car but do not attempt to remove it. It can rest on the rear crossmember at one end and be tied up with string at the other.

11 Undo and remove the two Allen screws holding the differential housing to the rear suspension crossmember. Allow the connecting tube to rest on the rear crossmember.

12 Place a jack under one of the rear crossmember supports (not the rear suspension crossmember) and allow it to support a little weight.

13 If a second jack is available place this under the other support.

14 Working inside the car undo and remove the three nuts which secure the supports that have just been jacked-up.

15 Lower the supports until the stop on the guide rod or the head of the bolt used instead bears against the floor (Fig. 7.5).

16 Undo and remove the four nuts holding the transmission tube

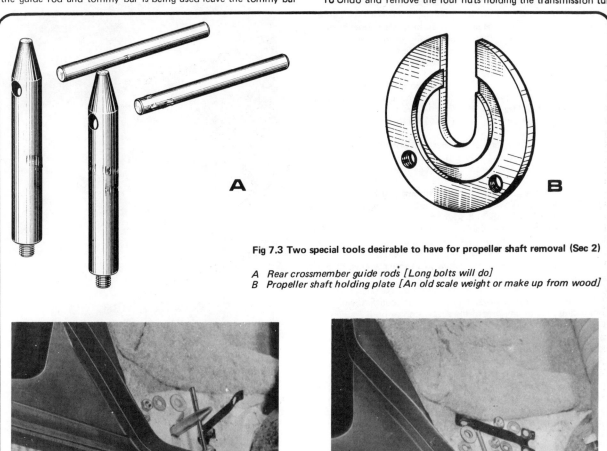

Fig 7.3 Two special tools desirable to have for propeller shaft removal (Sec 2)

A Rear crossmember guide rods [Long bolts will do]
B Propeller shaft holding plate [An old scale weight or make up from wood]

Fig 7.4 Guide rod [on bolt] in position (Sec 2)

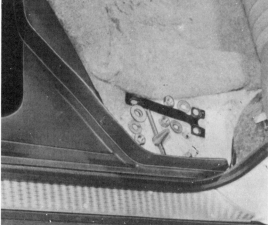

Fig 7.5 Guide rod [on bolt] lowered taking weight off rear crossmember (Sec 2)

to the differential housing. Draw the differential back, taking care that the propeller shaft does not come out of the tube as you do this. The idea is to leave the shaft in the tube supported at two points - the spline at the gearbox and the needle bearing in the middle of the tube (Fig. 7.6).

17 Remove the spring located in the end of the propeller shaft and put in a safe place.

18 Undo and remove the four Allen screws holding the transmission tube to the rear of the gearbox, withdraw the tube a little way and locate the holding plate in the groove in the propeller shaft. Fasten this plate to the tube flange (Fig. 7.7).

19 The transmission tube containing the propeller shaft can now be removed by drawing it forwards. It may be necessary to untie the exhaust pipe to do this (Fig. 7.8).

3 Propeller shaft (saloon models) - replacement

1 Generally speaking, refitting the propeller shaft is the reverse sequence to removal. There are several important points to be noted and these are given in the following paragraphs (Fig. 7.9).

2 Make sure that all mating surfaces are perfectly clean.

3 Start at the gearbox end. The holding plate should, of course, be fitted to the tube flange and this will keep the propeller shaft in position whilst being connected to the gearbox shaft. Just before doing this, smear the end with a little Castrol LM Grease. Once the splines have engaged, remove the holding plate, allowing the rear end of the transmission tube to rest on the rear crossmember. Bolt the flange to the gearbox, taking precautions to ensure that the propeller shaft does not move about too much within the tube. Use new Blockfor washers and tighten the screws to a torque wrench setting of 41-44 lb f ft (5.7-6.3 kg f m)(Fig. 7.10).

4 Turning to the other end of the shaft, do not forget to replace the spring. Grease it and insert it into the shaft. Smear the splines with Castrol LM Grease and engage them with the differential.

5 Bolt the flange of the tube to the differential housing using new Blocfor washers and tighten the nuts to a torque wrench setting of 41 - 44 lb f ft (5.7 - 6.3 kg f m).

6 The remainder of reassembly is now the reverse sequence to removal. Use new Blocfor washers on the two Allen screws which secure the differential housing to the rear suspension crossmember and tighten these screws to a torque wrench setting of 24 - 30 lb f ft (3.5 - 4.0 kg f m).

7 Refit the exhaust pipe assembly, using a new clamp gasket. Make sure that the exhaust pipe is not in contact with the connecting tube or any part of the suspension or body.

8 Finally, jack-up one of the rear crossmember supports, taking care as the studs approach the holes in the floor. Ease these through and continue raising the support until it makes contact with the floor. If a second jack is being used, repeat this operation for the second side. It then only remains to remove the guide rods or bolts, plug the guide holes with their plastic plugs, replace the flat washers on the studs, followed by a new tab washer and then the nuts which are tightened to a torque wrench setting of 27.6 - 30.4 lb f ft (3.8 - 4.2 kg f m) for models as follows:

504	A01-1 005	546
504	A02-1 003	649
504	A03 - Beginning of series	
504	B02-1 032	357
504	CO2-1 009	769

All cars produced later than those listed must have the nuts tightened to a torque wrench setting of 44.7 - 49.3 lb f ft (6.2 - 6.8 kg f m) (Fig. 7.11).

9 **Do not** forget to bend up the tab washers.

10 Apply a little Castrol LM Grease to the nipple linked to the propeller shaft bearing (Fig. 7.12).

Fig 7.6 Differential separated from connecting tube (Sec 2)

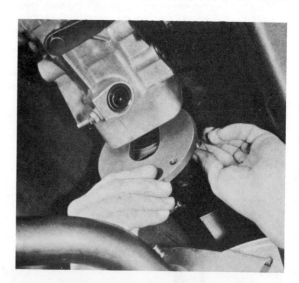

Fig 7.7 Fitting propeller shaft holding plate (Sec 2)

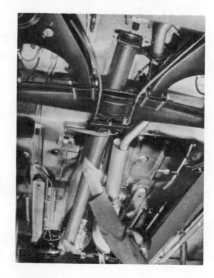

Fig 7.8 Lifting away propeller shaft assembly (Sec 2)

4 Propeller shaft and transmission tube (saloon models) - inspection

1 Before separating the shaft from the transmission tube, give the outside a good clean using paraffin or Gunk. Be careful that your cleaning operations do not allow dirt to enter the tube - a piece of rag wrapped round the propeller shaft where it emerges from the tube should prevent this.

2 When the tube and ends of the shaft are thoroughly clean, withdraw the shaft from the tube, being careful that no strain is placed on the needle bearing by too much lateral movement of the shaft.

3 Clean the shaft as necessary and inspect for signs of damage and wear - especially at the splines and at the centre where it is supported in the needle bearing.

4 Inspect the tube carefully for signs of damage. If it shows signs of having been damaged by driving over rocky ground it must be checked for out of true as described in the next paragraph.

5 To carry out this check, the tube must be placed between centres and the runout checked at the centre close to the grease nipple. The maximum permitted is 0.08 inch (2.0 mm). At the same time check the warping of the bearing surfaces, this should not exceed 0.002 inch (0.05 mm).

6 The propeller shaft should be treated in the same way; the maximum 'out of true' at the central bearing surface should not exceed 0.008 inch (0.2 mm).

7 It is unlikely that the average owner will be able to carry out these checks for himself, but there is nothing difficult about them and any reasonably equipped engineering works or garage should be able to do them. Whatever course of action is decided upon it is really only worthwhile if trouble is being experienced in the transmission system. Very often the propeller shaft is removed as part of some other job such as removing the gearbox or differential, and in this case, though it seems a pity not to have a quick look at the propeller shaft and tube, more elaborate checking is unnecessary.

5 Centre bearing (saloon models) - removal, inspection and replacement

1 The remarks made about checking the shaft and tube in the

Fig 7.9 Refitting propeller shaft to gearbox (Sec 3)

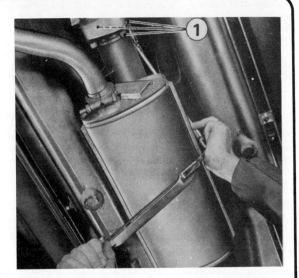

Fig 7.10 Tightening Allen screws at rear of gearbox (Sec 3)

1   Allen screws

Fig 7.11 Securing suspension crossmember to body (Sec 3)

Fig 7.12 Do not forget to grease propeller shaft centre bearing (Sec 3)

previous Section apply equally to the removal and checking of
the centre bearing. Unless vibration in the transmission has been
experienced or inspection of the propeller shaft has indicated
that all is not well it is simplest to leave this bearing alone.
However, it is not possible to inspect it properly unless it is
removed, and removal is not very difficult.

2 A drift will be required and this can be of brass about 0.8
inch (20 mm thick). Also something to drive it will be required.
This must be somewhat longer than the transmission tube and
should preferably have some means of holding the drift. A piece
of pipe would do or perhaps the wooden handle of a garden tool.

3 Before actually driving the bearing out, insert the drift at the
differential end and push it up against the bearing with the rod
to be used for drifting it out. Make a mark on this rod just where
it enters the tube so that when the new bearing is being fitted its
correct location in the middle of the bearing must line up with
the grease nipple.

4 Drive out the bearing until it leaves the tube at the gearbox
end (Fig. 7.13).

5 When the bearing is out of the tube, wash it thoroughly in
cleaning fluid giving it a final rinse with White Spirit. Examine it
carefully for signs of wear, blueing of the rollers or damage to
the cage. If it passes this test, smear it very lightly with oil and
put it on the propeller shaft in its correct position. Check for
play and if there is an appreciable amount the bearing should be
renewed.

6 To fit the bearing, carry out the removal procedure in reverse.
Lubricate the inside of the transmission tube with engine grade
oil, insert the bearing at the differential end being very careful
that it is fitted squarely. Start it off by tapping it very gently
with a soft faced hammer. Once inserted into the tube, drift it
along until the mark on the rod has been reached. At this stage
go very carefully checking through the grease nipple hole that
the groove in the bearing is correctly placed. Finally replace the
grease nipple. It is best not to grease the bearing until the propeller shaft is back into the tube. Do not forget to lubricate it
otherwise the bearing will fail within a short period of time.

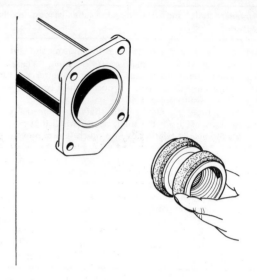

Fig 7.13 Propeller shaft centre bearing (Sec 5)

**6 Propeller shaft (automatic transmission and estate models) -
removal, overhaul and replacement**

There are slight differences in the propeller shaft assembly
fitted to cars with automatic transmission and also estate car
models. These differences in the main occur at the gearbox end
of the shaft. Refer to Section 8 of Chapter 13 for further
details.

Chapter 8 Rear axle and driveshafts

For modifications, and information applicable to later models, see Supplement at end of manual

Contents

Specifications

Type

Saloon	Hypoid bevel mounted on crossmember with driveshafts to rear wheels.
Estate models	Hypoid bevel mounted in conventional 'banjo' casing with halfshafts driving rear wheels.

Ratio

Carburettor models	3.89 : 1
Fuel injection models	3.78 : 1

Capacity ... ...

2.1 Imp pints (2.5 US pints, 1.136 litres)

Torque Wrench settings

	lb f ft	kg f m
Rear arm pivot nut	47	6.5
Damper lower nut	33	4.5
Damper upper nut	9	1.25
Hub/knuckle to suspension arm	29	4.0
Anti-roll bar link	33	4.5
Torque tube to differential housing	44.0	6.0
Differential to crossmember	27.1	3.75
Driveshaft nut	189	25

1 General description

The rear axle fitted comes in two forms depending on whether it is a Saloon or Estate car.

With Saloon car models the hypoid rear axle is suspended from a crossmember which is secured to the bodywork by flexible brackets. The transmission to the rear drive wheels is ensured by two "Glaenzer - spicer" shafts, each one fitted with two internal sliding velocity three pronged pot joints. The outer three pronged pot joint (wheel end) ensures the sliding action of the shaft and includes a spring which exerts constant pressure on the shaft. This combined with the design of the high sliding qualities of three pronged pot joints enables the length variation of the transmission, consecutive with the lateral movement of the rear suspension.

On Estate car models a more conventional system is used. A 'banjo' type rear axle is secured to the torque tube and drive from the differential unit to the rear wheels is via halfshafts. The axle is suspended from a crossmember which is secured to the body. Two tie rods are connected between the axle and torque tube.

Due to the need for special gauges and equipment the servicing and repair operations should be confined to those described in this Chapter.

Most of the detailed information given in this Chapter is applicable to Saloon models (independent suspension). When information is required for Estate car models (solid rear axle), then refer to Section 9 of Chapter 13.

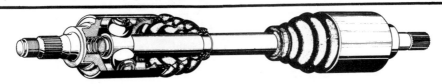

Fig 8.1 Driveshaft showing 'Pot' Joint

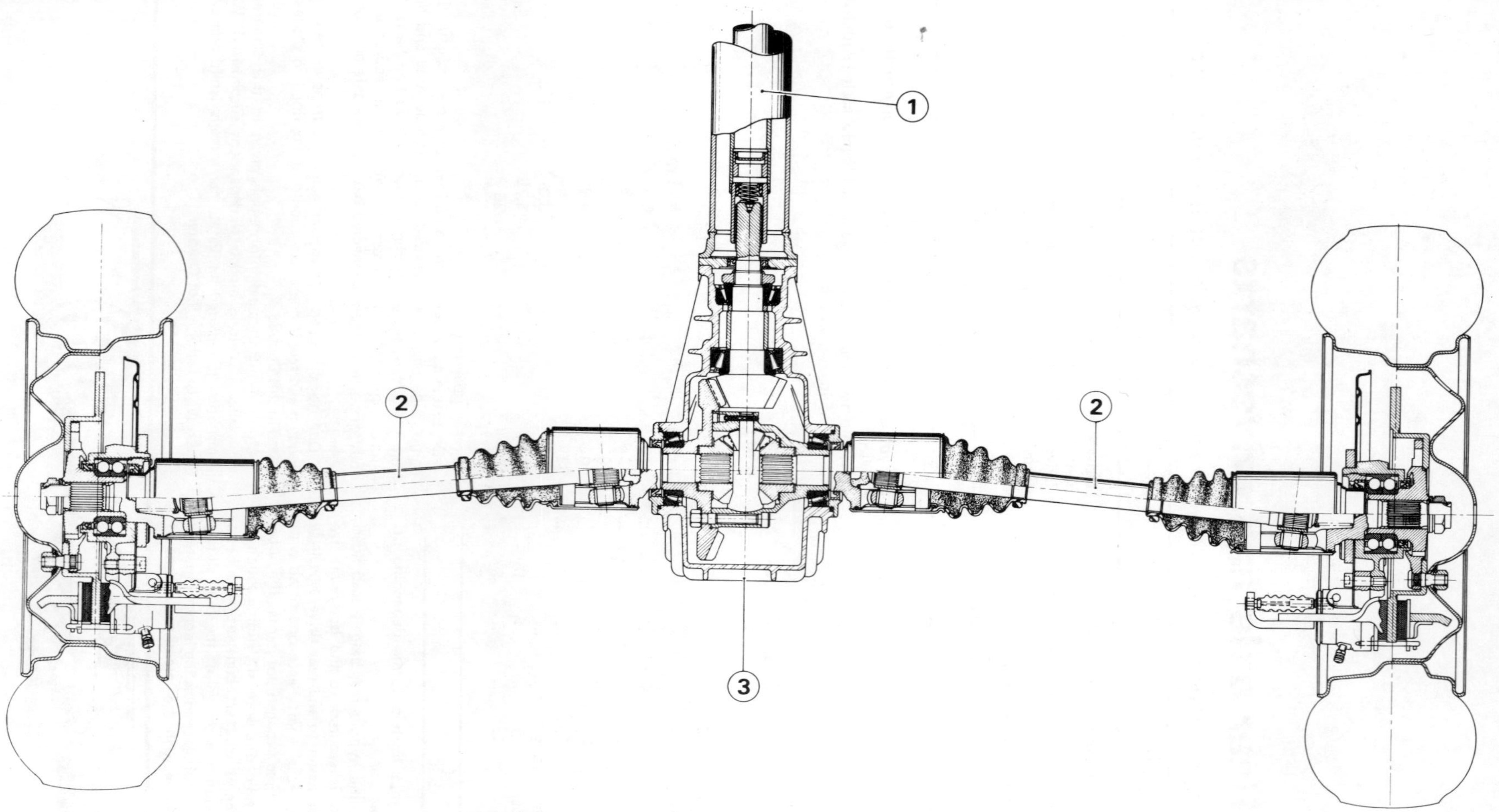

Fig 8.2 Cross-sectional view of rear axle assembly [Saloon models]

1 Longitudinal transmission or propeller shaft
2 Transverse transmission shafts
3 Sprung hypoid rear axle

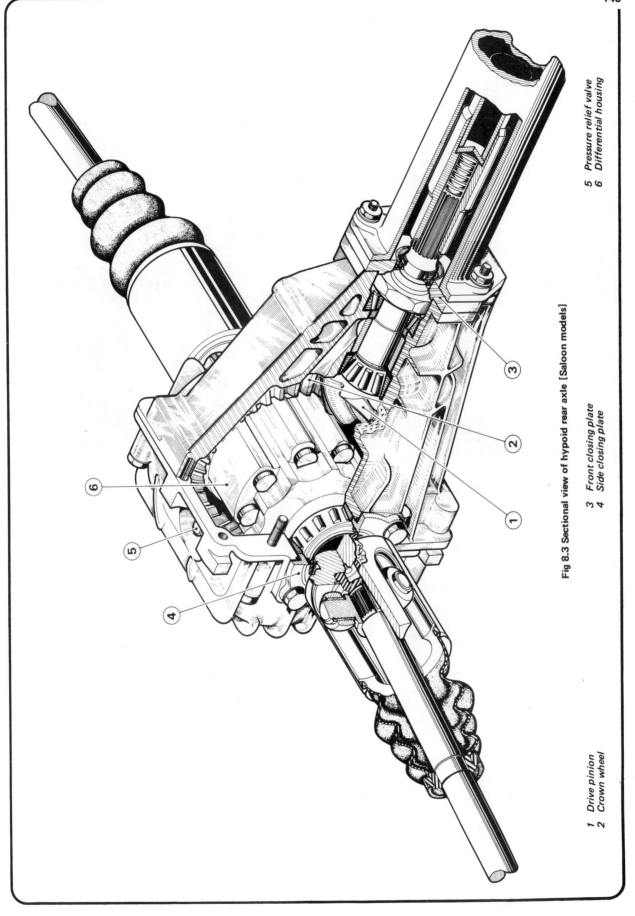

Fig 8.3 Sectional view of hypoid rear axle [Saloon models]

1 Drive pinion
2 Crown wheel

3 Front closing plate
4 Side closing plate

5 Pressure relief valve
6 Differential housing

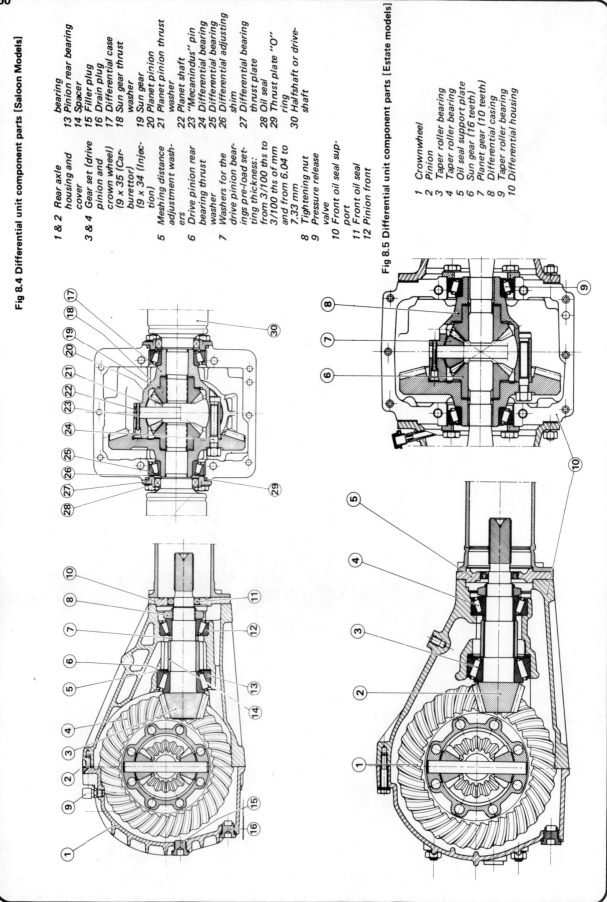

Fig 8.4 Differential unit component parts [Saloon Models]

1 & 2 Rear axle housing and cover
3 & 4 Gear set (drive pinion and crown wheel) (9 x 35 (Carburettor) (9 x 34 (Injection)
5 Meshing distance adjustment washers
6 Drive pinion rear bearing thrust washer
7 Washers for the drive pinion bearings pre-load setting thickness: from 3/100 ths to 3/100 ths of mm and from 6.04 to 7.33 mm
8 Tightening nut
9 Pressure release valve
10 Front oil seal support
11 Front oil seal
12 Pinion front bearing
13 Pinion rear bearing
14 Spacer
15 Filler plug
16 Drain plug
17 Differential case
18 Sun gear thrust washer
19 Sun gear
20 Planet pinion
21 Planet pinion thrust washer
22 Planet shaft
23 "Mecanindus" pin
24 Differential bearing
25 Differential bearing
26 Differential adjusting shim
27 Differential bearing thrust plate
28 Oil seal
29 Thrust plate "O" ring
30 Halfshaft or drive-shaft

Fig 8.5 Differential unit component parts [Estate models]

1 Crownwheel
2 Pinion
3 Taper roller bearing
4 Taper roller bearing
5 Oil seal support plate
6 Sun gear (16 teeth)
7 Planet gear (10 teeth)
8 Differential casing
9 Taper roller bearing
10 Differential housing

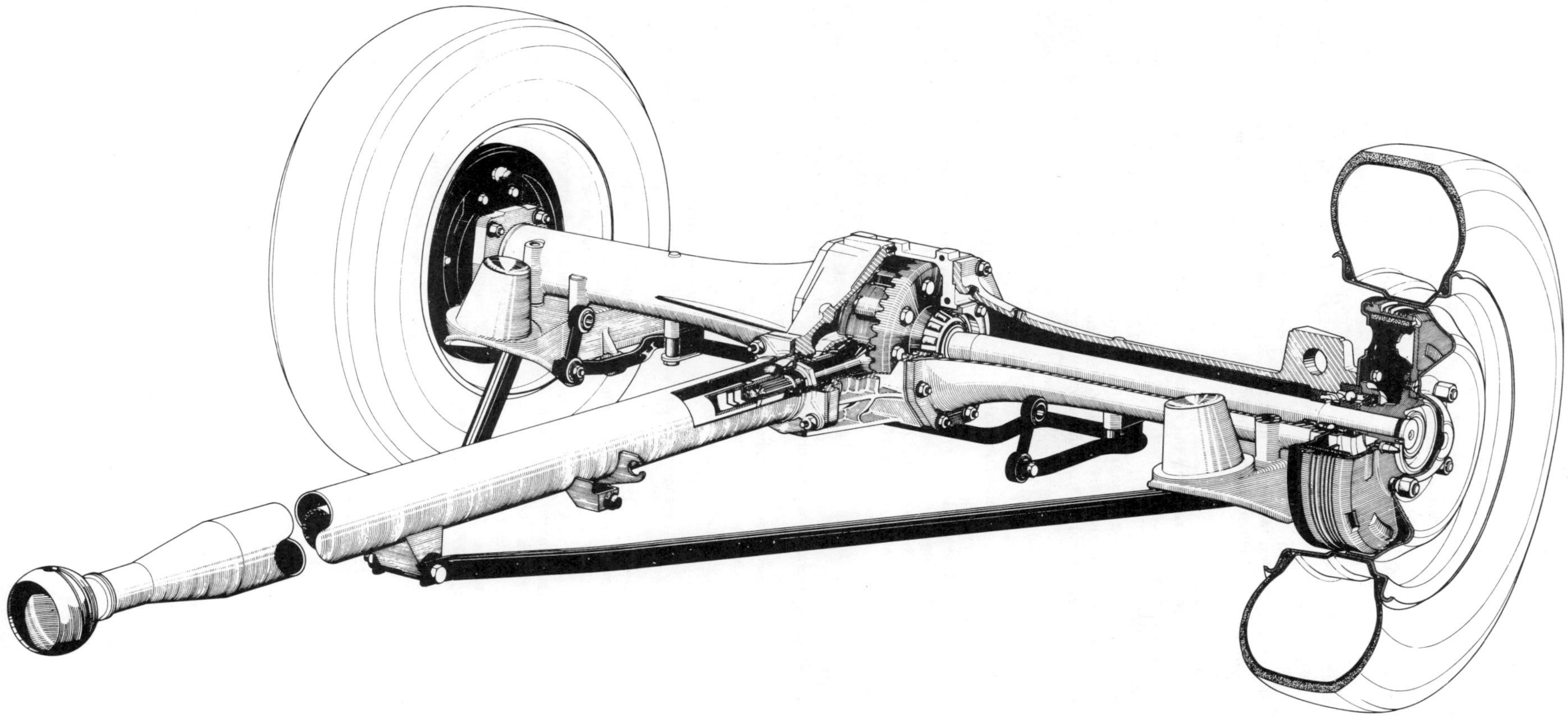

Fig 8.6 Rear axle assembly (Estate models)

2 Differential (Saloon models) - removal and replacement

Important: To remove the differential unit it is necessary to withdraw the left-hand driveshaft. However, this operation is also just possible if the right-hand driveshaft is removed.

1 Chock the front wheels, jack-up the rear of the car and support on firmly based axle stands. Remove the left-hand rear wheel.

2 Refer to Chapter 9, and remove the brake pads.

3 Undo and remove the brake caliper securing bolts (8 mm Allen socket).

4 Withdraw the brake caliper from the disc taking care not to bend the hose unnecessarily. Suspend the caliper using string or wire.

5 Refer to Chapter 9, and remove the disc.

6 Undo and remove the four Allen screws securing the hub carrier to the rear arm. For this use a socket spanner inserted in the hole provided in the hub for this purpose (Fig. 8.7).

7 Using two suitable threaded bolts positioned diagonally and a thrust plate withdraw the hub carrier and driveshaft assembly. By tightening the two bolts the carrier is removed from the rear arm (Fig. 8.8).

8 Remove the plug and drain the differential housing oil. Refit the drain plug.

9 Detach the brake compensator lever pivot from the underside of the body. Leave the lever suspended by its spring.

10 Undo and remove the four nuts that secure the connecting tube (torque tube) to the differential housing.

11 Undo and remove the two Allen screws that secure the differential housing to the suspension crossmember using a 10 mm Allen socket (Fig. 8.9).

12 Disengage the differential housing by pulling it to the rear, and then moving it to the left.

13 Recover the spring located in the rear end of the propeller shaft.

14 Refitting the differential unit is the reverse sequence to removal but the following additional points should be noted:

   a) Check the condition of the oil seals, located in the differential housing.
   b) Pack the space between the two lips of each seal with grease.
   c) Apply grease to the halfshaft splines.
   d) Do not forget to replace the spring in the end of the propeller shaft.
   e) Use new Blocfor washers behind the torque tube/ differential housing securing nuts. Tighten the nuts to a torque wrench setting of 43.5 lb f ft (6.0 kg f m).
   f) Secure the differential housing to the suspension crossmember using new Onduflex washers. Tighten the Allen screws to a torque wrench setting of 27.1 lb f ft (3.75 kg f m).
   g) Secure the knuckle to the rear arm using new Blocfor washers and tighten the Allen screws to a torque wrench setting of 29.0 lb f ft (4 kg f m).
   h) Do not forget to refill the differential housing with the correct grade of oil.

3 Differential (Convertible and Coupe models) - removal and replacement

Important: To remove the differential unit it is necessary for one of the driveshafts to be removed.

1 Chock the front wheels, jack-up the rear of the car and support on firmly based axle stands. Remove the left-hand rear wheel.

2 Remove the plug and drain the differential housing oil. Refit the drain plug.

3 Unhook the handbrake cable from the rear arm and disconnect the cable from the brake unit.

4 Remove the anti-roll bar link pivot.

5 Remove the suspension arm pivots.

6 Using a strong metal lever disengage the arm from the crossmember.

7 Carefully pull the arm/driveshaft assembly, so disengaging the shaft from the differential unit. Ensure that the oil seal is not damaged by the splined end of the shaft.

8 Do not remove the shock absorber as it will hold the coil spring in place. The driveshaft/arm assembly will remain suspended whilst the differential unit is removed.

9 Detach the brake compensator lever pivot from the underside of the body. Leave the lever suspended by its spring (Fig.8.10).

10 Remove the electric feed pump. Do not, however, disconnect it.

11 Undo and remove the four nuts that secure the connecting tube (torque tube) to the differential housing.

12 Undo and remove the two Allen screws that secure the differential housing to the suspension crossmember using a 10 mm Allen socket.

13 Carefully separate the differential from the connecting tube and withdraw the unit until the studs are approximately 15 mm from the flange.

14 Refer to Chapter 7, for information on the propeller shaft retaining plate.

15 Insert the plate between the differential and tube and secure it using a bolt in the top left-hand hole (Fig.8.11).

16 The differential unit may now be withdrawn completely.

17 Refitting the differential unit is the reverse sequence to removal but there are several points that require special note as described in the following paragraphs.

18 Check the condition of the oil seals located in the differential housing. Pack the space between the two lips of each seal with grease.

19 Apply grease to the halfshaft splines.

20 Do not forget to replace the spring in the end of the propeller shaft.

21 With the differential unit in position, use new Blocfor washers behind the torque tube/differential housing securing nuts. Tighten the nuts to a torque wrench setting of 43.5 lb f ft (6.0 kg f m).

22 Secure the differential unit to the crossmember using new counter plates and Blocfor washers. Tighten the Allen screws to a torque wrench setting of 27.1 lb f ft (3.75 kg f m).

23 Position the lips of the counterplates on the edges of the angle supports.

24 Pull the driveshaft/arm assembly outwards, compressing the sliding joints at the same time.

25 Engage the splined end of the shaft in the differential housing (Fig. 8.12).

26 Reposition the arm in the yokes on the crossmember, using a rod to line up the holes and insert the outer pivot first followed by the inner pivot. Fit the flat and new Nylstop nuts. **Do not** tighten the nuts yet.

27 Reconnect the anti-roll bar to its link. Fit a new Nylstop nut. **Do not** tighten the nuts yet.

28 Refit the roadwheel and lower the car to the ground. Two people should now sit in the rear seats then:

   a) Tighten the suspension arm pivot nuts to a torque wrench setting of 47 lb f ft (6.5 kg f m) (Fig. 8.26)
   b) Tighten the anti-roll bar link pivot nut to a torque wrench setting of 33 lb f ft (4.5 kg f m) (Fig. 8.27)

29 Finally, do not forget to refill the differential unit with the correct grade of oil.

4 Differential unit - overhaul

To dismantle, overhaul and reassemble the differential unit requires special tools as well as experience in working on these units. As this is considered to be outside the limits of a do-it-yourself motorist no information is given. If trouble has been

Fig 8.7 Removal of screws securing hub carrier to rear arm (Sec 2)

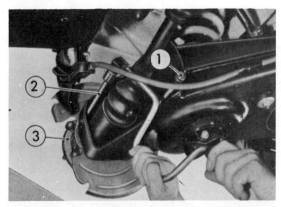

Fig 8.8 Removal of hub/carrier/drive shaft assembly (Sec 2)

1 and 2 Bolts
3   Thrust pad

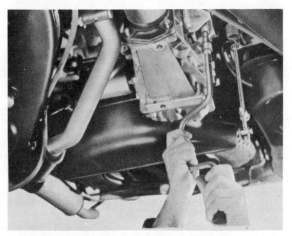

Fig 8.9 Removal of screws securing differential housing to suspension crossmember (Sec 2)

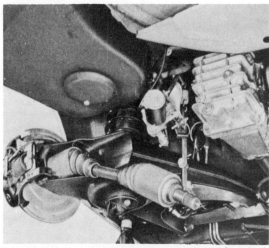

Fig 8.10 Brake compensator lever pivot detached from body (Sec 3)

Fig 8.11 Propeller shaft retaining plate (1) inserted between differential and torque tube (Sec 3) [See also Chapter 7]

Fig 8.12 Engaging splined end of shaft in differential housing (Sec 3)

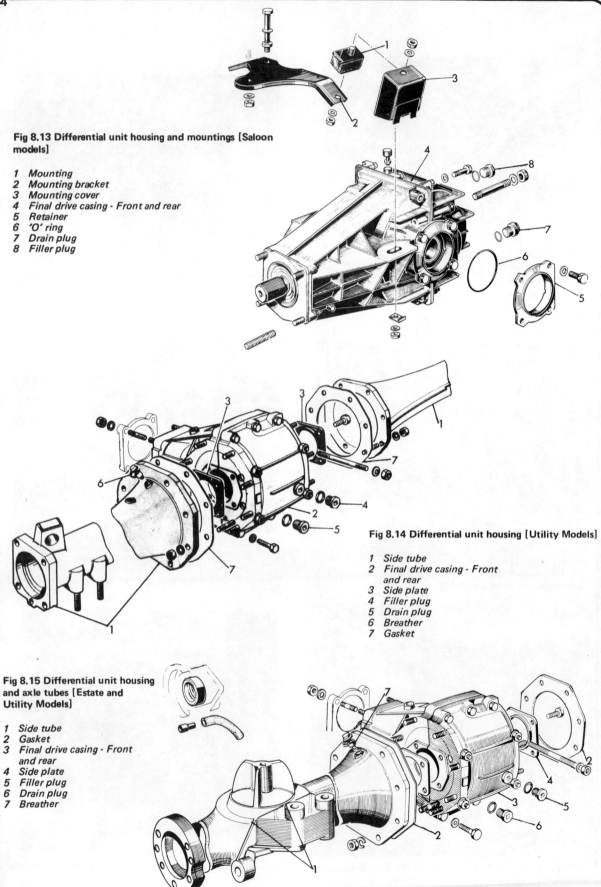

Fig 8.13 Differential unit housing and mountings [Saloon models]

1 Mounting
2 Mounting bracket
3 Mounting cover
4 Final drive casing - Front and rear
5 Retainer
6 'O' ring
7 Drain plug
8 Filler plug

Fig 8.14 Differential unit housing [Utility Models]

1 Side tube
2 Final drive casing - Front and rear
3 Side plate
4 Filler plug
5 Drain plug
6 Breather
7 Gasket

Fig 8.15 Differential unit housing and axle tubes [Estate and Utility Models]

1 Side tube
2 Gasket
3 Final drive casing - Front and rear
4 Side plate
5 Filler plug
6 Drain plug
7 Breather

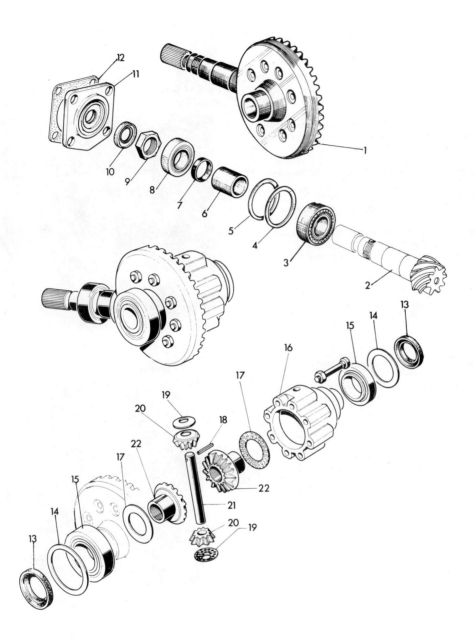

Fig 8.16 Differential unit component parts

1	Crownwheel pinion [Matched pair]	6	Spacer	11	Retainer	18	Roll pin
2	Pinion	7	Spacer	12	Gasket	19	Thrust washer
3	Bearing	8	Bearing	13	Oil seal	20	Planet pinion
4	Shim	9	Nut	14	Shim	21	Spindle
5	Thrust washer	10	Oil seal	15	Bearing	22	Sun gear
				16	Differential case		
				17	Thrust washer		

experienced with the differential unit it will probably be found to be better sense to obtain and fit a guaranteed overhauled unit as supplied by the local Peugeot garage.

5 Driveshafts (saloon models) - removal and replacement

1 Chock the front wheels, jack-up the rear of the car and support on firmly based stands. The stands should be placed under the suspension arms but do not release the jack completely. Remove the roadwheel.

2 A problem now arises because the hub nut must be unscrewed whilst the hub is held using a special tool but if not available one will have to be made up. **Do not**, however, just place a lever between two wheel studs. (The nut was originally tightened to a torque wrench setting of 189 lb f ft (27 kg f m) so be prepared for this) (Figs. 8.17 and 8.18).

3 Refer to Chapter 9, and remove the brake pads.

4 Open the brake line retaining clamp on the suspension rear arm (Fig. 8.19).

5 Undo and remove the Allen screws securing the caliper and lift the caliper from the disc taking care not to bend the hose unnecessarily. Suspend the caliper using string or wire.

6 Refer to Chapter 9, and remove the disc.

7 Undo and remove the four Allen screws securing the knuckle to the suspension arm. For this use a socket spanner inserted in the hole provided in the hub for this purpose (Fig. 8.20).

8 Using two suitable threaded bolts positioned diagonally and a thrust plate withdraw the hub carrier and driveshaft assembly. By tightening the two bolts the carrier is removed from the rear arm (Fig. 8.21).

9 Remove the backing plate and securing screws.

10 Remove the hub nut and washer.

11 The driveshaft may be removed from the hub knuckle using a large vice and soft faced hammer. However, if tight it will be necessary to resort to using a press.

12 To refit the driveshaft first make sure that all parts are thoroughly clean.

13 Mount the hub/knuckle assembly in a vice and smear a little Molykote 321 or similar grease onto the splines.

14 Engage the driveshaft into the hub and refit the washer and new nut. Tighten the nut hand-tight (Fig. 8.22).

15 Check that the sealing ring on the differential housing is in good order and then fill the gap between the seal lips with grease. Apply a little grease to the driveshaft splines (Fig. 8.23).

16 Engage the hub/knuckle/driveshaft assembly in its housing on the suspension arm.

17 Carefully introduce the driveshaft splined end into the differential housing.

18 Using new Blocfor washers secure the knuckle to the suspension arm tightening the Allen screws to a torque wrench setting of 29 lb f ft (4.0 kg f m).

19 Refit the brake disc, caliper and pads, this being the reverse sequence to removal (see also Chapter 9).

20 Refit the brake pipe to the suspension arm.

21 Using the same means for holding the hub as before (paragraph 2) hold the hub and tighten the driveshaft nut to a torque wrench setting of 189 lb f ft (25 kg f m). Lock the nut using a suitable punch.

22 Refit the roadwheel and finally check that the oil level in the differential housing is correct. Top-up if necessary.

6 Driveshafts (Convertible and Coupe models) - removal and replacement

1 Chock the front wheels, jack-up the rear of the car and support on firmly based stands. The stands should be placed under the rear crossmember. Remove the roadwheel.

2 A problem now arises because the hub nut must be unscrewed whilst the hub is held using a special tool as shown in Fig. 8.17. Try to borrow the correct tool but if this is not possible one will have to be made up. **Do not**, however, just place a lever between

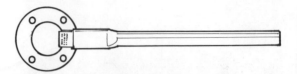

Fig 8.17 Special tool required to hold hub (Secs 5 and 6) [See text] (Sec 5)

Fig 8.18 Slackening hub nut (Secs 5 and 6)

1 Special tool

Fig 8.19 Location of brake line retaining clamp (Sec 5)

1 Clamp

Fig 8.20 Removal of knuckle to suspension arm securing screws (Sec 5)

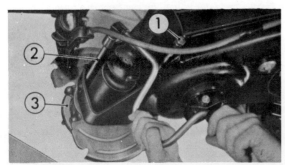

Fig 8.21 Removal of hub (steering knuckle/driveshaft assembly (Sec 5)

1 and 2 bolts
3   Thrust pad

Fig 8.22 Fitting hub nut (Sec 5)

1   Hub/knuckle assembly
2   Washer
3   Nut

Fig 8.23 Location of oil seal (Sec 5)

1   Oil seal

Fig 8.24 Removal of suspension arm inner pivot nut (Sec 6)

two wheel studs (The nut was originally tightened to a torque wrench setting of 189 lb f ft (25 kg f m) so be prepared for this). Do not remove the hub nut yet.

3   Unclip the handbrake cable from the rear arm and then disconnect the cable from the rear brake unit.

4   Remove the anti-roll bar link pivot.

5   Undo and remove the nuts from the suspension arm pivots (Fig. 8.24).

6   Using a suitable diameter drift carefully drive out the inner pivot first and then the outer pivot.

7   Do not remove the shock absorber as it holds the coil spring in place.

8   Using a suitable metal lever disengage the arm.

9   Compress the universal joints on the driveshaft and pull on the assembly to disengage the splined end of the shaft from the differential housing. Take care not to damage the differential oil seal with the splined end of the shaft.

10   Finally remove the hub nut and then using a universal puller and thrust pad draw the hub from the driveshaft (Fig. 8.25).

11   To refit the driveshaft first make sure that all parts are thoroughly clean.

12   Check that the sealing ring on the differential housing is in good order and then fill the gap between the seal lips with grease.

13   Coat the splines on the wheel end of the shaft with a little Molykote 321, or similar grease.

14   Engage the driveshaft in the hub, then fit the washer and new nut.

15   Grease the splines on the differential end of the shaft.

16   Carefully disengage the suspension arm as much as possible and compress the driveshaft universal joints.

17   Engage the splined end in the differential housing.

18   Carefully reposition the suspension arm in the yokes on the crossmember using a lever.

19   Refit the outer and then the inner pivots.

20   Refit the flat washers and new Nylstop nuts but do not tighten yet.

21   Reconnect the handbrake cable and secure it to the suspension arm.

22   Reconnect the anti-roll bar link using a new Nylstop nut. Do not fully tighten yet.

23   Using the same means for holding the hub as before (paragraph 2) hold the hub and tighten the driveshaft nut to a torque wrench setting of 189 lb f ft (25 kg f m). Lock the nut using a

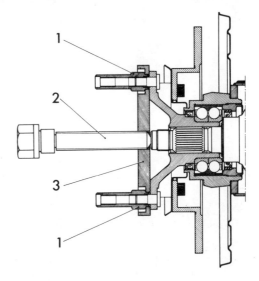

Fig 8.25 Use of universal puller to withdraw shaft form hub (Sec 6)

1   Nut on wheel stud   3   Universal puller body
2   Universal puller bolt

suitable punch.

24 Refit the roadwheel and lower the car to the ground. Two people should now sit in the rear seats, then:

   a) Tighten the suspension arm pivot nuts to a torque wrench setting of 47 lb f ft (6.5 kg f m) (Fig. 8.26)

   b) Tighten the anti-roll bar link pivot nut to a torque wrench setting of 33 lb f ft (4.5 kg f m) (Fig. 8.27)

25 Finally, do not forget to refill the differential unit with the correct grade of oil.

Fig 8.26 Tightening suspension arm pivot nut (Secs 3 and 6)

Fig 8.27 Tightening anti-roll bar link pivot nut (Secs 3 and 6)

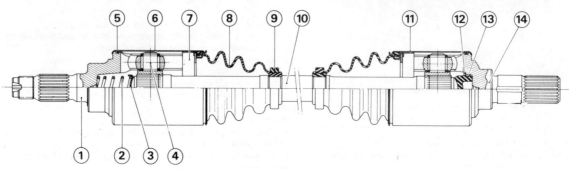

Fig 8.28 Driveshaft component parts (Sec 7)

1 Tulip	5 O - ring	9 Retaining ring	13 Stop
2 Spring	6 Cover. length 113 mm	10 Shaft	14 Tulip
3 Cup	7 Spacer	11 Cover: length 99 mm	
4 Journal and bearing Pack	8 Gaiter	12 Thrust washer	

Fig 8.29 Bending back end of cover (Sec 7)

Fig 8.30 Removal of cover (Sec 7)

Fig 8.31 Tape wrapped around bearing pack (Sec 7)

Fig 8.32 Removal of bearing pack using
a press (Sec 7)

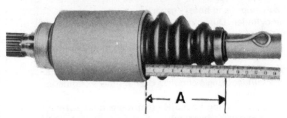

Fig 8.34 Final assembly of wheel side joint (Sec 7)

A = 88 mm

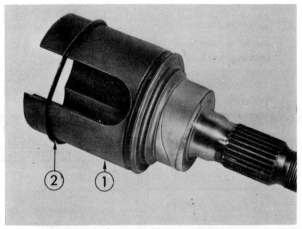

Fig. 8.33 Location of 'O' ring on tulip (Sec 7)

1   Tulip assembly
2   'O' ring

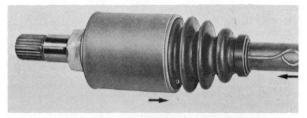

Fig 8.35 Final assembly of differential side joint (Sec 7)

7   Driveshafts - dismantling, overhaul and reassembly

1   Mount the driveshaft vertically in a vice.
2   Bind some adhesive tape around the oil seal bearing face of
the tulip to protect it from damage.
3   Using a pair of end cutters carefully bend back the cover (Fig.
8.29).
4   Disengage the cover by lightly tapping with a soft-faced
hammer (Fig. 8.30).
5   Remove the tulip by raising it vertically. On the wheel side
joint recover the spring and thrust cup.
6   Slide the gaiter down on the shaft as far as possible.
7   Bind some adhesive tape around the bearing pack. This is a
paired component and must not be sparated (Fig. 8.31).
8   Carefully remove as much grease as possible. **Do not** use any
solvents.
9   Using a large vice or press, extract the bearing pack. Don't
forget to hold the driveshaft or it will drop onto the floor. Note:
There is no need to remove the three punch marks on the shaft
as they will disappear during removal (Fig. 8.32).
10 Remove the protector and rubber ring.
11 Dismantling the differential end side joint is similar to that
for the wheel side.
12 Should both protectors need renewal there is no need to
remove both bearing packs. The protector for the second joint
can be removed over the end of the first joint.
13 Remove the 'O' ring from the tulip and then remove as much
grease as possible from inside the tulip. **Do not** use any solvents
(Fig. 8.33).
14 If the differential side tulip needs attention because of wear
or damage to the nylon stop, carefully cut this away using a
sharp chisel.
15 Using a screwdriver remove the retaining washer through the
cut in the nylon stop.
16 Remove the punch marks from the washer using a small
rotary file or stone.
17 Finally clean out the tulip really thoroughly so that no traces

of abrasive or metal are left behind.
18 Obtain the new protector assemblies and the correct amount
of grease (130 gms per side joint - Esso Ladex HPF2).
19 To reassemble, first fit the gaiter and spacer together. Grease
it and insert into the cover. Push the spacer in until it abuts.
20 Hold the shaft vertically in a vice and slide on the retaining
ring and previously assembled protector.
21 Refit the bearing pack to the shaft and using a tubular drift
drive it down the shaft until it abuts.
22 Check that the lower part of the bearing pack is flush with
the bottom of the shaft groove.
23 Make three equidistant punch marks, spreading the splines on
the shaft towards the hub of the bearing pack using a sharp
centre punch.
24 If the nylon stop has been removed refit it to the interior of
the tulip.
25 Insert the washer and then make three equidistant punch
marks, spreading the splines on the shaft towards the hub of the
bearing pack.
26 Insert 130 gms of grease into each side joint. Spread the
grease inside the tulip and gaiter.
27 Remove the adhesive tape from the bearing pack.
28 Place the cup and spring on the wheel end of the shaft.
29 Fit a new 'O' ring to the tulip and then refit the tulip.
30 The tulip cover must now be crimped. For this the use of a
press will make life far easier. With the spacer held in position
bend over the lip using a hammer.
31 Fit the retaining ring to the gaiter. Slide a piece of welding
wire or small electricians screwdriver between the gaiter and
shaft to release the air trapped. **Do not** puncture the gaiter.
32 Wheel side joint: Insert the shaft to obtain a dimension of **88
mm** as shown in Fig. 8.34. Remove the metal rod **without**
altering this position.
33 Differential side joint. With the metal rod located **under the**
gaiter insert the shaft into the tulip until it abuts. Then remove
the metal rod. (Fig. 8.35).
34 Finally check the operation of the joints by hand. They **must**
slide freely and no deformation must be present.

Chapter 9 Braking system

For modifications, and information applicable to later models, see Supplement at end of manual

Contents

Specifications

Type of system

Footbrake	Hydraulic, operating on all four wheels
Handbrake	Mechanical, cable operated to rear wheels only. Automatic adjustment

Front disc brakes

Type	2 piston Girling with floating armature
Disc diameter	10.75 in (273 mm)
Disc runout (maximum)	0.003 in (0.07 mm)
Disc thickness:	
New	0.5 in (12.75 mm)
Machined (minimum)	0.4 in (10.0 mm)
Width of braking track	2.2 in (56 mm)
Front pads	Ferodo EP 2430
Thickness (new)	0.472 in (12 mm)
Thickness (minimum)	0.1 in (2.5 mm) before warning light operates, if fitted
Front pad area	37 x 2 = 74 sq cm per wheel
Braking surface of the front discs	764 sq cm per wheel

Rear disc brakes

Type	2 piston Girling with floating armature
Disc diameter	10.75 in (273 mm)
Disc runout (maximum)	0.003 in (0.07 mm)
Disc thickness:	
New	0.442 in (11.25 mm)
Machined (minimum)	0.35 in (9 mm)
Rear pads	Ferodo EP 2430
Thickness (new)	0.472 in (12 mm)
Thickness (minimum)	0.1 in (2.5 mm) before warning light operates, if fitted
Rear pad area	25 x 2 = 50 sq cm per wheel
Braking surface area of rear disc	325 x 2 = 650 sq cm, per wheel

Rear drum brakes

Type	Hydraulic, with floating shoes
Drum diameter	11.03 in (280 mm)
Lining dimensions (per wheel):	
Leading shoe	11.03 x 2.36 in (280 x 60 mm)
Trailing shoe	9.76 x 2.36 in (248 x 60 mm)
Lining area (per wheel)	285 sq. cm
Rear lining swept area (per wheel)	527.5 sq. cm
Minimum lining thickness	0.06 inch (1.52 mm)

Master cylinder

Type	Single or Tandem
*Bore	0.81 in (20.6 mm)
Brake fluid reservoir	with level indicator

Subject to various modifications. Ensure identical replacement is obtained.

Wheel cylinders

Front disc piston diameter	2.126 in (54 mm)
Rear disc piston diameter	1.686 in (42.8 mm)
Rear drum piston diameter	0.866 in (22 mm)

Servo unit

Type	Bendix Mastervac
Application:	
LHD	Piston diameter 7.875 in (200 mm)
RHD	Piston diameter 6.889 in (175 mm)
Assistance ratio:	
LHD	3.3 : 1
RHD	2.8 : 1

Brake compensator

Type	Bendix

Stoplight control

Type	Mechanical switch

Torque wrench settings

	lb f ft	kg f m
Wheelnuts	43.5	6.0
Bleed screw	5 - 7	0.70 - 1.0
Caliper securing bolts (front)	51	7.0
Caliper securing bolts (rear)	31	4.25
Disc to hub Allen screws	34	4.75
Handbrake lever casing nuts	4.5	0.6
Outer cable retaining collar	7.25	1.0

---

1 General description

Disc brakes are fitted at all four wheels on most models covered by this manual; on a few models drum brakes are fitted to the rear wheels. This is in the main applicable to the Saloon (Luxe version) and utility vehicles. One point to note is that with the rear disc brakes fitted to convertible and coupe models the disc is located inside the hub.

The disc is of cast iron and is secured to the hub by four bolts. The caliper which is mounted over the disc and contains the pads incorporates two pistons mounted on one side of the disc. The pad on the other side of the disc is brought into contact with the disc by using an armature which slides in the caliper body.

Basically the rear disc brakes are similar to those fitted to the front with the exception that the brake pads are slightly smaller.

The rear drum brakes (when fitted) are of the leading/trailing shoe type and operated by a hydraulic wheel cylinder.

All four brakes are hydraulically operated via a pendant pedal positioned under the instrument panel. When the pedal is depressed a master cylinder, which is connected to the brake pedal, is brought into operation.

To assist the driver and reduce brake pedal pressures a vacuum servo unit is located between the brake pedal and master cylinder.

The master cylinder incorporates a brake fluid reservoir which supplies both the clutch and brake hydraulic circuits. On some models is a special float contact in the reservoir cap which is in circuit with a warning light on the instrument panel which comes on when the level of fluid is too low for safety. This warning light also indicates when the brake pads have reached their minimum thickness and also when the handbrake has been applied.

A brake hydraulic pressure compensating device is fitted into the system and this varies the front to rear brake line pressure. It is also attached to the rear suspension anti roll bar to accommodate differences in vehicle load. Basically it comprises a hollow piston having two different parts, each fitted with a sealing ring. A hollow plug with a slot on its front face is screwed to the piston to act as a guide for a regulator valve which is held on its seat by a spring. A metal link connects the device to the anti-roll bar by a spring and it is this which enables the hydraulic pressure

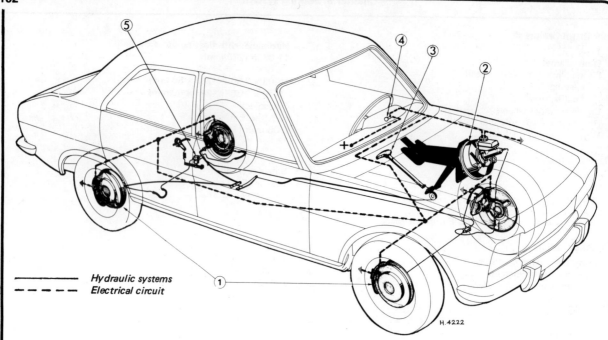

Hydraulic systems
------ Electrical circuit

Fig 9.1 Layout of braking system (Saloon model with discs front and rear

1 Disc brake units
2 Vacuum servo unit

3 Handbrake

4 Warning light

5 Braking compensator

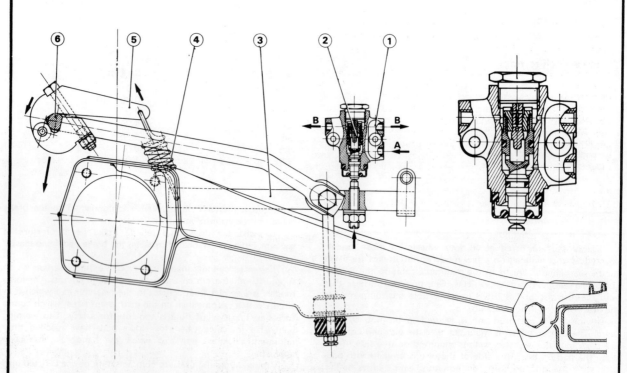

Fig 9.2 Principle of operation of brake compensator

1 Load actuated brake compensator
2 Compensator differential piston
3 Piston thrust lever
4 Lever control spring

5 Spring connecting link on the anti-roll bar
6 Anti-roll bar
A Fluid intake from master cylinder
B Fluid outlets towards rear left and right hand brakes

to the rear cylinders to be varied.

The mechanical handbrake system operates on the rear wheels only. The handbrake lever is attached to a long main cable, a compensator and two shorter side cables.

A self-adjusting mechanism is fitted to the rear wheel brakes to take up any excessive play and ensure the efficient operation of the handbrake for a long period of time. To operate the adjuster is simple, just depress the footbrake several times when the handbrake has been applied.

As disc brake systems are self adjusting in that as the lining material of the brake pads become worn, so hydraulic fluid will be drawn from the reservoir to supplement that already in the brake system, no means of manual adjustment is provided.

2 Bleeding the hydraulic system

1 Removal of all the air from the hydraulic system is essential to the correct working of the braking system, and before undertaking this, examine the fluid reservoir cap to ensure that the vent hole is clear. Check the level of fluid in the reservoir and top-up if required.

2 Check all brake line unions and connections for possible seepage, and at the same time check the condition of the rubber hoses.

3 If the condition of the caliper or wheel cylinders is in doubt, check for possible signs of fluid leakage.

4 If there is any possibility that incorrect fluid has been used in the system, drain all the fluid out and flush through with methylated spirits. Renew all piston seals and cups since they will be affected and could possibly fail under pressure.

5 Gather together a clean glass jar, a 12 inch (300 mm) length of tubing which fits tightly over the bleed screws and a tin of the correct brake fluid.

6 To bleed the system, fully release the handbrake, then remove the rubber cap and fit the tubing to one rear bleed screw.

7 Place the end of the tube in the clean jar which should contain sufficient fluid to keep the end of the tube underneath during the operation.

8 Open the bleed screw ¼ turn with a spanner and depress the brake pedal. After slowly releasing the pedal, pause for a moment to allow the fluid to recoup in the master cylinder and then depress it again. This will force air from the system. Continue until no more air bubbles can be seen coming from the tube. At intervals make certain that the reservoir is kept topped-up, otherwise air will enter at this point again.

9 Finally press the pedal down fully and hold it there whilst the bleed screw is tightened. To ensure correct seating it should be tightened to a torque wrench setting of 5 - 7 lb f ft (0.70 - 1.0 kg fm).

10 Repeat this operation on the second rear brake, and then the front brakes.

11 When completed check the level of the fluid in the reservoir and then check the feel of the brake pedal, which should be firm and free from any 'spongy' action, which is normally associated with air in the system.

12 It will be noticed that during the bleeding operation the effort required to depress the pedal the full stroke will increase because of the loss of vacuum assistance as it is destroyed by repeated operation of the servo unit. Although the servo unit will be inoperative as far as assistance is concerned it does not affect the brake bleed operation.

13 It should be noted that if the rear disc brakes have been removed or overhauled, the rear calipers must be refilled using a different procedure as follows.

14 Before refitting the disc pads, engage the special key in the groove on the piston as shown in Fig.9.4, pump the brake pedal, and bleed the caliper with the outer housing in contact with the disc.

15 Refit the disc pads and carry out the same procedure on the remaining rear caliper.

16 With all disc pads refitted, bleed the rear and front brakes as described earlier in this Section.

17 Top-up the brake fluid level as necessary, then with the engine running, check that the brake pedal has a positive action.

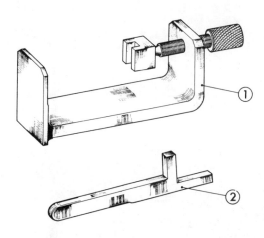

Fig. 9.3 Two special tools that are desirable to have when working on disc brakes (Sec 2)

1   *Clamp [Use a 'G' clamp and wood block if tool not available]*
2   *Key [Make up out of scrap metal]*

Fig 9.4 Key fitted to groove in piston
(Sec 2)

1   Key

Fig 9.5 Key pivoted through 1/8 turn
(Sec 2)

1   Key

Fig 9.6 Returning piston using clamp
(Sec 2)

1   Clamp

3 Hydraulic hoses (flexible) - inspection, removal and replacement

1 Inspect the condition of the flexible hydraulic hoses leading to the front and rear brakes. (photo)
2 If they are swollen, damaged or chafed, they must be renewed.
3 Wipe the top of the brake master cylinder reservoir and unscrew the cap. Place a piece of polythene sheet over the top and secure to make an airtight joint. This is to stop hydraulic fluid syphoning out during subsequent operations. If the cap is replaced the float contact could be damaged.
4 To remove a flexible hose wipe the union and any supports free of dust and undo the union nuts from the metal pipe ends.
5 Undo and remove the locknut and washer securing the flexible hose end to the bracket.
6 Unscrew the hose from the caliper or connector as applicable.

7 Refitting the flexible hose is the reverse sequence to removal. It will be necessary to bleed the brake hydraulic system as described in Section 2.

4 Disc brake pads (front) - removal, inspection and replacement

After high mileages, it will be necessary to fit replacement pads. It is important that the pads for both front brakes are renewed. Because of this brake pads are supplied in sets of four.
1 Chock the rear wheels, jack-up the front of the car and support on firmly based axle stands. Remove the roadwheel. (photo)
2 Disconnect the brake wear warning lead at the terminal connector. (photo)
3 Remove the brake pads thrust spring. (photo)
4 Undo and remove the nut and washer securing the pads retaining fork. (photo)

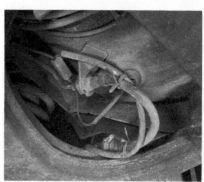

3.1 Rear brake hose

4.1 Front disc brake assembly

4.2 Disconnecting pad wear warning lead

4.3 Removing brake pads thrust spring

4.4 Removal of pads retaining fork securing nut and washer

4.5 Withdrawing pads retaining fork

4.6A Removing outer pad

4.6B Removing inner pad

Fig 9.7 Releasing pads with lever [or screwdriver] (Sec 4)

5 Withdraw the pads retaining fork. (photo)
6 The pads may now be removed (photos). Should the pads be difficult to remove it is permissible to release them using a screwdriver or lever placed squarely between the metal lips of the brake pads (Fig. 9.7).
7 Clean down the caliper and disc assembly and generally inspect for fluid leakage, wear or damage.
8 Measure the thickness of the pad lining and if it is badly worn the pads must be renewed.
9 If new pads are to be fitted push the piston into the bore using a block of wood and a 'G' clamp. To stop hydraulic fluid overflowing from the reservoir, slacken the caliper bleed screw.
10 Refitting the pads is the reverse sequence to removal but the following additional points should be noted:

  a) Fit the brake pads thrust spring with the arrow pointing upwards.
  b) Tighten the pads retaining fork securing nuts to torque wrench setting of 13 lb f ft (1.75 kg f m).
  c) Check the brake fluid level and top-up if necessary.
  d) Operate the brake pedal several times until a strong resistance is felt. This will ensure that the pads have settled correctly. Road test the car.

5 Disc brake caliper (front) - removal and replacement

1 Chock the rear wheels, apply the handbrake, jack-up the front of the car and support on firmly based axle stands. Remove the roadwheel.
2 Disconnect the brake wear warning lead at the terminal connector.
3 Disconnect the union of the flexible hose from the caliper body. Tape the end to stop loss of hydraulic fluid (Fig. 9.8).
4 Undo and remove the two bolts securing the caliper assembly to the front suspension member (Fig. 9.9).
5 It should now be possible to lift the caliper assembly from over the disc. If the pads are binding it is permissible to release them using a screwdriver placed squarely between the metal lips of the brake pads.
6 Refitting the caliper assembly is the reverse sequence to removal but the following additional points should be noted:

  a) Use new 'Blocfor' washers for the caliper securing bolts.
  b) Tighten the caliper securing bolts to a torque wrench setting of 51 lb f ft (7.0 kg f m).
  c) Reconnect the flexible hosing using new sealing washers.
  d) Refer to Section 2, and bleed the brake hydraulic system.

6 Disc brake caliper (front) - overhaul

If hydraulic fluid is leaking from the caliper it will be necessary to fit new seals or renew the caliper. Should brake fluid be found running down the side of the wheel or if it is noticed that a pool of fluid forms alongside one wheel or the level in the master cylinder reservoir drops excessively it is also indicative of seal failure.
1 Refer to Section 4, and remove the caliper pads.
2 Refer to Section 5, and remove the caliper.
3 Using a 'G' clamp and wooden block retract the pistons as shown in Fig. 9.11.
4 Remove the thrust spring from the armature.
5 Disengage the armature from the guide grooves in the caliper body.
6 Carefully remove the spring clips that secure the piston protectors (Fig. 9.12).
7 Remove the two protectors.
8 Carefully push the two pistons out of the cylinder.
9 Remove the nylon spacer from the piston on the armature side.
10 Using a non-metallic rod remove the sealing rings from the caliper cylinder body (Fig. 9.13).

Fig 9.8 Removal of front brake caliper - Hose and warning light lead detached (Sec 5)

Fig 9.9 Removal of front caliper securing bolts (Sec 5)

Fig 9.10 Front caliper partially dismantled (Sec 6)

1 Thrust spring 3 Pads retaining fork
2 Bolt 4 Pads

11 Thoroughly wash all parts in methylated spirits or clean hydraulic fluid. During reassembly new rubber seals must be fitted and these should be well lubricated with clean hydraulic fluid before fitment.

12 Inspect the piston and bore for signs of wear, score marks or other damage. If evident a new caliper assembly will be necessary.

13 To reassemble first clamp the cylinder body in a vice (use soft faces).

14 Well lubricate the rubber seals and position in the grooves inside the cylinder body.

15 Place the nylon spacer in the piston which will be fitted to the armature side.

16 Well lubricate the pistons and insert them one at a time into the cylinder body.

17 Fit the two protector rubbers and their spring clips. Note that the narrow clip must be on the disc side and the thicker clip to the armature side.

18 If the thrust plates have been removed refit them to the armature.

19 Place a piece of shim steel 0.008 in (0.20 mm) thick against each of the plates to facilitate their engagement in the grooves on the cylinder body (Fig. 9.14).

20 Engage the armature in the cylinder body grooves whilst compressing the thrust plates. When in position remove the two strips of shim steel.

21 Refit the thrust spring to the upper part of the armature.

22 Finally retract the pistons fully using the 'G' clamp and wooden block.

23 Reassembly is now complete and the unit is ready to refit to the car. The pads are then refitted as described in Section 4.

7 Brake discs and hub assembly (front) - removal and replacement

1 Refer to Section 5, and remove the caliper assembly. It is not necessary to disconnect the flexible hose if the caliper does not require attention. Suspend the caliper on wire or string to prevent straining the flexible hose.

2 Carefully remove the grease cap from the wheel spindle.

3 Unscrew and remove the hub nut and washer.

4 Grip the hub and disc assembly and pull it from the wheel spindle.

5 Thoroughly clean the disc and inspect for signs of deep scoring or excessive corrosion. If evident the surfaces may be refaced but leave this to the experts. It is desirable however to fit a new disc if at all possible.

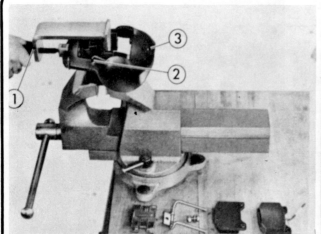

Fig 9.11 Returning pistons using clamp (Sec 6)

1 Clamp   3 Armature
2 Thrust spring

Fig 9.12 Front caliper final dismantling (Sec 6)

1 Spring clips   3 Piston
2 Protectors   4 Nylon spacer

Fig 9.13 Removal of sealing rings (Sec 6)

1 Sealing rings

Fig 9.14 Assembling thrust plates to armature (Sec 6)

1 Thrust plate   2 Shim stud

6 To remove the disc from the hub first mark the hub and disc assembly if the original parts are to be used.

7 Undo and remove the four securing Allen screws and part the disc from the hub (Fig. 9.15).

8 To reassemble first make sure that the mating faces are really clean and then refit the four Allen screws using new 'Blocfor' washers. Tighten to a torque wrench setting of 34 lb f ft (4.75 kg f m) (Fig. 9.16).

9 Grease the hub bearings and refit the assembly to the steering swivel.

10 Refit the washer with the inner shoulder against the inner race of the bearing.

11 Fit a new hub nut and pre-tighten to a torque wrench setting of 22 lb f ft (3 kg f m). Then back off the nut.

12 Retighten the nut to a torque wrench setting of 7.25 lb f ft (1 kg f m). **Do not** lock the nut yet.

13 It is now necessary to check for disc run-out. For this a dial indicator gauge or feeler pack is required.

14 Rotate the disc and check for run-out at a point approximately 1.0 in (25 mm) from the outer circumference. With a dial indicator this is easy but when using a feeler gauge pack this should be positioned between the backplate and disc at the caliper location (Fig. 9.17).

15 The maximum runout should not exceed 0.003 in (0.07 mm). If it does however, first remove the disc and hub assembly, part the two and check for dirt. Reposition the disc through a quarter of a turn relative to the hub.

16 Recheck for runout and when satisfactory lock the hub nut using a suitable punch.

17 Refit the caliper assembly as described in Section 5.

---

8 Disc brake pads (rear) - removal, inspection and replacement

After high mileages it will be necessary to fit replacement pads. It is important that the pads for both rear brakes are renewed. Because of this brake pads are supplied in sets of four.

1 Chock the front wheels, jack-up the rear of the car and support on firmly based axle stands. Remove the roadwheel.

2 Disconnect the brake wear warning lead at the terminal connector (photo), where fitted.

3 Undo and remove the bolt and nut securing the pads retaining fork and pad support. (photo) Lift away the pad support.

4 Withdraw the pads retaining fork. (photo)

5 The pads may now be removed (photos). Should the pads be difficult to remove it is permissible to release them using a screwdriver placed squarely between the metal lips of the brake pads.

6 Clean down the caliper and disc assembly and generally inspect for fluid leakage, wear or damage.

7 Measure the thickness of the pad lining and if it is badly worn the pads must be renewed.

8 To return the brake pistons for the rear brakes a special piston positioning key is required (Fig. 9.3). It should not be too difficult to manufacture an alternative.

9 Place the key in the inner brake pad position in such a manner that it is lodged in the groove on the piston.

10 Rotate the piston one eighth of a turn so as to bring the arm of the key against the angle of the brake pad guide, in order to release the automatic handbrake play take up device.

11 Remove the key and ensure that the handbrake lever on the piston is well down onto its nylon stop.

12 Push the piston into the bore using a block of wood and a 'G' clamp. To stop hydraulic fluid overflowing from the reservoir, slacken the caliper bleed screw.

13 Now return the piston to its initial positon using the key.

14 Refitting the pads is now the reverse sequence to removal but the following additional points should be noted:

a) When fitted, the brake pads thrust spring should be replaced with the arrow pointing upwards.

Fig 9.15 Front disc and hub assembly (Sec 7)

Fig 9.16 Refitting disc to hub (Sec 7)

Fig 9.17 Use of dial indicator gauge to check disc runout (Sec 7)

8.2 Disconnecting pad wear warning lead

8.3 Removal of pads retaining fork securing bolt and nut

8.4 Withdrawing pads retaining fork

8.5A Removing outer pad

8.5B Removing inner pad

Fig 9.18 Removal of rear caliper (Sec 9)

b) *Tighten the pads retaining fork securing bolt and new washer to a torque wrench setting of 13 lb f ft (1.75 kg f m).*
c) *Check the brake fluid level and top-up if necessary.*
d) *Operate the brake pedal several times until a strong resistance is felt. This will ensure that the pads have settled correctly. Road test the car.*

9 Disc brake caliper (rear) - removal and replacement

1 Chock the front wheels, jack-up the rear of the car and support on firmly based axle studs. Remove the roadwheel.
2 Disconnect the brake wear warning lead at the terminal connector, where fitted.
3 Disconnect the brake hydraulic fluid line and plug the ends to stop dirt ingress or loss of hydraulic fluid.
4 Disconnect the handbrake cable and outer casing.
5 Undo and remove the two bolts that secure the caliper and lift away from over the disc (Fig. 9.18). If the pads are binding it is permissible to release them using a screwdriver between the metal lips of the brake pads. As a last resort remove the pads, as described in Section 8.
6 Refitting the caliper assembly is the reverse sequence to removal but the following additional points should be noted:

a) *Use new 'Blocfor' washers for the caliper securing bolts.*
b) *Tighten the caliper securing bolts to a torque wrench setting of 31 lb f ft (4.25 kg f m).*
c) *Reconnect the handbrake and adjust as described in Section 23.*
d) *Refer to Section 2 and bleed the brake hydraulic system.*

10 Disc brake caliper (rear) - overhaul

If hydraulic fluid is leaking it will be necessary to fit new seals or renew the caliper. Should brake fluid be found running down the side of the wheel or if it is noticed that a pool of fluid forms alongside one wheel or the level in the master cylinder reservoir drops excessively it is also indicative of seal failure.
1 Refer to Section 8, and remove the caliper pads.
2 Refer to Section 9, and remove the caliper.
3 To return the brake pistons a special piston positioning key is required (Fig. 9.3). It should not be too difficult to manufacture an alternative.
4 Using the key rotate the piston until it abuts on the brake pad guide.
5 Using a 'G' clamp and wooden blocks return the pistons into the cylinder.
6 Detach and remove the thrust spring from the armature.
7 Slide the armature to disengage it from the grooves in the cylinder body.
8 Carefully remove the Truarc ring (Fig. 9.19) and then the handbrake lever return spring.
9 Raise the handbrake lever and recover the nylon spacer.
10 Carefully remove the spring clips that secure the piston protectors.
11 Remove the two protectors.
12 To remove the pistons, push on the "grooved" one and eject from the end of the bore.
13 Using a non-metallic rod, remove the sealing rings from the caliper cylinder body.
14 Thoroughly wash all parts in methylated spirits or clean hydraulic fluid. During reassembly new rubber seals must be fitted and these should be well lubricated with clean hydraulic fluid before fitment.
15 Inspect the piston and bore for signs of wear, score marks or other damage. If evident a new caliper assembly will be necessary.
16 To reassemble first clamp the cylinder body in a vice (use soft faces).
17 Well lubricate the rubber seals and position in the grooves inside the cylinder body.
18 Well lubricate the pistons and then referring to Fig. 9.20

insert piston (1) positioning the handbrake lever as shown.

19 Refit piston (2) with its groove inclined at one eighth of a turn from the vertical.

20 Fit the two protector rubbers and their spring clips. Note that the narrow clip must be on the disc side and the thicker clip to the armature side.

21 Raise the handbrake lever and position the nylon spacer on the piston.

22 If the thrust plate have been removed refit them to the armature.

23 Place a piece of shim steel 0.008 in (0.20 mm) thick against each of the plates to facilitate their engagement in the grooves on the cylinder body.

24 Engage the armature in the cylinder body grooves whilst compressing the thrust plates. When in position remove the two strips of shim steel.

25 Slide the handbrake return spring onto its pivot and hook over the two ends (Fig. 9.21).

26 Lock the spring on its pivot using a new 'Truarc' ring.

27 Refit the thrust spring onto the upper part of the armature.

28 Reassembly is now complete and the unit is ready for refitting to the car. The pads are then refitted as described in Section 8.

---

11 Brake discs and hub assembly (rear Type 1) - removal and replacement

---

1 The instructions given in this Section are applicable to models with the disc mounted *behind* the hub. For other models refer to Section 12. Note that a special Peugeot tool is required (Fig. 9.22).

2 Refer to Section 9, and remove the caliper assembly. It is not necessary to disconnect the flexible hose if the caliper does not require attention.

 a) Slacken the hose nut on the rear arm support and disengage the hose from it.
 b) Open the clamp that holds the brake line onto the rear arm.
 c) Detach the handbrake cable from the rear arm.
 d) Refer to Section 8 and remove the brake pads.
 e) Now remove the two caliper securing bolts and lift from over the disc.
 f) Suspend the caliper on wire or string to prevent straining the flexible hose.

3 Refer to Chapter 8, and remove the driveshaft.

4 Reposition the suspension arm in the crossmember yokes to give better access.

5 Using a suitable socket, 'T' bar and tube (or a similar arrangement) undo and remove the hub carrier nut. **Beware:** It is very tight as it is tightened to a torque of 181.25 lb f ft (25 kg f m).

6 Using a suitable thrust block and drift remove the hub and disc assembly (Fig. 9.22).

7 Thoroughly clean the disc and inspect for signs of deep scoring or excessive corrosion. If evident, the surfaces may be refaced but leave this to the experts. It is desirable however, to fit a new disc if at all possible.

8 To remove the disc from the hub first mark the hub and disc assembly if the original parts are to be re-used.

9 Undo and remove the four Allen screws and part the disc from the hub (Fig. 9.23).

10 To reassemble first make sure the mating faces are really clean.

11 Renew the deflector plate if it shows any trace of damage on the bearing faces (disc side or hub side).

12 Fit the four Allen screws using new 'Blocfor' washers. Tighten to a torque wrench setting of 33 lb f ft (4.5 kg f m) -

13 Refit the hub/disc assembly onto the arm and then using a long bolt, nut and large washers draw the assembly fully onto the arm. Remove the nut, washers and bolt (Fig. 9.24).

14 It is now necessary to check for disc runout. For this a dial indicator gauge or feeler gauge pack is required.

Fig 9.19 Removal of rear caliper handbrake lever (Sec 10)

1 Truarc ring	3 Handbrake lever
2 Lever return spring	4 Nylon spacer

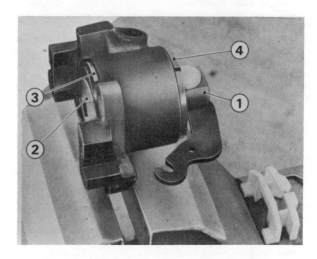

Fig 9.20 Initial reassembly of rear brake caliper cylinder (Sec 10)

1 Piston No. 1	3 Thin spring clip
2 Piston No. 2 [Note position of groove]	4 Thick spring clip

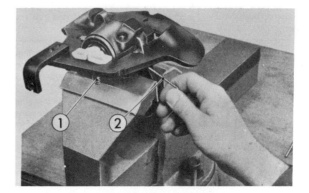

Fig 9.21 Final assembly of rear caliper (Sec 10)

1 Handbrake return spring   2 Thrust spring

15 Rotate the disc and check for runout at a point approximately 1 in (25 mm) from the outer circumference. With a dial indicator this is easy but when using a feeler gauge pack this should be positioned between the backplate and disc at the caliper location.

16 The maximum runout should not exceed 0.003 in (0.07 mm). If it does however, first remove the disc and hub assembly, part the two and check for dirt. Reposition the disc through a quarter of a turn relative to the hub.

17 Recheck for runout and when satisfactory fit a new hub carrier nut and tighten to a torque wrench setting of 181.25 lb f ft (25 kg f m). Lock the carrier nut using a suitable punch.

18 Refit the driveshaft and caliper assembly, this being the reverse sequence to removal.

12 Brake discs and hub assembly (rear Type 2) - removal and replacement

1 The instructions given in this Section are applicable to models with the disc mounted on the *outside* of the hub. For other models refer to Section 11.

2 Refer to Section 11, and follow the instructions given in paragraph 2.

3 Mark the position of the disc relative to the hub.

4 Undo and remove the one crosshead screw securing the disc to the hub (Fig. 9.25).

5 Lift away the disc and carefully clean the hub without removing it.

6 Thoroughly clean the disc and inspect for signs of deep scoring or excessive corrosion. If evident the surfaces may be refaced but leave this to the experts. It is desirable however to fit a new disc if at all possible.

7 To reassemble first make sure the mating faces are really clean.

8 Offer up the disc and secure with the crosshead screw. Also use two nuts on the wheel studs and tighten these to a torque wrench setting of 43.5 lb f ft (6 kg f m). (Fig. 9.26).

9 It is now necessary to check for disc runout. For this a dial indicator gauge or feeler gauge pack is required.

10 Rotate the disc and check for runout at a point approximately 1 in (25 mm) from the outer circumference. With a dial indicator this is easy but when using a feeler gauge pack this should be positioned between the backplate and disc at the caliper location.

11 The maximum runout should not exceed 0.003 in (0.07 mm). If it does however remove the disc and check for dirt. Reposition the disc through half of a turn relative to the hub.

12 Recheck for runout and when satisfactory the caliper can be refitted.

13 Drum brake shoes (rear) - inspection, removal and replacement

After high mileages, it will be necessary to fit replacement shoes with new linings. Refitting new brake linings to old shoes is not considered economic, or possible, without the use of special equipment. However, if the services of a local garage or workshop having brake re-lining equipment are available then there is no reason why the original shoes should not be successfully relined. Ensure that the correct specification linings are fitted to the shoes.

1 Chock the front wheels, jack-up the rear of the car and place on firmly based axle stands. Remove the roadwheel.

2 Release the handbrake, remove the brake drum retaining screw, and using a soft faced hammer on the outer circumference of the brake drum remove the brake drum.

3 If the brake drum is difficult to remove, back-off the adjusters on Utility models, or on self-adjusting brakes, remove the plugs from the backplates and use a screwdriver to press the

handbrake levers over the stop pins.

4 The brake linings should be renewed if they are so worn that the rivet heads are flush with the surface of the lining. If bonded linings are fitted, they must be renewed when the lining material has worn down to 0.06 inch (1.52 mm) at its thinnest part.

5 Depress each shoe holding down spring and detach the anchor plate located at the rear of the brake backplate.

6 Ease each shoe from its location slot in the fixed pivot and then detach the other end of each shoe from the wheel cylinder.

7 Note which way round and into which holes in the shoes the retracting springs fit and detach the retracting springs.

8 Lift away the front shoe followed by the operating link. (Fig.9.28).

9 Detach the handbrake inner cable from the rear shoe lever and lift away the rear shoe together with lever.

10 If the shoes are to be left off for a while place a warning on the steering wheel as accidental depression of the brake pedal will eject the pistons from the wheel cylinder.

11 If new shoes are being fitted the levers will have to be transferred.

12 Thoroughly clean all traces of dust from the shoes, backplates and brake drums using a stiff brush. It is recommended that compressed air is not used as it blows up dust which should not be inhaled. Brake dust can cause judder or squeal and therefore, it is important to clean out as described.

13 Check that the pistons are free in the cylinder, that the rubber dust covers are undamaged and in position and that there are no hydraulic fluid leaks.

14 Prior to reassembly smear a trace of Castrol PH Brake Grease on the shoe support pads, brake shoe pivots and on the ratchet pawl teeth, where fitted.

15 Reassembly is the reverse sequence to removal and provided that care was taken to note the location of each part as it was removed no problems will arise.

16 When all is together adjust the handbrake and shoe to drum clearance as described in Sections 23 and 16 respectively.

14 Wheel cylinder (rear drum brakes) - removal and replacement

If hydraulic fluid is leaking from the brake wheel cylinder, it will be necessary to dismantle it and replace the seals. Should brake fluid be found running down the side of the wheel, or if it is noticed that a pool of liquid forms alongside one wheel or the level in the master cylinder reservoir drops it is also indicative of failed seals.

1 Refer to Section 13 and remove the brake drums and shoes. Clean down the rear of the backplate using a stiff brush. Place a quantity of rag under the backplate to catch any hydraulic fluid that may issue from the open pipe or wheel cylinder.

2 Using an open ended spanner carefully unscrew the hydraulic pipe connection union to the rear of the wheel cylinder. To prevent dirt ingress tape the end of the pipe.

3 Undo and remove the two bolts and spring washers that secure the wheel cylinder to the backplate.

4 Withdraw the wheel cylinder from the front of the brake backplate.

5 Refitting the wheel cylinder, shoes and drums is the reverse sequence to removal. It will be necessary to bleed the brake hydraulic system as described in Section 2.

15 Wheel cylinder (rear drum brakes) - inspection and overhaul

1 With the wheel cylinder removed, thoroughly clean down and wipe dry with a non-fluffy rag.

2 Ease off each rubber dust cover and draw out the pistons, cup seals and spring. Note which way round the seals are fitted (Fig. 9.29).

3 Inspect the inside of the cylinder for score marks caused by impurities in the hydraulic fluid. If any are found, the cylinder and pistons will require renewal.

4 If the cylinder is sound, thoroughly clean it out with fresh

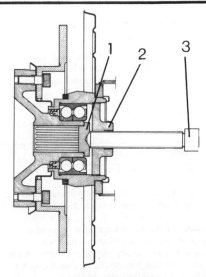

Fig 9.22 Removal of hub and disc assembly using special tool (Type I) (Sec 11)

1 Thrust pad   3 Special bolt
2 Extractor

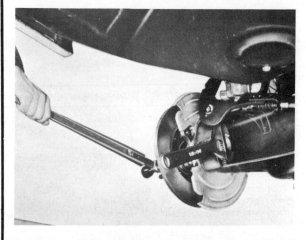

Fig 9.24 Drawing hub and disc assembly into position (Type 1) (Sec 11)

Fig 9.26 Refitting rear disc (Type 2) (Sec 12)

1 Hub nuts

Fig 9.23 Hub and disc assembly (Type 1) (Sec 11)

1 Disc   3 Hub
2 Deflector

Fig 9.25 Rear disc detached from hub (Type 2) (Sec 12)

1 Crosshead screw hole in hub flange

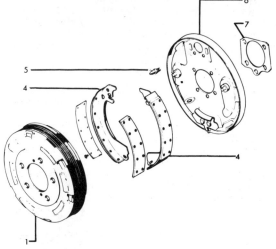

Fig 9.27 Rear drum brake shoes, drum and backplate (Sec 13)

1 Drum   6 Backplate
4 Shoe assembly   7 Gasket
5 Centering dowel

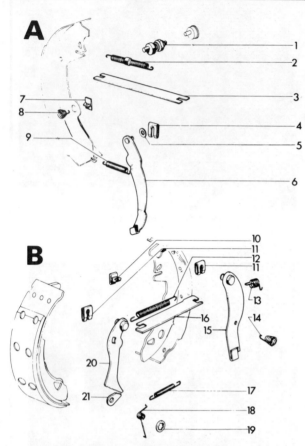

Fig 9.28 Rear drum brake shoe linkage A - Utility models B - Saloon models (Sec 13)

1 Adjuster	12 Spring
2 Spring	13 Spring
3 Operating link	14 Spring
4 Clip	15 Operating lever
5 Washer	16 Operating link
6 Operating lever	17 Spring
7 Anchor	18 Spring
8 Spring	19 Washer
9 Spring	20 Wear take up lever
10 Anchor	21 Pawl
11 Clip	

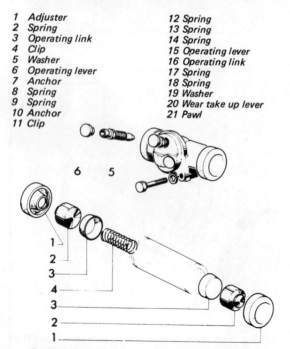

Fig 9.29 Rear drum brake wheel cylinder (Sec 15)

1 Rubber boot	4 Spring
2 Piston	5 Bleed screw
3 Cup seal	6 Cap

hydraulic fluid.

5 The old rubber seals will probably be swollen and visibly worn. Smear the new rubber seals with hydraulic fluid and fit the spring, cup seals, pistons and rubber dust cover to the wheel cylinder.

6 The wheel cylinder is now ready for refitting to the brake backplate.

16 Drum brakes (rear) - adjustment

Utility models

1 Chock the front wheels, release the handbrake completely, jack-up the rear of the car and support on firmly based axle stands.

2 The adjuster eccentric is located at the top of the backplate and it is recommended that all dirt is removed from the adjuster area. Lightly lubricate the adjuster with penetrating oil.

3 Make sure that the handbrake cables are not in tension so causing the brakes to be partially applied.

4 Turn the adjuster until the brake shoes make firm contact with the drum. Back-off the adjuster until the drum rotates without signs of binding.

5 A slight rubbing noise will probably be due to dust in the drum.

6 Repeat operations 4 and 5 for the second rear brake.

Saloon models

7 Adjustment is made automatically, each time the brake pedal is depressed. After fitting new shoes, pump the brake pedal several times to set the adjustment lever.

17 Master cylinder (single circuit) - removal and replacement

1 For safety reasons, disconnect the battery.

2 Wipe down the outside of the master cylinder and reservoir. Unscrew the reservoir cap.

3 With a clean glass jar ready detach the clutch master cylinder hydraulic fluid supply pipe from the underside of the reservoir. Catch the hydraulic fluid as it drains out from the reservoir.

4 Plug the end of the clutch master cylinder hydraulic fluid supply pipe with a pencil to stop loss of fluid or dirt ingress.

5 Undo and remove the union nut from the end of brake master cylinder.

6 Undo and remove the two nuts and washers securing the master cylinder to the vacuum servo unit.

7 The master cylinder and reservoir may now be lifted away. **Do not** allow brake fluid to contact any paintwork as it acts as a solvent.

8 Refitting the brake master cylinder is the reverse sequence to removal but the following additional points should be noted:

a) *If the rubber pipe is squeezed as it is connected to the reservoir and at the same time the reservoir is refilled it should not be necessary to bleed the clutch hydraulic system. However, should air be in the clutch pipe it will be necessary to bleed the system, as described in Chapter 5.*

b) *Bleed the brake hydraulic system, as described in Section 2*

18 Master cylinder (dual-circuit) - removal and replacement

Cars exported to some countries are fitted with a dual-line braking system. Models so fitted use a different master cylinder as will be seen from Figs. 9.31 and 9.33. Removal and refitting this master cylinder is basically the same as that for the single circuit type with the exception that one additional hydraulic pipe must be detached. Refer to Section 17, for full information.

19 Master cylinder (single circuit) - dismantling, examination and reassembly

If a replacement master cylinder is to be fitted, it will be necessary to lubricate the seals before fitting to the car as they have a protective coating when originally assembled. Remove the blanking plug from the hydraulic pipe union seat. Inject some clean hydraulic fluid into the master cylinder and operate the piston with a screwdriver several times so that the fluid spreads over all the internal working surfaces.

If the master cylinder is to be dismantled after removal proceed as follows.

1 Thoroughly clean the exterior of the master cylinder and reservoir and wipe dry with a non-fluffy rag.
2 Using a pair of circlip pliers remove the circlip from the end of the bore (Fig. 9.30).
3 The internal parts may now be removed in the followig order: plain washer, secondary cup, piston, disc (some models), main cup, and spring.
4 Examine the bore of the cylinder carefully for any signs of scores or ridges. If this is found to be smooth all over new seals can be fitted. If however, there is any doubt of the condition of the bore then a new master cylinder must be fitted.
5 If examination of the seals shows them to be apparently oversize, or swollen, or very loose on the pistons, suspect oil contamination in the system. Oil will swell these rubber seals and if one is found to be swollen it is reasonable to assume that all seals in the braking system will need attention.
6 Thoroughly clean all parts in clean hydraulic fluid or methylated spirits. Ensure that the ports are clear.
7 All components should be assembled wet after dipping in fresh brake fluid.
8 Carefully fit the internal parts in the following order: spring, main cup, disc (when fitted) piston and secondary cup, and plain washer.
9 Retain the fitted parts with the circlip located in the end of the bore.
10 Check that the piston is free to move by pushing with a screwdriver and then refit to the car.

20 Master cylinder (dual circuit - Lockheed) - dismantling, examination and reassembly

1 Refer to the introduction to Section 19.
2 Thoroughly clean the exterior of the master cylinder and reservoir and wipe dry with a non-fluffy rag.
3 Using a pair of circlip pliers remove the circlip from the end of the bore. Also unscrew the stop screw located on the underside of the master cylinder (Fig. 9.31).
4 The internal parts may now be removed in the following order: plain washer, primary piston and seals, spring, shaped washer, secondary piston and seals and finally a spring.
5 Inspect the master cylinder bore and seals, as described in Section 19, paragraphs 5, 6 and 7.
6 Carefully fit the internal parts in the reverse order to removal.
7 Retain the fitted parts with the circlip located in the end of the bore.
8 Replace the stop screw and new sealing 'O' ring.
9 Check that the pistons are free to move by pushing with a screwdriver and then refit to the car.

21 Master cylinder (dual circuit-Teves) - dismantling, examination and reassembly

The overhaul sequence is basically identical to that described in Section 20, but there are minor differences in the internal parts which are apparent upon comparision of Figs. 9.31 and 9.33. Provided that care is taken no problems will arise. One point worth noting however is that a range of reservoirs can be

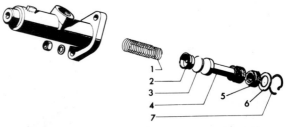

Fig 9.30 Exploded view of master cylinder (Sec 19)

1	Spring	5	Seal
2	Seal	6	Washer
3	Disc	7	Circlip
4	Piston		

Fig 9.31 Exploded view of master cylinder - (Lockheed - dual circuit) (Sec 20)

1	Sealing plug	7	Spring
2	Stop screw	8	Seal
3	Washer	9	Piston
4	Spring	10	Seal
5	Seal	11	Washer
6	Seals	12	Circlip

Fig 9.32 Selection of hydraulic fluid reservoirs fitted to Lockheed dual circuit master cylinder

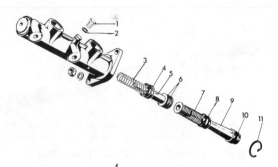

Fig 9.33 Exploded view of master cylinder - ('Teves' - dual circuit)

1	Stop screw	7	Spring
2	Washer	8	Seal
3	Spring	9	Piston
4	Seal	10	Seal
5	Piston	11	Circlip
6	Seals		

Fig 9.34 Hydraulic fluid reservoir fitted to 'Teves' dual circuit master cylinder

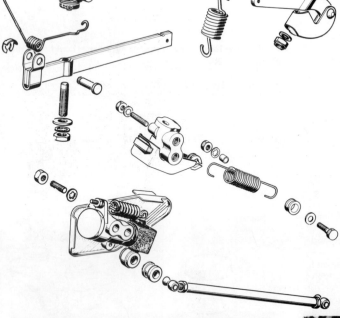

Fig 9.36 Weight hung on compensator lever

Fig 9.37 Feeler gauge inserted between adjuster screw and compensator piston

Fig 9.35 Exploded view of brake pressure regulator assembly

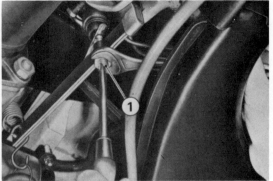

Fig 9.38 Compensator screw adjustment

1   Adjustment screw

Fig 9.39 Handbrake adjustment

1   Handbrake lever fully off
2   Control mechanism lever

fitted depending on local market requirements. These are shown in Figs. 9.32 and 9.34. For models originally fitted with a Lockheed tandem master cylinder the front and rear circuits connections must be reversed when fitting a Teves tandem master cylinder.

22 Compensator - adjustment

1 With the car on a ramp or over a pit, remove all luggage from the rear but leave the spare wheel in position. Ideally the fuel tank should be full - if not, add weight to compensate.
2 Hook an 11 lb (5 kg) weight on the upper rear extremity of the compensator lever, to the right of the existing notch (Fig. 9.36).
3 Insert a 1.4 mm (0.056 in) feeler gauge between the extremity of the adjuster screw and the compensator piston (Fig.9.37).
4 If adjustment is necessary slacken the locknut and adjust the screw until a tight sliding fit of the feeler gauge is obtained. Check that the compensator piston is pushed in completely (Fig. 9.38).
5 Tighten the locknut and remove the weight.

23 Handbrake - adjustment

1 Fully release the handbrake lever then, with the engine running, depress the footbrake pedal several times.
2 Switch off the engine.

Rear disc brake type

3 On models having a fascia-mounted handbrake lever, check that the caliper levers are in contact with the nylon pads, then adjust the nut on the cable equaliser so that the spring cup has a deflection of 0.039 to 0.056 in (1.0 to 1.5 mm). If the spring cup is worn unduly it must be renewed (photo).
4 On models having a central handbrake lever, loosen the locknuts on the ends of the cables and release the adjusting nuts until the caliper levers are just free from the nylon pads. Tighten the nuts half a turn each and retighten the locknuts; both adjusting nuts must protrude by equal amounts from the ends of the cables.

Rear drum brake type

5 Jack-up the rear of the car and support it on axle-stands.

23.3 Handbrake counter lever and control rod

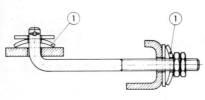
Fig 9.40 Cross section through traction rod (Sec 23)

1 Cup washers

24.1 Handbrake control cable attached to counter lever

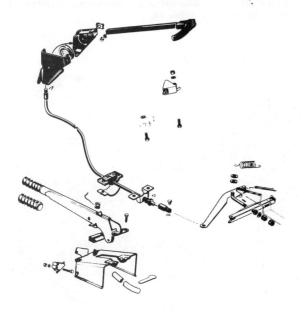
Fig 9.41 Handbrake assembly - (Saloon models)

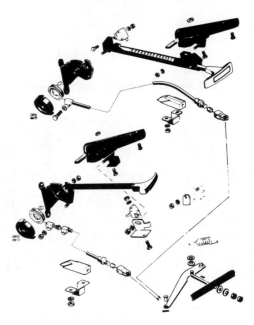
Fig 9.42 Handbrake assembly - (Cabriolet and Coupe models)

6 On models having a fascia-mounted handbrake lever, loosen the locknut on the equaliser beneath the floor. On models having a central handbrake lever, loosen the locknut on the equaliser behind the lever (inside the car).

7 Tighten the adjustment nut until the handbrake lever is fully on at 4 to 7 notches. Check that both wheels are free with the handbrake lever fully released, then tighten the locknut.

24 Handbrake primary cable - removal and replacement

1 Working under the car, disconnect the control cable yoke from its lever. (photo)

2 Remove the clamp and rubber union fixing the rear extremity of the primary outer cable to the car floor (Fig. 9.44).

3 Now working inside the car, raise the mat and underfelt from the gearbox tunnel.

4 Unclip the primary cable from under the front seat support.

5 Remove the clip that secures the plastic counter pulley protector.

6 Undo and remove the upper and lower handbrake lever case securing nuts and primary outer cable retaining collar nut (Fig. 9.45).

7 Detach the handbrake lever and case assembly from the top

and the move towards the counter pulley.

8 Remove the pulley and retaining collar from the lower support.

9 Push the handbrake lever fully into its case.

10 Unhook the cable from the lever.

11 Working under the car again pull the primary cable towards the rear through the opening in the rear floor of the car.

12 Recover the securing collar from the cable outer casing.

13 Refitting the handbrake primary cable is the reverse sequence to removal but the following additional points should be noted:

    a) *Tighten the upper and lower handbrake lever case securing nuts to a torque wrench setting of 4.5 lb f ft (0.6 kg f m).*

    b) *Tighten the outer cable retaining collar on the support to a torque wrench setting of 7.25 lb f ft (1 kg f m).*

25 Vacuum servo unit - removal and replacement

1 Slacken the clip securing the vacuum hose to the servo unit and carefully draw the hose from its union. (photo)

2 Remove the brake master cylinder as described earlier on in this Chapter.

3 Using a pair of pliers remove the spring clips in the end of the

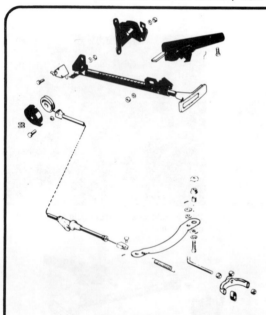

Fig 9.43 Handbrake assembly - (Utility models)

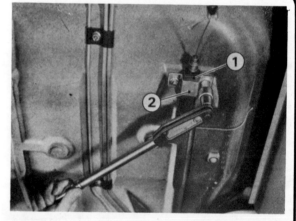

Fig 9.44 Detaching handbrake cable clamp from underside of body on Saloon models (Sec 24)

1 *Rubber seal*   2 *Clamp*

Fig 9.45 Handbrake lever and case removal (Sec 24)

1 *Collar nut*

25.1 Servo unit with vacuum hose detached

brake pedal to pushrod clevis pin. Lift away the clevis pin.

4   Undo and remove the nuts and springs washers that secure the servo unit to the bulkhead. Lift away the servo unit.

5   Refitting the servo unit is the reverse sequence to removal. It will be necessary to bleed the brake hydraulic system, as described in Section 2.

26 Vacuum servo unit - overhaul

It is very rare for a servo unit to develop an internal fault and therefore it should not need any maintenance or servicing.

However, should it develop a fault which has been confirmed after checking the vacuum hose and clips it is strongly recommended that a replacement unit be obtained and fitted. Normally these units are available on an exchange basis. No overhaul procedures are given because special tools are required and it is considered far more economical to fit a replacement unit rather than try to obtain a service kit and do the job oneself. The following two points should be noted:

a) *The unit is supplied with the master cylinder pushrod preset to a determined protrusion and this must not be altered under any circumstances.*

b) *The rod from the reaction disc must never be withdrawn because if the disc falls into the cylinder it cannot be refitted in its correct positon without dismantling.*

27 Hydraulic pipes and hoses - general

1   Periodically all brake pipes, pipe connections and unions should be carefully examined.

2   First examine for signs of leakage where the pipe unions occur. Then examine the flexible hoses for signs of chafing and fraying and, of course, leakage. This is only a preliminary part of the flexible hose inspection, as exterior condition does not necessarily indicate the interior condition, which will be considered later.

3   The steel pipes must be examined carefully and methodically. They must be cleaned off and examined for any signs of dents or other percussive damage, rust or corrosion. Rust and corrosion should be scraped off and, if the depth of pitting in the pipes is significant the pipes should be renewed. This is particularly likely in those areas underneath the car body and along the rear axle where the pipes are exposed to full force of road and weather conditions.

4   Rigid pipe removal is usually quite straightforward. The unions at each end are undone, the pipe and union pulled out, and the centre sections of the pipe removed from the body clips. The joints may sometimes be very tight. As one can only use an open-ended wrench and the unions are not large, burring of the flats is not uncommon when attempting to undo them. For this reason, a self-locking grip wrench is often the only way to unscrew a stubborn union.

5   Removal of flexible hoses is described in Section 3.

6   With the flexible hose removed, examine the internal bore. If it is blown through first, it should be possible to see through it. Any specks of rubber which come out, or signs of restriction in

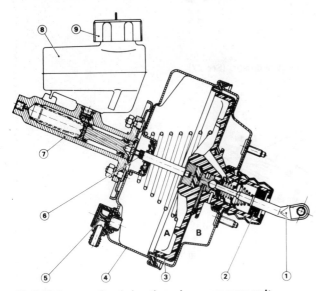

Fig 9.46 Cross sectional view through vacuum servo unit (Sec 26)

1   Pushrod
2   Air inlet filter
3   Separation diaphragm of chambers A and B of the Mastervac
  A - Chamber subhect to engine vacuum
  B - Chamber put into communication with atmospheric pressure
4   Vacuum servo unit
5   Vacuum retaining valve
6   Master cylinder pushrod
7   Master cylinder
8   Brake and clutch fluid reservoir
9   Reservoir cap with level indicator

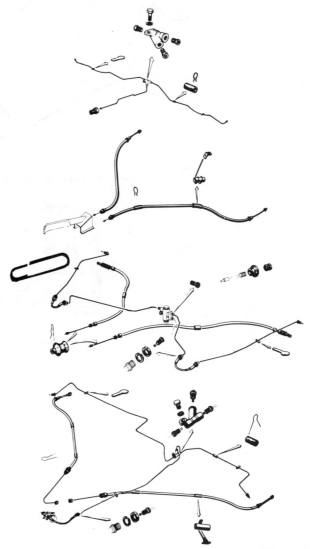

Fig 9.47 Rear brake pipes and cables (alternatives shown) (Sec 27)

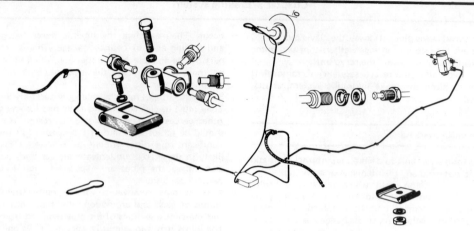

Fig 9.48 Front brake pipes and hoses (Single circuit) (Sec 27)

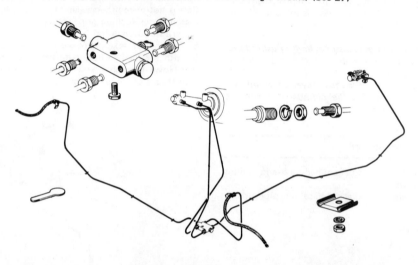

Fig 9.49 Front brake pipes and hoses (Dual circuit) (Sec 27)

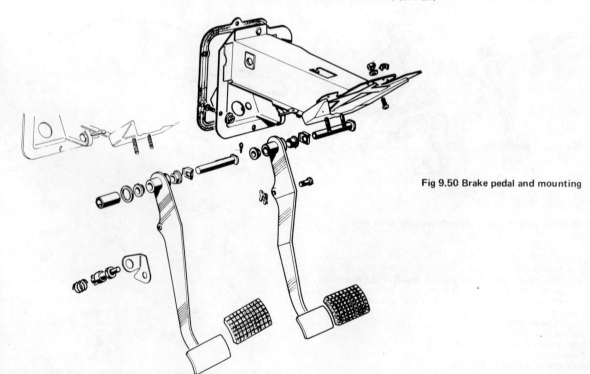

Fig 9.50 Brake pedal and mounting

the bore means that the rubber lining is breaking up and the hose must be renewed.

7 Rigid pipes which need renewal can usually be purchased from any Peugeot garage where they have the pipes, unions and special tools to make them up. All they need to know is the total length of pipe, the type of flange used at each end with the unions, and the length and thread of the union. It is a good idea to take the old pipe along as a pattern.

8 Replacement of the pipe is a straightforward reversal of the removal procedure. If the rigid pipes have been made up it is best to get all the bends in them before trying to install them. Also if there are any acute bends ask your supplier to put these in for you on a special tube bender - otherwise you may kink the pipe and thereby decrease the bore area and fluid flow.

9 With the pipes replaced it will be necessary to bleed the brake hydraulic system, as described in Section 2.

28 Fault diagnosis - braking system

Before diagnosing faults from the following chart, check that any braking irregularities are not caused by:

1 Uneven and incorrect tyre pressures
2 Incorrect 'mix' of radial and crossply tyres
3 Wear in the steering mechanism
4 Defects in the suspension
5 Misalignment of the chassis

Symptoms	Reason/s	Remedy
Pedal travels a long way before the brakes operate	Brake shoes set too far from the drums	Adjust the brake shoes to the drums.
Stopping ability poor, even though pedal pressure is firm	Linings and/or drums badly worn or scored	Dismantle, inspect and renew as required.
	One or more wheel hydraulic cylinders seized, resulting in some brake shoes not pressing against the drums	Dismantle and inspect wheel cylinders. Renew as necessary.
	Brake linings contaminated with oil	Renew linings and repair source of oil contamination.
	Wrong type of linings fitted (too hard)	Verify type of material which is correct for the car, and fit it.
	Brake shoes wrongly assembled	Check for correct assembly.
Car veers to one side when the brakes are applied	Brake linings on one side are contaminated with oil	Renew linings and stop oil leak.
	Hydraulic wheel cylinder(s) on one side partially or fully seized	Inspect wheel cylinders for correct operation and renew as necessary.
	A mixture of lining materials fitted between sides	Standardise on types of linings fitted.
	Unequal wear between sides caused by partially seized wheel cylinders	Check wheel cylinders and renew linings and drums as required.
Pedal feels 'spongy' when the brakes are applied	Air is present in the hydraulic system	Bleed the hydraulic system and check for any signs of leakage.
Pedal feels 'springy' when the brakes are applied	Brake linings not bedded into the drums (after fitting new ones)	Allow time for new linings to bed in after which it will certainly be necessary to adjust the shoes to the drums as pedal travel will have increased.
	Master cylinder or brake backplate mounting bolts loose	Retighten mounting bolts
	Severe wear in brake drums causing distortion when brakes are applied	Renew drums and linings.
Pedal travels right down with little or no resistance and brakes are virtually non-operative	Leak in hydraulic systems resulting in lack of pressure for operating wheel cylinders	Examine the whole of the hydraulic system and locate and repair source of leaks. Test after repairing each and every leak source.
	If no signs of leakage are apparent all the master cylinder internal seals are failing to sustain pressure	Overhaul master cylinder. If indications are that seals have failed for reasons other than wear all the wheel cylinder seals should be checked also and the system completly replenished with the correct fluid.
Binding, juddering, overheating	One or a combination of causes given in the foregoing sections	Complete and systematic inspection of the whole braking system.

Chapter 10 Electrical system

For modifications, and information applicable to later models, see Supplement at end of manual

Contents

Specifications

Battery

Type	Lead Acid
Earthed terminal	Negative (— ve)
Capacity	40, 45, 55 amp/hr depending on model and specification

Starter motor

Type	Ducellier 6.189A or Paris-Rhone D 8E. 76. Solenoid operated
Rotation (from driving end)	Clockwise
Average torque at 1000 rpm	0.72 kg f m
Current consumption (average torque)	280 amps

Alternator

Type	Ducellier 7529, 7556A or 7556B Paris-Rhone A 13 M 3, A 13R15 A13 R95 or A13 R120, SEV-Motorola A 14/30
Voltage	14
Rating	370W - 500 depending on type fitted
Rectification	Silicone diodes
Maximum speed	12,000 rpm

Regulator

Type	Ducellier 8364, 8349A or 8362A Paris-Rhone AYB 21, or AYA 21 SEV - Marchal VR 14

Windscreen wiper

Type	Bosch or SEV-Marchal
Number of speeds	2

Bulbs

Headlights	45/40W
Flashers	21W
Stop	21W
Reverse lights	21W
Panel lights	4W
Warning lights	2W
Interior lights	4W (Festoon Type)
Parking lights	14V. 0.25A

Fuses

Number of fuses	4 or 5 depending on model - see text

Torque wrench settings

	lb f ft	kg f m
Alternator pulley nut	29	4
Starter motor securing bolts	14	2

1 General description

The electrical system is of the 12 volt negative earth type and the major components comprise a 12 volt battery of which the negative terminal is earthed, an alternator which is driven from the crankshaft pulley, and a starter motor.

The battery supplies a steady amount of current for the ignition, lighting and other electrical circuits and provides a reserve of electricity when the current consumed by the electrical equipment exceeds that being produced by the alternator.

The alternator has its own integral regulator which ensures a high output if the battery is in a low state of charge or the demand from the electrical equipment is high, and a low output if the battery is fully charged and there is little demand for the electrical equipment.

When fitting electrical accessories to cars with a negative earth system it is important, if they contain silicone diodes or transistors, that they are connected correctly, otherwise serious damage may result to the components concerned. Items such as radios, tape recorders, electronic ignition systems, electronic tachometer, automatic dipping etc, should all be checked for correct polarity.

It is important that the battery positive lead is always disconnected if the battery is to be boost charged; also if body repairs are to be carried out using electric arc welding equipment the alternator must be disconnected otherwise serious damage can be caused to the more delicate instruments. Whenever the battery has to be disconnected it must always be reconnected with the negative terminal earthed.

2 Battery - removal and replacement

1 The battery is on a carrier fitted to the left-hand wing valance of the engine compartment. It should be removed once every three months for cleaning and testing. Disconnect the negative and then the positive leads from the battery terminals by undoing and removing the terminal nuts and bolts. Note that two cables are attached to the positive terminal.

2 Release the battery clamp and carefully lift the battery from its carrier and hold it vertically to ensure that none of the electrolyte is spilled.

3 Replacement is a direct reversal of this procedure. **Note:** Replace the positive lead before the negative lead and smear the terminals with the vaseline to prevent corrosion. **Never** use an ordinary grease.

3 Battery - maintenance and inspection

1 Normal weekly battery maintenance consists of checking the electrolyte level of each cell to ensure that the separators are covered by ¼ inch (6 mm) of electrolyte. If the level has fallen, top up the battery using distilled water only. Do not overfill. If a battery is overfilled or any electrolyte spilled, immediately wipe away the excess as electrolyte attacks and corrodes any metal it comes into contact with very rapidly.

2 If the battery has the Auto-fil device as fitted on original production of the car, a special topping up sequence is required. The white balls in the Auto-fil battery are part of the automatic topping up device which ensures correct electrolyte level. The vent chamber should remain in position at all times except when topping up or taking specific gravity readings. If the electrolyte level in any of the cells is below the bottom of the filling tube top-up as follows:

a) Lift off the vent chamber cover.

b) With the battery level, pour distilled water into the trough until all the filling tubes and trough are full.

c) Immediately replace the cover to allow the water in the trough and tubes to flow into the cells. Each cell will automatically receive the correct amount of water.

3 As well as keeping the terminals clean and covered with petroleum jelly, the top of the battery, and especially the top of the cells, should be kept clean and dry. This helps prevent corrosion and ensures that the battery does not become partially discharged by leakage through dampness and dirt.

4 Once every three months remove the battery and inspect the battery securing bolts, the battery clamp plate, tray and battery leads for corrosion (white fluffy deposits on the metal which are brittle to touch). If any corrosion is found clean off the deposit with ammonia and paint over the clean metal with an anti-rust anti-acid paint.

5 At the same time inspect the battery case for cracks. If a crack is found, clean and plug it with one of the proprietary compounds marketed by such firms as Holts for this purpose. If leakage through the crack has been excessive then it will be necessary to refill the appropriate cell with fresh electrolyte as detailed later. Cracks are frequently caused to the top of the battery case by pouring in distilled water in the middle of winter *after* instead of *before* a run. This gives the water no chance to mix with the electrolyte and so the former freezes and splits the battery case.

6 If topping-up the battery becomes excessive and the case has been inspected for cracks that could cause leakage, but none are found, the battery is being overcharged and the voltage regulator will have to be checked and reset.

7 With the battery on the bench at the three monthly interval check, measure the specific gravity with a hydrometer to determine the state of charge and condition of the electrolyte. There should be very little variation between the different cells and, if a variation in excess of 0.025 is present is will be due to either:

a) Loss of electrolyte from the battery at some time caused by spillage or a leak, resulting in a drop in the specific gravity of the electrolyte when the deficiency was replaced with distilled water instead of fresh electrolyte.

b) An internal short circuit caused by buckling of the plate or similar malady pointing to the likelihood of total battery failure in the near future.

8 The specific gravity of the electrolyte for fully charged conditions, at the electrolyte temperature indicated, is listed in Table A. The specific gravity of fully discharged battery at different temperatures of the electrolyte is given in Table B.

TABLE A — Specific gravity - battery fully charged

1.268 at 100° F or 38° C electrolyte temperature
1.272 at 90° F or 32° C   "   "
1.276 at 80° F or 27° C   "   "
1.280 at 70° F or 21° C   "   "
1.284 at 60° F or 16° C   "   "
1.288 at 50° F or 10° C   "   "
1.292 at 40° F or 4° C   "   "
1.296 at 30° F or -1.5° C   "   "

TABLE B — Specific gravity - battery fully discharged

1.098 at 100° F or 38° C electrolyte temperature
1.102 at 90° F or 32° C   "   "
1.106 at 80° F or 27° C   "   "
1.110 at 70° F or 21° C   "   "
1.114 at 60° F or 16° C   "   "
1.118 at 50° F or 10° C   "   "
1.122 at 40° F or 4° C   "   "
1.126 at 30° F or -1.5° C   "   "

4 Battery - electrolyte replenishment

1 If the battery is in a fully charged state and one of the cells maintains a specific gravity reading which is 0.025 or more lower than the others and a check of each cell has been made with a voltage meter to check for short circuits (a four to seven second test should give a steady reading of between 1.2 and 1.8 volts), then it is likely that electrolyte has been lost from the cell with the low reading at some time.

2 Top the cell up with a solution of 1 part sulphuric acid to 2.5 parts of water. If the cell is already fully topped up draw some electrolyte out of it with a pipette.

3 When mixing the sulphuric acid and water **never add water to sulphuric acid** — always pour the acid slowly onto the water in a glass container. **If water is added to sulphuric acid it will explode.**

4 Continue to top-up the cell with the freshly made electrolyte and then recharge the battery and check the hydrometer readings.

5 Battery - charging

1 In winter time when heavy demand is placed upon the battery, such as when starting from cold and much electrical

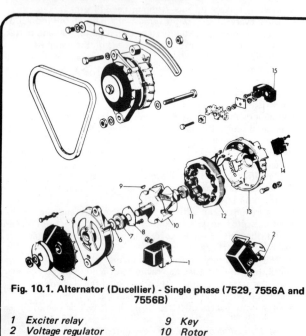

Fig. 10.1. Alternator (Ducellier) - Single phase (7529, 7556A and 7556B)

1 Exciter relay	9 Key
2 Voltage regulator	10 Rotor
3 Pulley	11 Bearing - rear
4 Fan	12 Stator
5 Front housing	13 Rear housing
6 Washer	14 Brush holder
7 Bearing - front	15 Cover
8 End plate	

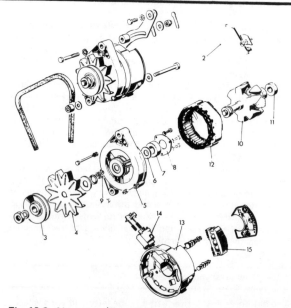

Fig. 10.2. Alternator (Ducellier) - Three phase (for caption see Fig. 10.1)

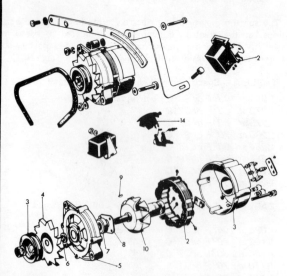

Fig. 10.3. Alternator (Paris-Rhone) - Single phase (for caption see Fig. 10.1)

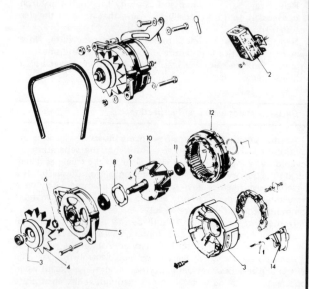

Fig. 10.4. Alternator (Paris-Rhone) - Three phase (for caption see Fig. 10.1)

equipment is continually in use, it is a good idea to occasionally have the battery fully charged from an external source at the rate of 3.5 to 4 amps.

2 Continue to charge the battery at this rate until no further rise in specific gravity is noted over a four hour period.

3 Alternatively, a trickle charger charging at the rate of 1.5 amps can be safety used overnight.

4 Specially rapid 'boost' charges which are claimed to restore the power of the battery in 1 to 2 hours are most dangeous as they can cause serious damage to the battery plates through overheating.

5 While charging the battery note that the temperature of the electrolyte should never exceed 100°F (37.8°C)

6 Alternator - general description

All models covered by this manual are fitted with alternators. The alternator generates alternating current (AC) which is rectified by diodes into direct current (DC) and is the current needed for charging the battery.

The main advantage of the alternator lies in its ability to provide a high charge at low revolutions. Driving slowly in heavy traffic with a dynamo invariably means no charge is reaching the battery. In similar conditions even with the heater, wiper, lights and perhaps radio switched on the alternator will ensure a charge reaches the battery.

The alternator is of the rotating field ventilated design and comprises principally a laminated stator on which is wound the output winding; a rotor carrying the field windings - each end of the rotor shaft runs in ball race bearings which are lubricated for life.

The rotor is belt driven from the engine through a pulley keyed to the rotor shaft. A fan adjacent to the pulley draws air through the unit. This fan forms an integral part of the alternator specification. It has been designed to provide adequate airflow with minimum noise, and to withstand the high stresses associated with the maximum speed. Rotation is clockwise when viewed from the drive end.

7 Alternator - maintenance

1 The equipment has been designed for the minimum amount of maintenance in service, the only items subject to wear being the bushes, and bearings.

2 Bushes should be examined after about 75,000 miles (120,000 km) and renewed if necessary. The bearings are pre-packed with grease for life, and should not require further attention.

3 Regularly check the fan belt tension and if slack adjust as described in Chapter 2.

8 Alternator - special procedures

Whenever the electrical system of the car is being attended to, or external means of starting the engine is used, there are certain precautions that must be taken otherwise serious and expensive damage can result.

1 Always make sure that the negative terminal of the battery is earthed. If the terminal connections are accidentally reversed or if the battery has been reverse charged the alternator diodes will burn out.

2 The output terminal on the alternator marked 'BAT' or B+ must never be earthed but should always be connected directly to the positive terminal of the battery.

3 Whenever the alternator is to be removed or when disconnecting the terminals of the alternator circuit always disconnect the battery earth terminal first.

4 The alternator must never be operated without the battery to alternator cable connected.

5 If the battery is to be charged by external means always disconnect both battery cables before the external charge is connected.

6 Should it be necessary to use a booster charger or booster battery to start the engine always double check that the negative cable is connected to negative terminal and the positive cable to positive terminal.

9 Alternator - removal and refitting

1 Disconnect the battery leads.

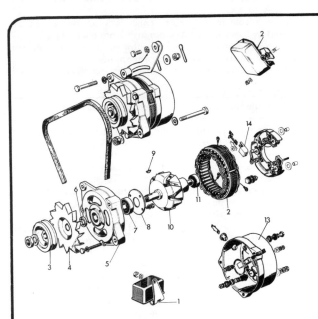

Fig. 10.5. Alternator (Paris-Rhone) - Three phase - alternative (for caption see Fig. 10.1)

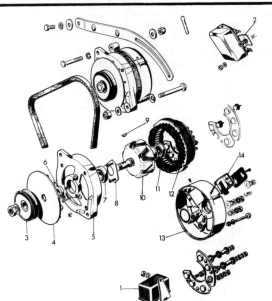

Fig. 10.6. Alternator (SEV) - Three phase (for caption see Fig. 10.1)

2 Note the terminal connections at the rear of the alternator and disconnect the plug, multi-pin connector or terminals. (photo)

3 Undo and remove the alternator adjustment arm bolt, slacken the alternator mounting bolts and push the alternator inwards towards the engine. Lift away the fan belt from the pulley.

4 Remove the remaining two mounting bolts and carefully lift the alternator away from the car.

5 Take care not to knock or drop the alternator otherwise this can cause irreparable damage.

6 Refitting the alternator is the reverse sequence to removal.

10 Alternator - fault diagnosis and repair

Due to the specialist knowledge and equipment required to test or service an alternator it is recommended that if the performance is suspect, the car be taken to an automobile electrician who will have the facilities for such work. Because of this recommendation, information is limited to the inspection and renewal of the brushes. Should the alternator not charge or the system be suspect the following points may be checked before seeking further assistance:

1 Check the fan belt tension, as described in Chapter 2.
2 Check the battery, as described in Section 3.
3 Check all electrical cable connections for cleanliness and security.

11 Starter motor - general description

The starter motor is of the pre-engaged type with a series parallel wound four pole, four brush motor fitted with a pre-engagement solenoid. Incorporated in the pinion assembly is a roller clutch which is able to transmit torque from the starter motor to the engine but not in the reverse direction thereby ensuring that the armature is not driven by the engine at any time.

The solenoid comprises a soft iron plunger, starter switch contacts, main closing winding (series winding) and a hold on winding (short winding). When the starter/ignition switch is operated both the coils are energised in parallel but the closing winding is shorted out by the starter switch contacts when they are closed.

12 Starter motor - testing on engine

1 If the starter motor fails to turn the engine when the switch is operated there are four possible reasons why:

a) The battery is discharged or faulty.
b) The electrical connections between switch, solenoid, battery and starter motor are somewhere failing to pass the necessary current from the battery, through the starter to earth.
c) The solenoid has an internal fault.
d) The starter motor is either jammed or electrically defective.

2 To check the battery, switch on the headlights. If they go dim after a few seconds the battery is discharged. If the lamps glow brightly next operate the ignition/starter switch and see what happens to the lights. If they do dim it is indicative that power is reaching the starter motor but failing to turn it. Therefore check that it is not jammed by placing the car in gear and rocking it to-and-fro. If it is not jammed the starter will have to be removed for examination. If the starter should turn very slowly go on to the next check.

3 If, when the ignition/starter switch is operated the lights stay bright, then the power is not reaching the starter motor. Check all connections from the battery to solenoid for cleanliness and tightness. With a good battery fitted this is the most usual cause of starter motor problems. Check that the earth cable between

9.2 Alternator with cables detached

the engine and chassis is also intact and cleanly connected. This can sometimes be overlooked when the engine is taken out.

4 If no results have yet been achieved turn off the headlights, otherwise the battery will soon be discharged. It may be possible that a clicking noise was heard each time the ignition/starter switch was operated. This is the solenoid switch operating but it does not necessarily follow that the main contact is closing properly. (If no clicking has been heard from the solenoid it is certainly defective). The solenoid contact can be checked by putting a voltmeter or bulb across the main cable connection on the starter side of the solenoid and earth. When the switch is operated there should be a reading or a lighted bulb. If not the switch has a fault.

13 Starter motor - removal and replacement

1 Disconnect the battery positive and negative leads from the terminals.

2 Make a note of the cable connections to the rear of the solenoid and detach the cable terminals from the solenoid.

3 Undo and remove the starter motor securing nuts, bolts and spring washers and lift away the starter motor.

4 Refitting the starter motor is the reverse sequence to removal.

14 Starter motor - dismantling, overhaul and reassembly

1 Such is the inherent reliability of the starter motor it is unlikely that a motor will ever need dismantling until it is totally worn out and in need of replacement. It is not a task for the home mechanic because although reasonably easy to undertake, the reassembly and adjustment before refitting is beyond his scope because of the need for specialist equipment. It would under all circumstances be realistic for the work to be undertaken by the specialist auto-electrician.

2 For the more ambitious, exploded diagrams of the range of starter motors fitted are supplied. (Figs. 10.7 to 10.10).

15 Starter motor drive pinion - inspection and repair

1 Persistent jamming or reluctance to disengage may mean that the starter pinion assembly needs attention. The starter motor should be removed first of all for inspection.

2 With the starter motor removed thoroughly remove all grime and grease with a petrol soaked rag, taking care to stop any

liquid running into the motor itself. If there was a lot of dirt this could be the trouble and all will now be well. The pinion should move freely in a spiral movement along the shaft against the light spring and return easily on being released. To do this the spiral splines should be completely clean and free of oil (oil merely collects dust and grime and gums up the splines). The spring should be intact.

3 If the preceding cleaning and check does not actually remove

the fault the starter motor will need to be stripped down to its component parts and a further check made. This, as has been explained in the preceding Section, is really beyond the scope of the home mechanic and should be left to the professional auto-electrician. Removal of the pinion itself from the armature is not difficult but requires skill and special tools to replace. If it is thought that the starter motor needs further inspection take it to the auto-electrician.

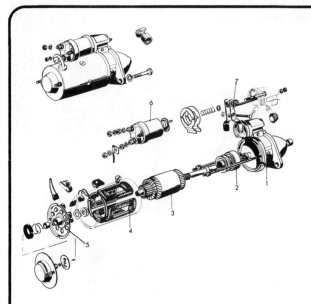

Fig. 10.7. Starter motor (Ducellier) - standard fitment

1	Drive end housing	5	Brush end plate
2	Starter drive	6	Solenoid
3	Armature	7	Actuating lever
4	Field coils		

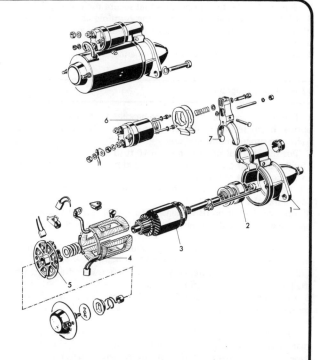

Fig. 10.8. Starter motor (Ducellier) - cold climate fitment (for caption see Fig. 10.7)

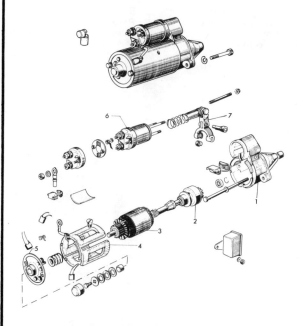

Fig. 10.9. Starter motor (Paris-Rhone) - Standard fitment (for caption see Fig. 10.7)

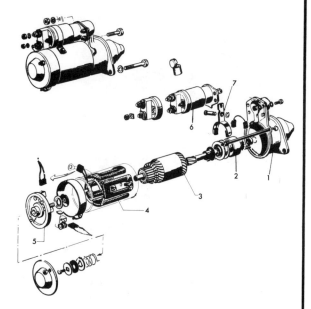

Fig. 10.10. Starter motor (Paris-Rhone) - Cold climate fitment (for caption see Fig. 10.7)

16 Headlight bulb - removal and replacement

1   It will be seen from Figs. 10.11, 10.12 and 10.13 that several types of headlight units have been fitted. In most cases access to the bulb is from the rear with the exception of those cars fitted with quartz-halogen bulbs when the light unit must be drawn forwards first to gain access to the terminal connection and bulb (Fig. 10.13).
2   Swing back the two spring clips that secure the bulb. (photo)
3   Withdraw the bulb and detach the terminal connector from it. (photo) Note the type of bulb fitted and replace it with one of the same type.
4   Refitting the bulb is the reverse sequence to removal.

17 Headlight - alignment

1   It is always advisable to have the headlights aligned on proper optical beam setting equipment but if this is not available the following procedure may be used.
2   Position the car on level ground 10 ft (3.048 metres) in front of a dark wall or board. The wall or board must be at right angles to the centreline of the car.
3   Draw a vertical line on the board or wall in line with the centreline of the car.
4   Bounce the car on its suspension to ensure correct settlement and then measure the height between the ground and the centre of the headlights.
5   Draw a horizontal line across the board or wall at this measured height. On this horizontal line mark a cross on either side of the vertical centreline the distance between the centre of the light unit and the centre of the car.
6   On models with quartz-halogen bulbs remove the rim securing screw and lift away each rim. The two adjuster screws are not visible on the rim.
7   With the remaining light units two adjusters are located at the rear of each unit. One at the top for vertical movement and the other halfway down the rim of the radiator side. This is for horizontal adjustment, see Fig. 10.14.

8   Switch the headlights onto full beam.
9   By careful adjusting of the horizontal and vertical adjusting screws on each light, align the centres of each beam onto the crosses which were previously marked on the horizontal line.
10 Bounce the car on its suspension again and check that the beams return to the correct positions. At the same time check the operation of the dip switch. Replace the headlight rims if removed.
11 Refer to Chapter 13 for details of beam height compensation for vehicle loading.

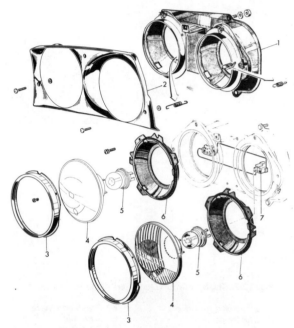

Fig. 10.12. Twin headlight unit assembly - Export (Saloon and utility vehicles)

1	Light unit body	5	Bulb
2	Outer rim assembly	6	Reflector mounting housing
3	Rim	7	Multi-pin connector assembly
4	Reflector		

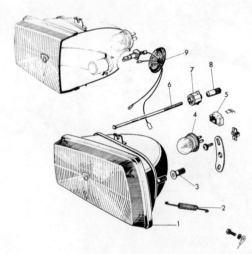

Fig. 10.11. Headlight assembly (Saloon and utility vehicles)

1	Light unit (complete)	6	Adjuster rod
2	Spring	7	Adjuster control
3	Adjuster screw - horizontal beam	8	Knob
4	Bulb	9	Parking light bulb and socket
5	Multi-pin plug		

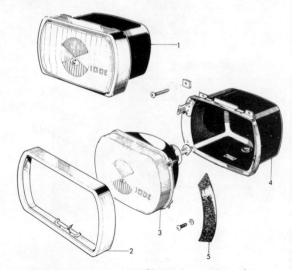

Fig. 10.13. Headlight unit (Cabriolet and Coupe)

1	Light unit (complete)	4	Light unit body
2	Rim	5	Gasket
3	Reflector assembly		

16.2 Headlight bulb retaining clips

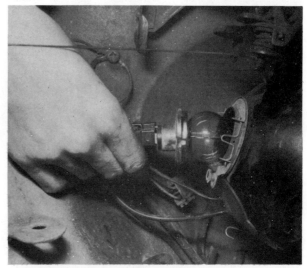

16.3 Headlight bulb removal

Fig. 10.14 Headlight beam adjusters - later type (Sec 17)

1	Vehicle load compensator	5	Horizontal adjuster
4	Vertical adjuster		

---

18 Front parking and direction indicator lights

The assembly fitted to the models covered by this manual is shown in Figs. 10.15 and 10.16.

Bulb renewal
1 To renew a light bulb it is not necessary to remove the light body.
2 Undo and remove the two screws securing the lens to the light body. Lift away the lens and gasket. (photo)
3 Depress the bulb and turn anti-clockwise to release the bayonet fitting. Withdraw the bulb.
4 Refitting the bulb and lens is the reverse sequence to removal.

Light body - removal and replacement
Saloon and Utility models
1 Undo and remove the two screws securing the lens to the light body. Lift away the lens and gasket.
2 Detach the two electric cables from the terminal connectors.
3 Carefully ease the light body forwards from its aperture. Recover the gasket. (photo)
4 Refitting the light body is the reverse sequence to removal.

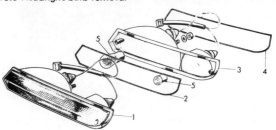

Fig. 10.15. Front light assembly (Saloon and utility vehicles)

1	Light unit (complete).	4	Gasket
2	Gasket	5	Bulb
3	Light unit body		

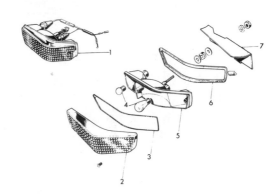

Fig. 10.16. Front light assembly (Cabriolet and Coupe)

1	Light unit complete	5	Light unit body
2	Lens	6	Gasket
3	Gasket	7	Shield
4	Bulb		

Cabriolet and Coupe models
1 Detach the two electric cables from the terminal connectors.
2 Undo and remove the two screws securing the lens to the light body. Lift away the lens and gasket.
3 Undo and remove the nut and washer securing the protector to the rear of the light body. Lift away the protector.
4 Undo and remove the second nut and washer from the stud at the rear of the light body.
5 Carefully ease the light body forwards from its aperture. Recover the gasket.
6 Refitting the light body is the reverse sequence to removal.

18.a2 Removal of lens exposing bulbs

18.b3 Removal of light body

19.1 Removal of rear light cluster lens

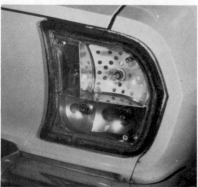

19.2 Four bulbs are used in the rear cluster

20.1 Rear number plate light location

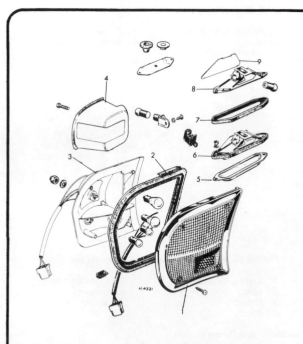

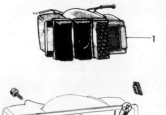

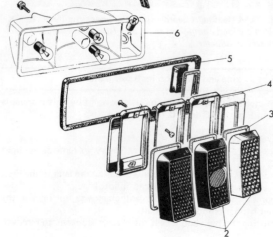

Fig. 10.17. Rear light cluster and number plate light assembly (Saloon)

Rear light cluster	Rear number plate light
1 Lens	5 Lens
2 Gasket	6 Body
3 Body	7 Gasket
4 Cover	8 Body
	9 Lens

Fig. 10.18. Rear light cluster assembly (Cabriolet and Coupe)

1 Light unit (complete)	4 Trim
2 Lens	5 Gasket
3 Gasket	6 Light body

19 Rear light cluster - removal and replacement

The assembly fitted to models covered by this manual are shown in Figs. 10.17, 10.18 and 10.19.

Bulb renewal
1 Undo and remove the screws that secure the lens assembly to the light body. Lift away the lens and gasket. (photo)
2 Depress the relevant bulb and turn anticlockwise to release the bayonet fitting. Withdraw the bulb. (photo)
3 Refitting the bulb and lens is the reverse sequence to removal.

Light body - removal and replacement
1 Detach the electric cables from the terminal connectors located inside the luggage compartment.
2 **Saloon models:** Undo and remove the nut and washer securing the light body and draw away from its aperture.
3 **Other models:** Undo and remove the screws securing the light body and draw away from its aperture.
4 Refitting the light body is the reverse sequence to removal.

20 Rear number plate light - removal and replacement

Bulb renewal
All models except Utility, Cabriolet and Coupe
1 Working inside the rear of the car detach the transparent covers and depress the bulb and turn anticlockwise to release the bayonet fitting. Withdraw the bulb. (photo)
2 Refitting the bulb is the reverse sequence to removal.
Utility models
1 Undo and remove the two screws securing the lens to the light body. Lift away the lens and gasket.
2 Depress the bulb and turn anticlockwise to release the bayonet fitting. Withdraw the bulb.
3 Refitting the bulb is the reverse sequence to removal.
Cabriolet and Coupe models
The rear number plate light is incorporated in the innermost end of each rear light cluster. Refer to Section 19, for full relevant information.

Light body - removal and replacement
All models except Utility, Cabriolet and Coupe
1 Working inside the rear of the car, detach the electric cables from the wiring harness.
2 Undo and remove the two securing nuts and washers. Lift away the light body.
3 Refitting the light body is the reverse sequence to removal.
Utility models
1 Undo and remove the nuts, washers and bolts securing the light body to the rear panel.
2 Detach the electric cables from the wiring harness and lift away the light body.
3 Refitting the light body is the reverse sequence to removal.
Cabriolet and Coupe models
The rear number plate light is incorporated in the innermost end of each rear light cluster. Refer to Section 19 for full relevant information.

21 Windscreen wiper blades - removal and replacement

1 To remove a windscreen wipe blade depress the tab and pull the blade from the arm.
2 Refitting the windscreen wiper blade is the reverse sequence to removal.

22 Windscreen wiper arms - removal and replacement

1 Before removing a wiper arm, turn the windscreen wiper switch on and off to ensure the arms are in their normal parked

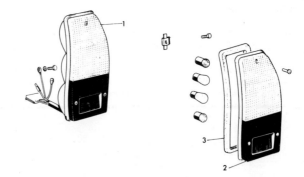

Fig. 10.19. Rear light cluster assembly (Utility vehicles)

1 Light unit (complete)   3 Gasket
2 Lens

Fig. 10.20. Number plate light assembly (Utility vehicles)

1 Lens cover   4 Bezel
2 Gasket   5 Lens
3 Bulb holder

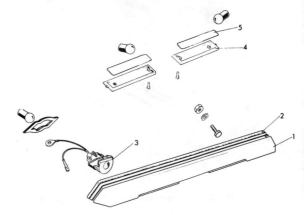

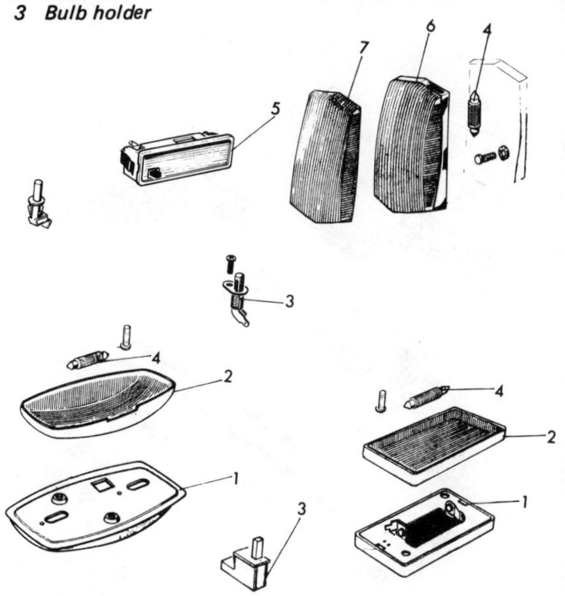

Fig. 10.21. Interior light assemblies

1 Light body   5 Light assembly (complete)
2 Lens   6 Light assembly (complete)
3 Switch   7 Lens
4 'Festoon' bulb

position with the blades parallel with the bottom of the windscreen.

2 To remove the arm, pivot the arm back and pull the wiper
arm head off the splined drive, at the same time easing back the
clip with a screwdriver.

3 When replacing an arm, place it so it is in the correct relative
parked position and then press the arm head onto the splined
drive until the retaining clip clicks into place.

23 Windscreen wiper mechanism - fault diagnosis and rectification

1 Should the windscreen wipers fail, or work very slowly, then
check the terminal connectors for security and make sure the
insulation of all the wiring is not damaged so causing a short
circuit. If this is in order then check the current the motor is
taking by connecting an ammeter in the circuit and turning on

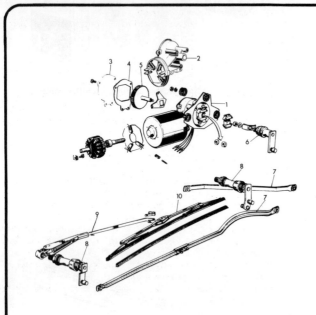

Fig. 10.22. Windscreen wiper assembly (Bosch 2 speed)

1	Motor and gearbox	6	Arm assembly
2	Gearbox housing	7	Operating links
3	End cover	8	Wiper arm spindle and
4	Gasket		housing
5	Gearwheel	9	Wiper arm
		10	Wiper blade

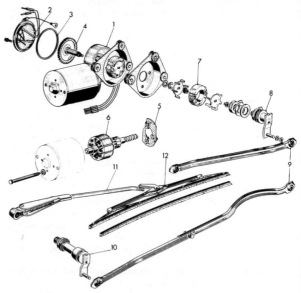

Fig. 10.23. Windscreen wiper assembly (Ducellier 2 speed)

1	Motor and gearbox	7	Limit switch cam
2	End cover	8	Arm assembly
3	Gasket	9	Operating links
4	Gearwheel	10	Wiper arm spindle and
5	Brush holder		housing
6	Armature	11	Wiper arm
		12	Wiper blade

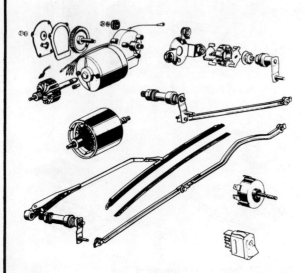

Fig. 10.24. Windscreen wiper assembly (SEV) (For caption see
Fig. 10.23)

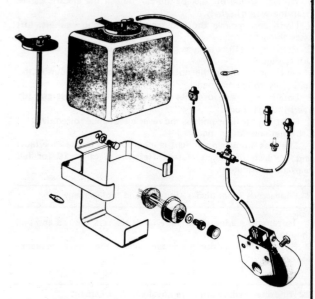

Fig. 10.25. Windscreen washer (Manual control)

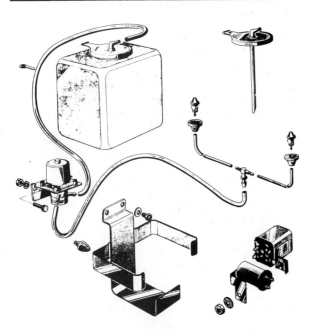

Fig. 10.26. Windscreen washer (Electric control)

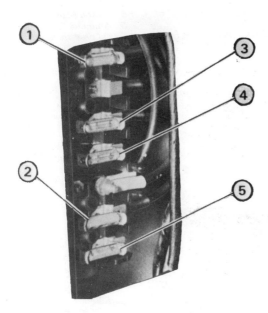

Fig. 10.27. Fuse block (Early models also family Saloon and Estate) (For caption see text)

the wiper switch. Consumption should be between 2 and 3 amps.

2 If no current is passing through the motor, check that the switch is operating correctly.

3 If the wiper motor takes a very high current check the wiper blades for freedom of movement. If this is satisfactory check the gearbox cover or linkage for damage.

4 If the wiper motor takes a very low current ensure that the battery is fully charged. Check the brush gear and ensure the brushes are bearing on the commutator. If not, check the brushes for freedom of movement and, if necessary, renew the tension springs. If the bushes are very worn they should be replaced with new ones. Check the armature by substitution if this part is suspect.

24 Horn - fault diagnosis and rectification

1 If the horn works badly or fails completely check the wiring leading to the horn. Make sure that all connections are clean and secure.

2 Using a test light check that current is reaching the horn and then ensure that the horn switch is operating correctly.

3 Check that the horn is secure on its mounting and that there is nothing lying on the horn body.

4 If all appears to be well test the horn and circuit by substitution.

25 Direction indicator light circuit - fault diagnosis and rectification

Should the flasher unit fail to operate, or work very slowly or rapidly, check out the circuit as detailed below before assuming that there is a fault in the unit.

a) *Examine the direction indicator light bulbs both front and rear, for broken filaments.*

b) *If the external flashers are working, but either of the internal flasher warning lights have ceased to function, check the filaments in the warning light bulb and replace with a new bulb if necessary.*

c) *If a flasher bulb is sound but does not work check all the flasher circuit connections with the aid of the relevant wiring diagram at the end of the Chapter.*

d) *With the ignition switched on check that the correct voltage is reaching the flasher unit.*

e) *Should all appear to be well then check the flasher unit by substitution.*

26 Fuses

The fuse box is located on the left-hand side of the dashboard. **Do not** renew a blown fuse until the cause is found and rectified. The circuits protected are as follows:

Early models (to approx 1971)

Fuse	Rating	Circuit
1 (Top)	5 amp	*Front and rear side lights* *Instrument panel lights* *Rear number plate light*
2	10 amp	*Horns* *Cigarette lighter* *Electric clock* *Interior lights* *Boot lights* *Parking lights*
3	10 amp	*Self-disengaging fan* *Stop lights* *Reverse lights* *Electric fuel pump (Fuel injection models)*
4	10 amp	*Flashing indicators* *Heater motor* *Thermal voltmeter* *Water thermometer* *Fuel gauge* *Oil pressure warning light* *Brake safety light* *Choke warning light (Carburettor models)*
5	10 amp	*Windscreen wiper motor*

Later models - Family Saloon and Estate

Fuse	Rating	Circuit
1 (Top)	5 amp	Front and rear side lights
		Side light warning light
		Dashboard lights
		Heater control lights
		Number plate light
	15 amp	Horns
		Cigarette lighter
		Clock
		Interior lights
		Glovebox light
		Rear roof light
	10 amp	Reverse light
		Stop light
		Self disengaging fan
	10 amp	Flashing indicators
		Oil pressure warning light
		Water temperature gauge
		Brake warning light
		Fuel gauge
		Choke warning light (Carburettor models)
	10 amp	Windscreen wiper
		Windscreen washer pump
		Heater fan

Later models - Station Wagon

Fuse	Rating	Circuit
1 (Top)	5 amp	Sidelight warning light
		Front and rear sidelights
		Dashboard lights
		Number plate lights
2	15 amp	Horn
		Roof light
3	10 amp	Flashing indicators
		Stop lights
		Oil pressure warning light
		Brake warning light
		Water temperature gauge
		Fuel gauge
4	10 amp	Windscreen wiper
		Heater fan

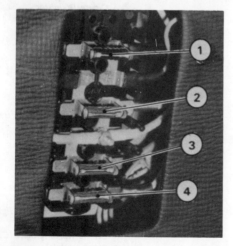

Fig. 10.28. Fuse block (Station wagon) (For caption see text)

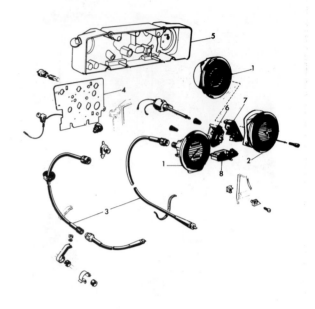

Fig. 10.29. Instrument cluster (Some Saloon models, family car and Estate)

1 Speedometer head
2 Clock
3 Speedometer cable (alternative also shown)
4 Printed circuit
5 Cluster housing
6 Ammeter
7 Oil pressure gauge
8 Fuel gauge

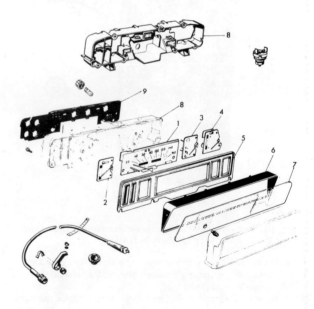

Fig. 10.30. Instrument cluster (Station wagon)

1 Speedometer head
2 Temperature gauge
3 Fuel gauge
4 Ammeter
5 Trim
6 Finisher
7 Lens
8 Cluster housing (alternative shown)
9 Printed circuit

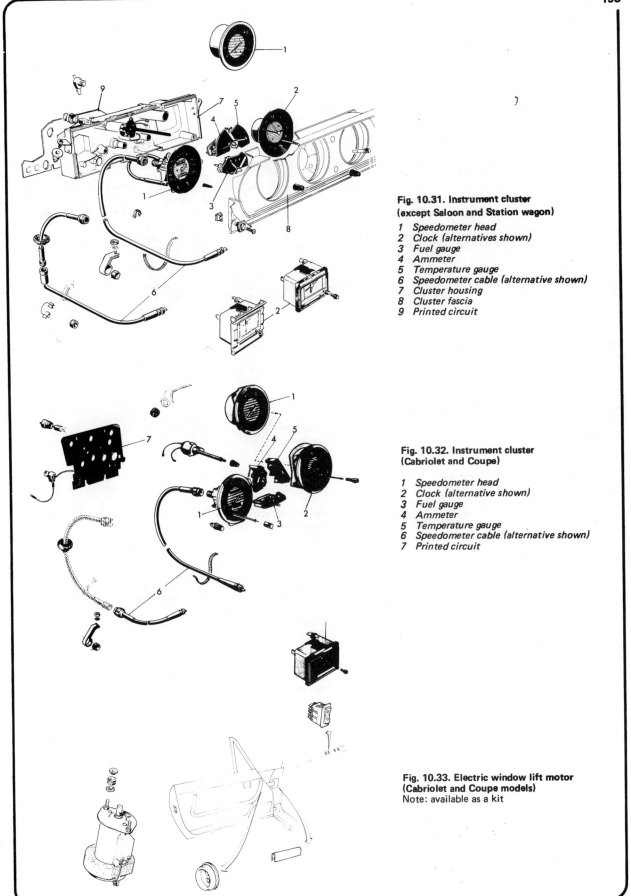

Fig. 10.31. Instrument cluster
(except Saloon and Station wagon)

1 Speedometer head
2 Clock (alternatives shown)
3 Fuel gauge
4 Ammeter
5 Temperature gauge
6 Speedometer cable (alternative shown)
7 Cluster housing
8 Cluster fascia
9 Printed circuit

Fig. 10.32. Instrument cluster
(Cabriolet and Coupe)

1 Speedometer head
2 Clock (alternative shown)
3 Fuel gauge
4 Ammeter
5 Temperature gauge
6 Speedometer cable (alternative shown)
7 Printed circuit

Fig. 10.33. Electric window lift motor
(Cabriolet and Coupe models)
Note: available as a kit

29 Fault diagnosis - electrical system

Symptom	Cause	Remedy
Starter motor fails to turn engine	Battery discharged	Charge battery.
	Battery defective internally	Fit new battery.
	Battery terminal leads loose or earth lead not securely attached to body	Check and tighten leads.
	Loose or broken connections in starter motor circuit	Check all connections and tighten any that are loose.
	Starter motor switch or solenoid faulty	Test and replace faulty components with new
	Starter motor pinion jammed in mesh with flywheel gear ring	Disengage pinion by turning squared end of armature shaft.
	Starter brushes badly worn, sticking, or brush wire loose	Examine brushes, replace as necessary, tighten down brush wires
	Commutator dirty, worn or burnt	Clean commutator, recut if badly burnt.
	Starter motor armature faulty	Overhaul starter motor, fit new armature
	Field coils earthed	Overhaul starter motor.
Starter motor turns engine very slowly	Battery in discharged condition	Charge battery
	Starter brushes badly worn, sticking, or brush wires loose	Examine brushes, replace as necessary, tighten down brush wires.
	Loose wires in starter motor circuit	Check wiring and tighten as necessary.
Starter motor operates without turning engine	Starter motor pinion sticking on the screwed sleeve	Remove starter motor, clean starter motor drive.
	Pinion or flywheel gear teeth broken or worn	Fit new gear ring to flywheel, and new pinion to starter motor drive.
Starter motor noisy or excessively rough engagement	Pinion or flywheel gear teeth broken or worn	Fit new gear teeth to flywheel, or new pinion to starter motor drive.
	Starter drive main spring broken	Dismantle and fit new main spring.
	Starter motor retaining bolts loose	Tighten starter motor securing bolts. Fit new spring washer if necessary.
Battery will not hold charge for more than a few days	Battery defective internally	Removal and fit new battery.
	Electrolyte level too low or electrolyte too weak due to leakage	Top up electrolyte level to just above plates
	Plate separators no longer fully effective	Remove and fit new battery.
	Battery plates severely sulphated	Remove and fit new battery.
	Fan/alternator belt slipping	Check belt for wear, replace if necessary, and tighten.
	Battery terminal connections loose or corroded	Check terminals for tightness, and remove all corrosion.
	Alternator not charging properly	Take car to specialist.
	Short in lighting circuit causing continual battery drain	Trace and rectify
	Regulator unit not working correctly	Take car to specialist.
Ignition light fails to go out, battery runs flat in a few days	Fan belt loose and slipping or broken	Check, replace and tighten as necessary.
	Alternator faulty	Take car to specialist.

Failure of individual electrical equipment to function correctly is dealt with alphabeitcally, item-by-item, under the headings listed below.

Fuel gauge		
Fuel gauge gives no reading	Fuel tank empty!	Fill fuel tank.
	Electric cable between tank sender unit and gauge earthed or loose	Check cable for earthing and joints for tightness.
	Fuel gauge case not earthed	Ensure case is well earthed.
	Fuel gauge supply cable interrupted	Check and replace cable if necessary.
	Fuel gauge unit broken	Replace fuel gauge.
Fuel gauge registers full all the time	Electric cable between tank unit and gauge broken or disconnected	Check over cable and repair as necessary.

Horn		
Horn operates all the time	Horn push either earthed or stuck down	Disconnect battery earth. Check and rectify source of trouble.
	Horn cable to horn push earthed	Disconnect battery earth. Check and rectify source of trouble.

Symptom	Cause	Remedy
Horn fails to operate	Blown fuse Cable or cable connection loose, broken or disconnected Horn has an internal fault	Check and renew if broken. Ascertain cause Check all connections for tightness and cables for breaks. Remove and overhaul horn.
Horn emits intermittent or unsatisfactory noise	Cable connections loose Horn incorrectly adjusted	Check and tighten all connections. Adjust horn until best note obtained.
Lights Lights do not come on	If engine not running, battery discharged Light bulb filament burnt out or bulbs broken. Wire connections loose, disconnected or broken Light switch shorting or otherwise faulty	Push-start car, charge battery Test bulbs in live bulb holder. Check all connections for tightness and wire cable for breaks. By-pass light switch to ascertain if fault is in switch and fit new switch as appropriate.
Lights come on but fade out	If engine not running battery discharged	Push-start car and charge battery (not automatics).
Lights give very poor illumination	Lamp glasses dirty Reflector tarnished or dirty Lamps badly out of adjustment Incorrect bulb with too low wattage fitted Existing bulbs old and badly discoloured Electrical wiring too thin not allowing full current to pass	Clean glasses. Fit new reflectors. Adjust lamps correctly. Remove bulb and replace with correct grade. Renew bulb units. Re-wire lighting system.
Lights work erratically - flashing on and off, especially over bumps	Battery terminals or earth connections loose Lights not earthing properly Contacts in light switch faulty	Tighten battery terminals and earth connection Examine and rectify. By-pass light switch to ascertain if fault is in switch and fit new switch as appropriate
Wipers Wiper motor fails to work	Blown fuse Wire connections loose, disconnected or broken Brushes badly worn Armature worn or faulty Field coils faulty	Check and replace fuse if necessary. Check wiper wiring. Tighten loose connections. Remove and fit new brushes. If electricity at wiper motor remove and overhaul and fit replacement armature. Purchase reconditioned wiper motor.
Wiper motor works very slowly and takes excessive current	Commutator dirty, greasy or burnt Drive to wheelboxes too bent or unlubricated Wheelbox spindle binding or damaged Armature bearings dry or unaligned Armature badly worn or faulty	Clean commutator thoroughly. Examine drive and straighten out severe curvature. Lubricate. Remove, overhaul, or fit replacement. Replace with new bearings correctly aligned Remove, overhaul, or fit replacement armature.
Wiper motor works slowly and takes little current	Brushes badly worn Commutator dirty, greasy, or burnt Armature badly worn or faulty	Remove and fit new brushes. Clean commutator thoroughly. Remove and overhaul armature or fit replacement.
Wiper motor works but wiper blades remain static	Driving cable rack disengaged or faulty Wheelbox gear and spindle damaged or worn Wiper motor gearbox parts badly worn	Examine and if faulty, replace. Examine and if faulty, replace. Overhaul or fit new gearbox.

Key to wiring diagrams. Due to the numerous model variants it is only possible to include a typical selection

A to Z	Connectors
A.C.	Cigarette lighter
A.C.S.	Seat belt buzzer
Al.	Distributor
Alt.	Alternator
Amp.	Ammeter
A.T.C.	Buzzer (ignition key indicator)
Av.	Horn
Bie.	Battery
Bo.	Coil
Br.	Terminal
C.A.	Horns switch
Cap.P.	Sensing head
C.C.E.	Electrovalve control box
C.Cli.	Direction indicators unit
C.E.V./L.V.	Windscreen washer/wiper switch
Cli.	Flasher
Com.	Light switch
Conac.	Double switch on scuttle
Cor.	Relay box (Corel)
Co.R.	Regulator condenser
Coup.	Coupler
Cr.	Connector
C.R.	Idling cut out
C.T.	Rev-counter
Dem.	Starter (Solenoid)
DIR.AV.	Flasher/Horn switch
Dyn.	Dynamo
E.C.	Luggage boot light
E.Ce.	Ashtray light
E.Cl.	Heater light
E.Co.	Controls light
E.I.	Interior light
E.I.D.	Interior RH light
E.I.G.	Interior LH light
E.P.B.D.	RH dashboard light
E.P.B.G.	LH dashboard light
E.P.P.	Registration plate light
E.V.	Windscreen wiper
E.Va.	Electrovalve
E.V.P.	Glovebox light
F (n)	Fuse
F.L.	Lateral lights
F.P..	Door indicator light
F.Pr.	Headlamp fuse
F.R.	Lateral flasher light
F.S.	Parking light
H.E.	Water and oil warning light
I.A.	Davauto or Neiman ignition switch
I.A.D.	Ignition anti-theft starter switch
I.C.F.	Brake warning light relay
I.Cli.	Direction indicators switch
I.C.P	Pressure drop switch
I.C.S.	Seat belt switch
I.D.	Four way flasher switch
I.E.C.	Luggage boot light switch
I.E.V.	Windscreen wiper switch
I.E.V./L.V.	Windscreen wiper/switch
I.E.V.P.	Glovebox light switch
I.F.M.	Handbrake switch
I.F.S.	Parking light switch
I.L.C.	Rear window heater switch
I.L.V.D.	RH window switch
I.L.V.G.	LH window switch
I.P.	Door switch
I.P.A.V.	Front door switch
I.P.A.R.	Rear door switch
I.P.M.	Neutral switch
I.P.P.	Passenger seat switch
I.P.R.	Reverse light switch
I.S.	Stop light switch
I.S.D.	Inhibitor switch
I.T.S.	Choke warning light switch
I.V.	Tail gate switch
I.V.Cl.	Heater fan switch
I.V.Cl.C.	Additional heater blower switch

J.R.	Fuel gauge
J.Tr.	Fuel gauge transmitter
L.	Side light
L.C.	Heated rear window
L.E.	Instrument panel light
L.V.D.	RH window motor
L.V.G.	LH window motor
M.	Earth (ground)
Ma.	Main beam flasher switch
M.C.A.	Brake assistance pressure switch
M.C.E.	Fuel pressure switch
M.C.F.	Brake circuit checking pressure switch
M.C.H.	Oil pressure switch
Mo.	Electric clock
P.B.	Inspection lamp socket
P.E.	Fuel pump
P.E.V.	Windscreen washer pedal
P.F.	Brake pad
Pl.	Roof light with switch
Pl.2.	Rear roof light
Pl.D.	RH roof light
Pl.G.	LH roof light
P.L.V.	Windscreen washer pump
Pl.R.	Relay plate
Pog.	Gear change lever with switch
P.R.	Reverse light
Pr.	Headlamp
Pr.C.	Dipped beam headlamp
Pr.H.	Halogen headlamp
Pr.R.	Main beam headlamp
P.T.	Temperature gauge transmitter
R.A.E.V.	Alternator and windscreen wiper relay
R.A.L.	Double headlamp flasher relay
R.A.P.	Anti-pollution device relay
R.Bie.	Battery master switch
R.C.S.	Seat belt relay
R.D.	Starter relay
Reg.	Regulator
R.E.V.	Windscreen wiper relay
R.F.E.V.	Fixed windscreen wiper relay
Rh.	Instrument panel light rheostat
Rh.Co.	Control light rheostat
Rh.V.Cl.	Heater fan rheostat
R.L.C.	Rear window heater relay
R.L.F.	Brake fluid reservoir (Nicovode)
R.Ph.	Main beam relay
R.Pr.	Headlamp relay
R.T.	Warning resistance
R.V.E.	Electric fan relay
S.	Stop light
T.	Windscreen wiper time switch
T.C.	Charge warning light
T.Cli.	Flasher warning light
T.C.S.	Seat belt warning light
T.D.	Four way flasher warning light
Te.E.	Water temperature warning light
T.E.	Fuel pressure warning light
T.H.	Oil pressure warning light
Th.E.	Water temperature gauge
Th.T.	Water temperature gauge thermo-switch
Th.V.D.	Fan thermo-switch
Th.V.D.E.	Fan thermo-switch (in water circuit)
Th.V.D.H.	Fan thermo-switch (in oil circuit)
Th.V.E.	Electro fan thermal switch
T.L.	Side light warning light
T.L.C.	Heated rear window warning light
T.Ph.	Main beam warning light
T.P.	Pre-heater warning light
T.S.	Choke warning light
T.S.F.	Brake safety warning light
T.V.	Gear change pattern
V.Cl.	Heater fan
V.Cl.C.	Additional heater blower
V.D.	Self-engaging fan
V.E.	Electric fan
+a.c.	Live after connection
+p.	Live

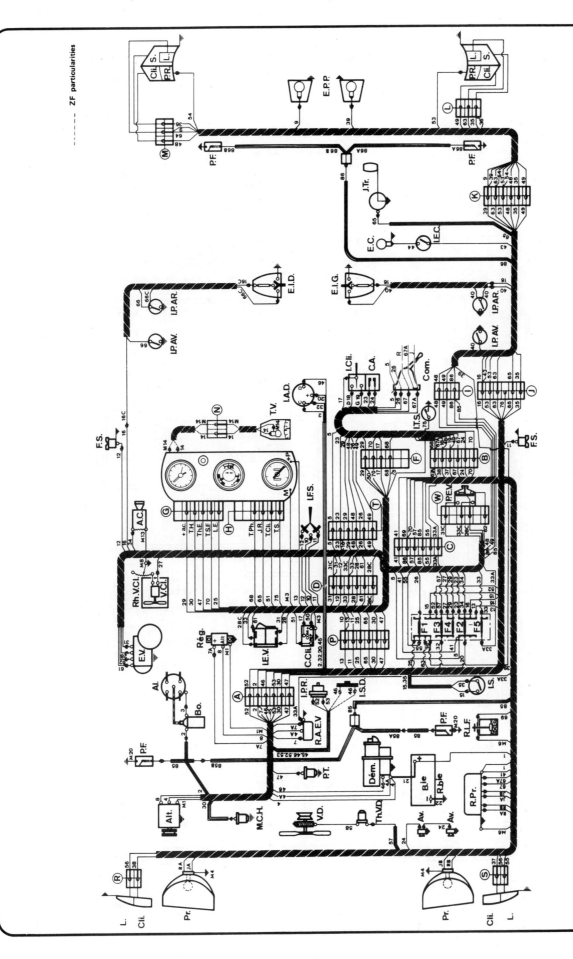

Wiring diagram — 504 Saloon, carburettor engine, December 1968 to July 1969

197

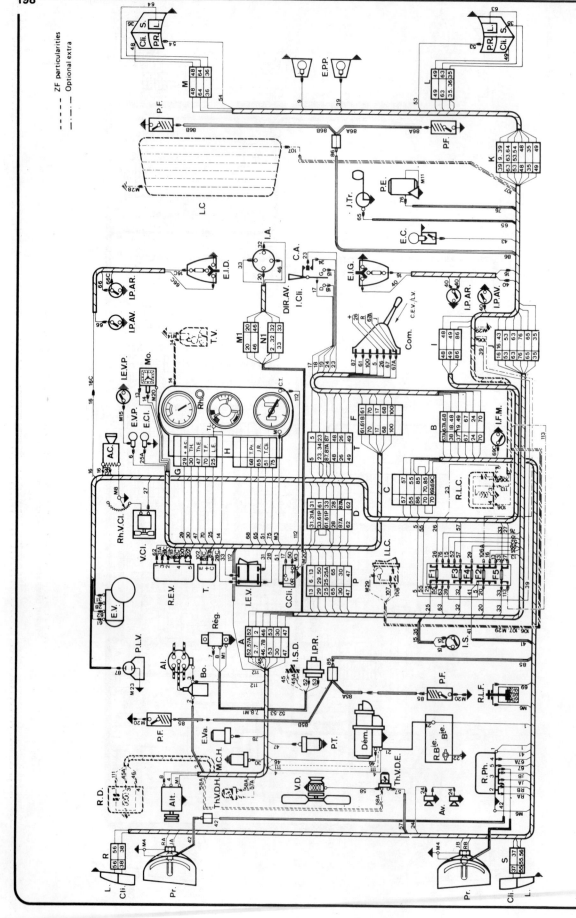

Wiring diagram — 504 Saloon, petrol injection, July 1970 to July 1972

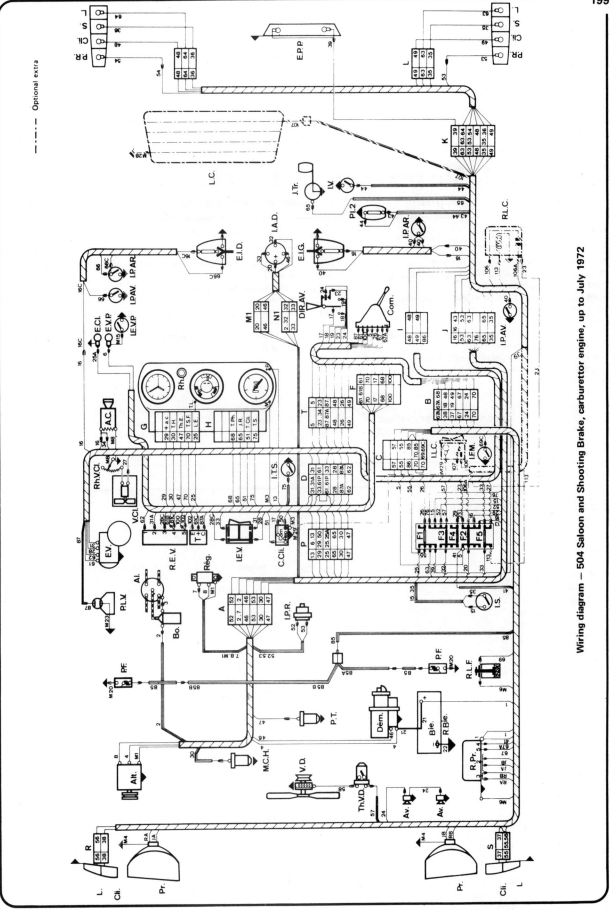

Wiring diagram – 504 Saloon and Shooting Brake, carburettor engine, up to July 1972

Chapter 11 Suspension and steering

For modifications, and information applicable to later models, see Supplement at end of manual

Contents

Specifications

Front Suspension

Type	Independent, with MacPherson struts, coil springs, telescopic dampers and anti-roll bar

Coil spring

	Free height	Reference
Model:		
504 A01		
504 A02	500 mm or 550 mm	Red/green or white/green
504 A03		
504 B02	426.5 mm	Red/yellow or green/blue
504 C02		

Coil diameter:	
Carburettor	6.417 in. (163 mm)
Automatic and fuel injection	6.426 in. (163.25 mm)
Wire diameter:	
Carburettor	0.512 in. (13.0 mm)
Automatic and fuel injection	0.523 in. (13.25 mm)
Number of active coils:	
Carburettor	7.2
Automatic and fuel injection	7.7

Dampers

Fluid type	Esso Oleofluid 40X
Capacity (approx)	0.5 pint (0.6 US pint, 0.3 litre)

Anti-roll bar

Diameter	26 mm

Wheel alignment*

*Car normally loaded with tools, oil, water and petrol

Castor	$2^\circ\ 40' \pm 30'$
Camber	$0^\circ\ 38' \pm 30'$
King pin inclination	$8^\circ\ 54' \pm 30'$
Toe-in	3 mm $\pm$ 1 mm

Rear Suspension

Type:

Saloon	Independent. Coil spring, trailing arms, telescopic dampers and anti-roll bar.
Utility models	Conventional 'banjo' axle with twin coil springs at either end. Telescopic dampers and anti-roll bar.
Anti-roll bar diameter	18 mm

Wheel alignment:

Toe-in	4.5 mm $\pm$ ½ mm
Camber	1° 0' $\pm$ 0° 40' 0° 20'

Steering

Type	Rack and pinion with two piece steering shaft.
Rack plunger free play	0.1 $\pm$ 0.05 mm (Max)
Plunger adjustment shims	0.10, 0.20, 0.50 mm
Steering wheel turns, lock to lock	4.5 turns
Steering radius (maximum)	5.5 M

Torque wrench settings

	lb f ft	kg f m
Front Suspension		
Hub to stub axle:		
Initial	22	3.0
Final	7.2	1.0
Triangle arm to suspension arm	33	4.5
Triangle arm to crossmember	33	4.5
Stub axle balljoint	33	4.5
Front suspension unit upper bolts	7.2	1.0
Wheel nuts	44	6.0
Anti-roll bar connecting link	33	4.5
Rear Suspension		
Shock absorber lower pivot	33	4.5
Shock absorber upper nylstop nut	9	1.25
Stub axle to suspension arm	29	4.0
Wheel nuts	44	6.0
Crossmember to body nuts (inner)	23.5	3.25
Crossmember to body nuts (outer)	See text.	
Final drive housing to crossmember	27	3.75
Rear arm pivot nuts	47	6.5
Anti-roll bar connecting link	9	1.25
Hub carrier Allen screws	29	4.0
Anti-roll bar link nut	33	4.5
Support block nut:		
Front	23.5	3.25
Rear	9	1.25
Intermediate support to crossmember	23.5	3.25
Crossmember front nuts	13	1.75
Crossmember rear nuts	23.5	3.25
Rear hub carrier nut	181	25
Steering		
Rack housing to crossmember	23.5	3.25
Trackrod balljoint	31	4.25
Pinion nut	11	1.5
Flexible coupling bolts and nuts	13	1.75
Steering wheel	33	4.5
Steering column to flector	7.2	1.0
Grease nipple to thrust plate	7.2	1.0
Thrust plate bolts	7.2	1.0
Rack eye locknut	25	3.5
Trackrod yoke to rack	33	4.5
Steering column closing plate	7.2	1.0
Handbrake outer cable clamp nuts	3.5	0.5
Steering column nuts	7.2	1.0
Cardan joint nut	7.2	1.0

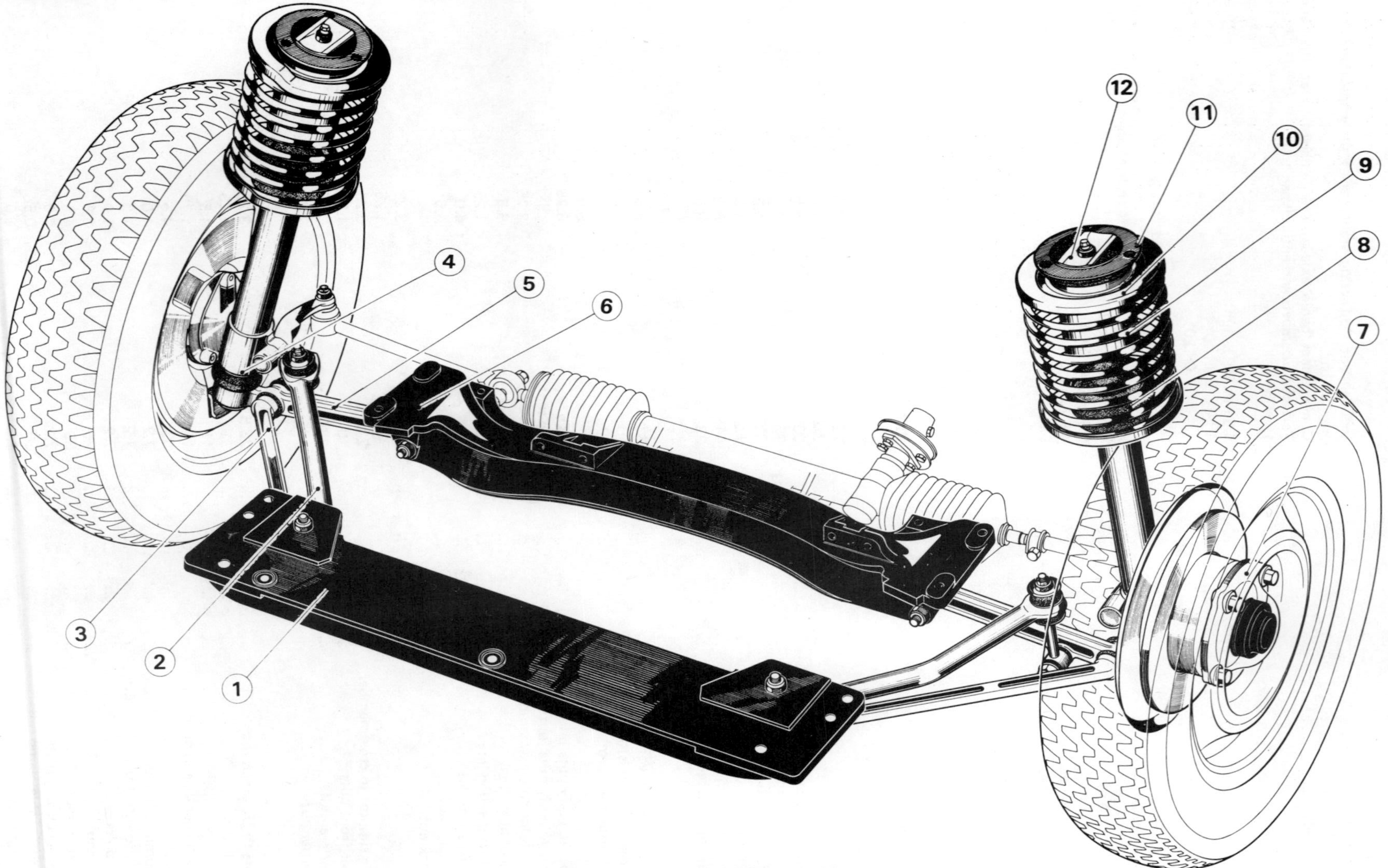

Fig. 11.1. Front suspension assembly

1 Front crossmember in steel sheet
2 Anti-roll bar
3 Triangle front arm

4 Steering knuckle with shock absorber
5 Triangle rear arm
6 Main crossmember in cast steel

7 Front hub
8 Rebound stop
9 Suspension spring

10 Upper spring seating cup
11 Upper flexible mounting
12 Rebound seating cup

1 General description

The front suspension on all models is fully independent with integral shock absorbers and coil springs.

It will be seen from Fig. 11.1 that a steel crossmember acts as a mounting for the engine as well as the rack and pinion steering gear. At the ends of the crossmember are transverse suspension links which pivot in bushes on the crossmember. The outer ends of the links are connected to the stub axles. Resilient 'Silentbloc' mountings are used.

A second crossmember located in front of the first crossmember is connected to the transverse suspension links by front triangle arms again mounted in 'Silentbloc' bushes.

When an anti-roll bar is fitted it is mounted on the front crossmember and connected to the transverse arms by a short link.

Two coil springs are mounted vertically and rest on the telescopic double acting shock absorber cylinders which are integral with the stub axles. At the lower end, each suspension unit is accurately positioned by the transverse suspension links and triangle arms. When fitted, the anti-roll bar links the two suspension units together.

The top end of the suspension units is attached to the body at the top wheel arch panels.

On models with independent rear suspension the final drive

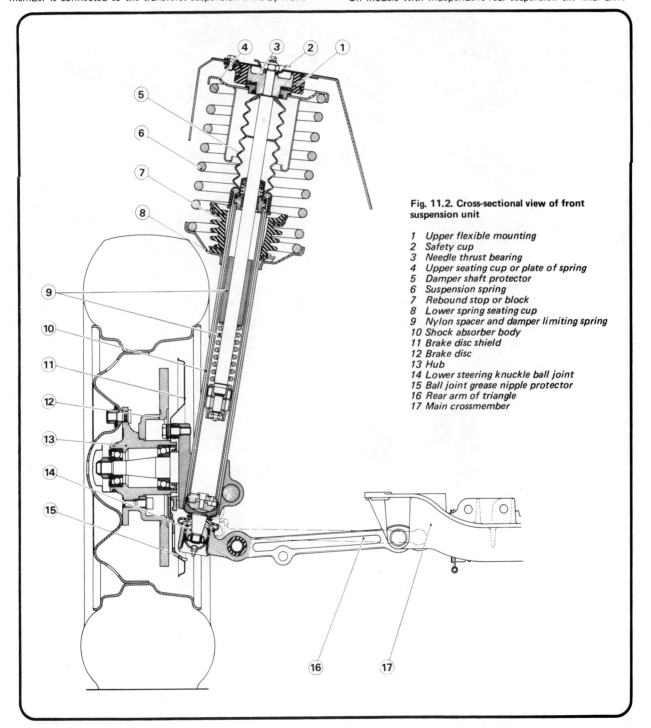

Fig. 11.2. Cross-sectional view of front suspension unit

1 Upper flexible mounting
2 Safety cup
3 Needle thrust bearing
4 Upper seating cup or plate of spring
5 Damper shaft protector
6 Suspension spring
7 Rebound stop or block
8 Lower spring seating cup
9 Nylon spacer and damper limiting spring
10 Shock absorber body
11 Brake disc shield
12 Brake disc
13 Hub
14 Lower steering knuckle ball joint
15 Ball joint grease nipple protector
16 Rear arm of triangle
17 Main crossmember

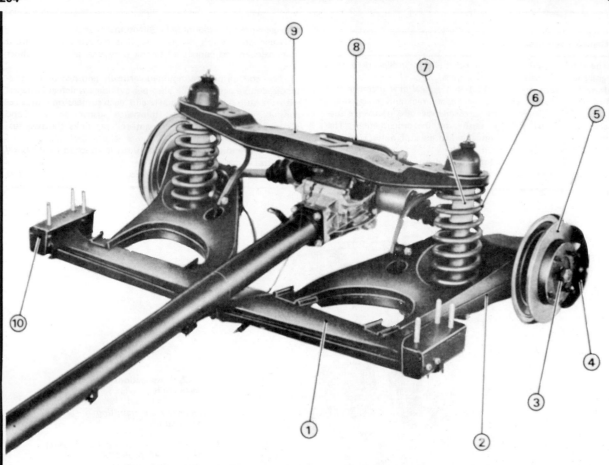

Fig. 11.3. Rear suspension assembly

1	Rear crossmember	4	Brake caliper	7	Rear shock absorber		crossmember
2	Rear arm	5	Brake disc	8	Anti-roll bar	10	Rear crossmember
3	Rear hub	6	Suspension spring	9	Rear suspension		support

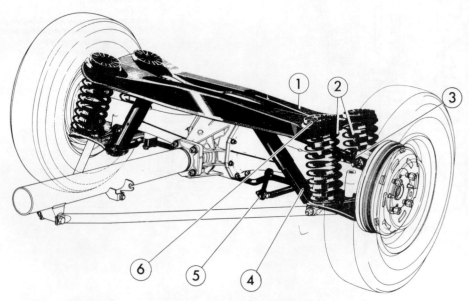

Fig. 11.4. Rear suspension assembly (utility models)

1	Rear suspension crossmember	3	Stabiliser bar	5	Rear anti-roll bar
2	Rear springs	4	Rear shock absorbers	6	Rear crossmember rubber block

and rear suspension assembly is supported by two pressed steel crossmembers which form a subframe. This is attached to the main body using resilient Silentbloc mountings. The front crossmember acts as a mounting for the trailing arms which carry the coil springs and dampers. These are located at their upper ends by the rear crossmember which is mounted at a higher level.

On Estate and Utility models a 'banjo' type rear axle is used. Twin coil springs are fitted at each end and lateral location is provided by two arms mounted towards the centre of the torque tube.

The steering gear used on all models is of the rack and pinion type. When the steering wheel is turned, the steering shaft, onto which is attached a helically toothed gear, also turns. This

gear is located in the steering gearbox which is mounted on the front crossmember.

The helically toothed gear, called the pinion, meshes with the rack which is located in a tubular housing. Gaiters are fitted at either end to contain the lubricant and exclude road dirt. When the pinion rotates the rack is caused to move transversely in the housing. Universal joints are fitted to each end of the rack and connect it to the trackrods. Movement of the rack causes the trackrods and steering arms on the front swivel hubs to move thereby giving movement to the front wheels.

The left-hand trackrod is of the adjustable type and an anti-theft steering lock is located on the steering shaft housing.

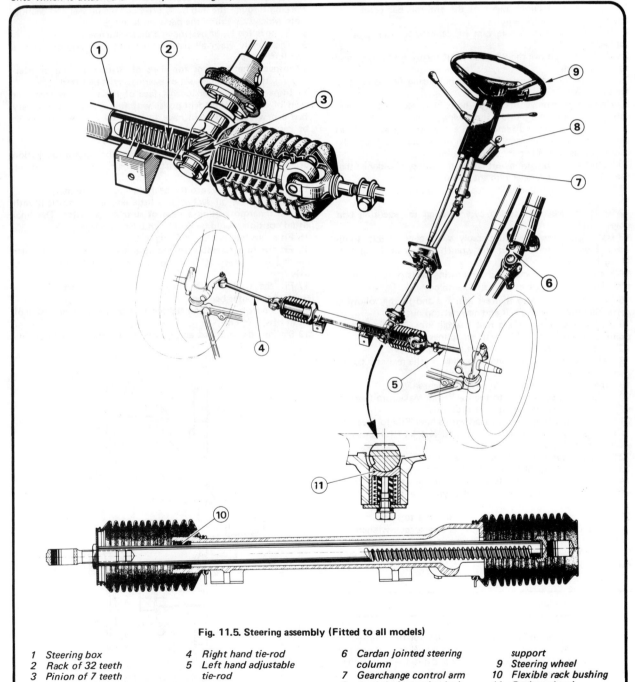

Fig. 11.5. Steering assembly (Fitted to all models)

1	Steering box	4	Right hand tie-rod
2	Rack of 32 teeth	5	Left hand adjustable tie-rod
3	Pinion of 7 teeth		

6	Cardan jointed steering column		support
7	Gearchange control arm	9	Steering wheel
8	Anti-theft steering lock	10	Flexible rack bushing
		11	Rack pushrod

2   Front suspension unit - removal and replacement

1   Chock the rear wheels, apply the handbrake, jack-up the front of the car and support on firmly based axle stands. Remove the roadwheel.

2   Refer to Chapter 9 and detach the disc brake caliper. There is no need to disconnect the hydraulic hose but suspend the caliper on string or wire.

3   Undo and remove the trackrod balljoint securing nut and using a universal balljoint separator release the balljoint taper. **Do not** 'shock' release the taper with two hammers unless new parts are to be fitted.

4   Remove the securing pivot of the anti-roll bar connecting link on the rear triangle arm.

5   Release the rear triangle arm by tapping to disengage the splined part.

6   Undo and remove the Silentbloc nut securing the front arm to the rear arm.

7   Support the weight of the wheel hub using blocks, or preferably, a jack.

8   Undo and remove the three bolts that secure the upper spring holder to the top of the inner wing panel.

9   Hold the spring and remove the blocks (or lower the jack) and remove the suspension unit from inside the wheel arch. Be careful because it is heavier than it looks.

10   To refit the suspension unit position the upper holder so that the safety cup lies parallel with the axis of the car.

11   Place the suspension unit on a trolley jack and move under the front wing.

12   Raise the assembly taking care to align the securing bolt holes.

13   Refit the three bolts preferably with new double tooth washers and tighten to a torque wrench setting of 7.2 lb f ft (1 kg f m).

14   Remove the jack and fit the following parts onto the front arm: Thrust washers, cup and half Silentbloc.

15   Fit the front arm to the rear arm eye and fit the following parts: Silentbloc second half and new nylstop nut.

16   Engage the pivot of the rear triangle arm. The head must point rearwards and be flush with the splines.

17   Fit a new nylstop nut but do not fully tighten yet.

18   Refit the anti-roll bar connecting link on the rear arm by engaging the pivot. The top must face rearwards.

19   Fit a washer and nut but do not fully tighten yet.

20   Reconnect the trackrod to the track arm. Make sure that the split pin hole is perpendicular to the rod axis.

21   Tighten the balljoint nut, fitted with a new 'Blocfor' washer, to a torque wrench setting of 33 lb f ft. (4.5 kg f m) and lock with a new split pin.

22   Refer to Chapter 9, and refit the disc brake caliper.

23   Refit the roadwheel and lower the car to the ground.

24   Working under the car (preferably over a pit or the front wheels supported on blocks under the tyres), refit the rear articulation joint.

25   Bounce the car up and down several times to settle the suspension and tighten the following nuts to a torque wrench setting of 33 lb f ft (4.5 kg f m): Pivot nut on the crossmember, Silentbloc nut, and finally, the nut securing the anti-roll bar connecting link to the rear arm.

3   Front suspension unit - overhaul

This job is not considered to be suitable for the do-it-yourself motorist as six special tools are required. Without these the coil spring cannot be removed in safety and also the unit cannot be dismantled or reassembled without damaging various parts. If the unit is in need of overhaul then it is far better for the local Peugeot garage to transfer the spring to a reconditioned or new unit.

4   Front hub - removal, overhaul and replacement

1   Chock the rear wheels, apply the handbrake, jack-up the front of the car and support on firmly based stands. Remove the roadwheel.

2   Refer to Chapter 9, and detach the disc brake caliper. There is no need to disconnect the hydraulic hose but suspend the caliper on string or wire.

3   Using a screwdriver remove the hub cap.

4   Unscrew the hub nut and withdraw the hub assembly.

5   Remove as much grease as possible.

6   Remove the hub nut cap 'O' ring seal.

7   To remove the inner bearing use a suitable tapered drift and working through the hub body drive out the oil seal and bearing. Note which way round the parts are fitted.

8   Remove the outer bearing in a similar manner.

9   Thoroughly wash all parts in paraffin and wipe dry using a non-fluffy rag.

10   Inspect the bearings for signs of rusting, pitting or overheating. If evident a new set of bearings must be fitted.

11   Inspect the oil seal journal face of the stub axle shaft for signs of damage. If evident polish with fine emery tape or if very bad a new stub axle will have to be fitted. This will of course be very expensive as it is incorporated in the front suspension unit.

12   To reassemble, carefully drift the new bearings into position using a suitable diameter drift. Make sure they are fitted the correct way round.

13   Work some grease into the bearings and hub assembly.

14   Smear a new oil seal with a little engine oil and fit it with the lip innermost using a tube of suitable diameter. The final fitted position should be flush with the hub flange.

15   Fit a new hub nut cap 'O' ring seal.

16   Fit the hub assembly to the stub and check that the inner bearing inner track is flush against the shoulder of the stub axle.

17   Fit the washer with the inner shoulder against the inner track of the outer bearing.

18   Fit a new hub nut and tighten to a torque wrench setting of 22 lb f ft (3 kg f m).

19   Slacken the hub nut and tighten to a torque wrench setting

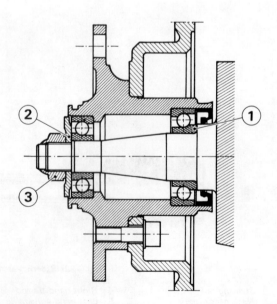

Fig. 11.6. Cross-sectional view of front hub (Sec. 4)

1   Inner race   *3   Hub nut*
2   Washer

of 7.2 lb f ft (1 kg f m).

20 Lock the nut in the two grooves provided using a suitable drift.

21 Insert a little grease into the hub nut cap and refit to the hub.

22 Refit the disc brake caliper, as described in Chapter 9.

23 Refit the roadwheel and lower the car to the ground.

5 Triangle rear arm - removal and replacement

To remove the triangle rear arm requires the use of seven special tools and it is therefore considered that this work be entrusted to the local Peugeot garage. To save cost the arm can be removed with the front suspension unit (see Section 2) and the assembly taken to the garage for them to carry out the necessary work.

6 'Silentbloc' or 'Metalastic' bushes - removal and replacement

1 The procedure for the removal and replacement of metalastic bushes is the same no matter from where they come on the car.

2 Drift the old bush out of its bore. This may be extremely difficult if the bush has distorted or broken up. However, it does not matter if the bush is damaged during removal as it is to be renewed.

3 Smear the new bush with soap or washing up liquid (on no account use oil or grease) and also its bore. This will ease replacement a great deal.

4 Tap the new bush into its bore with a soft faced hammer. Alternatively and more desirable use a bench vice as a press to face the bush into its bore. If movement is continuous the job is easier and there is little chance of the bush 'picking up' half way in.

7 Rear shock absorbers - removal and replacement

1 Working inside the car undo and remove the Nylstop nut at the top end of the shock absorber. It will be necessary to hold the shock absorber using a 5 mm open ended spanner. (Fig. 11.8).

2 Lift off the upper sheet metal cup and the rubber washer.

3 Now working under the car remove the lower securing pivot on the rear arm.

4 To remove the shock absorber from the car withdraw it through the hole provided in the rear arm.

5 To test the shock absorber alternatively compress the extend it throughout its full movement. If the action is jerky or weak, either it is worn or there is air in the hydraulic cylinder. Continue to compress and extend it and if the action does not become more positive a new shock absorber should be obtained. If the shock absorber is showing signs of leaking it should be discarded as it is not possible to overhaul it.

6 Check the rubber washers and bushes and if they show signs of deterioration a new set of rubbers should be obtained and fitted. Ideally this should be done every time the shock absorber is removed.

7 Fully extend the shock absorber rod and fit on the following parts: thrust cup, rod protector, centering cup, rubber washer, and nylon spacer.

8 Engage the shock absorber in its recess with the rod positioned in the suspension crossmember hole.

9 Fit the lower securing pivot using a new Blocfor washer and screw on the nut. Do not fully tighten yet.

10 Fit the following parts to the shock absorber rod: rubber washer, upper sheet metal cup with the raised edge facing upwards and the Nylstop nut. Tighten the nut to a torque wrench setting of 9 lb f ft (1.25 kg f m).

11 Tighten the shock absorber lower pivot securing nut to a torque wrench setting of 33 lb f ft (4.5 kg f m).

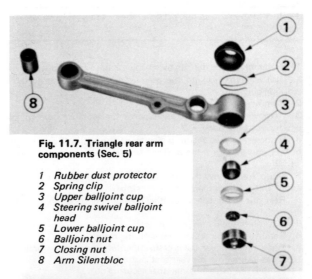

Fig. 11.7. Triangle rear arm components (Sec. 5)

1 Rubber dust protector
2 Spring clip
3 Upper balljoint cup
4 Steering swivel balljoint head
5 Lower balljoint cup
6 Balljoint nut
7 Closing nut
8 Arm Silentbloc

Fig. 11.8. Rear shock absorber top mounting (Saloon) (Sec. 7)

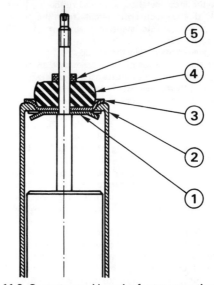

Fig. 11.9. Correct assembly order for top mounting (Saloon) (Sec. 7)

1 Thrust cup	3 Centering cup
2 Rod protector	4 Rubber washer
	5 Nylon spacer

8   Rear suspension upper crossmember - removal and replacement

1   Preferably place the car over a pit or on a ramp, but if these are not available jack-up the rear of the car to a comfortable working height.
2   Remove the roadwheels.
3   Remove the rear nut that secures the exhaust pipe to the underside of the body.
4   Remove the two securing clamps of the anti-roll bar flexible bushes and disengage the anti-roll bar from the bodywork. (Fig 11.10).
5   Undo and remove the two Allen screws that secure the differential unit to the suspension crossmember.
6   Rest the rear section of the connecting tube on the rear crossmember.
7   Slacken the rear arm pivot nuts.
8   Remove the petrol pipe rear securing clamp.
9   Place a jack under the crossmember left-hand lateral bracket.
10 Carefully remove the rear seat cushion.
11 Unlock the three crossmember securing nuts.
12 Undo and remove the front securing nut.
13 Prise up the lockwasher and remove the plastic plug from the guide hole.
14 Two long bolts and washers are now required. One must be screwed into each side of the suspension at the point of the guide holes. There must be a protrusion of about 3 inches (76.2 mm) into the car. Figs 7.4 and 7.5 (Chapter 7) show the special tool in use but bolts and large washers do just as well.
15 Remove the crossmember rear securing nuts and the thrust washers.
16 Carefully lower the crossmember until the bolt is supporting its weight.
17 Repeat the previously described sequence for the right-hand side of the crossmember.
18 Place chocks under the rear arms.
19 Refer to Section 7, and remove the two shock absorbers.
20 Carefully raise the rear of the car until the coil springs are completely detached.
21 Remove the springs and their upper rubber cups. (Fig. 11.11).
22 Undo and remove the suspension crossmember securing nuts from under the body.
23 Remove the sheet metal cups and the rubber washers.
24 Carefully disengage the crossmember from the bodywork and then pull it sideways to avoid contact with the final drive housing. (Fig. 11.12)
25 Finally remove the rubber thrust cups.
26 To refit the rear suspension upper crossmember first place the rubber thrust cups on the suspension crossmember. To facilitate positioning them smear with soap or washing up liquid.
27 Place the crossmember between the final drive housing and underside of body.
28 Secure the crossmember to the body using rubber washers, sheet metal cups, nuts and new Blocfor washers. Tighten the nuts to a torque wrench setting of 23.5 lb f ft. (3.25 kg f m) (Fig. 11.13).
29 Locate the rear spring upper rubber cup in the recess in the crossmember. For this it is suggested that some adhesive is used.
30 Place the springs between their upper and lower supports.
31 Carefully lower the rear of the car and position the springs in their upper cups.
32 Refer to Section 7, and refit the two rear shock absorbers. Do not tighten the lower securing nuts yet.
33 Refit the roadwheels and lower the car to the ground.
34 Place a jack under the right-hand lateral holder and raise the crossmember until it comes into contact with the floor.
35 Remove the bolt and washer and close the guide hole using the plastic plug.
36 Fit the following onto the studs in this order: flat washers, a new tab lock and securing nuts.
37 Tighten the nuts to a torque wrench setting of:

Fig. 11.10. Removal of anti-roll bar-to-body clamp (Sec. 8)

Fig. 11.11. Removal of coil spring (Sec. 8)

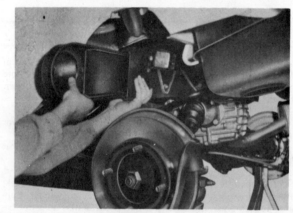

Fig. 11.12. Withdrawing crossmember through wheel arch (Sec. 8)

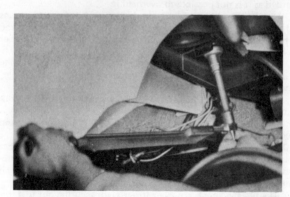

Fig. 11.13. Securing crossmember to body (Sec. 8)

a) up to serial numbers
504 A01 - 1005546
504 A02 - 1003649
504 B03 - All Cars   29 lb f ft (4 kg f m)
504 B02 - 1032357
504 C02 - 1009769
b) From the quoted serial numbers   47 lb f ft (6.5 kg f m)

38 Lock the nuts by bending the tab tongue over the nuts.
39 Repeat the sequence previously described for the second side.
40 Refit the rear seat cushion.
41 Secure the final drive housing to the suspension crossmember using two Allen screws fitted with new 'Blocfor' washers. Tighten to a torque wrench setting of 27 lb f ft (3.75 kg f m).
42 Smear a little rubber grease onto the anti-roll bar bushes.
44 Fit and secure the anti-roll bar to the underside of the body.
45 Refit the petrol pipe securing clamp.
46 Reconnect the rear portion of the exhaust pipe to the body.
47 With the car on the ground and two people sitting in the rear seats tighten the shock absorber lower pivot nuts to a torque wrench setting of 33 lb f ft (4.5 kg f m) and the nuts of the rear arm flexible bushes to 47 lb f ft (6.5 kg f m).

9 Rear suspension arms (saloon models) - removal and replacement

1 Refer to Chapter 8, and remove the driveshaft.
2 Raise the rear of the car and support it under each crossmember support.
3 Place a jack under the rear arm and raise the rear arm so that the shock absorber is not fully extended.
4 Remove the shock absorber, as described in Section 7.

5 Release the flexible hose from the lug on the rear arm by slackening the nut on hose and detaching from the lug. (Fig 11.14).
6 Unclip the handbrake cable from the rear arm (Fig. 11.15).
7 Undo and remove the nut that secures the anti-roll bar link under the rear arm.
8 Withdraw the metal cup and the rubber washer and immediately replace the nut to prevent the upper parts from falling inside the arm.
9 Unscrew the rear arm pivot nuts.
10 Carefully lower the jack until the suspension spring is fully extended.
11 Remove the spring and its upper rubber cup.
12 Finally withdraw the rear arm pivots and lift away the rear arm.
13 Check the rear suspension arm for damage or excessive corrosion and renew if evident. Inspect the bushes and if they have deteriorated, renew them as described in Section 6.
14 When refitting the rear suspension arm always use new 'Nylstop' nuts and 'Blocfor' or 'Orduflex' type washers.
15 To refit first position the rear arm in the corresponding yokes on the crossmember.
16 Insert a rod through the inner joint and fit the outer pivot into its housing (Fig. 11.16).
17 Withdraw the rod and fit the inner pivot into its housing.
18 Fit new 'Nylstop' nuts but do not fully tighten yet.
19 Place a jack under the rear part of the arm.
20 Smear the upper rubber spring cup with a little soap or washing up liquid. This will make its final positioning easier.
21 Place the spring in between its upper and lower mountings.
22 Carefully raise the arms taking care that the spring centres correctly in its housing. (Fig. 11.17) At the same time guide

Fig. 11.14. Flexible hose detached from lug on rear arm (Sec. 9)

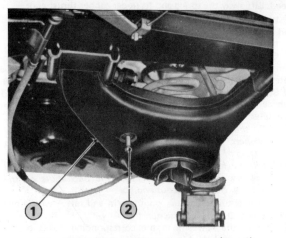

Fig. 11.15. Underside view of rear arm (Sec. 9)

1   Handbrake cable mounting   2   Nut

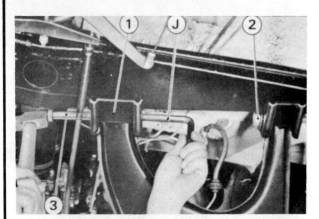

Fig. 11.16. Refitting rear arm (Sec. 9)

1   Inner pivot   3   Inner pivot bolt
2   Outer pivot   J   Rod

Fig. 11.17. Refitting rear spring (Sec. 9)

the anti-roll bar connecting link into position in the rear arm.

23 Refit the two rubber washers, the metal cup and the upper shock absorber securing nut.

24 Fit the shock absorbers lower mounting but do not fully tighten the lower nut yet.

25 Tighten the upper shock absorber nut to a torque wrench setting of 9 lb f ft (1.25 kg f m).

26 Lower and remove the jack from under the car.

27 Fit the rubber washer and metal cup onto the anti-roll bar connecting link. Tighten the nut to a torque wrench setting of 9 lb f ft (1.25 kg f m). (Fig. 11.18).

28 Refit the rear brake hose and handbrake cable to the rear arm.

29 Refit the driveshaft as described in Chapter 8.

30 Refit the roadwheel and lower the car to the ground.

31 With two people sitting in the rear seats tighten the shock absorber lower pivot nuts to a torque wrench setting of 33 lb f ft (4.5 ln f m) and the rear arm pivot nuts to 47 lb f ft (6.5 kg f m).

32 Finally check the oil level in the final drive housing and top-up if necessary.

---

10 Rear suspension arm (Convertible and Coupe models) - removal and replacement

1 Refer to Chapter 8, and remove the driveshaft.

2 Temporarily support the suspension arm with rods passed through the bushes and crossmember (Fig. 11.19).

3 The brake caliper should be removed as described in Chapter 9, and the rear hub and hub carrier if still in position.

4 Place a jack under the arm and raise it until the shock absorber is no longer at its maximum extension.

5 Refer to Section 7, and remove the shock absorber.

6 Lower the jack until the suspension spring is completely freed. Lift away the spring and its upper rubber thrust cup.

7 Withdraw the rods supporting the arm to the crossmember and lift away the arm.

8 If necessary remove the anti-roll bar link from the arm.

9 Check the rear suspension arm for damage or excessive corrosion and renew if evident. Inspect the bushes and if they have deteriorated they should be renewed as described in Section 6.

10 Before refitting, the suspension arm, the disc protector and hub carrier may be reassembled to the arm at this stage rather than later:

 a) *Fit the disc protector and hub carrier using new 'Blocfor' washers. Tighten the Allen screws to a torque wrench setting of 29 lb f ft (4 kg f m) - (Fig. 11.20).*

 b) *Fit the hub in the carrier using a long bolt, nut and washers. Tighten the bolt until the hub abuts on the bearing. Remove the nut and bolt.*

11 Fit the anti-roll bar link on the arm and retain with a new Nylstop nut. Do not fully tighten the nut yet.

12 Position the rear arm in the corresponding yokes on the crossmember and hold in position by temporarily inserting the two rods (Fig. 11.19).

13 Place a jack under the rear part of the arm.

14 Smear a little washing up liquid on the upper thrust cup to facilitate fitting.

15 Place the spring between its supports and raise the arm making sure that the spring seats correctly.

16 Fit the shock absorber upper rubber washers and metal cup and secure with a new Nylstop nut which should be tightened to a torque wrench setting of 9 lb f ft (1.25 kg f m).

17 Fit the shock absorber bottom pivot but do not tighten yet.

18 Lower the jack and remove it from under the car.

19 Withdraw the two rods holding up the arm and disengage the arms from the crossmember yokes.

20 Refit the driveshaft, as described in Chapter 8 and the rear brake, as described in Chapter 9.

21 Refit the roadwheel and lower the car to the ground.

22 With two people sitting in the rear seats the following attachments should be tightened to the required torque wrench settings:

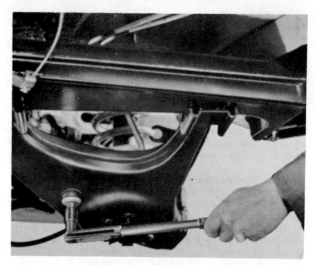

Fig. 11.18. Tightening anti-roll bar connecting link nut (Sec. 9)

Fig. 11.19. Suspension arm supported by two rods (J) (Sec. 10)

Fig. 11.20. Tightening disc protector and hub carrier Allen screws (Sec. 10)

a) *Arm pivot nuts: 47 lb f ft (6.5 kg f m).*
b) *Anti-roll bar link nut: 33 lb f ft (4.5 kg f m) (Fig. 11.21).*
c) *Shock absorber link pivot nut: 33 lb f ft (4.5 kg f m)*
d) *Rear arm to link: 9 lb f ft (1.25 kg f m).*

23 Finally check the oil level in the final drive housing and top-up if necessary.

11 Rear suspension lower crossmember - removal and replacement

1 Preferably, place the car over a pit or on a ramp, but if these are not available jack-up the rear of the car to a comfortable working height.
2 Remove the roadwheels.
3 Unscrew but do not remove the nuts that secure the rear brake flexible hoses to the supports on the underside of the rear floor panel. Carefully detach the hoses (Fig. 11.22).
4 Release the brake pipes from their supports.
5 Place a jack under the left-hand lateral crossmember support in contact with it.
6 Remove the rear seat cushion.
7 Unlock the three nuts that secure the crossmember.
8 Undo and remove the front securing nut.
9 Prise up the lock washer and remove the plastic plug from the guide hole.
10 Two long bolts and washers are now required. One must be screwed into each side of the suspension at the point of the guide holes. There must be a protrusion of about 3 inches (76.2 mm) into the car. Figs. 7.4 and 7.5 (Chapter 7) show the special tool in use but bolts and larger washers do just as well.
11 Remove the crossmember rear securing nuts and the thrust washers.
12 Carefully lower the crossmember until the bolt is supporting its weight.
13 Repeat the previously described sequence for the right-hand side of the crossmember.
14 Unhook the handbrake control lever return spring.
15 Straighten the handbrake cable stop tongues on the relay arm and slide the cable sideways out of the arm (Fig. 11.23 and 11.24).
16 Remove the lever and arm assembly.
17 Remove the protector covers and withdraw the brake cables from their respective guides on the crossmember (Fig. 11.25).
18 Support the weight of the body using jacks and wood packing under the outer sidemembers (sills) of the body at a pivot approximately 22 inches (560 mm) in front of the wheel arches.
19 Remove the inner rear arm pivots and slide in two rods to support its weight.
20 Remove the outer rear arm joints and slide out the two rods.
21 Using a lever disengage the left-hand rear arm joints followed by the right-hand rear arm joints.

Fig. 11.21. Tightening shock absorber link to rear arm securing nut (Sec. 10)

Fig. 11.22. Rear brake flexible pipe detached from support (Sec. 11)

Fig. 11.23. Straightening handbrake cable retaining tongues on the relay arm (Sec. 11)

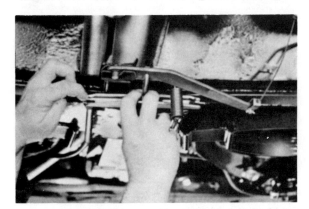

Fig. 11.24. Sliding cable out of arm (Sec. 11)

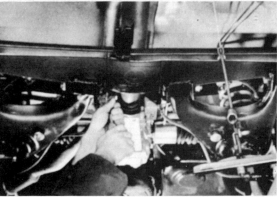

Fig. 11.25. Withdrawing handbrake cables from their guides (Sec. 11)

22 Support the crossmember so as to release the tension on the two bolts suspending the crossmember from the floor. Remove the two bolts (Fig. 11.26).

23 The crossmember may now be removed from under the car.

24 To refit the rear suspension lower crossmember position under the car and support using the two bolts and washers.

25 Using a lever reposition the rear arm pivots into the crossmember yokes (Fig. 11.27).

26 Insert rods through the pivots to take the weight of the rear arm.

27 Remove the inner rods and insert the pivots. Follow this by removing the outer rods and inserting the pivots. Fit new 'Nylstop' nuts on the pivots but do not fully tighten yet.

28 Raise the car and the rear and support under the crossmember lateral mountings.

29 Lower the rear of the car until the crossmember is against the underside of the body.

30 Remove the bolt and washer and close the guide hole using the plastic plug.

31 Fit the following onto the studs in the order of: flat washers, a new tab lock and securing nuts.

32 Tighten the nuts to a torque wrench setting of:

　a) up to serial number
　504A01 - 1005546
　504A02 - 1003649
　504B03 - All cars　　29 lb f ft (4 Kg f m)
　504302 - 1032357
　504C02 - 1009769
　b) From the quoted serial numbers 47 lb f ft (6.5 kg f m).

33 Lock the nuts by bending the tab tongues over the nuts.

34 Repeat the sequence previously described for the second side.

35 Refit the rear seat cushion.

36 Coat the rubber stop rings with a little washing up liquid and introduce the outer cable ends in their respective guides.

37 Refit the protector covers.

38 Refit the handbrake control equipped with new relay arm.

39 Carefully bend over the cable retaining tongues on the relay arm (Fig. 11.28).

40 Refer to Chapter 9, and adjust the handbrake.

41 Reconnect the flexible hoses to the supports on the underside of the rear floor panel.

42 Refit the rear wheels and lower the car to the ground.

43 With two people sitting in the rear seats tighten the rear arm pivot nuts to a torque wrench setting of 47 lb f ft (6.5 kg f m).

---

12 Rear suspension lower crossmember support - removal and replacement

1 Preferably, place the car over a pit or on a ramp, but if these are not available jack-up the rear of the car to a comfortable working height.

2 Remove the roadwheel.

3 Unscrew, but do not remove, the nut that secures the rear brake flexible hose to the support on the underside of the rear floor panel. Carefully detach the hose.

4 Unlock the rear support shouldered nut on the rear support block (Fig. 11.29).

5 Place a jack under the crossmember support and in contact with it.

6 Remove the rear seat cushion.

7 Unlock the three nuts that secure the crossmember.

8 Undo and remove the front securing nut.

9 Prise up the lock washers and remove the plastic plug from the guide hole.

10 A long bolt and washer is now required. It must be screwed onto the suspension at the point of the guide hole. There must be a protrusion of about 3 inches (76.2 mm) into the car. Remove the head of the bolt so that it acts as a stud. Figs. 7.4 and 7.5 (Chapter 7) show the special tool in use.

11 Undo and remove the crossmember rear securing nuts and thrust washers.

Fig. 11.26. Crossmember supported on blocks (Sec. 11)

Fig. 11.27. Fitting rear arm pivots into crossmember yokes with lever (Sec. 11)

Fig. 11.28. Bending over handbrake cable retaining tongues (Sec. 11)

Fig. 11.29. Unlocking rear support shouldered nut on the rear block (Sec. 12)

12 Carefully lower the crossmember until the guide bolt in detached from the body (Fig. 11.30).
13 Place a wooden block approximately 4 inches (10.16 cm) thick under the end of the rear crossmember.
14 Remove the guide bolt using a mole wrench.
15 The crossmember support may now be removed. (Fig. 11.31)
16 The cast alloy intermediate support together with its rubber blocks may be removed next.
17 If necessary replace the rubber blocks using new 'Onduflex' washers. Tighten the securing nuts to a torque wrench setting of 23.5 lb f ft (3.25 kg f m) for the front block and 9 lb f ft (1.25 kg f m) for the rear block.
18 To refit a rear crossmember support first secure the intermediate support to the crossmember using new star washers. Tighten the bolts to a torque wrench setting of 23.5 lb f ft (3.25 kg f m).
19 Next fit the crossmember support to the rubber blocks using new star washers and a new locking washer. Tighten the two front nuts to a torque wrench setting of 13 lb f ft (1.75 kg f m) and the rear nut to 23.5 lb f ft (3.25 kf f m). Lock by bending the tab washer tongues over the nut.
20 Fit the guide to the crossmember support, place a jack under the support and raise until the three crossmember studs are completely engaged.
21 Remove the guide and close the guide hole using the plastic plug.
22 Fit the following onto the studs in the order of: flat washers, a new tab lock and securing nuts.
23 Tighten the nuts to the recommended torque wrench setting. See Section 11, paragraph 32, for full information.
24 Lock the nuts by bending the tab tongues over the nuts.
25 Refit the roadwheel and lower the car to the ground.

13 Rear hub and carrier (Saloon models) - removal, overhaul and replacement

1 Refer to Chapter 8, and remove the driveshaft.
2 Unscrew the hub nut and set aside the washer.
3 Remove the driveshaft from the hub carrier using a soft faced hammer. If very tight it may be necessary to use a universal puller or even a press.
4 Hold the hub carrier assembly between soft faces in a bench vice. Using a spanner unlock and remove the hub carrier nut. Beware because it is very tight.
5 Using a universal puller and thrust pad located inside the hub draw off the hub from the carrier.
6 Using a suitable tapered drift remove the double bearing. Note which way round it is fitted.
7 Invert the hub carrier in the vice and lever out the oil seal, noting which way round it is fitted.
8 Inspect the bearing for signs of wear, damage or overheating and, if evident a new bearing must be obtained.
9 Whenever the hub is dismantled the nut with its two lipped oil seal and also the outer oil seal must be renewed. All new bearings are fitted with a nylon ring inserted in the inner track. This ring must be removed before fitting the bearing.
10 To reassemble, first fit the oil seal using a suitable diameter tubular drift. It should abut onto the nut.
11 Fit the bearing assembly into the carrier using a suitable diameter tubular drift. (Fig. 11.32).
12 Refit and tighten the carrier nut until it comes into contact with the bearing. Now tighten the nut to a torque wrench setting of 181 lb f ft (25 kg fm).
13 Lock the carrier nut using a centre punch in the notches provided.
14 Hold the nut in the vice on its two flat edges and place the carrier on the nut.
15 Insert the hub into the carrier and using a large nut and bolt draw on the hub until it abuts on the bearing.
16 Smear a little grease onto the driveshaft splines and insert into the hub and carrier.

Fig. 11.30. Suspension crossmember lowered (Sec. 12)

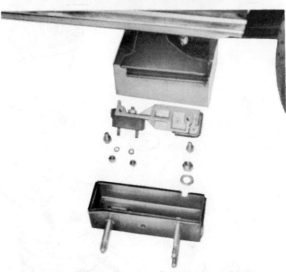

Fig. 11.31. Crossmember supports and attachments (Sec. 12)

Fig. 11.32. Fitting bearing into the carrier (Sec. 13)

17 Fit the washer and hand tighten a new hub nut. (Fig. 11.33).
18 Reassembly and refitting is now described in Chapter 8, and is a continuation of driveshaft replacement.

14 Rear hub and carrier (Convertible and Coupe models) - removal, overhaul and replacement

1 Refer to Chapter 8, and remove the driveshaft. For this the caliper will have to be removed (Chapter 9).
2 Using a suitable drift or other means remove the hub carrier nut from the end of the carrier. This is an internal nut so be prepared.
3 Using a universal puller and thrust pad detach the hub carrier assembly from the disc.
4 Undo and remove the four Allen screws that secure the hub carrier to the arm. Again using the universal puller detach the hub carrier.
5 Dismantling and reassembly of the rear hub, the hub carrier nut and oil seals is basically identical to that described in Section 13.
6 To refit the rear hub carrier first replace the disc brake

Fig. 11.33. Driveshaft being fitted to hub and carrier (Sec. 13)

1 Hub and carrier assembly   2 Washer
                                   3 Hub nut

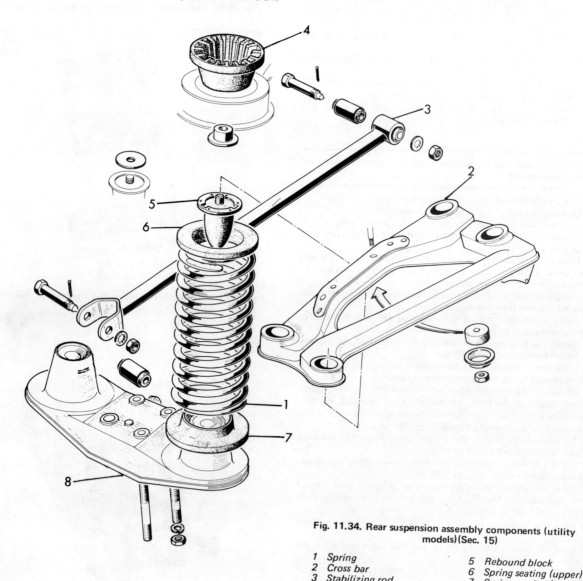

Fig. 11.34. Rear suspension assembly components (utility models)(Sec. 15)

1 Spring   5 Rebound block
2 Cross bar   6 Spring seating (upper)
3 Stabilizing rod   7 Spring seating (lower)
4 Butyl rest   8 Support

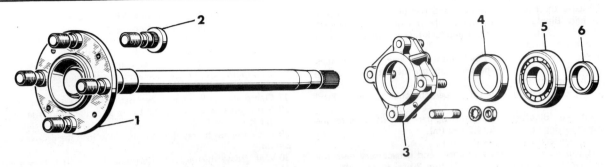

Fig. 11.35. Rear hub and halfshaft (utility vehicle)(Sec. 15)

1 Halfshaft	3 Retainer	5 Bearing
2 Wheel stud	4 Oil seal	6 Locking ring

protector and then engage the hub carrier in its housing on the arm.

7   Fit new Blocfor washers and tighten the four Allen screws to a torque wrench setting of 29 lb f ft (4 kg f m).

8   Assemble the hub to the hub carrier using a large bolt, nut and washers. The hub should abut against the bearing.

9   Reassembly is now a continuation of refitting the driveshaft. Refer to Chapter 8 for full information.

15 Rear suspension (Utility models) - removal, overhaul and replacement

The rear suspension system uses twin coil springs, one located either side of the axle 'banjo'. Unless special tools are available for holding the springs during the removal stages a very nasty accident could occur. For this reason no further information is given on rear suspension overhaul. Leave this to the local Peugeot garage. The work that can be carried out is as follows and will present no problems provided that the work is carried out methodically.

   a) *Removal and replacement of anti-roll bar.*
   b) *Removal and replacement of shock absorber (Section 7).*
   c) *Removal and replacement of rear axle (see also Chapter 7).*
   d) *Removal and replacement of rear brakes giving access to hub bearings.*

16 Steering rack and pinion - removal and replacement

1   Undo and remove the trackrod balljoint nuts at the wheel end of each trackrod.

2   Using a universal balljoint separator detach the trackrod ball pin ends from the steering arms.

3   Undo and remove the steering column/flector assembly bolt.

4   Undo and remove the two Allen screws securing the steering assembly to the front suspension crossmember. Note that on some models, these screws are pinned and, where this is the case, the pins must first be removed.

5   Insert a drift or punch (diameter 6 mm) in place of the flector bolt (Fig. 11.36).

6   Disengage the steering column by rocking the flector slightly using the drift or punch.

7   The steering rack and pinion assembly may now be lifted away from under the car.

8   To refit the steering rack and pinion assembly first position the steering wheel spokes vertically.

9   Place the front wheel which is opposite to the steering wheel in the 'straight-ahead' position.

10 Turn the other front wheel inwards as far as possible.

11 Centre the rack in the housing by counting the number of pinion turns from one full lock to the other full lock, halving the number of turns and setting the pinion to this number.

12 Temporarily reconnect the trackrod balljoint on the opposite side to the steering wheel.

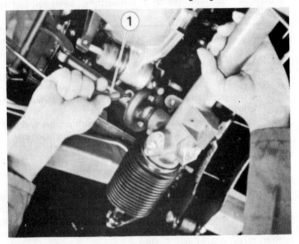

Fig. 11.36. Drift inserted in place of flector bolt (1) (Sec. 16)

Fig. 11.37. Aligning flector clamp with splined end of steering column (Sec. 16)

13 Rotate the steering flector ¼ of a turn to align the flector clamp with the splined end of the steering column (Fig. 11.37).

14 Insert the drift or punch into the bolt hole on the flector collar.

15 Insert the steering column end in the flector collar by rocking the flector slightly using the centre punch or drift as a lever.

16 Next secure the steering assembly to the crossmember and tighten the screws to a torque wrench setting of 23.5 lb f ft (3.25 kg fm).

17 Secure the steering column in the flector using a new nut, bolt and 'Blocfor' washer. Tighten the nut to a torque wrench setting of 7.2 lb f ft (1 kg fm) and lock by spreading the end of the bolt (Fig. 11.38).

18 Reconnect the trackrod balljoint on the steering wheel side. Check the alignment of the two flats on the balljoint housing and the connecting yoke.

19 Position the balljoint pin holes perpendicular to the trackrod axis.

20 Fit new 'Blocfor' washers and tighten the nuts to a torque wrench setting of 31 lb f ft (4.25 kg fm).

21 Fit new split pins to lock the nuts.

22 It will now be necessary to check and if necessary reset the front wheel alignment. Refer to Section 20 for further information.

17 Steering rack and pinion - dismantling, overhaul and re-assembly

1 Wash the outside of the rack and pinion assembly using paraffin or a proprietary cleaner and wipe dry with a non-fluffy rag.

2 Mount the assembly horizontally between soft faces in a bench vice.

3 Mark the position of the flector collar with the rack in the straight ahead position.

4 Remove the four rubber rack gaiter securing clips and push the two gaiters away from the centre of the steering assembly.

5 Unlock and remove the two trackrod yoke pivots.

6 Remove the two trackrods and the rack eye on the opposite side to the pinion. For this clamp the rack directly between soft faces in a vice and slacken the locknut.

7 Then remove the rack plunger plate securing bolts and washers. Lift away the plunger retaining plate complete with grease nipple and nylon stop, the plunger spring, rack plunger, bearing sealing cup, pinion nut and finally the pinion together with its thrust washer and 'O' ring.

8 The rack may now be withdrawn from the pinion side.

9 Remove the flexible bush retaining circlips. Withdraw the bush and the two steel thrust washers.

10 Remove the pinion bearing retaining circlips. Dip the steering box in boiling water to loosen the bearing. Lift out the bearing.

11 The steering rack is now fully dismantled. Clean all the parts in paraffin and wipe dry with a non-fluffy rag (Fig. 11.39).

12 Thoroughly inspect the rack and pinion teeth for signs of wear, cracks or damage. Check the ends of the rack for wear, especially where it moves in the bushes.

13 Examine the rubber gaiters for signs of cracking, perishing or other damage - if evident new gaiters must be obtained.

14 Inspect the rack eyes and yoke pivots for wear - if evident, new parts will be necessary. Any other parts that show wear or damage must be renewed.

15 Should it be necessary to renew the pinion bush it should be drifted out into the steering box with a suitable diameter drift.

16 To fit the new bush heat the steering box in boiling water and then carefully but quickly insert the new bush tapping, if necessary, with a soft faced hammer.

17 Grease the end bearing and immerse the end of the steering box in boiling water for a few minutes. Carefully but quickly insert the bearing into its housing, pressing on the outer race.

18 Fit the retaining circlip.

19 Fit into the housing on the opposite end to the pinion, the inner thrust washer, the flexible bush complete with two rubber rings, the outer thrust washer and the circlip.

20 Well grease the rack and flexible bush. Insert the rack into the box from the pinion side.

21 Temporarily thread the second eye onto the rack together with its locknut. Lightly tighten the locknut.

22 Push the rack until the locknut comes into contact with the steering box.

23 Well grease the pinion. Fit the 'O' ring and thin metal thrust washer to the pinion housing.

24 Place the pinion into its bore. The nut locking groove must be away from the plunger housing.

25 Starting from the vertical position of the pinion flange, rotate it to the left through about 20° (Fig. 11.40).

26 Push in the pinion until it abuts its bearing. The pinion flange should now be vertical with the locknut still in contact with the extremity of the steering box.

27 Clamp the pinion flange between soft faces in a bench vice.

28 Screw on a new nut and tighten to a torque wrench setting of 11 lb f ft (1.5 kg f m).

29 Lock the nut by tapping the nut collar into the groove on the pinion.

30 Well grease the bearing housing and then fit a new sealing cup, tapping it into place with a soft faced hammer.

31 Assemble the thrust plate by first refitting the grease nipple. Tighten to a torque wrench setting of 7.2 lb f ft (1.0 kg f m). Then the shim pack and the nylon stop (Fig. 11.41).

32 Well grease and then place the plunger and spring in its housing in the steering box.

33 Secure the thrust plate assembly with the two bolts and new 'Blocfor' washers. Tighten the bolts to a torque wrench setting of 7.2 lb f ft (1.0 kg f m).

34 Remove the eye from the rack on the opposite end to the pinion.

35 Fit the rack rubber gaiter.

36 Refit and adjust the rack eye to a distance of 20 - 21 mm between the locknut and shoulder of the eye (Fig. 11.42).

37 Align the moveable eye with the fixed eye using two 12 mm diameter rods, inserted in the inner rings of the 'Silentblocs'.

38 Tighten the locknut firmly but not excessively.

39 Turn the pinion to release the rack from the housing and clamp the rack horizontally in the vice again.

40 Tighten the eye locknut to a torque wrench setting of 25 lb f ft (3.5 kg f m).

41 Position the yoke of the trackrod on the pinion side of the rack.

42 Place the trackrod in line with the rack. The head of the bolt should be on the same side as the pinion flange.

43 Use a new tab washer and tighten the bolt to a torque wrench setting of 33 lb f ft (4.5 kg f m). Bend the tab washer up around the bolt head.

44 Fit the rack gaiter on the pinion side so that the larger axis is perpendicular to the bearing faces of the mounting flanges on the steering box on the main crossmember. The prongs of the clips must face the lower part of the steering box when fitted to the car.

45 Check and, if necessary, adjust the distance between the shoulders of the yoke and balljoint housing on the pinion side trackrod to 180 mm. Equalise the distance between the shoulders and the adjuster rod. Retighten the two clamp bolts (Fig. 11.43).

46 Fit the rack gaiter on the opposite end to the pinion. Refit the one piece trackrod onto the rack and position the trackrod so it is in line with the rack (paragraph 37).

47 Fit a new tab washer and tighten the bolt to a torque wrench setting of 33 lb f ft (4.5 kg f m). Bend the tab up around the bolt head.

48 Fit four new 'Blockfor' washers and bolts to the flector. The heads of the bolts should be towards the steering box.

49 Position the plates on both sides of the flector with the holes forming a cross.

50 Secure the flector to the pinion flange.

51 Centre the rack relative to the steering box so that it is in the straight-ahead position.

52 Fit the clamp to the flector using the reference marks made during dismantling. In the 'straight-ahead' position the bore of the collar bolt hole must be parallel to the rack.

53 The thrust faces of the pinion flange and the collar should be in contact with the flector through the holes in the plates. Tighten the four nuts to a torque wrench setting of 13 lb f ft (1.75 kg f m).

54 Lock the bolts by spreading the threads with a cold chisel.

55 Do not forget to refill with lubricant before fitting to the car.

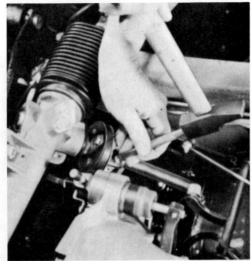

Fig. 11.38. Locking flector bolt by spreading with chisel (Sec. 16)

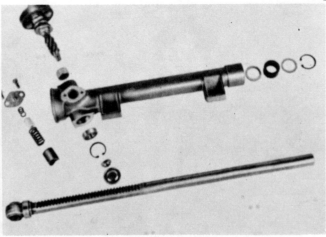

Fig. 11.39. Steering rack and pinion dismantled (Sec. 17)

Fig. 11.40. Rotating pinion flange through 20º (Sec. 17)

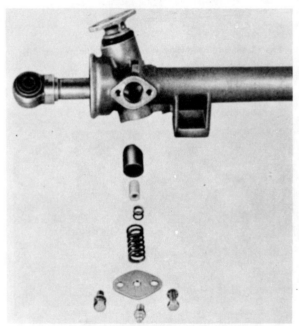

Fig. 11.41. Thrust plate and relative components (Sec. 17)

Fig. 11.42. Correct positioning of rack eye (Sec. 17)

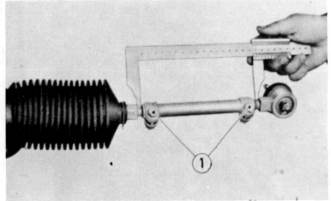

Fig. 11.43. Pinion side track rod initial adjustment (Sec. 17)

1 Clamp bolts

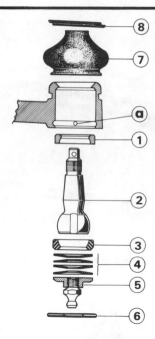

Fig. 11.44. Exploded view of track rod balljoint (Sec. 18)

1 Steel half cup
2 Ball head
3 Nylon half cup
4 Belleville washers
5 Balljoint cover
6 Spring clip
7 Rubber boot
8 Clip
a Hole

Fig. 11.45. Steering column gearchange rods (Sec. 19)

1 Upper control rod   3 Bolt
2 Selector rod

Fig. 11.46. Location of gearchange control rods retaining pin clip (1) (Sec. 19),

Fig. 11.47. Removal of pin using parallel pin punch (Sec. 19)

Fig. 11.48. Removal of clamp bolt (Sec. 19)

Fig. 11.49. Withdrawing the upper steering column assembly (Sec. 19)

18 Trackrod balljoints - dismantling and reassembly

1   With the trackrod removed from the car, clamp it in a vice.
2   Remove the clip and the rubber gaiter.
3   Carefully disengage the spring clip retaining the balljoint cover using a pin punch inserted in the hole provided.
4   The following parts should next be removed: the balljoint cover, the belleville washers, the lower nylon half cup, the ball head and finally the upper steel half cup.
5   Reassemble is the reverse sequence to dismantling. Do not forget to grease, preferably before refitting.

19 Steering column - removal and replacement

1   For safety reasons, disconnect the battery.
2   Detach the upper gearchange control rod and then the selector rod from its lever (Fig. 11.45).
3   Undo and remove the bolt from the flector.
4   Remove the lower shell from the steering column.
5   Move the clip that retains the pin assembling the gearchange control rods in an upwards direction (Fig. 11.46).
6   Using a 6 mm diameter drift remove the pin (Fig. 11.47).
7   Undo and remove the clamp bolt from the lower collar of the steering column cardan joint (Fig. 11.48).
8   Carefully slide the lower part of the steering column downwards until it abuts the flector.
9   Make a note of and disconnect the Neiman anti-theft wires. There are also three connectors on the steering column wiring harness to be detached.
10 Remove the two bolts that secure the handbrake lever support under the dashboard.
11 Undo and remove the four bearing nuts of the column. These are also located under the dashboard.
12 Simultaneously, release the two parts of the gearchange control rod and the steering column.
13 Lower the handbrake lever support to enable the freeing of the wiring harness of the steering column.
14 Withdraw the upper steering column assembly (Fig. 11.49).
15 Withdraw the lower bar of the steering column as far as possible and disengage it towards the interior of the car.
16 Remove the handbrake outer cable stop clamp. This will enable the handbrake return lever to be withdrawn relative to the scuttle (Fig. 11.50).

17 Undo and remove the four nuts that secure the steering column closing plate to the scuttle.
18 Disengage the handbrake lever support from its securing studs to enable the freeing of the closing plate.
19 Finally remove the lower gearchange control plate and its gasket. (Fig. 11.51).
20 Refitting the steering column assembly is the reverse sequence to removal. The following additional points should however be noted:

   a) If damaged renew the closing plate gasket.
   b) Tighten the closing plate nuts to a torque wrench setting of 7.2 lb f ft (1.0 kg f m).
   c) Tighten the handbrake outer cable clamp securing nuts to a torque wrench setting of 3.5 kb f ft (0.5 kg f m).
   d) Well grease the lower steering column bush which is fitted into the sealing plate before fitting the lower steering column rod.
   e) Tighten the four steering column nuts to a torque wrench setting of 7.2 lb f ft (1.0 kg f m).
   f) Tighten the cardan joint nut to a torque wrench setting of 7.2 lb f ft (1.0 kg f m). Always use a new nut. Lock by spreading the end of the bolt.
   g) Tighten the column to flector nut to a torque wrench setting of 7.2 lb f ft (1.0 kg f m). Always use a new nut, bolt and 'Blocfor' washer. Lock by spreading the end of the bolt.
   h) Refer to Chapter 6, and adjust the gearchange control rods.

20 Front wheel alignment

The front wheels are correctly aligned when they are turning in at the front by 3 mm. It is important that this measurement is taken on a centre line drawn horizontally and parallel to the ground through the centre line of the hub. The exact point should be in the centre of the sidewall of the tyre and not on the wheel rim which could be distorted and therefore give inaccurate readings.

The adjustment is effected at the left-hand trackrod but is one job best left to the local Peugeot garage as accurate alignment requires the use of special equipment. If the wheels are not in alignment tyre wear will be heavy and uneven and the steering will be stiff and unresponsive.

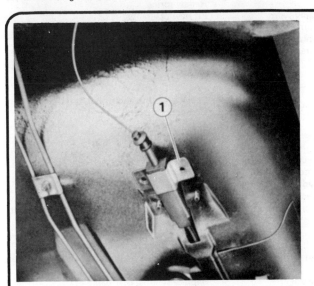

Fig. 11.50. Handbrake outer cable stop clamp (Sec. 19)

Fig. 11.51. Removal of lower gearchange control assembly (Sec. 19)

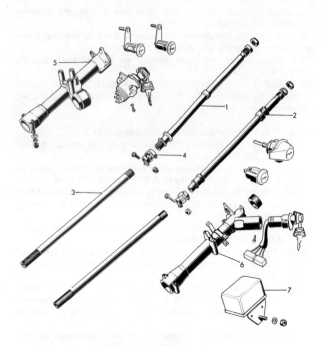

Fig. 11.52. Steering shaft assemblies

1   Upper steering shaft (early)
2   Upper steering shaft (later)
3   Lower steering shaft
4   Cardan joint
5   Steering column outer assembly
6   Steering column outer assembly (alternative)
7   Steering lock buzzer

Fig. 11.53. Steering wheel assemblies (Two alternatives shown)

21 Fault diagnosis - suspension and steering

Symptom	Cause	Remedy
Steering feels vague, car wanders and floats at speed	Tyre pressures uneven	Check pressures and adjust as necessary
	Dampers worn	Test, and replace if worn
	Spring broken	Renew spring
	Steering gear balljoints badly worn	Fit new balljoints
	Suspension geometry incorrect	Check and rectify
	Steering mechanism free play excessive	Adjust or overhaul steering mechanism
	Front suspension and rear axle pick-up points out of alignment	Normally caused by poor repair work after a serious accident. Extensive rebuilding necessary.
Stiff and heavy steering	Tyre pressures too low	Check pressures and inflate tyres
	No grease in swivel pins	Grease thoroughly
	No oil in steering gear	Top up steering gear
	No grease in steering and suspension balljoints	Grease thoroughly
	Front wheel toe-in incorrect	Check and reset toe-in
	Suspension geometry incorrect	Check and rectify
	Steering gear incorrectly adjusted too tightly	Check and re-adjust steering gear
	Steering column badly misaligned	Determine cause and rectify (usually due to bad repair after severe accident damage and difficult to correct)
Wheel wobble and vibration	Wheel nuts loose	Check and tighten as necessary
	Front wheels and tyres out of balance	Balance wheels and tyres and add weights as necessary
	Steering balljoints badly worn	Replace steering gear balljoints
	Hub bearings badly worn	Remove and fit new hub bearings
	Steering gear free play excessive	Adjust and overhaul steering gear
	Front springs weak or broken	Inspect and overhaul as necessary

Chapter 12 Bodywork and fittings

For modifications, and information applicable to later models, see Supplement at end of manual

Contents

1 General description

The combined body and underframe is of all steel welded construction. This makes a very strong and torsionally rigid shell. Various body styles are available but may be generally divided into Saloon (Sedan) and Estate Wagon (Break) styles.

Due to the design of the body a considerable degree of protection to the driver and passengers is offered in the event of an accident. Also body panel renewal is straightforward provided that normal bodywork repair equipment is available.

During production the bodyshell is treated using a special electrolytic process to assist in corrosion protection.

2 Maintenance - bodywork and underframe

1 The condition of your car's bodywork is of considerable importance as it is on this that the second-hand value of the car will mainly depend. It is much more difficult to repair neglected bodywork than to renew mechanical assemblies. The hidden portions of the body, such as the wheel arches, the underframe and the engine compartment are equally important, although obviously not requiring such frequent attention as the immediately visible paintwork.
2 Once a year or every 12,000 miles, it is a sound scheme to visit your local main agent and have the underside of the body steam cleaned. All traces of dirt and oil will be removed and the underside can then be inspected carefully for rust, damaged hydraulic pipes, frayed electrical wiring and similar maladies. The car should be greased on completion of this job.
3 At the same time the engine compartment should be cleaned in a similar manner. If steam cleaning facilities are not available then brush a proprietary cleanser over the whole engine and engine compartment with a stiff paint brush, working it well in where there is an accumulation of oil and dirt. Do not paint the ignition system, and protect it with oily rags when the cleanser is washed off. As the cleanser is washed away it will take with it all traces of oil and dirt, leaving the engine looking clean and bright.

4 The wheel arches should be given particular attention as under-sealing can easily come away here and stones and dirt thrown up from the roadwheels can soon cause the paint to chip and flake, and so allow rust to set in. If rust is found, clean down the bare metal with wet and dry paper, paint on an anti-corrosive coating, and renew the paintwork and undercoating.
5 The bodywork should be washed once a week or when dirty. Thoroughly wet the car to soften the dirt and then wash the car down with a soft sponge and plenty of clean water. If the surplus dirt is not washed off very gently, in time it will wear the paint down as surely as wet and dry paper. It is best to use a hose if this is available. Give the car a final wash down and then dry with a soft chamois leather to prevent the formation of spots.
6 Spots of tar and grease thrown up from the road can be removed by a using a rag dampened with petrol/gasoline.
7 Once every six months, or every three months if wished, give the bodywork and chromium trim a thoroughly good wax polish. If a chromium cleaner is used to remove rust on any of the car's plated parts remember that the cleaner also removes part of the chromium, so use sparingly.

3 Maintenance - upholstery and carpets

1 Remove the carpets or mats and thoroughly vacuum clean the interior of the car every three months or more frequently if necessary.
2 Beat out the carpets and vacuum clean them if they are very dirty. If the upholstery is soiled apply an upholstery cleaner with a damp sponge and wipe off with a clean dry cloth.

4 Maintenance - PVC external roof covering

Under no circumstances try to clean any external PVC roof covering with detergents, caustic soaps or spirit cleaners. Plain soap and water is all that is required, with a soft brush to clean dirt that may be ingrained. Wash the covering as frequently as the rest of the car.

This sequence of photographs deals with the repair of the dent and paintwork damage shown in this photo. The procedure will be similar for the repair of a hole. It should be noted that the procedures given here are simplified — more explicit instructions will be found in the text

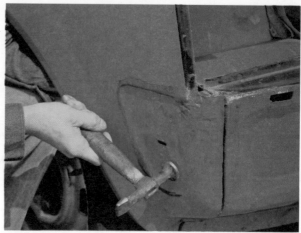

In the case of a dent the first job — after removing surrounding trim — is to hammer out the dent where access is possible. This will minimise filling. Here, the large dent having been hammered out, the damaged area is being made slightly concave

Now all paint must be removed from the damaged area, by rubbing with coarse abrasive paper. Alternatively, a wire brush or abrasive pad can be used in a power drill. Where the repair area meets good paintwork, the edge of the paintwork should be 'feathered', using a finer grade of abrasive paper

In the case of a hole caused by rusting, all damaged sheet-metal should be cut away before proceeding to this stage. Here, the damaged area is being treated with rust remover and inhibitor before being filled

Mix the body filler according to its manufacturer's instructions. In the case of corrosion damage, it will be necessary to block off any large holes before filling — this can be done with aluminium or plastic mesh, or aluminium tape. Make sure the area is absolutely clean before ...

... applying the filler. Filler should be applied with a flexible applicator, as shown, for best results; the wooden spatula being used for confined areas. Apply thin layers of filler at 20-minute intervals, until the surface of the filler is slightly proud of the surrounding bodywork

Initial shaping can be done with a Surform plane or Dreadnought file. Then, using progressively finer grades of wet-and-dry paper, wrapped around a sanding block, and copious amounts of clean water, rub down the filler until really smooth and flat. Again, feather the edges of adjoining paintwork

The whole repair area can now be sprayed or brush-painted with primer. If spraying, ensure adjoining areas are protected from over-spray. Note that at least one inch of the surrounding sound paintwork should be coated with primer. Primer has a 'thick' consistency, so will find small imperfections

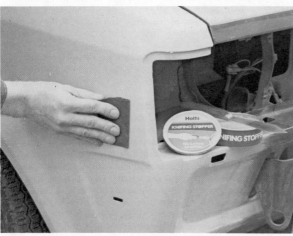

Again, using plenty of water, rub down the primer with a fine grade wet-and-dry paper (400 grade is probably best) until it is really smooth and well blended into the surrounding paintwork. Any remaining imperfections can now be filled by carefully applied knifing stopper paste

When the stopper has hardened, rub down the repair area again before applying the final coat of primer. Before rubbing down this last coat of primer, ensure the repair area is blemish-free – use more stopper if necessary. To ensure that the surface of the primer is really smooth use some finishing compound

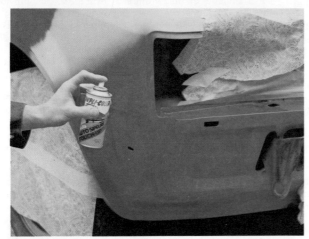

The top coat can now be applied. When working out of doors, pick a dry, warm and wind-free day. Ensure surrounding areas are protected from over-spray. Agitate the aerosol thoroughly, then spray the centre of the repair area, working outwards with a circular motion. Apply the paint as several thin coats

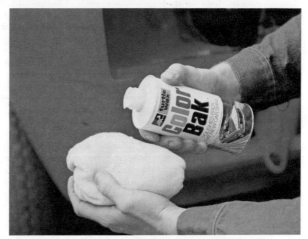

After a period of about two weeks, which the paint needs to harden fully, the surface of the repaired area can be 'cut' with a mild cutting compound prior to wax polishing. When carrying out bodywork repairs, remember that the quality of the finished job is proportional to the time and effort expended

5   Minor body damage - repairs

See also photo sequences on pages 222 and 223.

Repair of minor scratches in the car's bodywork

If the scratch is very superficial, and does not penetrate to the metal of the bodywork - repair is very simple. Lightly rub the area of the scratch with a paintwork renovator (eg; T-Cut), or a very fine cutting paste, to remove loose paint from the scratch and to clear the surrounding bodywork of wax polish. Rinse the area with clean water.

Apply touch-up paint to the scratch using a thin paint brush; continue to apply thin layers of paint until the surface of the paint in the scratch is level with the surrounding paintwork. Allow the new paint at least two weeks to harden, then, blend it into the surrounding paintwork by rubbing the paintwork in the scratch area with a paintwork renovator (eg; T-Cut), or a very fine cutting paste. Finally apply wax polish.

An alternative to painting over the scratch is to use Holts Scratch-Patch. Use the same preparation for the affected area; then simply, pick a patch of a suitable size to cover the scratch completely. Hold the patch against the scratch and burnish its backing paper; the patch will adhere to the paintwork, freeing itself from the backing paper at the same time. Polish the affected area to blend the patch into the surrounding paintwork.

Where a scratch has penetrated right through to the metal of the bodywork, causing the metal to rust, a different repair technique is required. Remove any loose rust from the bottom of the scratch with a penknife; then apply rust inhibiting paint (eg; Kurust) to prevent the formation of rust in the future. Using a rubber or nylon applicator fill the scratch with body-stopper paste. If required, this paste can be mixed with cellulose thinners to provide a very thin paste which is ideal for filling narrow scratches. Before the stopper paste in the scratch hardens, wrap a piece of smooth cotton rag around the tip of a finger. Dip the finger in cellulose thinners and then quickly sweep it across the surface of the stopper-paste in the scratch; this will ensure that the surface of the stopper-paste is slightly hollowed. The scratch can now be painted over as described earlier in this Section.

Repair of dents in the car's bodywork

When deep denting of the car's bodywork has taken place, the first task is to pull the dent out, until the affected bodywork almost attains its original shape. There is little point in trying to restore the original shape completely, as the metal in the damaged area will have stretched on impact and cannot be reshaped fully to its original contour. It is better to bring the level of the dent up to a point which is about 1/8 inch (3 mm) below the level of the surrounding bodywork. In cases where the dent is very shallow anyway, it is not worth trying to pull it out at all.

If the underside of the dent is accessible, it can be hammered out gently from behind, using a mallet with a wooden or plastic head. Whilst doing this, hold a suitable block of wood firmly against the outside of the dent. This block will absorb the impact from the hammer blows and thus prevent a large area of bodywork from being 'belled-out'.

Should the dent be in a section of the bodywork which has double skin or some other factor making it inaccessible from behind, a different technique is called for. Drill several small holes through the metal inside the dent area - particularly in the deeper sections. Then screw long self-tapping screws into the holes just sufficiently for them to gain a good purchase in the metal. Now the dent can be pulled out by pulling on the protruding head of the screws with a pair of pliers.

The next stage of the repair is the removal of the paint from the damaged area, and from an inch or so of the surrounding 'sound' bodywork. This is accomplished most easily by using a wire brush or abrasive pad on a power drill, although it can be done just as effectively by hand using sheets of abrasive paper. To complete the preparations for filling, score the surface of the bare metal with a screwdriver or the tang of a file, or

alternatively, drill small holes in the affected area. This will provide a really good 'key' for the filler paste.

To complete the repair see the Section on filling and respraying.

Repair of rust holes or gashes in the car's bodywork

Remove all paint from the affected area and from an inch or so of the surrounding 'sound' bodywork, using an abrasive pad or a wire brush on a power drill. If these are not available a few sheets of abrasive paper will do the job just as effectively. With the paint removed you will be able to gauge the severity of the corrosion and therefore decide whether to replace the whole panel (if this is possible) or to repair the affected area. Replacement body panels are not as expensive as most people think and it is often quicker and more satisfactory to fit a new panel then to attempt to repair large areas of corrosion.

Remove all fittings from the affected area except those which will act as a guide to the original shape of the damaged bodywork (eg;headlamp shells etc). Then, using tin snips or a hacksaw blade, remove all loose metal and any other metal badly affected by corrosion. Hammer the edges of the hole inwards in order to create a slight depression for the filler paste.

Wire brush the affected area to remove the powdery rust from the surface of the remaining metal. Paint the affected area with rust inhibiting paint; if the back of the rusted area is accessible treat this also.

Before filling can take place it will be necessary to block the hole in some way. This can be achieved by the use of one of the following materials: Zinc gauze, Aluminium tape or Polyurethane foam.

Zinc gauze is probably the best material to use for filling a hole. Cut a piece to the approximate size and shape of the hole to be filled, then position it in the hole so that its edges are below the level of the surrounding bodywork. It can be retained in position by several blobs of filler paste around its periphery.

Aluminium tape should be used for small or very narrow holes. Pull a piece off the roll and trim it to the approximate size and shape required, then pull off the backing paper (if used) and stick the tape over the hole; it can be overlapped if the thickness of one piece is insufficient. Burnish down the edges of the tape with the handle of a screwdriver or similar, to ensure that the tape is securely attached to the metal underneath.

Polyurethane foam is best used where the hole is situated in a section of bodywork of complex shape, backed by a small box section (eg; where the sill panel meets the rear wheel arch - most cars).The usual mixing procedure for this foam is as follows: Put equal amounts of fluid from each of the two cans provided in the kits, into one container. Stir until the mixture begins to thicken, then quickly pour this mixture into the hole, and hold a piece of cardboard over the larger apertures. Almost immediately the polyurethane will begin to expand, gushing frantically out of any small holes left unblocked. When the foam hardens it can be cut back to just below the level of the surrounding bodywork with a hacksaw blade.

Having blocked off the hole the affected area must now be filled and sprayed - see Section on bodywork filling and respraying.

Bodywork repairs - filling and re-spraying

Before using this Section, see the Sections on dent, deep scratch, rust hole, and gash repairs.

Many types of bodyfiller are available, but generally speaking those proprietary kits which contain a tin of filler paste and a tube of resin hardener (eg; Holts Cataloy) are best for this type of repair. A wide, flexible plastic or nylon applicator will be found invaluable for imparting a smooth and well contoured finish to the surface of the filler.

Mix up a little filler on a clean piece of card or board - use the hardener sparingly (follow the maker's instructions on the pack), otherwise the filler will set very rapidly.

Using the applicator, apply the filler paste to the prepared area; draw the applicator across the surface of the filler to achieve the correct contour and to level the filler surface. As soon as a contour that approximates the correct one is achieved, stop working the paste - if you carry on too long the paste will become sticky and begin to 'pick-up' on the applicator.

Continue to add thin layers of filler paste at twenty-minute intervals until the level of the filler is just 'proud' of the surrounding bodywork.

Once the filler has hardened, excess can be removed using a Surform plane or Dreadnought file. From then on, progressively finer grades of abrasive paper should be used, starting with a 40 grade 'wet-and-dry' paper. Always wrap the abrasive paper around a flat rubber, cork, or wooden block - otherwise the surface of the filler will not be completely flat. During the smoothing of the filler surface the 'wet-and-dry' paper should be periodically rinsed in water - this will ensure that a very smooth finish is imparted to the filler at the final stage.

At this stage the 'dent' should be surrounded by a ring of bare metal, which in turn should be encircled by the finely 'feathered' edge of the good paintwork. Rinse the repair area with clean water, until all the dust produced by the rubbing-down operating is gone.

Spray the whole repair area with a light coat of grey primer - this will show up any imperfections in the surface of the filler. Repair these imperfections with fresh filler paste or body-stopper, and once more smooth the surface with abrasive paper. If bodystopper is used, it can be mixed with cellulose thinners to form a really thin paste which is ideal for filling small holes. Repeat this spray and repair procedure until you are satisfied that the surface of the filler, and the feathered edge of the paintwork are perfect. Clean the repair area with clean water and allow to dry fully.

The repair area is now ready for spraying. Paint spraying must be carried out in a warm, dry, windless and dust free atmosphere. This condition can be created artificially if you have access to a large indoor working area, but if you are forced to work in the open, you will have to pick your day very carefully. If you are working indoors, dousing the floor in the work area with water will 'lay' the dust which would otherwise be in the atmosphere. If the repair area is confined to one body panel, mask off the surrounding panels; this will help to minimise the effects of a slight mis-match in paint colours. Bodywork fittings (eg; chrome strips, door handles etc) will also need to be masked off. Use genuine masking tape and several thicknesses of newspaper for the masking operation.

Before commencing to spray, agitate the aerosol can thoroughly, then spray a test area (an old tin, or similar) until the technique is mastered. Cover the repair area with a thick coat of primer; the thickness should be built up using several thin layers of paint rather than one thick one. Using 400 grade 'wet-and-dry' paper, rub down the surface of the primer until it is really smooth. While doing this, the work area should be thoroughly doused with water, and the wet-and-dry paper periodically rinsed in water. Allow to dry, before spraying on more paint.

Spray on the top coat, again building up the thickness by using several thin layers of paint. Start spraying in the centre of the repair area and then using a circular motion, work outwards until the whole repair area and about 2 inches of the surrounding original paintwork is covered. Remove all masking material 10 to 15 minutes after spraying on the final coat of paint. Allow the new paint at least 2 weeks to harden fully, then, using paintwork renovator (eg; T-Cut) or a very fine cutting paste, blend the edges of the new paint into the existing paintwork. Finally, apply wax polish.

6 Major body damage - repair

1 Because the body is built on the monocoque principle, major damage must be repaired by a competent body repairer with the necessary jigs and equipment.
2 In the event of a crash that resulted in buckling of body panels, or damage to the roadwheels the car must be taken to a Peugeot dealer or body repairer where the bodyshell and suspension alignment may be checked.
3 Bodyshell and/or suspension mis-alignment will cause excessive wear of the tyres, steering system and possibly transmission. The handling of the car will also be affected adversely.

7 Hinges, door catches and locks - maintenance

1 Oil the hinges of the bonnet, boot and doors with a drop, or two, of light oil, periodically. A good time is after the car has been washed.
2 Oil the bonnet release catch pivot pin and the safety catch pivot pin, periodically.
3 Do not over-lubricate door latches and strikers. Normally a little oil on the end of the rotary pinion spindle and a thin smear of high melting point grease on the striker pinion teeth and shoe spring plunger are adequate. Make sure that before lubrication they are wiped thoroughly clean and correctly adjusted. The excessive use of ordinary grease will result, more likely, in badly stained clothing!

8 Doors - tracing rattles and rectification

1 Check first that the door is not loose at the hinges and that the latch is holding it firmly in position. Check also that the door lines up with the aperture in the body.
2 If the hinges are loose or the door is out of alignment it will be necessary to detach it from the hinges.
3 If the latch is holding the door correctly it should be possible to press the door inwards fractionally against the rubber weatherstrip. If not, adjust the striker plate.
4 Other rattles from the door would be caused by wear or looseness in the window winder, the glass channels and sill strips, or the door handles and remote control arm; all of which are described in following Sections.

9 Front door trim panel (Saloon) - removal and replacement

1 Using a hook made from welding wire located between the window regulator handle and its thrust cup, withdraw the spring clip. (Fig. 12.1)
2 Note the position of the door handle with the glass in the raised position and remove the handles and thrust cup.
3 Remove the inner door opening control lever.

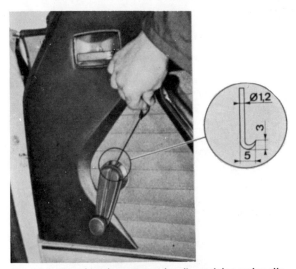

Fig. 12.1. Use of hook to remove handle retaining spring clip (Sec. 9)

4   Remove the armrest.
5   Undo and remove the interior door locking button.
6   Disengage the clips securing the upper padded panel using a wide bladed screwdriver.
7   Raise the upper panel and lift away. (Fig. 12.2)
8   Again using a wide bladed screwdriver disengage the clips and lift away the lower trim panel.
9   Refitting the lower and upper trim panels is the reverse sequence to removal.

10 Front door window winder regulator (Saloon) - removal and replacement

1   Refer to Section 9, and remove the front door trim panel.
2   With the window in the raised position, undo and remove the four nuts and washers securing the mechanism to the door inner panel.

Fig. 12.2. Removal of door trim upper panel (Sec. 9)

Fig. 12.3. Removal of window winder regulator (Sec. 10)

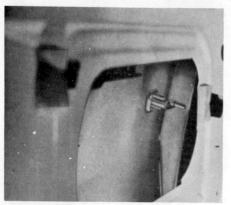

Fig. 12.5. Door outer lock (Sec. 11)

3   Hold the glass in the raised position, push the mechanism in and disengage the rollers from the slide. To do this, work towards the rear of the mechanism.
4   The mechanism may now be withdrawn through the upper aperture. (Fig. 12.3)
5   Refitting the window regulator is the reverse sequence to removal but it will be necessary to adjust its final fitted position, as described in the following paragraphs.
6   Check the free-movement of the glass paying particular attention to excessive play or hard spots.
7   Lower the glass fully and slacken the lower slide securing nut on the inner door panel. This is the bottom nut nearest to the door hinge.
8   Move the slide into contact with the bottom of the glass and tighten the nut.

11 Front door lock (Saloon) - removal and replacement

1   Refer to Section 9, and remove the interior trim panel.
2   Disconnect the control link at the lock end.
3   Undo and remove the three door lock securing screws. (Fig 12.4)
4   Lift away the guide plate.
5   Insert the key into the lock and slide the lock downwards until the locking crank disengages from the catch.
6   Pivot the lock around the slide support and withdraw the lock.
7   To remove the outer lock carefully withdraw the lock stop fork and disengage in an outward manner. (Fig. 12.5).
8   Refitting the door lock is the reverse sequence to removal. Check the operation of the lock mechanism and the condition of all the return springs. Apply a little grease to all the pivots.

Fig. 12.4. Removal of door lock securing screws (Sec. 11)

1   Control link   2   Guide plate

Fig. 12.6. Door lock assembly (Sec. 11)

12 Front door window (Saloon) - removal and replacement

1 Refer to Section 10, and remove the window winder regulator.
2 With the window in the raised position lift it towards the front so as to disengage it from its slides.
3 With the glass in this position draw it upwards and out through the outer side of the door aperture. (Fig. 12.7)
4 Should the glass need to be renewed due to damage or other reasons clean the glass support mounting.
5 Obtain a new rubber section and smear with a little washing up liquid.
6 Fit the support mounting to the glass so that the extremity of the mounting is 9½ in. (242 mm) from the rear of the glass.
7 Refitting the glass and support mounting is the reverse sequence to removal.

13 Front door trim - outer window seal (Saloon) - removal and replacement

1 Refer to Section 9, and remove the door trim panel.
2 Check the condition of the outer seal as it must not have any cracks or permanent distortion.
3 To remove the trim, insert a screwdriver between the plastic clips and the inner edges of the trim.
4 Ease the trim upwards starting at the front end. (Fig. 12.8).

5 Refitting the outer window seal is the reverse sequence to removal. Always fit the plastic clips to the door panel first and then push the trim into position.

14 Rear door trim panel (Saloon) - removal and replacement

Refer to Section 9, for full information

15 Rear door window winder regulator (Saloon) - removal and replacement

1 Refer to Sections 14 and 9, and remove the rear door trim panel.
2 Raise the glass and hold in this position.
3 Undo and remove the four nuts and washers securing the mechanism to the door inner panel.
4 Push the mechanism inwards, then backwards until the shaft appears in the elongated hole in the interior door panel. (Fig 12.9)
5 Using the handle turn the mechanism to the maximum raised position. Remove the handle.
6 Push the mechanism inwards again and move it forwards so as to disengage the rollers from the slide.
7 Withdraw the mechanism through the upper rear opening in the interior door panel. (Fig. 12.10)
8 Refitting the window regulator is the reverse sequence to

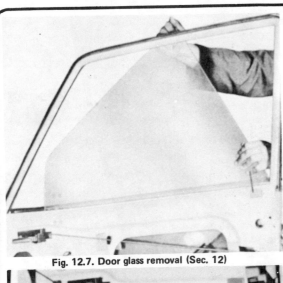
Fig. 12.7. Door glass removal (Sec. 12)

Fig. 12.8. Door trim outer window seal removal (Sec. 13)

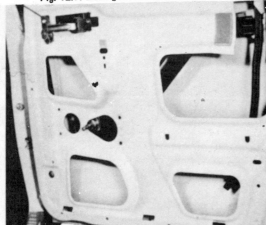
Fig. 12.9. Window regulator assembly moved rearwards in door (Sec. 15)

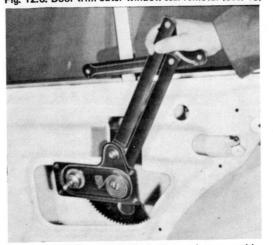
Fig. 12.10. Final removal of window regulator assembly (Sec. 15)

removal. Apply a little grease to all moving parts and before actually inserting into the door, position the quadrant to obtain a distance of ¼ in. (6 mm) between the two arms.

16 Rear door lock (Saloon) - removal and replacement

Refer to Section 11, for full information.

17 Rear door window (Saloon) - removal and replacement

1   Refer to Section 14 and 9, and remove the rear door trim panel.
2   Undo and remove the three screws that secure the rear slide support.
3   Remove the upper glass slide by carefully unclipping it from the middle and working outwards. (Fig. 12.11)
4   Raise the glass fully and disengage the slide from the lower part of the rear support.
5   Remove the lower part of the rear slide support by pivoting it forwards, pushing the top forwards and finally disengaging the support downwards. (Fig. 12.12)
6   Refer to Section 15, and remove the regulator assembly.
7   Lower the glass as much as possible and then push the upper slide support forwards. (Fig. 12.13)

8   Remove the slide support by lifting up from the door.
9   The glass may now be removed by holding in its normal position and lifting outwards through the door aperture.
10 Should the glass need to be renewed due to damage or other reasons clean the glass support mounting, carefully.
11 Obtain a new rubber section and smear with a little washing up liquid.
12 Fit the support mounting to the glass so that the extremity of the mounting is ¾ in. (18 mm) from the rear of the glass.
13 Refitting the glass and support mounting is the reverse sequence to removal.

18 Rear door fixed window (Saloon) - removal and replacement

1   Refer to Section 17, and remove the door glass.
2   Push the fixed window towards the front of the door and withdraw the glass together with its seal. (Fig. 12.14)
3   Refitting the fixed window is the reverse sequence to removal.

19 Rear door trim outer window seal (Saloon) - removal and replacement

Refer to Section 13, for full information.

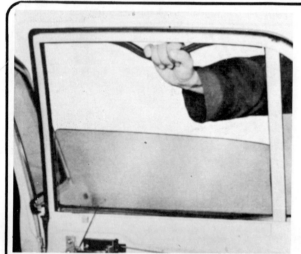

Fig. 12.11. Removal of upper glass slide (Sec. 17)

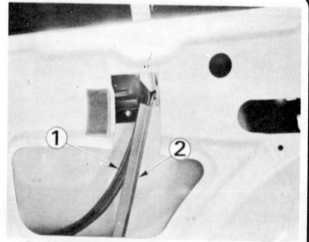

Fig. 12.12. Slide disengaged from rear support (Sec. 17)
1   Slide   2   Rear support

Fig. 12.13. Pushing upper slide support forwards (Sec. 17)

Fig. 12.14. Rear door fixed window removal (Sec. 18)

20 Front door trim panel (Convertible and Coupe) - removal and replacement

1 Fully lower the window and then raise it by 5/8 to ¾ in. (15 to 20 mm).
2 For safety reasons, disconnect the battery.
3 Using a screwdriver carefully remove the uppermost door panel trim.
4 Remove the door handle and trim.
5 Remove the door lock trim.
6 Carefully raise the ends of the plastic strip to expose the arm rest securing screws. Undo and remove these screws. (Fig. 12.16)
7 Remove the arm rest by sliding it upwards and recover the plastic thrust cups.
8 Undo and remove the four screws securing the armrest lower trim panel bracket to the door inner panel. (Fig. 12.17)
9 Also undo and remove the lower trim panel securing screws.
10 Disconnect the door courtesy light leads.
11 Carefully detach the door trim panel using a wide bladed screwdriver and recover the clip protectors.
12 If necessary remove the waterproof panel.
13 Refitting the door trim panels is the reverse sequence to removal.

21 Front door window winder regulator (Convertible and Coupe) - removal and replacement

1 Refer to Section 20, and remove the door trim panel.
2 Place a tool clip over the window winder drum to retain the cable onto the drum. (note a clip is supplied with each new drive).
3 Place a block of wood under the glass so as to support its weight. This will give better access to the cable clamps.
4 Remove the two cable clamps and components.
5 Remove the adjustable idler pulley.
6 Disengage the cable from the four pulleys.

Fig. 12.15. Front door trim panel (Sec. 20)

1 Door panel trim   3 Lock trim
2 Door handle and trim

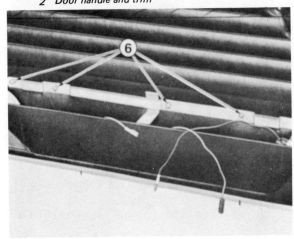

Fig. 12.17. Lower trim panel bracket screws (1) (Sec. 20)

Fig. 12.16. Armrest securing screws (Sec. 20)

1 Screws   2 Plastic insert

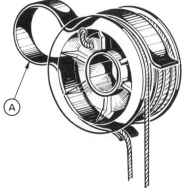

Fig. 12.18. Clip (A) fitted to window winder drum (Sec. 21)

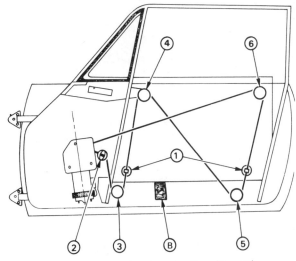

Fig. 12.19. Layout of cable and pulleys (Sec. 21)

1 Cable clamp   3 - 6 Pulleys
2 Idler pulley   B   Wood block

7   Make a note of and disconnect the motor feed cables.

8   Undo and remove the three nuts that secure the motor to the door panel. Carefully remove the motor and cable assembly through the lowermost opening in the door inner panel.

9   Should it be necessary to dismantle the motor assembly first undo and remove the nuts that secure the motor to the winding mechanism.

10 Separate the motor from the mechanism.

11 Undo and remove the three bolts holding the mechanism to the mounting frame.

12 Separate the mechanism from the frame and recover the flexible washer, drum with the cable and the flexible drive seal.

13 To reassemble first ensure that the cable is well wound on the drums and retained by a tool clip.

14 Make sure that the support shaft of the crank is perfectly inset.

15 Raise the mechanism cover and check the condition of the pinions. Make sure they are well greased.

16 Mount the drum on the mechanism shaft.

17 *Left-hand door:* Position the cable wound ¼ of a turn (a) against the mechanism and position the strands (a) and (b) in such a way that they pass between the spacers (7) and (8) of the frame (4)

18 *Right-hand door:* Position the cable wound ¼ of a turn (a) away from the mechanism and position the strands (a) and (b) in such a way that they pass between the spacers (7) and (9) of the frame (4) (Fig. 12.23).

19 Place the flexible washer on the shaft.

20 Fit the flexible drive seal.

21 Assemble the mechanism (3) and frame (4) making sure of the correct positioning of the cable.

22 Replace the flexible motor mounting blocks on the frame.

23 Assemble the motor and frame positioning the motor to give accessibility to the connectors when the motor is mounted in the door.

24 Ensure that the silencing collar is in position on the motor body.

25 To refit first mount the motor and cable assembly on the door inner panel and secure with the three bolts.

26 Reconnect the electric cables.

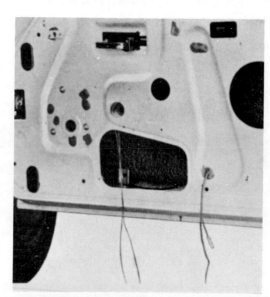

Fig. 12.20. Motor cables detached from door (Sec. 21)

Fig. 12.21. Motor and drive mechanism (Sec. 21)

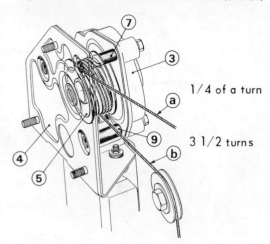

1/4 of a turn

3 1/2 turns

Fig. 12.22. Cable wound on drum - left hand door (Sec. 21)

(a) and (b) cable
3   Winder mechanism
4   Frame
7   Spacer
8   Spacer

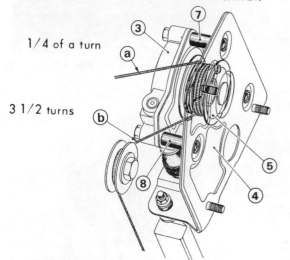

1/4 of a turn

3 1/2 turns

Fig. 12.23. Cable wound on drum - right hand door (Sec. 21)

(a) and (b) cable
3   Winder mechanism
4   Frame
7   Spacer
9   Spacer

27 Engage the cable (b) on the pulleys in the order of (3), (4), (5) and (6). Take great care that the cable (a) linking the drum to the pulley (6) passes in front of the other part of the cable (Fig. 12.24).

28 Fit the adjustable idler pulley (2) and tension the cable.

29 Remove the clip (A) from the drum.

30 In the event of unwinding of the cable refit it to the drum after removing the motor and cable assembly.

31 Lower the windows to obtain access to the cable securing holes.

32 Secure the cable to the windows, using the clamps in the order (7) - (14) (Fig. 12.25).

33 **Do not** tighten the cable yet but lower the window until it abuts on the wooden block.

34 Press the window against the front guide and moderately tighten the cable assembly.

35 Connect the battery up temporarily and operate the window raising motor to move the window up and down several times. Make sure the glass slides freely.

36 It should be noted to prevent damage to the motor a thermal cut out operates when the window is fully up, or down.

37 With the window fully up or down one of the two cable strands must be wound at least ¼ of a turn around the drum. If necessary alter the window position to obtain this condition.

38 Finally tighten the cable clamps.

39 If the motor operates in the reverse order to that indicated by the switch, turn the switch round in its housing without disconnecting it.

40 Refer to Section 20, and refit the door trim panel.

22 Front door window (Coupe) - removal and replacement

1 Refer to Section 20, and remove the door trim panel.

2 Fit a tool clip over the window winder drum to retain the cable onto the drum. (note a clip is supplied with a new drive).

3 Place a block of wood under the glass so as to support its weight. This will give better access to the cable clamps.

4 Remove the two clamps and recover the components.

5 Remove the adjustable idler pulley.

6 Disengage the cable from pulleys (3) (4) (5) and (6) (Fig. 12.24).

7 Leave the cable hanging through the lower opening in the door panel.

8 Remove the door trims and then undo and remove the two screws that secure the deflector control (7). (Fig. 12.27).

9 Slacken the nut (8) so as to release the bracket (9) of the lever (10).

10 Remove the lever (10) by disengaging it towards the front and then reclose the deflector.

11 Raise the window and hold it in this position with some

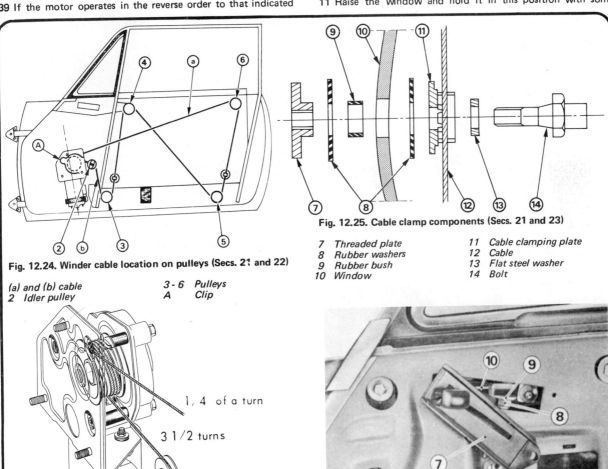

Fig. 12.24. Winder cable location on pulleys (Secs. 21 and 22)

(a) and (b) cable
2 Idler pulley

3 - 6 Pulleys
A Clip

Fig. 12.25. Cable clamp components (Secs. 21 and 23)

7 Threaded plate
8 Rubber washers
9 Rubber bush
10 Window

11 Cable clamping plate
12 Cable
13 Flat steel washer
14 Bolt

1, 4 of a turn

3 1/2 turns

Window fully lowered

Fig. 12.26. Cable strands on drum with window fully lowered (Sec. 21)

Fig. 12.27. Deflector control (Sec. 22)

7 Deflector control plate
8 Nut

9 Bracket
10 Lever

strong adhesive tape.

12 Undo and remove the screws (11 - 14) (Fig. 12.28) and re-cover the tubular spacer from the screw (12).

13 Remove the front guide screw (15).

14 Unclip the lower part of the window guide (16) and remove its securing screw. (Fig. 12.29)

15 Carefully remove the frame/deflector assembly.

16 To refit first check that the control cable is in good condition. Any signs of fraying necessitates replacement of the cable and drum. Also the five pulleys must show no signs of wear and rotate freely.

17 Check the exterior trim/window seal and replace if necessary.

18 Position the window in its frame and hold using strong adhesive tape.

19 Fit the frame - window/deflector assembly taking care not to damage the exterior window seal.

20 Secure the frame to the door using the screws (11 - 14) (Fig 12.28) but do not fully tighten yet. Also do not forget the spacer on screw number (12).

21 Check the frame position and if necessary adjust it until the rear upright is parallel to the door port.

22 Tighten the screws (11 - 14) fully.

23 Secure the frame at the bottom using the screws (15) and (16) (Fig. 12.30).

24 Refit the cable onto the pulleys and secure it to the window in the manner described in Section 21.

25 Refit the deflector control by passing the lever through the slot and position the rubber seal.

26 Raise the lever in the plastic pivot support making sure that the bracket engages in the cutaway on the lever. Tighten the pivot nut.

27 Adjust the support making use of the elongated holes to obtain complete closing of the deflector.

28 Refit the door trims and then referring to Section 20 refit the door trim panel.

23 Front door window (Convertible) - removal and replacement

1 Refer to Section 20, and remove the door trim panel.

2 Chock the window to gain access to the cable clamps.

3 Remove the two clamps and recover the components.

4 The window together with its mobile slide may now be removed from the door.

5 Should it be that the cable does not require renewal it is not necessary to remove the mechanism components.

6 Before refitting check the control cable is in good condition. If it is frayed the cable and control drum must be renewed.

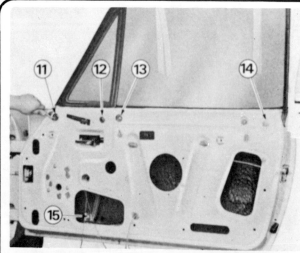

Fig. 12.28. Window guide attachment locations (Sec. 22)

11 - 15   Screws

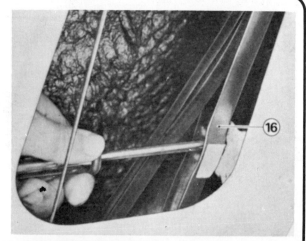

Fig. 12.29. Unclipping lower part of window guide (16) (Sec. 22)

Fig. 12.30. Frame attachments at bottom of door (Sec. 22)

15 - 16   Screws

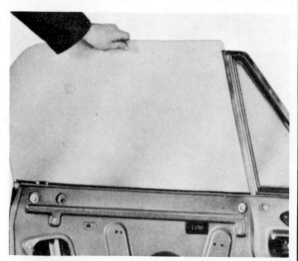

Fig. 12.31. Door glass removal (convertible) (Sec. 23)

7 The five pulleys should not show any signs of wear. If the cable tension is incorrect it should be re-tensioned.

8 Check the exterior window trim and seal. If damaged renew.

9 Also check the condition of the two nylon lugs on the mobile slide and the upper stops on the inside of the panel. Any parts worn or damaged should be renewed.

10 Grease the rear guide and then fit the mobile slide equipped with its seal and nylon lugs onto the window.

11 Tighten the screw after inserting the rubber bush and washer between the threaded plate and the glass.

12 Engage the glass in the front and rear guide at the same time taking care not to damage the seal and trim or the nylon stops. If necessary adjust the rear guide.

13 Position the window so that the cable clamp holes are accessible.

14 Secure the cable using the clamps assembled in the order of (7 - 14) (Fig. 12.25). But do not tighten the clamps yet.

15 Lower the window onto its stops and hold the window against the front guide. Now tighten the clamps.

16 Connect the battery and operate the window raising motor to move the window up and down several times. Make sure that the glass slides freely.

17 It should be noted to prevent damage to the motor a thermal cut-out operates when the window is fully up or down.

18 With the window fully up or down one of the cable strands must be at least ¼ of a turn around the drum. If necessary correct the position of the window and fully tighten the clamps.

19 Operate the window again to check for free-movement.

20 Make quite sure that the heads of the clamp bolts are in contact with the stops when the top of the glass is flush with that the deflector. If necessary adjust by moving the stops. (Fig. 12.34).

21 Refit the door trim panel as described in Section 20.

---

24 Front door deflector windows (Convertible and Coupe) - removal and replacement

1 Refer to Section 20, and remove the door trim panel.

2 Undo and remove the screws securing the lever frame to the door inner panel.

3 Slacken the nut securing the control lever bracket.

4 Remove the lever by disengaging it in a forward manner.

5 Remove the deflector pivot nut, bracket, plastic support,

Fig. 12.32. Location of upper stop (1) (Sec. 23)

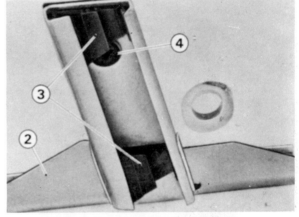

Fig. 12.33. Mobile slide assembly (Sec. 23)

2 Mobile slide	3 Nylon lugs
	4 Screw

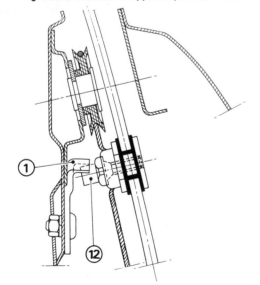

Fig. 12.34. Location of clamp relative to stop (Sec. 23)

1 Stop	2 Clamp bolt

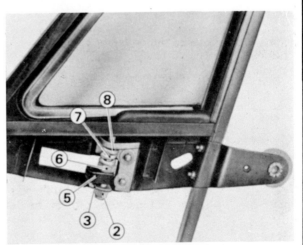

Fig. 12.35. Deflector pivot assembly (Sec. 24)

2 Nut	6 Tension adjuster nut
3 Bracket	7 Spring
5 Plastic support	8 Washers

tension adjuster nut, spring and washers. (Fig. 12.35)

6 Slacken the two lower guide nuts and lower the guide as far as possible.

7 Press on the deflector so as to disengage the upper hinge.

8 The deflector may now be removed upwards from the door. Recover the steel and plastic washers.

9 Refitting the deflector window is the reverse sequence to removal. Should any adjustment be necessary use the elongated

holes in the control lever frame.

25 Windscreen glass - removal and replacement

This operation is best left to specialists as it is a job which although easy for a specialist who is used to handling glass can present problems for a do-it-yourself owner attempting this type of work for the first time.

Chapter 13 Supplement:
Revisions and information on later models

Contents

1 Introduction

This Supplement contains information which is additional to, or a revision of, material contained in the first twelve Chapters of this Manual. The following Sections follow the same order as the Chapters to which they relate. The Specifications are all grouped together for convenience, but they follow Chapter order.

It is recommended that before any particular operation is undertaken, reference be made to the appropriate Section(s) of the Supplement. In this way any changes to procedure or components can be noted before referring to the main Chapters.

2 Specifications

The specifications listed here are revised or supplementary to the main specifications given at the beginning of each Chapter.

Engine
Valve timing (with 0.7 mm valve clearance)

1969 USA XM engine	As previous (see Chapter 1)		
XN1 and XM7 engines to October 1972:			
Inlet opens	1°	BTDC
Inlet closes	36°	ABDC
Exhaust opens	33°	BBDC
Exhaust closes	5° 30'	ATDC

USA engines up to and including 1972:

Inlet opens	4°	ATDC
Inlet closes	34°	ABDC
Exhaust opens	34°	BBDC
Exhaust closes	4°	BTDC

XN1 and XM7 engines, October 1972 onwards and XN1 USA 1973:

Inlet opens	2°	ATDC
Inlet closes	39°	ABDC
Exhaust opens	30°	BBDC
Exhaust closes	$8^{\circ}\,30'$	ATDC

Fuel injection engines KF6 and KF5:

Inlet opens	$1^{\circ}\,30'$	BTDC
Inlet closes	36°	ABDC
Exhaust opens	$35^{\circ}\,30'$	BBDC
Exhaust closes	9°	ATDC

XN2 engine to October 1972:

Inlet opens	$2^{\circ}\,30'$	BTDC
Inlet closes	42°	ABDC
Exhaust opens	36°	BBDC
Exhaust closes	7°	ATDC

XN2 engine October 1972 onwards:

Inlet opens	$0^{\circ}\pm3^{\circ}$	TDC
Inlet closes	$44^{\circ}\,30'$	ABDC
Exhaust opens	$33^{\circ}\,30'$	BBDC
Exhaust closes	$9^{\circ}\,30'$	ATDC

Fuel system
Air cleaner

Type (some models, from chassis no. 1 904 001)	Temperature-controlled

Carburettor

Type	Zenith 35/40 INAT or Solex 32/35 TMIMA

Zenith 35/40 INAT

	Up to May '75		May '75 onwards	
	Primary	Secondary	Primary	Secondary
Venturi	22	28	22	28
Main jet	X112.5	X130	X112.5	X130
Correction jet	150	110	150	90
Emulsion tube	9R	4N	9R	4N
Idling jet	45	—	45	—
Idling air jet	120	—	120	—
Pump injector tube	0.5	0.5	0.5	0.5
Pump piston bleed hole	0.30 mm	0.65 mm	0.30 mm	0.65 mm
Enrichment valve	40	—	40	—
Progression jet	—	50	—	50
Needle valve	2		2	
Float	8.5 g		8.5 g	

Solex 32/35 TMIMA

	Manual transmission		Automatic transmission	
	Primary	Secondary	Primary	Secondary
Venturi	24	27	24	27
Main jet	122.5 ± 2.5	140 ± 2.5	120 ± 2.5	140 ± 2.5
Correction jet	155 ± 10	130 ± 10	155 ± 10	130 ± 10
Emulsion tube	x3	x2	x3	x2
Idling jet	46 ± 5	40 ± 5	42 ± 5	40 ± 5
Idling air bleed	$160\pm10+80$	150	$160\pm10+80$	150
By-pass	0.6 x 5	110	0.6 x 5	110
Constant CO jet	30 ± 5	—	30 ± 5	—
Constant CO air jet	125 ± 10	—	125 ± 10	—
Pump injector	40 ± 5	50 ± 5	40 ± 5	50 ± 5
Needle valve	1.7 (ball type)		1.7 (ball type)	
Float	5.2 g		5.2 g	
Economiser petrol jet	—	80 ± 10	—	80 ± 10
Enricher petrol jet	60 ± 10	—	60 ± 10	—

Ignition system
Spark plug type

XM and XN1 engines	AC 42XLS, Champion N9Y, Marchal GT34.5H, Champion N288
XM7 engines	AC C44XL, Champion N7Y, Marchal 35HS
XM.KF6 engines (fuel injection)	Champion N6Y, Marchal GT34HD
XM.KF5 engines (fuel injection)	AC 41-2XLS, Champion N6Y, Marchal GT34HD
XN2 engines	AC 42XLS, Champion N9Y

Spark plug electrode gap ... ... 0.020 in (0.5 mm) on XM.KF6 engine, 0.024 in (0.6 mm) on all other engines

Ignition coil type
Carburettor engines ... ... Ducellier 2789A, SEV Marchal 3H 12V Bosch E12V 0221 123 012 Femsa B1 12.55

Fuel injection engines:
To chassis no. 2 231 088 ... ... Ducellier 2781A, 2761B
From chassis no. 2 231 089 on ... ... Ducellier 3805A

Note: *Models for high humidity countries are fitted with a Ducellier 2791A coil with a ballast resistor circuit*

Transistorized ignition ... ... AC-Delco

Distributor advance curves
Carburettor versions:
XM, XM7 engines and 8.35 : 1 compression ratio XN1 engines
up to chassis nos. 1 757 900(A11), 1 756 072(A13), 1 756 113
(F13), 1 758 054(F11), 1 758 054(D11) M48
All remaining XN1 engines except 7.6 : 1 compression ratio
from chassis no. 2 401 000 ... ... M78
7.6 : 1 compression ratio engines from chassis no. 2 401 000 M48

Fuel injection versions:
XM.KF6, XM.KF5 engines M53
XN2 engines up to chassis no. 1 766 128 ... ... M53
XN2 engines from chassis no. 1 766 129 to 2 401 000 ... M77
XN2 engines from chassis no. 2 401 001 on M95
XN1 engines fitted with transistorized ignition M78DE

Distributor type
Engines fitted with transistorized ignition ... ... Ducellier 525 181

Ignition timing
Transistorized ignition ... ... 8° BTDC

Gearbox (manual)
Ratios
First ... ... 3.667 : 1 (0.2727)
Second ... ... 2.170 : 1 (0.4608)
Third ... ... 1.409 : 1 (0.7098)
Top ... ... 1.000 : 1 (1.0)
Reverse ... ... 3.747 : 1 (0.2669)

Automatic transmission
Type
From chassis no. 2 727 386 ... ... ZF 3HP 22

Fluid capacity (total) ... ... 9.0 to 9.3 Imp pt (5.1 to 5.3 litres/5.4 to 5.6 US qt)

Fluid capacity (after draining) ... ... 3.3 to 3.7 Imp pt (1.9 to 2.1 litres/2.0 to 2.2 US qt)

Rear axle and driveshafts
Rear axle ratio
Coupe/Convertible models ... ... 3.70 : 1

Braking system
Front brake discs
Disc thickness:
Minimum after machining ... ... 0.443 in (11.25 mm)
Wear limit ... ... 0.423 in (10.75 mm)

Rear brake discs

	Girling Mk I	Girling MK III
Disc thickness:		
New	0.394 in (10 mm)	0.472 in (12 mm)
Minimum after machining	0.354 in (9 mm)	0.433 in (11 mm)
Wear limit	0.335 in (8.5 mm)	0.413 in (10.5 mm)

Rear drum brakes

	Long models	L models
Drum diameter	11.024 in (280 mm)	10.039 in (255 mm)
Maximum diameter after machining	11.063 in (281 mm)	10.079 in (256 mm)
Wear limit	11.083 in (281.5 mm)	10.098 in (256.5 mm)

Lining dimensions:
Leading shoe (504 L models) ... ... 10.51 x 1.77 in (267 x 45 mm)
Trailing shoe (504 L models) ... ... 8.62 x 1.77 in (219 x 45 mm)

Torque wrench settings (braking system)

	lbf ft	kgf m
Bleed screw	9	1.25
Front disc Allen screw	36	5.0
Disc pad fork Allen screw	12.7	1.75
Rear hub bearing nut	181	25
Brake caliper bolt (front)	51	7.0
Rear disc Allen screw	36	5.0
Brake caliper bolt (rear - disc inside hub)	31	4.25
Brake caliper bolt (rear - disc outside hub)	36	5.0
Driveshaft nut	181	25

Electrical system
Battery capacity

Cold climate and ambulance	60 amp hr

Starter motor

Type (to November 1971)	Ducellier 6189 or Paris-Rhone D8E (76, 96, 122, or 124)
Type (November 1971 onwards)	Ducellier 6190 or Paris-Rhone D9E9

Alternator

Type	Ducellier, Paris-Rhone, SEV Marchal, or Femsa
Output	350W to 750W depending on model and climate

Regulator

Type	Ducellier, Paris-Rhone or SEV Marchal. (Femsa and SEV Marchal alternators fitted to models from chassis no. 2 821 313 incorporate integral electronic regulators)

Steering
Rack plunger (manual steering)

Free play (without grease nipple)	0.0004 to 0.0024 in (0.01 to 0.06 mm)

Power steering

Hydraulic fluid type	Esso B11216
Capacity	1.1 Imp pt (0.65 litres/0.7 US qt)
Plunger adjustment shims	0.10, 0.20, 0.50 mm
Rack plunger free play	0.10 ± 0.05 mm

Power steering torque wrench settings

	lbf ft	kgf m
Track-rod end	27	3.75
Ram retaining nut	39.8	5.5
Steering gear mounting	23.5	3.25
Flexible coupling nuts	14.5	2.0
Pinion nut	12.7	1.75
Grease nipple	7.2	1.0
Thrust plate bolt	7.2	1.0
Clevis locknut	57.9	8.0
Link through-bolt	32.5	4.5
Track-rod clamps	7.2	1.0
Union nut (rigid)	10.8	1.5
Clevis through-bolt	32.5	4.5
Union nut (hose)	16.3	2.25

Wheels and tyres
Wheel type:

To October 1978 (saloons) and May 1978 (utility)	5J 14 4/35 (for tubed tyres)
From October/May 1978	5J 14 FH 4/35 (for UK), 5½J 14 (for tubeless tyres, USA)

Tyre sizes:

504 GL	**175SR14**
504 TI	**175HR14**
504 Estate	**185SR14**

Pressures - lbf/in^2 (bar):	Saloon	Estate
Front	23.2 (1.6)	23.2 (1.6)
Rear (unladen)	27.6 (1.9)	36.3 (2.5)
Rear (laden)	27.6 (1.9)	46.4 (3.2)

Note: *For high speed motoring increase these pressures by 2.9 lbf/in^2 (0.2 bar)*

Wheel torque wrench setting
Wheel nuts:

	lbf ft	kgf m
Steel wheels	44	6.0
Alloy wheels	60	8.3

Air conditioning system

Radiator filler cap opening pressure	14.2 lb/in^2 (1.0 kg/cm^2) - colour code green

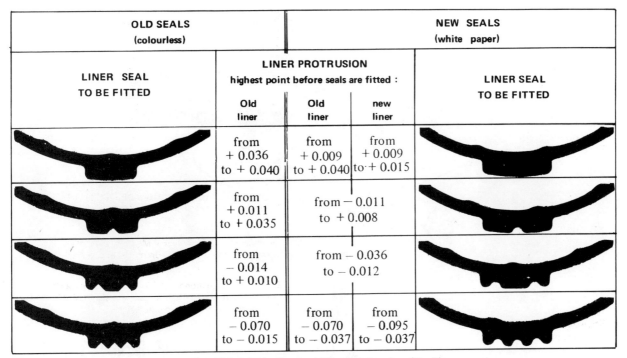

OLD SEALS (colourless)				NEW SEALS (white paper)
LINER SEAL TO BE FITTED	LINER PROTRUSION highest point before seals are fitted :			LINER SEAL TO BE FITTED
	Old liner	Old liner	new liner	
	from + 0.036 to + 0.040	from + 0.009 to + 0.040	from + 0.009 to + 0.015	
	from + 0.011 to + 0.035	from − 0.011 to + 0.008		
	from − 0.014 to + 0.010	from − 0.036 to − 0.012		
	from − 0.070 to − 0.015	from − 0.070 to − 0.037	from − 0.095 to − 0.037	

Fig. 13.1 Cylinder liner seal identification chart (Sec 3)

3 Engine

Modifications

1 With the introduction of the Zenith 35/40 INAT carburettor (see Section 5), the XN1 engine has received a number of modifications. The inlet ports and inlet valve seats in the cylinder head have been modified, and the compression ratio increased to 8.8 to 1. The camshaft sprocket is of different dimensions in order to give different valve timing. XN2 engines also have similar modifications.

2 Because of these modifications, it is essential to obtain the correct components for the engine being worked on. The identical modifications apply to engines fitted with the Solex 32/35 TMIMA carburettor.

Cylinder liners - renewal

3 As from chassis no. 2 889 629, modified liners are fitted, together with thicker liner seals. New liners have a sealing shoulder which is reduced in height by 0.001 in (0.025 mm) compared with the earlier type.

4 Both old and new type liners are interchangeable, but the new type seals must always be fitted. The liner protrusion checking dimensions together with the type of new liner seal to be fitted are shown in Fig. 13.1. The old seals are distinguished from the new type by being colourless, whereas the new seals are of white paper.

4 Cooling system

Modifications

1 As from chassis no. 2 717 290, some models fitted with automatic transmission and air conditioning, and those models operated in extreme condition territories, are fitted with a reinforced polyamide fan having a diameter of 13.78 in (350 mm). Models operated in extreme condition territories are also equipped with a fan cowl and a radiator matrix incorporating copper finning; an electric fan motor is fitted to some models.

2 When the new type radiator is fitted, it is imperative also to fit the larger reinforced fan.

Radiator - removal and refitting

3 On models fitted with a radiator cowl as described in paragraph 1, the cowl must be detached from the radiator before removing the radiator from the engine compartment.

Thermostat - removal and refitting

4 On vehicles fitted with XM7, XN1, XNA and XN2 engine types, the method of thermostat location may be different from that shown in Chapter 2.

5 Fig. 13.2 shows the early and later methods of location. The later, modified thermostat is fitted within the water pump body and incorporates a leak pin which allows system venting and rapid engine warm up.

6 To remove the thermostat, partially drain the cooling system (see Chapter 2), disconnect the hose from the pump and remove the housing with thermostat.

7 Before fitting the thermostat, check that the leak pin is free to move. Refitting is the reverse sequence of removal. After replenishing the cooling system, run the engine and check for leaks from any disturbed connections.

Cooling system - bleeding

8 The cooling system must be bled of all air during replenishment. Some vehicles will be fitted with bleed screws to assist this operation and details of their location and use can be obtained from your Peugeot dealer.

9 To bleed a system which does not incorporate bleed screws, disconnect the carburettor heating pipe and wait until the coolant flowing from it is free of air bubbles before reconnecting it. Check for leaks.

Heater - removal and refitting

10 The heater unit should not normally give trouble, but if removal is necessary, first drain the cooling system as described in Chapter 2. Read the first two paragraphs of Section 12, Chapter 2.

11 To expose the heater, pull away the trim which surrounds it. The trim is easily removed if grasped firmly on each side and pulled sharply away.

12 Various types of heater units are fitted to the Peugeot 504 and whichever type is found to be fitted, removal will have to

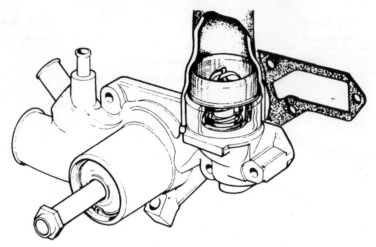

OLD TYPE ARRANGEMENT

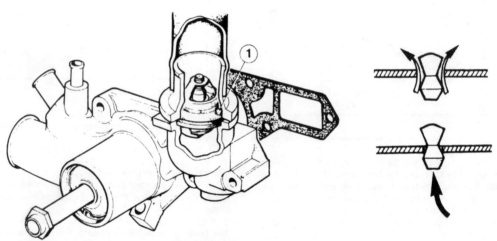

NEW TYPE ARRANGEMENT

be carried out in a logical and orderly manner. If necessary, label any hose or electrical connections for reference when fitting. Once released from its mountings, manoeuvre the unit towards the left-hand side and clear of the console. Take care to prevent coolant spilling from the unit.

13 Refitting is a reverse sequence of removal whilst noting the following points. Renew any hose which is damaged or perished. Do not allow the unit to hang from any hose or wire and check for correct routing of the same. Select 'maximum heat' on the heater controls before filling and bleeding the cooling system.

5 Fuel system

Air cleaner - adjustment

1 Where the air cleaner housing incorporates a manual 'summer/winter' adjuster, check that this is correctly set for the time of year, otherwise engine performance will be adversely affected. From chassis no 1 904 001, some vehicles are fitted with temperature-controlled air cleaners. Figs. 13.3 to 13.6 show the types fitted.

Temperature-controlled air cleaner - testing and adjustment

2 On the type having an external return spring, remove the mixer box from the end of the air cleaner. On all other types remove the cover and filter element.

Fig. 13.2 Old and new thermostat arrangements (Sec 4)

1   Leak pin

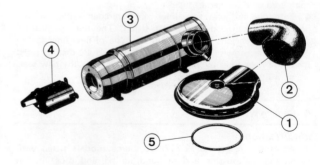

Fig. 13.3 Air cleaner fitted from chassis No 1 904 001 to 2 018 428 (Sec 5)

1	Inlet cover	4	Mixer
2	Hose	5	Seal
3	Body		

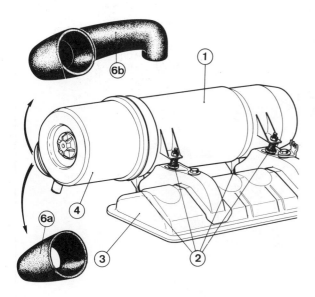

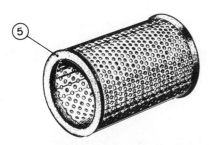

Fig. 13.4 Air cleaner fitted from chassis No 2 018 429 (XN1 engine) and 2 142 001 (XM7) engine to 2 448 431 (Sec 5)

1	Body	5	Element
2	Mounting	6a	Hose
3	Rocker cover	6b	Hose
4	End cover		

3 Check that the control flap is not jammed and can be moved easily from the open to closed positions.

4 Immerse the temperature sensitive element in water at a temperature of 18 to 20°C (64.4 to 68°F) for 5 minutes, and check that the control flap is in the fully closed position (ie, admitting warm air only). Check also that there is no endplay on the operating rod.

5 If the test in paragraph 4 is not completed successfully, proceed as described in paragraph 6 or 7.

External return spring type

6 Remove the temperature sensitive element and, using vernier calipers, adjust the end screw to obtain a dimension of 1.67 ± 0.02 in (42.3 ± 0.4 mm) (see Fig. 13.7). Refit the element, leaving the retaining screws loose, then immerse the element in water at 18 to 20°C (64.4 to 68°F) for 5 minutes. Hold the flap in the closed position and slide the element along until the operating rod endplay is eliminated; then tighten the retaining screws with the element still immersed in the water. With the water heated to between 33 and 37°C (91.4 and 98.6°F), the control flap must be fully open (ie admitting air through the main inlet).

Other types

7 Refer to Figs 13.8 and 13.9. Loosen the locknut or screw attaching the element to the operating rod and immerse the element in water at 18 to 20°C (64.4 to 68°F) for 5 minutes. With the element still immersed, hold the control flap in the closed position and turn the element (locknut type), or move the operating rod (screw type), until there is no endplay on the operating rod. Tighten the locknut or screw, then check that the control flap is fully open (ie admitting air through the main inlet) with the water heated to between 33 and 37°C (91.4 and 98.6°F).

Zenith 35/40 INAT carburettor
Description

8 As from chassis no. 1 904 001, models fitted with the XN1 engine are equipped with the Zenith 35/40 INAT carburettor. Models up to chassis no. 2 701 987 (Saloon) and 2 679 910 (Estate) have a fully electric automatic choke whereas models after these chassis numbers have an electric automatic choke linked with coolant temperature control. The secondary barrel throttle valve on both carburettors is vacuum-operated by an externally-mounted vacuum capsule.

9 The component parts of the carburettor are shown in Figs. 13.10 and 13.11.

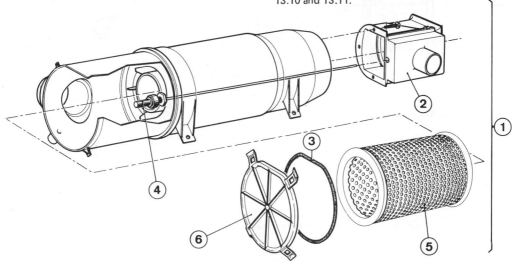

Fig. 13.5 Air cleaner fitted from chassis no 2 448 432 onwards - Quillery type (Sec 5)

1	Cleaner assembly	3	Seal	5	Element
2	Mixer	4	Capsule	6	End cover

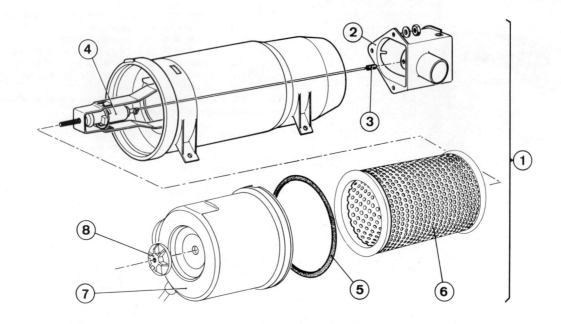

Fig. 13.6 Air cleaner fitted from chassis No 2 496 253 onwards - Lautrette type (Sec 5)

1	Cleaner assembly	3	Buffer	5	Seal	7	End cover
2	Mixer	4	Capsule	6	Element	8	Nut

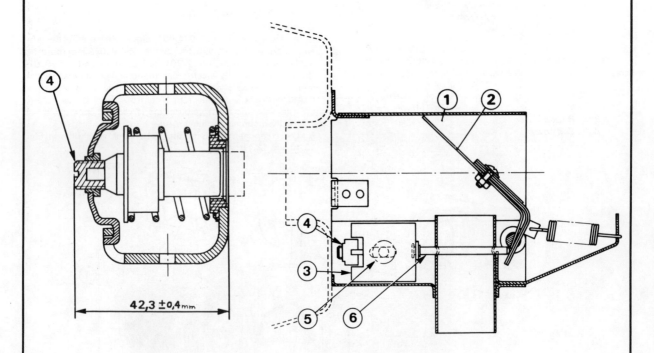

42,3 ±0,4mm

Fig. 13.7 External return spring type temperature controlled air cleaner components (Sec 5)

1	Mixer	3	Element	5	Retaining screws
2	Control flap	4	Adjusting screw	6	Operating rod

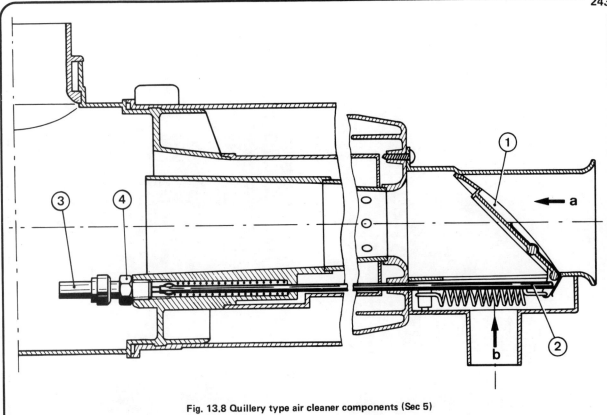

Fig. 13.8 Quillery type air cleaner components (Sec 5)

1	Control flap	3	Element	a	Cold air
2	Operating rod	4	Locknut	b	Hot air

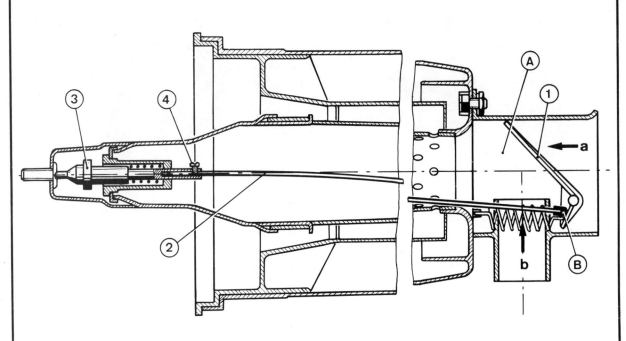

Fig. 13.9 Lautrette type air cleaner components (Sec 5)

1	Control flap	3	Element	A	Mixer	a	Cold air
2	Operating rod	4	Adjusting screw	B	Buffer	b	Hot air

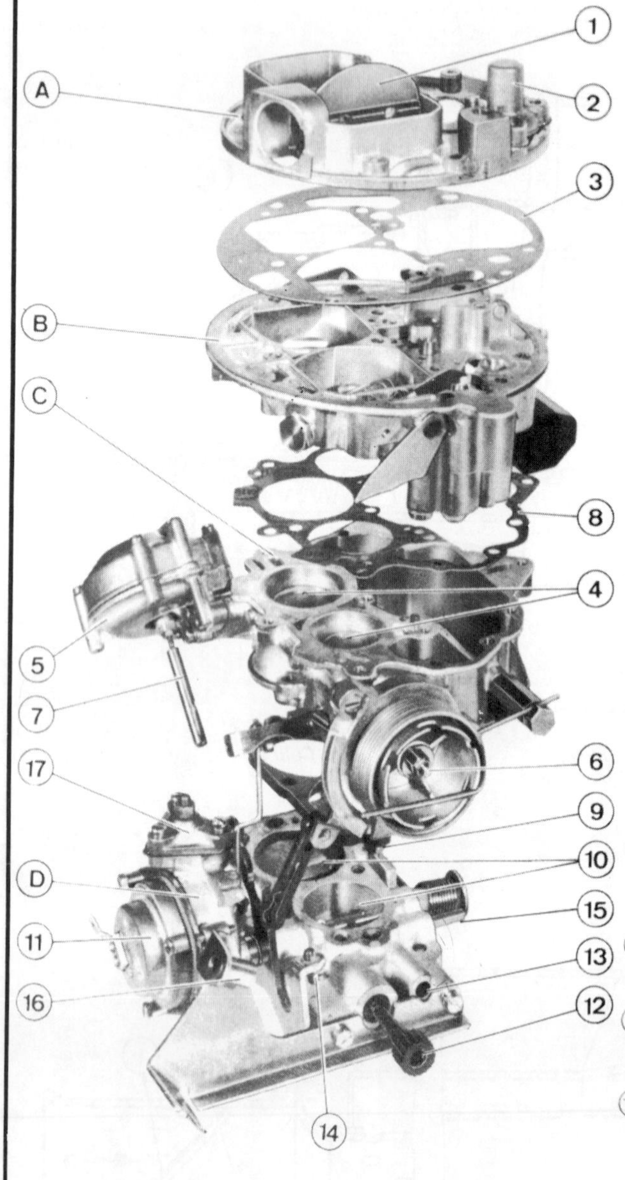

Fig. 13.10 Exploded view of Zenith 35/40 INAT
carburettor (Sec 5)

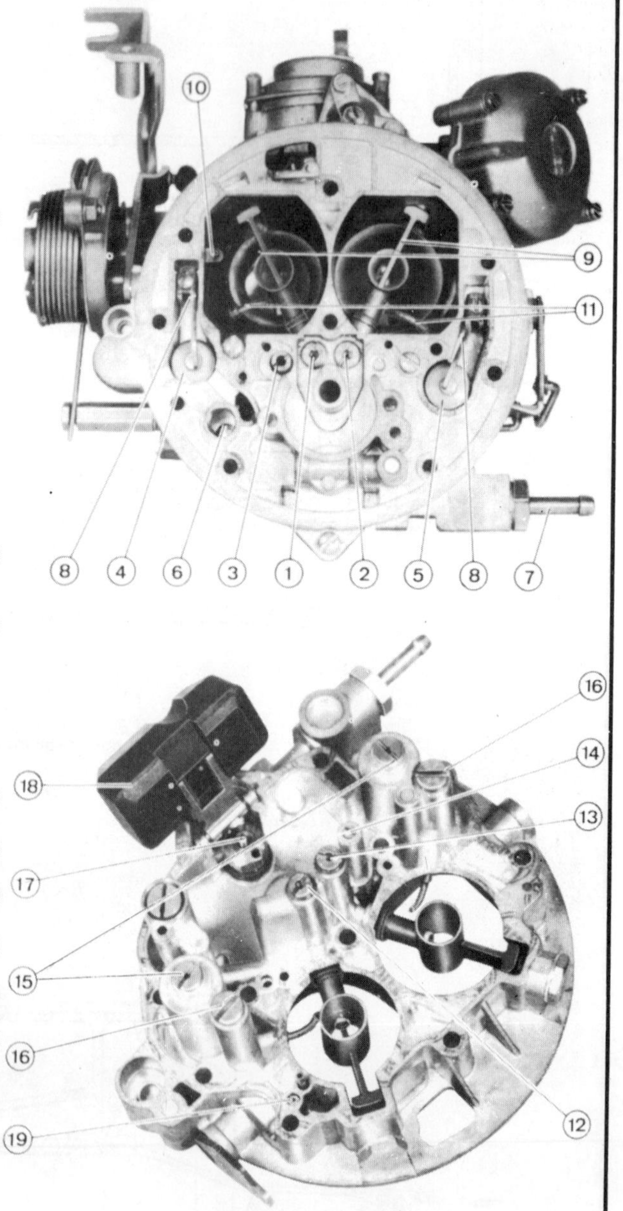

Fig. 13.11 Zenith 35/40 INAT carburettor cover
components (Sec 5)

A	Top plate	8	Gasket	
B	Cover	9	Insulated pillar	
C	Body	10	Throttle valves	
D	Throttle housing	11	Automatic choke	
1	Choke valve	12	CO adjustment screw	
2	Enrichment valve	13	Mixture screw	
3	Gasket	14	Throttle stop screw	
4	Venturis	15	Distributor vacuum	
5	Secondary throttle		connection	
	operating capsule	16	Cable mounting	
6	Throttle drum	17	Anti-flood device	
7	Rod			

1	Primary air correction jet	9	Spray nozzles	
2	Secondary air correction jet	10	Supplementary air jet	
3	Idling jet	11	Pump injectors	
		12	Primary main jet	
4	Primary accelerator pump	13	Secondary main jet	
5	Secondary accelerator pump	14	Progression jet	
		15	Suction valves	
6	Enrichment valve	16	Discharge valves	
7	Fuel intake	17	Needle valve	
8	Levers	18	Float	
		19	Calibrated orifice	

Idling adjustment

10 Read paragraphs 61 and 62. Run the engine until it reaches its normal operating temperature.

11 Adjust the throttle stop screw (Fig. 13.12) to give an engine speed of 950 rpm; if possible use a tachometer to make an accurate adjustment.

12 Locate the mixture screw and, using a self-tapping screw, remove the tamperproof cap. Turn the screw to obtain the maximum engine speed, then back off the throttle stop screw to reset the engine speed to 950 rpm.

13 Screw in the mixture screw until the engine speed drops to 900 rpm, then fit a new tamperproof cap.

14 If an exhaust gas analyser is being used, the mixture screw must be adjusted to give a CO percentage of 1.5 to 2.5, and a CO_2 percentage of at least 10.

Primary throttle fast idle opening adjustment

15 Run the engine until normal operating temperature is reached and the choke valve is fully open.

16 Remove the air filter and open the primary throttle.

17 Shut the choke valve and then release the throttle. The throttle valve will be held in the fast idle position and, if the choke valve is released, it will return to its fully open position.

18 Connect a tachometer to the engine then start it and check that it turns at 2800 rpm. Do not touch the accelerator pedal or the throttle valve will return to its normal idling position.

19 If the fast idle speed is incorrect, remove the automatic choke cover and adjust the screw (see Fig. 13.13).

Accelerator pump nozzle adjustment

20 Refer to Fig. 13.14 and check that the nozzles are in the correct position; if not, carefully bend them as necessary.

Throttle valve initial setting

21 After removing or overhauling the carburettor, the throttle valves must be adjusted to their initial settings as described in paragraphs 22 to 25 before refitting the carburettor.

22 Fully open the throttle, hold the choke valve in its fully open position, and then release the throttle.

23 Remove the tamperproof cap (if fitted) from the throttle stop screw, and back off the screw until the throttle valve in the primary barrel is fully closed.

24 The throttle valve must now be opened by 2° 10'; to do this either obtain the special tool from a Peugeot garage or, alternatively, attach a piece of card to the throttle drum and mark the angle with a protractor. After the adjustment, fit a new tamperproof cap.

25 To adjust the secondary throttle valve, loosen the locknut and adjust the stop screw so that the faintest glimmer of light is visible past the secondary throttle valve and barrel wall. Check that a 0.05 mm (0.002 in) feeler gauge can just be inserted into the gap, then tighten the locknut, see Fig. 13.15.

Automatic choke adjustment

26 Remove the automatic choke cover, fully open the primary throttle valve, then close the choke valve and release the throttle valve.

Fig. 13.12 Zenith 35/40 INAT carburettor - screw location (Sec 5)

Va *Throttle stop screw*   W *Mixture screw*

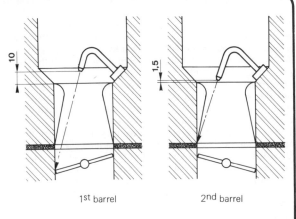

Fig. 13.14 Zenith 35/40 INAT carburettor - primary and secondary accelerator pump nozzle adjustment (Sec 5)

Dimensions in mm

Fig. 13.13 Zenith 35/40 INAT carburettor - screw location (Sec 5)

1 Fast idle adjusting screw

Fig. 13.15 Zenith 35/40 INAT carburettor (Sec 5)

A *Secondary throttle initial opening dimension*
2 *Locknut*
3 *Adjustment screw*

27 Turn the operating lever inside the automatic choke body so that the choke valve is held shut, then use a feeler gauge to check that the clearance between the lever and the anti-flood plunger is between 0.004 and 0.008 in (0.1 and 0.2 mm). If necessary, adjust the lever position by loosening the intermediate rod clamp screw with an Allen key.

28 With the anti-flood plunger pressed upwards, turn the choke lever anti-clockwise until it is in contact with the plunger. Using a drill, check that the clearance between the lower edge of the choke valve and the barrel wall is 0.138 in (3.5 mm). If necessary, loosen the locknut and adjust the screw located on the top of the anti-flood device.

29 Refit the automatic choke cover making sure that the bi-metallic spring engages with the choke operating lever.

30 To check the electric heating of the bi-metallic spring, first check that the choke valve is fully shut (ambient temperature of 18 to 20°C). Switch on the ignition without starting the engine; the choke valve should open to a maximum of 0.315 in (8.0 mm).

Fuel filter renewal

31 At intervals of approximately 9 000 miles (15 000 km) the in-line fuel filter fitted in the carburettor supply hose must be renewed. Make sure that the arrow points towards the carburettor inlet when fitting the new filter.

Solex 32/35 TMIMA carburettor
Description

32 As from chassis no. 2 648 401 all models with 8.8 to 1 compression ratio engines, except those with air conditioning, are equipped with a Solex 32/35 TMIMA carburettor. The carburettor is also fitted to all models with 8.0 to 1 compression ratio engines as from chassis no. 2 698 501. The automatic choke is controlled by a wax capsule activated by the engine coolant The secondary throttle valve is operated via a linkage from the primary throttle valve in an elongated hole; the secondary valve does not commence to open until the primary valve is approximately two-thirds open.

33 The component parts of the carburettor are shown in Fig. 13.16.

Idling adjustment

34 The procedure is identical to that for the Zenith carburettor described in paragraphs 10 to 14, and the location of the screws is shown in Figs. 13.17 and 13.18.

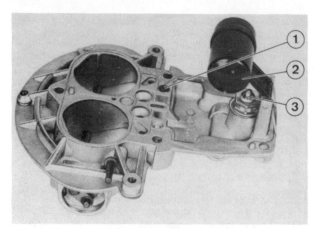

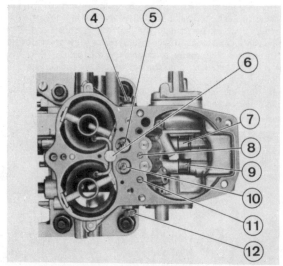

Fig. 13.16 Solex 32/35 TMIMA carburettor main components (Sec 5)

1	Economiser circuit	8	CO jet
	O-ring seal	9	Secondary main jet
2	Float	10	Secondary air correction jet
3	Needle valve		
4	Primary idling jet	11	Economiser jet
5	Primary air correction jet	12	Secondary idling jet
6	Pump injectors	13	Primary barrel enrichener jet
7	Primary main jet		

Fig. 13.17 Solex 32/35 TMIMA carburettor - screw location (Sec 5)
Va Idle adjusting screw

Fig. 13.18 Solex 32/35 TMIMA carburettor - screw location (Sec 5)
W Mixture screw

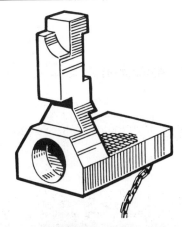

Fig. 13.19 Solex 32/35 TMIMA carburettor automatic choke setting gauge (Sec 5)

Fig. 13.20 Solex 32/35 TMIMA carburettor automatic choke adjustment (Sec 5)

1 Locknut	*2 Adjusting screw*

Fig. 13.21 Solex 32/35 TMIMA carburettor automatic choke adjustment (Sec 5)

X 0.079 in (2.0 mm)	*3 Adjusting screw*

Automatic choke adjustment
Note: *Adjustment is only possible if Peugeot tool no. 80143 is available. If not available, leave this adjustment to your dealer.*
Fig. 13.19 shows the special tool.
35 Run the engine until normal operating temperature is reached.
36 Disconnect the inlet hose from the carburettor.
37 Using tool no. 80143, locate it on the automatic choke roller with the arm against the carburettor body. The top edges of the choke valves should now be 0.177 in (4.5 mm) from the barrel walls; this dimension can be checked using a suitable drill, see Fig. 13.20.
38 If the dimension checked in paragraph 37 is incorrect, loosen the locknut on the anti-flood device and adjust the screw as necessary.
39 With the engine at operating temperature, check that the dimension X in Fig. 13.21 is 0.079 in (2.0 mm). If not, adjust the screw (3) as necessary.
40 Locate the tool no. 80143 on top of the carburettor body, then tighten the screw (3) until the tool cutout engages with the roller. To adjust the screw, insert a screwdriver through the hole provided.

41 Unhook the spring from the upper pin and allow the engine (warm) to idle, then push the lower pin downwards as far as possible. With a tachometer connected, the engine speed should increase and stabilize at 3200 ± 50 rpm (automatic transmission) or 3800 ± 50 rpm (manual transmission). If this is not the case, turn the adjusting screw as necessary without removing the clip, see Fig. 13.22.
42 Reconnect the spring, and refit the cover and inlet hose.

Accelerator pump nozzle adjustment
43 Refer to Fig. 13.23 and check that the nozzles are in the correct position; if not, carefully bend them as necessary.

Float level setting
44 To check the float level setting, the cover must be removed from the carburettor.
45 Hold the cover vertically with the float assembly hanging from the fulcrum pin, with light pressure on the needle valve ball. With the gasket removed, the distance from the top of the float to the cover face must be 31 ± 1 mm (1.22 ± 0.04 in). Use vernier calipers to make the check, and also make sure that the float is parallel to the cover face.
46 If the dimension obtained in paragraph 45 is too great, progressively tighten the needle valve to a maximum of 18 lbf in (2.5 kgf m) until the dimension is correct; tightening the needle valve by 18 lbf in (2.5 kgf m) reduces the float height by approximately 0.013 in (0.32 mm). If necessary, reduce the washer thickness.
47 If the dimension obtained in paragraph 45 is too small, renew the needle valve washer and tighten the valve initially to 11 lbf in (1.5 kgf m). *Note that when checking the dimension, the float seam must not be taken into consideration.*
48 Refit the carburettor cover making sure that the economiser rubber O-ring is fitted in the recess.

Throttle valve initial setting
49 After removing or overhauling the carburettor, the throttle valves must be adjusted to their initial settings as described in paragraphs 50 to 53 inclusive before refitting the carburettor.
50 First, remove the tamperproof caps (if fitted) and back-off the two stop screws until both throttles are fully closed.
51 Detach the intermediate rod from the automatic choke lever.
52 The primary throttle valve must now be opened by 1° 30', and the secondary throttle valve by 9° 15'. To do this, either obtain the special tool from a Peugeot garage or alternatively mark the angles on a piece of card and attach the card to the throttle levers; use a protractor to obtain the correct angles.
53 After the adjustment, fit two new tamperproof caps and reconnect the intermediate rod.

Idle step-up valve adjustment
54 Some models fitted with an air conditioning system have a step-up valve fitted to the carburettor in order to retain the normal idling speed of the engine when the air conditioning compressor is in operation.
55 To adjust the valve, first run the engine until it reaches the normal operating temperature.
56 Adjust the idling speed without the compressor in operation as described in Chapter 3; idling speed is normally 900 rpm.
57 Connect a lead from the battery positive (+) terminal to the compressor feed terminal, and unscrew the cap from the end of the valve.
58 Start the engine and, using a screwdriver, adjust the valve until the engine idle speed is 900 rpm.
59 Stop the engine, and refit the cap.
60 Remove the lead from the compressor and battery.

Idling adjustment - precautions (all carburettor types)
61 Depending on operating territory and production date, the idle mixture adjustment screw may be 'tamperproofed' by means of a plastic cap or seal, which must be destroyed in order to make an adjustment. The object of fitting the seal is to discourage (and to detect) adjustment by unqualified or unskilled operators.

Fig. 13.22 Solex 32/35 TMIMA carburettor fast idle adjustment (Sec 5)

4	Spring	6	Adjusting screw
5	Pin		

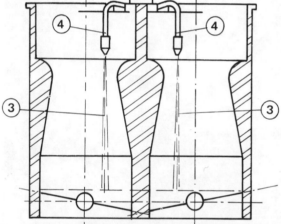

Fig. 13.23 Solex 32/35 TMIMA carburettor accelerator pump nozzle adjustment (Sec 5)

3	Spray direction	4	Nozzles

62 If you wish to remove a tamperproof seal, satisfy yourself that you are not breaking any local or national anti-pollution laws by so doing. If the vehicle is still under warranty, be aware that you may be in breach of the warranty conditions. Fit a new seal on completion where this is required by law.

6 Ignition system

Distributor dwell angle - adjustment
1 As from chassis no. 2 848 962 all models equipped with XM7 and XN1 engines are fitted with a new type distributor on which the dwell angle can be adjusted with the engine running. The distributor can be identified by the plastic hinged flap located by one of the distributor cap retaining clips, see Fig. 13.24.
2 Removal and refitting operations are identical to those given in Chapter 4, but make sure that the adjustable contact point is mounted centrally in its support plate.
3 To adjust the dwell angle, lift the plastic cap and insert a 3 mm Allen key into the adjustable contact point, see Fig. 13.25.

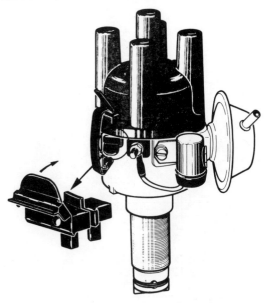

Fig. 13.24 Distributor - showing plastic flap location for external dwell angle adjustment (Sec 6)

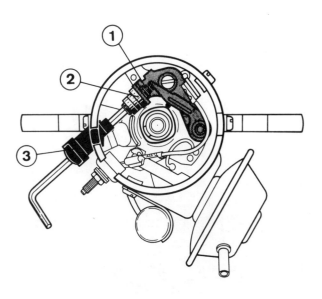

Fig. 13.25 External dwell angle adjustment distributor - components (Sec 6)

1	Adjustable contact point	3	Plastic cap (Allen key inserted)
2	Support plate		

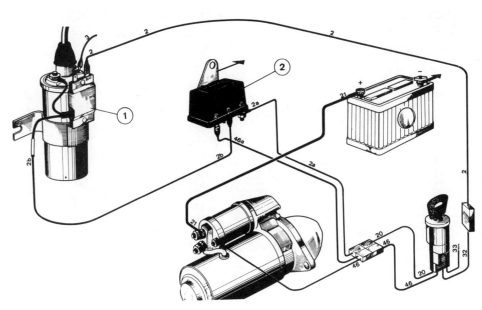

Fig. 13.26 Ballast resistor ignition system components (Sec 6)

1	Resistor	46a	Starter solenoid +	2b	Feed to coil when
2	Relay	2a	Continuous +		operating the starter

Ballast resistor

4 As from July 1974 models destined for high humidity countries are fitted with a ballast resistor ignition circuit. The main components and circuit of the system are shown in Fig. 13.26.

5 The coil is designed to operate at less than 12 volts and under normal engine running, a resistor ensures that the primary circuit receives the necessary voltage. However, during starting, the resistor is by-passed through a relay, and full battery voltage is supplied to the coil. This increases the intensity of the spark at the spark plug and therefore facilitates easy starting. Normal voltage is restored when the starter motor is switched off.

6 Since the coil and resistor are matched, they must be renewed together if faulty.

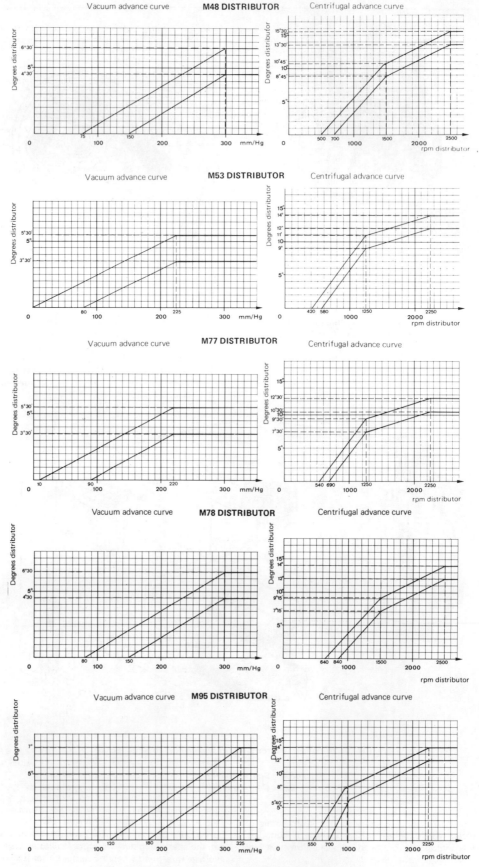

Fig. 13.27 Distributor advance curves (see Specifications)

Transistorized ignition system
Description and precautions

7 Figs. 13.28 to 13.30 show the types of distributor fitted to vehicles equipped with transistorized ignition system. As well as the distributor, the system contains a coil/amplifier assembly. The system should require virtually no maintenance or adjustment. It is not recommended that the distributor is dismantled beyond the limits of the operations described in the following sub-Sections.

8 The voltage produced by a transistorized ignition system is much higher than that from a conventional system, and therefore the following precautions should always be observed:

(a) When checking the engine speed, use only an HT type tachometer
(b) Switch off the ignition before removing any of the components
(c) Disconnect the system when arc welding
(d) Do not work in close contact with a working system if medically equipped with a cardiac pacemaker

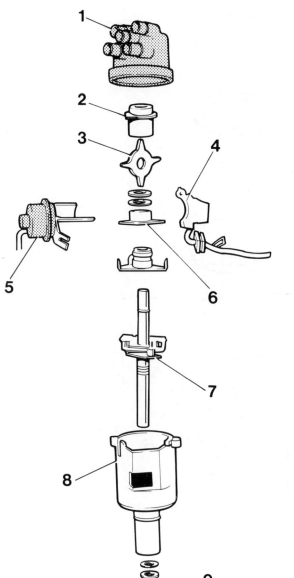

Fig. 13.28 Exploded view of transistorized distributor (Sec 6)

1	Cap	6	Base-plate
2	Rotor arm	7	Centrifugal advance
3	Polarity wheel	8	Body
4	Electro-magnetic coil	9	Drive dog
5	Vacuum advance capsule		

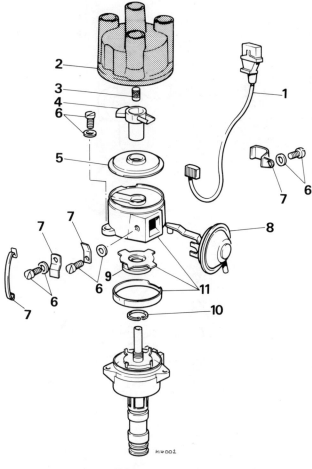

Fig. 13.29 Exploded view of transistorized distributor - Ducellier type (Sec 6)

1	Electrical connector	7	Clip
2	Cap	8	Vacuum advance capsule
3	Brush		
4	Rotor arm	9	Coil (ignition)
5	Dust shield	10	Clip
6	Screw and washer	11	Pick-up coil module

HT current check

9 Remove the distributor cap and turn the engine until the polarity wheel is positioned with an arm either side of the coil core.

10 Switch on the ignition, then disconnect the HT lead from the distributor cap and hold it approximately 0.40 in (10 mm) from the cylinder head with a pair of well-insulated electrician's pliers.

11 Touch the coil core with the tip of a screwdriver, then withdraw the screwdriver; a spark should occur between the HT lead and the cylinder head. If not, check the system as described in the following sub-Section. Refer to Fig. 13.31 for the system circuit diagram.

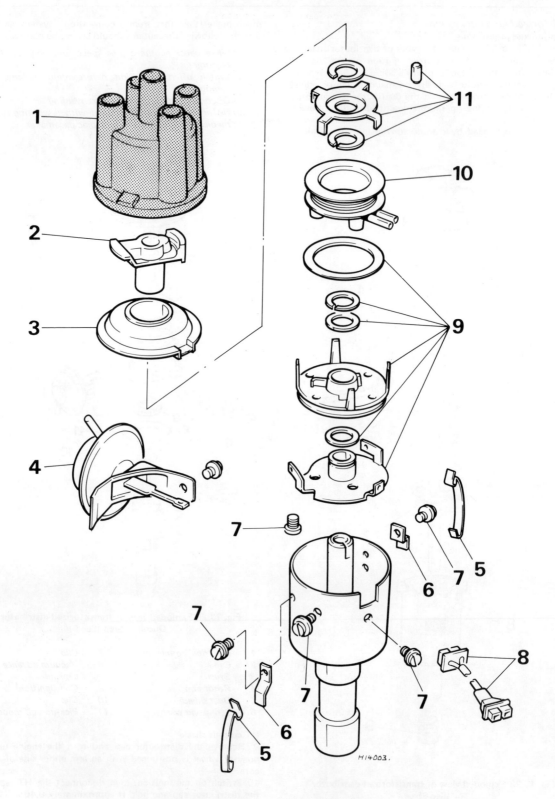

Fig. 13.30 Exploded View of transistorized distributor - Bosch type (Sec 6)

1	Cap	5	Clip	9	Pick-up coil module
2	Rotor arm	6	Clip	10	Ignition coil
3	Dust shield	7	Screw	11	Retainer
4	Vacuum advance capsule	8	Electrical connector		

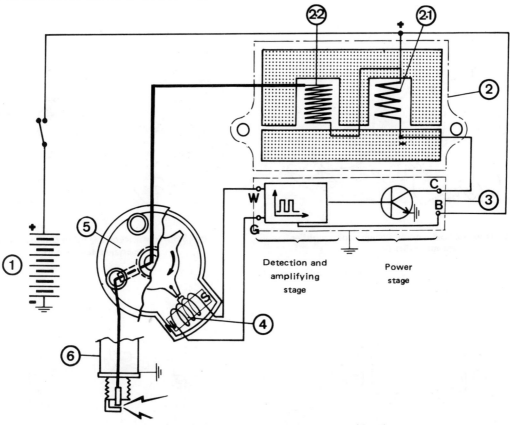

Fig. 13.31 Transistorized ignition circuit diagram (Sec 6)

1	Battery	3	Amplifier module	5	Distributor
2	Coil (2.1 primary coil, 2.2 secondary coil)	4	Magnetic impulse generator	6	Spark plug

Magnetic impulse generator check and renewal

12 With the ignition switched off, disconnect the impulse generator plug from the coil/amplifier assembly.

13 Connect an ohmmeter across the two plug contacts and check that the resistance is between 900 and 1100 ohms. Make sure that the plug contacts are not corroded, otherwise an incorrect reading will be obtained.

14 To check the impulse generator coil insulation, connect the ohmmeter across one plug contact and a chassis earthing point; the reading must be infinity,

15 Renew the impulse generator if the tests in paragraphs 13 and 14 prove it to be faulty. First remove the distributor cap, rotor arm, and plastic cover.

16 Unscrew the two magnet/coil retaining screws, and the screw on the side of the distributor body. Lift the connector from its slot and withdraw the impulse generator.

17 Refitting is a reversal of removal, but the air-gap between the polarity wheel and coil core must be adjusted before tightening the retaining screws. To adjust, turn the engine until a polarity wheel arm is pointing towards the coil core. Using a non-magnetic feeler gauge (i.e. of brass) set the coil core 0.01 to 0.02 in (0.30 to 0.50 mm) from the polarity wheel arm, then tighten the retaining screws, see Fig. 13.32.

Coil/amplifier check and renewal

18 Note Figs. 13.33 and 13.34. Check that current is reaching the coil by connecting a 12 volt test lamp and leads from the positive (+) terminal to a chassis earthing point. The lamp should glow with the ignition switched on.

19 With the positive terminal connected to the coil, disconnect the negative (−) terminal lead and connect a 12 volt test lamp

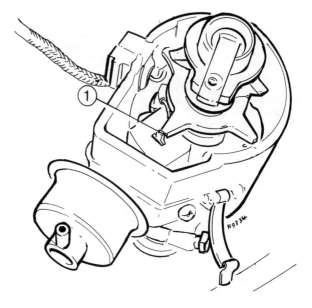

Fig. 13.32 Transistorized ignition system - air gap check (Sec 6)

1   Coil core

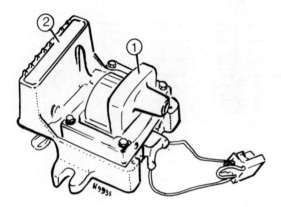

Fig. 13.33 Transistorized ignition system - coil/amplifier assembly (Sec 6)

1   *Ignition coil*   2   *Alloy base housing amplifier module*

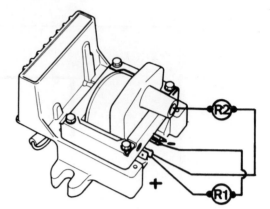

Fig. 13.35 Transistorized ignition coil - terminals and resistance test (Sec 6)

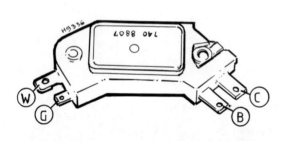

Fig. 13.34 Transistorized ignition system - amplifier module (Sec 6)

G   *To impulse generator*   W   *To impulse generator*
B   *To coil feed*   C   *To coil negative (−) terminal*

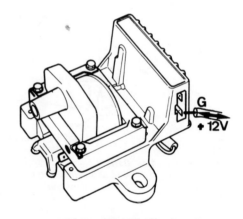

Fig. 13.36 Transistorized ignition system - amplifier module test (Sec 6)

and leads from the coil negative terminal to earth. The lamp should glow with the ignition switched on. If it does not glow, the coil primary circuit may be broken or the amplifier module transistor short-circuit.

20 The coil may be checked for open-circuit using an ohmmeter. Refer to Fig. 13.35 and check that the resistance R1 is between 0.48 and 0.61 ohms, and resistance R2 is between 9000 and 11 000 ohms; disconnect the amplifier module leads during this test.

21 To test the amplifier module, first disconnect the impulse generator plug and the HT lead at the distributor cap. Hold the HT lead approximately 0.40 in (10 mm) from the cylinder head with well-insulated electrician's pliers, then switch on the ignition.

22 Connect a lead from the battery positive terminal, and touch the remaining end on the G terminal of the amplifier module several times (see Fig. 13.36). A spark should occur between the end of the HT lead and the cylinder head each time the lead contacts the G terminal.

23 If the coil/amplifier assembly is proved faulty, it may be renewed by disconnecting the electrical wiring and removing the retaining screws. Make sure that a good earth is made between the base and the body when refitting the assembly. If the amplifier module is renewed separately, the new unit must be coated with the silicon grease provided, in order to ensure adequate heat transfer to the base.

Ignition timing

24 Stroboscopic timing should be carried out as described for the equivalent mechanical breaker system.

25 Checking and adjusting the dwell angle is not required with breakerless distributors. The ignition timing itself should rarely need adjusting, except overhaul or renewal of the distributor or related engine components.

Distributor removal and refitting

26 This procedure is as described for the equivalent mechanical breaker type.

Distributor dismantling and reassembly

27 Reference to Figs. 13.28 to 13.30 will show to what extent the distributor can be dismantled.

28 Work carefully and in a logical order when dismantling, keeping conditions of utmost cleanliness. Renew any defective components; if in doubt ask your Peugeot dealer before rejecting a component. Note the instructions given for renewal of the magnetic impulse generator (where applicable) during reassembly.

Fault diagnosis

29 Total ignition failure or misfiring may be due to loose or disconnected wires or plugs, or to component malfunction. Misfiring may also be due to the same faults on the HT side as

those described in Chapter 4, Section 11.

30 Do not remove plug caps whilst the engine is running in an attempt to locate a misfire. Personal electric shock and/or damage to the coil insulation may result.

31 Testing of the ignition system units should be left to a Peugeot dealer or automobile electrician. Beware of haphazard testing by substitution - a fault in one component may damage other units.

32 If sealing compound is observed to have spilled from the coil cap, displacing the sealing plug, both the coil and the control unit should be renewed.

33 It is possible for the ignition system to malfunction when in close proximity to certain types of VHF radio transmitters. Consult your Peugeot dealer if this is a problem.

Cassette distributor

Description

34 To improve efficiency of the ignition system, the distributor fitted to some later vehicles has a cassette arrangement incorporated in place of the conventional contact breaker points, see Fig. 13.37. With the conventional points, the spark passing between the rotor arm and the distributor cap jumps sideways which means that if there is any side play in the distributor spindle, the spark appearing at each spark plug will vary in strength. With the cassette, the spark jumps vertically thereby obviating any variation caused by spindle movement.

Contact breaker points check

35 The condition of the contact breaker points within the cassette can be determined by measuring the resistance across them with the gap closed. If the voltage reading obtained exceeds 0.2 volts, then suspect a fault. Apart from points in bad condition, faults may include the low tension wire between the HT coil and distributor being defective, a defective earth between the distributor body and the engine or an internal fault in the distributor.

Contact breaker points adjustment

36 There are two methods of checking and adjusting the gap between the contact breaker points. The most accurate method is by using a dwellmeter to determine the dwell angle, which is

Fig. 13.37 Exploded view of cassette type distributor (Sec 6)

the angle through which the distributor cam turns between the instance of closure and opening of the contact breaker points during one ignition cycle. A reduction of the points gap will increase the dwell angle and vice versa, see Fig. 13.38.

37 With the dwellmeter attached to the ignition system in accordance with the manufacturer's instructions, measure the dwell angle. This angle must be as specified. If the correct type of meter is available, then measure the dwell percentage, which must also be as specified. If necessary, refer to the relevant sub-Section for dwell adjustment.

38 The second method of adjustment requires the manufacture of a special tool, that is a length of metal bar with a diameter of 0.667 in (16.96 mm). Insert this tool into the centre of the cassette in place of the drive spindle and then adjust the points gap to 0.016 in (0.40 mm) by using a feeler gauge.

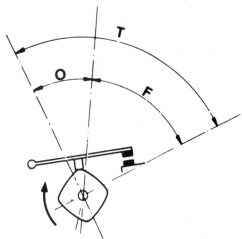

Fig. 13.38 Dwell angle identification (Sec 6)

T Total angle (90°)	F Dwell angle (57°)
O Angle of opening (33°)	

Contact breaker points renewal

39 The contact breaker points form an integral part of the cassette. Figs. 13.39 and 13.40 show removal of the cassette from the distributor and disconnection of the cassette from the vacuum capsule.

40 New cassettes are preset by the manufacturer and require no further adjustment. Take care when fitting the cassette over the cam, to make sure that the contact heel is not damaged by coming into contact with the apex of a cam. When refitting the rotor arm, ensure that it is fully home in the drive spindle and that the complete cassette/condenser assembly is fully home in the distributor body. Recheck all electrical connections after assembly. Reset the initial ignition timing.

Dwell angle and percentage adjustment

41 Making this adjustment is simply a matter of using a 3 mm Allen key in a method similar to that shown in Fig. 13.25. Carry out adjustment with the engine idling. Turn the key clockwise to increase dwell or anti-clockwise to decrease dwell.

Cassette distributor (SEV-Marchal alternative)

42 By comparing the exploded views of both distributors, it will be seen that the Marchal distributor bears some resemblance to that type shown in the preceding test. Changing the cassette is therefore a similar operation to that previously described; Figs. 13.41 and 13.42 show the detail differences and points to note.

43 Fig. 13.43 shows the method of contact breaker point adjustment. Do not loosen the screw A; simply insert the flat of a small screwdriver into the triangular cutout shown and turn the screwdriver to effect adjustment.

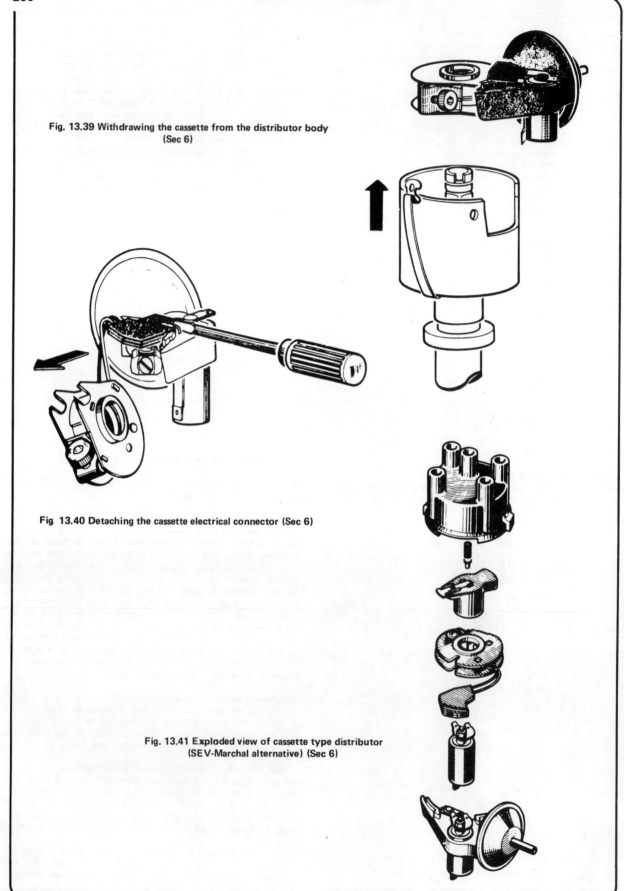

Fig. 13.39 Withdrawing the cassette from the distributor body
(Sec 6)

Fig 13.40 Detaching the cassette electrical connector (Sec 6)

Fig. 13.41 Exploded view of cassette type distributor
(SEV-Marchal alternative) (Sec 6)

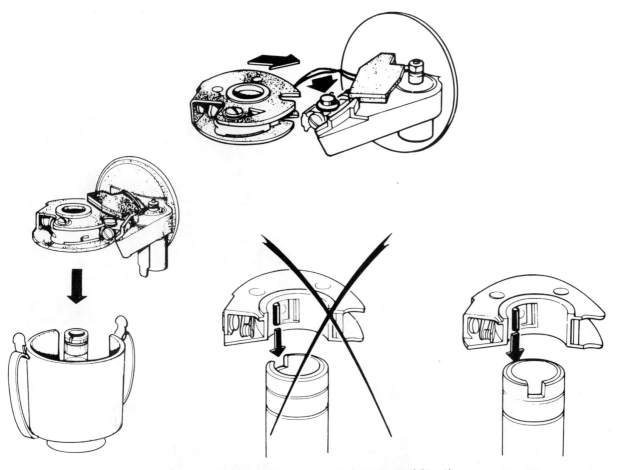

Fig. 13.42 Fitting a replacement cassette (SEV-Marchal) (Sec 6)

7 Manual gearbox and automatic transmission

Manual gearbox - overhaul
1   When renewing gears, it is essential to ensure that a correct replacement is obtained, as there are a number of variations between models. Some gears have an annular groove cut into the teeth to distinguish them, and where this is the case, the new gear must have the same identification.

Automatic transmission - description
2   As from chassis no. 2 727 386 a new version of the automatic transmission is fitted as given in Specifications. The main external difference is that the fluid sump has been lowered by 0.087 in (22.0 mm) to improve fluid cooling and circulation. The procedures given in Chapter 6 still apply, and the fluid level can be checked with the transmission warm or cold.

8 Propeller shaft

General description
1   Whereas Chapter 7 relates to vehicles equipped with independent rear suspension, the following text covers those vehicles equipped with a solid 'banjo' type rear axle. Here the gearbox attachment is slightly different because the propeller shaft and torque tube must move up and down to cater for suspension movement. The torque tube is therefore allowed to pivot on a spherical bearing bolted to the rear face of the gearbox. A universal joint is also fitted to the rear of the gearbox mainshaft. Figs. 7.1 (B) and 7.2 of Chapter 7 show the component parts of the 'banjo' axle propeller shaft.

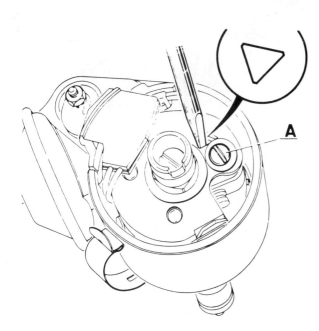

Fig. 13.43 Adjusting the contact breaker points
(SEV-Marchal) (Sec 6)

Shaft and torque tube - removal and refitting

2 The procedure for removing the propeller shaft from a vehicle equipped with a solid 'banjo' type rear axle is rather more difficult than that described in Chapter 7.

3 It is first necessary to remove the complete rear axle assembly from the car. This is necessary to provide sufficient clearance to enable the propellor shaft and torque tube to be moved rearwards and thus disengaged from the gearbox.

4 With the rear axle removed, disconnect the exhaust system from its mounting and from the joint at the exhaust manifold, and lower the system to the ground.

5 At the rear of the gearbox remove the two rubber vibration damper blocks (if fitted), and also the exhaust bracket if still in position (photo).

6 Undo and remove the four socket-headed bolts securing the torque tube spherical bearing to the rear of the gearbox (photo).

7 Carefully slide the torque tube and propeller shaft rearwards and out of engagement with the gearbox universal joint splines. Lower the assembly to the ground and out from under the car.

8 Refitting the shaft and torque tube assembly is basically the reverse sequence of removal. Note the instructions given in Chapter 7 and remember to grease the front spherical bearing.

Shaft and torque tube - inspection

9 All information contained in Section 4 of Chapter 7 is applicable to vehicles equipped with a solid 'banjo' type rear axle. In addition, the spherical bearing at the front of the torque tube should be inspected by undoing the two socket-headed bolts and separating the bearing halves (photo). Renew the bearing seal if flattened or damaged.

8.6 Torque tube spherical bearing to gearbox mounting bolts

8.5 Vibration damper blocks at rear of gearbox

8.9 Torque tube spherical bearing components

Fault diagnosis

Symptom	Reason(s)
Vibration	Wear in propeller shaft splines Torque tube distorted Excessive propeller shaft run-out Centre bearing worn Front universal joint worn (where applicable)
Knock or clunk when taking up drive	Wear in propeller shaft splines Front universal joint worn *See also Section 9 'Fault diagnosis - rear axle'*

9 Rear axle

General description

1 Further to the information given in Chapter 7, the solid 'banjo' type of rear axle will now be found fitted to Saloon, Estate and Family Estate models, see Fig. 13.44 and Fig. 8.6 of Chapter 8. The following text gives the servicing procedures for the solid rear axle.

Rear axle - removal and refitting

2 Jack up the rear of the car and support the body on axle stands.

3 Undo the rear axle drain plug and allow the oil to drain into a suitable container. When all the oil has drained, refit and tighten the drain plug.

4 Disconnect the handbrake cables from the rear brake shoes and brake backplates. Remove the wire clips securing the cables to the axle tie-rods and lower the cables to the ground.

5 Disconnect the tension spring from the brake compensator and the bracket on the torque tube.

6 Using a brake hose clamp or self-gripping wrench with suitably protected jaws, firmly clamp the flexible rear brake hose. This will prevent loss of hydraulic fluid when the hose is disconnected.

7 Now undo and remove the rigid metal brake pipe union from the end of the hose, and then detach the hose from the bracket on the torque tube. Plug or tape over the disconnected ends to prevent dirt ingress.

8 Undo and remove the nuts securing the anti-roll bar links to each side of the axle casing and then detach the links from the axle (photo).

9 Extract the split pin and undo and remove the nut and bolt securing the Panhard rod to the axle casing.

10 Place a sturdy jack under the centre of the axle and jack it up slightly. Ensure that the axle is well supported and not likely to slip off.

11 Undo and remove the shock absorber lower mounting nuts and thrust pads (photo).

12 Carefully lower the axle until all tension is released from the coil road springs. When they are completely free, lift them out of their locations in the body crossmember and axle.

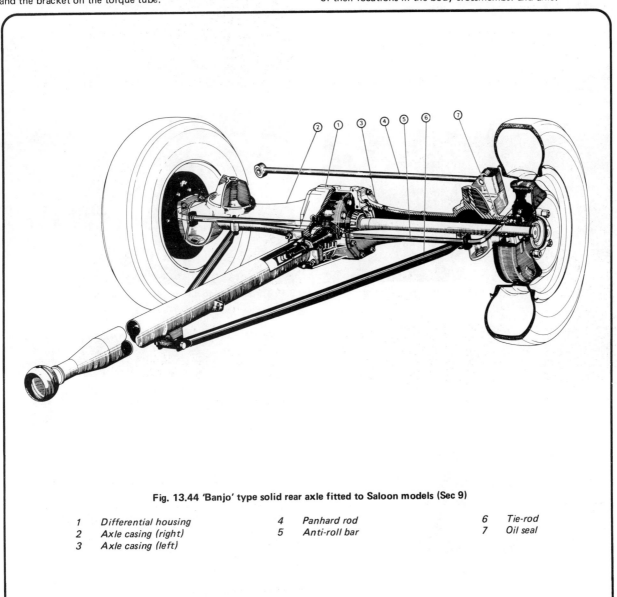

Fig. 13.44 'Banjo' type solid rear axle fitted to Saloon models (Sec 9)

1	Differential housing	4	Panhard rod
2	Axle casing (right)	5	Anti-roll bar
3	Axle casing (left)		
		6	Tie-rod
		7	Oil seal

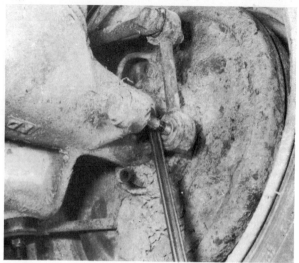

9.8 Removing anti-roll bar links from rear axle

9.11 Removing shock absorber lower nut, washer and thrust block

9.13 Removing axle tie-rod to torque tube retaining bolt

9.14 Torque tube to differential housing retaining nuts

9.15 Disengaging rear axle from torque tube

9.21a Withdraw the halfshaft . . .

9.21b . . . and secure the backplate with an old nut and bolt

9.22 The halfshaft and bearing assembly

13 Undo and remove the nut and bolt securing the two axle tie-rods to the torque tube (photo).

14 Undo and remove the four nuts and washers securing the torque tube to the front of the differential housing (photo).

15 Make a final check that everything is disconnected and then lower the axle until there is just sufficient clearance to move it rearward and out of engagement with the torque tube (photo). As the axle comes free, ensure that the propeller shaft slides off the differential pinion splines and stays behind in the torque tube. Take care also that the preload spring in the end of the propeller shaft does not fall out unnoticed.

16 Once the axle is clear of the propeller shaft, it can be fully lowered and withdrawn from under the car.

17 Refitting the rear axle is the reverse sequence to removal bearing in mind the following points:

(a) *Ensure that the preload spring is in place in the propeller shaft before reconnecting it to the differential housing*

(b) *Bleed the rear brakes on completion of the installation (Chapter 9)*

(c) *Refill the rear axle with the specified grade of oil*

(d) *Observe the correct torque wrench settings during refitting.*

Halfshafts - removal and refitting

18 Jack up the rear of the car and support it on axle stands. Remove the appropriate rear roadwheel.

19 Undo and remove the retaining screws, release fully the handbrake and then withdraw the brake drum. If it is tight, tap its circumference with a soft-faced mallet.

20 Undo and remove the seven nuts, at the rear of the brake backplate, that secure the halfshaft outer bearing and brake backplate to the axle flange.

21 The halfshaft can now be removed from the axle by tapping the wheel hub flange with a soft-faced mallet. **Note:** *After withdrawing the halfshaft, the brake backplate will remain in position on the axle supported only by the brake hydraulic pipe. To avoid straining the pipe temporarily attach the backplate to the axle flange using a scrap nut and bolt (photos).*

22 Should the outer halfshaft bearing or oil seal require renewal, this work should be entrusted to your Peugeot dealer, as a press and other special tool are needed to remove the bearings (photo).

23 Refit the halfshaft in the reverse sequence to removal, ensuring that the mating surfaces are perfectly clean and new gaskets are used where applicable. Remember to check and if necessary top up the rear axle oil level on completion of fitting.

Fault diagnosis

24 The following information applies to vehicles which have either a solid rear axle or independent rear suspension fitted.

Symptom	Reason(s)
Vibration	Worn driveshaft pot joints
	Worn halfshaft or driveshaft bearings
	Excessive run-out or distortion of driveshafts
	Wheels out of balance
	Defective tyre
Noise	Insufficient lubricant
	Excessive wear of gears or bearings
Clunk on acceleration or deceleration	Incorrect mesh of crownwheel and pinion
	Worn driveshaft pot joints
	Worn halfshaft or driveshaft splines
	Worn drive pinion splines
	See also Section 8 'Fault diagnosis - propeller shaft'
Oil leakage	Defective or worn pinion, side cover or halfshaft oil seal
	Blocked differential housing breather

10 Braking system

Hydraulic fluid - renewal

1 The brake hydraulic fluid must be renewed every 24,000 miles (40,000 km) or every 2 years, whichever comes first.

Hydraulic system - bleeding

2 Where it is found impossible to free the hydraulic system of air, then it will be necessary to take advice from your Peugeot dealer who may advise the use of pressure bleeding equipment supplied by Peugeot.

3 Where the vehicle is equipped with a rear load sensitive valve, ensure that the vehicle weight is on the road wheels before bleeding the system. Alternatively, use a length of wire or cord to hold the valve open, thus ensuring a full flow of fluid to the rear brake system. Do not forget to remove any wire or cord on completion.

4 On the type of system where the brake reservoir supplies fluid to the clutch system, take care when maintaining the clutch system not to allow the fluid level in the reservoir to drop so far as to allow air into the brake system.

Front and rear disc brakes

Brake pad refitting

5 To prevent any tendency to squeak, the outer surface of new disc pads should be coated with a special compound available from a Peugeot dealer. The friction material of the pads must be protected with masking tape while the outer surface is sprayed with the compound from the aerosol. After the compound is dry (approximately 1 hour), remove the masking tape and fit the pads.

6 The spring retaining clips holding the disc pads in position on later models incorporate a hole instead of an arrow to indicate the top of the clip.

7 On some models, an Allen screw instead of a nut secures the pad retaining fork to the caliper. When installing this screw, coat the threads with a liquid locking agent and tighten it to the new specified torque.

Brake disc refitting

8 When installing the Allen screws which secure the brake disc to the hub assembly, coat the threads with a liquid locking agent before tightening them to the torque loading specified in Chapter 9.

Brake caliper refitting

9 When refitting the disc brake caliper, coat the threads of the retaining bolts with a liquid locking agent before tightening them to the torque loading specified in Chapter 9.

Caliper assemblies - 1980 on

10 Figs. 13.45 and 13.46 show the Girling brake caliper assemblies fitted to vehicles from 1980 on. These assemblies differ from preceding types in that the slides on which the frames move are widened and the tension plates are replaced by a sliding circular-section spacer. The pad retaining method has been modified and each slide is lubricated with a 'high temperature' metallic paste.

11 **Caution:** *Girling caliper assemblies of different types are similar in appearance.* When renewing a caliper, ensure that the one to be fitted matches the one removed. Do not mix caliper types on one axle; the difference in composition of the brake pads between types will mean that the brakes pull unevenly.

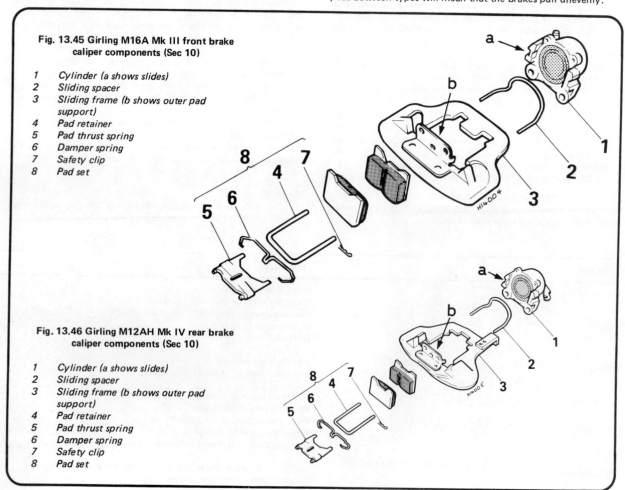

Fig. 13.45 Girling M16A Mk III front brake
caliper components (Sec 10)

1   Cylinder (a shows slides)
2   Sliding spacer
3   Sliding frame (b shows outer pad
     support)
4   Pad retainer
5   Pad thrust spring
6   Damper spring
7   Safety clip
8   Pad set

Fig. 13.46 Girling M12AH Mk IV rear brake
caliper components (Sec 10)

1   Cylinder (a shows slides)
2   Sliding spacer
3   Sliding frame (b shows outer pad
     support)
4   Pad retainer
5   Pad thrust spring
6   Damper spring
7   Safety clip
8   Pad set

12 Where the caliper frame is found to have partially seized, then dismantle the caliper, clean the sliding surfaces and coat them thinly with Molykote 321 R (obtainable from your Peugeot dealer). The same surfaces should then be coated with Molykombin paste before reassembly.

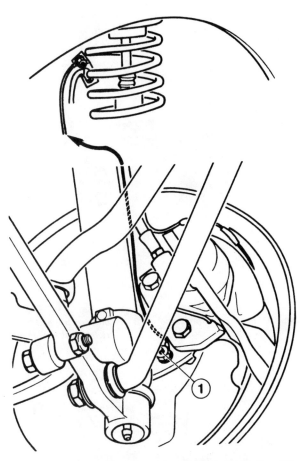

Fig. 13.47 Earthing the brake pad wear warning light (Sec 10)

1   Shield securing bolt

Front disc brakes
Brake pad wear warning light
13 Where the vehicle is fitted with a pad wear warning light and renewal of one or both of the front suspension units becomes necessary, then check that the warning circuit remains correctly earthed.
14 It is probable that new front suspension units will have Teflon-coated piston rings which cannot be relied upon to complete the earth circuit, in which case an earth wire will have to be routed from the stub axle to brake pipe dip as shown in Fig. 13.47. This will necessitate replacing the shield securing bolt with a longer item.

Rear disc brakes
Brake disc and hub removal and refitting
15 Two types of rear hub assemblies are described in Chapter 9. However, later models are equipped with a further type having the discs mounted behind the hub but with an access hole in the flange. A special Peugeot tool will be required for dismantling and reassembly.
16 Remove the caliper assembly without disconnecting the hose as described in Chapter 9.
17 Prevent the hub from rotating and unscrew the driveshaft nut, see Fig. 13.48.
18 Insert a socket through the access hole and unscrew the hub retaining bolts.
19 Using a puller attached to the wheel studs, press the driveshaft through the hub, then withdraw the hub and disc assembly.
20 Mount the assembly in a vice and unscrew the bearing housing nut; the special Peugeot tool will be required to do this, see Fig. 13.49.
21 Using a suitable puller, press the drive flange and disc from the hub. The disc can now be separated from the drive flange (4 bolts), and the bearing removed from the hub with a soft metal drift.
22 Clean all components and examine them for wear and deterioration; renew them as necessary.
23 Start refitting by assembling the disc to the drive flange, making sure that the access hole is aligned in both components. Coat the threads of the retaining Allen screws with a liquid locking agent and install the special lockwashers before tightening them to the specified torque.

Fig. 13.48 Removing the driveshaft nut (Sec 10)

Fig. 13.49 Using the special tool to remove the rear hub drive flange (Sec 10)

| 1 | Thrust pad | 2 | Extractor | 3 | Special bolt |

24 Renew the oil seals, then drive the bearing into the hub and tighten the bearing housing nut to the specified torque; do not lock it at this stage.

25 Press the drive flange and disc into the hub using the special Peugeot tools.

26 Mount the bearing housing in a vice and check the disc run-out with a dial gauge (refer to Chapter 9).

27 Lock the bearing housing nut by staking, then assemble the drive flange over the driveshaft. Coat the bearing housing bolts with a liquid locking agent before tightening them to the specified torque.

28 Tighten the driveshaft nut to the specified torque then refit the brake caliper as described in Chapter 9.

Brake caliper overhaul

29 When refitting the piston to the rear brake caliper, use the special key to set the piston as shown in Fig. 13.50. Mk 1 calipers are fitted to cars having a 0.40 in (10 mm) thick brake disc, and Mk III calipers are fitted to cars having a 0.47 in (12 mm) thick brake disc.

Brake pad renewal

30 Where the vehicle is fitted with a self-adjuster mechanism, note the following information before attempting to fit new brake pads.

31 Before returning the brake pistons to allow the fitting of new pads, refer to Fig. 13.51 and rotate each direct piston through 45° so that it disengages the rod ratchet teeth from the pawls of the self-adjuster. Upon returning the brake pistons, rotate each direct piston back through 45° to re-engage the ratchet and pawl mechanism.

32 **Warning:** *Failure to observe the above procedure will result in the pawls becoming damaged beyond repair.*

33 After pad renewal, check that the handbrake lever returns fully to its off position. With the handbrake off, separate the footbrake pedal several times. As the pedal is operated, an assistant listening at each wheel should hear the self-adjuster click until reaching full adjustment.

Handbrake adjustment

34 Handbrake adjustment is correct if the lever moves through 7 to 13 notches on its quadrant without any 'dead' travel.

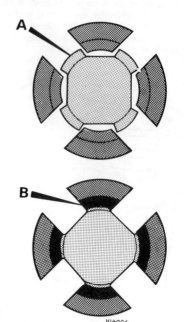

Fig. 13.51 Setting the rear brake self-adjusting mechanism (Sec 10)

A   *Direct piston disengaged from ratchet post*   B   *Direct piston and ratchet post realigned*

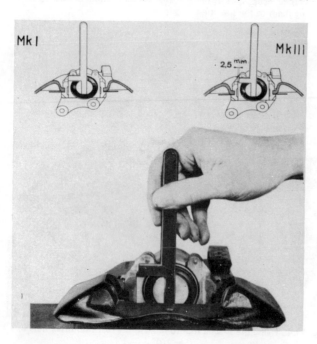

Fig. 13.50 Setting the rear brake caliper pistons (Sec 10)

Fig. 13.52 Adjusting the handbrake (rear disc brakes) (Sec 10)

1	Mechanism control lever	4	Adjusting nut
2	Nylon pad	J	Caliper lever to nylon pad clearance
3	Locknut		

Adjustment must be checked if there is excessive slack in the operating cables (lever travel excessive) or the clearance between the caliper levers and nylon pads (J in Fig. 13.52) amounts to more than 0.02 in (0.5 mm).

35 Before attempting handbrake adjustment, park the vehicle on an area of flat and level ground; the vehicle must be resting on all four wheels. There should be no air in the hydraulic system and the handbrake cables must be checked for seizure. If necessary, renew or lubricate the cables. Start the engine and press hard on the footbrake pedal several times to 'bed down' the brakes. Stop the engine and commence adjustment.

36 Refer to Fig. 13.52 and loosen the locknut on each cable; Screw in both adjusting nuts, a little at a time and in even amounts, until the caliper levers are just clear of their nylon pads (maximum clearance - 0.02 in). Now unscrew each adjusting nut by one half a turn and retighten its locknut.

37 Operate the handbrake lever several times, checking that it moves through the permissible travel. Recheck the lever to pad clearance at each caliper. If either of these checks prove unsatisfactory, then repeat adjustment.

Rear drum brakes (manually adjusted)

Brake adjustment

38 Further to the information given in Section 16 of Chapter 9, it may be found that instead of the one adjuster mentioned, there are two of the same. Where this is the case, repeat the procedure given for the first adjuster on the second.

Compensator - adjustment

39 The compensator described in Chapter 9 is the Bendix type. Some vehicles are equipped with a Teves type compensator as shown in Fig. 13.53.

40 To adjust the compensator, jack-up the rear of the car and support it with axle-stands placed beneath the underframe so that the wheels are free of any load.

41 Press the compensator lever towards the torque tube as far as possible and check that the control spring is free of any tension. If necessary, loosen the adjusting nut and reposition the bolt, then tighten the nut.

42 Lower the car to the ground.

43 Estate models are equipped with two alternative types of compensator - a) rod restrained and b) spring restrained.

44 To adjust the rod restrained type, position the car over a pit or a ramp. Insert the wedge (tool no. 0.0806) between the body underframe and the front of the differential housing (see Fig. 13.54).

45 Obtain the adjustment gauge (tool no. 80803) and check that it fits in the holes on the compensator. If not, loosen the

locknuts and adjust the compensator rod as necessary. Do not attempt to adjust the spring position, see Fig. 13.55.

46 Remove the wedge and gauge from the car.

47 To adjust the spring restrained type, first check whether the spring has a blue identification mark or not.

48 Position the car over a pit or on a ramp, and insert the wedge (tool no. 0.0806) between the body, underframe and the front of the differential housing, see Fig. 13.56.

49 Using vernier calipers, measure the distance from the spring retaining bracket to the tip of the compensator lever, first with the lever moved away from the torque tube but without the spring tensioned, and then with the lever pressed towards the torque tube. The difference between these two dimensions must be 0.047 to 0.087 in (1.2 to 2.2 mm) for plain spring systems, and 0.087 to 0.126 in (2.2 to 3.2 mm) for blue spring systems.

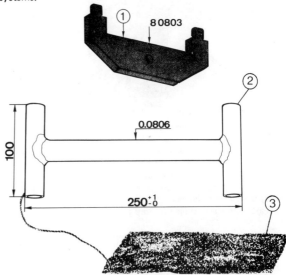

Fig. 13.54 Special tools for compensator adjustment on Estate models (Sec 10)

| 1 | Gauge | 3 | Warning flag |
| 2 | Wedge | | |

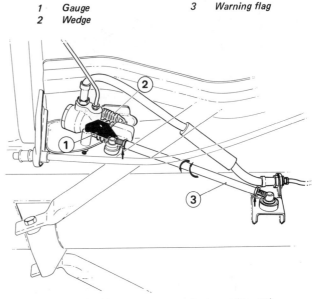

Fig. 13.55 Checking compensator adjustment (Sec 10)

| 1 | Gauge | 3 | Adjustable rod |
| 2 | Spring | | |

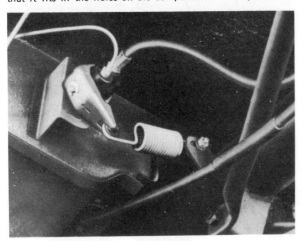

Fig. 13.53 Teves type brake compensator (Sec 10)

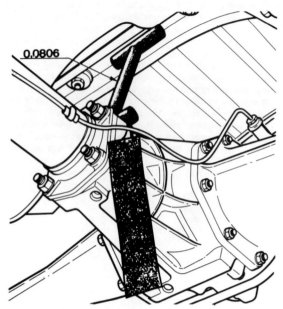

Fig. 13.56 Brake compensator wedge location (Sec 10)

50 If adjustment is necessary, set the caliper to 0.067 in (1.7 mm) for plain spring systems and 0.106 in (2.7 mm) for blue spring systems. Loosen the adjustment nut and position the bolt so that the spring is not under any tension while holding the lever at the correct distance.

51 Tighten the adjusting nut and remove the wedge from the car.

Secondary brake - description

52 On some late models fitted with air conditioning and a front bench seat, a secondary brake is fitted in place of a handbrake. The brake is foot operated but incorporates a hand release lever mounted beneath the fascia panel.

Brake pedal - removal and refitting

53 Working underneath the dashboard, remove the spring clip from the end of the brake pedal-to-vacuum servo unit pushrod clevis pin, using a pair of pliers. Lift out the clevis pin.

54 At the top of the brake pedal, remove the split pin or nut from the brake pedal pivot pin and slide out the pin. Space is extremely limited in this area, and removal of the split pin or nut and pivot pin is a fiddly operation requiring a good deal of patience.

55 Having removed the pivot pin, carefully lower the brake pedal out from under the dash and recover the bushes, washers and spacer (if fitted).

56 Examine the bushes for wear, and check that the pivot pin is a slide fit in them with very little side play. Renew the bushes or pivot pin if worn.

57 Refitting the brake pedal is the reverse sequence to removal. If necessary, refer to Fig. 13.57 for the correct fitted position of bushes etc.

Stop-light switch - removal and refitting

58 The stop-light switch is located on a bracket beneath the dashboard and is activated by movement of the brake pedal (photo).

59 To remove the switch, disconnect the electrical connections and then slacken the two switch retaining locknuts.

60 Remove the locknut nearest the brake pedal and then lift out the switch.

61 To refit the switch, place it in position on the mounting bracket and loosely refit the locknuts. Reconnect the electrical

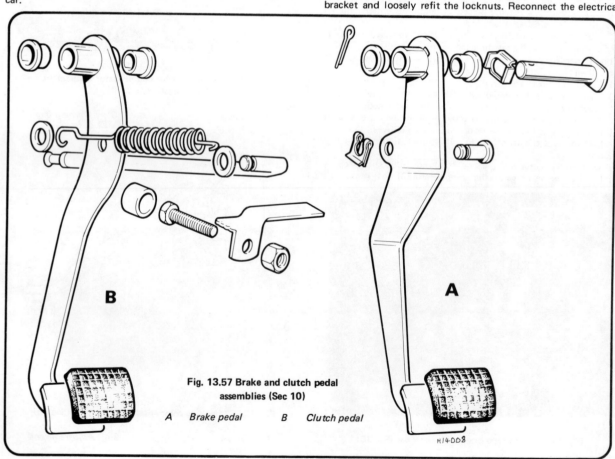

Fig. 13.57 Brake and clutch pedal assemblies (Sec 10)

A   Brake pedal   B   Clutch pedal

B

A

H14008

10.58 Brake pedal assembly and stop-light switch (arrowed)

leads to the switch.

62 Depress the brake pedal just sufficiently to take up the free play of the servo unit and master cylinder. With the pedal in this position, adjust the switch by repositioning the locknuts so that the stop-lights are just illuminated.

11 Electrical system

Voltage regulator
Remote-mounted type

1 All vehicles manufactured before 1978 have a voltage regulator which is mounted on the rear bulkhead of the engine bay.

This unit is set during manufacture and should require no further attention. However, should it prove defective then it must be renewed as a complete unit.

Integral electronic type

2 From chassis no 2 821 313 some vehicles are fitted with Femsa and SEV-Marchal alternators which incorporate an integral electronic regulator. Figs. 13.58 and 13.59 show the circuitry for each alternator type.

3 A resistor casing replaces the remote-mounted regulator previously fitted, but this has no regulator function, its purpose being to excite the alternator.

Headlights
Unit removal and refitting

4 Should it be necessary to renew a headlight unit, then advice will have to be sought from your Peugeot dealer. The procedure for removal and refitting of a unit will obviously depend on the type fitted, see Figs. 10.11, 10.12 and 10.13 of Chapter 10.

5 Should advice be unobtainable, then approach the task of removal with care. Do not attempt to separate components without checking that all fasteners are removed. It may be necessary to remove the radiator grille and raise the bonnet to gain access to fasteners. Note the fitted position of all component parts for reference when refitting. On completion of refitting, refer to Chapter 10 and realign the headlights.

Beam height/vehicle load compensation

6 When carrying heavy loads in the vehicle, it is necessary to avoid dazzling oncoming drivers by lowering the headlight beams. This can be done by turning the outer section of the beam height vertical adjuster to the position shown in Fig. 13.60.

Windscreen wiper motor - removal and refitting

7 The windscreen wiper motor is located beneath the grilled panel which separates the rear of the bonnet from the windscreen. To remove this panel, raise the bonnet and separate the

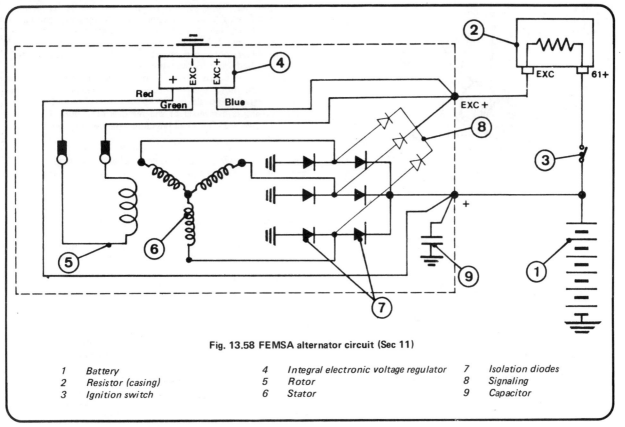

Fig. 13.58 FEMSA alternator circuit (Sec 11)

1	Battery	4	Integral electronic voltage regulator	7	Isolation diodes
2	Resistor (casing)	5	Rotor	8	Signaling
3	Ignition switch	6	Stator	9	Capacitor

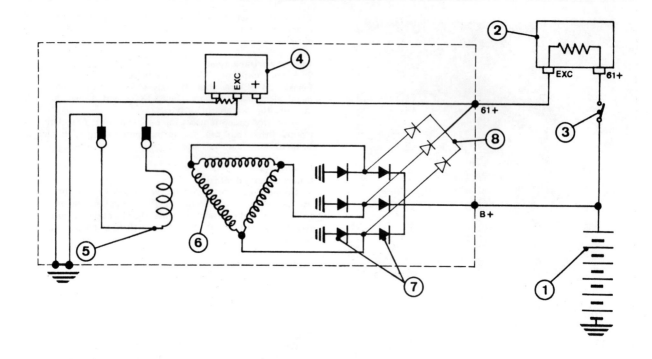

Fig. 13.59 SEV-Marchal alternator circuit (Sec 11)

1	Battery	4	Integral electronic voltage	6	Stator
2	Resistor (casing)		regulator	7	Isolation diodes
3	Ignition switch	5	Rotor	8	Signaling

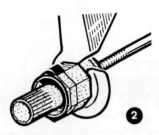

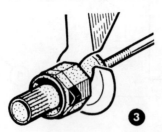

Fig. 13.60 Beam height/vehicle load compensation (Sec 11)

2	Vehicle unladen (or light load)	3	Vehicle laden (heavy load)

seal from the front edge of the panel to expose its retaining bolts. Remove the bolts, lift the front of the panel and ease it from position, taking care not to damage the paintwork of bonnet or panel.

8 The wiper motor can now be unbolted from its mountings and detached from its operating linkage, see Figs. 10.22, 10.23 and 10.24 of Chapter 10. Disconnect the battery before un-plugging the motor electrical connections. Clean each connector and note its fitted position.

9 Refitting is a reversal of the removal procedure. Grease the linkage pivots before reconnecting. Renew the panel seal if perished or split.

Rear screen wiper motor - removal and refitting

10 Fig. 13.61 shows the screen wiper assembly fitted to the tailgate of some Estate models.

11 To remove the wiper motor, first refer to Chapter 10 and remove the wiper arm, followed by any seal and/or nut. Raise the tailgate and release the trim from its lower half to expose the motor.

12 Disconnect the battery and unplug the motor electrical connections. Clean each connector and note its fitted position. Unbolt the motor from its mountings and ease it clear of the tailgate.

13 Refitting is a reversal of the removal procedure. Renew any seal which is split or perished.

Econoscope

14 Later vehicles have an Econoscope system fitted, the component parts of which are shown in Fig. 13.62 and the circuitry of which is shown in Fig. 13.63.

15 The system consists of two main components, a vacuum operated pick-up and a warning light unit. The pick-up detects engine vacuum level and relays a signal to the warning lights which are mounted on the instrument panel. The warning lights

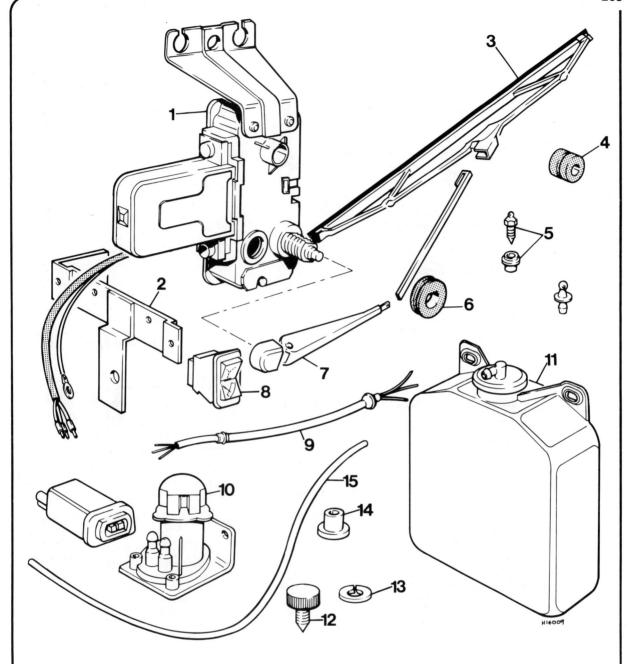

Fig. 13.61 Rear screen wiper assembly (Sec 11)

1	Motor and gearbox	6	Spacer seal	11	Reservoir
2	Bracket	7	Wiper arm	12	Screw
3	Wiper blade	8	Switch	13	Sealing washer
4	Buffer	9	Wiring harness	14	Spacer/nut
5	Washer jet	10	Pump	15	Washer tube

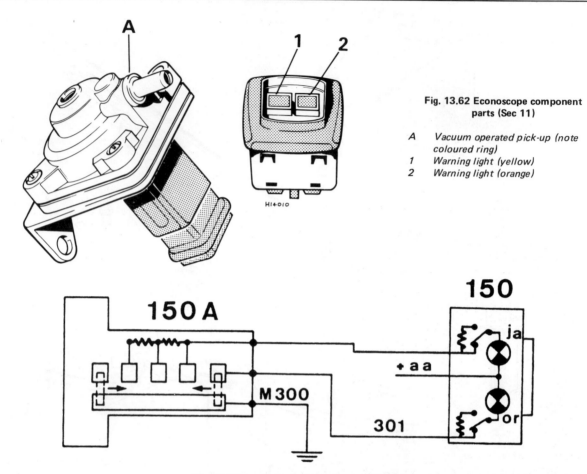

Fig. 13.62 Econoscope component parts (Sec 11)

A   Vacuum operated pick-up (note coloured ring)
1   Warning light (yellow)
2   Warning light (orange)

Fig. 13.63 Econoscope circuit diagram (Sec 11)

150	Warning light unit	+aa	Accessory feed	Ja	Warning light (yellow)
150A	Pick-up unit	3a		Or	Warning light (orange)

are coloured yellow and orange.

16 If neither of the warning lights is illuminated, this indicates to the driver that he is driving economically. If the yellow light illuminates, then fuel consumption is increasing. The yellow light passes through three degrees of brightness until the orange light illuminates, indicating that fuel consumption is excessive.

17 When obtaining a replacement pick-up unit, ensure that it is the correct type. The unit must have an orange ring (as opposed to brown, blue or black) fitted around its vacuum take-off spigot.

Mobile radio equipment - interference-free installation

Some Peugeot 504 models will not have a radio or aerial fitted as standard equipment. Where this is the case, then read the following text carefully before selecting and fitting any type of in-car entertainment unit.

Aerials - selection and fitting

The choice of aerials is now very wide. It should be realised that the quality has a profound effect on radio performance, and a poor, inefficient aerial can make suppression difficult.

A wing-mounted aerial is regarded as probably the most efficient for signal collection, but a roof aerial is usually better for suppression purposes because it is away from most interference fields. Stick-on wire aerials are available for attachment to the inside of the windscreen, but are not always free from the interference field of the engine and some accessories.

Motorised automatic aerials rise when the equipment is switched on and retract at switch-off. They require more fitting space and supply leads, and can be a source of trouble.

There is no merit in choosing a very long aerial as, for example, the type about three metres in length which hooks or clips on to the rear of the car, since part of this aerial will inevitably be located in an interference field. For VHF/FM radios the best length of aerial is about one metre. Active aerials have a transistor amplifier mounted at the base and this serves to boost the received signal. The aerial rod is sometimes rather shorter than normal passive types.

A large loss of signal can occur in the aerial feeder cable, especially over the Very High Frequency (VHF) bands. The design of feeder cable is invariably in the co-axial form, ie a centre conductor surrounded by a flexible copper braid forming the outer (earth) conductor. Between the inner and outer conductors is an insulator material which can be in solid or stranded form. Apart from insulation, its purpose is to maintain the correct spacing and concentricity. Loss of signal occurs in this insulator, the loss usually being greater in a poor quality cable. The quality of cable used is reflected in the price of the aerial with the attached feeder cable.

The capacitance of the feeder should be within the range 65 to 75 picofarads (pF) approximately (95 to 100 pF for Japanese and American equipment), otherwise the adjustment of the car radio aerial trimmer may not be possible. An extension cable is necessary for a long run between aerial and receiver. If this adds capacitance in excess of the above limits, a

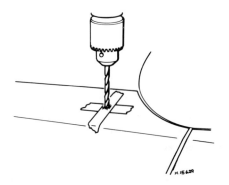

Fig. 13.64 Drilling the bodywork for aerial mounting (Sec 11)

connector containing a series capacitor will be required, or an extension which is labelled as 'capacity-compensated'.

Fitting the aerial will normally involve making a 7/8 in (22 mm) diameter hole in the bodywork, but read the instructions that come with the aerial kit. Once the hole position has been selected, use a centre punch to guide the drill. Use sticky masking tape around the area for this helps with marking out and drill location, and gives protection to the paintwork should the drill slip. Three methods of making the hole are in use:

(a) Use a hole saw in the electric drill. This is, in effect, a circular hacksaw blade wrapped round a former with a centre pilot drill.

(b) Use a tank cutter which also has cutting teeth, but is made to shear the metal by tightening with an Allen key.

(c) The hard way of drilling out the circle is using a small drill, say 1/8 in (3 mm), so that the holes overlap. The centre metal drops out and the hole is finished with round and half-round files.

Whichever method is used, the burr is removed from the body metal and paint removed from the underside. The aerial is fitted tightly ensuring that the earth fixing, usually a serrated washer, ring or clamp, is making a solid connection. *This earth connection is important in reducing interference.* Cover any bare metal with primer paint and topcoat, and follow by underseal if desired.

Aerial feeder cable routing should avoid the engine compartment and areas where stress might occur, eg under the carpet where feet will be located. Roof aerials require that the headlining be pulled back and that a path is available down the door pillar. It is wise to check with the vehicle dealer whether roof aerial fitting is recommended.

Loudspeakers

Speakers should be matched to the output stage of the equipment, particularly as regards the recommended impedance. Power transistors used for driving speakers are sensitive to the loading placed on them.

Before choosing a mounting position for speakers, check whether the vehicle manufacturer has provided a location for them. Generally door-mounted speakers give good stereophonic reproduction, but not all doors are able to accept them. The next best position is the rear parcel shelf, and in this case speaker apertures can be cut into the shelf, or pod units may be mounted.

For door mounting, first remove the trim, see Chapter 12, and then select a suitable gap in the inside door assembly. Check that the speaker would not obstruct glass or winder mechanism by winding the window up and down. A template is often provided for marking out the trim panel hole, and then the four fixing holes must be drilled through. Mark out with chalk and cut cleanly with a sharp knife or keyhole saw. Speaker leads are then threaded through the door and door pillar, if necessary drilling 10 mm diameter holes. Fit grommets in the

holes and connect to the radio or tape unit correctly. Do not omit a waterproofing cover, usually supplied with door speakers. If the speaker has to be fixed into the metal of the door itself, use self-tapping screws, and if the fixing is to the door trim use self-tapping screws and flat spire nuts.

Rear shelf mounting is somewhat simpler but it is necessary to find gaps is the metalwork underneath the parcel shelf. However, remember that the speakers should be as far apart as possible to give a good stereo effect. Pod-mounted speakers can be screwed into position through the parcel shelf material, but it is worth testing for the best position. Sometimes good results are found by reflecting sound off the rear window.

Unit installation

The Peugeot 504 has a dash panel aperture specifically designed to take a radio/audio unit. This aperture is located directly beneath the heater controls or to one side of them (depending on model type) and is fitted by a plastic panel which can be unclipped. Select a unit which will fit the aperture.

Offer the unit into the aperture after removal of the knobs (*not* push buttons) and the trim plate. In some cases a special mounting plate is required to which the unit is attached. It is worthwhile supporting the rear end in cases where sag or strain may occur, and it is usually possible to use a length of perforated metal strip attached between the unit and a good support point nearby. In general it is recommended that tape equipment should be installed at or nearly horizontal.

Connections to the aerial socket are simply by the standard plug terminating the aerial downlead or its extension cable. Speakers for a stereo system must be matched and correctly connected, as outlined previously.

Note: *While all work is carried out on the power side, it is wise to disconnect the battery earth lead.* Before connection is made to the vehicle electrical system, check that the polarity of the unit is correct. Most vehicles use a negative earth system, but radio/audio units often have a reversible plug to convert the set to either + or − earth. *Incorrect connection may cause serious damage.*

The power lead is often permanently connected inside the unit and terminates with one half of an in-line fuse carrier. The other half is fitted with a suitable fuse (3 or 5 amperes) and a wire which should go to a power point in the electrical system. This may be the accessory terminal on the ignition switch, giving the advantage of power feed with ignition or with the ignition key at the 'accessory' position. Power to the unit stops

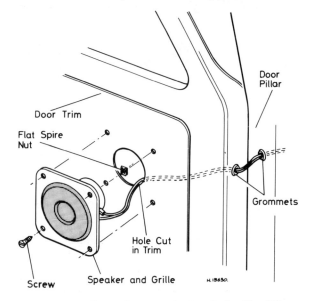

Fig. 13.65 Door-mounted speaker installation (Sec 11)

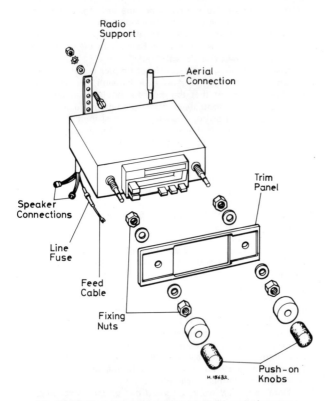

Fig. 13.66 Mounting component details for radio/cassette unit (Sec 11)

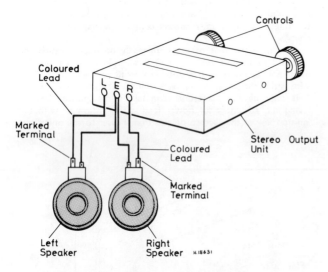

Fig. 13.67 Speaker connections must be correctly made as shown (Sec 11)

when the ignition key is removed. Alternatively, the lead may be taken to a live point at the fusebox with the consequence of having to remember to switch off at the unit before leaving the vehicle.

Before switching on for initial test, be sure that the speaker connections have been made, for running without load can damage the output transistors. Switch on next and tune through the bands to ensure that all sections are working, and check the tape unit if applicable. The aerial trimmer should be adjusted to give the strongest reception on a weak signal in the medium wave band, at say 200 metres.

Interference

In general, when electric current changes abruptly, unwanted electrical noise is produced. The motor vehicle is filled with electrical devices which change electric current rapidly, the most obvious being the contact breaker.

When the spark plugs operate, the sudden pulse of spark current causes the associated wiring to radiate. Since early radio transmitters used sparks as a basis of operation, it is not surprising that the car radio will pick up ignition spark noise unless steps are taken to reduce it to acceptable levels.

Interference reaches the car radio in two ways:

(a) by conduction through the wiring.
(b) by radiation to the receiving aerial.

Initial checks presuppose that the bonnet is down and fastened, the radio unit has a good earth connection (*not* through the aerial downlead outer), no fluorescent tubes are working near the car, the aerial trimmer has been adjusted, and the vehicle is in a position to receive radio signals, ie not in a metal-clad building.

Switch on the radio and tune it to the middle of the medium wave (MW) band off-station with the volume (gain) control set fairly high. Switch on the ignition (but do not start the engine) and wait to see if irregular clicks or harsh noise occurs. Tapping the facia panel may also produce the effects. If so, this will be due to the voltage stabiliser, which is an on-off thermal switch to control instrument voltage. It is located usually on the back of the instrument panel, often attached to the speedometer. Correction is by attachment of a capacitor and, if still troublesome, chokes in the supply wires.

Switch on the engine and listen for interference on the MW band. Depending on the type of interference, the indications are as follows:

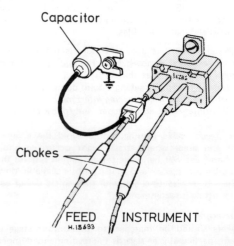

Fig. 13.68 Voltage stabiliser interference suppression (Sec 11)

A harsh crackle that drops out abruptly at low engine speed or when the headlights are switched on is probably due to a voltage regulator.

A whine varying with engine speed is due to the alternator. Try temporarily taking off the fan belt - if the noise goes this is confirmation.

Regular ticking or crackle that varies in rate with the engine speed is due to the ignition system. With this trouble in particular and others in general, check to see if the noise is entering the receiver from the wiring or by radiation. To do this, pull out the aerial plug (preferably shorting out the input socket or connecting a 62 pF capacitor across it). If the noise disappears it is coming in through the aerial and is *radiation noise*. If the noise persists it is reaching the receiver through the wiring and is said to be *line-borne*.

Interference from wipers, washers, heater blowers, turn-indicators, stop lamps, etc is usually taken to the receiver by wiring, and simple treatment using capacitors and possibly chokes will solve the problem. Switch on each one in turn (wet the screen first for running wipers!) and listen for possible interference with the aerial plug in place and again when removed.

Note that if most of the vehicle accessories are found to be creating interference all together, the probability is that poor aerial earthing is to blame.

Component terminal markings

Throughout the following sub-sections reference will be found to various terminal markings. These will vary depending on the manufacturer of the relevant component. If terminal markings differ from those listed below, then consult your Peugeot dealer.

Alternator	Alternator terminal (thick lead)	Exciting winding terminal
Delco Remy	+	EXC
Ducellier	+	EXC

Ignition coil	Ignition switch terminal	Contact breaker terminal
Delco Remy	+	−
Ducellier	BAT	RUP

Voltage regulator	Voltage input terminal	Exciting winding terminal
Delco Remy	BAT/+	EXC
Ducellier	BOB/BAT	EXC

Suppression methods - ignition

Suppressed HT cables are supplied as original equipment by manufacturers and will meet regulations as far as interference to neighbouring equipment is concerned. It is illegal to remove such suppression unless an alternative is provided, and this may take the form of resistive spark plug caps in conjunction with plain copper HT cable. For VHF purposes, these and 'in-line' resistors may not be effective, and resistive HT cable is preferred. Check that suppressed cables are actually fitted by observing cable identity lettering, or measuring with an ohmmeter - the value of each plug lead should be 5000 to 10 000 ohms.

A 1 microfarad capacitor connected from the LT supply side of the ignition coil to a good nearby earth point will complete basic ignition interference treatment. *NEVER fit a capacitor to the coil terminal to the contact breaker - the result would be burnt out points in a short time.*

If ignition noise persists despite the treatment above, the following sequence should be followed:

(a) Check the earthing of the ignition coil; remove paint from fixing clamp.
(b) If this does not work, lift the bonnet. Should there be no change in interference level, this may indicate that the bonnet is not electrically connected to the car body. Use a proprietary braided strap across a bonnet hinge ensuring a first class electrical connection. If, however, lifting the bonnet increases the interference, then fit resistive HT cables of a higher ohms-per-metre value.
(c) If all these measures fail, it is probable that re-radiation from metallic components is taking place. Using a braided strap between metallic points, go round the vehicle systematically - try the following: engine to body, exhaust system to body, front suspension to engine and to body, steering column to body (especially French and Italian cars), gear lever to engine and to body (again especially French and Italian cars), Bowden cable to body, metal parcel shelf to body. When an offending component is located it should be bonded with the strap permanently.
(d) As a next step, the fitting of distributor suppressors to

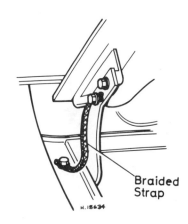

Fig. 13.69 Braided earth strap between bonnet and body (Sec 11)

each lead at the distributor end may help.
(e) Beyond this point is involved the possible screening of the distributor and fitting resistive spark plugs, but such advanced treatment is not usually required for vehicles with entertainment equipment.

Electronic ignition systems have built-in suppression components, but this does not relieve the need for using suppressed HT leads. In some cases it is permitted to connect a capacitor on the low tension supply side of the ignition coil, but not in every case. Makers' instructions should be followed carefully, otherwise damage to the ignition semiconductors may result.

Suppression methods - alternator

Alternators should be fitted with a 3 microfarad capacitor from the + main output terminal (thick cable) to earth. Additional suppression may be obtained by the use of a filter in the supply line to the radio receiver.

It is most important that:

(a) Capacitors are never connected to the field terminals of the alternator.
(b) Alternators must not be run without connection to the battery.

Suppression methods - voltage regulator

The voltage regulator used in conjunction with an alternator will be one of three types:

(a) Vibrating contact regulators separate from the alternator. Used extensively on continental vehicles.
(b) Electronic regulators separate from the alternator.
(c) Electronic regulators built-in to the alternator

In case (a) interference may be generated on the AM and FM (VHF) bands. For some cars a replacement suppressed regulator is available. Filter boxes may be used with non-suppressed regulators. But if not available, then for AM equipment a 2 microfarad or 3 microfarad capacitor may be mounted at the voltage terminal marked BOB or BAT of the regulator. FM bands may be treated by a feed-through capacitor of 2 or 3 microfarad.

Electronic voltage regulators are not always troublesome, but where necessary, a 1 microfarad capacitor from the regulator + terminal will help.

Integral electronic voltage regulators do not normally generate much interference, but when encountered this is in combination with alternator noise. A 1 microfarad or 2 microfarad capacitor from the warning lamp terminal to earth should cure the problem.

274

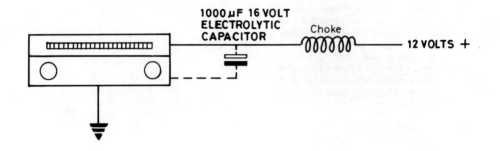

1000 μF 16 VOLT ELECTROLYTIC CAPACITOR

Choke

12 VOLTS +

Fig. 13.70 Line-borne interference suppression (Sec 11)

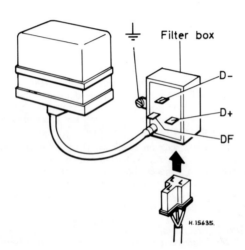

Filter box

D–

D+

DF

H.15635.

Fig. 13.71 Typical filter box for vibrating contact voltage regulator (alternator equipment) (Sec 11)

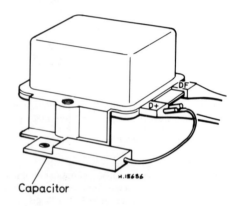

Capacitor

H.15686

Fig. 13.72 Suppression of AM interference by vibrating contact voltage regulator (alternator equipment) (Sec 11)

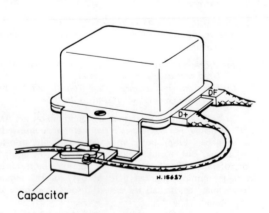

Capacitor

H.15637

Fig. 13.73 Suppression of FM interference by vibrating contact voltage regulator (alternator equipment) (Sec 11)

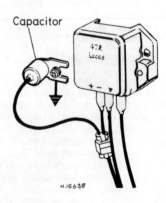

Capacitor

H.15638

Fig. 13.74 Electronic voltage regulator suppression (Sec 11)

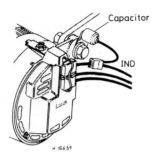

Fig. 13.75 Suppression of interference from electronic voltage regulator when integral with alternator (Sec 11)

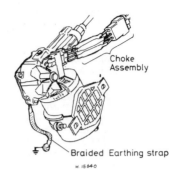

Fig. 13.76 Wiper motor suppression (Sec 11)

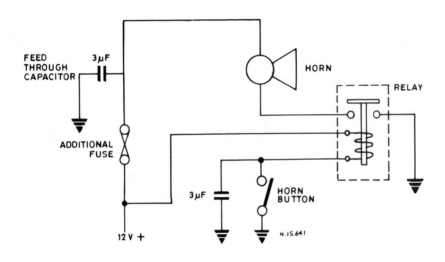

Fig. 13.77 Use of relay to reduce horn interference (Sec 11)

Suppression methods - other equipment

Wiper motors - Connect the wiper body to earth with a bonding strap. For all motors use a 7 ampere choke assembly inserted in the leads to the motors.

Heater motors - Fit 7 ampere line chokes in both leads, assisted if necessary by a 1 microfarad capacitor to earth from both leads.

Electronic tachometer - The tachometer is a possible source of ignition noise - check by disconnecting at the ignition coil CB terminal. It usually feeds from ignition coil LT pulses at the contact breaker terminal. A 3 ampere line choke should be fitted in the tachometer lead at the coil CB terminal.

Horn - A capacitor and choke combination is effective if the horn is directly connected to the 12 volt supply. The use of a relay is an alternative remedy, as this will reduce the length of the interference-carrying leads.

Electrostatic noise - Characteristics are erratic crackling at the receiver, with disappearance of symptoms in wet weather. Often shocks may be given when touching bodywork. Part of the problem is the build-up of static electricity in non-driven wheels and the acquisition of charge on the body shell. It is possible to fit spring-loaded contacts at the wheels to give good conduction between the rotary wheel parts and the vehicle frame.

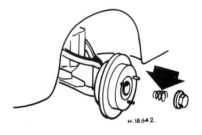

Fig. 13.78 Use of spring contacts at wheels (Sec 11)

Changing a tyre sometimes helps - because of tyres' varying resistances. In difficult cases a trailing flex which touches the ground will cure the problem. If this is not acceptable it is worth trying conductive paint on the tyre walls.

Radio/cassette case breakthrough

Magnetic radiation from dashboard wiring may be sufficiently intense to break through the metal case of the radio/cassette player. Often this is due to a particular cable routed too close and shows up as ignition interference on AM and cassette play and/or alternator whine on cassette play.

The first point to check is that the clips and/or screws are fixing all parts of the radio/cassette case together properly. Assuming good earthing of the case, see if it is possible to re-route the offending cable - the chances of this are not good, however, in most cars.

Next release the radio/cassette player and locate it in different positions with temporary leads. If a point of low interference is found, then if possible fix the equipment ·in that area. This also confirms that local radiation is causing the trouble. If re-location is not feasible, fit the radio/cassette player back in the original position.

Alternator interference on cassette play is now caused by radiation from the main charging cable which goes from the battery to the output terminal of the alternator, usually via the + terminal of the starter motor relay. In some vehicles this cable is routed under the dashboard, so the solution is to provide a direct cable route. Detach the original cable from the alternator output terminal and make up a new cable of at least 6 mm^2 cross-sectional area to go from alternator to battery with the shortest possible route. *Remember - do not run the engine with the alternator disconnected from the battery.*

Ignition breakthrough on AM and/or cassette play can be a difficult problem. It is worth wrapping earthed foil round the offending cable run near the equipment, or making up a deflector plate well screwed down to a good earth. Another possibility is the use of a suitable relay to switch on the ignition coil. The relay should be mounted close to the ignition coil; with this arrangement the ignition coil primary current is not taken into the dashboard area and does not flow through the ignition switch. A suitable diode should be used since it is possible that at ignition switch-off the output from the warning lamp alternator terminal could hold the relay on.

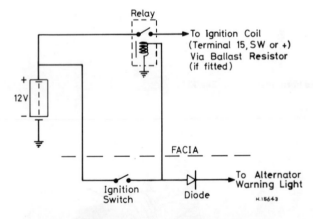

Fig. 13.79 Use of ignition coil relay to suppress case breakthrough (Sec 11)

Connectors for suppression components

Capacitors are usually supplied with tags on the end of the lead, while the capacitor body has a flange with a slot or hole to fit under a nut or screw with washer.

Connections to feed wires are best achieved by self-stripping connectors. These connectors employ a blade which, when squeezed down by pliers, cuts through cable insulation and makes connection to the copper conductors beneath.

Chokes sometimes come with bullet snap-in connectors fitted to the wires, and also with just bare copper wire. With connectors, suitable female cable connectors may be purchased

from an auto-accessory shop together with any extra connectors required for the cable ends after being cut for the choke insertion. For chokes with bare wires, similar connectors may be employed together with insulation sleeving as required.

VHF/FM broadcasts

Reception of VHF/FM in an automobile is more prone to problems than the medium and long wavebands. Medium/long wave transmitters are capable of covering considerable distances, but VHF transmitters are restricted to line of sight, meaning ranges of 10 to 50 miles, depending upon the terrain, the effects of buildings and the transmitter power.

Because of the limited range it is necessary to retune on a long journey, and it may be better for those habitually travelling long distances or living in areas of poor provision of transmitters to use an AM radio working on medium/long wavebands.

When conditions are poor, interference can arise, and some of the suppression devices described previously fall off in performance at very high frequencies unless specifically designed for the VHF band. Available suppression devices include reactive HT cable, resistive distributor caps, screened plug caps, screened leads and resistive spark plugs.

For VHF/FM receiver installation the following points should be particularly noted:

(a) Earthing of the receiver chassis and the aerial mounting is important. Use a separate earthing wire at the radio, and scrape paint away at the aerial mounting.

(b) If possible, use a good quality roof aerial to obtain maximum height and distance from interference generating devices on the vehicle.

(c) Use of a high quality aerial downlead is important, since losses in cheap cable can be significant.

(d) The polarisation of FM transmissions may be horizontal, vertical, circular or slanted. Because of this the optimum mounting angle is at 45° to the vehicle roof.

Citizens' Band radio (CB)

In the UK, CB transmitter/receivers work within the 27 MHz and 934 MHz bands, using the FM mode. At present interest is concentrated on 27 MHz where the design and manufacture of equipment is less difficult. Maximum transmitted power is 4 watts, and 40 channels spaced 10 kHz apart within the range 27.60125 to 27.99125 MHz are available.

Aerials are the key to effective transmission and reception. Regulations limit the aerial length to 1.65 metres including the loading coil and any associated circuitry, so tuning the aerial is necessary to obtain optimum results. The choice of a CB aerial is dependent on whether it is to be permanently installed or removable, and the performance will hinge on correct tuning and the location point on the vehicle. Common practice is to clip the aerial to the roof gutter or to employ wing mounting where the aerial can be rapidly unscrewed. An alternative is to use the boot rim to render the aerial theftproof, but a popular solution is to use the 'magmount' - a type of mounting having a strong magnetic base clamping to the vehicle at any point, usually the roof.

Aerial location determines the signal distribution for both transmission and reception, but it is wise to choose a point away from the engine compartment to minimise interference from vehicle electrical equipment.

The aerial is subject to considerable wind and acceleration forces. Cheaper units will whip backwards and forwards and in so doing will alter the relationship with the metal surface of the vehicle with which it forms a ground plane aerial system. The radiation pattern will change correspondingly, giving rise to break-up of both incoming and outgoing signals.

Interference problems on the vehicle carrying CB equipment fall into two categories:

(a) Interference to nearby TV and radio receivers when transmitting.

(b) Interference to CB set reception due to electrical equipment on the vehicle.

Problems of break-through to TV and radio are not frequent, but can be difficult to solve. Mostly trouble is not detected or reported because the vehicle is moving and the symptoms rapidly disappear at the TV/radio receiver, but when the CB set is used as a base station any trouble with nearby receivers will soon result in a complaint.

It must not be assumed by the CB operator that his equipment is faultless, for much depends upon the design. Harmonics (that is, multiples) of 27 MHz may be transmitted unknowingly and these can fall into other users' bands. Where trouble of this nature occurs, low pass filters in the aerial or supply leads can help, and should be fitted in base station aerials as a matter of course. In stubborn cases it may be necessary to call for assistance from the licensing authority, or, if possible, to have the equipment checked by the manufacturers.

Interference received on the CB set from the vehicle equipment is, fortunately, not usually a severe problem. The precautions outlined previously for radio/cassette units apply, but there are some extra points worth noting.

It is common practice to use a slide-mount on CB equipment enabling the set to be easily removed for use as a base station, for example. Care must be taken that the slide mount fittings are properly earthed and that first class connection occurs between the set and slide-mount.

Vehicle manufacturers in the UK are required to provide suppression of electrical equipment to cover 40 to 250 MHz to protect TV and VHF radio bands. Such suppression appears to be adequately effective at 27 MHz, but suppression of individual items such as alternators/dynamos, clocks, stabilisers, flashers, wiper motors, etc, may still be necessary. The suppression capacitors and chokes available from auto-electrical suppliers for entertainment receivers will usually give the required results with CB equipment.

Other vehicle radio transmitters

Besides CB radio already mentioned, a considerable increase in the use of transceivers (ie combined transmitter and receiver units) has taken place in the last decade. Previously this type of equipment was fitted mainly to military, fire, ambulance and police vehicles, but a large business radio and radio telephone usage has developed.

Generally the suppression techniques described previously will suffice, with only a few difficult cases arising. Suppression is carried out to satisfy the 'receive mode', but care must be taken to use heavy duty chokes in the equipment supply cables since the loading on 'transmit' is relatively high.

278

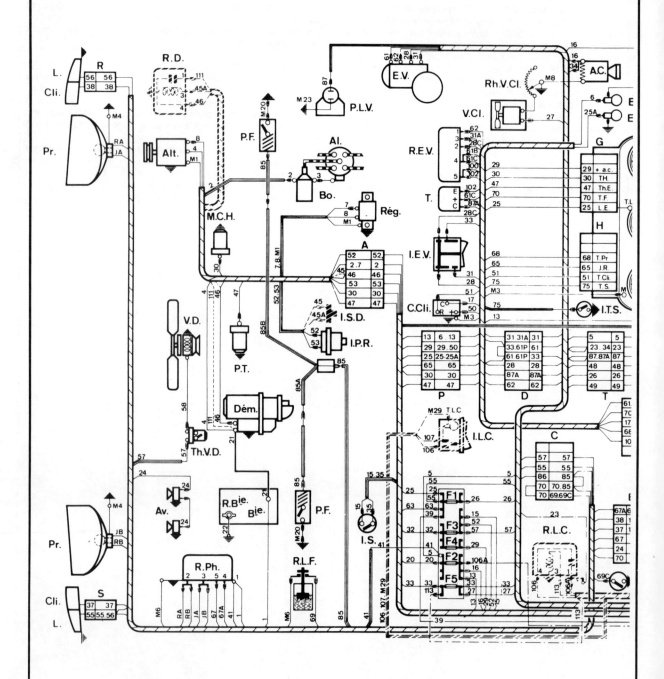

Fig. 13.80 Wiring diagram - 504 Saloon, carburettor engine, July 1970 to July 1972. For key see page 196

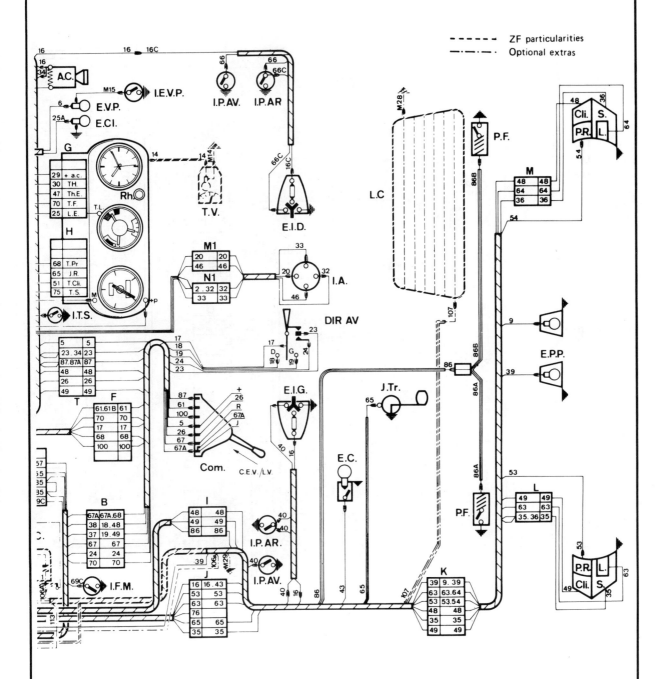

Fig. 13.80 Wiring diagram - 504 Saloon, carburettor engine, July 1970 to July 1972 (continued). For key see page 196

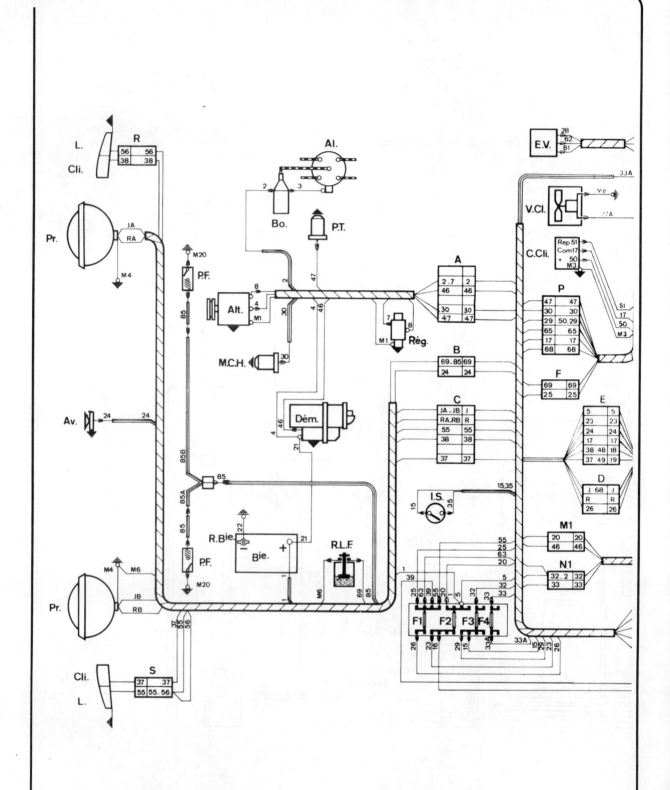

Fig. 13.81 Wiring diagram - 504 Station Wagon, carburettor engine, up to July 1972. For key see page 196

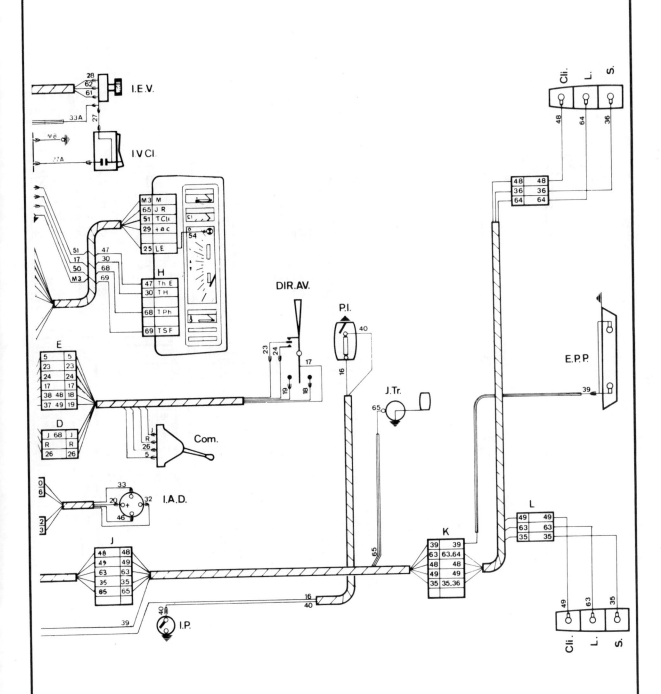

Fig. 13.81 Wiring diagram - 504 Station Wagon, carburettor engine, up to July 1972 (continued). For key see page 196

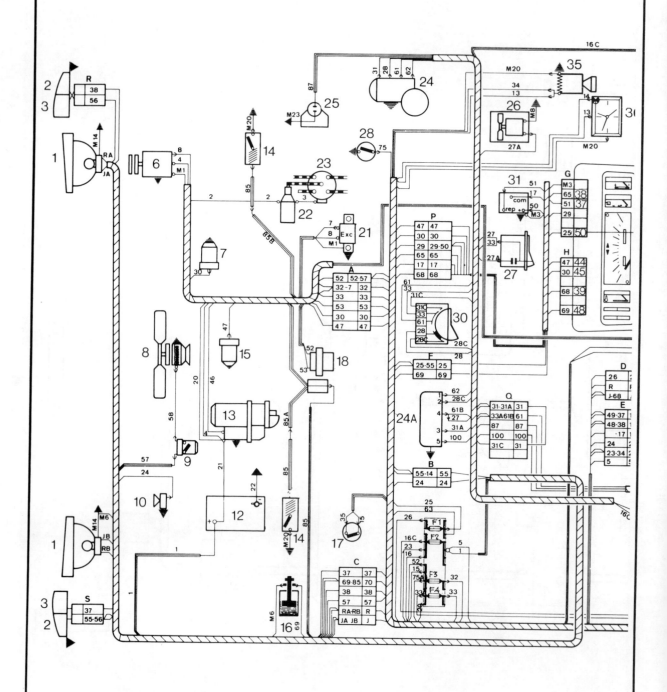

Fig. 13.82 Wiring diagram - 504 L Saloon, carburettor engine, July 1972 to July 1973. For key see pages 304 and 305

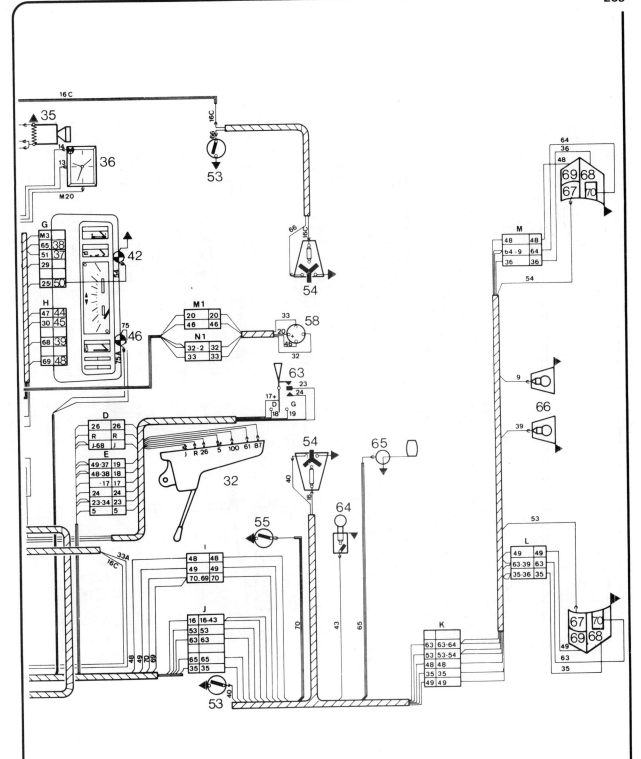

Fig. 13.82 Wiring diagram - 504 L Saloon, carburettor engine, July 1972 to July 1973 (continued). For key see pages 304 and 305

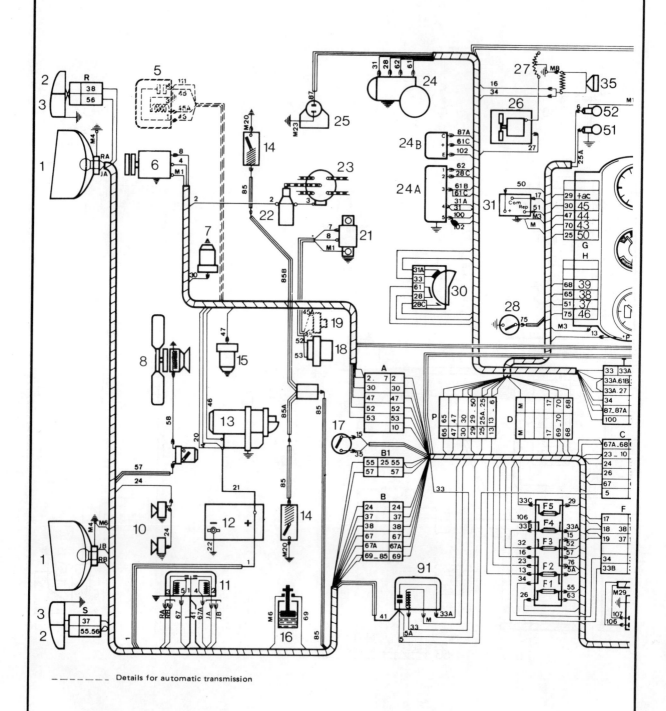

284

Fig. 13.83 Wiring diagram - 504 GL Saloon, carburettor engine, July 1973 to July 1974. For key see pages 304 and 305

- - - - - Details for automatic transmission

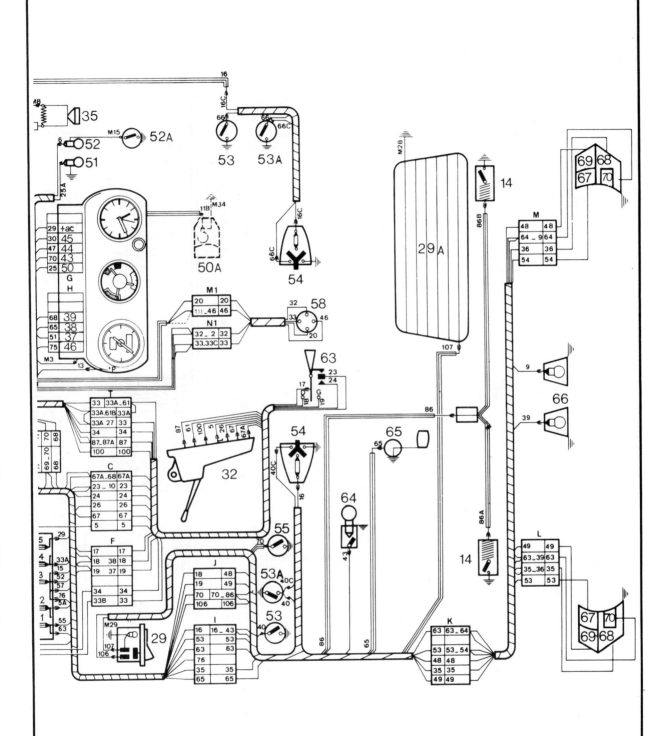

Fig. 13.83 Wiring diagram - 504 G L Saloon, carburettor engine, July 1973 to July 1974 (continued).
For key see pages 304 and 305

286

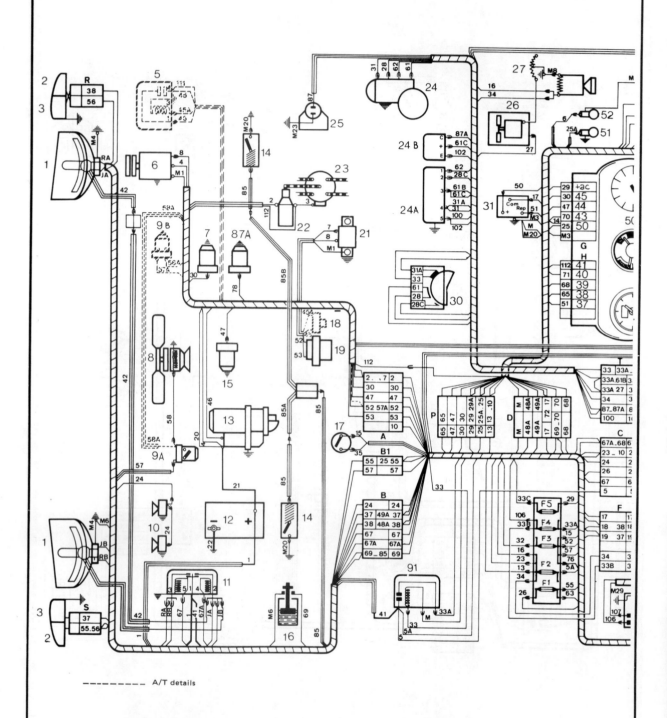

Fig. 13.84 Wiring diagram - 504 TI Saloon, fuel injection, July 1974 to July 1975. For key see pages 304 and 305

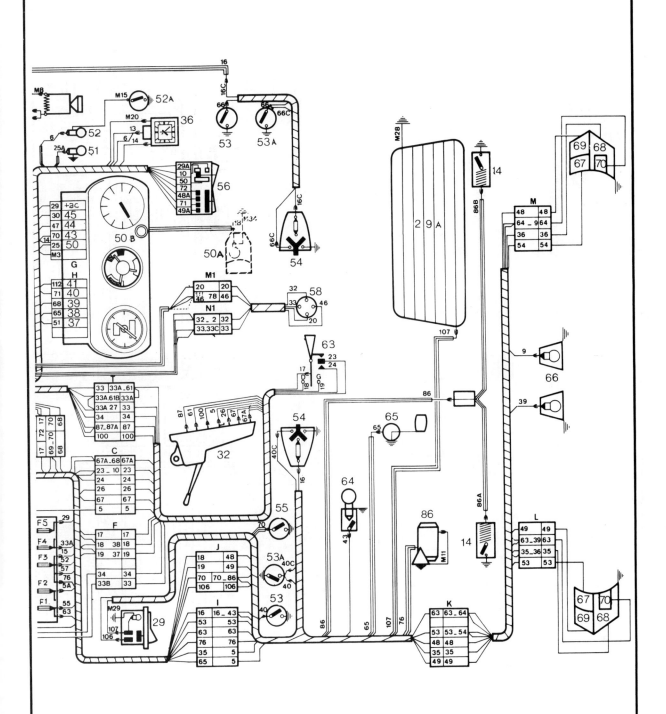

Fig. 13.84 Wiring diagram - 504 TI Saloon, fuel injection, July 1974 to July 1975 (continued). For key see pages 304 and 305

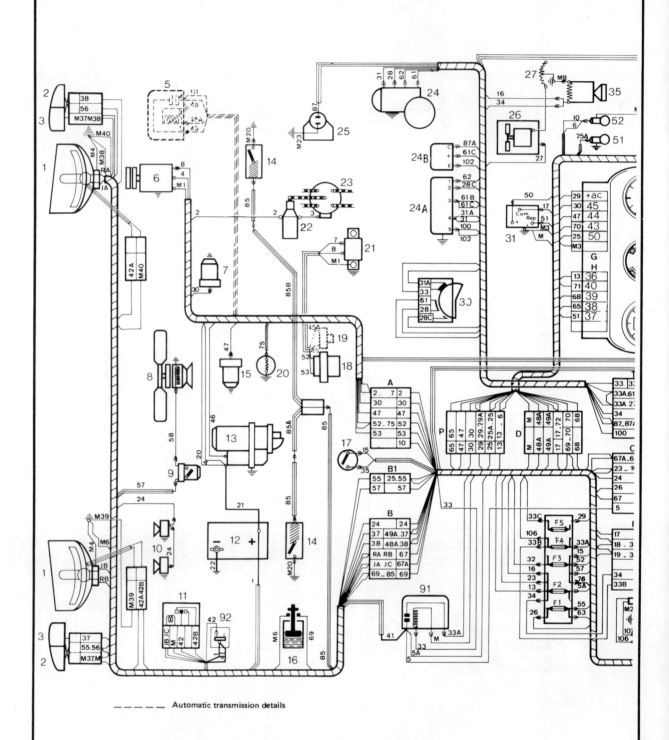

----- Automatic transmission details

Fig. 13.85 Wiring diagram - 504 GL Family Estate and Estate, carburettor engine, July 1975 to July 1976.
For key see pages 304 and 305

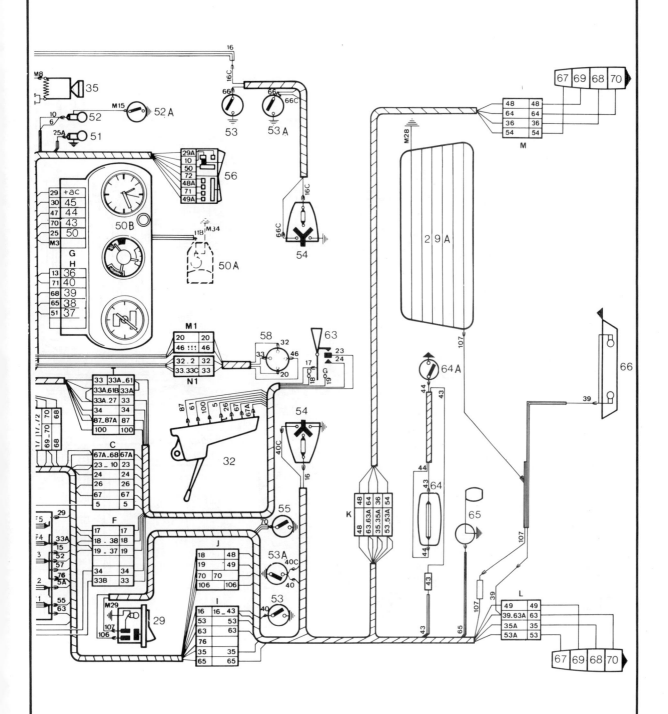

Fig. 13.85 Wiring diagram - 504 GL Family Estate and Estate, carburettor engine, July 1975 to July 1976 (continued). For key see pages 304 and 305

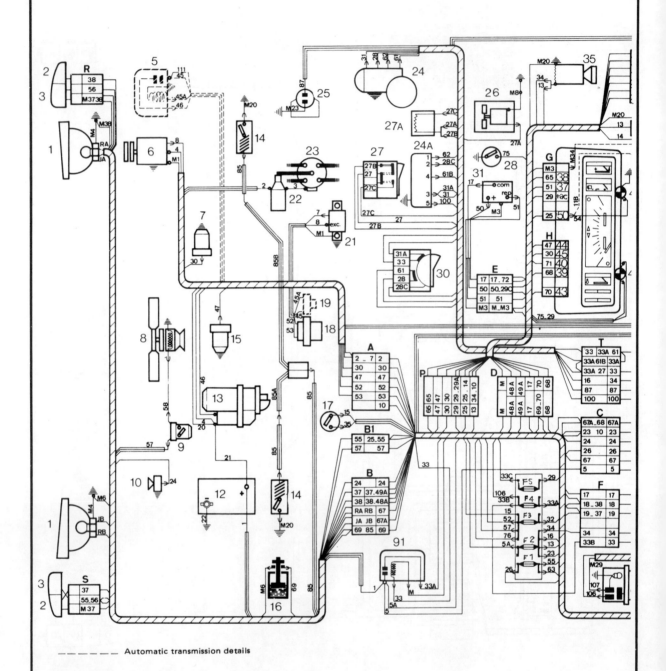

Fig. 13.86 Wiring diagram - 504 L Saloon, carburettor engine, July 1975 to July 1976. For key see pages 304 and 305

– – – – – Automatic transmission details

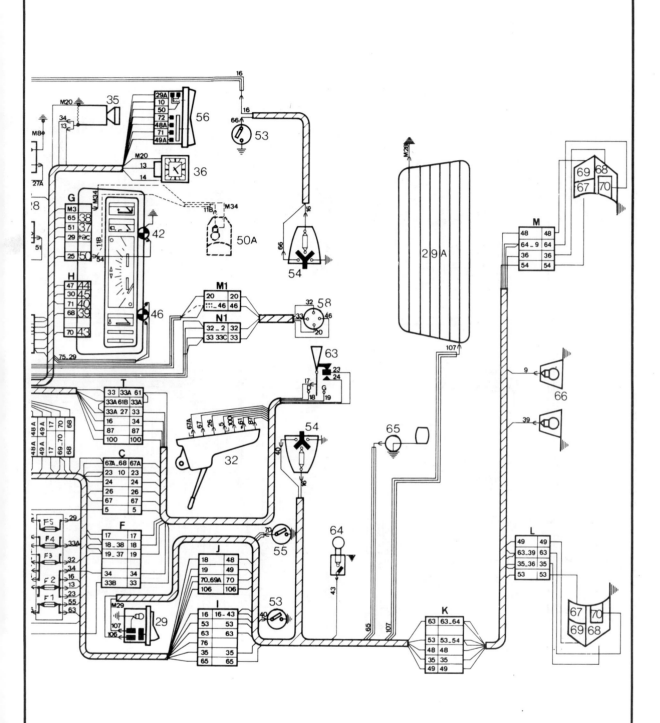

Fig. 13.86 Wiring diagram - 504 L Saloon, carburettor engine, July 1975 to July 1976 (continued)
For key see pages 304 and 305

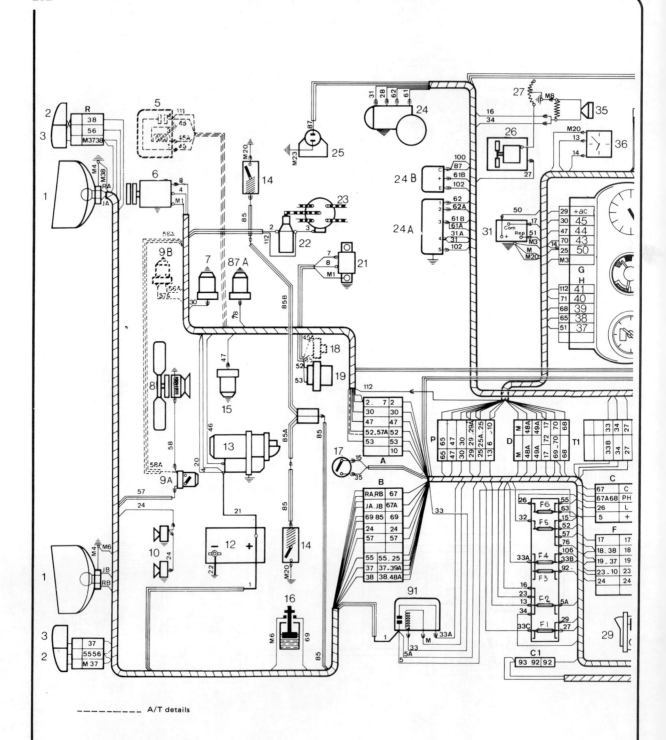

Fig. 13.87 Wiring diagram - 504 TI Saloon, fuel injection, July 1976 to July 1979. For key see pages 304 and 305

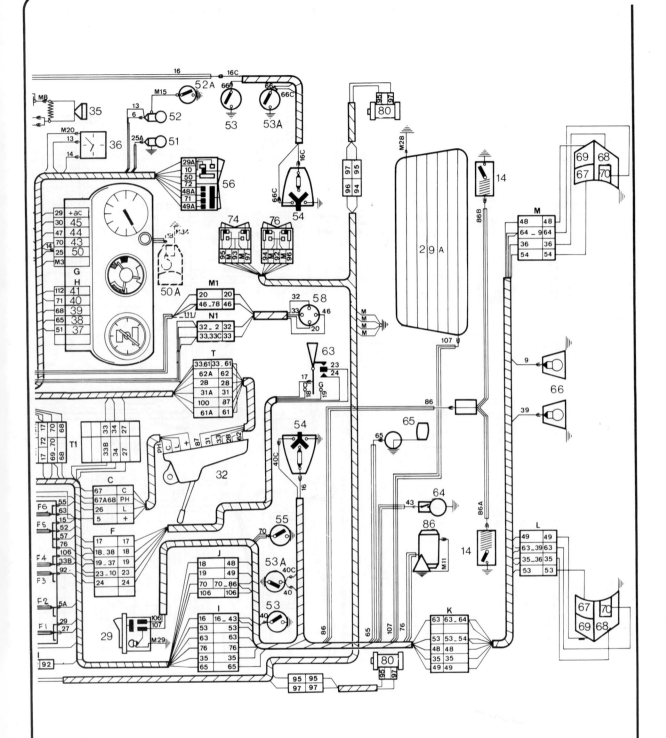

Fig. 13.87 Wiring diagram - 504 TI Saloon, fuel injection, July 1976 to July 1979 (continued).
For key see pages 304 and 305

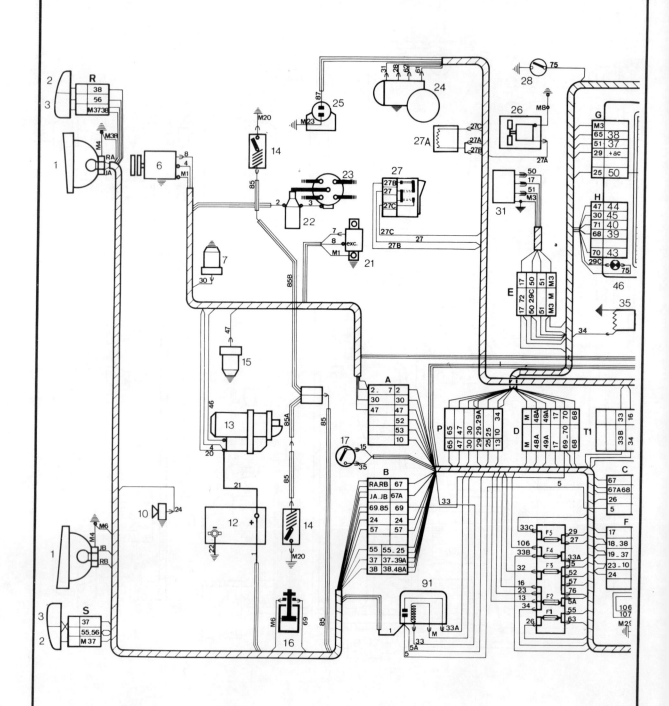

Fig. 13.88 Wiring diagram - 504 L Estate, carburettor engine, July 1976 to July 1978. For key see pages 304 and 305

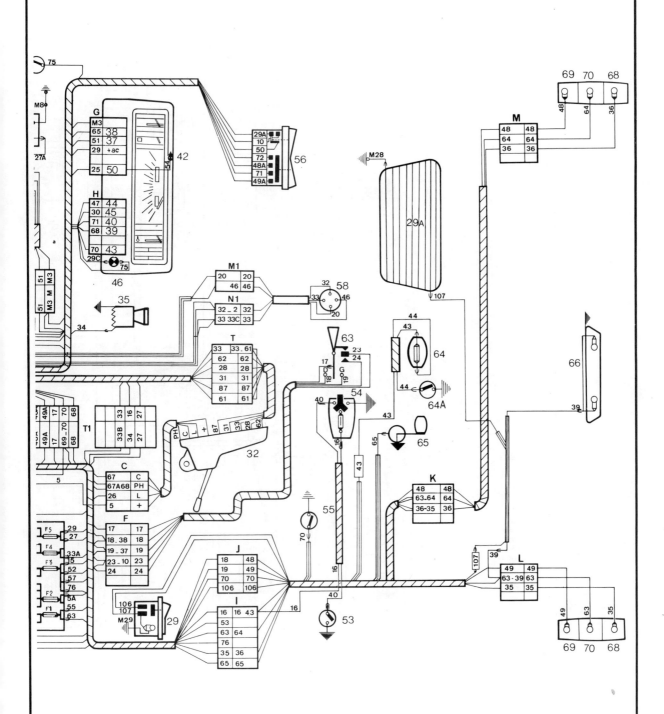

Fig. 13.88 Wiring diagram - 504 L Estate, carburettor engine, July 1976 to July 1978 (continued). For key see pages 304 and 305

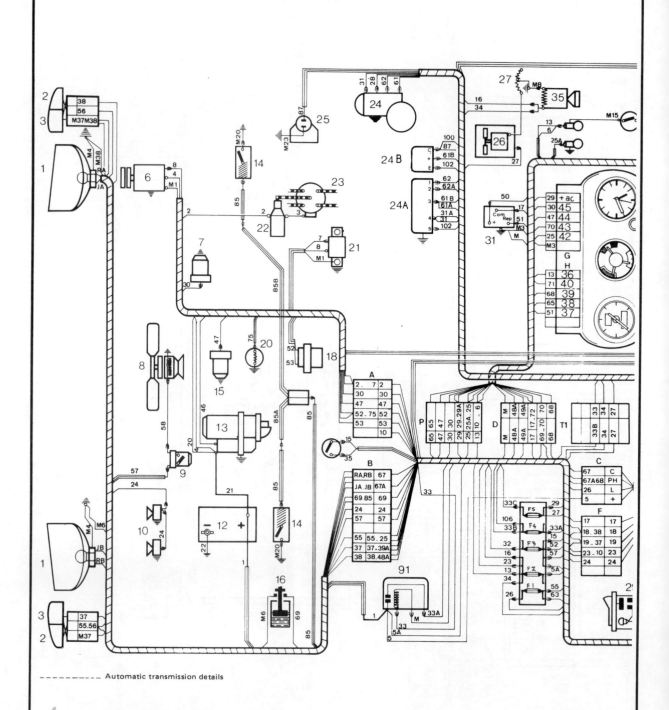

Automatic transmission details

Fig. 13.89 Wiring diagram - 504 GL Saloon, carburettor engine, July 1977 to July 1979. For key see pages 304 and 305

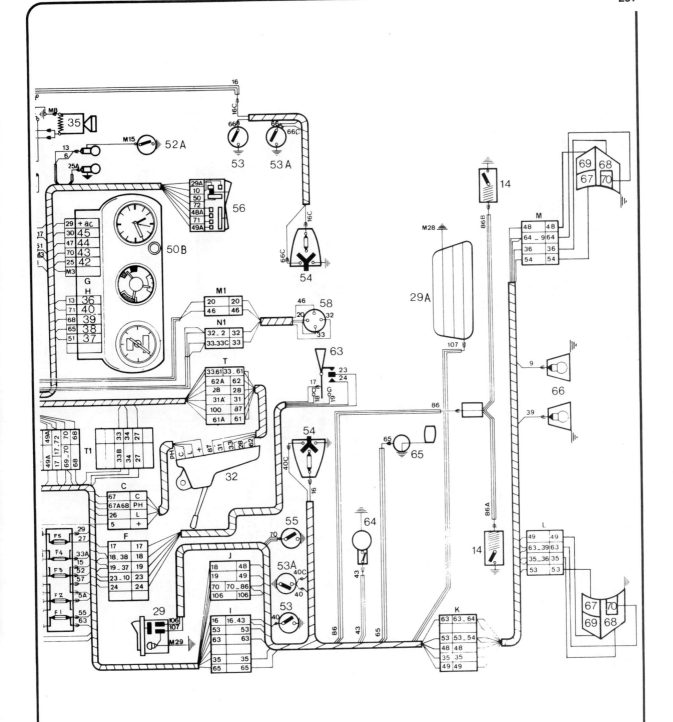

Fig. 13.89 Wiring diagram - 504 GL Saloon, carburettor engine, July 1977 to July 1979 (continued).
For key see pages 304 and 305

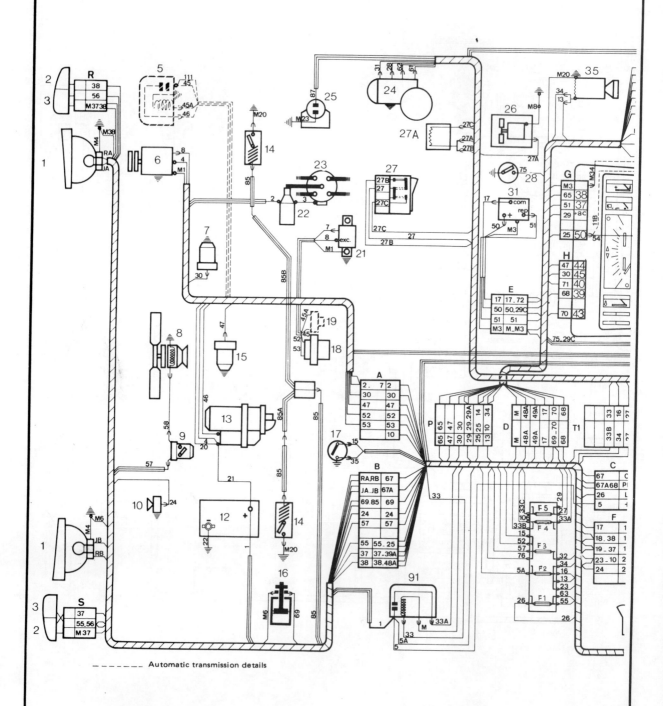

Automatic transmission details

Fig. 13.90 Wiring diagram - 504 L Saloon, carburettor engine, July 1976 to July 1978. For key see pages 304 and 305

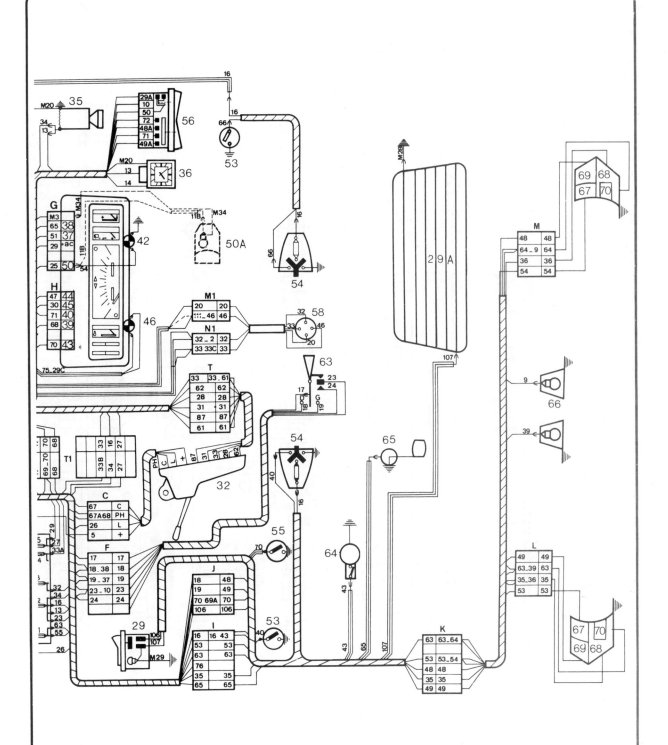

Fig. 13.90 Wiring diagram - 504 L Saloon, carburettor engine, July 1976 to July 1978 (continued).
For key see pages 304 and 305

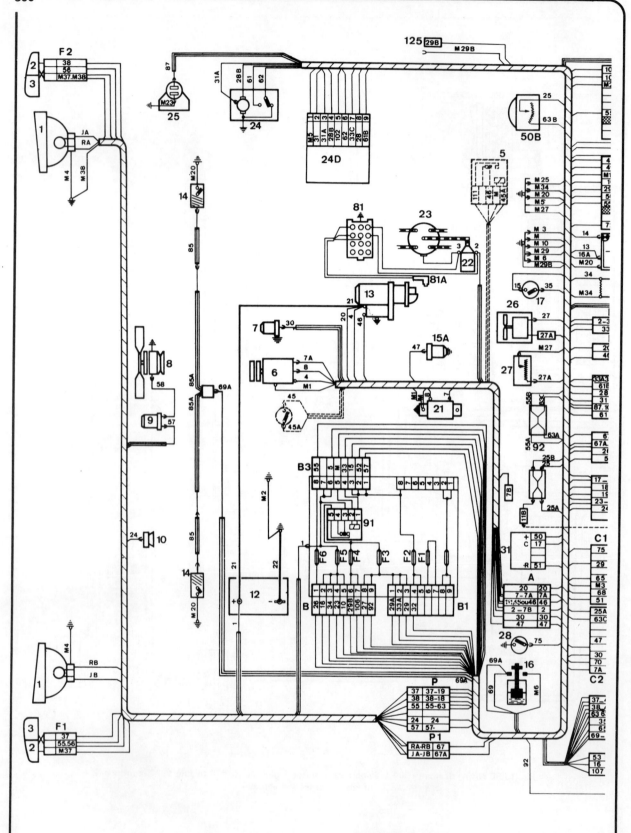

Fig. 13.91 Wiring diagram - 504 GR/SR Saloon and Estate, November 1979 to January 1982. For key see pages 304 and 305

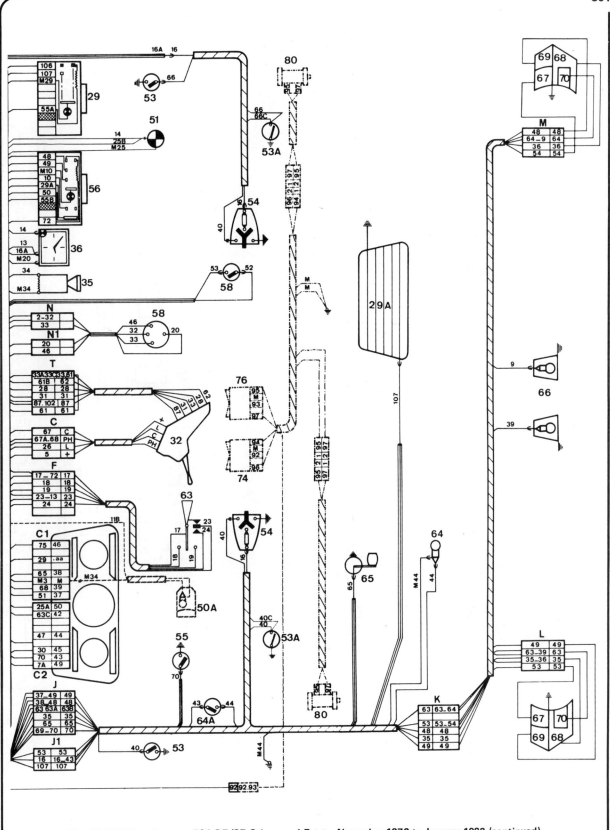

Fig. 13.91 Wiring diagram - 504 GR/SR Saloon and Estate, November 1979 to January 1982 (continued).
For key see pages 304 and 305

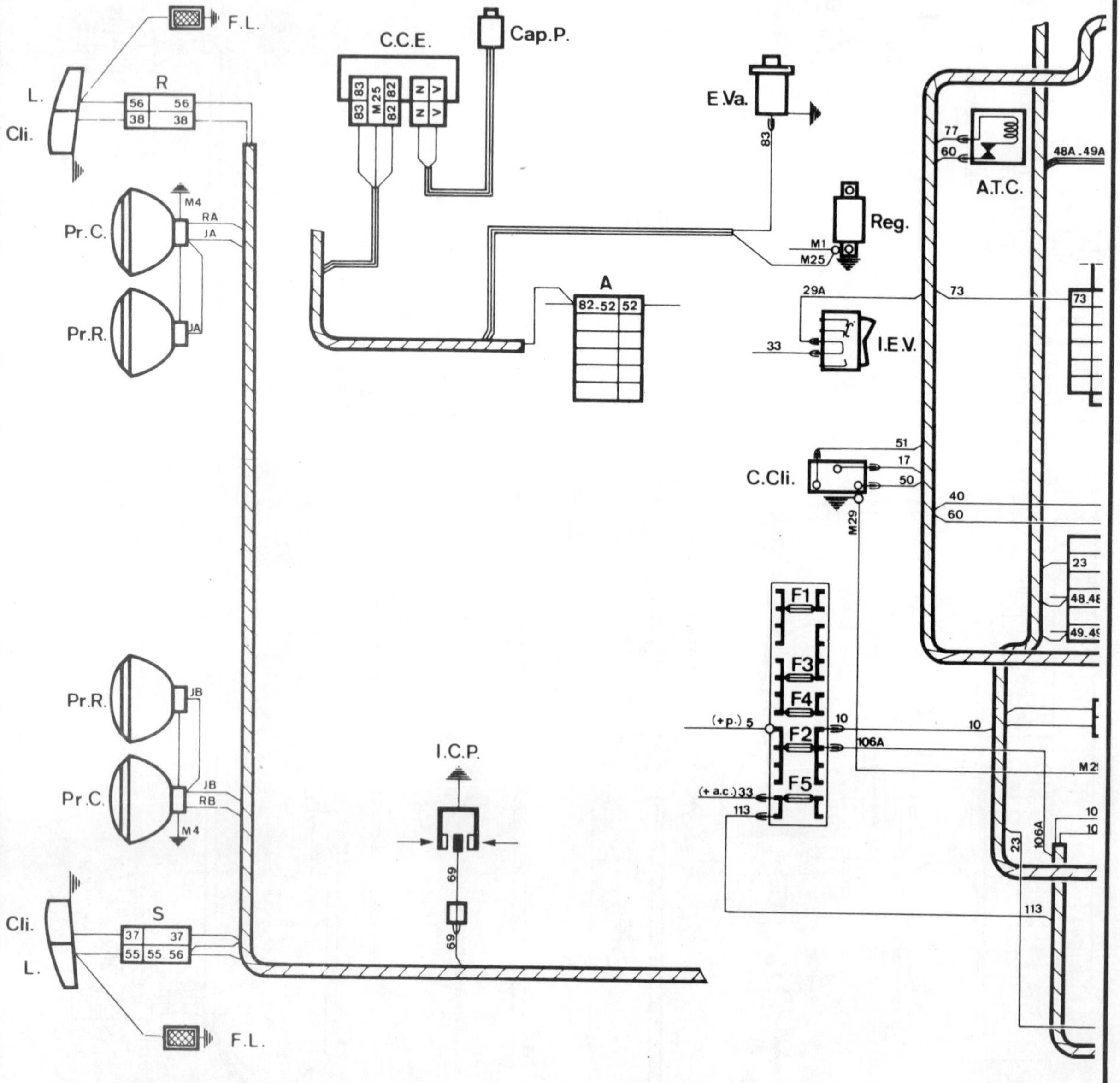

Fig. 13.92 Wiring diagram - Differences for USA models. For key see page 196

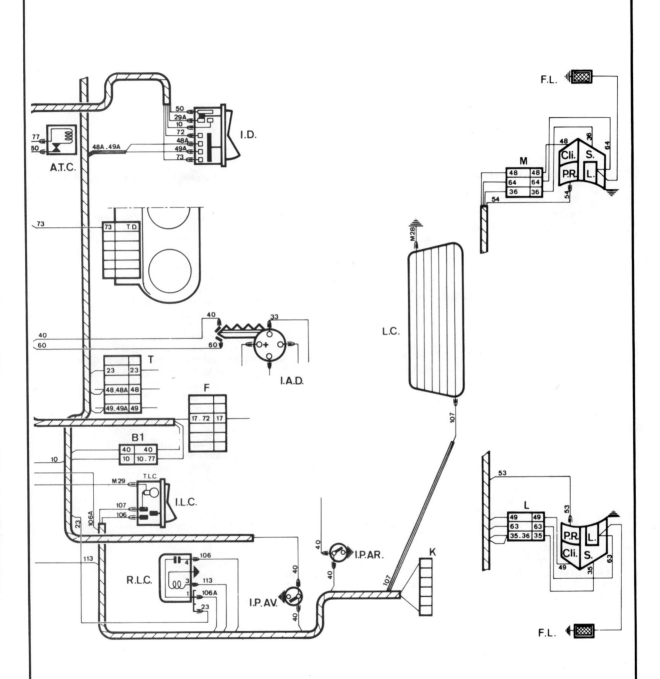

Fig. 13.92 Wiring diagram - Differences for USA models (continued) For key see page 196

Key to wiring diagrams on pages 282 to 301. Due to numerous model variants it is only possible to include a typical selection

1	Headlight
2	Front direction indicators
3	Front sidelights
4	Direction indicators relay
5	Starter relay
6	Alternator
7	Oil pressure switch
8	Electro-magnetic or motor driven fan
8A	Motor driven fan relay
9	Thermal switch for electro-magnetic fan or motor driven fan
9A	Thermal switch in water circuit for electro-magnetic fan
9B	Thermal switch in oil circuit for electro-magnetic fan
10	Horn
10A	Seat belt audible warning signal (USA)
10B	Seat belt warning tell-tale (USA)
10C	Seat belts warning system switch (USA)
11	Headlights relay
12	Battery
12A	Battery cut-out terminal
13	Starter
14	Brake pad electrode
15	Water temperature transmitter
15A	Water temperature thermostat
15B	Water temperature tell-tale switch or water temperature tell-tale
16	Brake fluid reservoir
17	Stoplights switch
18	Reversing light switch
19	Starter inhibitor switch
20	Carburettor idling circuit - cut-out resistor
21	Regulator
22	Ignition coil
22A	Coil relay
22B	Coil resistor

22C	Coil resistor relay (USA and Sweden)
23	Distributor
24	Front screen wiper
24A	Screen wiper relay
24B	Screen wiper time
24C	Rear window wiper
25	Front screen washer pump
25A	Rear window washer pump
26	Car heater blower
26A	Car heater blower to rear
26B	Car heater blower switch
27	Heater blow switch, or rheostat
27A	Rheostat resistors, or heater blower resistor
27B	Switch for car heater blower to rear
28	Switch to choke tell-tale
28A	Choke actuating motor (USA)
28B	Choke thermostat (USA)
29	Heated rear window switch
29A	Heated rear window
30	Screen wash/wipe switch
30A	Rear window wash/wipe switch
31	Direction indicators unit
32	Lights-screen wash/wipe dual purpose switch
33	Headlights flasher relay
34	Sidelights
35	Cigarette lighter
36	Clock
37	Direction indicators tell-tale
38	Fuel gauge
38A	Reserve fuel tell-tale
39	Headlights tell-tale
40	Hazard warning tell-tale
41	Tachometer
42	Sidelights tell-tale
43	Brakes system warning light

43A	Brakes system warning light control diode
44	Water temperature tell-tale or water temperature gauge
45	Oil pressure tell-tale
46	Choke tell-tale
47	Oil and water tell-tale
49	Charge indicator
50	Facia lighting
50A	Gearplate
50B	Facia lighting rheostat
50C	Lighting to switches
51	Heater controls lighting
51A	Console lighting
51B	Console lighting rheostat (USA)
52	Glove compartment lighting
52A	Glove compartment lighting switch
53	Front door light switch
53A	Rear door light switch
54	Vehicle interior lights
54A	Below facia lighting
55	Handbrake tell-tale switch
56	Hazard warning switch
57	Sliding roof panel switch
57A	Sliding roof panel motor
57B	Sliding roof panel max. travel cut-out
57C	Sliding roof panel safety cut-out
58	Ignition/anti-theft lock
58A	Ignition switch warning buzzer (USA)
63	Direction indicators/horns dual purpose switch
64	Boot or tailgate light
64A	Boot or tailgate light switch
65	Fuel tank unit (with or without reserve fuel tell-tale switch)
65A	External resistor to fuel tank unit
66	Rear numberplate light

67	Reversing lights
68	Stop lights
69	Rear direction indicators
70	Rearlights
71	Tailgate light switch
72	Open door warning light
73	Rear LH window winder switch
74	Front LH window winder switch
75	Cut-out switch for rear windows and cigarette lighter
76	Front RH window winder switch
77	Rear RH window winder switch
78	Rear LH window winder switch
79	Rear RH window winder switch
80	Window winder motor
80A	Window winder motor relay
86	Fuel pump
87	Solenoid valve
87A	Switch to solenoid valve
88	Sensor
89	Electronic control unit
90	Rear foglights
90A	Rear foglights switch
90B	Rear foglights tell-tale
91	Relay
91A	Seat belts timer relay (USA)
92	Terminal
93	Multiple junction box
94	Conductive tailgate stay
95	Brakes system pressure switch
96	Brake pedal travel switch
97	Headlights wash/wipe switch
98	Headlights washer pump
99	Headlights wiper motor
100	Oil pressure drop warning light

12 Suspension and steering

Power steering
Description
1   The main component parts of the power steering system are shown in Fig. 13.93. Modifications which were made in late 1979 are shown in Fig. 13.94.

2   The system is controlled by a rotary valve located on the steering gear pinion, which feeds hydraulic fluid from a belt-driven pump to an hydraulic ram. The ram provides assistance to the steering rack movement.

3   Maintenance consists of periodically checking the level of the fluid in the reservoir mounted on the pump. To do this, remove

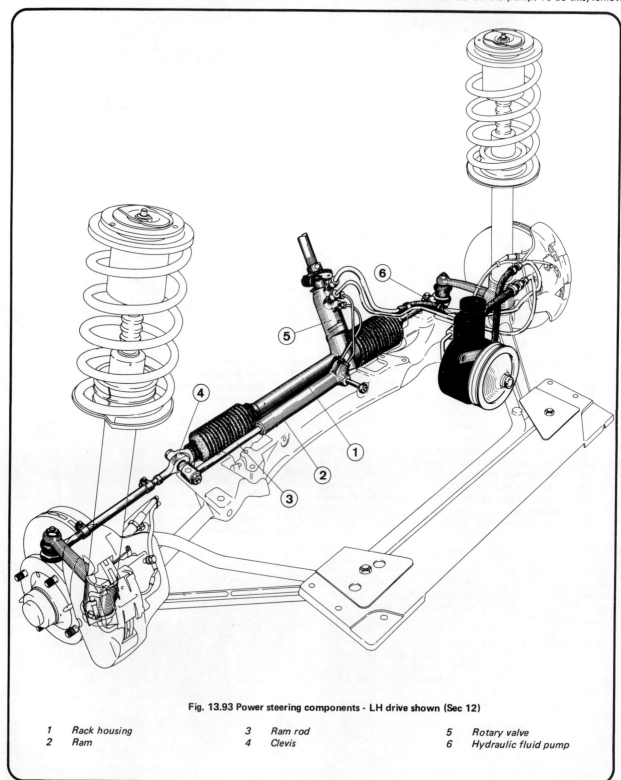

Fig. 13.93 Power steering components - LH drive shown (Sec 12)

1	Rack housing	3	Ram rod	5	Rotary valve
2	Ram	4	Clevis	6	Hydraulic fluid pump

OLD TYPE ARRANGEMENT

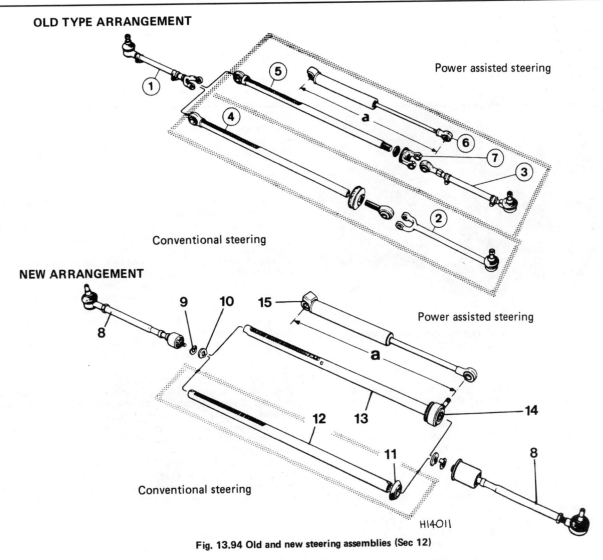

NEW ARRANGEMENT

H14011

Fig. 13.94 Old and new steering assemblies (Sec 12)

1	LH track rod	6	Ram (a = 545.5 mm, fully extended)
2	RH track rod (manual)	7	Clevis (power)
3	RH track rod (power)	8	RH or LH track rod
4	Rack (manual - 34 tooth)	9	Lock washer
5	Rack (power - 32 tooth)		

10	Stop washer
11	Lock stop (manual)
12	Rack (manual - 34 tooth)
13	Rack (power - 32 tooth)
14	Clevis (power)
15	Ram (a = 510.7 mm, fully extended)

the filler cap and level probe. The level will depend on the temperature of the fluid as indicated on the probe (see Fig. 13.95); top up the system if necessary using only the approved fluid. At the same time check and adjust the tension of the pump drivebelt.

Steering gear removal and refitting
4 Jack up the front of the car and support it with axle stands.
5 Disconnect the battery negative terminal.
6 Remove the reservoir cap, disconnect the pump bottom hose, and drain the hydraulic fluid into a suitable container. Move the rack from lock-to-lock to ensure that all the fluid is drained.
7 Disconnect the pump supply (upper) hose.
8 Detach the steering column flexible coupling and the track-rod ends.
9 Detach the safety clips and the steering gear mounting bolts, then unscrew the ram-to-crossmember retaining nut, see Fig. 13.96.

Fig. 13.95 Power steering fluid reservoir level probe and cap (Sec 12)

Fig. 13.96 Power steering ram mounting nut (1) location (Sec 12)

10 Withdraw the power steering gear rearwards, together with the two hoses.

11 Refitting is the reverse of removal, but tighten the retaining nuts and bolts to the specified torque, and refill the system as follows. Pour 0.5 Imp pt, (0.3 litre, 0.3 US qt) into the reservoir, and slowly turn the steering from lock-to-lock with the engine stopped. Fill the reservoir and start the engine, then turn the steering from lock-to-lock. Finally top up the fluid and check the wheel alignment.

Pump drivebelt adjustment

12 Loosen the pump adjustment nut and release all tension from the drivebelt.

13 With a pencil, make two marks on the outer surface of the drivebelt exactly 3.93 in (100 mm) apart.

14 Refit the drivebelt with the two marks between the pulleys,

then tension the belt until the distance between the marks is 4.0 in (101.5 mm) for a used belt, or 4.04 in (102.5 mm) for a new belt.

15 Tighten the adjustment nut.

Steering gear overhaul

16 Before starting work, check that the special tools and press mentioned in the following paragraphs are available if required.

17 Thoroughly clean the exterior of the steering gear with paraffin and wipe dry, whilst observing the necessary fire precautions.

18 Mount the steering gear in a soft metal vice and disconnect the ram pipe unions from the ram only.

19 Refer to Fig. 13.94 and identify the type of rack and track rod assembly fitted.

20 On the older arrangement, unscrew the through bolt and remove the ram, bolt, spacer and the free track rod.

21 Remove the remaining track rod and bellows after removing the bellows retaining rings, then detach the link by unscrewing the pivot bolt.

22 Unscrew the clevis after moving back the remaining bellows and loosening the locknut, then remove the retaining rings, locknut, and bellows from the steering gear.

23 On the new arrangement, remove the ram and retaining nut and pull the ram free of the clevis pin. It may be necessary to use a small two-legged puller to achieve this. The clevis is an interference fit on the rack.

24 Where necessary (see Fig. 13.97), knock back the tab of each lock washer before unscrewing each track rod from the rack whilst noting the number of turns.

25 In both cases, lay the removed components out in a logical order and keep them identified side-for-side to ensure correct refitting. Where applicable, do not attempt to loosen the ram rod locknut as this is preset at the factory.

26 Mount the steering gear in a vice with the pinion uppermost, then detach the thrust plate with the grease nipple and withdraw the plunger components.

27 Remove the pinion bearing cover and unscrew the retaining nut while holding the flexible coupling stationary.

28 Unscrew the control valve retaining bolts and lower the rack until it can be retained by a metal rod inserted through the eyelet.

29 Carefully tap the pinion and control valve assembly from the housing with a hide or plastic mallet.

30 If necessary, detach the flexible coupling from the pinion.

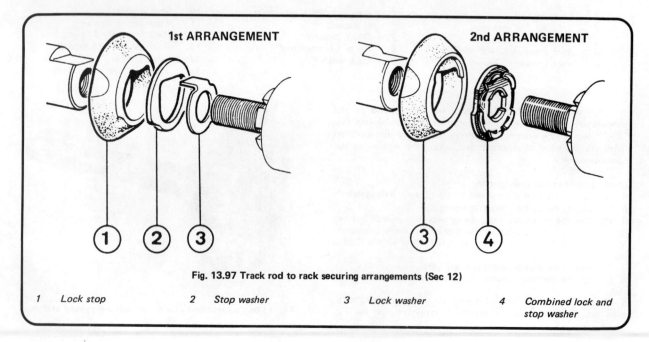

Fig. 13.97 Track rod to rack securing arrangements (Sec 12)

| 1 | Lock stop | 2 | Stop washer | 3 | Lock washer | 4 | Combined lock and stop washer |

31 Withdraw the rack from the housing.
32 Remove the circlip and drive out the pinion bearing with a soft metal punch, see Fig. 13.98.
33 Clean all components and examine them for wear and deterioration. The pinion bearing and all self-locking nuts must be renewed at every overhaul together with all bellows retaining rings, lockwashers, and the bearing cover.
34 Where applicable, silentbloc bushes can be renewed by using a press or a home-made extractor; make sure that the new bushes are positioned centrally in the eye. Soapy water will facilitate fitting the bushes. See Fig. 13.99.
35 If the control valve is faulty, the seals may be renewed as follows. First extract the circlip and pull the pinion from the housing; do not drive out the pinion from the coupling end.
36 Remove the thrust washer and seal, then place the rotor/pinion to one side in a clean area.
37 Extract the circlip, scraper seal, and oil seal from the valve

housing. Clean all components in methylated spirit.
38 Fit the new seals in the reverse order of removal, but first dip them in fresh hydraulic fluid. Make sure that the closed ends of the oil seals face outwards, see Fig. 13.100.
39 Start reassembly by checking that the pinion bearing is a good fit on the end of the pinion, then drive the bearing fully into the rack housing with a soft metal punch.
40 Pack grease into the bearing and into the rack housing bore. Refit the retaining circlip.
41 Mount the housing in a vice. Grease the rack and insert it into the housing, retaining it in position with a metal rod inserted through the eyelet. Make sure that the rack teeth face the pinion bore.
42 Fit the flexible coupling and position it as shown in Fig. 13.101.
43 Insert the pinion into the housing with the flange of the control valve offset anti-clockwise by approximately 60°. When

Fig. 13.98 Removal of circlip retaining pinion bearing (1) in rack housing (Sec 12)

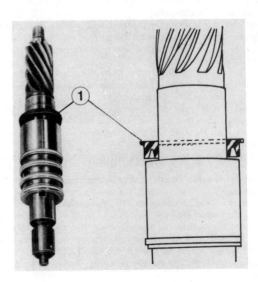

Fig. 13.100 Power steering control valve pinion/rotor seal location (1) (Sec 12)

Fig. 13.99 Correct fitted position of steering rack bush (old type) (Sec 12)

Fig. 13.101 Pinion position before fitting to rack housing (Sec 12)

a Control valve outlets

the pinion is fully engaged with the rack and the flanges are aligned, the flexible coupling should be in the position shown in Fig. 13.102.

44 Insert and tighten the control valve retaining bolts.

45 The rack plunger free play adjustment must now be made, see Fig. 13.103. To do this, install the plunger, spring, and thrust plate on the housing and attach a dial gauge with the probe inserted through the grease nipple hole and in contact with the plunger.

46 Turn the pinion and move the rack from side-to-side, then position the rack at the point where the dial gauge registers the highest reading. Tap the housing lightly to make sure that the correct reading is obtained.

47 Zero the dial gauge and retain the rack in the same position with a suitable clamp; a jubilee clip and steel plate will be sufficient.

48 Install and tighten the pinion nut to the specified torque while holding the coupling stationary.

49 Fill the housing cavity with grease and fit the bearing cover.

50 Lever the rack against the plunger as far as possible and note the reading on the dial gauge.

51 Remove the plunger components and, using a straight-edge, check that a gap exists between the end of the plunger and the nylon stop inside. Select shims and fit them on the nylon stop until the gap is eliminated.

52 Deduct 0.004 in (0.10 mm) from the reading obtained in paragraph 50 and add a further number of shims of the resulting thickness to the shims in paragraph 51.

53 Install the plunger components with the selected shims to the rack housing, making sure that the shims are located over the grease nipple thread and that the components are lubricated with grease.

54 Tighten the thrust plate retaining bolts to the specified torque.

55 Remove the jubilee clip if fitted, then move the rack fully into the housing.

56 With the older arrangement fit the bellows, locknut, and clevis to the end of the rack.

57 Adjust the position of the clevis so that the eye centre is 25.551 in (649 mm) from the eye centre at the opposite end of the rack with the eyes horizontal, see Fig. 13.104, then tighten the locknut and refit the bellows retaining rings with the bellows vertical.

58 Fit the link to the opposite end of the rack with the flat facing the rear, and the bolt head to the rear, see Fig. 13.105. Tighten the bolt and bend the locking plate to secure.

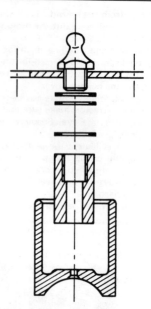

Fig. 13.103 Cross sectional view of steering gear plunger without spring (Sec 12)

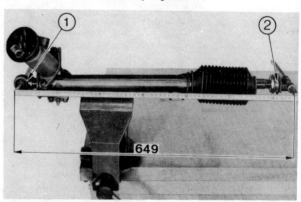

Fig. 13.104 Adjusting steering rack length (old type) (Sec 12)

1   Rubber bush   2   Clevis

Fig. 13.102 Inserting pinion control valve assembly into rack housing (Sec 12)

b   Control valve flange

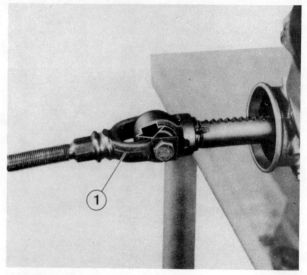

Fig 13.105 Power steering link (1) and pivot bolt backplate (old type) (Sec 12)

59 Temporarily screw the track rod end onto the link and adjust it so that the distance between the link bolt centre and the track rod end centre is 10.969 in (278.6 mm) (Fig. 13.106).
60 Tighten the outer clamp bolt and measure the distance from the link to the track rod with vernier calipers; note this dimension, see Fig. 13.107.
61 Unscrew the track rod and fit the remaining bellows, securing it with the retaining ring and twisted wire.
62 Screw on the track rod until the previously noted dimension is obtained, then tighten the clamp bolt.
63 Fit the remaining track rod assembly with the inner link boss uppermost. Insert the through-bolt through the ram rod eye and tighten the self-locking nut.
64 Adjust the track rod so that the distance between the link pivot bolt centre and the track rod end centre is 10.969 in (278.6 mm), then tighten the clamp bolts.
65 With the new arrangement, if the clevis has been pulled from the rack, then it should now be pressed back into its original position. If trouble is experienced during this operation, then ask advice from your Peugeot dealer. The clevis must be a good interference fit.
66 Renew the tab washers or the combined lock/stop washers, as necessary. Refit each track rod, checking that each one screws in the original number of turns until it bears on the lock washer. Check tighten to a torque loading of 36 lbf ft (5 kgf m) and where necessary, bend over the tab of the lock washer into one of the balljoint casing slots.
67 In both cases, insert the retaining bolt, then reconnect the ram pipe unions to the ram; locate the spacer over the retaining bolt.

Steering column removal and refitting
68 Disconnect the battery negative terminal.
69 Unscrew and remove the flexible coupling clamp-bolt.
70 Detach the steering column lower shroud and disconnect the wiring.
71 Unscrew the retaining nuts and withdraw the column from inside the car.
72 To refit the column, first position the roadwheels in the straight-ahead position.
73 Install the column and engage it with the flexible coupling; tighten the column retaining nuts.
74 Make up a key to the dimensions shown in Fig. 13.108 and insert it in the slot beneath the column (see Fig. 13.109).

75 With the key in position, tighten the flexible coupling clamp-bolt, then remove the key.
76 Reconnect the wiring and refit the lower shroud.
77 Reconnect the battery negative terminal.

Pump modifications
78 From mid 1980, the threaded attachments of the power steering pump are metric sizes instead of the British sizes previously used.
79 When obtaining replacement fittings, make sure they have threads which are compatible to the pump body. Normally, a sticker applied to the filler pipe body will indicate that the pump has metric threads.

Fig. 13.107 Checking track rod adjustment before fitting bellows (old type) (Sec 12)

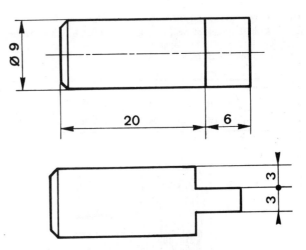

Fig. 13.108 Power steering column adjusting key dimensions (Sec 12)

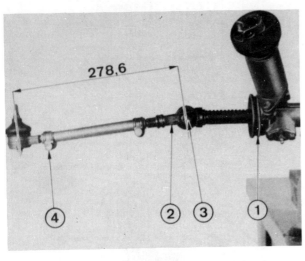

Fig. 13.106 Track rod initial adjustment dimension (old type) (Sec 12)

1	Bellows retaining ring	3	Pivot bolt
2	Clevis	4	Clamp bolt

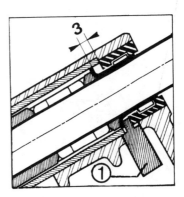

Fig. 13.109 Adjusting power steering column position with key (1) (Sec 12)

80 Fig. 13.110 shows the old and new pipe end fittings. These fittings are not interchangeable so care must be taken to change the pipe when renewing an old pump as only the metric pump is now supplied.

Manual steering

Rack and pinion removal and refitting
81 The clamp bolt securing the flexible coupling to the steering column is now fitted with a nylon insert locknut. Renew this nut if removed, and tighten it to 10.8 lbf ft (1.5 kgf m). Similar nuts are also fitted to the track-rod ends on later models; these must also be renewed if removed, and tightened to 27 lbf ft (3.75 kgf m).

Rack and pinion overhaul
82 The pinion on later models is fitted with a lipped seal instead of an O-ring and thrust washer (see Fig. 13.111). When refitting this type, the pinion flange must be vertical, with the rack centralised.
83 The pinion retaining nut on later models is self-locking. Renew this nut when removed and, when installing the pinion, tighten it to 25.3 lbf ft (3.5 kgf m).
84 The flexible coupling nuts on later models are self-locking. Renew these nuts after removing them, and tighten the new nuts to 14.5 lbf ft (2.0 kgf m).
85 Some models are fitted with a steering rack without a grease nipple for periodic lubrication. The grease used in this type is special, and cannot be mixed with normal multi-purpose grease. It is therefore important, when working on this type of steering gear, to obtain the correct grease from a Peugeot dealer.

Rack plunger adjustment
86 The steering rack plunger components may be of two types as shown in Fig. 13.112, depending on whether a grease nipple is fitted to the thrust plate. The plunger free play on each type is different (see Specifications) and the adjustment procedures are as follows.
87 *On the steering gear with a grease nipple,* install the plunger and spring in the housing, then tighten the thrust plate into position with the grease nipple removed.
88 A dial gauge must now be fitted to the housing with the probe touching the plunger through the grease nipple hole, see Fig. 13.113.
89 Turn the pinion to move the rack from side-to-side and then position the rack at the point where the highest reading is obtained; zero the dial gauge at this point.
90 Using a lever (see Fig. 13.114), lift the rack and note the reading on the dial gauge.
91 Remove the plunger from the housing and use a straight edge to check that a gap exists between the end of the plunger and the nylon stop fitted inside, see Fig. 13.115.
92 Using the adjustment shims (see Chapter 11), eliminate the gap noted in the previous paragraph.
93 Subtract 0.004 in (0.10 mm) from the reading obtained in paragraph 90, then add further shims of this value to those in the previous paragraph.
94 Install the plunger components on the steering gear and tighten the retaining bolts and grease nipple.
95 *On the steering gear without a grease nipple,* install the plunger and spring into the housing and tighten the special dial gauge into position.
96 Turn the pinion to move the rack from side-to-side, and position the rack at the point where the highest reading is obtained; zero the dial gauge at this point.
97 Lever the rack as shown in Fig. 13.116 and note the reading on the dial gauge.
98 Deduct 0.0013 in (0.035 mm) from the reading obtained in the previous paragraph, and select shims nearest to this value to obtain the specified free play.
99 Remove the dial gauge, fit the shims, and install the thrust plate.

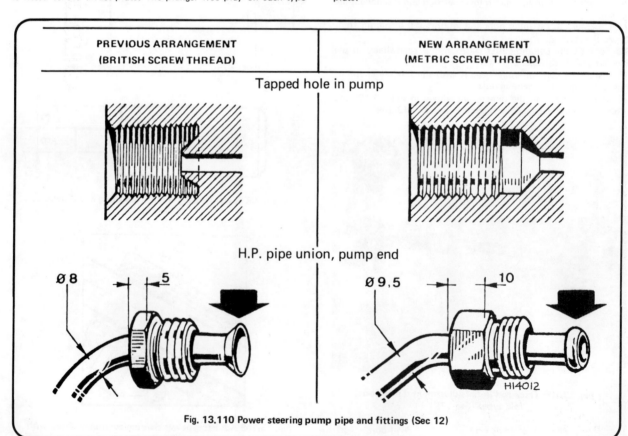

PREVIOUS ARRANGEMENT (BRITISH SCREW THREAD)	NEW ARRANGEMENT (METRIC SCREW THREAD)

Tapped hole in pump

H.P. pipe union, pump end

Fig. 13.110 Power steering pump pipe and fittings (Sec 12)

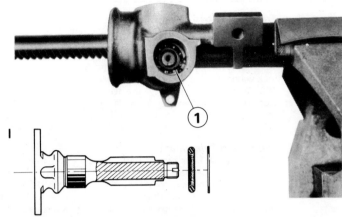

Fig. 13.111 Alternative steering gear pinion and
seal arrangements (Sec 12)

1   Early   2   Late

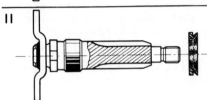

Fig. 13.112 Alternative steering gear plunger
arrangements (Sec 12)

1   Early   2   Late

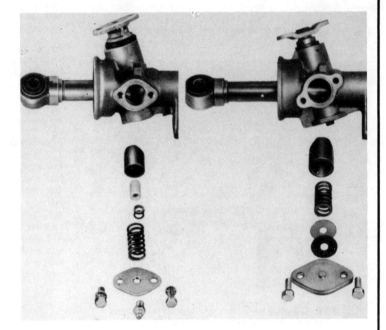

Fig. 13.113 Checking steering gear plunger free play -
grease nipple type (Sec 12)

Fig. 13.114 Using a lever to check rack movement (Sec 12)

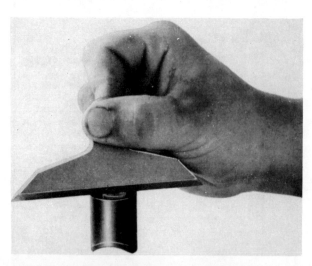

Fig. 13.115 Checking steering gear plunger to nylon stop clearance with a straight-edge (Sec 12)

Fig. 13.116 Checking steering rack movement - no grease nipple type (Sec 12)

Track rod removal and refitting

100 Figs. 13.117 and 13.119 show the later type of track rod attachment. The later rods have a balljoint which replaces the previously used flexible coupling method of attachment.

101 Removal is simply a matter of knocking back the tab of the lock washer (where fitted) and unscrewing the rod from the rack.

102 Before refitting, renew the tab washer or combined lock/stop washer as necessary. Screw in the track rod and tighten it to a torque loading of 36 lbf ft (5 kgf m). Where necessary, bend over the locking tab into one of the balljoint casing slots.

Front wheel alignment

103 Where the later type of track rods are fitted, then carry out front wheel adjustment as shown in Fig. 13.117.

104 With the locknut loosened, one turn of the track rod will equal a 0.12 in (3 mm) change in wheel alignment. On completion of adjustment, retighten the locknut to a torque loading of 32.5 lbf ft (4.5 kgf m) and move the balljoint casing back to a horizontal plane, but first note the following instructions.

105 On manual steering, carry out adjustment on one rod by up to one half a turn; above that, evenly distribute adjustment between both rods.

106 On power steering, carry out adjustment by equal amounts on both track rods.

Roadwheels - fitting

106 The wheel holding nuts should be tightened to the torque settings given in the Specifications Section of this Chapter. *Under no circumstances should an air powered wrench be used to tighten the wheel nuts.*

107 Where alloy wheels are fitted, recheck the nuts for correct tightness after 100 miles (160 km) have been covered.

Front hub - overhaul and adjustment

108 Some late models are equipped with tracer roller bearing front hubs instead of the previous ball bearing type. The overhaul and adjustment procedure for this type is as follows.

109 Jack up the front of the car and support it on axle stands. Remove the roadwheel.

110 Remove the caliper and suspend it with a piece of wire (see Chapter 9).

111 Remove the hub grease cap and unscrew the hub nut. The hub assembly can now be removed but if the bearing inner races are tight on the stub axle, a puller will be needed.

112 If the inner bearing seizes on the stub axle when the hub is

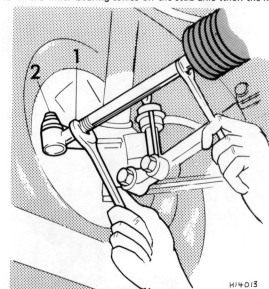

Fig. 13.117 Adjusting wheel alignment - later type track rods (Sec 12)

1   Locknut   2   Balljoint casing

Fig. 13.118 Using a puller to remove the front hub inner bearing (Sec 12)

removed, remove it with a puller and recover the oil seal. Remove the bearings and oil seal from the hub, see Fig. 13.118.

113 Wash the bearings in paraffin and wipe dry, then examine them for damage and deterioration. Renew them if necessary.

Clean the stub axle and check that it is not damaged; pay particular attention to the threads, as if these are unserviceable, the steering swivel must be renewed. Check that the bearing inner races are a sliding fit on the stub axle, and if necessary polish them with emery tape. Check the oil seal and renew it, if necessary. Check the bearing outer races and if necessary drive them out of the hub with a soft metal drift.

114 Start reassembly by driving the bearing outer races into the hub. Grease the inner bearing and locate it on its outer race, then tap the oil seal into the hub with its closed end facing out of the hub. Grease the outer bearing and smear a little grease onto the lip of the oil seal. Pack a little grease into the hub cavity.

115 Locate the outer bearing in the hub then slide the hub assembly onto the stub axle.

116 Fit the safety washer and screw on a new axle nut. Using a torque wrench, tighten the nut to 29 lbf ft (4.0 kgf m) whilst rotating the hub.

117 Loosen the axle nut then retighten it to 7.23 lbf ft (1.0 kgf m).

118 Refit the brake caliper with reference to Chapter 9.

119 The axle nut must now be turned anti-clockwise by approximately 40°, but in order to obtain the correct setting it will be necessary to use the Peugeot tool no. 8 0616.

120 Stake the axle nut in two places to lock it, then refit the hub grease cap and wheel, and lower the car to the ground.

Rear hub and carrier - removal and refitting

121 On models having rear discs mounted behind the hub, but with an access hole in the drive flange, the procedure for removing and refitting the rear hub is identical to that for removing and refitting the rear brake disc given in Section 10 of this Chapter.

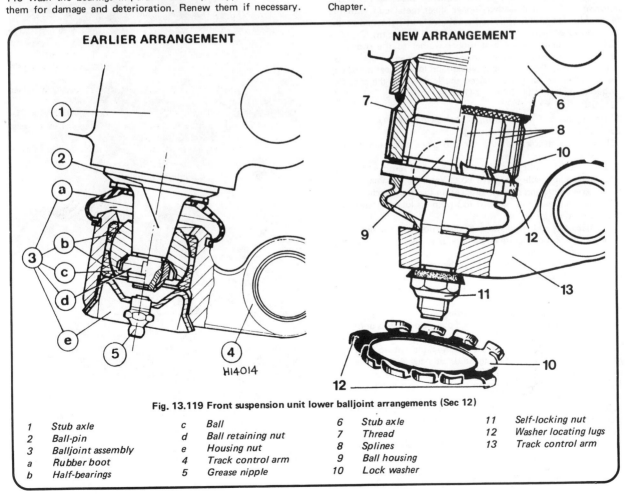

Fig. 13.119 Front suspension unit lower balljoint arrangements (Sec 12)

1	Stub axle	c	Ball	6	Stub axle	11	Self-locking nut
2	Ball-pin	d	Ball retaining nut	7	Thread	12	Washer locating lugs
3	Balljoint assembly	e	Housing nut	8	Splines	13	Track control arm
a	Rubber boot	4	Track control arm	9	Ball housing		
b	Half-bearings	5	Grease nipple	10	Lock washer		

Front suspension unit - removal and refitting

122 On later models, the suspension unit lower balljoint shown in Chapter 11 has been superseded by a new type. Fig. 13.119 shows the differences between the early and later assemblies.

123 Before attempting removal of the balljoint housing, check that a new item is easily obtainable. Both the housing and lock-washer must be renewed as a matter of course. A special tool no. 8 0616 F is available for balljoint removal. Ask your Peugeot dealer how this tool is used. It will be necessary to break off the two diametrically opposite tabs from the lock washer before removing the housing.

124 When fitting a new housing, lubricate its threads before insertion. Check that the tabs of the new lock washer are correctly aligned with the housing during fitting and tighten the housing to 125 lbf ft (17 kgf m). Tighten the track control arm to a torque setting of 33 lbf ft (4.5 kgf m).

Rear shock absorbers - removal and refitting

125 Section 7 of Chapter 11 refers mainly to the removal and refitting of shock absorbers fitted as part of an independent rear suspension system. The following text deals with those shock absorbers fitted to vehicles equipped with a solid 'banjo' type rear axle.

126 Carry out paragraphs 1 and 2 of Section 7, Chapter 11. Paragraphs 3 and 4 are not applicable; instead from beneath the car, remove the lower locknut, sheet metal cup and rubber washer (photo). Lift the shock absorber to clear the lower mountings and lower it out from beneath the vehicle.

127 Carry out the test, inspection and refitting procedures given in paragraphs 5, 6, 7 and 8 of Section 7. Complete re-fitting as follows.

128 From inside the car, fit the following parts to the shock absorber rod: rubber washer, upper sheet metal cup with the raised edge facing upwards, and a new locknut tightened to the specified torque wrench setting of 9 lbf ft (1.25 kgf m).

129 Fit the centring cup and rubber washer to the shock absorber, and then engage the lower mounting with the lug on the axle casing. Fit the rubber washer and lower sheet metal cup followed by the locknut. Tighten the locknut to the specified torque wrench setting of 9 lbf ft (1.25 kgf m).

Rear suspension (solid 'banjo' rear axle system)

Panhard rod - removal and refitting

130 Jack up the rear of the car and place axle stands under the rear axle.

131 Extract the split pins and then undo and remove the nuts, and where applicable the pivot bolts, securing the Panhard rod to the axle casing and support bracket on the underbody.

132 Carefully ease the Panhard rod from its location and withdraw it from under the car.

133 Check the rod for damage or distortion and the bushes for wear. If the bushes require renewal refer to Section 6 of Chapter 11.

134 Refitting the Panhard rod is the reverse sequence to removal. Tighten the mountings to the specified torque wrench settings of 23 lbf ft (3.2 kgf m) and always use new split pins.

Rear anti-roll bar - removal and refitting

135 Jack up the rear of the car and place axle stands under the rear axle.

136 Undo and remove the nuts securing the anti-roll bar connecting links to the mounting studs at each end of the axle casing (photo).

137 Using a stout screwdriver, ease the connecting links off the mounting studs.

138 Now undo and remove the bolts securing the two anti-roll bar mounting blocks to the under body (photo).

139 The anti-roll bar can now be withdrawn from under the car.

140 If necessary, undo and remove the nuts and bolts and lift the connecting links off the anti-roll bar.

141 Examine the parts for damage or distortion and for wear of the rubber bushes. Renew any suspect components.

12.126 Shock absorber lower mounting

12.136 Rear anti-roll bar connecting link

12.138 Anti-roll bar to body mounting block

142 Refitting the anti-roll bar is the reverse sequence to removal. Ensure that the mountings are tightened to the specified torque wrench settings.

13 Bodywork and fittings

Air conditioning

1 Some late models for operation in certain territories are fitted with an air conditioning unit, comprising a condenser mounted at the front of the car, a belt-driven compressor, a receiver, an evaporator, and a blower unit.

2 The oil-filled compressor is driven from the crankshaft pulley and incorporates a magnetic-type clutch.

3 Servicing of the system is outside the scope of the home mechanic as special equipment is necessary to evacuate and recharge the refrigerant. If a fault occurs, the repair is best entrusted to a suitably-equipped Peugeot dealer or refrigeration engineer.

4 Maintenance of the system should be confined to the following operations:

(a) *Periodically adjust the tension of the drivebelts. To do this, loosen the mounting nuts, allow the spring to tension the belts, then tighten the nuts*

(b) *Periodically check the security of all hoses and electrical connections*

(c) *Periodically brush away any flies or dirt from the condenser fins, using a soft brush*

(d) *During winter months, operate the system for a few minutes each week in order to lubricate the compressor.*

Sliding roof

5 Any maintenance which is required on the sliding roof mechanism should be left to your Peugeot dealer who will have the knowledge and equipment necessary to effect a satisfactory repair.

6 Scratches on the paint surface of the roof will normally indicate misalignment. Misalignment will also contribute to leakage, as will seal failure.

Dashboard - removal and refitting

7 The dashboard arrangement fitted to the Peugeot 504 has

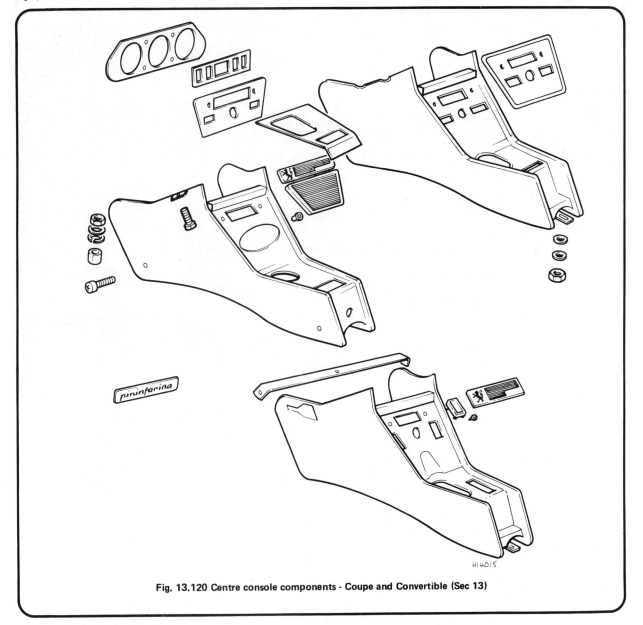

Fig. 13.120 Centre console components - Coupe and Convertible (Sec 13)

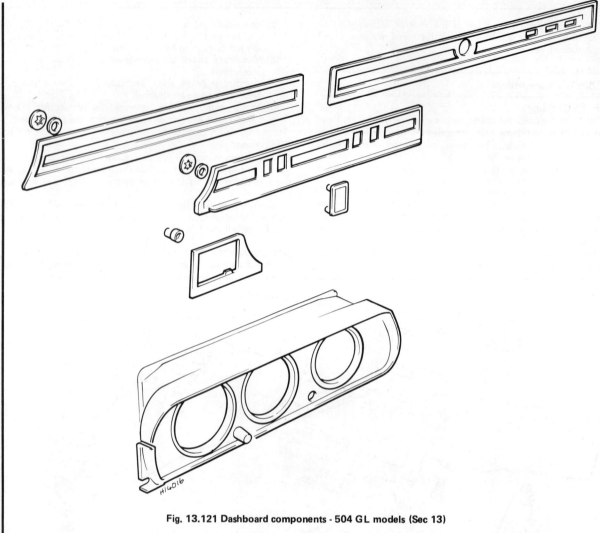

Fig. 13.121 Dashboard components - 504 GL models (Sec 13)

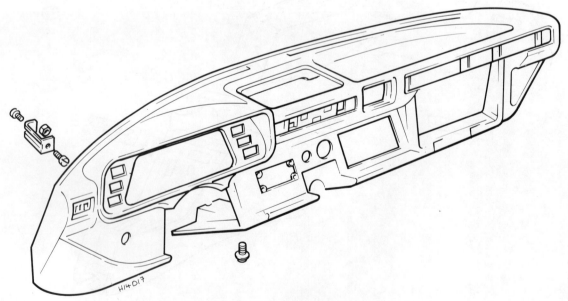

Fig. 13.122 Dashboard components - 504 GR models (Sec 13)

remained straightforward in design and is therefore relatively simple to remove. Commence by sitting in the centre of the front seat(s) and sharply forcing the front edge of the dashboard cover upwards with the heel of each hand. Once free of its retaining clips, the cover can be eased clear of the dashboard to reveal the facia retaining bolts.

8 The remaining main section of trim, that which surrounds the heater, can be removed by grasping it firmly on each side and pulling it sharply away.

9 *If it is intended to disturb any electrical connections to facilitate removal of the facia or instruments, then the battery must first be disconnected.* Note the fitted position of all connections for reference when refitting.

10 Proceed with removal of the facia whilst working in a systematical and logical manner. Do not attempt to force apart components, but look for hidden fasteners. If necessary, refer to the accompanying figures (Figs. 13.120 to 13.123) when dismantling the assembly.

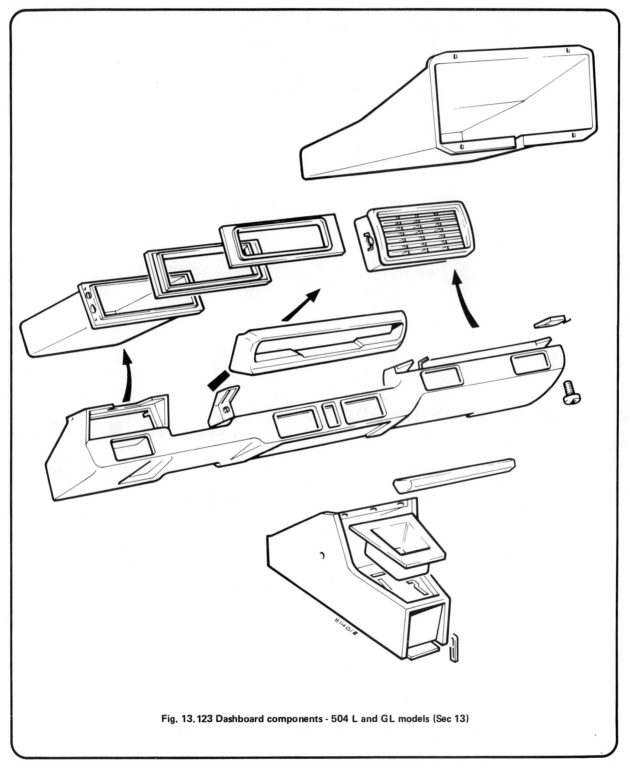

Fig. 13.123 Dashboard components - 504 L and GL models (Sec 13)

General dimensions and weights

Overall length
Saloon ... ... 4480 mm (176.3 in)
Estate and Family Estate 4803 mm (189.1 in)

Overall width ... ... 1695 mm (66.7 in)

Overall height
Saloon ... ... 1460 mm (57.5 in)
Estate and Family Estate ... ... 1550 mm (61.1 in)

Wheelbase
Saloon ... ... 2740 mm (107.9 in)
Estate and Family Estate ... ... 2900 mm (114.1 in)

Front track ... ... 1420 mm (55.9 in)

Rear track
Saloon ... ... 1330 mm (52.4 in)
Estate and Family Estate ... ... 1360 mm (53.5 in)

Turning circle
Saloon ... ... 10 220 mm (402.3 in)
Estate and Family Estate ... ... 10 760 mm (423.6 in)

Kerb weight
Saloon ... ... 1210 kg (2671 lbs)
Family Estate ... ... 1375 kg (3031 lbs)
Estate ... ... 1325 kg (2921 lbs)

General repair procedures

Whenever servicing, repair or overhaul work is carried out on the car or its components, it is necessary to observe the following procedures and instructions. This will assist in carrying out the operation efficiently and to a professional standard of workmanship.

Joint mating faces and gaskets

Where a gasket is used between the mating faces of two components, ensure that it is renewed on reassembly, and fit it dry unless otherwise stated in the repair procedure. Make sure that the mating faces are clean and dry with all traces of old gasket removed. When cleaning a joint face, use a tool which is not likely to score or damage the face, and remove any burrs or nicks with an oilstone or fine file.

Make sure that tapped holes are cleaned with a pipe cleaner, and keep them free of jointing compound if this is being used unless specifically instructed otherwise.

Ensure that all orifices, channels or pipes are clear and blow through them, preferably using compressed air.

Oil seals

Whenever an oil seal is removed from its working location, either individually or as part of an assembly, it should be renewed.

The very fine sealing lip of the seal is easily damaged and will not seal if the surface it contacts is not completely clean and free from scratches, nicks or grooves. If the original sealing surface of the component cannot be restored, the component should be renewed.

Protect the lips of the seal from any surface which may damage them in the course of fitting. Use tape or a conical sleeve where possible. Lubricate the seal lips with oil before fitting and, on dual lipped seals, fill the space between the lips with grease.

Unless otherwise stated, oil seals must be fitted with their sealing lips toward the lubricant to be sealed.

Use a tubular drift or block of wood of the appropriate size to install the seal and, if the seal housing is shouldered, drive the seal down to the shoulder. If the seal housing is unshouldered, the seal should be fitted with its face flush with the housing top face.

Screw threads and fastenings

Always ensure that a blind tapped hole is completely free from oil, grease, water or other fluid before installing the bolt or stud. Failure to do this could cause the housing to crack due to the hydraulic action of the bolt or stud as it is screwed in.

When tightening a castellated nut to accept a split pin, tighten the nut to the specified torque, where applicable, and then tighten further to the next split pin hole. Never slacken the nut to align a split pin hole unless stated in the repair procedure.

When checking or retightening a nut or bolt to a specified torque setting, slacken the nut or bolt by a quarter of a turn, and then retighten to the specified setting.

Locknuts, locktabs and washers

Any fastening which will rotate against a component or housing in the course of tightening should always have a washer between it and the relevant component or housing.

Spring or split washers should always be renewed when they are used to lock a critical component such as a big-end bearing retaining nut or bolt.

Locktabs which are folded over to retain a nut or bolt should always be renewed.

Self-locking nuts can be reused in non-critical areas, providing resistance can be felt when the locking portion passes over the bolt or stud thread.

Split pins must always be replaced with new ones of the correct size for the hole.

Special tools

Some repair procedures in this manual entail the use of special tools such as a press, two or three-legged pullers, spring compressors etc. Wherever possible, suitable readily available alternatives to the manufacturer's special tools are described, and are shown in use. In some instances, where no alternative is possible, it has been necessary to resort to the use of a manufacturer's tool and this has been done for reasons of safety as well as the efficient completion of the repair operation. Unless you are highly skilled and have a thorough understanding of the procedure described, never attempt to bypass the use of any special tool when the procedure described specifies its use. Not only is there a very great risk of personal injury, but expensive damage could be caused to the components involved.

Jacking and towing

To change a wheel in an emergency, use the jack supplied with the vehicle. Ensure that the roadwheel nuts are slackened before jacking up the car, and make sure that the arm of the jack is fully engaged with the body bracket, and that the base of the jack is standing on a firm level surface. Chock at least one of the wheels remaining in contact with the ground.

The jack supplied with the vehicle is not suitable for use when raising the vehicle for maintenance or repair work. For these operations use a trolley, hydraulic or heavy duty screw type jack, located under the front or rear crossmember, or rear axle casing. Always supplement the jack with the axle stands or blocks before working beneath the car.

If your vehicle is being towed, make sure that the tow rope is attached to one of the towing eyes or the front crossmember. If the vehicle is equipped with automatic transmission, ensure that the selector lever is in the 'N' position and do not exceed 30 mph (50 km/h). If towing a car equipped with automatic transmission for a distance greater than 25 miles (40 km), add 1 litre (1.76 pints, 2.1 US pints) of the recommended automatic transmission fluid to the unit.

When towing a trailer or caravan, ensure that the maximum towing weight permissible for the type of vehicle being used is not exceeded. Your Peugeot dealer will give information on towing weights and speeds and will also be able to supply any tow bar equipment.

Vehicle jack in position at front and rear of car

Safety first!

Professional motor mechanics are trained in safe working procedures. However enthusiastic you may be about getting on with the job in hand, do take the time to ensure that your safety is not put at risk. A moment's lack of attention can result in an accident, as can failure to observe certain elementary precautions.

There will always be new ways of having accidents, and the following points do not pretend to be a comprehensive list of all dangers; they are intended rather to make you aware of the risks and to encourage a safety-conscious approach to all work you carry out on your vehicle.

Essential DOs and DON'Ts

DON'T rely on a single jack when working underneath the vehicle. Always use reliable additional means of support, such as axle stands, securely placed under a part of the vehicle that you know will not give way.

DON'T attempt to loosen or tighten high-torque nuts (e.g. wheel hub nuts) while the vehicle is on a jack; it may be pulled off.

DON'T start the engine without first ascertaining that the transmission is in neutral and the parking brake applied.

DON'T suddenly remove the filler cap from a hot cooling system – cover it with a cloth and release the pressure gradually first, or you may get scalded by escaping coolant.

DON'T attempt to drain oil until you are sure it has cooled sufficiently to avoid scalding you.

DON'T grasp any part of the engine or exhaust without first ascertaining that it is sufficiently cool to avoid burning you.

DON'T syphon toxic liquids such as fuel, brake fluid or antifreeze by mouth, or allow them to remain on your skin.

DON'T inhale brake lining dust – it is injurious to health.

DON'T allow any spilt oil or grease to remain on the floor – wipe it up straight away, before someone slips on it.

DON'T use ill-fitting spanners or other tools which may slip and cause injury.

DON'T attempt to lift a heavy component which may be beyond your capability – get assistance.

DON'T rush to finish a job, or take unverified short cuts.

DON'T allow children or animals in or around an unattended vehicle.

DO wear eye protection when using power tools such as drill, sander, bench grinder etc, and when working under the vehicle.

DO use a barrier cream on your hands prior to undertaking dirty jobs – it will protect your skin from infection as well as making the dirt easier to remove afterwards; but make sure your hands aren't left slippery.

DO keep loose clothing (cuffs, tie etc) and long hair well out of the way of moving mechanical parts.

DO remove rings, wristwatch etc, before working on the vehicle – especially the electrical system.

DO ensure that any lifting tackle used has a safe working load rating adequate for the job.

DO keep your work area tidy – it is only too easy to fall over articles left lying around.

DO get someone to check periodically that all is well, when working alone on the vehicle.

DO carry out work in a logical sequence and check that everything is correctly assembled and tightened afterwards.

DO remember that your vehicle's safety affects that of yourself and others. If in doubt on any point, get specialist advice.

IF, in spite of following these precautions, you are unfortunate enough to injure yourself, seek medical attention as soon as possible.

Fire

Remember at all times that petrol (gasoline) is highly flammable. Never smoke, or have any kind of naked flame around, when working on the vehicle. But the risk does not end there – a spark caused by an electrical short-circuit, by two metal surfaces contacting each other, or even by static electricity built up in your body under certain conditions, can ignite petrol vapour, which in a confined space is highly explosive.

Always disconnect the battery earth (ground) terminal before working on any part of the fuel system, and never risk spilling fuel on to a hot engine or exhaust.

It is recommended that a fire extinguisher of a type suitable for fuel and electrical fires is kept handy in the garage or workplace at all times. Never try to extinguish a fuel or electrical fire with water.

Fumes

Certain fumes are highly toxic and can quickly cause unconsciousness and even death if inhaled to any extent. Petrol (gasoline) vapour comes into this category, as do the vapours from certain solvents such as trichloroethylene. Any draining or pouring of such volatile fluids should be done in a well ventilated area.

When using cleaning fluids and solvents, read the instructions carefully. Never use materials from unmarked containers – they may give off poisonous vapours.

Never run the engine of a motor vehicle in an enclosed space such as a garage. Exhaust fumes contain carbon monoxide which is extremely poisonous; if you need to run the engine, always do so in the open air or at least have the rear of the vehicle outside the workplace.

If you are fortunate enough to have the use of an inspection pit, never drain or pour petrol, and never run the engine, while the vehicle is standing over it; the fumes, being heavier than air, will concentrate in the pit with possibly lethal results.

The battery

Never cause a spark, or allow a naked light, near the vehicle's battery. It will normally be giving off a certain amount of hydrogen gas, which is highly explosive.

Always disconnect the battery earth (ground) terminal before working on the fuel or electrical systems.

If possible, loosen the filler plugs or cover when charging the battery from an external source. Do not charge at an excessive rate or the battery may burst.

Take care when topping up and when carrying the battery. The acid electrolyte, even when diluted, is very corrosive and should not be allowed to contact the eyes or skin.

If you ever need to prepare electrolyte yourself, always add the acid slowly to the water, and never the other way round. Protect against splashes by wearing rubber gloves and goggles.

When jump starting a car using a booster battery, for negative earth (ground) vehicles, connect the jump leads in the following sequence: First connect one jump lead between the positive (+) terminals of the two batteries. Then connect the other jump lead first to the negative (–) terminal of the booster battery, and then to a good earthing (ground) point on the vehicle to be started, at least 18 in (45 cm) from the battery if possible. Ensure that hands and jump leads are clear of any moving parts, and that the two vehicles do not touch. Disconnect the leads in the reverse order.

Mains electricity

When using an electric power tool, inspection light etc, which works from the mains, always ensure that the appliance is correctly connected to its plug and that, where necessary, it is properly earthed (grounded). Do not use such appliances in damp conditions and, again, beware of creating a spark or applying excessive heat in the vicinity of fuel or fuel vapour.

Ignition HT voltage

A severe electric shock can result from touching certain parts of the ignition system, such as the HT leads, when the engine is running or being cranked, particularly if components are damp or the insulation is defective. Where an electronic ignition system is fitted, the HT voltage is much higher and could prove fatal.

Fault diagnosis

Introduction

The vehicle owner who does his or her own maintenance according to the recommended schedules should not have to use this section of the manual very often. Modern component reliability is such that, provided those items subject to wear or deterioration are inspected or renewed at the specified intervals, sudden failure is comparatively rare. Faults do not usually just happen as a result of sudden failure, but develop over a period of time. Major mechanical failures in particular are usually preceded by characteristic symptoms over hundreds or even thousands of miles. Those components which do occasionally fail without warning are often small and easily carried in the vehicle.

With any fault finding, the first step is to decide where to begin investigations. Sometimes this is obvious, but on other occasions a little detective work will be necessary. The owner who makes half a dozen haphazard adjustments or replacements may be successful in curing a fault (or its symptoms), but he will be none the wiser if the fault recurs and he may well have spent more time and money than was necessary. A calm and logical approach will be found to be more satisfactory in the long run. Always take into account any warning signs or abnormalities that may have been noticed in the period preceding the fault – power loss, high or low gauge readings, unusual noises or smells, etc – and remember that failure of components such as fuses or spark plugs may only be pointers to some underlying fault.

The pages which follow here are intended to help in cases of failure to start or breakdown on the road. There is also a Fault Diagnosis Section at the end of each Chapter which should be consulted if the preliminary checks prove unfruitful. Whatever the fault, certain basic principles apply. These are as follows:

Verify the fault. This is simply a matter of being sure that you know what the symptoms are before starting work. This is particularly important if you are investigating a fault for someone else who may not have described it very accurately.

Don't overlook the obvious. For example, if the vehicle won't start, is there petrol in the tank? (Don't take anyone else's word on this particular point, and don't trust the fuel gauge either!) If an electrical fault is indicated, look for loose or broken wires before digging out the test gear.

Cure the disease, not the symptom. Substituting a flat battery with a fully charged one will get you off the hard shoulder, but if the underlying cause is not attended to, the new battery will go the same way. Similarly, changing oil-fouled spark plugs for a new set will get you moving again, but remember that the reason for the fouling (if it wasn't simply an incorrect grade of plug) will have to be established and corrected.

Don't take anything for granted. Particularly, don't forget that a 'new' component may itself be defective (especially if it's been rattling round in the boot for months), and don't leave components out of a fault diagnosis sequence just because they are new or recently fitted. When you do finally diagnose a difficult fault, you'll probably realise that all the evidence was there from the start.

Electrical faults

Electrical faults can be more puzzling than straightforward mechanical failures, but they are no less susceptible to logical analysis if the basic principles of operation are understood. Vehicle electrical wiring exists in extremely unfavourable conditions – heat, vibration and chemical attack – and the first things to look for are loose or corroded connections and broken or chafed wires, especially where the wires pass through holes in the bodywork or are subject to vibration.

All metal-bodied vehicles in current production have one pole of the battery 'earthed', ie connected to the vehicle bodywork, and in nearly all modern vehicles it is the negative (–) terminal. The various electrical components – motors, bulb holders etc – are also connected to earth, either by means of a lead or directly by their mountings. Electric current flows through the component and then back to the battery via the bodywork. If the component mounting is loose or corroded, or if a good path back to the battery is not available, the circuit will be incomplete and malfunction will result. The engine and/or gearbox are also earthed by means of flexible metal straps to the body or subframe; if these straps are loose or missing, starter motor, generator and ignition trouble may result.

Assuming the earth return to be satisfactory, electrical faults will be due either to component malfunction or to defects in the current supply. Individual components are dealt with in Chapter 10. If supply wires are broken or cracked internally this results in an open-circuit, and the easiest way to check for this is to bypass the suspect wire temporarily with a length of wire having a crocodile clip or suitable connector at each end. Alternatively, a 12V test lamp can be used to verify the presence of supply voltage at various points along the wire and the break can be thus isolated.

If a bare portion of a live wire touches the bodywork or other earthed metal part, the electricity will take the low-resistance path thus formed back to the battery: this is known as a short-circuit. Hopefully a short-circuit will blow a fuse, but otherwise it may cause burning of the insulation (and possibly further short-circuits) or even a fire. This is why it is inadvisable to bypass persistently blowing fuses with silver foil or wire.

Spares and tool kit

Most vehicles are supplied only with sufficient tools for wheel changing; the *Maintenance and minor repair* tool kit detailed in *Tools and working facilities*, with the addition of a hammer, is probably sufficient for those repairs that most motorists would consider attempting at the roadside. In addition a few items which can be fitted without too much trouble in the event of a breakdown should be carried. Experience and available space will modify the list below, but the following may save having to call on professional assistance:

Spark plugs, clean and correctly gapped
HT lead and plug cap – long enough to reach the plug furthest from the distributor
Distributor rotor, condenser and contact breaker points
Drivebelt(s) – emergency type may suffice
Spare fuses
Set of principal light bulbs
Tin of radiator sealer and hose bandage
Exhaust bandage
Roll of insulating tape
Length of soft iron wire
Length of electrical flex
Torch or inspection lamp (can double as test lamp)
Battery jump leads
Tow-rope
Ignition waterproofing aerosol
Litre of engine oil
Sealed can of hydraulic fluid
Emergency windscreen
'Jubilee' clips
Tube of filler paste

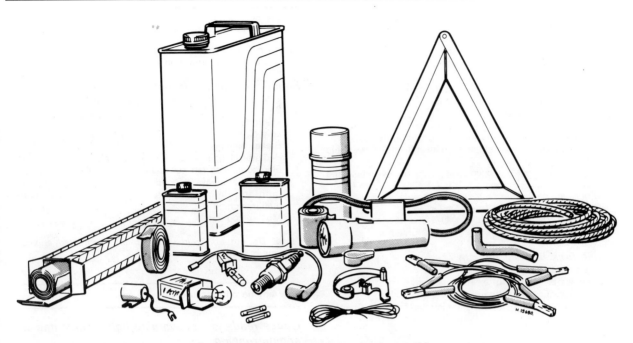

Carrying a few spares can save you a long walk!

If spare fuel is carried, a can designed for the purpose should be used to minimise risks of leakage and collision damage. A first aid kit and a warning triangle, whilst not at present compulsory in the UK, are obviously sensible items to carry in addition to the above.

When touring abroad it may be advisable to carry additional spares which, even if you cannot fit them yourself, could save having to wait while parts are obtained. The items below may be worth considering:

Throttle cables
Cylinder head gasket
Alternator brushes
Fuel pump repair kit
Tyre valve core

One of the motoring organisations will be able to advise on availability of fuel etc in foreign countries.

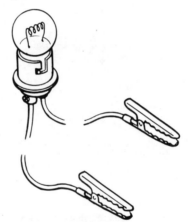

A simple test lamp is useful for checking electrical faults

Engine will not start

Engine fails to turn when starter operated
Flat battery (recharge, use jump leads, or push start)
Battery terminals loose or corroded
Battery earth to body defective
Engine earth strap loose or broken
Starter motor (or solenoid) wiring loose or broken
Automatic transmission selector in wrong position, or inhibitor switch faulty
Ignition/starter switch faulty
Major mechanical failure (seizure)
Starter or solenoid internal fault (see Chapter 10)

Starter motor turns engine slowly
Partially discharged battery (recharge, use jump leads, or push start)
Battery terminals loose or corroded
Battery earth to body defective
Engine earth strap loose
Starter motor (or solenoid) wiring loose
Starter motor internal fault (see Chapter 10)

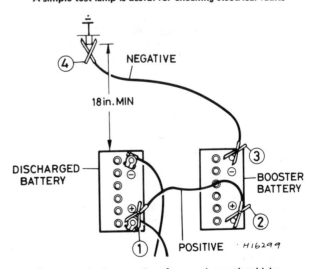

Jump start lead connections for negative earth vehicles - connect leads in order shown

Starter motor spins without turning engine
Flat battery
Starter motor pinion sticking on sleeve
Flywheel gear teeth damaged or worn
Starter motor mounting bolts loose

Engine turns normally but fails to start
Damp or dirty HT leads and distributor cap (crank engine and check for spark)
Dirty or incorrectly gapped distributor points (if applicable)
No fuel in tank (check for delivery at carburettor)
Excessive choke (hot engine) or insufficient choke (cold engine)
Fouled or incorrectly gapped spark plugs (remove, clean and regap)
Other ignition system fault (see Chapter 4)
Other fuel system fault (see Chapter 3)
Poor compression (see Chapter 1)
Major mechanical failure (eg camshaft drive)

Engine fires but will not run
Insufficient choke (cold engine)
Air leaks at carburettor or inlet manifold
Fuel starvation (see Chapter 3)
Ballast resistor defective, or other ignition fault (see Chapter 4)

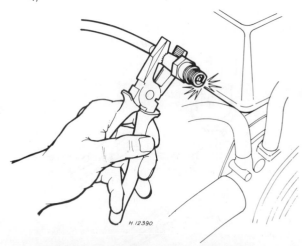

Crank engine and check for spark. Hold lead with an insulated tool!

Engine cuts out and will not restart

Engine cuts out suddenly – ignition fault
Loose or disconnected LT wires
Wet HT leads or distributor cap (after traversing water splash)
Coil or condenser failure (check for spark)
Other ignition fault (see Chapter 4)

Engine misfires before cutting out – fuel fault
Fuel tank empty
Fuel pump defective or filter blocked (check for delivery)
Fuel tank filler vent blocked (suction will be evident on releasing cap)
Carburettor needle valve sticking
Carburettor jets blocked (fuel contaminated)
Other fuel system fault (see Chapter 3)

Engine cuts out – other causes
Serious overheating
Major mechanical failure (eg camshaft drive)

Engine overheats

Ignition (no-charge) warning light illuminated
Slack or broken drivebelt – retension or renew (Chapter 2)

Ignition warning light not illuminated
Coolant loss due to internal or external leakage (see Chapter 2)
Thermostat defective
Low oil level
Brakes binding
Radiator clogged externally or internally
Electric cooling fan not operating correctly
Engine waterways clogged
Ignition timing incorrect or automatic advance malfunctioning
Mixture too weak

Note: *Do not add cold water to an overheated engine or damage may result*

Low engine oil pressure

Gauge reads low or warning light illuminated with engine running
Oil level low or incorrect grade
Defective gauge or sender unit
Wire to sender unit earthed
Engine overheating
Oil filter clogged or bypass valve defective
Oil pressure relief valve defective
Oil pick-up strainer clogged
Oil pump worn or mountings loose
Worn main or big-end bearings

Note: *Low oil pressure in a high-mileage engine at tickover is not necessarily a cause for concern. Sudden pressure loss at speed is far more significant. In any event, check the gauge or warning light sender before condemning the engine.*

Engine noises

Pre-ignition (pinking) on acceleration
Incorrect grade of fuel
Ignition timing incorrect
Distributor faulty or worn
Worn or maladjusted carburettor
Excessive carbon build-up in engine

Whistling or wheezing noises
Leaking vacuum hose
Leaking carburettor or manifold gasket
Blowing head gasket

Tapping or rattling
Incorrect valve clearances
Worn valve gear
Worn timing chain or belt
Broken piston ring (ticking noise)

Knocking or thumping
Unintentional mechanical contact (eg fan blades)
Worn fanbelt
Peripheral component fault (generator, water pump etc)
Worn big-end bearings (regular heavy knocking, perhaps less under load)
Worn main bearings (rumbling and knocking, perhaps worsening under load)
Piston slap (most noticeable when cold)

Conversion factors

Length (distance)

	X		=		X		=
Inches (in)	X	25.4	= Millimetres (mm)		X	0.0394	= Inches (in)
Feet (ft)	X	0.305	= Metres (m)		X	3.281	= Feet (ft)
Miles	X	1.609	= Kilometres (km)		X	0.621	= Miles

Volume (capacity)

	X		=		X		=
Cubic inches (cu in; in³)	X	16.387	= Cubic centimetres (cc; cm³)		X	0.061	= Cubic inches (cu in; in³)
Imperial pints (Imp pt)	X	0.568	= Litres (l)		X	1.76	= Imperial pints (Imp pt)
Imperial quarts (Imp qt)	X	1.137	= Litres (l)		X	0.88	= Imperial quarts (Imp qt)
Imperial quarts (Imp qt)	X	1.201	= US quarts (US qt)		X	0.833	= Imperial quarts (Imp qt)
US quarts (US qt)	X	0.946	= Litres (l)		X	1.057	= US quarts (US qt)
Imperial gallons (Imp gal)	X	4.546	= Litres (l)		X	0.22	= Imperial gallons (Imp gal)
Imperial gallons (Imp gal)	X	1.201	= US gallons (US gal)		X	0.833	= Imperial gallons (Imp gal)
US gallons (US gal)	X	3.785	= Litres (l)		X	0.264	= US gallons (US gal)

Mass (weight)

	X		=		X		=
Ounces (oz)	X	28.35	= Grams (g)		X	0.035	= Ounces (oz)
Pounds (lb)	X	0.454	= Kilograms (kg)		X	2.205	= Pounds (lb)

Force

	X		=		X		=
Ounces-force (ozf; oz)	X	0.278	= Newtons (N)		X	3.6	= Ounces-force (ozf; oz)
Pounds-force (lbf; lb)	X	4.448	= Newtons (N)		X	0.225	= Pounds-force (lbf; lb)
Newtons (N)	X	0.1	= Kilograms-force (kgf; kg)		X	9.81	= Newtons (N)

Pressure

	X		=		X		=
Pounds-force per square inch (psi; lbf/in²; lb/in²)	X	0.070	= Kilograms-force per square centimetre (kgf/cm²; kg/cm²)		X	14.223	= Pounds-force per square inch (psi; lbf/in²; lb/in²)
Pounds-force per square inch (psi; lbf/in²; lb/in²)	X	0.068	= Atmospheres (atm)		X	14.696	= Pounds-force per square inch (psi; lbf/in²; lb/in²)
Pounds-force per square inch (psi; lbf/in²; lb/in²)	X	0.069	= Bars		X	14.5	= Pounds-force per square inch (psi; lbf/in²; lb/in²)
Pounds-force per square inch (psi; lbf/in²; lb/in²)	X	6.895	= Kilopascals (kPa)		X	0.145	= Pounds-force per square inch (psi; lbf/in²; lb/in²)
Kilopascals (kPa)	X	0.01	= Kilograms-force per square centimetre (kgf/cm²; kg/cm²)		X	98.1	= Kilopascals (kPa)

Torque (moment of force)

	X		=		X		=
Pounds-force inches (lbf in; lb in)	X	1.152	= Kilograms-force centimetre (kgf cm; kg cm)		X	0.868	= Pounds-force inches (lbf in; lb in)
Pounds-force inches (lbf in; lb in)	X	0.113	= Newton metres (Nm)		X	8.85	= Pounds-force inches (lbf in; lb in)
Pounds-force inches (lbf in; lb in)	X	0.083	= Pounds-force feet (lbf ft; lb ft)		X	12	= Pounds-force inches (lbf in; lb in)
Pounds-force feet (lbf ft; lb ft)	X	0.138	= Kilograms-force metres (kgf m; kg m)		X	7.233	= Pounds-force feet (lbf ft; lb ft)
Pounds-force feet (lbf ft; lb ft)	X	1.356	= Newton metres (Nm)		X	0.738	= Pounds-force feet (lbf ft; lb ft)
Newton metres (Nm)	X	0.102	= Kilograms-force metres (kgf m; kg m)		X	9.804	= Newton metres (Nm)

Power

	X		=		X		=
Horsepower (hp)	X	745.7	= Watts (W)		X	0.0013	= Horsepower (hp)

Velocity (speed)

	X		=		X		=
Miles per hour (miles/hr; mph)	X	1.609	= Kilometres per hour (km/hr; kph)	X	0.621	= Miles per hour (miles/hr; mph)

Fuel consumption*

	X		=		X		=
Miles per gallon, Imperial (mpg)	X	0.354	= Kilometres per litre (km/l)		X	2.825	= Miles per gallon, Imperial (mpg)
Miles per gallon, US (mpg)	X	0.425	= Kilometres per litre (km/l)		X	2.352	= Miles per gallon, US (mpg)

Temperature

Degrees Fahrenheit = (°C x 1.8) + 32   Degrees Celsius (Degrees Centigrade; °C) = (°F - 32) x 0.56

*It is common practice to convert from miles per gallon (mpg) to litres/100 kilometres (l/100km), where mpg (Imperial) x l/100 km = 282 and mpg (US) x l/100 km = 235

Index

Printed by
J H Haynes & Co Ltd
Sparkford Nr Yeovil
Somerset BA22 7JJ England